Otto Zoeckler

The Cross of Christ

Studies in the history of religion and the inner life of the church

Otto Zoeckler

The Cross of Christ
Studies in the history of religion and the inner life of the church

ISBN/EAN: 9783337253837

Printed in Europe, USA, Canada, Australia, Japan

Cover: Foto ©Lupo / pixelio.de

More available books at **www.hansebooks.com**

THE

CROSS OF CHRIST:

STUDIES IN THE HISTORY OF RELIGION AND THE INNER LIFE OF THE CHURCH.

BY THE REV.
OTTO ZOECKLER, D.D.,
PROFESSOR OF THEOLOGY IN GREIFSWALD.

TRANSLATED, WITH THE CO-OPERATION OF THE AUTHOR,
BY THE
REV. MAURICE J. EVANS, B.A.

"Crux Christi unica est eruditio verborum Dei, theologia sincerissima."
LUTHER, on Psalm vi. 11.

London:
HODDER AND STOUGHTON,
27, PATERNOSTER ROW,
MDCCCLXXVII.

[*All Rights Reserved.*]

AUTHOR'S PREFACE.

A MONOGRAPH of the Cross in the form of an octavo volume of almost five hundred pages will appear to some a hazardous undertaking; to others, it may be, a monstrosity. He who has seen the three bulky quarto volumes of Gretser's gigantic work will perhaps doubt the possibility of adding anything thereto of a nature to complement or correct that which has been said by him. On the other hand, he who is unacquainted with the abundance of problems connected with the history of worship and of art, and even of civilisation and morals, presenting themselves in this domain, will regard it as hardly comprehensible that a volume, even of the size of the present one, should be composed upon this subject, without its contents being afflicted with the bane of tedious dryness, or with the pedantry of an ingeniously trifling miniature painting.

We hope, from the nature and contents of our work, to be sufficiently justified against objections on either side. A mere hasty glance at the sketch of the Literature appended to this Preface will be enough to correct the impression of those —of the one class or of the other—who doubt as to the necessity for fresh investigations upon our subject, and specially as to the timeliness of a survey of the researches devoted to this subject. To the seriously reflecting mind, however, not merely that side of the subject bearing on the archæology of cultus and art—of which the very great fulness in particular, is forcibly illustrated by our compendious list of the works already written upon it,—but also its significance for a deeper penetration into the innermost essence of Christianity, and for a right apprehension of highly important religious and social problems of the present day, can hardly remain long a thing unperceived. The cross as "the emblem of Christianity universally," as the symbolic "representation of the one great truth, out of which a multitude of truths may be developed,"[1] is only apparently on a level with a number of other religious emblems, the study of which can call forth no interest beyond that of an art-historical or liturgical examination. It may be that a false externalising, specially in the Church of the Middle Ages, has attached itself to the reverence manifested towards the cross. An exact and critical detailing of these superstitious extravagances and mystical playings of the imagination may more than once run the risk of producing a wearying or even repelling effect. Nevertheless there is inherent in *this* particular sign a stronger power of attraction than in any of the other symbols of Christianity. The externalising and corrupting influence upon the essence and life of our religion proceeding from it, from the time of Constantine and Helena, was followed in the period of the Reformation by a purifying and spiritualising process, which, equally with that process of degeneration, took its point of departure in the original expression of believing and enthusiastic attachment to the symbol of redemption. The Catholic devotion to the Cross, and the Evangelical preaching of the Cross, have their roots in the same soil. The implement of torture, transformed from an abhorred symbol of the curse into a rock of salvation for all peoples, is the common sacrificial altar of both, alike of that half of Christendom which has returned to the poor rudimentary ordinances of the world (Gal. iv. 3 ; Col. ii. 8, 20), and of that which by virtue of a truly spiritual apprehension and embodiment of the idea of the cross of

[1] K. Chr. W. Bähr.

Jesus (Matt. xvi. 24), is raised above the danger of relapse into a heathen or Jewish externality. Nor does it in the present day deny its place of honour and of power, either in the Romish, or in the Greek, or in the Evangelical Church; and it will continue to maintain its central and uniting significance for the totality of the Church until the end of the days.

A delineation, briefly presenting in its leading features the historic course of development which gave rise successively to these main forms and phases of the religion of the Cross, may, on account of the beauty and grandeur of its object, be regarded as secured against the suspicion of micrologic dulness. The history of the Cross necessarily presents a reflected image of the history of Christianity itself, and indeed a more instructive and important one than any other similar contemplation, under the veil of an emblem, of the rise and growth of our religion hitherto, which might in any way be attempted. Specially upon a closer examination of its preparatory history —in the remarkable and partly enigmatical airy reflections which, in the form of so many a cruciform symbol upon the art monuments of the pre-Christian as of modern Heathendom, serve as heralds and precursors of the cultus of the Cross in the Christian Church—does our subject awaken interest in every one at all endowed with historic culture, and a sense for the appreciation of higher ethical endeavours and problems. The title "Contribution to the Philosophy of History," pertains with unquestionable right to a treatment of the subject designed and executed from such standpoint ; even though from time to time an indispensable entering into the details of the controversies with regard to the archæology of worship or of art, as also an examination of the more important phenomena of the dogmatic or mystic-ascetic literature bearing upon our subject, should occasion many deviations from the mode of treatment ordinarily prevailing in works on the philosophy of history.

We might also, looking not so much at the plan and mode of treatment as at the nature of its contents, have ventured to designate our book an "Apology for Christianity." For a history of the glorifying of the Cross by the forms of cultus and the art-formations of the Church, but also not less by the manifold products of the practical following of Christ upon the *via regia crucis*, is in itself, without any apologetic addition or rhetorical art, an effective defence of Christianity. And the more vigorously and incisively we, in presenting this history, employ the critical standard which the Evangelical standpoint of faith places in our hand; the more carefully all glorification of the sensuous and external side of the symbol of redemption, in the sense of an unsound romanticism or of a hazy natural-philosophic mystery, remains excluded; the more emphatically, on the other hand, the intransitory religious-ethical core and centre of the same is presented in bold relief, and is set forth in its ever radiant clearness, its irresistible power of attraction, its solace and peace-diffusing operations, among Christians of all confessions: so much more distinctly will be brought out that which the Cross preaches in the present day, alike to the scornful despisers as to the salvation-loving friends of the religion of Jesus, and at the same time with the elenctic will also the apologetic significance of this preaching become apparent, amidst the conflict of the powers of our age.

We hope that, on account of the paramount interest which the subject presents on more than one side, the studies and literary notes, bearing more upon the learned details of our investigations, which we have collected in the form of a number of excurses at the end of our work,—some of these only slightly connected with the main object of our examination, (Nos. III., IV. and VII.,)—will meet with a not unfriendly reception at the hand of the majority of our readers.

GREIFSWALD, *July*, 1875.

TRANSLATOR'S PREFACE.

THE Christian conception of the Cross of Christ is that of the world's altar of reconciliation, on which the sacrifice of the God-man is the antitype and substance, not only of the typical expiations of the Old Covenant, but also of all those shadowy expiations which occupy so prominent a place in the history of all ancient peoples. The supreme affection which the Church has always cherished for the symbol of the Cross is thus an affection which has for its object, not the instrument of death in itself, but the Divine Saviour who in grace hung thereon. The Church in all ages has rejoiced to extol the love of Him who redeemed her with His blood. In our author's volume the paramount influence of this affection upon the Church's thought and life is traced through the successive ages of her history. So early as the time of the Apostles, the grace of her Redeemer finds its meet commendation in Christian song. One of the earliest hymns of the Cross is that communicated by the Apostle Paul:

"If we have died with Him, we shall also live with Him;
If we suffer, we shall also reign with Him:
If we deny Him, He also will deny us;
If we believe not, yet He abideth faithful,
He cannot deny Himself."

Who can tell to what extent such calm and peaceful songs of the Christians on that memorable Sunday preceding the battle of the Milvian Bridge affected the perturbed mind of Constantine, and disposed him to accept as a token of deliverance the sign which on the next day appeared to him in the sky? The songs, too, of the Church in the Mediæval Age, and in later times, still celebrate with the same ardour the same inexhaustible theme.[1] A translation of some of these is given in the following pages (pp. 316, 317, 323, and 371), the poetic rendering of which in English is due to the kindness of a lady who has bestowed great pains on the preserving of the metre of the original. Of *English* hymn-writers perhaps none have surpassed Kelly on this theme, particularly in his hymn

"Glory, glory everlasting,
Be to Him who bore the cross!"

Scarcely later than the Church's first efforts in song to the praise of the Crucified are the first symbolic representations of the blessings obtained through redemption in Christ. Figures like those delineated on p. 201 of this work—without the Greek letters—were observed by the Rev. Hugh Macmillan upon certain rings in the Museum at Naples. As the rings upon which these emblems were engraved were taken from the ruins of Pompeii (overwhelmed by the eruption of Vesuvius, A.D. 79), they must have dated at the latest from the third quarter of the first century. "The same symbols," he says, in a recent article in the *Family Treasury*,[2] "which we find in the Roman Catacombs,—the palm-branch, the sacred fish, the monogram of Jesus, the dove,—are unmistakably represented on these rings. Some of them are double, indicating that they were used by married persons; one has the palm-branch twice repeated; another exhibits the palm and anchor; a third has a dove with foliage in its

---

[1] An excellent monograph on one of the earlier encomiasts of the cross was published at the close of 1876 by Kemink and Son, Utrecht: *Johannes Damascenus*, etc., which gives a sketch of this Father as a theologian, a preacher, and a poet. The author is Dr. F. H. J. Grundlehner, a young theologian of the Utrecht School.

[2] Sept. 1877.

bill; and one ring has the Greek word *Elpis*—Hope—inscribed upon it."

With the vision of Constantine and the discovery of the supposed wood of the Cross by Helena, another era dawns upon the Church, one in which bitter suffering is exchanged for the favour of the secular powers. The history of Helena's discovery is involved in the greatest obscurity. Eusebius himself does not indeed directly mention this event; but, in a letter of Constantine to Macarius, preserved by Eusebius (*Life of Constantine*, iii. 30), this emperor speaks of the recovery of the Cross as of a fact universally acknowledged. For by the expression "token *of the most sacred passion* of the Redeemer, which had been so long buried under the earth," it would seem evident beyond doubt that only the wood of the True Cross can be meant, and not the sepulchre, the place of which was *never* lost sight of. What we no longer possess, however, is the evidence on which such a man as Cyril affirmed without hesitation that the cross of the Lord was still in existence in his time. All, therefore, that can now be said on the question is summed up by our author under the head of Chapter IV. of this work.

The shrinking on the part of the early Christians from directly depicting the instrument of their Lord's passion is well known: the earliest representation of the so-called Latin Cross in the Catacombs is said to belong to the time of Pope Damasus (366—384). One of the earliest representations of the Crucifixion in stone of those now existing is that known as the Camus Cross, on the summit of the ridge of Downie, near Monikie, N.B. This monument is about six feet in height, and bears upon its west or obverse side the figure of the Saviour extended upon the cross, and under His feet what appears to be a very large footboard. Beneath is a figure of Mary weeping. On the other side is a figure supposed to represent a priest with a book upon his breast. The whole cross is covered with sculptured figures, said to represent angels, priests with their books, and a centaur, but very difficult to decipher. According to the old Scottish chroniclers, *e.g.*, Boece or Boyce in his *Scotorum Historiæ* (1527), this cross was erected to mark the grave of the Danish General Camus, slain in flight after the battle of Barrie, 1010. Inasmuch as the family of Boyce had long before his time been connected with Panbride, in the immediate neighbourhood, his account in the main is the more worthy of credit.[1] Some magnificent crosses at and near Meigle in Perthshire, and Glamis and Aberlemno in Forfarshire, are connected by tradition with the murder of the erewhile victor at Barrie, Malcolm II., a quarter of a century later (about 1034). A more pacific association, on the other hand, with the wayside crosses of the Middle Ages, is that of the rest afforded to the weary traveller by means of the seats ordinarily raised at the foot. To this friendly custom of placing seats under the cross, the old Welsh proverb owes its origin: "Where there is a cross, there is wont to be a resting-place."

The opposition to the use of crosses and crucifixes which had already arisen early in the ninth century, and found its representatives in Claude of Turin, the Albigenses, and later the theologians of the Reformed Church, is perhaps to be regarded as but a natural and healthful reaction against a heathenish adoration of the material cross, so generally exhibited on the part of the more worldly and superstitious of the adherents of Rome. At any rate, though sometimes carried beyond due limits, it could not be called a blind or unreasoning opposition to the emblem of redemption, and still less an opposition to the *doctrine* of redemption itself. Luther, too, sometimes expresses his indignation against the

---

[1] The account of Boyce received confirmation in some of its more important particulars, on the opening of the grave by order of Sir Patrick Maule of Panmure, about the year 1620.

abuse of crosses and crucifixes, to the obscuring of the doctrine of salvation, as strongly as any of those above mentioned. And we must remember that the charge of Manichean doctrines brought against the Albigenses rests almost entirely on the testimony of their opponents, and does not appear to be critically well supported. Nevertheless the more conservative position taken up by the Lutheran Church towards the emblem of Christ's redemptive death is historically justified by the abundance of consolatory literature of the Cross yielded by that Church in the Reformation age, and the glorious succession of Hymns of the Cross which she has continued to yield even to the present day. The true corrective to every form of abuse of the Cross will be found in the vigorous and loving presentation of its real significance, as the emblem of redemption and consolation through the Crucified, and this the Evangelical Church of Germany has afforded in no stinted measure. Nor has the important truth of sanctification through the Cross been altogether overlooked, as connected with the doctrine of redemption, in accordance with 1 Cor. i. 30.

The Church may yet have to acquire by a fresh experience of the world's hostility a deeper sense of her oneness with Christ in sufferings and glory. The saying of the stout-hearted Godfrey de Bouillon in 1099, when offered the crown of Jerusalem, may eight centuries later come to express the feeling of the whole Church: "I desire not to wear a crown of gold where Christ wore a crown of thorns." Then the hour of her triumph will not tarry. To commend, in the meantime, the fulness of consolation and life which comes to us through the cross of atonement is the aim of the present volume, addressed as it is, more especially, to "the quiet ones in the land."

The examination in detail of the points advanced in the text is reserved for the Appendices, which moreover are interesting as (in the words of a German reviewer) " affording a glance into the workshop of the author." The historic and archæological value of No. VI. in particular will be seen to be very considerable; and, indirectly, its doctrinal value in relation to the history of the Lord's passion and resurrection, not less so. A general index and a few short notes included within square brackets have been added to the English edition. The former chronologically arranged in the interest of the general reader. Thanks to the great care exercised in the printing, the book has been preserved exceptionally free from errors for a work of such varied references.

M. J. E.

29*th Sept.*, 1877.

CONTENTS.

	PAGE
AUTHOR'S PREFACE	v
TRANSLATOR'S PREFACE	ix
MONOGRAMMATIC LITERATURE ON THE CROSS, AND THE SIGN OF THE CROSS	xvii
INTRODUCTION	xxvii

CHAP. I. THE CROSS IN THE PRE-CHRISTIAN AND EXTRA-CHRISTIAN RELIGIONS:
  A. AS THE SYMBOL OF BLESSING . . . 1
  B. AS THE SYMBOL OF THE CURSE . 46

CHAP. II. THE CROSS UPON CALVARY . . 85
  A. ACCORDING TO THE DECLARATIONS OF THE GOSPELS . . 88
  B. ACCORDING TO THE TESTIMONY OF THE APOSTOLIC DISCOURSES AND WRITINGS 99

CHAP. III. THE CROSS OF CHRIST IN THE PRE-CONSTANTINE CHURCH AND THEOLOGY 109

CHAP. IV. CONSTANTINE'S VISION OF THE CROSS, AS THE STARTING-POINT FOR THE SENSUOUS-EXTERNAL ADORATION OF THE CROSS IN THE MIDDLE AGES . . 136

CHAP. V. THE CROSS IN THE CHURCH OF THE MIDDLE AGES 152
  A. THE EXERTION OF THE *POWER* OF THE CROSS IN THE MISSIONARY ACTIVITY OF THE CHURCH 155
  B. THE GLORIFYING OF THE *MAJESTY* OF THE CROSS IN THE CULTUS OF THE CHURCH 161
  C. THE UNFOLDING OF THE *BEAUTY* OF THE CROSS IN ECCLESIASTICAL ART 180
  D. THE AFTER-EXPERIENCE OF THE *PAINS* OF THE CROSS IN ASCETICISM 227
  E. THE SOUNDING OF THE *DEPTHS* OF THE CROSS IN THEOLOGY, ESPECIALLY IN THE MYSTICAL THEOLOGY . . . 239

CHAP. VI. THE CROSS IN THE THEOLOGY AND CHURCH OF
THE REFORMATION 268
 A. THE SPIRITUALISING OF THE IDEA OF THE CROSS BY THE
 THEOLOGY OF THE REFORMATION 270
 B. THE TRANSFORMATION OF THE CULTIC USE OF THE CROSS, IN
 ACCORDANCE WITH THE REFORMATIONAL SPIRITUALISING
 OF ITS IDEA, AND THE CONTROVERSIES WITH ROMISH
 THEOLOGIANS RELATING THERETO 295
 C. THE IDEA OF THE CROSS IN MODERN ART, RELIGIOUS POETRY,
 AND SPECULATION 310
CHAP. VII. THE CROSS IN THE PRESENT AND FUTURE OF
THE CHURCH 346

APPENDIX.

EXCURSE I. ON THE PURELY ORNAMENTAL USE OF THE SYMBOL OF
THE CROSS UPON PRE-CHRISTIAN MONUMENTS . . 373

II. EARLIER AND LATER OPINIONS WITH REGARD TO THE
SYMBOLIC MEANING OF THE EGYPTIAN ANSATE CROSS 379

III. PARADISE, ACCORDING TO EARLIER AND MORE RECENT
OPINIONS 382

IV. AGAINST THE ASSERTION OF AN ENTIRE IRRELIGIOUS-
NESS ON THE PART OF CERTAIN NATIONS . . . 393

V. IS IT POSSIBLE THAT CHRIST WAS CRUCIFIED UPON A
THREE-ARMED CROSS? 401

VI. THE SINGLE EXTERNAL CIRCUMSTANCES AND PROCEED-
INGS IN THE WORK OF CRUCIFIXION 409

VII. HISTORY OF THE EXPOSITION OF EPHES. III. 18, AS COM-
PARED WITH JOB XI. 8, 9, AND PSALM CXXXIX. 8—10 419

VIII. JOHN SCOTUS ERIGENA AND FULBERT OF CHARTRES AS
SINGERS OF THE CROSS 426

IX. THE SIGN OF THE RETURNING SON OF MAN . 429

MONOGRAPHIC LITERATURE ON THE CROSS AND THE SIGN OF THE CROSS.[1]

COMPREHENSIVE MONOGRAPHIC DISCUSSIONS.

*† JAC. GRETSER, S. J., de Cruce Christi rebusque ad eam pertinentibus libri iv. Ingolstadii, 1598. 4to. Tom. ii., *ibid.*, 1600. Tom. iii., *ibid.*, 1605.

*† ———— de Cruce Christi, t. i., nunc tertia editione multis partibus auctus, ut ferme novum opus videri possit. Ingolst., 1608. 4to [Also in *J. Gretseri opp.*, Ratisbon., 1734 sqq., t. i.—iii.]

AND. BAUDIS (jun.), Crux Christi ex historiarum monumentis constructa. Viteb. [*i.e.*, Vienna], 1669. 4to.

CHR. LUD. SCHLICHTER, De cruce apud Judæos, Christianos, et Gentiles signo salutis. Halæ, 1733. 4to.

* WILLIAM HASLAM, The Cross and the Serpent, being a brief history of the triumph of the Cross through a long series of ages, in prophecy, types, and fulfilment. Oxford, 1849.

W. R. ALGER, History of the Cross, Boston (U.S.), 1858.

J. P. BERJEAU, History of the Holy Cross, London, 1863.

H. DANA WARD, History of the Cross, London, 1871.

W. C. PRIME, Holy Cross. A history of the Wood known as the True Cross. New York and London, 1877.

POLEMIC WRITINGS AGAINST AND IN FAVOUR OF THE CULTIC USE OF THE CROSS.

* GUILLAUME FAREL, Du vray usage de la croix de Jésus Christ, et de l'abus et de l'idololatrie commise autour d'icelle. Genève, 1560. 12mo.

[Nouv. édn., suivi de divers écrits du même auteur, Genève, 1865, 8vo.]

---

[1] Those writings marked with an asterisk are treated with more or less of detail, or are at least mentioned in the course of our dissertation. The works of Romish authors are indicated by a †.

xviii MONOGRAPHIC LITERATURE.

† MARTIN EISENGREIN (Convert from Protestantism, Vice-Chancellor of the Univ. of Ingoldstadt; † 1578), Von dem Zeichen des heil. Kreuzes, dass es ein recht christlicher, uralter, apostolischer, und in Gottes Wort gegründeter Gebrauch, auch nütz und gut sei. Ingolstadt, 1572. 4to.

† ALFONSUS CIACCONIUS, Libellus de signis sanctissimæ crucis, *i.e.*, de variis crucis apparitionibus, priscis et novis. Rom., 1591. 4to.

† ALANUS COPUS, De Cruce.

† ARNOLD. MERMANNUS († 1578), De veneratione ss. reliquiarum. Id. : De rogationibus. (Lovan., 1566.)

† AUGUSTIN. FIVIZANIUS, Libri iii. de more summo Pontifici crucem præferendi, Rom., 1592.

[These three are cited by Gretser, De cruce, t. i.]

* JOH. ARNDT, Iconographia : gründlicher und christlicher Bericht von Bildern, ihrem Ursprung, rechtem Gebrauch und Missbrauch im A. u. N. Test. . . . Von den Ceremonien oder Zeichen des Creutzes, auch von der äusserlichen Reverentz und Ehrerbietung gegen den hochgelobten Namen Jesu Christi, unseres einiger Erlösers und Ehrenkönigs, 1596. 4to.

* CONRAD. DECKER, De staurolatria Romana, libb. ii. Hanov., 1617. 8vo.

† JAC. BOSIUS (Mediolanensis, eques ord. Melitens., flor. circ. 1610), Crux triumphans et gloriosa. Antverp., 1617.

* EZECH. SPANHEIM, Discours sur la Croix de notre Seigneur. Genève, 1655.

* JOANN. DALLÆUS, Adversus Latinorum de cultus religiosi objecto lib. v., cont. argumenta contra Latinam de religioso crucium cultu traditionem propria. [Tom. ii., p. 704—789, ed. Genev., 1665. 4to.]

CHR. WILDVOGEL, De venerabili signo Crucis. Jenæ, 1690. 4to.

J. A. SCHMID, De crucis dominicæ per Helenam, Constantini matrem, inventione. Helmstad., 1714.

CH. GODOFR. RICHTER (G. H. Zeibich), Dissertatio de signo crucis e templis nostris eliminando. Viteb., 1735. 4to.

* J. JUL. CHR. F(ULDA), De crucis signaculo, Christianorum precum comite destinato. Lips., 1759. (Contained in VOLBEDING'S *Thes. commentatt. selectarum*, tom. i., p. 372 sqq.)

ARCHÆOLOGY OF THE CROSS OF CHRIST, OR OF THE HISTORY OF THE PASSION.

*† JUSTUS LIPSIUS, De cruce libb. iii., ad sacram profanamque historiam utiles, una c. notis, Antverp., 1595. 12mo. (Also Amstel., 1670; Vesal. [Wesel], 1675 ; Antverp., 1694, etc.)

MONOGRAPHIC LITERATURE. xix

† JOSEPH MARIA CARRACIOLI (Cleric. reg. Neapolit., † 1656), Dissert. de titulo crucis e sacræ et profanæ historiæ monumentis.

*† NICQUET, Titulus s. crucis, seu historia et mysterium tituli crucis. Par., 1648; Antverp., 1670. (Also contd. in the collection: *Authores de cruce*, tom. iv., Lugd. Bat., 1695. 12mo.)

* CLAUD. SALMASIUS († 1653), De cruce, Epistolæ iii. ad Bartholinum, in THOM. BARTHOLINI *diss. de latere Christi aperto*, Lugd. Bat., 1646.

* THOM. BARTHOLINUS (Medic. reg. Dan., † 1680), De cruce Christi hypomnemata iv. Havn., 1651; Amstel., 1670.

*† BARTHOLD. NIHUSIUS, De Cruce, epistola ad Thom. Bartholinum. Colon., 1647.

*† CORNEL. CURTIUS, Augustinianus, De clavis dominicis lib. Antverp., 1634.

[The three last also combined in the collection *Justi Lipsii et aliorum de Cruce opuscc.*, Vesal., 1675.]

HENR. MÜLLER, Historia passionis, crucifixionis et sepulturæ Domini nostri J. Christi, notis theologico-historico-criticis illustrata. Rostoch., 1661.

[See on this work O. KRABBE, *H. Müller und seine Zeit* Rostock, 1866.]

HENR. KIPPING († 1678), Lib. de cruce et cruciariis, in *Exercitatt* xxxv., Brem., 1679.

ANTON. BYNÆUS, De morte J. Christi commentarius amplissimus. Lib. iii. Amstel., 1691—1698. Also in German: Gekreutzigter Christus, etc. Cassel, 1701.

EMUNDUS MERILLIUS, J. C., Notæ philologicæ in passionem Christi. Roterod., 1693.

ANT. BALT. WALTHER, Juristisch-historische Betrachtungen über das Leiden und Sterben Jesu Christi, etc. Bresl. and Leipzig, 1738.

JOH. VAL. HENNEBERG, Philol.-histor. u. krit. Commentar üb. d. Geschichte der Leiden und des Todes Jesu. Leipz., 1822.

* J. H. FRIEDLIEB, Archäologie der Leidensgeschichte. Bonn, 1843.

JOH. WICHELHAUS, Versuch eines ausführlichen Commentars zu d. Geschichte des Leidens J. Christi nach den vier Evv. Halle, 1855 (never completed).

*† JOS. LANGEN, Die letzten Lebenstage Jesu. Freiburg in Br. 1864.

A. CH. A. ZESTERMANN, Die bildliche Darstellung des Kreuzes u. der Kreuzigung Christi. (Zwei Programme der Thomasschule.) Leipz., 1867, 1868. 4to.

*† PH. DEGEN, Das Kreuz als Strafwerkzeug und Strafe der Alten, Aachen, 1873. (Progr.) 4to.

*† CARL FRIEDRICH, Kritischer Rückblick auf die Literatur über die Geschichte und Archäologie des Kreuzes. (*Bonn Theol. Literaturbl.*, 1875, Nos. 17—19.)

ART-HISTORY OF THE CROSS AND CRUCIFIX.

*† GRETSERI de cruce, tom. iii., lib. 1.: *De numismat. crucigeris;* lib. ii.: *De inscriptionibus crucigeris.*
*† BARTHOLOM. RICCI, *S. J.* († 1613), Triumphus Jesu Christi crucifixi, cum iconibus martyrum (auct. A. Collaert). Antverp., 1614.
MENCKENII, Diatribe de monogrammate Christi. (In *Decad. dissertatt. Acad. Lips.*, 1734, iii., p. 85 sqq.)
† PHIL. DE VENUTIS (Venutus), De cruce Cortonensi diss. Liburni, 1731.
† DOM. GIORGI (Georgius), De monogrammate Christi Domini. Rom., 1738.
† PAOLO PACIAUDI, De veteri Christi crucifixi signo et antiquis crucibus, quæ Ravennæ sunt, dissert. (in Gori: *Symbolæ literariæ*, t. iii., 1748, p. 211).
† L. ANT. MURATORI., Diss. 21: de cruce Nolana (in *Antiqu. Ital.*, t. ii.)
JO. E. IMM. WALCH, De antiqua cruce stationali ærea inaurata diss. (in *Miscell. Lips. nov.*, vol. ix., p. 1, Lips., 1752).
† STEPH. BORGIA, De cruce Vaticana. Rom., 1779.
† ———, De cruce Veliterna. Rom., 1780.
* F. MUENTER, Sinnbilder und Kunstvorstellungen der alten Christen. Altona, 1825. (S. 68 ff.)
† DIDRON, Manuel d'Iconographie chrétienne. Paris, 1845.
† ———, Annales archéologiques, Par. 1844, sqq. (*passim*).
*† J. B. DE ROSSI, Inscriptiones christianæ urbis Romæ sept. sæculo antiquiores. Rom., 1857 sqq. Id.: De christianis titulis Carthaginiensibus. Par., 1858.—Id.: De christ. monumentis IXΘYN exhibentibus. Par., 1855. (Both originally in PITRA, *Spicilegium Solesmense*, tom. iii., iv.)
† GARRUCCI, Il crocifisso graffito in casa dei Cesari. Rom., 1857.
* FERD. BECKER, Das Spottcrucifix der römischen Kaiserpaläste aus dem Anf. des 3 Jahrhdts., erläutert. Bresl., 1863.
* E. AUS'M WEERTH, Das Siegeskreuz der byzantinischen Kaiser Constantin VII. Porphyrogenitus u. Romanus II., etc., etc., erläutert. Bonn, 1866. (Large fol.)
*† P. J. MUENZ, Archäol. Bemerkungen über das Kreuz, das Monogramm Christi, die altchristlichen Symbole, das Crucifix. Frankft. a. M., 1867.
*† J. STOCKBAUER, Kunstgeschichte des Kreuzes. Die bildl. Darstellung

des Erlösungstodes Christi im Monogramm, Kreuz, u. Crucifix. Schafihausen, 1870.
* F. PIPER, Der Baum des Lebens. (*Evangel. Kalend.* Jahrg., 1863, S. 17—94.)
LLEWELLYNN JEWITT, The Cross, in Nature and in Art. (Eight papers, illustrated, in the *Art Journal*, 1874.)
ALFRED RIMMER, Ancient Stone Crosses of England. Lond., 1875.
* RICHARD MORRIS, Legends of the Holy Rood; Symbols of the Passion and Cross. Poems, in old Engl. of the xi., xiv., and xv. Centuries. Lond., 1871.
* E. SCHROEDER, Van dem holte des hilligen Creuzes. Middle Low-Germ. poem; edited with Germ. introduction, notes, and glossary. Erlang., 1869.
*† A. BIRLINGER, Die deutsche Sage, Sitte, u. Literatur in Predigt und Legendenbüchern. (Austrian *Vierteljahrschr. f. Kath. Theologie*, Bd. xii., 1873, ii., iii.)
* A. MUSSAFIA, Sulla legenda del legno della croce. Vienna, 1870.
* A. FREYBE, Der Karfreitag in der deutschen Dichtung. Gütersloh, 1877. [A companion volume to MORRIS' *Legends of the Holy Rood.*]

ARCHÆOLOGY OF THE PRE-CHRISTIAN RELIGIOUS CROSS-SYMBOLS.

* L. DASSOVIUS, Signa crucis gentis Hebrææ, Kil. 1695.
J. CH. HARENBERG, Exercitatio de Crucis signo, symbolo salutis frontibus Israelitarum imponendo, ad Ezech. ix. 4. (In the *Bibl. Brem. hist.-philol. theol., Class.*, vi., fasc. 6.)
CHR. L. SCHLICHTER, De cruce apud Judæos, Christ., et Gentiles. (Vid. supra.)
*† M. LETRONNE, Examen archéologique de ces deux questions: 1. La croix ansée égyptienne a-t-elle été employée par les Chretiens d'Egypt pour exprimer le monogramme du Christ? 2. Retrouve-t-on ce symbole sur des monuments antiques étrangers à l'Egypte? in the *Mémoires de l'Acad. des Inscriptions et Belles-Lettres*, tome xvi., 1846, p. 236 sqq.
RAOUL-ROCHETTE, De la croix ansée, ou d'un signe qui lui ressemble considerée principalement dans ses rapports avec le symbole égyptien sur des monuments étrusques et asiatiques. (*Ib.*, p. 285 sqq.)
HUZARD, Observations sur l'origine et la signification du symbole appelé la croix ansée. (*Ib.*, tom. xvii.)
L. MUELLER, Ueber Sterne, Kreuze, und Kreise als religiöse Symbole der alten Culturvölker. Copenhagen, 1864.

* ED. RAPP, Das Labarum und der Sonnencultus. (In the *Jahrbb. des Vereins von Alterthumsfreunden im Rheinlande*. Double part, xxxix., xl.) Bonn, 1866.
* GABR. DE MORTILLET, Le Signe de la Croix avant le Christianisme. Paris, 1866.

  ERNST VON BUNSEN, Das Symbol des Kreuzes bei allen Nationen, und die Entstehung des Kreuz-Symbols der Chr. Kirche. Berlin, 1876.

DEVOTIONAL AND THEOSOPHIC-MYSTIC LITERATURE.[1]

* JOANN. CHRYSOSTOMI de Cruce et Latrone homil. duo. (*Opp.*, t. ii., p. 402—421, ed. Montf.)
* ———— de Cœmeterio et Cruce. (*Ib.*, p. 396 sqq.)
* AMBROSII de Cruce Serm. 55 et 56. (*Opp.*, t. iii., p. 280 sqq.)
* LEONIS MAGN. Serm. xix. de passione Domini. (In MIGNE'S *Patrologia*, Ser. i., t. 54, p. 313—384.)
* ———— Serm. de persecutione et cruce ferenda, s. de quadrages. Serm. ix. (*Ib.*, p. 294 sqq.)
* NICETÆ Paphlag., Orat. in exaltat. ven. Crucis. (In COMBEFIS, *Auctar. Bibl. patrum novissim.* Par. 1672, i., p. 440 sqq.)

  Pseudochrysostomi Homilia in venerab. ac vivificam crucem. (In *Opp. Chrys.*, ed. Montf., t. ii., p. 820 sqq.)
* Variorum orationes encomiasticæ de inventione S. Crucis, item de exaltatione et de adoratione S. Crucis. (Alexand. monach., Georg. Hamartolos, Sophron. Hierosol., Andreas Cretens., Joseph. Thessalonicens., etc.) [In GRETSERI de Cruce, t. ii.]
* RHABANUS MAURUS, De laudibus S. Crucis. (*Opp.*, t. i., p. 133—294, ed. Migne.)
* Pseudo-Anselmi De mensuratione Crucis.
* BONAVENTURA, Lignum vitæ. (*Opp.*, t. v., p. 393 sqq., ed. Venet., 1754.)
* BERTHOLD OF REGENSBURG, Sermon : Von dem hêren kriuze. (PFEIFFER, *Berthold*, etc. 1862, Bd. i., S. 537—548.)
* ANGELA OF FOLIGNO, Theologia Crucis. ("Die Theologie des Kreuzes J. Christi"—in G. TERSTEGEN, *Auserlesene Lebensbeschreibungen heiliger Seelen*, Bd. ii., St. 5, K. 13.)

  Comp. her *Vita* by Arnoldus (in AA. SS. Boll., t. i., 4 Jan.), and specially her *Passus spirituales*, etc., c. 10, therein given. Also *B. Angela de Fulignio, ostendens veram viam, qua possumus sequi vestigia Redemptoris*. Colon., 1601. Also, Der heil. Angela v. Foligno Geschichte und Unterweisungen in deutscher Bearbeitung von Lammertz. Cöln., 1851.

---

[1] We confine ourselves to the mention of such works as expressly indicate by their title their relation to the cross, taken in a material or a purely spiritual-mystical sense.

* THOMÆ A KEMPIS, Serm. de cruce quotidie tollenda in relig. assumpta. (Sermon. ad Novit., part. iii.)
  [Serm., tom. i., p. 67—76, ed. Sommal.]
* ——— Concio seu meditatio de cruce Jesu, quam pro nobis ipse portavit ; *item*, De merito dominicæ passionis et dignitate s. crucis. (Concion. s. meditatt. Nos. 23 and 24.)
  [Tom. ii., p. 205 sqq., 208 sqq., ed. Somm.]
* HIERNON. SAVONAROLA, Il trionfo della Croce, 1497. Triumphus crucis sive de veritate fidei, libb. iv., recens in lucem edit. Lugd. Bat., 1633. 12mo.
* M. LUTHER, Feine christl. Gedanken der alten heil. Väter und Lehrer der Kirche, dass ein Christ das Kreuz, so ihm von Gott aufgelegt ist, mit Geduld tragen solle. 1530. (*Erlang. edn.*, Bd. lxiv., S. 298 ff.)
* ———, Sermonen von Kreuz und Leiden. (*Erl. Ausg.*, xvii., 40 ff. ; xx., 309 ff.)
* ———, Predigten am Kreuzerfindungstage und am Kreuzerhebungstage. (*E. A.*, xv., 333 ff. ; 455 ff.)
* PH. MELANCTHON, Loc. de calamitatibus et de cruce, et de veris consolationibus. (In the Loci comm. tert. ætat., *Corp. Ref.*, t. xxi., p. 934 sqq.)
* JOH. BRENTIUS, Etlich Tractetli (1528): Wie das Holz des Kreuzes behauen und am weichsten angegriffen werden soll, u. s. f. (In J. HARTMANN, *Joh. Brenz, Leben und ausgewählte Schriften*, S 322 ff.)
  [On other works of Brenz, Urban. Rhegius, etc., falling under this head, see Chap. VI., pp. 286—290.]
* JOH. CALVINUS, De crucis tolerantia, quæ est pars abnegationis sui. (De souffrir patiemment la croix, qui est une partie de renoncer à nous mesmes) : *Instit. Relig. Christ.*, lib. iii., ch. 8, ed. 1559 sqq.
* PETRI MARTYRIS, De cruce et afflictionibus perferendis. (*Loci comm. theolog.*, Basil., 1580. Loc. xii., tom. i., p. 1193—1212.)
  LUD. LAVATER (Bullinger's Son-in-law, † 1586), De crucis tolerantia. Tigur., seq. ann.
  LEONARD. CULMANN, An crux expediat vel noceat (in loc. Joh. xvi. 7 : Expedit ut ego vadam). Norimb., 1550. 8vo.
† JOHN MARSHALL, Treatise of the Cross. Antv., 1564.
† ———, A Reply to Mr. Calfhill's Blasphemous Answer against the Treatise of the Cross. Lovan., 1566.
  A. GREYFENBERG, Die Lehre vom Creutz der Christen in 4 Haubtartikel geteilet und zu Wittenberg in fünf Predigten ausgelegt. Wittenberg, 1567.
  CHRIST. VISCHER, Trostschrift, wie sich ein Christ in allerlei Creutz trösten solle. Schmalkalden, 1570.

M. SCULTETUS, Warer Christen Creutz. In diesen kümmerlichen Zeiten allen hochbetrübten vnd vilgeplagten Creutzträgern zu Unterricht und Trost beschrieben. Zerbst, 1592. 8vo.

† JAC. GRETSERI, Hortus S. Crucis. Ingolst., 1610, 1630, etc.

† ———, *Signa crucis*, d. i. ein lustiger und nützlicher Tractat von dem Zeichen des heil. Creutzes, aus dem Lat. verdeutscht durch Carolum Stengelium. Ingolst., 1612.

† MATTH. TYMPIUS, Creutz-Fähnlein. Münster, 1619. 4to.

JOH. HEERMANN († 1647 at Lissa), *Crux Christi* oder die schmerzreiche Marterwoche unseres Heilands, 1618. (New edn., Ruppin, 1861.)

———, *Heptalogus Christi*, oder die sieben Worte am Kreuz, 1619. (Berlin, 1856.)

THOM. DRAXONIS (Draxe, or Drake, of Warwick, † 1616), Synopsis consolatoria, s. spiritualia et selectissima Consilia, remedia, et lenimenta adversus crucem. Francof., 1618. 8vo.

CHARLES DRELINCOURT († 1669), Le triomphe de l'Eglise sous la Croix. Genève, 1630.

† LOUIS GRANDIS, Les perfections de Dieu connues par la Croix. Par. 1642.

* JOACHIM BETKIUS, Mysterium crucis oder Erinnerung derer Geheimnissen und Krafft des Creutzes Christi. Berlin, 1637. Frankf., 1646 and 1647.

J. J. RUED, Seelen-Apoteck, oder Labsal und Erquickung in allerhand Creutz und Trübsalen. Nürnberg, 1653.

JOH. HEMMING, Jesu Christi meditatio sacra de passione Christi simulque de crucis ligno et signo eiusque usu et abusu. Han., 1657. 4to.

AND. DAN. HABICHHORST († 1704), De crucifixione Christi satisfactoria in medio malefactorum facta, ex ratione Is. liii., Ps. xxii., etc. Gryphiswald., 1681. 4to.

* CHR. SCRIVER, Seelenschatz, oder von der menschlichen Seele hoher Würde, tiefem und kläglichem Sündenfalle, Busse und Erneuerung durch Christum, göttlichem heiligen Leben, vielfältigem Kreuze und Trost im Kreuz, etc., etc. Magdeburg, 1681, 1692. Magd. and Leipzig, 1737, and frequently.

* PH. GOTTL. SPENER, Das Kreuz. (Sermons on John xvi. 16—23, in "Evangelischer Glaubenstrost aus den göttlichen Wohlthaten," etc. Frankfurt, 1694.)

J. QUIRSFELD, Geistliches Myrrhengärtlein, versetzt mit 50 traurigen Cypressen, worunter die geängstigte Seele in allerlei Creutz und Widerwärtigkeiten mit Christo ihr tröstliches Gesprch häält. Leipzig, 1696.

Geistliche Kranken-Apothek, d. i. christliche Unterweisung, wie Kranke und Sterbende ihr Kreuz geduldig tragen können. Stuttgart, 1703.

CH. A. HAUSEN, *Theologia paracletica generalis et specialis*, oder gründliche Erklärung von der Christen Kreuz und Trost in Predigten. 2 vols. Dresden, 1706, 1723.

LUCK. STOECKEL, Creutzschule der gläubigen Kinder Gottes. Oppenheim, 1611.

* PHIL. KEGEL, Geistliche Kampfschul, welcher maassen ein christl. Ritter die Mühseligkeit dieses Lebens erdulden soll, etc. Leipzig, 1616.

THOM. TILANDRI, *Schola crucis et lucis* in etlichen Predigten. Rostock, 1616. 4to.

BEN. HEFTERI, Schola crucis, Antverp., 1629.

———, Via regia crucis, *ib.*, 1654.

* VALENTIN WUDRIAN, Schola crucis. Creuzschul. Stralsund, 1641; Bremen, 1641, (and often elsewhere). Also Latin : Schola crucis et tessera Christianismi, Lüneburg, 1666.

* HEINR. MUELLER, Creutz, Buss, und Betschule, vorgestellet von David im 143 Psalm und der Gemeine Christi zu St. Marien in Rostock in zweijährigen Bett-Stunden geöffnet. Rostock, 1661. 12mo. Third edn., *ib.* 1665. (Also republished there 1671, 1674; Frankf., 1668, 1671, 1674, 1687, and frequently besides.)

* JOH. OLEARIUS, Christliche Geduldschule sammt herzerquickendem Troste. Halle, 1668.

FRANCISCI SIMEONIS, *Gymnasium Crucis*. Creutzschule, gerichtet auf die sonntägliche Evangelia. Hamburg, 1670.

JOH. FEINLER, Wahrer Christen Creutz-Schul. Naumburg, 1676.

JOH. WEIDNER, Gläubiger Kinder Gottes Kreuzschule. Augsburg, 1731.

* MAGN. FRIEDR. ROOS, Kreuzschule, oder Anweisung zu einem christlichen Verhalten unter dem Leiden. Tübingen, 1779. Stuttg., 1857. (7th edn., 1875.)

* MYSTÈRE DE LA CROIX affligeante et consolante, mortifiante et vivifiante, humiliante et triomphante, de Jésus-Christ et de ses Membres. Par un disciple de la Croix de Jésus. 1732. Nouv. édit. Lausanne, 1791. (German : Das Geheimniss des Kreuzes Jesu Christi und seiner Glieder. Leipzig, 1782.)

* JOH. FRIEDR. V. MEYER, Das Kreuz Christi. *Blätter f. höh. Wahrheit*, Bd. vii. (Smaller collection, Bd. ii., S. 438 ff.)

* GOTTFR. MENKEN, Ueber die eherne Schlange und das symbol. Verhältniss derselben zur Person und Geschichte Jesu Christi. 1812. (Gesamm. Schriften, Bd. vi., S. 351 ff. Bremen, 1858.)

MONOGRAPHIC LITERATURE.

* FRANZ THEREMIN, Das Kreuz Christi, 4 vols. Berlin, 1828—1841.
* F. W. KRUMMACHER, Der Leidende Christus. Ein Passionsbuch. Bielefeld, 1854. (Also English: The Suffering Saviour. 8th edition.)
* B. A. LANGBEIN, Das Wort vom Kreuze. Sermons delivered in the years 1857—1860. 4 vols. Leipzig.

E. SCHEELE, Das Kreuz J. Christi. Passions- und Osterpredigten. Halle, 1857.

(Under this head also fall the numerous published discourses of more recent times on "The Seven Words of Jesus upon the Cross," by F. Arndt, 1842; F. W. Langer, 1842; Ph. Bridel, Lausanne, 1851; W. Löhe, 1859; H. Dalton, 1871; C. J. Vaughan, Lond., 1875, etc.)

CÆSAR MALAN, The True Cross. London, 1838. Latest edn., 1872.

E. DE PRESSENSÉ, The Mystery of Suffering. Lond., 1869.

D. GRESWELL, *Colloquia Crucis.* Lond., 1871.

* A. B. MACKAY, The Glory of the Cross. 2nd edn. Lond., 1877.
* R. M'CHEYNE EDGAR, The Philosophy of the Cross. Lond., 1874. 8vo.

INTRODUCTION.

> "Faith of the cross, thou only combinest, in one
> Wreath, the twofold palm at once of meekness and strength."

IT was a phenomenon pertaining to the outward circle of the salutary operations of Christianity, in which Schiller thus recognised the unique character of Christianity itself. The proud spectacle of the Knights of the Hospital of St. John, adorned and defended by the sign of redemption, taught him to understand the profound combination—nowhere else recurring in history—of lowliness and majesty, by which our religion has for nearly two thousand years celebrated its triumphs. More deeply still would he have comprehended our religion—and that not as a "combining of humility and strength" displayed once for all, but as one constantly and powerfully exerting itself—if he had been able to derive his knowledge of it, not from an admiring reflection upon the deeds of those knights, wrought under the banner and in the armour of the cross, but from a believing contemplation of the Crucified One Himself, and from a loving self-absorption in the mystery of His sufferings. The fact that this latter way remained closed to him, affects not, or not essentially, the truth of that which he did learn. Christianity presents a synthesis of weakness and strength, of dying and living, of self-humiliation and exaltation, such as has never been attained in any other religion. And the cross is the emblem of this its peculiar essence, an emblem of so much the more apt significance, and so much the more effective operation, in proportion as the historic fact which imparts to it its significance, is seen to be of a more serious and real nature, and the more perfectly all poetic caprice and fantastic combination has been excluded in raising it to be the symbol of that religion which is to hold sway over the world.

The cross is the deeply significant symbol of the Christian faith, and yet religious significance attaches to it not merely within the bounds of Christianity. It is not so exclusively an emblem of faith in Christ as to appear, beyond the sphere thereof, only in the form of ordinary embellishment, as a meaningless ornament or an unimportant thing of chance. The cross plays an important part as a religious symbol, even in the history of the pre-Christian and extra-Christian religions. We meet with it under various modifications, alike of its external form and character as also of its import, among the extra-Christian nations of antiquity as of the present day, of the Old as of the New World. Rude and barbarous peoples of the torrid as of the temperate zones, and representatives of almost every stage of heathen civilisation—Greeks and Romans, dwellers by the Nile, as by the Ganges, Godavery, and Indus, aborigines of the new discovered North, Central, and South America, and islanders of the South Sea—have placed this mysterious symbol upon their monuments. Only in rarer cases can a purely mundane (*profan*), significance be shown to attach to these cruciform signs which adorn the monuments of heathendom. The entire absence of any kind of religious import appears in the case of most of them more difficult of supposition, than their destination to some kind or other of cultic end—though this end may often remain scarcely discernible, or may in the course of time have fallen into oblivion, and the cruciform figure in question may thus have sunk down almost to a mere ornament, or garniture without significance.[1] Nay, a certain general identity of nature in the religious significance of these extra-Christian

---

[1] See Appendix I. : ON THE PURELY ORNAMENTAL USE OF THE SYMBOL OF THE CROSS UPON PRE-CHRISTIAN MONUMENTS.

cross-symbols with that of our religion is susceptible of proof. They are either, as in the majority of cases, emblematic of BLESSING, and thus express a religious consciousness directed positively to the Divine, and thence beneficially affected and satisfied; or they are symbols of the CURSE, and thus serve only to express a consciousness disposed in a negatively religious manner, one which remains unreconciled and obdurate under the experience of the Divine wrath against sin. The two forces, that of the curse and that of the blessing, that of death and that of life, of wrath and of grace, brought into immediate oneness in the Cross of Christ, regularly diverge from each other in the typical phenomena of the pre-Christian religious life; yea, they appear almost always abruptly severed, and opposed the one to the other, so that it is *either* divinely blessing (agathodæmonic) powers, *or* hellishly condemning and destroying ones (cacodæmonic, typhonic), which seem to manifest themselves therein. A shadowy expectation that the place of the curse might and would one day become the place where the fountain of blessing and salvation is opened for the suffering, God-estranged humanity, does not appear clothed in any other form than in one extremely obscure and indefinite, either in Heathendom or even in Judaism. To the height of a clear prophetic prescience it does not appear developed even in the case of the most enlightened men of God under the Old Covenant.

A preparatory consideration of these varied pre-Christian forms and characters of the cross as a religious symbol is seen to be the more indispensably necessary, in proportion as they have frequently been uncritically reviewed, and inasmuch as unfounded conjectures—whether in favour of, or adverse to, the absolute value of Christianity and its character as a revelation—have not seldom been attached to them. From the time that the erratic philosopher of Norwich, Sir Thomas Browne (b. 1605, d. 1682),—by means of his *Religio Medici* (1642), and his *Enquiries into Vulgar and Common Errors* (1646), one of the most influential pioneers of the British Scepticism or Deism—in his quixotic treatise, *The

Garden of Cyrus (1658),[1] presented an uncritical combination of an incredibly large number of cruciform figures, from heathen and Jewish sources, and, half with mystic, half with sceptical intent, sought to demonstrate everywhere the presence of his favourite symbol of the Quincunx

* *
*
* *

in such wise that, in the words of S. T. Coleridge, he would find "quincunxes in heaven above, quincunxes in earth below, quincunxes in the mind of man, quincunxes in tones, in optic nerves, in roots of trees, in leaves, in everything,"[2] from that time a great deal, even if not excessively much that is untenable and one-sided, has been written upon the sign of the cross, as this appears beyond the bounds of Christendom. Some, after the example of Gibbon, the historian of "The Decline and Fall of the Roman Empire," have censured with bitter scorn as absurd and useless the seeking of cruciform figures "in almost every object of art or nature," on the part of the Church Fathers and later Christian authors. With others, as in the case of the English clergyman William Haslam (1849), the American W. R. Alger (1858), the French writer De Mortillet (1866), the danger of an over-hasty apologetic tendency, carried to the length of the fantastic, has not been wholly avoided in this domain. Haslam, for example, in all earnestness represents the cross, too, as being revealed to our first parents immediately after the fall, along with the promise of the ultimate victory of the seed of the woman over the serpent, and as the means of this victory. He speaks of a formal prophecy of the cross within and without the sphere of Old Testament revelation, and maintains that the cross was, in these predictions of the first age, just as now in Christendom, "the external sign of a

[1] [Originally appended to his *Hydrotaphia, or Urn Burial* (1658).]
[2] Compare the eighth edition of the wonderful book, "The Garden of Cyrus; or the Quincuncial Lozenge, or Network Plantations of the Ancients, artificially, naturally, mystically considered," contained in the new edition of the works of Sir Thomas Browne. (Bohn's edition, London 1852, vol. ii.)

hidden mystery, connected with Divine promise." Noah was acquainted with the cross as a sacred sign before the time of the dispersion of the nations—yea, even before the flood. Even Adam was acquainted with the cross; even to him there was communicated by the Almighty a knowledge of this sacred sign.[1] In opposition to such extravagances of a mystically trifling uncritical apologetics, the pre-Christian sign of the cross is scarcely at all mentioned in many writings in which we should expect to meet with it; *e.g.*, in the well-known work of H. Lüken, "The Traditions of the Human Race, or the Primitive Revelation of God among the Heathen," (2 Aufl., 1869), in which the subject is only once touched upon, and then by no means discussed in the thorough manner and with the amount of critical consideration which it merits. Others, as the investigations of the French Academicians Letronne and Rochette, hereafter to be frequently cited, the meritorious dissertation of Ed. Rapp, on "The Labarum and the Sun Worship," and the learned programmes of Dr. A. Ch. A. Zestermann on "The Figurative Representation of the Cross or the Crucifixion of Christ,"[2] call attention to only a part of the various forms and relations under which the Cross plays a part in the history of pre-Christian civilisation and religion; thus indirectly themselves invite to a complementing of that which they present, in the interest of a general comprehension in one of the whole of the examples falling under the point of view of the pre-Christian religious representation of the Cross.

Such general review must therefore prepare the way for our

---

[1] Rev. W. HASLAM, *The Cross and the Serpent, being a brief History of the Triumph of the Cross through long Series of Ages*, etc. (Oxford, 1849,) p. 885, p. 127. Of a like character, but more sober, Rev. W. R. ALGER, *History of the Cross*, Boston, 1858, as also GABRIEL DE MORTILLET, *Le Signe de la Croix avant le Christianisme*, Paris, 1866. With the latter, of whose interesting and beautifully illustrated work we shall speak more fully in Appendix I., many points of agreement are presented by F. DE ROUGEMONT, *Le peuple primitif*, i. 267 sqq.

[2] i. Abth., *Das Kreuz vor Christus* (48 pp. 4to). ii. Abth., *Die Kreuzigung bei den Alten* (52 pp. 4to), Leipzig, 1867, 1868. Upon this work of ZESTERMANN the Aachen Realschulprogramm of Dr. PH. DEGEN is almost entirely based.

subsequent contemplation of the Cross within the limits of Christendom, historically and in relation to the philosophy of history. Of the two lines of the representation of the symbol of redemption, the positively and the negatively religious, or the agathodæmonic and the cacodæmonic—until the time of Christ constantly diverging lines—we proceed, in the first place, to the nearer examination of the former.

THE CROSS OF CHRIST.

I.

The Cross in the Pre-Christian and Extra-Christian Religions.

A. *AS THE SYMBOL OF BLESSING.*

AS a religious positive symbol, one indicative of salvation and blessing, the cross would seem to exist in the case of a great number of heathen nations of the Old World and the New. Yet the more special significance of the different cruciform emblems of heathendom remains to a great extent still veiled in darkness, and gives rise to various questions and doubts. And so far as they cannot, as here and there in India, in the South Sea Islands, and in the New World, be regarded as traceable to the influence of Christian ideas, they at all events appear as *purely cosmical* emblems, serving for the representation of the mere powers of nature, or as symbols of idolatrous worship, and bear no sort of mark of revelation, no sign of having their home in the suprasensuous world.

As belonging to the class of the inadequate and external rudimentary ordinances of the world (Gal. iv. 3, 9), appears especially the cruciform religious emblem of the ancient EGYPTIANS, the so-called Ansate cross (*crux ansata*), improperly called also the "Key of the Nile,"—a term the signification of which is liable to be misapprehended. (Figs. 1, 2, 3.)

Fig. 1.    Fig. 2.   Fig. 3.

Those Christian Egyptians living towards the close of the fourth century who were versed in the hieroglyphics, when consulted as to the meaning of this sign, attached to it the signification of "the life to come." Such was their judgment as given on the occasion of the discovery of this sign, together with other sacred hieroglyphs, upon the stones of the temple of Serapis, destroyed in the time of Bishop Theophilus (390 or 391)—a discovery which had excited the astonishment of the Christian multitude engaged upon the work of destruction.[1] But this metaphysical signification of the symbol can certainly only be regarded as a derived one, belonging to a later more spiritualised phase in the development of the ancient Egyptian religion. The more modern Egyptology, from the time of Champollion, has asserted for the hieroglyph of the Ansate cross simply the signification of "Life" (Earl. Egypt. and Copt. *anch*).[2]

But even this seems to have sprung from a still more concrete and sensuous meaning; perhaps that which the hieroglyph in question had as a symbol of Osiris or the sun. According to Macrobius, the Egyptians, when they would hieroglyphically depict Osiris, were "wont to draw the picture of a staff with an eye above it; because the ancients called the sun the eye of God."[3] And for the fact that the so-depicted sun-god Osiris was not essentially different from

[1] Socrates, *H. E.*, v. 17. Compare the shorter account of Sozom., vii. 15; Theodoret, v. 22; Ruffinus, ii. 26, 29.

[2] Uhlemann, *Handbuch der Ges. ägypt. Alterthumskunde*, i., "Gesch. der Aegyptologie." S. 108 f. Cp. Letronne, *La Croix Ansée*, in the *Mém. de l'Académie des Inscriptions*, T. xvi. (1846), pt. ii., p. 236; as also Raoul Rochette, *ibid.*, p. 286 sqq.

[3] Macrob., *Saturn.*, i. 20: Osirim Ægyptii ut solem esse asserant, quoties hieroglyphicis literis suis exprimere volunt, insculpunt sceptrum inque eo speciem oculi exprimunt, etc.

Serapis—and that, accordingly, the frequent occurrence of the sign in question upon the walls of the Serapeion must have referred to none other than the god of this temple— we have a direct testimony in Marcianus Capella.[1] Of the single constituent parts of the mystic symbol, the ring or circle may in itself have been designed to indicate the sun— as is indeed expressly testified by Clemens Alexandrinus.[2] The longer perpendicular lines may have designated the perpendicularly descending rays of the noonday sun; the shorter horizontal line beneath the circle, the horizontal rays of the rising sun of morning and the setting sun of evening.[3] Placed in the hand of a human figure, the sign might denote the divine dignity of the person; conferred upon a king, it might imply that eternal life, or exaltation into the blissful communion of the gods, was granted to him. The mere sign T, moreover, without any image of the sun resting upon it, occurs upon the Egyptian monuments, *e.g.*, on the breast of a mummy in the British Museum; sometimes also as growing out of the heart of a man, and apparently denoting the hope of a divine reward or of the life to come. It must, however, be remembered that the foregoing attempt at interpretation is only one among many; and we do not venture to characterise it as an absolutely certain and trustworthy one. Egyptian hieroglyphic art possesses also several other cruciform signs, which—alike because no deeper mystic signification attaches to them, as because they are met with much less frequently in the hieroglyphic texts than the almost constantly recurring Ansate cross—can scarcely be reckoned as among those crosses of the ancient world which have a religious significance, although some of them express

[1] *De Nuptiis Mercurii et Philologiæ*, ii. 191:
   Te Serapin Nilus Memphis veneratur Osirim,
   Dissona sacra Mithram Ditemque ferumque Typhonem, etc.

[2] *Strom.*, v. 4, p. 657, Pott. ἥλιον γοῦν γράψαι βουλόμενοι κύκλον ποιοῦσι.

[3] So at least Rapp, *Das Labarum*, etc., S. 123 f., with whom Zestermann, i., S. 7, agrees. Others, indeed, explain the Ansate cross in an essentially different manner; cp. Appendix II.: EARLIER AND LATER OPINIONS WITH REGARD TO THE SYMBOLIC MEANING OF THE EGYPTIAN ANSATE CROSS.

in a very distinct manner the form of the sacred symbol of Christianity. Such are Figs. 4, 5, 6, 7, 8; this last a deter-

minative, signifying "town," "inhabited place." Only one of these figures, the symbol of the Nilometer (Νειλομέτριον, Νειλοσκοπεῖον) (Fig. 9), consisting of an upright bar with four cross-bars, appears to have expressed a deeper religious conception. This sign, occurring as the attribute of the god Ptah, appears to have been symbolic of the fourfold character of the world's zones and of the elements, but at the same time also of the four stages of the spiritual life and of the soul's migrations (metempsychosis).[1] Taken in itself, indeed, it was certainly only a simplifying figurative representation of those pillars erected in the Nile at different places, *e.g.*, at Syene, Elephantine, Koptos, Memphis, Mendes, Chois, etc., portioned off into cubits, feet, and inches, by means of which the rising or falling of the waters of the sacred stream was observed. It is indicative of the peculiarly Egyptian character of this symbol that it does not recur with other nations of antiquity; while the Ansate cross, though ordinarily in a form differing in one respect or other from the Egyptian type, appears as pretty generally diffused throughout the art symbolics of the nations of Citerior Asia as well. For the opposite opinion of Letronne, who sought to show that the *crux ansata* was an exclusively Egyptian symbol, was presently refuted by Rochette with superior archæological learning.[2]

As concerns the cruciform emblems of the ancient religions

---

[1] Compare as regards these hieroglyphic signs, H. Brugsch, *Hieroglyphische Grammatik*, Leipzig, 1872. On the signification of the Nilometer according to Passalaqua, cp. Carrière, *Die Kunst im Zusammenhang der Culturentwicklung*, etc., i. 199.

[2] *De la Croix Ansée*, etc., as before, pp. 288 sqq.

of CITERIOR ASIA, among these predominates the figure (Fig. 10), with the subordinate forms (Figs. 11, 12, 13), etc.

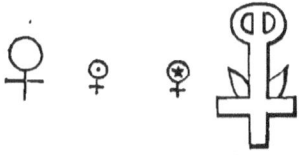

Fig. 10. Fig. 11. Fig. 12. Fig. 13.

This appears, notwithstanding the circular form of its ring, and the little distance between the under edge thereof and the horizontal line of the cross, pretty similar to the Egyptian Ansate cross. Egyptian monuments, too, on some occasions represent entirely the figure of Citerior Asia, as conversely in single rare cases there is found upon monuments of Citerior Asia the Egyptian form (Fig. 14). Moreover, the sign ♀

Fig. 14.

presents itself amidst entirely similar circumstances and surroundings as in the figurative representations of the Egyptians. Gods carry it in their hands; especially does the Assyrian Venus, or Istar, standing upon a lion, bear the emblem (in the third and most complicated of the above secondary forms) in her left hand, while with her right she supports herself upon a staff with crescent-shaped handle.[1] Upon a Babylonian cylinder it is held forth or presented to the figure of a king or god, by a man in the posture of adoration. Here and there the separation of the upper and lower elements of the figure recur: thus upon a stele from Khorsabad, where an eagle-headed man holds in his right hand the ring, in his left the cross or Tau.[2] From this the essential identity of the sign with the Egyptian one becomes evident, even as to its mystic signification, which assuredly, even with the people of the Euphrates, the Phœnicians, etc.,

---

[1] Compare the well-known representation of the Assyrian Venus (of Pterium) in Layard's *Nineveh and its Remains*, Fig. 82 ; also, *e.g.*, in Riehm's *Handwörterbuch des bibl. Alterthums*, Art. "Astarte" (S. 113).

[2] Botta, *Monumens de Ninevé*, vol. ii., p. 158; cp. Layard, Fig. 23 (Riehm, Fig. B, S. 114).

was no other than that of "Life." Specially, and for the most part indeed, does this sign seem to have been consecrated in the religions of Citerior Asia to the goddess of love and fruitfulness, that Babylonian-Assyrian Istar, the Phœnician Astarte, the mother of the gods in the worship of Asia Minor —the Artemis too of Ephesus, for example. The well-known ♀ use of the form (Fig. 15) as a sign of the planet Venus

Fig. 15.

has also in any case arisen from this primitive religious symbolisation, on the part of the eastern nations, with regard to the goddess of love; whether the origin of this astronomical semiology is to be sought in Egypt or on the banks of the Euphrates.[1]

Besides this ansate cruciform figure, which—in distinction from the Egyptian Ansate cross, and with reference to its ordinary use among astronomers and almanac makers, even in the present day, as a symbol of Venus—we may speak of as Venus' looking-glass, the monuments of the Assyrians, Persians, Phœnicians, and peoples of Asia Minor, display a yet simpler cruciform figure (Figs. 16, 17, 18, 19) as a religious

Fig. 16.   Fig. 17.   Fig. 18.   Fig. 19.

emblem, occurring partly alone, partly in combination with the other. It is the sacred sun-wheel with the four radii, which are depicted either with their circumference, or separate from it in the figure of an equal-armed cross—similar to the Maltese cross—the emblem of the all-pervading and all-quickening power of the sun, glittering upon the breasts of images representing Assyrian kings, sometimes borne as an ear-ornament by persons of royal rank, frequently

---

[1] Compare in general Raoul Rochette, in the dissertation against Letronne, as before referred to, *Mém. de l'Acad. des Inscriptions*, etc. On the work of Fel. Lajard, *Observations sur l'Origine et la Signification du Symbole appellé la Croix Ansée*, Par. 1847, which belongs to this part of our subject, but is to be received with caution, cp. Appendix II., No. 6.

also (on monuments of Nineveh and Persepolis) placed in connection with the winged figure of a ferver, which then appears depicted within the four-spoked sun-wheel.[1] From the Babylonian-Assyrian cultus-tradition and art, this symbol proceeded eastward to the Persians, westward to the Phœnicians, by which latter it was transplanted partly to Asia Minor, partly to the islands of the Mediterranean. Thus a gigantic cross of this kind, hewn in the solid rock on the island of Malta, as likewise some similar ones on Gozzo, is said not to date from the time of the Knights of St. John, but to have a Phœnician (!) origin.[2] Coins from Marathus in Phœnicia, from Cyprus, Cilicia, Lycia, etc., present, in addition to the Asiatic Ansate cross, though more rarely than this last-mentioned one, the equal-armed cross.[3] Upon coins of the Philistine Gaza, upon Phœnician vases and stone monuments, frequently in Asia Minor,—yea, according to Schliemann, upon several of the vases of Hissarlik, belonging to the supposed "Trojan antiquities," there occurs (in addition to these) that cruciform emblem which we shall farther on learn to know as the sacred Swastika (Sçavistica) sign among the nations of Farther Asia on the one hand, and the Etruscans and Celts on the other, and which, like the sign (Fig. 20), ┼ is perhaps to be regarded

Fig. 20.

as a simplification or abbreviating variation of the sun-wheel (Fig. 21).   ⊕

Fig. 21.

As a third cross-shaped symbol of Assyrian or Babylonian origin may the strange mystic miraculous-tree be regarded, which is to be found engraven upon numerous monuments of

---

[1] Layard, *Nineveh*, Fig. 79 a, b, cp. Figs. 11, 59.
[2] So also [Walter Wilkins] the learned writer of the article on "the pre-Christian Cross" in the *Edinburgh Review*, Jan. 1870 (p. 234), who, however, is often uncritical, and given to over-statement.
[3] See the representatives in Rochette, *l. c.* Pl. ii., No. 1—19, and in Rapp, *Das Labarum*, etc. Taf. ii. Cp. also Perrot, *Voyage en Bithynie*, etc., Pl. ix.

ancient Nineveh, alike in the cylinder, as in the embroidery of the garments of human figures.[1]

Fig. 22.

Inasmuch as there is characteristically apparent, amidst the manifold tastefully and laboriously wrought ornamentations of this peculiar figure (Fig. 22), a threefold crossing of the perpendicularly rising stem by horizontal branches extending to the right and to the left, it displays a certain distant resemblance to the Nilometer, which presents an upright rod crossed by four bars. Yet that the tree-like character of the figure preponderates is evident from the further mutual intersection and intertwining of the net-shaped boughs, and the termination of the same in flower-like ornaments, encircling the whole figure as a fringe, and regularly fifteen in number. Though, it is true, no definite tree or plant in nature, neither the cypress, nor the tamarisk, nor the palm, etc., can be assigned as the type of this the conventional product of the imagination. As regards its religious significance, its reference to the tradition of Paradise, and its connection—yea, its original identity—with the Old Testament Tree of Life, appears to be indisputable. This is especially evident from the occurrence of the figure upon the clay coffins excavated in Warka, the ancient *Erech* (Gen. x. 10), and now preserved in the British Museum. On these the figure appears to have been imitated from models belonging at any rate to a very early antiquity, and must necessarily express a reference to eternal life, and the blissful communion with the gods in the other world.[2] The mythological tradition and religious art of the ancient Persians knows the same symbol as the tree of Hom (Homa), and depicts it in like manner as the Baby-

---

[1] Depicted in Layard's *Nineveh*, Fig. 33; as in Piper's dissertation, "Der Baum des Lebens," *Evangel. Kalender*, 1863, S. 23.

[2] Compare Schrader, "Semitismus und Babylonismus," in Heft i. of the *Jen. Jahrbb. für protestant. Theol.*, 1875, S. 124 f.—Cp. also what is said below, at the close of this chapter.

Ionian-Assyrian monuments, though not without considerable deviation on particular points. Thus there do not appear with them worshipping priests standing at the two sides of the tree, but ordinarily—as on that beautiful Sassanidic vase of silver in the Paris Museum—two erect lions arranged crosswise.[1] More important deviations from the typical scheme of a triple cross, which lies at the foundation of the Babylonian-Persian form of the Tree of Life, are presented in the sacred tree of the Indian monuments; especially in the traditional representation as Bodhi-tree (Tree of Knowledge or Wisdom), *i.e.*, as that *Ficus religiosa*, under which Sakya Mouni, absorbed in devout meditations, is said to have raised himself to the dignity of a Buddha.[2] An analogy with that associating of the Tree of Life with the idea of wisdom, which obtains, too, in the Old Testament (Prov. iii. 18, and often), as well as in other religious traditions of antiquity, is certainly to be traced here. But no relation to the religious-symbolical representation of the cross is to be sought in connection with this sacred tree of the Buddhist monuments.

INDIA, however, and especially BUDDHISTIC INDIA, otherwise abounds in primitive symbols of the cross, of different form and significance. The Ansate cross or Nile-key, especially, is, according to the statements of English investigators, to be seen, with peculiar modification, upon certain ancient representations of Brahma, Vishnu, and Siva ; the Nile-key-like symbol *Tshakra*, held in the hands of these divinities, is said to imply "dominion," " majesty," and, especially where it occurs as an attribute of Vishnu, to symbolise the eternal, ever-increasing dominion of this god over the lower world of earth.[3] Huge rude stone crosses, supposed to have been of

---

[1] Compare Lenormant, in the *Mélanges d'Archéologie*, T. iii.. p. 124. Piper, a. a. O., S. 79.

[2] Lassen, *Indische Alterthumskunde*, 2 Aufl., Bd. ii., S. 75.

[3] Comp. *Edinb. Review*, Jan. 1870, p. 232. On the magical operations ascribed by the worshippers of Vishnu to this Tshakra cross, frequently employed as an amulet, or put to similar uses, the reviewer observes : "It is a curious fact, that his obsequious follower attaches as many virtues to it, as does the devout Romanist to the Christian Cross."

pre-Christian origin, are said to have been discovered in various places of Citerior India. So on the banks of the Godavery, not far from Nirmul, and here in the immediate vicinity of certain cromlechs, the well-ascertained pre-Christian antiquity of which must, it is said, force us to a corresponding conclusion with regard to the period to which the crosses belong. On the other hand, however, no less an authority than Fergusson, the best-qualified judge on the question of ancient Indian culture and art history, has expressed himself in favour of the view that both kinds of monuments, the cromlechs as well as the crosses, were alike raised during the Middle Ages, by a dolmen-forming tribe under Christian influence.[1] With greater certainty may we regard the gigantic granite monoliths in the form of a cross, discovered by Mulheran in the Vindhya district of Central India, in the year 1869, as dating from a pre-Christian period.[2] A particularly prominent part is played by the sign of the cross, mostly indeed in a somewhat curved type, as Swastika cross (*croix pattée*, footed cross of the French archæologists, Fig. 23), among the BUDDHISTS of Hither and Farther India. It is not indeed an object of adoration, but yet a specially favourite religious symbol of this sect. Originally it seems to have denoted for them the four corners or quarters of the world; and this indeed, in the first place, in the more complete form of the sun-wheel (Fig. 24), which seems to indicate the four heavenly regions traversed by the sun's course—*i.e.*, the four points of the compass—of which the Swastika appears to be a later abbreviating transformation, effected by the omission of the greater part of the four arcs.[3] Much less easily defended does the other explanation of the

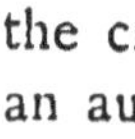

Fig. 23.

Fig. 24.

---

[1] J. Fergusson, *Rude Stone Monuments in all Countries*. London, 1872.

[2] Comp. *Edinb. Rev.*, l. c., p. 253 sqq., where a more complete description is given of this cruciform monolith, on the authority of the photographic views of Colonel Meadowes Taylor.

[3] So rightly the English Chinese scholar Beal, (in a lecture delivered by him at Plymouth in the winter of 1874,) resting upon the support of his translation of the Abhinishkramana-Sûtra, one of the earliest sources for the life of Buddha, from the Chinese.

Swastika cross appear—an explanation which can be true
only with regard to a part of the Buddhists, and that of comparatively late formation—which represents it as the mystic
shibboleth of the "western Paradise." This land of bliss
(Sukhâvati), said to have been designated by Buddha himself
as lying in the far west, forms a main feature in the belief of
the more northerly Buddhists, in Northern India, Cashmere,
Tibet, etc., who relate wonderful things about this land, supposed to extend beyond the limits of the visible world, as
the dwelling-place of the immortal sage Amitâbha, and the
blissful companions of his immortality. Especially does the
dogmatic tradition of the northern Buddhists, attached to this
worship of Amitâbha, delight to paint with the highest colouring of the eastern imagination the seven pools situated in the
centre of this wonderland, the precious properties of their
waters, the glory of their bottom sparkling with sand of gold
and with gems, the fragrant perfume of the lotos flowers
cradling on their surface, the bewitchingly sweet notes of the
beauteous birds hovering over them. All this it does, certainly not without the design of presenting an alternative to
the popular conception of the *Nirvâna*-belief on the part of
the other Buddhists; but precisely therein it betrays its later
origin, which does not indeed extend back beyond the fifth
Christian century, and consequently by no means excludes
the possibility of a co-operation of Christian influences in its
formation.[1] Older than this northern Buddhism, yea according to some as old as the Buddhistic belief itself, and at any
rate dating back by some centuries before the first days of
the Christian history, is the sect of the Jainas in northern
Central India, especially south of the Jumna, in Rajpootana,
Scindia, etc. In the bosom of this sect there seems to have
especially flourished a mystic-philosophic worship of the
cross, the professors of which—the so-called Tirthankars, or
"purified ones"—are said, on account of the high degree of
importance they attached to the Swastika cross as a symbo-

[1] Comp. Ernst J. Eitel, *Buddhism: its Historical, Theoretical, and Popular Aspects*. London, 1873.

lisation of their atheistic and, as is alleged, also immoral, libertine principles, leading to the indulgence of every sensuous excess, to have been known also as simply Swastikas. The sign of the cross appears consequently in their case to have been the symbol of a cosmical or worldly bias in the worst sense of the word—of a radical secularism. Then they fell again into three separate sects, supposed to have been founded by the three deified sages, Suparusnath, Sitalanath, and Arnath, and distinguished by the special modifications of the Swastika cross, of which they availed themselves as emblems. For while the followers of Suparusnath, the Swastikas properly so called, who form the oldest and strongest body of the "purified ones," designated themselves by the simplest and most generally diffused type of this cross (that above depicted), the sect of the Srivatsa, founded by the second of these sages, bore the emblem (Fig. 25), and the party founded by Arnath the yet more artificial and complicated sign (Fig. 26). Yet another emblem, to be found on the monuments of the Jaina sect, which displays at least a certain distant resemblance to a cross, is the so-called "Tree of Knowledge," *Kalpa Vritsh*, represented as an immense thick stem, in the form of a human head, with not altogether disagreeable features. From the top of the skull grow two longer branches drooping over the two sides, while a third and smaller branch, crowned with a blossom-like head, rises erect. This strange figure bears no distinct form of the cross, any more than it displays—as has been assumed—a very definite resemblance to the sacred Bodhi-tree of the Buddhists. On the other hand, the fact may be regarded as solidly established that Buddhism has employed the cross, and indeed the abovementioned simplest and most original Swastika cross, with the cosmical significance above attached to it (as an image of the world or earth), as an ideal architectural element in its imposing temple-structures of Hither and Farther India. For, on the one hand, the great Pagoda Bindh Madhu, at Benares, destroyed in the seventeenth century by the Great Mogul Aurungzebe, was, according to the testimony of the French traveller Tavernier (1675), constructed on the plan of a colossal cross, and as it is said a diagonal, or St. Andrew's cross (Fig. 27).[1] On the other hand, first Mouhot and then Ad. Bastian, about the middle of the present century, found, in the course of their travels in Farther India, the great Buddhist temples of Cambodia—and especially the mighty pagoda of Nakhon Vat or Ongkor Vat—not merely variously adorned upon its gates and walls with cruciform figures, but also expressing in its general outlines, as well as in matters of detail, the " Prasat," or form of the cross; in such wise that its corridors always intersect each other at right angles.[2]

Fig. 27.

Outside of India too, so far as Buddhist influences extend, the presence of the crosses characteristic of Buddhism, specially of the Swastika cross, was to be looked for. And it is said, in fact, that these have been discovered in certain parts of Tibet and China, yea even in Japan—in the latter country appearing, *e.g.*, upon the breast of the idol Xaka, the Buddha reformer of Japan—and still farther to the north.[3] Yet with regard to several of the instances in point, the suspicion of Christian influence is not excluded, especially where the sign bears less resemblance to the Swastika than to the ordinary Christian type of the cross, and where moreover the proof is wanting for the pre-Christian antiquity of the monuments in question. The Catholic Missionary-Bishop Faurie, who testifies to the religious use of the sign of the cross among certain tribes of the province of Kui-tshëu in Southern China, and gives an account of sacrifices presented before great crosses erected at the entrances of villages, and

---

[1] *Voyages de Tavernier*, t. iv., p. 149. Comp. *Edinb. Rev.*, as before, p. 249.
[2] Ad. Bastian, *A Visit to the Ruined Cities and Buildings of Cambodia* (London, 1866), p. 7. "The Prasat, the distinguishing feature of these exotic stone monuments of Cambodia, *forms always a cross*, with the corridors dissecting each other at right angles."
[3] Stockbauer, *Kunstgeschichte des Kreuzes*, S. 91. *Edinb. Rev.*, p. 238 ff., Rapp, *das Labarum*, etc., S. 126. The latter will see in the Chinese sign for five  a religious significance. Hardly with sufficient reason.

of coloured crosses wrought into the garments, of marking the foreheads of the dead with a cross in ashes, etc., may certainly be right in explaining these customs as of Christian origin. At any rate the fact that the said tribes, according to his account, attach to the cross the name of a "great patriarchal ancestor, Saviour, and protector," by no means suffices to prove a heathen origin to this superstitious reverence of the cross, and a Buddhistic one in particular. For of such idolatrous worship of the cross neither in Buddhistic tradition in general, nor specially that among the Siamese or other races of Farther Asia akin to these races of Southern China, do any evidences exist. Whether the symbol of the cross in use among the Kamschatdales, of which Humboldt on one occasion makes mention,[1] and the sign of the cross upon the magic drums of Samoiedan and Lappian priests,[2] and other matters of a like nature in Northern Asia and Europe, are to be traced to Buddhistic or to Christian influences, or—like those supposed Swastika signs which Schliemann reports having discovered on the vases excavated by him in Hissarlik, and other things similar—are to be reckoned as belonging to the class of independent inventions of heathendom in the course of its natural growth, must remain undecided, owing to the insufficiency of the information we possess with regard to the phenomena in question. To some of the forms belonging to this category we shall have occasion to return at a later stage.

Involved in great obscurity is the origin and significance of that Labarum cross of ANCIENT BACTRIA, which, though unquestionably of pre-Christian origin, yet displays a surprising resemblance to the Labarum of Constantine, and possibly may have served as a model for the cross-adorned standard of the first Christian emperor. The form in which this symbol appears on coins of the Bactrian king Hippostratus (circ. A.C. 130), (Figs. 28, 29,) is distinguished from that ordinarily found

---

[1] Comp. A. v. Humboldt, in the *Examen crit. de l'Histoire de la Géographie du Nouveau Continent*, ii., 354. Rochholz, *Altdeutsches Bürgerleben*, S. 184.

[2] Cp. *Magazin f. d. Literat. des Auslands*, 1873, No. 13.

upon the coins of Constantine the Great by the fact that the

Fig. 28.   Fig. 29.

upright staff (furnished with the ear, or handle) (Fig. 30) does not in the latter rise above the sides of the square figure, but within the same passes through the diagonal cross (Figs. 31,

Fig. 30.   Fig. 31.   Fig. 32.   Fig. 33.

32, 33). A similar figure to that of these Bactrian coins is borne also on the coins of the Egyptian Ptolemies, as also on some Attic tetradrachms of a later period (Figs. 34, 35).

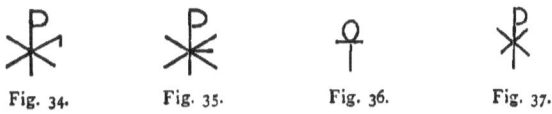

Fig. 34.   Fig. 35.   Fig. 36.   Fig. 37.

In like manner does the sign (Fig. 36) found upon silver coins of Mithridates of Pontus, bear some approach to this form.[1] Now since this variously modified pre-Christian figure (Fig. 37) occurs in essentially the same form, with the ear or handle rising above the square, upon Roman coins too of Constantine, and the succeeding emperors until the time of Arcadius, we are warranted in maintaining in reality the perfect identity of the Labarum of that kingdom of the Hellenic diadochoi (successors of Alexander) with that of the Christianised Roman Empire. The direct imitation of the former by the latter, or at any rate the falling back of Constantine in some way upon that former sign as a precedent, thus becomes probable. (Compare below, Chapters III. and IV.) Is perhaps the Egyptian Ansate cross, as a symbol of the sun shedding its life-giving beams upon the earth, or as also the hieroglyph of everlasting life, to be regarded as the common archetype of both? An extending of the symbol of such ex-

---

[1] Stockbauer, S. 87, and the authorities there cited.

ceedingly frequent occurrence upon the Egyptian monuments to that kingdom on the Upper Oxus—distant indeed from Egypt, but from the time of Alexander the Great and Seleucus remaining for a considerable time in a constant relation of culture with the world of Citerior Asia, and even with the land of the Nile—is not in itself at all inconceivable, any more than emblems and customs derived from Egyptian forms of worship need surprise us in imperial Rome, the meeting-place of all the possible superstitions of the East.[1] But the form of the Egyptian Ansate cross is essentially different from that of the Labarum cross, whether the pre-Christian one of the East, or the Christian-Roman cross of Constantine, in that the Tau form (Fig. 38) of the staff supporting the ring or handle remains unalterably fixed, Fig. 38. whilst the Labarum—in all its modifications, at any rate of the earlier pre-Constantine period[2]—ever displays a diagonal cross, the so-called St. Andrew's Cross (*crux decussata*, or *decussis*), ✕ bisected by a perpendicular line, ansate (*i.e.*,
Fig. 39.
furnished with a handle) at the top. This diagonal cross, in which the Greek must recognise the lines of his letter χ, the Roman those of his numeral X, forms the true characteristic of the Labarum ; whilst for the various modifications of the ansate cross, or Nile-key, the characteristic is the intersection of a perpendicular line by a horizontal one, thus an upright cross. The view of Rapp, with whom Zestermann agrees,[3]

---

[1] Comp. Raoul Rochette in his argument before referred to (*Mém.*, Tom. xvi., 2, pp. 360 sqq.)

[2] On the form (Fig. 40) which occurs as a merely graphic monetary sign upon some coins of Herod the Great (Madden, *Hist. of Jewish Coinage*, pp. 83, 85, 87), and, later, frequently as a Christian monogram upon inscriptions and coins under the successors of Constantine the Great—for the first Fig. 40. time upon an inscription of the year 355, then pretty frequently upon coins of Valentinian I., see below, Chapter III.

[3] Zestermann, i., 7 f. "In the lands more northerly situated, as Bactria in Asia, Gaul and Britain in Europe, the sun never stands at the zenith. It sends forth at every season of the year, only slanting, diagonal rays, which fall from S.E. to N.W., or from S.W. to N.E., according to the position of the sun. These rays, placed in a quadrangle, the earliest image of the world, form, with the image of

that the combination of the diagonal cross with the above-
mentioned ansate perpendicular line in the Bactrian Labarum
is to be regarded as emblematical of the northern zone of the
earth, enlightened by the obliquely falling rays of the sun—
so that the handle or half-circle denotes the sun, and the
square crossed by the two diagonals the world (the *orbis
quadratus*)—appears to us to have something forced about it,
and to be wanting in sufficient positive support. In connection with this hypothesis, the difficulty remains unexplained,
why the sun is not represented as the centre or starting-point
of the so-called rays, which cross each other, but appears
raised above their point of intersection. It is moreover a
question whether the representation of the world under the
form of a square was specially practised among the ancient
heathen nations of Central Asia, as the Bactrians, Northern
Indians, etc. A development of the figure (Fig. 41) from that
other figure (Fig. 42), of which the very early use among the

Fig. 41.   Fig. 42.

nations of the region in question is so much better attested—
see above, p. 10—can scarcely be supposed. The simplest
explanation of the Bactrian and Ptolemaic Labarum cross, as
of the various secondary forms thereof, is that which sees in
them only graphic signs or abbreviations, having reference to
words such as χρυσός, or ἄρχων, etc. See the examples given
in Chapter III.

We come to the pre-Christian symbols of the cross in
EUROPE. Upon urns and vases of ancient ETRURIA, as
the sun, which, sometimes half (Fig. 43), sometimes whole (Fig. 44), stands at the
top of the perpendicular ray above the world, the figure (Figs. 45, 46), which in

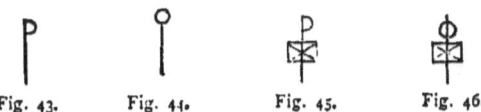

Fig. 43.   Fig. 44.   Fig. 45.   Fig. 46.

Asia and Europe—so far as the Egyptian form of worship had not, as on the
coasts of the Mediterranean, introduced the Egyptian symbol of the sun—was the
emblem of the sun-worship," etc. Cp. Rapp, S. 123 f.

well as in the neighbouring districts of Upper Italy, it is well known that cruciform characters have been observed, as indeed those in the form of the Swastika cross—such as very manifestly appear, *e.g.*, upon a mortuary urn of Etruscan work, discovered remarkably enough at Shropham (Norfolk), England, where they occur as an ornament in about twenty-fourfold repetition; as likewise upon a beautiful golden fibula of the Vatican Museum, etc.—as also those resembling the equal-armed Greek cross, of varied form (Figs. 47—52).

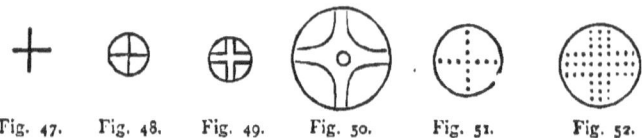

Fig. 47.   Fig. 48.   Fig. 49.   Fig. 50.   Fig. 51.   Fig. 52.

The essentially ornamental character of these last figures, which appear too upon other vessels and implements of Etruscan (? or Celtic) origin, *e.g.*, not seldom upon the pommels of dagger or sword hilts, is indeed—from the frequency of their occurrence, and the variety of modification adopted with regard to them—not to be doubted. To this extent, however, Mortillet, who would claim for them a religious symbolical signification, may be right, viz., that these signs too were certainly in their origin designed to serve for the expression of certain religious ideas. The same is also no doubt the case with that beautiful silver vase from an ancient sepulchre at Cære (in Etruria), where the form of the sign pretty much resembles that of the Egyptian Nile-key, but still more resembles that of the Cilician coins in the abbreviated form of the Venus' looking-glass, as given below (Fig. 53); and moreover—by the fact that it appears depicted on the hind quarter of a horse—gives rise to the supposition that we have in this case a representation of a highly valuable horse (of Corinthian breed) marked with the sign of the Koppa, a κοππατίας, or ἵππος κοππαφόρος, the mark of which in the present instance had been changed, with a view to ornamentation or out of religious motives, from the ordinary (Fig. 54) into the more graceful (Fig. 55). Other forms of a different kind are displayed by these emblems upon the terra-cotta vases of Alba Longa, of which the cruciform symbols are probably to be regarded as emblems

Fig. 54.   Fig. 55.

of Libitina or Persephone, the terrible queen of the shades.[1] At any rate we may conclude that very early relations of religious culture between the most artistic and civilised people of ancient Italy and the peoples of the East find a significant expression in those Etruscan symbols of the cross, even though with regard to many details of these relations we can come to no certain results.

The same is the case with the cruciform or wheel-shaped signs occurring upon coins of the ancient GAULS, *i.e.*, such as represent the figures (Figs. 56 and 57), of which some are

Fig. 56.   Fig. 57.

shown from the neighbourhood of Bourges, of Arthenay, and of Choisy-le-Roi.[2] Likewise is it the case with other traces of a mystic-superstitious use of the sign of the cross, within the domain of research into Celtic and Celtiberian antiquities, such as, *e.g.*, the peculiarly formed ancient armorial bearings of the Isle of Man and of Sardinia ; also the remarkable combination of cross and half-moon (Fig. 58), shown upon what is said to be an ancient coin of the Iberian city of Asido, now Medina Sidonia, in the south of Spain.[3] Fig. 58. To this category belong further the T-shaped symbols with

---

[1] Millin, *Galerie Mythologique*, pl. cxxxi. and cxxxv. Comp. *Edinb. Review*, l. c., 238 sqq.

[2] Lelewel. *Études numismatiques* (cited in Rauch, *die Einheit des Menschengeschlechts*, Augsb., 1873, S. 321), "La croix est un symbole plus ancien dans le type gaulois ; elle se retrouve dans les différens coins empreints du symbolisme, dans le coin de l'Armorique, des Andecaves, et elle est sur la monnaie en argent, qui se rattache aux frontières des Biturigis." Comp. too Mionnet, Supplément. i., pl. vi., n. 25 ; as also engravings of Ancient British and Gallic coins in *Art Journal*, June 1874, p. 185.

[3] J. Zobel de Zangronitz, in the *Zeitschrift der deutschen morgenl. Gesellsch.*, Bd. 17 (1863), S. 337 ff. expresses no doubt as to the pre-Christian origin and character of this coin described by him. In reality, also many ancient Gallic

which, according to an ancient tradition, the Druids used to mark in different places the bark of their sacred trees—gigantic and fair-grown forest trees, to which they were wont, by removing all the other limbs up to two opposite ones of special magnitude, to give the form of a colossal cross or of a man with outstretched arms.[1] It has even been sought to refer to this category the sign ⊤ or otherwise ┼, and similar emblems, upon old church bells, inasmuch as they have been explained as magical signs for warding off evil spirits, thus as remains of old heathen superstition which had crept in again during the Middle Ages.[2] The signs of the god Thor, engraved upon Runic monuments of ZEALAND and SCANDINAVIA (Thor's hammers),—along with which is also found, remarkably enough, the Swastika symbol, and that sometimes in the artistically interlaced form (Fig. 59), belong moreover to this class.[3] Not less so do the crosses upon different North German monuments, *e.g.*, that in the wall of a sepulchral apartment hewn out in a hill at Niedleben, near Halle, close by which were also delineations of plants and weapons; where a piece of perforated amber, a bronze celt, and moreover flint implements,[4] were likewise found in the same sepulchral chamber.

Fig. 59.

coins, *e.g.*, one drawn by De Mortillet, found near Choisy-le-Roi, display entirely similar cruciform emblems, along with star-shaped and, as it is said, crescent-shaped ones. (De Mortillet, *Signe de la Croix*, p. 153.) For other symbols belonging to this class, see Eug. Hucher, Symbolisme des plus anciennes médailles gauloises (in the *Revue Numismatique*, 1850, 1852, 1855).

[1] Maurice says (*Indian Antiquities*, vol. vi., p. 49), "It is a fact, not less remarkable than well-attested, that the Druids in their groves were accustomed to select the most stately and beautiful tree as an emblem of the deity they adored, and having cut off the side branches, they affixed two of the largest of them to the highest part of the trunk, in such manner that these branches extended on each side like the arms of a man, and, together with the body, presented the appearance of a huge cross: and in the bark in several places was also inscribed the letter tau." Comp. also Alger, *History of the Cross*, pp. 11 sqq.

[2] *Edinb. Rev.*, l. c., p. 239.

[3] Stephens, *The Old Northern Runic Monuments* (London, 1860), p. 674.

[4] F. de Rougemont, *The Bronze Age, or the Semites in the West*. [Page 410 ff. of the German edition.]

A pre-Christian and specifically heathen origin could hardly, however, be proved with absolute certainty in the case of any of these crosses upon northern or Germanic monuments. Those of the Runic stones, especially, are admitted to date only from the Christian period, and seem in great part to have originated under the influence of Christian models. On the other hand, no reasonable doubts can be entertained as to the ancient heathen origin of the Scandinavian-Germanic Tree of the World, or Tree of Life, the ash Yggdrasill, notoriously the counterpart of the sacred trees alike of Eastern and of Celtic mythology. Rightly does so cautious an examiner as Jacob Grimm—with all the importance which he attaches to the manifold points of resemblance between this ancient northern myth and the legends of the Middle Ages concerning the wood of the cross—nevertheless give as his judgment, "I cannot possibly believe that the myth of Yggdrasill, in all its greater fulness of form, proceeded from this ecclesiastical conception of the cross. Rather must the conjecture be permitted that floating heathen traditions of the Tree of the World were soon after the introduction of Christianity accommodated in Germany, France, or England, to an object of Christian faith, just as heathen temples and sites were turned into Christian ones."[1]

AFRICA, too, displays in its various lands, with the exception of Egypt and the districts immediately bordering thereupon (*e.g.*, the Libyan desert and Nubia), hardly any other examples of the adoration of the cross than those which are of Christian origin. So the custom of the princes of Mussorongho, on the Loango coast, of wearing as an ornament rosaries, sometimes with a cross attached to them (tosairo), a custom distinctly pointing back to the former Christian dominion of the Portuguese; besides which, also, the ceremony of crossing oneself, with other customs of a like origin, has been preserved—spite of the fetich-idolatrous heathenism into which in other respects this tribe has sunk back.[2] Rather

[1] *Deutsche Mythologie*, ii., 758 (second edition).
[2] Ad. Bastian, *Die deutsche Expedition an der Loango-Küste*, etc., Bd. i., 1874, S. 282.

might even the cross held in honour by the present heathen inhabitants of the island of Socotra, the so-called Bedouins, as a religious symbol in their places of worship, be of pre-Christian origin ; for besides it, there serve to them as objects of adoration the moon, and an idol with a serpent's head. But, on the other hand, much pleads for the supposition of a mixed character to their religion, made up of scanty remains of a former Christianity of St. Thomas, along with Arabian-Sabæan heathenism.[1]

Scarcely can such an independent significance be attached to that which is related concerning the religious uses made of the cross upon some of the OCEANIC ISLANDS, as to justify us in speaking of Polynesian crosses as a separate and original branch of the domain of extra-Christian forms of religion here under review. Among the various figures, unquestionably in their origin of religious significance, with which the aborigines of several islands are wont to tattoo themselves, occur, among several other types, *e.g.*, imitations of plants and animals, arabesque-like lines, squares, etc., as also cruciform designs ; without, however, these latter playing any prominent part.[2] The colossal statues of Hermes-like form discovered upon Easter Island, now placed in the British Museum, bear upon their reverse side roughly chiselled cruciform figures.[3] The possibility of these marks being the work of later Christian visitors to the lonely island, can of course hardly be denied. If, however, we are to see in them the efforts of native talent, perhaps of the same age and of a similar character to the remarkable hieroglyphic figures

---

[1] W. Germann, "das Christenthum auf Socotora." in the *Zeitschr. für histor. Theologie*, 1874, H. ii., S. 256.

[2] Comp. Waitz, *Anthropol. der Naturvölker*, Bd. vi., pp. 38 ff. See especially p. 32, where the inhabitants of the isle of Anaa (belonging to the Paumotu Archipelago) are spoken of as "tattooing themselves with cruciform lines, while the inhabitants of Rarotonga adopted as their models crosses and squares side by side." On the religious significance, originally belonging to the practice of tattooing in general, comp. Wuttke, *Die Entstehung der Schrift*, Bd. i., Leipzig, 1872.

[3] *Edinb. Rev.*, l. c., p. 231, note.—A representation of the stone monuments in question, in Christmann and Oberlander, *Oceanien*, etc. (Leipzig, 1873), ii., S. 285.

upon some wooden tablets of the same island,[1] then we are most naturally led to regard the supposed religious motive which underlies them as not of originally Polynesian origin, but as having migrated thither from the shores of America, thus to be interpreted in the same way as the different forms of the pre-Christian worship of the cross among the aborigines of the New World. The same will be the case with many other traces of a veneration for the cross on the part of the heathen inhabitants, discovered upon the islands of Micronesia, *e.g.*, upon the Radack Islands, the Mulgrave Archipelago, etc. Some things, too, of this kind must be set down as of directly Christian origin ; such as, *e.g.*, the flag captured a few years ago from the heathen Maori in New Zealand, of which the cross can hardly have been anything else than an imitation of the Christian emblem well known to the natives.

On the cross as a pre-Christian symbol in the religious customs of the aborigines of AMERICA, we have remarkable accounts from the time of the historians who recorded the discovery and occupation of the lands and islands of the New Continent ; and since that time a not inconsiderable literature has sprung up.

Among the more recent authorities upon this subject are to be mentioned Squier,[2] a North American writer, and the German J. G. Müller.[3] The territory over which this remarkable phenomenon presents itself extends in pretty equal proportion throughout South, Central, and North America. As regards CENTRAL and SOUTH AMERICA, its existence is attested by Spanish historians even of the sixteenth century, such as Las Casas, Herera, Gomara, Peter Martyr, Garcilaso de la Vega : almost all of these start with the presupposition of very early Christian influences, especially the missionary activity of the Apostle Thomas, as underlying this pheno-

---

[1] Oberländer, *Oceanien*, S. 286.
[2] G. Squier, *The Serpent Symbol in America*, p. 98 sqq. Comp. his *Nicaragua*, p. 493, and often elsewhere.
[3] J. G. Müller, *Geschichte der amerikanischen Urreligionen*, S. 371, 421, 496 ff.

menon. Even though they erred in this respect, yet the credibility of that which they relate concerning the traces of a peculiar worship of the cross on the part of the aborigines, as already existing when the Spanish conquerors arrived, can hardly be called in question. The opinion expressed by Stephens in his works on Central America and Yucatan, that the crosses regarded with religious homage were introduced by the Spaniards themselves, deserves to be mentioned only as a literary curiosity.[1] The sense in which the Indians of South and Central America rendered to the cross religious homage, or at least made a religious use of it, seems to have been everywhere essentially the same. It is the fructifying nature-power of the regions of earth and air, and especially the rain, which was adored south as well as west and north of the Sea of the Antilles under the symbol of the cross. This signification of a rain-god seems to have been attached to the great cross, consisting of a single crystal jasper, which, according to Garcilaso's testimony, was held sacred by the Incas of Peru; so likewise was it the case with several other stone crosses of South American aborigines as far as Paraguay; as also with those wooden or stone crosses which they were wont in Cumana to lay upon new-born children in order to scare away the evil spirits. The great rope-cross, consisting of two cords stretched above the surface of a pool or river, at whose point of intersection the Muysca Indians were wont to cast into the water their offerings, consisting of fruits, precious oil, and jewels, had unquestionably a like significance.[2] Upon the island of Cozumel, in Yucatan, there was worshipped, under the form of great crosses of stone, or even wood, a divinity of rain or of fer-

[1] J. L. Stephens, *Incidents of Travel in Central America, Chiapas*, etc. (London, 1842), ii., 20 (of the German edition). Idem, *Incidents of Travel in Yucatan*, ii., 359 (of the German edition).

[2] Comp. *Edinb. Rev.*, p. 233, as well as the work of Brinton, *Myths of the New World* (1869), therein cited. Brinton advances in this work still farther than Müller; inasmuch as he regards the cross of the old Mexicans and other primitive American races as significant not only of rain and fertility, but also (as was the case with the Egyptians) of eternal life or immortality.

tility. Such was also the case in Chiapas and other regions of Central America, as about the celebrated ruins of Palenque, in the vicinity of which there has been discovered a figurative representation having reference to this divinity of rain, which shows above the fantastically decorated (scrolled) cross a bird —symbol of the higher region of air—as well as right and left of the same two human figures who appear to be looking upon the cross and presenting to it a child as a sacrifice.[1] Similar crosses, having (above) birds over them, and (below) an apparatus for sacrifice on the right and on the left, are also sometimes found depicted on ancient pre-Mexican MSS. Thus there is to be seen upon the last page of a manuscript now existing in Hungary, in the possession of a Mr. Fejérvary, a T-shaped cross of this kind, in the midst of which, moreover, appears depicted a sanguinary divinity![2] The worship in general offered by the ancient Mexicans to their cruciform rain-gods does not appear to have been of an unbloody kind. The favour of Centeotle, the "daughter of heaven and goddess of corn," they sought, we are told, to propitiate by annually in the spring nailing a young man or maiden to a cross, and transfixing this victim with arrows. Like this Mexican Ceres or Proserpine, the principal god of the Toltecs, Quetzalcoatl, a divinity of the air—whose mantle is represented as "entirely besprinkled with crosses"—is said also to have been worshipped under the symbol of the cross. According to the statement of the Toltec historian Ixtlilxochitl in Terneaux, this national god of his tribe "introduced the sign of the cross and the adoration of it." It was then called "god of rain and of health, and tree of sustenance and of life." Among the localities of Mexico and Central America in which this worship under the form of a cross of the divinity of air and rain existed, are further specially to

---

[1] A representation of this cruciform Tree of Life, or of the World—said to be called in Mexican *Tonacaquahuitl*, "Tree of our flesh"—is given by Stephens; comp. also Squier, Nicaragua, p. 493.—We shall have occasion to return to this subject farther on, in our treating of the cross as the Symbol of the Curse.

[2] Klemm, *Culturgeschichte*, v., 142 f. Comp. Müller, as before.

be mentioned Queretaro, Oaxaca, Guatulco, the island of St. Ulloa (celebrated on account of its great white marble cross), the island of Zaputera in Lake Nicaragua, as well as the province of Mixteca.

As to the other parts of NORTH AMERICA besides Mexico, an early Indian worship of the cross is vouched for as concerns Florida and the northern districts bordering thereupon, as far as Cibola, by Castaneda;[1] as regards the territory about Hudson's Bay, by the accounts of Protestant and Catholic missionaries, who found the adoration of a wondrous tree of the cross—as a symbol of fertility, or even as an instrument of magical operation—widely diffused among the Indian hordes of these northern regions.[2] A Christian origin in the case of many of these North American customs may be shown to be the most probable supposition. Especially to those tribes living in the vicinity of the Atlantic coast might there be brought by the Northmen, or perhaps by Irish navigators of the Middle Ages, along with other signs of Western civilisation, also the sacred symbol of Redemption. The venerable old man who once, we are told, delivered the province of Gaspé, south of the mouth of the St. Lawrence, from an epidemic by the application of the cross, and enjoined upon those healed reverence for this symbol, together with other religious customs, can hardly have been any other than a Christian herald of the faith coming from Europe; although the descendants of his converts, when recently discovered anew by French missionaries, had relapsed again into heathenism, and were worshipping the sun along with the cross.[3] We may for the elucidation of the fact in question recall to mind the account of the missionary journey to Vinland, undertaken about the year 1120 by the Greenland bishop, Erich Gnupson; we may, on the ground of Scandinavian and Iceland traditions of yet earlier

[1] In Terneaux, comp. ix., 165 ; also in Washington Irving, *Conquest of Florida*, ii., 206.
[2] *Missionsbilder* (Calw u. Stuttgart, 1864 ff.) Heft, v., S. 58 f.
[3] Maltebrun, "Newest Description of America," p. 145 of the Germ. edn. Comp. also Rauch, *Einheit d. Menschengeschl.*, S. 363.

date, believe in the existence of a Christian "Land of White Men" (Hvitramannaland), on the coast between Virginia and Florida;[1] we may perhaps extend the influence of these Christian expeditions of Western Europe during the Middle Ages even to the southern west coast of America, and suppose that Brazil too and the bordering lands were not unvisited by them. But to refer back the whole of the traces of the worship of the cross among the various primitive nations of the New World exclusively to *this* source, remains under any circumstances a scientific impossibility. In addition to the influences exerted by the Christian world, we must here assume the action also of pre-Christian influences. And the more uncertain the character of everything appears, which is conjectured regarding the colonisation of the New World by civilised nations of the pre-Christian Old World who had come in from the East; the more isolated the discoveries such as that of Dr. Lund at Bahia, in Brazil, in the year 1839, which is said to have embraced the fragments of a Runic stone table, as well as a statue of the god Thor and a Thor's hammer (together with gloves and magic girdle) ;[2] and the less there is afforded in reality a satisfactory explanation of the earlier American civilisation—whether regarded in general or in relation to the phenomenon in which we are specially interested—by such isolated phenomena, which seem indeed to testify to an influence of the ancient Scandinavians upon the development of civilisation in America, or even by the supposed traces of former Phœnician expeditions to the west coast of North or South America, which it is asserted some-

---

[1] We are, in fact, compelled to believe in the existence of such a Christian land there, by that which the Skrellings or Eskimos narrated concerning the customs of its occupants to the Northmen, who settled in Vinland. There were, said they, in the south, beyond Chesapeake Bay, "white men, who went about in long white garments, and carried before them poles upon which cloths were hung, and cried out with a loud voice." This fresh and faithful description on the part of the natives of Christian processions, (comp. Humbolt, *Kosm.*, ii., S. 71,) vouches at the same time, in a pretty direct manner, for the frequent religious use of crosses among these Christian settlers on the middle west coast of North America.

[2] *Ausland*, 1840, s. 652. Wernicke, *Geschichte der Welt*, 5th edn., Bd. ii., S. 660.

times present themselves;[1] so much the more inevitably are we impelled to the necessity of seeking the explanation of such abundant traces of a heathen-religious use of the cross, as in particular those of ancient Mexico, Peru, and Central America, in the influences of a primitive culture extending from eastern Asia ; thus to take into account the employment of similar symbols, perceptible as early as the Buddhistic epoch, and perhaps even in the pre-Buddhistic period of east Asiatic history, as the origin and foundation of the corresponding American phenomena. The supposition of an independent growth of these customs upon purely American soil, we need not by any means entirely exclude in connection with this view. When it is asserted by modern ethnologists, such as Peschel, von Hellwald, Fr. Müller, etc., not indeed of the American races themselves—whom they believe to have migrated out of the old world into America many thousands of years ago, while still in a condition of absolute barbarism—but yet of their earlier development in civilisation, that this was of a perfectly independent nature and origin ; we must assent to this view as just, if not with regard to all the forms of worship and of art now under review, at least with regard to some of them. Squier too, in his views expressed with regard to the development of the ancient American civilisation in general, and with regard to the Indian worship of the cross, the tree, and the serpent, in particular, is favourable to the supposition of a decidedly native origin. Yucatan is regarded by him as the central seat and primeval hearth whence the whole of the symbols and symbolical rites in question spread to the north and to the south. Yet he has in thus concluding perhaps in many respects proceeded too far, and has not sufficiently taken into account the striking agreement between these phenomena and those most nearly akin to them in the Old World.[2]

[1] On the question of an acquaintance with America on the part of the Phœnicians, comp. an article by the author: *Pseudomoabitisches und Pseudophönikisches*, in the *Beweis des Glaubens*, 1874, II. 11, S. 495 ff.

[2] For the criticism of this view of Squier, so far as it specially represents Yucatan

Our general survey of the evidence for the use of the cross, in the pre-Christian and extra-Christian religions, as a symbol of blessing, *i.e.*, as an object or means of direct devotional homage, and of corresponding importance for religious art, is now brought to a close. The multiplicity of the phenomena under review is great. A tracing of them back to one common origin and starting-point can hardly be regarded as a thing possible. Even as concerns their outward form of delineation, these symbols differ from each other in a very marked manner. Let us only recall to mind the principal and most characteristic types of the simpler kind:

without taking into account the different figures of the Tree of Life—peculiarly modified, sometimes in one direction, sometimes in another—among the Assyrians, Persians, Indian Buddhists, Celts, American Indians, etc. An historical derivation of all these figures from one primal form of the simplest order, serving as the basis to them all, appears to us an absolutely insoluble problem, comparable to the quadrature of the circle. The fanciful art of genealogising displayed by a Häckel might perhaps at best prove equal to supplying us with the means of constructing the all-embracing family tree which should present to us as springing forth, all and separately, from one root, the Nile-key and the Swastika cross, the Bactrian-Ptolemaic Labarum, and the old northern Runic cross, or Thor's hammer (fylfot).

As however the forms, so also do the significations of these heathen cross symbols, differ most considerably; so that a

as the starting-point of all the ancient civilisation in America, comp. a writer, in other respects one in principle with Squier, Hellwald, "Zur Geschichte des alten Yukatan," *Ausland*, 1871, S. 243. For the rest, Arth. Schott, *ibid.*, p. 900 ff., who derives from the serpent-worship of the Mayas and other central-American tribes convincing proofs of a primal connection of civilisation with Asia. Similarly Rauch, *as before*, S. 173 ff., 266 ff.

summing-up of them all under one fundamental or primal idea, cannot possibly be accomplished save by means of a critical act of violence or of speculative arbitrariness. And yet it seems to us, on the other hand, inadmissible to discard on principle every attempt at gaining a certain common point of view, if not for all of the phenomena coming under review, at least for one or other part thereof. Evidently nothing is gained and nothing is explained by such generalities as that " the cross is a symbol chosen merely as the result of accident ;" or that " such symbols, like a disease, are transmitted from generation to generation."[1] Indistinct and mystical— and moreover only applicable to a smaller portion of the actually occurring cases of a religious use of the cross in heathendom—appears the view of Mortillet, according to which the four forms of the cross-symbols of ancient monuments are all to be derived from the practice of one primal, widely extended secret sect, the followers of a purer and more spiritual kind of worship, who refrained from the ordinary conceptions and rites of idolatry, and as such are to be looked upon as more direct precursors of Christianity. In itself the great diversity of the symbolism of the cross in different lands, the radically dissimilar character of the emblems in question, as well as that of the accompanying circumstances under which they arise, speaks against such an hypothesis.[2] Unquestionably some of the significations which, according to ancient tradition and also according to modern archæological investigation, underlie the religious use of the symbol, were diffused more widely than merely over the district of one tribe or the religion of one nation. The crosses of the American aborigines would seem—so far as they are not to be looked upon as introduced by Christians coming into that continent—for the greater part to harmonise in the signification of a *rain*-god or fructifying power of nature. To proceed farther than this, and assume with J. G. Müller that the idea of " Peace," or with Brinton that of

---

[1] Comp. *Magaz. f. d. Literatur des Auslands*, 1873, No. 13, 1.
[2] For a critique of Mortillet's work, comp. Appendix I.

"Life and Immortality," is symbolised by the greater number of them, is hardly to be justified.[1] The concrete historical points of attachment for such metaphysical exaltation of the notion expressed by them of an external salutary power of nature, are too greatly wanting. But beyond the limits of America, this significance of the cross-symbols pointing to divinities of fruitfulness and of rain is less prominent. Even among the natives of that continent in which we might expect more than anywhere to meet with it—namely, Africa—there is scarcely a trace of it to be found. On the other hand, the primal and fundamental signification peculiar to the most favourite cruciform figure of the Egyptians, the Ansate cross, that of the life-giving *Sunlight*, seems to have enjoyed a pretty widespread reception. To suppose with Rapp and others that it was universally diffused throughout the ancient world, and to derive from it all the modifications of the cross among the heathen of Asia and of Europe, however greatly diverging in form from this—*e.g.*, the ancient Bactrian Labarum—is certainly not at all admissible. Yet assuredly that wheel-shaped cross of the Assyrian-Babylonian monuments, and originally also the Indian Swastika cross, may have expressed a reference to the worship of the sun. So too some of the symbols belonging to this class current among the Celts and ancient northern peoples may have expressed the same reference. But in addition to this relation to the sun, there were also some other peculiar relations of the cross-worship among the ancient nations of the eastern civilised world, which can be only artificially and with violence referred back to that of the sun-worship. This is seen in the

[1] Comp. Müller, *Amerik. Urreligionen*, S. 499; as well as Brinton, *Myths of the New World*, p. 96: "As the emblem of the winds, who dispense the fertilising showers, it is emphatically the tree of our life, our subsistence, and our health. It never had any other meaning in America; and if, as it has been said, the tombs of the Mexicans were cruciform, it was perhaps with reference to a resurrection, and to a future life as portrayed under this symbol, indicating that the buried body would rise by the action of the four spirits of the world." etc. Rightly does the critic of the *Edinburgh Review* (p. 234) speak of this interpretation as "involving a little too much;" but himself maintains the idea of a renewing of life or rejuvenescence as common to the different American forms of the cross-worship.

Tree of Life of the peoples of the Euphrates, of the Persians, and the Indians, and in the Venus' Looking Glass of the Assyrians, Phœnicians, races of Asia Minor, Greeks, etc. It may be that a mode of interpretation which gives a deeper and more spiritual religious meaning would be able to derive and develop from all, or at least from almost all of these forms of the ancient cross-worship, a like sublimated idea, as "*everlasting life*," *immortality*, or *resurrection*. It is possible that such method of developing the deeper idea was actually practised here and there, by priestly sages, upon the banks of the Nile, as of the Euphrates and Ganges; upon the Eranian as upon the Tibetian plateaus; yea, perhaps even upon the highlands of Anahuac, and in the lands of the Mayas and the Incas. But then surely this took place only as a result of later abstraction, and by giving play to a religious-philosophic speculation similar to that which moulded the childishly simple nature-belief of the ancient Indians in the time of the Vedas into Brahmaism; or that which formed out of the gods and hero-myths of the Homeric and post-Homeric Hellenism the doctrine of the Orphic and Pythagorean mysteries. There is, in accordance with our whole previous exposition of these symbols, no room for supposing that the different forms of the pre-Christian cross-worship originally proceeded from the idea of everlasting salvation, or of the future life—as an original foundation common to them all—which, in proportion to the greater or less degree of preference with which sometimes the one, sometimes the other form of its symbolisation has been cultivated, had developed itself into different secondary modes of conception and presentation.

Moreover, the remarkable endeavour on the part of the British scholar, in the *Edinburgh Review*—already so often referred to by us—to show that not the notion of life, or immortality, or sun, or rain, etc., but rather that of *Paradise*, is the common foundation and starting-point for all the different forms of the heathen cross-worship, can hardly be regarded as successful. This article, which displays admirable religious-historic lore, but yet is characterised rather by a bold flight of the imagination than by a sober consistency in the maintenance of truly philosophic principles, prepares the way for the attaining of this Paradise-theory, by tracing back the whole of the symbols of the cross in the Old World and the New, in the first place, to three fundamental conceptions of a sensuous or material kind, and then comprehending these three under the one idea of Paradise, or the original blissful abode of mankind. For he proceeds from the assumption that (1), as is shown by the cross-worship of all the American tribes, and, moreover, of the Egyptians, the Babylonians (?), and the ancient Indians—among whom is especially worshipped under the symbol of the cross, Vishnu, the water-divinity who holds sway over all rivers and lakes,—the fructifying and refreshing natural power of *water* formed a first main element of symbolisation for the ancient heathen representatives of the mystic superstition in question. He assumes further (2), again relying upon the support of ancient Indian, Babylonian-Assyrian, and Persian, but also upon that of Celtic, Northern, and American documents, that the conception of a luxuriously verdant and blossoming *tree*, which bears sweet fruit, or the nearly allied idea of some other fresh and living product of the vegetable kingdom, as, for instance, a lotus flower—underlies the various cruciform emblems. Or he seeks (3), appealing for support specially to the Ansate cross of the Babylonians—sometimes conically formed in its lower part, and then, as it is alleged, standing in special relation to the service of Astarte or Venus—as well as to that which is somewhat akin, namely, the phallic symbols of different peoples, to show that the idea of a *hill* or *mountain* is likewise frequently involved in that of the worship of the cross; and to prove the existence of a number of cruciform monuments— in addition to the pagodas of India, the pyramids of Egypt, etc. —especially of the class of the so-formed megaliths, dolmens or cromlechs,[1] as symbolisations of the mythic mountain of the gods, the abode of the blessed. In combining these three relative main allusions of the symbolism of the cross,

---

[1] Comp. above, p. 10.

i.e., such as do not appear generally and universally, but only over a more limited extent of territory, into one general conception, that, namely, of the high-lying region of Paradise, watered with streams, and furnished with precious fruit trees, he believes he has attained to the common primal and fundamental notion underlying all such religious emblems of antiquity. The water crosses, tree crosses, and phallus (!) crosses, or hill crosses, serve him as elements for the construction of this remarkable hypothesis, in which naturally the symbol of the mountain or hill, as the birthplace of the streams and home-land of the trees of life, plays a leading part. Some striking points of contact with the well-known traditions of Paradise, or the mountain of the gods, among ancient nations, certainly lend support to this fanciful construction. Thus the round, sweet festival cake, ornamented with a cross, borne by the Egyptian worshippers of Isis, which as an hieroglyph had, according to Wilkinson, a signification equivalent to "cultivated land," "garden," and consequently could in reality be looked upon as an image of Paradise, presented under the form of a cross. So too do the four rivers of Paradise, according to the, on this point, unanimous traditions of the Semites, the Persians, Indians, Chinese, and Germans—to which fourfold character the four arms of the cross, especially in that ancient Indian and Babylonian-Assyrian form (Fig. 60) seem to point. More than this, Fig. 60. that tradition of the Buddhists of Northern India, to which allusion has before been made, expressly characterises the Swastika cross as an emblem of the "western Paradise." To this Indian testimony, accordingly, our Essayist particularly appeals in favour of his hypothesis. "If, in conclusion," he says, "any reader entertains a lingering doubt respecting the real object and purpose of the symbol of the cross, . . . if this long series of coincidences, this immense accumulation of facts, all, as we have endeavoured to show, converging to a single point, is insufficient to convince any reader of its true significance, we can only remind him once more of the fond expectations, the typical philosophy of the existing races of mankind; refer

him to the most primitive and learned people in the East—
'Those heirs of all the ages in the foremost file of time'—
appeal to the united testimony of Buddhists and Brahmins (?), who together constitute nearly half the population of the world, and from whom he may learn that the decussated figure, whether in a simple or a complex form, symbolises the traditional happy abode of their primeval ancestors— that 'Paradise of Eden towards the East,' as we find it expressed in the Hebrew." [1]

We are unable to own ourselves converts to the belief in Paradise, in this new and peculiar form. However highly we rate the significance of the traditions of Paradise or the golden age, among so many ancient peoples, as a venerable reminiscence of the primitive period of our race, and as an important testimony to the character of revelation which belongs to the Biblical Monotheism in general,[2] it seems to us inadmissible to institute between these Paradise traditions and the pre-Christian heathen cross-worship—not merely occasional and isolated points of contact, but—a *thorough* historic and genetic connection; thus, as our Essayist does, to place every form and stamp of that symbolism of the cross in more or less direct relation to the tradition of a blissful primitive dwelling-place of man and starting-point of the human development. Among the Indians the custom may have been formed at an early period of indicating the notion of Paradise by the sign (Fig. 61) and (Fig. 62), or a similar figure.

Fig. 61.   Fig. 62.

But not even among them were these conventional Semiotics universally accepted: that "the combined testimony of Buddhists and Brahmins" pleads in favour thereof, is an altogether baseless assertion on the part of our Essayist. Besides the relation to Paradise, other significations of the Swastika cross

---

[1] *As before*, p. 254 f.
[2] Comp. our article upon Lüken's "Traditionen des Menschengeschlechts," in the *Beweis des Glaubens*, 1869, S. 463 ff.; especially S. 467.

have come into vogue; of these, that which refers it to the sun's path in the ecliptic, and to the four cardinal points, is possibly an older and more original interpretation than that which explains it of Paradise. The latter interpretation even appears, as was shown above, not entirely free from the suspicion of being an importation from the Christian west; inasmuch as it is probably not of earlier date than the fourth or fifth century of the Christian æra. Moreover, this very tradition of the northern Buddhists, which places the garden indicated under the form of the cross to the west (of them)— and to this extent is in harmony with the Hebrew tradition of the "Garden of Eden in the East"—speaks not of four, but of seven waters of Paradise. Conversely, in those types of the Paradise tradition which expressly emphasise the number four in connection with the rivers, as something essential and of profound import, there is no trace, or next to none, to be seen, of a tendency to the symbolisation of these four rivers by the four arms of a cross. Then, again, the majority of the more widely-diffused forms of the cross present in general no clearly perceptible relation to Paradise, and are much more easily explicable in any other sense than precisely one favourable to the hypothesis of our Essayist. Only the Tree of Life among the peoples of the Euphrates, the Persians, the Celts, etc., seems—as will presently be further shown—to include a reference to the tradition of Paradise. And just this belongs to the number of symbols which do not directly and clearly express the figure of a cross, but only, as it were, distantly and in a veiled manner—as a *crux dissimulata*. Of those symbols more clearly comprised under the form of a cross, the Egyptian Nile key far more naturally admits of a reference to the sun-worship, than to Paradise with its streams. Even in the case of a spiritualising interpretation of this symbol, the old traditional reference to everlasting life may indeed be very readily made out; but that to the past glory of Paradise, only with difficulty and in an artificial manner. The alleged "conical form," or phallus relation, of symbols like the Nile key upon Babylonian or other farther

Asiatic monuments is, however, something altogether precarious, perhaps only accidental. If it is really present as an important fact, it is much more likely to contain a reference to the Venus worship of these lands than to any reminiscences of the Paradisiac "mountain of the gods" of the first age.[1] The same is the case with the cruciform symbols of the Americans and other peoples—symbols which, in their primary and perhaps only signification, convey the idea of rain and fruitfulness. If in addition to this more immediate another and deeper one must be conceded to them, then as such the notion of "life, future life, immortality," is on the average fully as suitable as that of a lost Paradise, and in the majority of cases much more so. As a rule, however—since, in not a few cases, even the thought of immortality or the hope of a blissful life beyond the grave, is not to be recognised with sufficient clearness as an object of the symbolisation—in the case of the majority of the symbols in question we shall be justified only in claiming as their deeper signification that of "life," or "deliverance," or "blessing" in general. The attempt, in the article above frequently mentioned, to bring to a point this notion of religious well-being or blessing in the historically concrete notion of Paradise, could succeed only by dint of a violent drawing together and pressing into one of a great number of dissimilar elements and heterogeneous relations, with the result of thus forming a thoroughly artificial unity, and one entirely wanting in historic truth.

Still less capable of defence is the attempt already made by many—*e.g.*, after the example of Ghillany, by F. Nork in his Etymologisch-symbolisch-mythologisches Realwörterbuch —of tracing back the whole of the pre-Christian religious symbols of the cross to the phallus-worship—the immoral rites presented to the rude powers of nature, among many ancient peoples. As regards the Ansate cross of the Egyptians and inhabitants of Farther Asia, this hypothesis may possibly be advanced with at least a certain show of truth. But its application to the great variety of remaining forms,

[1] Comp. Appendix II., No. 5.

which here come under review, is an impossibility. A few attempts made with this end in view would not only call forth most break-neck operations in respect to etymological and archæological criticism, but would demand as their indispensable requirement an imagination of such a kind that its possessor is hardly to be envied.

It is a multiplicity of cosmical views and conceptions, no single primal idea, from which the symbolics of the cross in heathendom have arisen. A number of dissimilar conceptions was the only possible foundation for the complex of emblematical representations here under review; and the more so, since THE VISIBLE CREATION—from the objects of which the activity of the non-revealed religions in general receives its impulse to the formation of its myths and dogmas, and moreover derives its models—PRESENTS IN NONE OF ITS DOMAINS A FIGURE BEARING A STRIKING RESEMBLANCE TO A CROSS. The cross is nowhere reflected in nature in any remarkably prominent or frequently recurring manner. It appears scarcely more distinctly incorporated in the terrestrial or celestial world of phenomena around us, or more perceptible to the eye in nature, than, *e.g.*, the mystery of the Trinity; of which the cosmical reflections constantly present themselves, less as sensible signs than as relations of triplicity—thus more as triple harmonies than as triangles or triads.[1] A. v. Humboldt expressed his surprise that the most distinct and at the same time most striking of all the cruciform figures of the visible cosmos—the Southern Cross, which adorns the starry heavens of the Tropics—*was never*, either in classical antiquity, or in the earlier centuries of Christendom up to the time of the great discoveries and of the Reformation, *at all recognised as a cruciform figure;* that Ptolemy, with great lack of æsthetical perception, ranged it under the hind feet of the constellation of the Centaur; that the Christian anchorites of the Thebaid in the fourth and fifth centuries, who had such

---

[1] See the author's *Theologia naturalis*, p. 660 ff. The views there developed concerning the reflection of the Holy Trinity in the kingdom of nature and of mind, are espoused in their essential particulars by Kahnis, *Lutherische Dogmatik*, I. 368 of the new edition.

excellent opportunities for witnessing it, do not appear to have noticed such resemblance; that Dante, in the celebrated passage of the Purgatorio[1] in which he expresses his acquaintance with that wondrously brilliant phenomenon, indicates it only by the expression "four stars" (quattro stelle); that even Amerigo Vespucci, in the year 1501, is able only to speak of four resplendent stars which formed a rhomboidal figure (una mandorla), and that only with the epoch-making years of the Reformation, 1517 and 1520, in the person of the Florentine Corsali, and in that of Pigafetta, the companion of Magelhaen in his circumnavigation of the globe, the recognition of the cruciform character of this fair constellation appears to have been made.[2] That which especially surprises him in all this, is the fact that the said constellation— "although the form of the cross is so strikingly presented in it, and so remarkably *individualises itself*, in separation" from that of the other constellations—yet first became of importance in the study of nature, and in the devotional contemplation of nature, as the representation of the cross, only in modern times. Even in this case, scarcely so urgent a necessity impels us to fill up the outline of these four stars into a quincunx, and to look upon this as a figure of the cross, as in the star-cross of the northern hemisphere, the "Swan" of the older astronomers; although in the case of the latter constellation the less brilliant lustre of the stars, and the diversion of the eye by the transcending magnitude of its immediate neighbours, such as Vega, have prevented the early and general attention of religiously disposed observers of the marvels of the heavens being drawn to it. In reality, the observing of one or other of these constellations can hardly thus have formed the first impelling motive for one out of the many instances above enumerated of the adoration of the cross on the part of the ancient heathen. Much rather must we suppose that, either the sun or some brightly luminous planet or other, particularly Venus, served as the

---

[1] Canto I., v. 22—24.
[2] *Kosmos*, II., 205 ff.

prototype for certain characteristic forms of the pre-Christian symbolism of the cross; so that in this way the cross really presented itself as, according to the expression of Hamann, "a star deprived of its rays;" served thus as an abbreviature of the formal representation of a star or sun, and appears to have been derived from the natural phenomenon underlying it, rather by the process of mental abstraction than that of direct imitation. Still more difficult would it appear to be to find scientific justification for the attempt, presently to be spoken of, on the part of Böhme and Baader, to conceive of lightning or fire (light) as a power manifesting itself under the form of a cross; or to make good the supposition that some definite kind of natural existence, belonging to the sphere of the organic or inorganic earthly creation, was immediately represented by the symbolism of the cross in the pre-Christian age. The form of the cross is not presented in a striking manner, and with sufficiently frequent recurrence, either in the mineral kingdom or in the animal or vegetable creation, for it to have given occasion to the formation of symbolic figures, such as those above described, of the Nile key, Swastika symbol, labarum, etc. Nay, it appears absolutely rare, and only exceptionally as a sharply defined and "separately individualised" figure, in those realms of nature. The staurolith, a granite whose crystals have assumed a peculiarly regular cross-formation, the harmatom or crossstone, and the chiastolith or hlospath—with beautiful quincunx-like design—are minerals of comparatively rare occurrence, and are formed in part by abnormal growths in the process of crystallisation. The same may be said too of the double or streaked pyritoid sometimes occurring in the pyrites, the so-called iron cross, and other intersecting or radiated crystals.[1] In the vegetable kingdom, too, there is presented—spite of the frequency of such names, and the pretty common occurrence of such classes as the cross-fern, cross-flower (milk-wort), cross-wort, cross-thorn (buckthorn),

[1] Comp. Naumann, *Elemente der Mineralogie* (3rd edn.), S. 281, 311, 324; Oken, *Naturgeschichte*, I. S. 400.

cross-pink, etc.—but very rarely an externally sharply defined conformity to the cruciform type, perceptible at a distance. [This applies still more to the salutary order of the cruciferous plants.] And in the animal kingdom, the species which are cross-shaped, or which bear a cruciform design, are comparatively rare, and in any case not very conspicuous. The arctic or cross-fox, this sufficiently rare, black-striped variety of the ordinary fox, the Brazilian cross-frog (*Sapo*), and the cross-adder, surely hardly afford an explanation for the existence of such a religious symbolism as that above considered in its most prominent examples; and certainly still less so, such smaller members of the animal kingdom as the beautifully marked beetle, *Carabus crux major*, and the *C. crux minor*, the cross-spider, cross-medusa, etc. Or may the mystic conception, in favour with the Fathers from the time of Justin and Tertullian, which sees in the flight of birds, yea, even in the swimming of fish and the bounding of deer, the shadowing forth of the cross, in reality have been formed even before the death of the Redeemer on the cross had become a positive fact of salvation? Could an interpretation so artificial, one so much the product of reflection, and importing so much into the symbol, have indeed sprung up upon pre-Christian soil?[1] It would thus surely be more natural to account for the origin of the cross-symbolism of the heathen worship, by the existence of that cross, which as an ideal form underlies the figure of a normally developed man, standing erect with outstretched arms—of which, according to the Church Fathers, the sculptors among the ancients made use as a standard in the formation of their images of the gods, and the Roman soldiers as a stand on which to hang up their trophies![2] But it is evident that by such a supposition, not a single one of the emblems with which we are acquainted—

---

[1] Görres (*Christliche Mystik*, I. 37) still commends the profoundness and aptness of this mode of view, according to which "the bird flies in the form of a cross, when now—with head thrown forward and wings outstretched—he with tail and feet directs his flight to the goal before his eye"; according to which, moreover, in this form "the fish cleaves the waves, the hart springs over the mountains," etc.

[2] Minucius Felix, *Octav.*, c. 29; Tertullian, *Apologet.*, c. 16.

Nile key, labarum, Swastika cross, etc.—would be rightly interpreted, *i.e.*, interpreted in accordance with its true historic signification. In this way we should, at any rate, be just as far from attaining the end of a sound and really satisfactory explanation for the phenomena with which we are occupied, as though we should assume as the primal and fundamental ground thereof, the double or treble axis-crosses of the mineral crystal forms, and would thus credit their childishly simple authors in hoary antiquity with a knowledge of crystallography.

Only of one characteristic main type in this province do we feel justified in supposing that here a direct imitation of nature had actually taken place. Inasmuch as the TREE OF LIFE of ancient Aryan and Semitic tradition is to be reckoned among the symbols of the cross in the wider sense, we must certainly assume as the originating cause of the adoption of this special form, or at least as a co-operating factor in this result, a frequent imitation of concrete models in nature—thus fruit trees dispensing life and blessing; as in Citerior Asia the date palm, in India the sacred fig, or banian tree, the banana, etc. Such noble models and masterpieces in the vegetable creation served as a welcome revival and refreshing for the ideal original figure of the Tree of Life, which from the time of Paradise had here remained, now in the more faint, now in the more distinct reminiscence of the peoples, an object of their longing. To this, therefore, does the creative fancy and plastic art in the realm of the earliest religious development especially attach itself; from its annually renewed glorious putting forth of foliage, blossoming, and fruit-bearing, the ancients must have mainly derived the thought of clothing, in a bodily form, that paradisiac ideal of longing, which also gradually became the inspiring ideal of the future, the emblem of everlasting life (comp. Ezek. xlvii. 12; Rev. ii. 7, xxii. 2 ff.) Even in recent times, a grateful admiration of the blessing diffused by such wondrous trees of the tropical climes as the banana, the bread-fruit tree, the mango, and above all the productive palm species, has brought vividly before the mind of Christian travellers and missionaries the Tree of Life of the Biblical Paradise-tradition. Appellations like that of *Musa paradisiaca* for the banana of India, or *Arbol del Vida* for the Maurica palm of the Orinoco lands, testify to this ;[1] in like manner the enthusiastic descriptions, alike of single specially blessing-fraught species of palms—such as the date palm, the cocoa palm, the palmyra palm—as of the order of palms in general, with which we meet in every class of works on natural science.[2] Ordinarily, too, the question as to the origin of the palms in these lands is wont to be regarded as of surpassing importance for that calculation of probability, not seldom attempted in modern historic-anthropologic and archæological works, having as its aim the determining of what was most likely the primal home or place of creation of the human race. To the tropical world, or at least to those regions bordering on the tropics which produce, in addition to cereals, also palms, and thus, according to Grisebach's expression, "combine in themselves the conditions of vegetation of the temperate and the tropical zones," are these Paradise-seekers of natural science, as a rule, not less favourably disposed than the majority of

---

[1] "*Arbol del Vida*" is the name given by the Jesuit Gumilla, in his *Orinoco illustrado*, to the glorious Maurica palm (Hartwig, *die Tropenwelt*, 462).—On the name *Musa paradisiaca* or *Pomum paradisi*, as Christian appellations of the Banana fig (Malab. *Pala*), comp. Oken, *Naturgesch.*, III. 1, 517—520.

[2] See, *i.a.*, N. Böhner's "Kosmos: Bibel der Natur," II. 249 ff. "The majestic forms of the palms proclaim in the history of the development of our planet the dawn of a new creative day. ... They are in the primeval world the precursors of man. They ... stood in no need of human culture; they once adorned the paradise of mankind, and, like a faithful nurse, offered to the new created man the first maternal milk. Our undertone of longing for the palms is perhaps a remnant of love inherited from our first parents, who were nourished by them, as the new-born child at the breast of a tender mother. In the paradisiac regions of the earth, where the rays of the tropical sun call forth from the soil a luxurious wealth of ever-verdant plants, the palms lift their glorious heads far above the topmost branch of the primeval forest, lovely images of grace and dignity, a precious adornment of the footstool of God's feet. The noble simplicity of their forms, the symmetrical organisation of their structure, the majesty of their growth, the beauty of their leafy crown, the excellence of their fruits, give to this family of palms an exalted stamp, and render it comprehensible that men from the earliest times have chosen these favourite trees as the symbol of peace, of love, and of triumphant joy." Comp. also what was said by Celsius, *Hierobotanicon*, II. p. 445 sqq.

those who base their speculations, on this subject too, mainly on the intimations of Holy Scripture alone; for the latter are by their researches led to take essentially the same route as the former—namely, to the more southerly lands of Asia, possibly also to Africa, not however to Europe, and in Asia not so far northwards as, *e.g.*, the lands watered by the Oxus.[1]

The palms may serve us as guides in determining the character, and in general also the locality, of the paradisiac primeval abode of our race. It must not, however, be forgotten, in connection with this inquiry, that the monuments of the history of religion amongst the most ancient civilised nations, do not specially and exclusively copy the palm when they would represent the Tree of Life, the emblem of the longing for Paradise and the hope of immortality. As was above shown, the figure of the symbol varies in accordance with the conventional laws which have become a regulative authority for the priesthood of the several lands —in India, reflecting rather the form of the sacred fig-tree; in Persia, more resembling the palm; in Babylonia, offering a fantastic combination of cypress, tamarisk, and date-palm; in Egypt, reminding of the lotus plant or the *persea*; among the Celts, in form approaching an oak;[2] among the Scandinavians, an ash; among the American tribes, again, other forest trees; and yet nowhere forming simply a copy, a mere imitation, from these types in the living world of plants. The same is true of the palm-like figures upon the inner walls of the temple of Solomon (1 Kings vi. 29); these symbols expressing, like the figures of the cherubim, the joyful and peaceful character of the sanctuary of Old Testament worship, of which the form may have been closely allied to that of the Trees of Life upon the Babylonian or Persian monuments.[3] These are all ideal conceptions,

---

[1] Compare Appendix III. PARADISE, ACCORDING TO EARLIER AND MORE RECENT OPINIONS.

[2] [The DERWEN, tree *par excellence* of the Celts. A word from the same root as the Greek words *drūs* and *doru*, and the English *tree*.]

[3] Bähr, *Der salomonische Tempel*, S. 122 ff.; Keil, *Biblische Archäologie*, S. 131 ff.

symbols, not exact copies of the paradisiac Tree of Life. And just as little as they present the figure of a definite tree in the full lifelike character of the actual tree, just so little, on the other hand, comes forth in full distinctness the figure of the cross, to which it is sought to reduce its form, or at least the skeleton outline of its branches. Neither as regards their signification, referred backwards to the Tree of Life in Paradise, nor as referred forwards to the life-giving sign of redemption, are they clear and distinct types, or do they belie their character of *cruces dissimulatæ*, of only half-consciously or almost unconsciously expressed prophetic signs. They appear, accordingly, to be most closely related to those profounder myths of Classic and Teutonic antiquity in which dwell, as it were, only obscure traces of a Divine primitive revelation at the beginning of history, and likewise only an indistinct, half-slumbering, half-dreaming consciousness of the range of its prophetic import, as pointing to the new and better religion of the future.

This one thing we accordingly recognise, in the above-cited interpretation of the cross-symbols of Heathendom in reference to Paradise, as just and applicable: in the midst of the great abundance and almost confusing multiplicity of these emblems, there exists at least *one*, certainly one of those least directly and clearly expressing the form of the cross, to which a retrospective reference to the blissful first home of mankind cannot be denied. Surrounded by a considerable number of cruciform figures, which serve as truly cosmical emblems for the symbolisation of now this, now that external phenomenon of nature or power of the elements, without however presenting any nearer relation to revelation, notwithstanding their more or less striking resemblance to the New Testament symbol thereof, the Tree of Life rises lonely and significantly on high, as a profound hieroglyph of actual import of revelation, as a memorial of former blessed communion of men with God upon the soil of a still virgin-pure earthly creation, as yet not desecrated by human sin. To its full extent, indeed, the significance of this symbol for the history of religion and for apologetics can be appreciated only after we have gained a position whence to overlook those institutions, emblems, and customs of the pre-Christian heathendom which typify the cross of the Lord as a symbol of the curse (Gal. iii. 13), as a scene of the judgment upon the sin of mankind. For only then shall we be in a position to enter more fully into the question whether, beside the Tree of Life, the Tree of Knowledge has not also cast its (long after) baneful shadow upon the development of the ancient heathen life of civilisation. We thus now come to consider the pre-Christian cross in the second place, as the Symbol of the Curse.

b. AS THE SYMBOL OF THE CURSE.

A complete and exhaustive survey of the wide-reaching field of the various applications, as the instrument of torture and punishment, which the cross has found in pre-Christian antiquity, cannot be made our aim. To this subject—with which the epoch-making work of Justus Lipsius, *De Cruce*, was already mainly occupied, so early as 1595—numerous and thorough treatises have been devoted, of which the list contained in the above-mentioned programmes of Zestermann and Degen may be looked upon as on the whole complete.[1] With regard, therefore, to the details of this part of our subject, we refer the reader, once for all, to the statements of these our predecessors, especially the two last named. Supplementary additions to the briefly recapitulating course of their investigations will be necessary in the main only on a single point—the question, namely, to what extent and how widely there was, consciously or unconsciously, a religious significance attached to that cross which was employed as the instrument of punishment or of torture; so that thus our connecting of the same with those crosses expressing the positive conception of blessing and of life may be shown to be justified.

An unconditional rejection of the supposition that a certain religious significance was attached to the punishment of the

[1] Compare our account of the literature given at the beginning of this work.

cross, appears at once inadmissible, for the very reason that all acts of imposing or executing punishment, among all peoples, rest originally upon a religious basis. A clear and definite consciousness of the fact that the punishment of human wrong-doing by human magistracy rests upon Divine authorisation, and is executed by virtue of Divine will or law—thus in God's name—has indeed preserved itself in antiquity only in that nation in whose bosom lived on undimmed the remembrance of that primevally revealed will of God, "Whoso sheddeth man's blood, by man shall his blood be shed" (Gen. ix. 6). Here in patriarchal times, the father of the family (Gen. xxxviii. 24), later, however, under the law, the nation, the totality of the heads of families in the theocratic community, exercised the right of imposing and inflicting punishment, and in particular the punishment of death (jus vitæ necisque), by virtue of Divine authority, or in God's stead (Exod. xx. 12 ff.; Levit. xx. 2 ff.; Deut. xiii. 6 ff.; xvii. 2 ff.) Thus here, and here only, could arise that knowledge which has passed over to the New Testament revelation, and through this has become the common possession of Christian men, the knowledge expressed by Paul, in Rom. xiii. 4, that the magistracy is "God's minister, an avenger for wrath upon him that doeth evil." Nevertheless, however little there exists beyond the sphere of revelation, any clear recognition of this Divine origin of the right of punishing, yet equally indubitably are there to be found even here, everywhere upon primitive heathen soil, certain religious references in the principles cherished and carried out in the punishment of transgressions. However the right of punishment may be theoretically maintained, whether on the so-called theory of retribution, or the theory of determent or repression, or the theory of prevention, or that of amendment, etc., in any case, the whole administration of criminal justice has to be regarded as a special element in the maintenance of public right. The preservation of the life of the State against violent infraction and breach of its legal ordinances, forms the ground and aim of all measures of criminal law.[1] All state life, however, alike among civilised nations as among the ruder children of nature, has been developed upon a religious basis, and is seen to rest in its earliest beginnings upon some conceptions, however obscure and defective, of a Godhead and a Divine retribution in the world beyond the grave, as well as to be provided with certain religious customs—expiatory and sacrificial rites, consecrations, prayers, etc.—maintained as the common possession of all members of a nation or state.[2] There are no peoples absolutely without a religion: where such might seem to be the case, this cannot possibly be regarded as having been their original condition; much more probable is the supposition that religious ideas and customs earlier present among them have perished.[3] So far as the nature of these germs, however imperfect still, of a community of life in religion or worship among nations, may be more accurately tested by the method of historical examination, these include in themselves, in a manner more or less clearly recognisable, a definitely religious character in the measures aiming at the punishment of transgressors and offenders against the common weal. Among all peoples—not merely the people of God of the old covenant (Exod. xxi. 13 ff.; Num. xxxv.; Deut. xix.)—the exaction of blood revenge was looked upon as something sacred, Divinely sanctioned, and lying at the root of Divine legislation. Even where the doctrine of the unpermitted character of avenging self-help, as a presumptuous invasion of the Divine prerogative of vengeance (Levit. xix. 18), was a thing unknown, and the carrying into execution of the blood-revenge was left to

---

[1] Ulrici, *Grundzüge der prakt. Philosophie*, I. 369 ff.; 411 f.
[2] Comp. the beautiful proofs adduced by Max Müller (*Introduction to the Science of Religion*, London, 1873) on the common character of all religions in their earliest stage of development, consisting in certain more general fundamental properties and names of the Godhead, such as strength, brightness, purity, greatness, goodness, etc., as well as in the use of the soteriological-ethical notions of sacrifice, prayer, altar, sin, virtue, spirit, body, etc.—"the outward framework of the incipient religions of antiquity."
[3] See Appendix IV. AGAINST THE ASSERTION OF AN ENTIRE IRRELIGIOUSNESS ON THE PART OF CERTAIN NATIONS.

the passionate zeal of the members of the family, it was nevertheless sacred conceptions and principles, for the most part mingled with all kinds of religious superstitions, in accordance with which the said actions were regulated.[1] Partly from the customs of blood-revenge, partly from the State control devoted to them, partly from the other measures designed to keep watch over the execution of private revenge, or against yet wilder attacks upon the life, property, and general security of the individual—as these were gradually developed in the smaller or greater extent of the community—does criminal justice everywhere appear to have proceeded; so that it nowhere denies its original close connection and interweaving with religious conceptions.[2] In this way is to be explained the ancient Hellenic view and treatment of every punishment as a political satisfaction or revenge ($\tau\iota\mu\omega\rho\iota\alpha$), which the State exacts of the offender, in the name of all, for the violated majesty of the law; for the accomplishment of which end—especially when it is a case of the expiation of the crime of bloodshed—sacrifices or lustrations are also called for, for the appeasement of the injured gods. Still more clearly does this religious element appear in the penal law of the ancient Romans, in which especially the rite of the solemn proscription (*sacratio capitis*) attaching to transgression against the security of the common weal, as well as that of the trial for high treason (*judicium perduellionis aut parricidii*), are of essentially religious import, and include the idea of a necessary propitiation of the offended gods by means of sacrifice. Yea, all death punishment among the Romans appears, from this point of view, to be a propitiatory sacrifice; as indeed the fundamental significance of the word most generally employed in the judicial language of the Romans for execution, *supplicium*, conveys no other notion than that of a sacrifice or prayerful offering to the incensed Divinity.

---

[1] Comp. Oehler, *Theologie des Alten Testaments*, i. 376 ff., and the literature there mentioned.

[2] Comp. the Lexicons, s.v. *supplicium*, *sacrare*, etc. Also the article "Strafe, Strafrecht," etc., in H. Wagener's *Staats und Gesellschafts Lexicon*, xx. S. 54 ff.

In ancient Germanic law, religious ideas of this kind play substantially the same significant part; as is shown by the notions of proscription, placing under ban (*Verfehmung*), wer-gild (blood-fine), the frequent use of ordeals, the severe criminal justice maintained by the priests in time of war, etc. Almost all other nations too, barbarous and civilised, of more ancient and more modern time, especially eastern nations of such comparatively high degree of civilisation as the Egyptians, Persians, Indians, and Chinese, manifest in various ways in their forms of justice the prevalence of such religious conceptions.[1]

After what has been said, it will be expected that the punishment of crucifixion too, which belongs to the oldest and most widely-spread forms of death punishment, must originally have had a religious significance; though it may be that in the course of time this significance receded so far into the background, and was so greatly lost sight of, that the said mode of execution might perhaps appear to bear no other than a merely profane character. It is true that—spite of the original signification of the Latin *supplicium* = sacrifice, sacrificial offering—we cannot suppose that the crucifixion of the transgressor was in general regarded and treated as a sacrifice properly so called. To this mode of regarding it, defended, *e.g.*, by Stockbauer, in his otherwise very meritorious work on the cross,[2] there are wanting all more direct grounds of confirmation. That the Phœnicians and Carthaginians sometimes presented to the sun-god Baal, who stood with arms outstretched after the form of a cross (?), human victims in the same posture of the cross, whom they burnt in his honour, is a mere conjecture unsupported by facts. Just as little is the assertion that the son of the King of Moab (who, according to 2 Kings iii. 27, was offered as a burnt-offering upon the wall of Kir-haraseth) was burnt in the form of a cross, even distantly favoured by the sacred text.

---

[1] This is seen in the instructive expositions of Saint René Taillandier, "L'Histoire du Droit de Punir," in the *Revue des Deux Mondes*, 15th Nov., 1874.

Kunstgeschichte dss Kreuzes, S. 2 ff.

And the instance related by Justin (xviii. 7) of the affixing of Cartalo, son of the Carthaginian general Maleus, upon a great cross within sight of the besieged city of Carthage, bears, according to the distinct account of that historian, not the character of a propitiatory sacrifice offered to Baal, but was simply the effect of an outburst of anger on the part of the enraged general on account of the supposed disobedience or attempted defection of his son. The hypothesis of a sacrifice, as a whole, encounters insuperable difficulties in the fact that the characteristic act of burning—a necessary element of all sacrificial acts—is never mentioned in connection with crucifixions or hangings. As the punishment of the cross is regularly presented as an independent form of execution complete in itself, never as a mere preliminary to other forms of the death-punishment, so in like manner does it nowhere appear as an act preparatory to a subsequent burning of the person crucified or hanged. On the contrary, the *continuing to hang unburned* of the person attached (living or dead) to the cross or stake, forms the true characteristic of this mode of punishment, the object of which seems especially to have been to expose the body of the executed to the air for corruption, and to the birds and dogs for a prey.[1]

In order to form a correct judgment as to the nature and signification of this terrible custom, it is indispensable that we keep duly before our mind this object in its infliction—an object appearing everywhere, and with the greatest clearness precisely in the earliest antiquity. Crucifixion, as well as its collateral forms of impalement, hanging, etc., is essentially and principally *a dishonouring exposure of the executed to become a prey to the birds of the air and the beasts of the field.* It is, as to its primary significance, A HEAPING OF INSULT UPON THE EXECUTED, A BRANDING WITH INFAMY. Among the more artificial modes of carrying into execution this primitive custom of revenge and punishment—of which men-

---

[1] [In this sense Josephus, *Antt.* vi. 14. 8, speaks of the Philistines as crucifying the bodies of Saul and Jonathan by the walls of Bethshan—τὰ δὲ σώματα ἀνεσταύρωσαν πρὸς τὰ τείχη τῆς Βηθσὰν πόλεως.]

tion is made almost countless times even in Homer's songs, and of which the simplest execution consisted in the vengeance inflicted by Creon upon Polynices, of leaving the body of the slain to remain unburied upon the open field,[1]— crucifixion is one of those most frequently occurring, as well as one of the oldest. Yea, as crucifixion in the widest sense —*i.e.*, as hanging upon some kind of stake or tree, even though it be not shaped like a cross[2]—the custom is scarcely less old indeed than that simple casting of the body upon the open field; it is, moreover, a common possession of all barbarous and warlike nations, of which no one to this day has been without its tree of ill omen, its stake of infamy and suffering.

Is the terrible custom one of Semitic (Hamito-Semitic), especially Phœnician-Carthaginian origin? This has been frequently asserted, and, so far as there is implied by this crucifixion nothing more than the affixing to a T, or cross-shaped piece of timber or scaffolding, perhaps not without justice; for no absolutely convincing proof can be adduced to the contrary, and the Carthaginians at any rate made a particularly extensive use of this cross in the narrower sense of the term. It seems, too, as we shall hereafter have to show more in detail, to have passed from them to the Romans. But if we take the idea of crucifixion in that wider sense denoted by the etyma, and by the ordinary usage of the classical languages with regard to the words in question—specially with regard to the words *crux, cruciare, crucifigere*, which lie immediately at the root of our "cross," "crucify"—according to which "hanging," "impaling,"

---

[1] The well-known Homeric οἰωνοῖσιν or θήρεσσιν ἕλωρ καὶ κύρμα γενέσθαι, *e.g.*, Il. v. 488; Od. iii. 271; v. 473; cp. Il. i. 5; viii. 379; xxii. 335; xxiv. 411. Soph., *Antig.* 29, 205; *Aj.* 817. Æsch., *Sept.* 1071; *Suppl.* 781, etc. The same form of speech occurs also frequently in the Old Test. : Comp. Deut. xxix. 26; Ezek. xxix. 5; as well as Goliath's threat to David, 1 Sam. xvii. 44.

[2] For an illustration of such crucifixion in the wider sense, accompanied by circumstances of unusual atrocity, as practised by the Turks, see the engraving in the *Graphic* of Sept. 16, 1876. p. 265. It represents three Servian soldiers bound to trees, and slowly consumed by fires kindled at their feet. The engraving is from a photograph taken on the spot.

"transfixing on a stake," and similar notions were also comprehended under them,[1] then the assertion of an exclusively Semitic origin to this custom appears to be altogether unsupported, since its existence in this more general form can be shown at least just as early, if not earlier, among non-Semitic nations, as among such Semites (more accurately speaking, Semitised Hamites), as the Phœnicians and Carthaginians, or even the Babylonians and Assyrians. The chaining of Prometheus to the rocky wall of the Caucasus, in order that the eagle of Zeus might prey upon him, has been represented as an instance of punishment by crucifixion in the most distant primeval age, and certainly not without warrant. For, apart from the fact that later Greek poets and prose writers describe the suffering imposed upon the hero with expressions which otherwise indicate "crucifixion" —Æschylus, *e.g.*, with ἀνασκολοπίζεσθαι, Lucian with ἀνασταυροῦσθαι—the whole act of punishment or revenge bears at any

---

[1] *Crux*, with its derivatives and composites, is most likely to be referred back —with the assumption of the middle form *cruc-c* or *cran-c*, to the *çram*, which in Sanscrit signifies to be tortured, *dolore vexari; crux* itself by no means denotes exclusively the cross in the narrower sense, but appears in the earlier Latinity as equivalent to *patibulum*, gibbet, or *stipes*, stake, etc. In like manner *cruciare* with Plautus, etc., still by no means denotes specially "crucify," but only "to torture," "to put to the rack." Similarly the Greek σταυρός, of which the primitive signification was that of "pale" or "stake" [still used of a stake in Jos., *B. J.* iii. 7. 19: σταυροῖς ἑδραίοις], from which that of the synonyms σκόλοψ and σανίς (post) does not essentially differ, and of which the derivatives σταυροῦν, ἀνασταυροῦν, etc., signify in the first place only "torture," "torment." (Zestermann, i. 13 f., 15 f.) [The origin of the word *crux* (Welsh *croes*) is probably to be sought in the Celtic root CRO-G = suspendere (? Greek ΚΡΕΜ in κρεμάννυμι), a root which exists in the Cymric, the Gaelic, the Irish, the Manx, and the Armoric. *Crogi*, in the first named of these languages, is the generic expression for "hang," (*e.g.*, Psalm cxxxvii. 2), and *croch* or *crogbren* is the Celtic equivalent for the gallows. The name of this instrument of execution would naturally be learnt by the Romans in their earlier intercourse with the Gauls, and—like *caballus* (ceffyl)—would be adopted from the latter before the use of the Carthaginian instrument was introduced. For an instance of the early use of σταυροῦν in the sense of hanging (?) on a gallows, see LXX. of Esther vii. 9. Instances, on the other hand, of the use of κρεμαννύναι, or suspendere in the sense of crucifying, are common: Luke xxiii. 39; Lam. v. 12, as comp. with Jer. xxxix. 6 *b.*] Fick (*Vergl. Wörterb. der indogerman. Sprachen*, 3rd ed., Götting. 1874, i. 813), derives *crux* from a supposed root "skark," signifying "to fold the arms," etc., "to go aslant."

rate the same meaning as does the affixing of an ordinary, not suprahuman-titanic transgressor, to a stake or gibbet. The rock of Prometheus deserves indeed so to be called, even as it has been termed with reference to the deeper meaning of the tradition which transfigures it: a "gigantic stone cross, which stands forth prophetically above the enchantment of Hellenic cycles of tradition."[1] While this myth of old Hellenic time, yea in its germ perhaps even of a pre-Hellenic period, affords an indirect but significant voucher for the high antiquity of the practice of crucifixion in the wider sense, among the GREEKS and the nations of Citerior Asia bordering upon them; and the common epos of this Hellenic-Asiate complex of nations, the Iliad, equally shows —in the account of the fight for the body of Patroclus—an acquaintance with the closely allied custom of impaling;[2] so again for EGYPT the presence of the like practice of hanging is already attested in the Old Testament by the history of Joseph. For the death-punishment which Joseph, by means of his power of interpreting dreams, predicts to the chief baker, and which was executed on him within three days, consists in "hanging on a tree."[3] This custom of hanging, too, is to be looked upon as genuinely Egyptian, as are all the other characteristic traits in this narrative—*e.g.*, the carrying of the baskets upon the head, the pressing out of the grapes into the king's cup, etc. The cross in the wider sense, as a stake or gibbet, appears accordingly to be known and employed in the land of Ham, so early as the first half of the second millennium before Christ, previous to the immigration of the Israelites.

[1] So Rocholl, *Hannöv. Vorträge über den zweiten Artik. des Glaubens;* 1872, ii. 16. Comp. also Luthardt, *Apolget. Vorträge*, iii. 194.

[2] Il. xviii. 176, the messenger of the gods, Iris, exhorts Achilles to hasten to the conflict for the body of his fallen friend; for "powerfully does the heart impel Hector 'to set upon a stake' the head of Patroclus"—κεφαλὴν πῆξαι ἀνὰ σκολόπεσσιν.

[3] Gen. xl. 19—23, הָלָה עַל עֵץ (Vulg., suspendere in cruce; Luth., an den Galgen henken). Of a real living tree, we can hardly think. Comp. the expositors *in loc.* Manetho also attests the practice of hanging as a form of punishment common among the Egyptians. (*Apostelesm.*, iii. 195 sqq.) [Josephus has here ἀνασταυροῦν, *Antt.* ii. 5. 3.]

To these traces of the practice of crucifixion in the wider sense amongst an Indo-Germanic and a Hamitic people—traces in all probability reaching back almost as far as the third chiliad before Christ—there may be added the much more numerous and direct accounts which testify to the imposition of this very form of punishment among the Semites of the south-western district of Asia, from the middle of the second chiliad before Christ. Among the ASSYRIANS it must have been customary specially in the form of impalement—*i.e.*, the driving of a sharpened stake through the cavity of the stomach (about the region of the heart), and the placing of this beam in an upright position with the body of the transfixed upon it; for the pictorial representation of a besieged city, upon one of the monuments of Nineveh, displays three such naked bodies impaled upon stakes, in such fashion that the head and arms hang down upon one side of the stake, the lower part of the body and legs on the other.[1] To what extent this representation testifies to a very ancient custom, or whether only to a custom belonging to a later epoch of the Babylonian-Assyrian history, may perhaps remain undetermined. With regard to the neighbouring family of the Euphrates peoples to the west, namely, the HEBREWS, it is shown by most distinct accounts in the Pentateuch and the prophetic books of sacred history that the custom, closely akin, of hanging the bodies of those executed, or of foes who were slain, prevailed among them as early as the age of Moses and Joshua. " Take all the heads (chiefs) of the people and hang them up before the Lord against the sun," is the command of Jehovah to Moses, when he was incensed at the apostacy of Israel to the impure worship of Baal Peor." The execution of this sentence consisted, according to what follows, in the impure offenders being "slain "—*i.e.*, put to death with the sword, or, as in the case of that couple

---

[1] See Bonomi, *Nineveh and its Palaces*, p. 276, Fig. 162. Also Layard, *Nineveh and its Remains*, ii. 374, and engraving on p. 369. For crucifixion (or impalement?) as an ancient Assyrian custom, comp. further Diodorus, ii. 1 ; with regard to the later Babylonians, also Herodotus, iii. 159.

[2] Numbers xxv. 4.

transfixed by Phinehas, with the spear—and then "hanged before the sun," *i.e.*, hung up upon a tree or stake. In the same manner must we suppose the execution of the King of Ai to have taken place, since Joshua "hanged him on a tree until eventide," as likewise that of the five Canaanitish kings captured in the cave at Makkedah, who, after their necks had been trodden under the feet of the captains, were slain and hanged on five trees until the evening.[1] The leaving suspended only until the evening, when accordingly the bodies were to be taken down and buried, "that the land be not defiled," here took place in accordance with the precept of Deuteronomy (Deut. xxi. 22 f.) How, in presence of these such distinct passages of the law and of the oldest book of history, any could deny the existence among the Israelities of punishment by the cross,[2] is comprehensible only when the punishment of the cross is recognised in the narrower sense exclusively, and the hanging upon trees, stakes, and such-like forms are entirely excepted from the notion of crucifixion— a position which, according to our previous exposition, appears to be alike grammatically and historically untenable. The form of the tree of shame here just as little affects the essence of the matter, as does the question whether the person to be subjected to this outrage was hanged upon it as a corpse or while still living. What was at first indeed executed only on those already dead, may in the course of time, and under the corrupting influence of the barbarous manners of surrounding nations, also have been extended to the living. Even in the case of the "hanging up before the Lord" of seven men of the house of Saul (2 Sam. xxi. 6), perpetrated by the Gibeonites, under David and with David's sanction, at Gibeah

[1] Joshua viii. 29; x. 24—27. The Heb. verb employed in these two passages is הָלָה, "to hang up;" whereas Num. xxv. 4, we have הוֹקִיעַ (from יָקַע, to dislocate) "to disjoint," "stretch out"—the same expression as is used in 2 Sam. xxi. 6, perhaps also with a somewhat similar meaning, that of a crucifixion properly so called. See below. [Fürst gives as the radical meaning of this verb, "to fix firmly;" so "to fasten (to a stake)," "to impale."]

[2] So Causobon; and, after him, Bormitius, Winer, art. "Kreuzigung," Zestermann, i. 10 f. Otherwise already Chaufepié, and, among the more modern exegetes, Bertheau and Keil.

of Saul,[1] the Biblical expression is such that a hanging of men yet living—and indeed as the verb employed in the original, "to stretch out," seems to imply, stretched out as upon a cross, thus perhaps upon actual crosses—appears to be involved in it.[2] Inasmuch as the non-Israelitish but Amorite origin of the Gibeonites is expressly declared at the beginning of this narrative (xxi. 2), and inasmuch as, in the carrying into execution of this cruel act, they did not hold themselves bound to the observance of that Deuteronomical precept which requires the taking down of the hanged on the evening of the day, but suffered them to hang there many days and nights—so that Rizpah, the mother of two of these Saulites, was moved to become a faithful guardian to them against the wild beasts of the field and the birds of the air (ver. 10)—the whole proceeding appears, we confess, as only partially and indirectly an act of judicial punishment among the Hebrews : the theocratic king concurs in this action, not as properly speaking enjoining it, but as permitting, as conceding to a Canaanitish vassal-people the observance of their own custom.[3] But may not something of a similar kind have been repeated within the history of Israel itself, even without the co-operation of such partially foreign influences ? May not, especially in time of war, when even much more terrible punishments were often imposed,[4] also the nailing of living beings to trees, stakes, or scaffolds —in imitation of the practice of the neighbouring peoples, or in revenge for the enormities they had committed—some-

---

[1] 2 Sam. xxi. 5—9.
[2] Comp. note [1] on the preceding page. The LXX. excellently translate יָקַע, in 2 Sam. xxi. 6, 9. by ἐξηλιάζειν; in Num. xxv. 4, on the other hand, less accurately by παραδειγματίζειν. The Vulgate has, Num. xxv. 4, *suspendere*; on the other hand, 2 Sam. xxi. 6, 9, *crucifigere*. (As it has also, in connection with Pharaoh's baker, Gen. xl. 19, once " suspendere *in cruce*.")
[3] Compare the instructive observations of Keil *in loc.*, in the second edition of his *Bibl. Comm. on the Books of Samuel*.
[4] Think of the tearing with saws and teethed sledges, and burning in brick-kilns, inflicted by David upon the Ammonites, 2 Sam. xii. 31 ; 1 Chron. xx. 3 ; as also of the hurling down of 10,000 Edomites from the rock by the command of Amaziah, 2 Chron. xxv. 12.

times have taken place? The account of the actual execution of a sentence of this kind is first expressly given us with regard to the Maccabæan king Alexander I., Jannæus (died B.C. 79), who once, after the taking of the rebellious city of Bethome, caused no fewer than 800 of the Jews there captured to be nailed to the cross, and for the augmentation of the punishment caused the wives and children of the crucified to be cut down before their eyes.[1] The supposition that similar enormities, though perhaps in less inhuman form, have been perpetrated from time to time among the Jews, cannot indeed be opposed by any very valid arguments; since the law of Deut. xxi. 23 most unequivocally testifies to the custom of hanging transgressors upon a tree of the curse as a constituent element in their criminal practice from the earliest time; and since the neighbouring race of PHŒNICIANS, closely related to them by the community of language, certainly practised this custom from the beginning of the last chiliad before Christ—if not even earlier—as is shown by the previously observed frequency of its occurrence among their colonists the *Carthaginians.* As concerns these last, the ferocity with which they were wont to inflict this punishment—not rarely aggravated by the addition of exquisite tortures—as well upon prisoners of war (as, *e.g.*, it is alleged, upon Regulus in the first Punic war) as upon domestic slaves, and above all upon many of their generals, has become proverbial.[2] It is a Punic slave whom Plautus represents as replying to one who was threatening him with crucifixion, "Threaten me not! I know the cross will be my grave; for there have all my ancestors been buried—father,

---

[1] Josephus, *Antiq.*, xiii. 14. 2. That the act of Alexander is here characterised as πάντων ὠμότατον ἔργον, and as a δίκη ὑπὲρ ἄνθρωπον, does not justify the conclusion Winer (*ut supra*) would deduce from it, in favour of his theory of the non-existence of the punishment of crucifixion in general among the Jews. Not in the crucifying of the 800 in itself, but in the slaying of their wives and children before their eyes, does the historian see something unparalleled and before unheard-of.

[2] Cp. Justin, xviii. 7 (see above); Valerius Maximus, ii. 7; Polyb., i. 24. 6; Livy, xvii. Epit. As regards Regulus in particular, Silius Ital., ii. 343.

grandfather, great-grandfather, and great-great-grandfather."[1] As this saying, so do the other express accounts of the infliction of crucifixion among the Carthaginians, not extend back beyond the commencement of the third century before Christ. What pleads for a much higher antiquity of this usage is the fact of its exceeding frequency and popularity, as well as the significant fact that the North-African neighbouring people of the BARCÆANS in Cyrenaica, already—according to a statement of Herodotus—knew and practised the custom of impalement or crucifixion (ἀνασκολοπίζειν) so early as the sixth century before Christ.[2]

For the extraordinarily widespread, yea almost unlimited prevalence of the punishment of the cross in the widest sense, among the better known pre-Christian peoples, evidence is afforded, moreover, by the to a large extent well-supported ancient accounts which attest it. For the INDIANS there are those referring to a time so early as that of the conquests of Semiramis, who—in Diodorus, ii. 18—scornfully threatens the Indian king Stabrobates with a nailing to the cross; for the Turanian people of the SCYTHIANS, to the north of Media, those referring to a period six hundred years before Christ, at the time of the Median king Cyaxares: as concerns the MEDES and PERSIANS, there are those vouching for its existence among them under the kings of the line of the Achæmenides, in the sixth and fifth centuries; for the people of MAGNA GRÆCIA, its presence is attested in Sicily at the time of the Elder Dionysius of Syracuse, about the year B.C. 400, and often after that time; for the MACEDONIANS, under Alexander the Great and his successors; even for the ancient BRITONS and the FRIESLANDERS, whose custom, attested by Tacitus, for the first century of our æra, of hanging their captives upon crosses or gibbets, unquestionably points

---

[1] *Miles Gloriosus*, ii. 4. 19:
    Noli minitari: scio crucem futuram mihi sepulcrum.
    Ibi mei majores sunt siti, pater, avos, proavos, abavos.

[2] Herod., iv. 202: Pheretime, queen of Barce, causes the murderers of her son Arcesilaus, whom the victorious Persians had delivered up to her, "to be impaled around the wall," ἀνεσκολόπισε κύκλῳ τοῦ τείχεος.

back to an existence thereof in earlier ages.[1] As concerns the ROMANS, crucifixions in the wider sense present themselves even in the history of their kings. The account in Livy, given in connection with the history of the Horatii, of a hanging upon a "tree of ill omen," no doubt refers to one which was effected by means of a cord, not by nailing, but nevertheless implies clearly enough an execution bearing the character of a punishment on the gallows,—a shameful death by hanging. And as it reminds of the "hanging upon the tree" of the Old Testament, so also does the proceeding of Tarquinius Priscus, of which Pliny bears testimony, who in the construction of the Cloaca Maxima caused the bodies of those who had committed suicide in order to escape the labour imposed upon them, to be attached to the cross as a warning to the other labourers,[2] in some degree resemble the above-mentioned ancient Hebrew custom. In its later prevailing form, as an execution carried out mainly upon slaves and of those guilty of the graver offences—such as mutinous soldiers, subjects taken in revolt, highway robbers, etc., but never upon Roman citizens[3]—crucifixion amongst the Romans declares with sufficient clearness its Punic origin, as a custom

---

[1] Mention is made of crucifixion, or similar forms of execution, among the *Indians*, Diod., ii. 18; among the *Scythians*, Justin, ii. 5; among the *Medes*, Herod., i. 128; among the *Persians*, Herod., iii. 125; iv. 43; vii. 33, 194; ix. 78, 120; also *Ctesiæ excerpt.*, 5; Thucyd., i. 110; Cic., *de Finib.*, v. 30; cp., Ezra vi. 11; Esther vii. 9 f.; among the *Syracusans* under Dionysius I., Diodorus, xiv. 53. 5; among the *Macedonians* under Alex. the Gr., Curtius R., iv. 4. 17 (execution of 2,000 Tyrians, after the taking of this city, by nailing to the cross, Curt., vii. 11. 28; ix. 8. 16); among the Macedonian troops under the Ptolemies in Egypt., Justin, xxx. 2; among the *Frieslanders* in the time of Tiberius, Tacit., *Ann.*, iv. 72; among the *Britons* in the time of Nero, A.D. 61, Tacit., *Ann.*, xiv. 33. [So Josephus uses σταυρός and ἀνασταυροῦν, *Antt.* xi. 6. 10, 11.]

[2] Liv., i. 26. Caput obnubito, arbori infelici reste (*with a cord*) suspendito; cp. Senec., *Ep.* ci., illud infelix lignum.—Pliny, H. N., 36. 15. Novum remedium invenit ille rex (Tarq. Prisc.), ut omnium ita defunctorum figeret crucibus corpora spectanda civibus simul et feris volucribusque laceranda. Comp. what has been said above (p. 55 f.) as to the crucifixion of dead bodies among Jews and Greeks.

[3] Cicero, *Verr.* 55, 66; Horace, *Serm.* i. 3. 82; Juvenal, vi. 219; Josephus, *Bell. Jud.*, v. 17. 1; *Antt.*, xvii. 10. 10; xx. 6. 2; Appulejus, *Metam.*, iii. p. 64, ed. Bipont. ; Capitolius, *Pertin.*, 8; Lampridius, *Alex. Sever.*, 23; etc.

which had extended to them by virtue of the commercial relations with Carthage during the first ages of the republic. And it is precisely this Roman custom of crucifixion, adopted from the Carthaginians, which first brings out with great distinctness the use of the four-armed cross, properly so called, ┿ to which we thus owe the idea and name of that which ┃ we now term crucifixion in the narrower sense.

A considerable diversity exists in the forms and mode of employing those implements of torture which are comprehended under the general appellation of crosses or instruments of crucifixion. The earliest and simplest form was without doubt that merely of an erect STAKE, to which offenders were nailed or hanged. To this stake—the place of which might also often be occupied by the stem of a tree; and which was itself briefly designated as the "tree"[1]—the person to be hanged was attached, either after previous execution or while yet living, usually in such wise that alike the feet and the arms (folded together above the head, and thus representing with the upright stake the form of a Φ) were fastened—it is doubtful as regards the latter whether through the hands—to the cross, each by one large nail. The appellations current in the classical languages for this primitive form of the cross—designated by Lipsius the *crux simplex*—are, in Greek, σταυρός[2] or σανίς, *post*, as also σκόλοψ, *pale* or *stake;* in Latin, *crux* or *stipes*, which latter expression may denote alike the stem of a living tree, as also a stake, stock, or log prepared from it. This mode of crucifixion was originally customary among all nations. Among those belonging to the historic period, that of the Persians, especially, seems to have frequently practised it; for Herodotus, in his accounts of Persian executions, occasionally makes use of such expressions as " nail to a plank " (σανίς) or " hang."[3]

[1] Liv., i. 26 (see note [2] on preceding page) ; Deut. xxi. 22 (Gal. iii. 13) ; Josh. viii. 29 ; x. 24. 27 ; etc.
[2] From the root σταƒ=στα, thus related to ἵστημι ; comp. Zestermann, i. 13, n. 21.
[3] So vii. 33 : 'Ἀρκταΰκτην ἄνδρα Πέρσην λαβόντες ζῶοντα πρὸς σανίδα προσδιεπασ-

Beside the post for hanging, there stands, as of not much later date in point of origin, but—as applied to the living— certainly a more terrible and violent means of crucifixion, the POINTED STAKE for transfixing the criminal, the instrument of impalement or transpiercing. It is that implement depicted upon the monuments of Nineveh, and thus existing among the ancient Assyrians, and employed by them and the neighbouring peoples, more especially in wars, for the impaling of fallen foes, in some cases also of living prisoners; and not less that stake of which the Iliad makes mention, in its account of the battle for possession of the fallen Patroclus, as being in ordinary use on the Trojan side, for fixing the head thereupon. To the Greek expression σκόλοψ, originally beyond doubt denoting specially *this* instrument, corresponds the Latin *acuta crux* ("pointed cross," "pointed stake") in Seneca.[1] The refined cruelty of impaling living persons, as this writer knew it, and as it is still described by Hesychius in the fourth century,[2] as consisting in the transfixing of the body along the whole length of the spine, "as in the case of fish roasted upon spits," is practised among many barbarian peoples even to the present day. The Khan of Khiva is said to have employed this terrible mode of punishment especially against Christians and Shi'ahs, using indeed a carriage for the impelling of the pointed stake into the body, as yet lying in a horizontal position firmly bound upon another carriage, as well as cords fastened to the legs of those impaled, in order to draw down the body more deeply after the erection of the stake, and thus to complete the work of impalement. Among the Mohammedan Negro races of the Joliba, at Ilori,

σάλευσαν. Comp. ix. 120. With justice does Zestermann maintain that these σανίδες of the Persians are *square* posts, or thick planks; cp. Passow and Pape, *s.v.*

[1] *Ep.* ci. Inde illud Mæcenatis turpissimum votum, quo et debilitatem non recusat et—novissime *acutam crucem*, dummodo inter hæc mala spiritus prorogetur.

[2] Hesych.: σκόλοψιν ὡς ὀπτῶσιν . . . . ὀξύνοντες ξύλον διὰ ῥάχεως καὶ τοῦ νώτου, καθάπερ τοὺς ὀπτωμένους ἰχθῦς ἐπὶ ὀβελίσκων. Comp. Seneca, *Consol. ad Marc.*, c. 20: alii per obscœna stipitem egerunt, etc. (Through the back, and along the spine.)

in West Africa, Gerhard Rohlfs in 1867 came upon a number of unfortunate creatures thus impaled, suspended upon their lance-like stakes high in the air.[1]

The transition from the stake and the pointed stake, as the two main forms of the *crux simplex*, to the cross properly so called, the COMPOSITE CROSS, *crux compacta* of Lipsius, is formed especially by the instrument of death of the nature of a pillory, employed by the Romans for the punishment of slaves, the cross-beam, or *patibulum*, and again by the fork, *furca*. The former, corresponding to the radical signification of patibulum = cross-bar of a gate, was a simple, beam-like, thick piece of wood, of oblong form, which was placed across the upper part of the victim's breast, and to the ends of which his arms—as widely as possible extended—were firmly attached. The man thus bound was then driven through the streets of the town, followed by the hangman, who scourged his back, to the place of execution. There he was drawn up by means of cords, which were fastened to the cross-beam, to an upright stake, in order thus to be devoted to a lingering death. So also the *furciferi*, or bearers of the "fork"—a combination of two cross-beams (resembling the rest for a carriage shaft), in the form $\times$, which must be borne upon the back, the hands being all the while firmly bound to the two lower ends of the beams, thus presenting a complicated variation from the straight cross-beam—were followed by the executioner, by whom they were scourged, not however to be finally hanged upon the cross, but to sink down exhausted by the heavy and torturing burden, and to yield up the spirit under the blows of the

His account is published in the "Daheim," 1873, No. 39. Also in his book of travels, "Quer durch Afrika," 1874, ii. 258. Comp. also Oberländer, *Westafrika* (Leipzig, 1874), S. 248 f. [A similar case of impalement was witnessed in Bosnia during the summer of 1876, inter alios, by Canon Liddon and Rev. M. Maccoll. Perfectly well-authenticated instances of impalement by the Turks in Servia also occurred during the same period. See, *e.g.*, Canon Liddon's letter to *Daily News* of January 12, 1877; confirmed by letter of Heinrich Renner in *Daily News* of February 6. For more recent cases see the letter of Mr. Gladstone, *ibid.*, May 22.]

scourger.[1] The names of these two Roman instruments of torture, although without doubt originally bearing a different signification, came gradually to be looked upon as synonyms with *crux*. *Patibulum* especially became quite the ordinary synonym for *crux*, with which, from the time of Cicero and Cæsar, it became almost an exact equivalent—an expression which in this later usage corresponds pretty nearly to our "Gallows."[2] This manifestly in consequence of the fact that the cross-beam was now fastened to the upright stake, the beam to which it was formerly raised, previously to the commencement of the execution, and the cross thus composed was laid upon the shoulders of the condemned, that he might bear it to the place of execution.

The *furca*, too, may in some cases, after having been borne to the place of execution, have been erected there, as a cross or gibbet, and thus have been made use of for branding with ignominy the death of the sufferer, as well as for the public exposure of his body. Definite historic accounts, however, of such employment of this instrument of torture can be adduced neither from the ancient Roman authors nor from Christian writers; and thus all that has been advanced by later writers from the time of J. Lipsius, and illustrated by pictorial representations, concerning execution on crosses of a furca-like form, rests entirely upon an uncertain basis. Neither for the form ╳ nor for that of a Greek Y—which latter, moreover, many Christian artists have made the basis of their representation of the crucified Saviour—do the annals of Roman criminal justice, or the

---

[1] See the lucid and convincing statements in Zestermann, i. 18-23, by which the, in many cases indistinct and baseless, explanations of the *patibulum* and the *furca* on the part of earlier writers find their thorough refutation—particularly the arbitrary identification of the two in Lipsius, *De Cruce*, iii. 3, and in Forcellini, *Lexicon*, s.vv., with whom, among more recent authors, agrees Keim, *Gesch. Jesu v. Nazara*, iii. 397.

[2] Tacitus, *e.g.*, employs indifferently *cruci affigere* (*Ann.* xv. 44), and *patibulo affigere* (*Ann.* iv. 72). Comp. also Cicero, *In Pison.* 78, *cruci suffigere*, with Appulej., *Metam.*, vi. 130; *patibulo suffigere*.—On ἴκριον as a (later Greek) synonym of *patibulum*, comp. Zestermann, i. 14.

Acts of the Martyrs of the early Church afford any kind of authorisation.[1] In like manner the so-called ST. ANDREW'S CROSS, or diagonal cross, X, cannot be shown to be a Roman instrument. That the Apostle Andrew was put to death on such a cross, at Patras in Achaia, is related only by very late and uncertain authorities.[2] The practice of criminal law among the Romans knows nothing of any but upright standing crosses, no such *cruces decussatæ;* and the frequent occurrence of the X as a monogram or abbreviation of the name of Christ upon early Christian monuments, does not justify us in the conclusion that the cross was frequently, or even at all, employed in this form for the torture of Christians in the times of persecution. Nevertheless a passage of Josephus, to the effect that during the Jewish war the Roman soldiers sometimes varied the forms of crucifixion in the case of their captives,[3] renders the occasional employment of the diagonal cross a thing in itself quite possible, yea even not improbable. Beyond the limits of the Roman Empire, too, this form of the cross must even earlier have been called into requisition here and there, for the purposes of executions, as its use has been retained, *e.g.*, in Ulterior India, up to the present day. The English traveller J. Talboys Wheeler, a few years ago, from the deck of the steamer on which he was traversing the Irawady,

[1] Only after the abolition of crucifixion as a death-punishment, under the Christian emperors of the fourth or fifth century (according to Aurel. Victor, *De Cæs.*, 41, Sozom., i. 8, and others, under Constantine the Great; but probably not until somewhat later), there came into use a fork-like gibbet, shaped like a Y, and called *furca*, as a Roman instrument of execution. In the pre-Constantine period, the employment of this Y-shaped *furca* cannot be shown to have taken place. Representations of the Saviour as hanging upon a cross of this form are first met with in the later Middle Ages. Agincourt, *Hist. de l'Art: Peinture*, tab. ci. 14, presents an instance, taken from a painting in the chapel of St. Sylvester, at Rome, belonging to the year 1248. Stockbauer, p. 292, gives this, and also adds a few later examples of the same kind.

[2] Neither the *Martyrol. Rom.*, under date of 30th Nov., nor Hippolytus, nor Paulinus of Nola (*Carm.*, 24, 406), speak of the martyrdom of St. Andrew as having taken place upon such diagonal cross.

[3] *B. J.*, v. 11, 1: προσήλουν δ' οἱ στρατιῶται τοὺς ἁλόντας ἄλλον ἄλλῳ σχήματι. Comp. also the words of Seneca, *Consol. ad Marc.*, c. 20, cited in a following note.

witnessed in the neighbourhood of Ava the horrible spectacle of a human being nailed to a X-shaped cross raised on the bank of the stream. And Adolf Bastian saw representations among the sculptures of the Buddhist sanctuary Nakhon Vat, in Cambodia, of scenes from hell, of a nature to set one's hair on end—tortures of ever-increasing ghastliness, "until at last, the transgressors were fixed, with hands *and feet* outspread, upon crosses (? thus surely upon X crosses), and stuck all over the body with nails."[1]

As in the case of the St. Andrew's cross, so in that of the three-armed (Egyptian) cross, known as ST. ANTHONY'S CROSS, T, the *crux commissa* of Lipsius, it cannot be shown with distinctness that it was ever a Roman implement of execution. It may, of course, have happened that in those executions with the *patibulum* in the earlier period of the Republic, the transom, with the offender attached thereto, may have been drawn up to the very top of the upright pole, so as to form with this a T; yet certainly this proceeding would offer greater mechanical difficulties than would the uncompleted elevation, from which resulted the form ✝. Only as an exceptional case, therefore, would the nailing to the three-armed or T cross take place among the Romans; whether it did so more frequently among other nations of antiquity, is a question not very easy of solution. Certainly the appellation "Egyptian cross" is, like the tradition that St. Anthony wore upon his mantle and on the top of his staff a T symbol, of entirely late origin, and without historic value.[2] So from the well-known typology of the Church Fathers, who look upon the Greek Tau as letter and numeral—also in the passage Ezek. ix. 4—as a prophecy having reference

---

[1] *Ausland*, 1874, No. 41 (S. 810). Bastian, *Die Völker des östl. Asien*, iv. 99.

[2] Many pictorial representations place a T-shaped walking-stick in the hand of St. Anthony, or show him beating down the devil by means of such cross-handled stick. Wessely, *Iconographie Gottes und der Heiligen* (Leipzig, 1874), S. 76, ventures on the gratuitous conjecture that "the letter T here indicates Theos (God)." Why not in this case a Θ? Rather may we perhaps assume an after-influence of the ancient Egyptian Nile-key.

to Christ, can nothing certain be concluded as regards the form of the ancient cross of execution. But when Lucian in one of his humorous writings represents men as pronouncing a curse upon Cadmus, because in addition to the other letters of the alphabet he invented also the T, this model for the terrible tree of smart employed by the tyrants,[1] we have in these words—because the form indicated is certainly not that of the ancient Greek or the Phœnician character, but the form of the T common in Lucian's time— surely a hint in favour of the three-armed cross being in use at least side by side with the four-armed. So, too, the T cross, as the most insensible and natural modification of the prevailing type, can hardly have been wanting among the "crosses of various kinds, now shaped in this way, now in that," of which Seneca speaks on one occasion.[2] And if Church Fathers so late as Gregory the Great and Isidore of Seville, at the beginning of the seventh century, appear to have no knowledge of crosses for the purpose of execution in the form of a T,[3] nothing definite can be deduced therefrom with regard to earlier times; and the more so, since their testimony is in direct opposition to that of Lucian, who lived four centuries earlier. That among peoples who were

[1] Lucian, Δίκη φωνηέντων, ed. Becker, i. 61, τῷ γὰρ τούτου (τοῦ Ταῦ) σώματι φασι τοὺς τυράννους ἀκολουθήσαντες καὶ μιμησαμένους αὐτοῦ τὸ πλάσμα, ἔπειτα σχήματι τοιούτῳ ξύλα τεκτήναντας ἀνθρώπους ἀνασκολοπίζειν ἐπ' αὐτά.—A "slavishly exact imitation" (Zestermn., i. 25), need by no means be implied by μιμησαμένους in this place. Certainly Lucian had, at any rate, before his mind a T, not the old Greek form ╪, as the subject of this imitation; on which account the above inference is sufficiently warranted.

[2] *Consol. ad Marc.*, 20: Video istic cruces *non unius quidem generis*, sed aliter ab aliis fabricatas, etc. As special instances of these variously formed "crosses" are mentioned, no doubt, only hangings in an inverted form (*capite conversos in terram suspendere*—a form of suffering well known as that which, according to the ordinary tradition, the Apostle Peter underwent), impalement throughout the length of the body, and "stretching out the arms upon the gallows." But this very "*brachia patibulo explicuerunt*" can hardly be limited to crucifixion upon the †-formed cross.

[3] Gregor. Magn., *Moral. in Job*, c. 39. Isidor., *Comm. in lib. Judic.*, c. 5.— For additional remarks on these passages, as upon the testimony (in part contradictory to them), given by Paulinus of Nola in favour of the T form of many execution-crosses (*Poem.*, xxvii.), see under Appendix V.

farther removed from the Roman civilisation of the west, as some American peoples, more especially the Mexicans, T-shaped crosses were employed as instruments of death or of torture, appears an indisputable conclusion from certain facts already mentioned in the preceding division of this chapter.

The most ordinary figure of the cross of execution in the last pre-Christian time—and consequently the one which possesses by far the strongest claims to be regarded as having been made use of in the crucifixion of the Lord—is the FOUR-ARMED UPRIGHT CROSS ✝, the *crux immissa* of Lipsius' terminology, or *Christian* cross, as it may be at once termed, in accordance with the tradition almost exclusively prevalent in Patristic literature and the whole of ecclesiastical art. Whether the pre-Christian use of this form of the cross can be supposed to have extended so widely beyond the limits of the Roman empire and criminal justice as Zestermann has sought to show; whether the above-mentioned crucifixions among the Scythians, the Medes, Egyptians, Syrians, Macedonians, Syracusans, etc., are all to be conceived of as a nailing to a four-armed cross, so that thus hardly any other than the Assyrians and Persians are to be excluded from the number of the ancient peoples who made use of this instrument of execution—on these points a number of doubts and queries certainly arise.[1] But at all events the form of the execution-cross in prevailing use amongst the Carthaginians during the latest period of their independent existence, which passed over from them to the Romans, and by the legions of Rome was extended—until towards the commencement of the imperial age—over the whole of the ancient civilised world, was no other than the four-armed. And for the fact that this form of the implement of crucifixion, or that at least forms more or less closely resembling it, were current among the most diverse heathen nations of Ulterior Asia, those too most distantly removed from the influence of the civilised life of the peoples of the Mediterranean, and even among the

[1] See Appendix V.

peoples of the New World, we may accept—though not without some critical caution and reserve—the testimonies of Catholic missionaries with respect to the crucifixions practised among the Malays of the Molucca islands, among the Japanese, and even among the Mexicans of the seventeenth century.

If we now cast a retrospective glance upon these manifold forms of the infliction of the death-punishment of the cross in the wider and the narrower sense ; if, especially, we represent to ourselves once more the most generally occurring forms of the cross of execution, or gibbet, from the most primitive *crux simplex*, down to the *crux immissa* of the latest Roman period :

and take into account, moreover, the different modes of procedure—now milder, now more severe—in connection with the executions made upon it, then at any rate the conviction forces itself upon us, that this mode of punishment as a whole belongs to those which are the severest conceivable, and that the instruments for its accomplishment well deserve the name of *cruces*, " instruments of torture ;" that, nevertheless, among those seven or eight different forms of the cross of execution, that which eventually became most widely spread, and certainly also was employed in the case of the Redeemer, the form † *can by no means be regarded as necessarily and in itself the most cruel and terrible one of all.* The cross in the narrower sense, the Roman four-armed cross of the Gospel history, cannot be spoken of without further explanation as the most severe, *i.e.*, the means of execution producing the most intense and acute suffering. Several of those other *cruces*, which the inventive faculty of the Romans

---

[1] Comp., in addition to Gretser, *De Cruce*, i. c. 24, Cornel. Hazart, S.J., *Kirchen-Geschichte*, 3rd edit. (Wien u. Muenchen, 1727), Pt. i., *passim*. Contains various woodcuts representing martyrs crucified on †-shaped crosses ; *e.g.*, p. 179, such martyrdom on the island of Ternate (Moluccas) ; p. 420, several such in the Japanese islands ; cp. 439, etc. On the crucifixions among the Mexicans at the time of the discovery of the New World, see below (p. 76).

and other nations of antiquity, ever fertile and unwearied in the discovery of new forms of suffering and torture, has devised, of which many have survived to the most recent times in the barbarian justice of ruder tribes, must have been adapted to produce death not less painful. Thus the impalement, or piercing through the body lengthwise, described by Seneca and Hesychius, as indeed the *furca* in its earlier mode of infliction as a scourging to death of the fugitive laden with the fork, must have effected the same result; not to speak of other instruments of torture, not falling under the general conception of "crosses," as the threshing sledge or the heated brick-kilns of the orientals, the burning on stakes, the laceration by wild beasts in the circus, or the terrible mode of execution still practised in China, called Lingchih, and consisting in the gradual hacking of the body in pieces. It is true Cicero, in his oration against Verres, several times speaks of crucifixion as the "worst, supreme, most cruel," or "odious," form of punishment,[1] and without doubt he has before his mind the execution upon the four-armed cross; thus crucifixion in the narrowest and most usual acceptation. But that this mode of execution was never equalled or surpassed in severity by any other, is certainly an inference unwarranted by these expressions. For, on the one hand, we must take into account the rhetorical colouring and excited character of these descriptions, which did not allow time for the careful pondering of the expressions chosen, or for a calmly reflecting comparison of the execution described with others. And, on the other hand, later juristic authorities, such as Paullus and the digests of Justinian, place various other modes of execution, as belonging with this to the category of "supreme punishments" (summa supplicia), expressly on a level with it: the former of these, burning, beheading, and casting to the wild beasts in the circus; the latter, burning and beheading.[2] It is evident, therefore, that

---

[1] *Verr.*, v. 66, 169: Servitutis extremum summumque supplicium; v. 66, 165: Crudelissimum taeterrimumque supplicium.

Paulli, *Sent.* 5, t. 17, 3: Summa supplicia sunt crux, crematio, decollatio;

the expression "highest" or "supreme punishment" here, as already in Cicero, is to be taken only in a relative sense, and by no means is it to be understood as indicating the extreme of torture and of pain.

That which undoubtedly was looked upon as culminating in the punishment of the cross, was the element of shame, of dishonour, and of infamy upon the condemned which attached to it. Crucifixion was—herein Cicero is perfectly right, and in harmony with the Biblical view of it [1]—*tæterrimum supplicium*, the *most odious* form of punishment, the climax of shame which could be attached to one judicially or extrajudicially visited, the ancient equivalent for that which was termed, in the legal phraseology of the Middle Ages, the "wheel or gallows"—*the punishment in which the reproach or ignominy heaped upon the condemned rose to the height of malediction*. In proof of the specially ignominious character of this death of the cross, which mainly distinguished it from those other less disgraceful forms of the *summum supplicium*—burning alive, beheading, and tearing to pieces by wild beasts, we may more particularly urge the fact already mentioned, that it was essentially a punishment for slaves, or a kind of execution inflicted upon robbers, rebels, deserters of the colours—occasionally also on poisoners, falsifiers of documents, or violators of the person.[2] Further, the fact that precisely those condemned to the cross, the *cruciarii*, were subjected to insults of a preparatory and supplementary kind, such as the compelling to drag forth the instrument of torture on which they were to die, the scourging, the urging forward with the ox-goad, the depriving of all the garments, the affixing of

---

t. 23, 17 : Magicæ artis conscios summo supplicio affici placuit. *i.e.*, bestiis objici aut cruci suffigi. Comp. *Digest.*, 48, 19, de poenis, Num. 28 : Summum supplicium esse videtur ad furcam (= crucem) damnatio, item vivi crematio, . . . item capitis amputatio, etc.

[1] See Deut. xxi. 22 f.; Gal. iii. 13.

[2] Comp. that saying of Cicero : *Servitutis* extr. summumque suppl., cited in a previous note, as well as the words by which it is immediately followed : Facinus est vinciri civem Romanum ; scelus, verberari ; prope parricidium, necari ; *quid dicam, in crucem tolli?* Verbo satis digno tam nefaria res nullo modo dici potest. Other authorities to a like effect see mentioned on p. 60, note [2].

a tablet to the uppermost arm of the cross, setting forth the offence with which they were charged, and other such like accompaniments.[1] And not less the custom still occasionally observed, even in the time of the emperors, of nailing corpses (as well as living beings) to crosses, in order even in death to brand them with infamy, as those deprived of honourable burial and exposed to the ravages of wild beasts and birds of prey.[2] Finally, the direct testimonies, not only of a Cicero but also of a number of Christian writers belonging to the age of imperial Rome, and certainly acquainted with Roman customs, all which agree in designating precisely this mode of execution as one more than all others disgraceful and dishonouring.[3]

The crucified one appears as accursed, one rejected from human society with every demonstration of passionate abhorrence, as an outcast and refuse of men. It may be asked whether the instrument of suffering on which this punishment was inflicted did originally present a conscious or unconscious imitation of that baneful tree, the partaking of whose fruit in opposition to the Divine command became for the first parents of our race the cause of their expulsion from Paradise? Indistinct reminiscences of this fatal catastrophe in the primeval age may have perpetuated themselves amongst the most ancient peoples, and gradually have led to the formation of the custom of exposing the most execrable or the most hated transgressors upon such very trees or stakes, or upon tree-like or, finally, cruciform scaffolds, as the prey of corruption or of the wild beasts; the scaffolds at the same time serving as imitations or memorials of the hated Tree of Knowledge. Points of attachment for such a supposition are

[1] Further details in Zestermann. ii. 24 ff. Degen, S. 26 f. ; 28 f.

[2] See that which has been said above.—Instances of the affixing of those already put to death (or at least of their heads) upon crosses, taken from the last days of the Republic and the time of the Empire, will be found : Sueton., *Cæs.* 74 (case of the Cilician pirates) ; Herodian, iii. 8. 2 ; Xiphilin. *Excerpt. ex Dion.* xxi. ; Severus (p. 315, ed. Steph. 1592), etc.

[3] See especially Paul, Phil. ii. 8. and the author of the Epistle to the Hebrews, xii. 2. Also Arnobius, i. 36, 40, 41 ; Lactantius. *Instit.*, iv. 26 ; Chrysost., *in Joann.*, Hom. 85, 2.

not altogether wanting. The expression, dating back from the earliest antiquity of the Hebrew language and civilisation, "to hang on a tree" (in which *ēts*, "tree," is ambiguous—and may equally denote either a tree or a stake or gallows), as likewise that ancient Roman title, "*arbor infelix*," "tree of misfortune," or "ill-omen," are perhaps to be explained in the sense above indicated. The connection, too, in which the mythological tradition of many peoples places a certain sacred tree with a dragon or serpent as emblems of evil or the power of death, must here be recalled to memory. Not only the tree of the world, Yggdrasil of the Northlanders and Germans, gnawed at its roots by the serpent Nidhoegr, belongs to this class of representations. Upon ancient Egyptian sarcophagi also, as well as upon Tyrian coins, we sometimes see depicted a mysterious tree with fruit-bearing boughs, and round it a serpent coiled. A snake dwelling in a fruit-bearing tree was worshipped by the Caribbees of Central America, as the dispenser of rain and fertility. Traditions of the Tree of Knowledge and of a "dragon from the deep," who first taught Fo-hi the distinction of the sexes, are handed down in the earliest religious writings of the Chinese. For the earlier history of Indian Buddhism, Fergusson has contributed from the topes of Sankhi and Amravati, covered as they are with remarkable sculptures, a rich abundance of monumental evidence for the worship of trees and serpents, here practised in very close connection.[1] Even in the domain of the Fetich religions of ruder tribes, are found here and there rites in which we are tempted to see a faint reminiscence of the misery-bringing Tree of Knowledge. Thus that superstitious custom of the negroes of Central Africa, attested by Burton, which consists in driving a nail into a so-called "devil's tree," or hanging a rag upon it, in order to heal or charm away a

---

[1] Fergusson, Tree and Serpent Worship, pl. xxiv., xxvi., etc. Cp. with regard to the Chinese, Lüken, *as before*, S. 98; to the Caribbees, Müller, *as before*, S. 131. Further, Hammer-Purgstall, *Fundgruben des Orients*, Bd. v.; Wägner, *Die Nordisch-germanische Vorzeit*, i. 48 ff. On Tree Worship in general; E. B. Tylor, *Early History of Mankind and of Civilisation*, ii. 216—230 (of Germ. edn. 1873), W. Mannhardt, *Der Baumcultus der Germanen*, etc. (1875).

disease, by exorcising the evil spirit of the disease.[1] Many of the instances previously mentioned of the worship of sacred trees, *e.g.*, among the ancient Celts, or the North and South American Indians, may likewise to some extent be ranged under this head. As, indeed, the notions "curse" and "blessing" insensibly blend with each other in the mysterious region of idolatrous tree-worship, no less than in that of serpent-worship—in which the conception of the serpent as agathodæmon or cacodæmon, most closely verge the one on the other—and as in general a confused mingling of the reminiscences of the Tree of Knowledge and the Tree of Life in Paradise seems to have taken place. We can here only just glance at this sinister domain—with which are frequently associated sacrificial rites of an inhuman character—namely, of the dæmonolatrous, and even directly devil-worshipping superstition of heathen nations in ancient and modern times. A further investigation thereof could besides yield an essential advantage to the cause of our investigation, if those earlier ideas and customs with which we are concerned, which can be with certainty referred to the pre-Christian age, were only presented in greater plenty. But it is for the most part only elements of later phases of development of the said religions of barbarous or civilised peoples, with which we become acquainted in the above-mentioned sphere.

The whole question as to the echoes of primitive traditions of Paradise and the Fall remains, from its very nature, to a great extent involved in obscurity. Whether, indeed, perfectly clear and certain results are to be obtained regarding the significance in relation to the past of the objects of heathen tree and

---

[1] Burton, *Central Africa*, ii. p. 352. Comp. E. B. Tylor, ii. 148 f. (of the German edition), where attention is also drawn to the kindred superstitious customs which have been perpetuated among the Germanic peoples until recent times; such as the nailing or hanging of supposed causes of sickness upon the trunk of a tree, etc. [For a notice of the practice, still common in Palestine, of hanging rags upon trees "as acknowledgments, or *as deprecatory signals and charms*," comp. Thomson, "Land and the Book," p. 442; Andrew Bonar, "Narrative of a Mission to the Jews," p. 298.]

cross worship, appears at best doubtful, especially when we take into consideration the more or less veiled form in which the account of the garden of Eden and its two trees is handed down to us in Holy Scripture, as well as the effectually blinding influence of sin and the worship of the creature upon the religious consciousness of mankind after the time of Paradise. More important than the question as to the origin of the phenomena under review, is, it seems to us, that as to their *end* and *aim*. A typical and prophetic relation, though only a mediate one, to the cross of the Redeemer, on the part of these symbols of the cross in Heathendom, themselves indicative of misery and the curse, must, it appears to us, be of necessity admitted; even as we perceived, in the emblems of a like kind indicative of salvation and blessing, a similar typical relation to the cross. *The world-renewing fact of the cancelling of the curse which had descended from Adam, by means of the blessing brought about by the second Adam upon the altar of the cross on Calvary, has been proclaimed aforehand by a twofold series of shadowy types, brighter ones and darker, in the pre-Christian history.* As we saw shadowed forth in the cross-figures of positive religious significance, the agathodæmonic figures of the cross, before considered, the positive salvation-bringing and transforming power of the redemptive sufferings on the cross; so also these very sufferings on their negative side—inasmuch as these indicated the utmost effect of the sinful principle of evil in mankind in the slaying of the sacred body of the God-man, and at the same time the removal of the tree of the curse and of death which rested upon our race—were reflected in the dark succession of idols and symbols of the curse, of a cacodæmonic cross-worship of the heathen world. Even the various implements of execution and of torture comprised under the general notion of *crux*, of which the religious significance originally attached to them had in the course of time disappeared, must be regarded as types of that cross on Calvary, the instrument of torture and of death for the Son of Man, but on this very account the means of deliverance for humanity. In more pregnant measure, however, is a typical activity having this end in view to be ascribed to those crosses of suffering (and rites connected with crucifixion) in the ancient world, to which was consciously attached a deeper religious import, as being the places of the propitiatory sacrifices for the averting of the wrath or conciliating the favour of Divine powers. That, among the numerous and diverse pre-Christian rites of crucifixion, there were also expiatory ones, can scarcely admit of dispute. The character of a sacrificial act in the proper sense of the term was borne indeed, as we have already shown, by no act of crucifixion, at any rate among the better known civilised peoples of ancient history. But that there were no expiatory rites connected with the religious symbolism of the cross, that the positive religious and the negative religious significance of the cross—its blessing and its curse-denoting import, beyond the pale of Christianity—were *constantly divergent*,—in other words, that the cross of the Lord, as an instrument of suffering and of the curse, was *never* and nowhere an object of prophetic presentiment and typical foreshadowing: this opinion, advanced in the *Edinburgh Review*, by the essayist to whom reference has already often been made, cannot, in presence of so many significant facts of the pre-Christian history of religion, by any means be maintained. The essayist himself alludes to that bloody right of expiation practised among the Mexicans already referred to—a rite consisting in the nailing of a young man or maiden to a cross, and piercing the victim through with arrows.[1] In other respects, too, the religious customs of the Mexicans and Yucatese seem to have included some single similar acts of expiation by blood, performed *upon* crosses or in presence of them. Before that remarkable Tree of Life, Tonacaquahuitl, a child appears— according to the representation of the monument of Palenque

[1] *Edinb. Rev.*, 1870, i. p. 233; cp. p. 229. The remark in the latter passage. "that the instrument of torture—the σταυρός or infamous tree—was never symbolised at any time, that is, in any pre-Christian age," certainly goes too far, and fails of doing justice to such cases as that brought forward in the former of these places, or as those to be adduced by us farther on.

—to have been presented as an offering; and an idol dripping with blood hangs upon the T-shaped gigantic cross, as it is depicted in some ancient Mexican manuscripts.[1] If, as is the case with so many of the monuments and traditions of the history of religion in America, falling within our province, we cannot perhaps entirely exclude a suspicion pointing to Christian influences;[2] and if the well-known Krishna legend of the Hindoos—which, *inter alia*, has to relate of Vishnu, incarnate as Krishna, that he offered himself upon a cross—appears still less free from such suspicion, but rather looks like a Hindoo transformation of the Gospel narrative, borne beyond the Indus during the first centuries of our æra by disciples of St. Thomas or by some other Christians;[3] yet there still remain abundant traces of an actually expiatory design in the employment of the cross in the cross-worship and in the customs of crucifixion among the nations of the extra-Christian world, against the originality of which no solid objections can be raised. That cross tree of the Celtic Druids, stripped of its foliage and boughs—consecrated at the time of full moon, in the midst of their sacred oak groves, as a special symbol of the Godhead —appears indeed to have served predominantly as an emblem of salvation and blessing, but certainly witnessed also many a bloody human sacrifice, of which the cruel ritual of this priesthood demanded such numbers, offered beneath its bare arms. And the "images of enormous size," which, as is already related by Cæsar, were among the same people filled with human beings of all kinds—with transgressors condemned to death, but also with innocent victims,—and were then set on fire, to be consumed as a gigantic burnt-

---

[1] See above, p. 25.
[2] Even the Spaniards in Cortez' time thought the after-operation of the preaching of Christianity in India, once undertaken by the Apostle Thomas, was to be recognised in the customs to which we now refer. (Lüken, *u.s.*, S. 78.)
[3] See the work of the learned Hindoo, Bholanauth Chunder, *Travels of a Hindoo to various parts of Bengal and Upper India*, Lond. 1869. vol. ii.. p. 25, in which this view of the Krishna legend as a plagiarism from early Christian sources is emphatically maintained.

offering or expiatory sacrifice, seem to have been, hardly other than the preceding, sacred oaks mutilated into stumps or pillars of half cruciform, half human shape.[1] It may appear significant that, in the description of this terrible custom, Cæsar twice makes use of that very expression, *supplicium*, of which the primitive meaning "sacrifice," opens up such an instructive insight into the ancient Roman conceptions of expiatory sacrifice and infliction of death, as notions closely bordering the one on the other—yea, as originally covering each other.—Even to the ancient Indians also, spite of the probably not original character of that Krishna myth, certain expiatory rites in connection with their veneration of cruciform emblems, may not have been altogether strange. The prevalence of agonising scenes of crucifixion amidst the representations of the Buddhistic hell upon temple ruins of Ulterior India, as well as the custom still practised in that very region of executing transgressors upon the cross of St. Andrew, seems to point to this conclusion.[2]

More clearly and unambiguously still do we find the meaning of the pre-Christian cross, as significant alike of curse and of blessing, expressed in the mysterious type of the serpent, raised by Moses upon a pole in the wilderness (Num. xxi. 8, 9). A partial connection of this emblem, placed by the Lord Himself in direct typical relation to His sacrificial death upon the cross of Calvary (John iii. 14), with the serpent and tree worship of the Egyptians, must without doubt be admitted; although Moses caused it to be raised, assuredly with no idolatrous intention, as a symbol of salvation addressed to the faith of the Jews then bitten by the fiery serpents of the wilderness, and by this very fact afforded a symbol prophetically pointing forward to the Saviour of the world, the Redeemer from the

---

[1] Cæs. *B. G.*, vi. 16. 4: "Alii immani magnitudine simulacra habent, quorum contexta viminibus membra vivis hominibus complent, quibus succensis circumventi flamma exanimantur homines. Supplicia eorum qui in furto, in latrocinio, aut aliqua noxa sint comprehensi, gratiora diis immortalibus esse arbitrantur; sed cum ejus generis copia defecit, etiam ad innocentium supplicia accedunt."

[2] See above, p. 66.

ruin of sin and of death.¹ An idolatrous significance was afterwards attached by the people to this symbol, inasmuch as, like their Canaanitish neighbours, and especially the Phœnicians, addicted as they were to the worship of trees and serpents, they offered incense to a brazen image of a serpent, called "Nehushtan" (*Brass-god*), until Hezekiah broke this idol to pieces (2 Kings xviii. 4).—That in certain practices of the Mosaic sacrificial ritual, in which the figure of the cross, or at least something bearing a distant resemblance to it, is represented, there is contained a divinely appointed and intended series of types, pointing to the offering of atonement one day to be presented on Calvary, has been often asserted in the contemplations of earlier theologians upon this domain.² Especially the paschal lamb, transfixed in the form of a cross upon the spit, as well as the movement with the different parts of the sacrifice (of those, too, presented by the Levites at their anointing) in the direction of the four points of the compass, in the so-called "waving," has been often looked upon in the light of such prophetic act, pointing forward to the death of the Lord upon the cross. Hardly, however, is this view justified; since neither the law itself nor the prophetic literature of the Old Covenant presents any utterance favouring it. Nor is there found in the New Testament any reference to those customs as of Messianic import, as we must assuredly expect would be the case—especially in such books as the Epistle to the Hebrews—if they really belonged to the cycle of the genuine typical pre-representations of the work of redemption.

On the other hand, there seems to be actually present a coinciding under the Old Testament of the two significations

¹ Comp. already *Wisdom of Sol.* xvi. 6, 7: σύμβολον σωτηρίας .... οὐ διὰ τὸ θεωρούμενον, ἀλλὰ διὰ τὸν πάντων σωτῆρα. ["A sign of salvation . . . not by the thing that he saw, but by Thee, that art the Saviour of all."] Not, indeed, the deeper Messianic-prophetic meaning, but yet the providential institution of this mysterious symbol, as well as the distinction between it and the idols of Gentile ophiolatry, is here rightly perceived. To teach us to understand this prophetic action in its full significance, the word of the Lord to Nicodemus was necessary.

² Compare, *inter alios*, G. Möbius, *De Agno Paschali*, i. p. 50, and L. Dassovius, *Signa Crucis Gentis Hebrew*, Kil., 1695.

of the cross-symbol, as indicative of the blessing and the curse in the important passage, Ezek. ix. 4. If, then, a delivering sign, in the form of a Tau or cross, is to be imprinted upon the brow of certain God-fearing inhabitants of Jerusalem at the time of a severe judgment impending over the city, this in reality has the appearance of a prophetic pointing forward to the delivering power of the redeeming death of Christ, once to be accomplished. For this Tau, of Ezekiel, is certainly in any case not without significance, and a figure of mere arbitrary choice; like that sign of subscription once spoken of by Job (Job xxxi. 35).[1] As a symbol imprinted on the forehead, shaped like a T, or rather like a ┬ (an ancient Hebrew letter Tau), it is designed not only to mark out its bearers from among the multitude, but also specially to designate them as devoted (inscribed) to Jehovah, as slaves of the Lord (*servi literati, inscripti*). It appears thus, then, of Messianic-prophetic import, inasmuch as in this sign upon the forehead is depicted the instrument of the curse and of suffering, on which the Saviour was destined one day to suffer, and to work out the redemption of the world. A higher providential ordering of events on the part of that God who disposes all things—under the Old Testament not less than under the New—for the salvation of man will here hardly be lost sight of by the believing student of history. To explain the cruciform shape of the delivering sign as the result of a mere play of accident appears —if we presuppose belief in the presence of a Divine guidance and control in the sacred history—much more difficult, yea, more unreasonable, than to derive this agreement between typical sign and fulfilling antitype, here also, as in the case of so many other agreements, and especially that which takes place in connection with the brazen serpent, from the counsel

---

[1] See, for example, my *Comm. on Job*, in loc. (Lange's series). Singularly, but certainly arbitrarily, Tayler Lewis, in his Anglo-American edition of my Commentary, p. 133, supposes the expression יָת, Job xxxi. 35, to stand (as the last letter) for the whole alphabet, and then to signify farther, "that which is written," "a writing." Much more to the point is the comparison, instituted by us, with the Arabic *Tiwá*, "brand," "mark."

of the three-one God, previously considering and wisely ordaining all things that come to pass.[1] An unconscious prophecy, no doubt, is this to be termed in one respect; since the full bearing, and the special significance in the history of the fulfilment, of that which according to God's eternal plan of salvation should be proclaimed aforehand by the delivering sign upon the forehead, assuredly lay beyond the horizon of the priestly seer. And still less than the prophet himself, did the pre-Christian people of God in the ages succeeding him recognise the profound meaning of this remarkable prophecy—*that* in it which pointed to the centre of the Messianic work of salvation. For nowhere does the pre-Christian Jewish literature show any trace of that Messianic sense of the same, which only the Fathers of the Christian Church, from the time of Tertullian, Origen, and Jerome, have vindicated for it, in opposition to the interpretation based on a superficial refining away and conjectural appreciation as of no importance, which sees in the Tau only the equivalent of "Sign"—such as we meet with in the versions of Aquila and Symmachus no less than that of the LXX. (Alexandrine version).[2] Like so many an other Old Testament prophecy relating to the Lord and His work of salvation, this utterance of Ezekiel also could be rightly understood and interpreted only after the time of its fulfilment.[3] In so far as pious Apocalyptists and prophetically gifted bearers of the Spirit of God of the last period before

---

[1] Comp. Schmieder in v. Gerlach's *Bibelw.*, *in loc.*, as also Schröder *in loc.* (Commentary on Ezekiel in Lange's series.)

[2] The LXX. understood ת as the exact equivalent of "sign" ($\delta \delta s \ \sigma \eta \mu \epsilon \hat{\iota} o \nu \ \dot{\epsilon} \pi \grave{\iota} \ \tau \grave{\alpha} \ \mu \acute{\epsilon} \tau \omega \pi a \ \tau \hat{\omega} \nu \ \dot{\alpha} \nu \delta \rho \hat{\omega} \nu$), thus excluding from the passage, as does once more the modern naturalistic Exegesis [Gesenius, Hitzig, etc.], every reference to a $+$ or T-like shape of the sign. Thus did also Aquila, who nevertheless, according to Origen (comp. *Fragm. vet. Interpret. Græc.*, p. 587) had in the first edition of hi version reproduced the word by $\theta a \hat{\upsilon}$; so did Symmachus in like manner. Theodotian, on the other hand, made the first advance towards the Christian interpretation of the passage in reference to the cross, by his version: $\sigma \eta \mu \epsilon \iota \acute{\omega} \sigma \iota \nu \ \tau o \hat{\upsilon} \ \theta a \hat{\upsilon} \ \dot{\epsilon} \pi \grave{\iota} \ \tau \grave{\alpha} \ \mu \acute{\epsilon} \tau \omega \pi a \ \tau \hat{\omega} \nu \ \dot{\alpha} \nu \delta \rho \hat{\omega} \nu$. Comp. Tertull., *adv. Marc.*, iii. 22; Cyprian, *Testimon. adv. Jud.*, ii. 22; Origen, *in Ezech.*, Opp., t. iii., p. 424; Jerome, *in Ezech.*, ix. 4; and *Esai.* lxvi.; Isidorus, *Origin.*, i. 3, 9; etc.

[3] Scarcely can the Roman custom of denoting any one (*e.g.*, a soldier) as living, by the sign T—as dead, by the sign Θ, have any connection with the *tau* of the

Christ—like those waiting for Israel's consolation (Luke ii, 25, 38), or like John the Baptist (John i. 29, 36)—recognised beforehand the necessity for the redeeming suffering of the Messiah, and were able to express that which they had contemplated in the Spirit concerning Him, in profound words of prophecy, like that of the "sign which should be spoken against," or that of the "Lamb of God which taketh away the sin of the world"—in so far, indeed, may prophetic utterances like Isaiah liii., or Psalm xxii., or Dan. ix. 24 ff., but hardly such as that passage of Ezekiel, have served to them as Biblical treasuries and pole-stars. The Spirit of Old Testament prophecy wrought of necessity more from within outwards, and by inner preparation and enlightenment of the heart, than by means of a very great plenitude of external symbols—*i.e.*, symbols having reference to the external historical manner of accomplishing the work of salvation. These latter have nowhere and never been wanting to the Divine pædagogia for Christ ; neither in the Mosaic and pre-Mosaic, nor in the prophetic epoch of the Old Covenant. But the revealing of their deeper meaning, and the leading into the full and ripened understanding of them, must remain reserved for the time when, after the setting up of the New Covenant, the Spirit should be given without measure into the hearts of believers, and the concealing veil of the law should be taken away from their eyes.

Several other alleged instances of direct prediction of the sufferings of Christ on the cross, in Old Testament books or in extra-Biblical writers, to which the Church Fathers were wont to attach a special importance in their Apologies directed against heathen or Jews, are entirely of an apocryphal

passage in question. (On the custom itself, see, on the one hand, Pers., *Sat.*, iv. 13 :

Et potis es, nigrum vitio præfigere Theta ;

and, on the other, Isidorus, *Orig.*, i. 23, p. 40, ed. Lindem : " T nota in capite versiculi posita *superstitem* designabat.") Rather might we suppose a connection with the Egyptian ansate cross, which signifies "life." But Raoul Rochette, *u.s.*, p. 289, rightly rejects this supposition too, leaving it doubtful whether we must credit the testimony of Isidorus regarding this custom.

AS THE SYMBOL OF THE CURSE. 83

order. They are to be reduced either to instances of an interpolation into the text, of Christian origin, as, *e.g.*, the much-cited addition "from the tree," ἀπὸ τοῦ ξύλου, which a number of MSS. of the Septuagint are said to have read in Psalm xcvi. 10;[1] or—as the alleged prophecy as to the dominion of the world on the part of the crucified Christ, which used to be discovered in a passage of Plato's Timæus—to instances of an allegorising interpretation and an arbitrary importing of Christian historic-philosophic speculation.[2] For the purpose of obtaining a more accurate acquaintance with the apologetic treatment of the question, and with the whole scientific method of the Church theology of the first centuries, these examples of Messianic argumentation, digressing as they do into an uncritical method, are exceedingly instructive; while they are in themselves scientifically valueless, and wanting

[1] It was beyond doubt MSS. of the LXX., interpolated by a Christian hand and in the interests of Christianity, which read in Psalm xcv. 10 (Psalm xcvi. of the Greek): ὅτι ὁ κύριος ἐβασίλευσεν ἀπὸ τοῦ ξύλου, and from which not only Greek Church Fathers (Barnabas, *Ep.*, c. 8, 5; Justin, *Dial. c. Tryph.*, p. 298; Cyril of Jerus., etc.), but also the Christian west (*Itala*, ex ligno; Tertull., *adv. Marc.*, iii. 19, 2; *adv. Jud.*, c. 11; Augustine, *Enarr. in Ps.*, p. 714; *lib. quæst.*, 64; Pseudo-Ambrosius, *Comm. in 1 Cor.* xv.; Leo M., *Serm* 4 *de pass.;* Greg. M., *Hom.* vi. *in Ezech.*, etc.) received this addition, and employed it apologetically against Heathen and Jews. If the interpolation had really been of pre-Christian origin, it must have been traced back to the same Alexandrine-Jewish speculation on the paradisiac Tree of Life—which was not pervaded by any deeper Messianic meaning, and in particular had no reference to the atoning death of Christ—which gave rise to allusions to this very Tree of Life also in the books of Enoch (xxiv. 4 f.; xxv. 5) and 4 Esr. (viii. 52). Comp. Müller, *Erklär. des Barnabasbr.*, S. 213 f. The same is the case with the apocryphal addition to Jerem. xi. 19: "Venite, conjiciamus lignum in panem ejus" (Itala), which figures in the writings of many Fathers, *e.g.*, Tertull., *adv. Marc.*, iii. 18 f.; iv. 40; Cyril, *Catech.*, xiii., etc., as a prophecy concerning the cross of Christ; as with the interpolation of the passage 4 Esr. v. 5, adduced by Barnabas, *Ep.*, c. 12: ὅταν ξύλον κλιθῇ καὶ ἀναστῇ, καὶ ὅταν ἐκ ξύλου αἷμα στάξῃ (cp. Müller, *l.c.*, p. 272). In the same manner several passages of the Sibylline oracles belong to this category, especially l. v. v. 257 *sq.* (p. 600 Gall.), and l. viii. v. 245, of which last we shall have to treat more fully hereafter.

[2] Justin, *Apol.*, i. p. 92, interprets the words of Plato, having reference to the diffusion of the world-soul, or Divine νοῦς, through all the world (*Tim.*, p. 36), ἐχίασεν αὐτὸν ἐν τῷ παντί, as relating to the lifting up of Christ upon the cross; whereas the χιάζειν is here intended simply to speak of a spreading out to the four points of the compass.

in any solid historic foundation. They can be just as little accepted as actual predictions concerning the person and work of the Redeemer, as can those cruciform figures of the Jewish Cabbalists—figures which have had their rise indeed under Christian influences—the names of the ten *Sephiroth* (Divine attributes, or forms of revelation) grouped together in such wise as to represent a tree, with roots, stem, and crown, or else an erect human being: a form in which the philosophy of the Middle Ages, and especially modern Theosophy, from the time of Agrippa v. Nettesheim and Jacob Böhme downwards, would find contained the mystery of the Trinity and that of Redemption.[1]

[1] We shall return subsequently to the more detailed treatment of the staurosophic speculations of modern mysticism. As a typical preformation of the cross does our Edinburgh Reviewer also regard the cabbalistic sephiroth-tree of Jewish mysticism. ("The Pre-Christian Cross," p. 242.)

II.

The Cross upon Calvary.

ALL the curse and the blessing, all misery of death and glory of life, which had been spread abroad through the pre-Christian humanity, appear in the cross of Christ, concentrated in the most wondrous image of the religious and moral development of our race. In the uplifted banner of salvation, which is to the Jews an offence, to the Gentiles a folly, we see all at once intersecting each other the two lines of the sinful corruption of man and the Divine call of grace: lines running side by side with each other, in abiding separation, throughout all previous ages. They intersect each other in rugged, sharp opposition, and with such mighty impact that the dark line of the sin-curse is pierced to the heart with deadly effect by the bright line of salvation. The health-giving Tree of Life, towards which the longing of all nations had been directed through the ages, and the poisonous Tree of Knowledge, fruitful in misery, before whose arrows they had trembled, and under whose death-shade they had sighed: they here appear wondrously formed into one; and over that figure leafless and bare, but beaming with the blessed hope of salvation, stands written in the fiery characters of Divine revelation, *Death is swallowed up in victory!* The Life itself is here become death, the blessing a curse, the Holy One of God, become sin—for ever to annihilate the dominion of sin and of death.

From early times in the Church, some have endeavoured to explain the common antitype of the two trees of Paradise uplifted on Calvary, in such wise that the cross itself should be seen to be foreshadowed in the Tree of Knowledge, and on the other hand the Crucified One hanging thereupon, in the Tree of Life.[1] And in reality this essay at interpretation contains a deep truth, abundantly attested by Holy Scripture, of the Old Testament as of the New. Christ Himself *is* the real Tree of Life; the prototype of that wondrous tree from whose salvation-bringing sight and enjoyment mankind had been removed in consequence of sin, without ever being able to lose the memory of it. He is called indeed in the Old Testament—as the eternal, heavenly Wisdom of God—a "Tree of Life" (Prov. iii. 18); even as, with regard to His human nature and origin, He is called a "rod out of the stem of Jesse," and a "branch out of his roots" (Isa. xi. 1). And He calls Himself in the New Testament the "true Vine" (John xv. 1 ff.); He speaks of Himself as the "green tree," which must suffer instead of the dry wood, properly destined for fuel (Luke xxiii. 31). The green wood, the gloriously blossoming fruit-laden palm tree (Psalm i. 3; xcii. 12), is hanged upon the dry bare tree of the curse (Gal. iii. 13); He consecrates this precisely thereby as a place of blessing, grows into one with it, as a gladdening, world-renewing Tree of Life, at whose roots gushes forth the fountain of everlasting life, whose fruit affords to every one the true and ever-satisfying food, and whose leaves are for the healing of the nations (Rev. ii. 7; xxii. 2). All that which had expressed itself in the pre-Christian world in efforts after the ideal or real [*i.e.*, by means of *types*] representation in religious symbolism of the Tree of Life as the compendium of all blessedness, finds here its fulfilment, its Divine ratification, in a blessing extending exceeding abundantly beyond all

---

[1] Christ Himself (not for instance His cross) is taken as the antitype of the Tree of Life, by Barnabas, *Ep.*, c. 12, init. (comp. above, p. 83); Justin, *Dial.*, c. 86; Origen *in Joh.*, tom. xx. § 29; Methodius, *Conviv.* x. *virgg.*, Orat. ix. c. 3; Greg. of Nyssa, *Orat.* iv. *in resurrect.*; Epiphanius, *Homil. in Sabb. magno* (Opp. t. ii. p. 274); Anastas Sinaita, *Anagog. contempl. in Hexaëm.*, l. viii., etc.—Of modern writings favouring this view are especially to be mentioned James Hamilton, *Emblems from Eden*, chapter i., "The Tree of Life;" and Piper, "Der Baum des Lebens" (*Evang. Kalender*, 1863), S. 39 ff.

previous dimly realised conception and even longing. They are all of them unreal shadows, these Trees of Life of the extra-Christian religions, vain and empty phantoms, compared with the Tree of Life of reality, the blessing-distilling tree of the curse on Calvary, on which He, in whom all the promises of God are Yea and Amen, pours forth His sacred heart's blood! It is certainly a superficial view on the part of modern writers of the philosophy of history, that the Tree of Life and the Tree of Knowledge are (even according to the Biblical account!) one and the same.[1] And equally to be rejected as this speculation, in direct and flagrant contradiction as it is with all exegetical truth, appears that confused mingling of the two symbols, such as was met with above in the case of several extra-Christian religions, as in that of the Chinese, Indian-Buddhist, and Celtic; a confusion shared also by several gnostic sects of the early Christian age, inasmuch as precisely the transgression of the Divine prohibition in Paradise was regarded by them as an important step in advance, and a source of blessing.[2] But in the cross of Calvary the Tree of Life and the Tree of Knowledge do certainly appear comprehended in one deeply significant prototypal unity; and in this unity shall we find the explanation of the fact that the religion of the cross presents in absolute fulness and perfection these two things: a theoretical foundation of truth of the highest solidity, and a morally renewing effect of more wondrous nature and power

---

[1] So, *e.g.*, Christ. Kapp (in Carrière, *Aesthetik*, i. S. 354): "The open eye sees growing up in history the Tree of Life and Knowledge, the ash Yggdrasil," etc. Entirely different the sentiment of Byron in *Cain*, where he puts into the mouth of his hero the words,

The tree of life
Was withheld from us by my father's folly,
While that of knowledge, by my mother's haste,
Was pluck'd too soon; and all the fruit is death.

[2] The mystic speculation of the Ophites is greatly occupied with the Tree of Life and the anointing proceeding from it, of which the Son is partaker. But it therein identifies the Tree of Life with the Tree of Knowledge, just as it perceives in the seducing serpent the blessing-fraught principle of Wisdom. Comp. Celsus, in Origen, κατὰ Κέλσου, vi. 33, 34; Epiphanius, *Haer.*, 37; also Keim, *Celsus wahres Wort*, S. 86, 89.

than that of *any* other religion. On this account the cross of the Saviour appears, even for the general contemplation of the philosophy of history, or for the æsthetical study of the history of civilisation, "the axis for the history of the world, as for the history of the soul," and He Himself "the copula, the connecting middle in the period of the judgment." He, "the purest among the mighty, and the mightiest among the pure, who with His pierced hand removed kingdoms out of their place, and the stream of the ages out of its bed, and still continues to exert dominion over time"—He is and remains the centre of all history, and of all historic life and cognition.[1]

The mystery of the cross is the mystery of mysteries; to seek to exhaust its depths is to seek to exhaust the depths of the whole Divine Revelation.[2] That which is here primarily incumbent upon us is the bringing out of that knowledge concerning the significance of the cross, for the world and for the kingdom, which can be derived from the immediate statements in regard to it found in the Holy Scriptures of the New Testament. We begin with the contemplation of the Messianic testimonies of the God-man concerning Himself, viewed in their connection with the respective facts of the Gospel history; and thus contemplate the cross and the death of the Lord on the cross, in the first place, *in the light of the declarations of the Gospels themselves.*

A. *ACCORDING TO THE DECLARATIONS OF THE GOSPELS.*

That which Symeon and John the Baptist, the last out-lying representatives of that prophetic development which had the Lord as its object, condensed into those brief but profoundly pregnant words, of inexhaustible import: the negative (sin-bearing, death-overcoming) and the positive

[1] Carrière, *Aesthetik*, S. 364 f., and, further, the words of Jean Paul there cited.
[2] Mackay, *The Glory of the Cross* (Lond. 1874), p. 2 ff.

(raising, Divine life-infusing) side of His redeeming activity, *that*, too, He certainly also confirms Himself from time to time, in utterances of like prophetic-enigmatic brevity, *e.g.*, that of the sign of Jonas (Matt. xii. 39; xvi. 4), of the breaking down of the temple and raising it again (John ii. 19, 22), of the lifting up of the Son of Man (John viii. 28). But in the majority of the declarations regarding the accomplishment of His work of suffering, He unfolds more distinctly and fully the import of this cross, and the relations of His sufferings to the same, so that far-reaching conclusions are to be derived, either from His words themselves or from the connection in which they were spoken. We distinguish three groups of such declarations:

1. Those which bring into relief the PROPHETIC-TYPICAL significance of the suffering on the cross. To this class belongs, not only that direct requirement of the taking up of one's cross, and following behind Him (Matt. x. 38), but —as is shown by the recurrence of these very words in Matt. xvi. 24—in general each of the solemn predictions of His death and resurrection, of which the Gospel history records altogether four (Matt. xvi. 21; xvii. 22; xx. 18; xxvi. 2, and parallel places). Farther, the declaration concerning the object contemplated in the sending of the Son of Man, who came not to be ministered unto, but to minister, and to give His life a ransom for many (Matt. xx. 26 f.); the saying concerning the necessity that the corn of wheat should fall and die, as the condition of its bringing forth fruit (John xii. 24 f.), as well as several of the words spoken in the parting discourses to the disciples recorded in John; such as John xiii. 15 f.: "An example have I given you," etc.; and xv. 13: "Greater love hath no man than this, that a man lay down his life for his friends," etc.—As these utterances lay special emphasis upon the sufferings of the God-man, as the glorifying completion and sealing of the prophetic testimony, or of the Redeemer's ministry of teaching during the days of His flesh, so there exists, again, a further series of sayings of the Lord having relation to His cross, in

2. Those which bring into relief the PRIESTLY, or sin-expiating and mediatorial significance of the Passion. Christ died for us, not merely as our example, but also as our atonement—as the vicarious sacrifice for our guilt. His suffering on the cross is an exemplary suffering *before* us, but also a representative suffering *instead of* us; as it calls for willing imitation, so does it at the same time demand the response of adoring love towards Him who was wounded for our transgressions and bruised for our iniquities. As the good Shepherd giveth His life for His sheep, so has He in our stead surrendered Himself a prey to the foe (John x. 15). He suffered Himself to be numbered among the transgressors, when in our place He went to the death of shame, the green tree in the stead of the dry (Luke xxiii. 31, 37); when He gave His soul a ransom, a holy, precious redemption price for many (Matt. xx. 28; cp. xvi. 26). In sublime high-priestly intercession sanctifying Himself, *i.e.*, consecrating Himself to death (John xvii. 19) for His own, He suffered Himself—like the serpent set up by Moses in the wilderness —to be lifted up as a delivering sign of the curse (John iii. 14). Precisely, hereby, did He become the priestly Mediator of a new covenant, who is able to give His flesh as the true meat, and His blood as the true drink, to the dearly purchased members of His kingdom (Matt. xxvi. 26, and parallels).—Along with the priestly side of His Divine-human work, these latter utterances bring into relief also the concluding and completing work which He continues unto eternity, as exalted to the right hand of God in heaven; they form the immediate transition to

3. Those utterances respecting the relations of the Passion to the KINGLY dignity of the Lord. For the radiance, too, of His kingly dignity shines forth out of the night of His sufferings, and glorifies the dark cloud of shame and abasement which was permitted for a little while to gather over Him. His deepest humiliation, to the death of slaves and malefactors, becomes immediately "glorifying" (John xiii. 31 f.), an "exaltation" (John viii. 28), and that an

exaltation fraught with blessed effects for all that believe in Him (John iii. 14 f.), for all who allow themselves to be drawn to Him as His own (John xii. 31 f.) In the midst of the abasement and reviling on the part of Gentiles and Jews, He expressly calls Himself a king (John xviii. 33—36), He points triumphantly to the testimonies of His kingly dignity and judicial glory proceeding from a higher world—a dignity and a glory which He will soon render manifest to the whole world (Matt. xxvi. 64; comp. xvi. 28; xxiv. 30 ff.; xxv. 31 ff.; John v. 22, 28; vi. 40, 54). And just as little as He shrinks from these claims to the highest and most glorious place of authority in the kingdom of God (comp. Matt. xxviii. 18—20), just so little does He relinquish the kingly high-priestly prerogative of pardon and of blessing. Even on the cross does He exercise this, His Divine kingly right towards those who had cursed Him (Luke xxiii. 43); and already before had He characterised precisely His going hence as a blessing-fraught coming to His people (John xiv. 23, 28; xvi. 22), precisely His dying as the way to the bringing forth much fruit, *i.e.*, to the presenting of His flesh for the life of the world (John vi. 51 f.; xii. 24), precisely the offering up of His faithful shepherd soul as the means for the bringing in of the other sheep, and the uniting of all in one flock under one shepherd (John x. 16). Thus the place of His execution is seen to be the scene of His exaltation to the glory of a Divine kingship. Unto salvation for all who believe in Him does it there become manifest that He suffered not merely *before* us, and *instead of* us, but also *for* us—that His suffering was not merely a prophetic-typical, and a high-priestly atoning one, but, in addition to all this, also a royally blessing, kingdom-founding, world-transforming suffering.

To these declarations of the Lord concerning the significance of His suffering, corresponds—according to the testimonies of the four Evangelists, here especially complementing each other in fullest harmony, and producing the impression of the strictest historical fidelity—THE ACTUAL

UNFOLDING OF THE HISTORY OF HIS PASSION. No step of the ascent of suffering, even up to the summit of the skull-place, remains untrodden by Him; even to the last drop must the bitter cup of suffering which the hand of the Father presents to Him, be drained. In all its fearfulness does the most horrible of all death-punishments, the *crudelissimum tæterrimumque supplicium* of the Romans, rage itself out upon His pure body. All that the crafty malignity of the arch-enemy of mankind had been able to compress of the nature of exquisite torture into this product of the ingenuity in the infliction of punishment among Carthaginians and Romans; all that was contained of a Satanic and deadly nature in this magnified copy and offset of the woe-fraught Tree of Knowledge, must be experienced by Him in its whole extent, be endured by Him unto the entire quenching of His earthly light of life.[1]

No pang is spared Him which this terrible mode of execution brings with it: but He suffers it all with the patience of a lamb which is brought to the slaughter. The insolent stroke upon the face, in the examination before Annas (John xviii. 19 ff.), and the furious blows with which the Jewish councillors, under the presidency of Caiaphas—vieing in this with their menials—presumed to outrage His sacred body (Mark xiv. 65), are followed in the court before Pilate by the scourging (Matt. xxvii. 26), which, ruthlessly inflicted at a post, formed according to the practice of criminal justice among the Romans the regular introduction and prelude to the approaching execution.[2] In this case there is added, as a further species of maltreatment, the crowning with a wreath woven out of the prickly branches of a thorn bush (Matt. xxvii. 29)—a crowning which not only was expressive of insult and derision, but also assuredly wounded with

[1] Mori voluit pro nobis, parum dicimus; crucifigi dignatus est: usque ad mortem crucis obediens factus, elegit extremum et pessimum genus mortis, qui omnem fuerat ablaturus mortem: de morte pessima occidit omnem mortem.—Aug., *Tract. 36 in Joann.*

[2] The "terrible preface" to the death of the cross (Keim, *Gesch. Jesu*, 3 Bearb., S. 333). Compare below, Appendix VI.

piercing smart. The bearing of the cross—that is, certainly, not merely its cross-beam or *patibulum*, but the whole of the great and heavy implement of death[1]—occasions, even at half of the distance to the place of execution, the sinking down in a fainting condition of that body, already so terribly weakened and exhausted by the blows of the lash. A Jew at the moment passing that way, Simon of Cyrene, is compelled by the rude soldiery to take from the Lord the burden become too heavy for Him, and to bear it up to Calvary. Large and terrible nails, proverbial for their hardness and firmness,[2] are driven—after the setting up of the cross, and the raising of the condemned upon it to the height of the transverse beam, as well as after the preparatory binding of Him to this transverse beam with cords[3]—through both hands, and certainly also through the feet of the crucified; as these latter were placed one upon the other and transfixed with one common nail.[4] What tortures must be endured in consequence of this cruel proceeding—tortures arising from the inflammation of the blood-trickling wounds in the hands and feet, from the rush of blood to the head and inner parts thus occasioned, from the terrible agony of not being able

---

[1] This in opposition to Cobet (*Mnemosyne*, viii., p. 276), who supposes only the *patibulum*, or cross-bar, to have been borne by the condemned to the place of execution—a view which he supports mainly by an appeal to a fragment of Plautus, preserved in Nonius Marcellus, p. 221 : *patibulum ferat per urbem, deinde affigatur*. With justice does Zestermann urge, on the other hand, that after the time of Cicero *patibulum* appears to be fully equivalent to *crux*, and that the expression *crucem portare*, familiarly occurring in the Fathers from the second century downwards (Tertull., Jer., etc.), cannot possibly denote merely "carrying the horizontal beam of the cross;" but must rather signify a bearing of the whole cross, composed of upright beam and transom. Whence else the so crushing weight of which Luke (xxiii. 26) testifies?—Keim, *u.s.*, p. 336, seeks still to uphold Cobet's view in opposition to the convincing reasoning of Zestermann, without, however, advancing anything decisive in favour of his position. Comp. further, Appendix VI.

[2] Horace, *Carm.*, i. 35, 18:

        Clavos *trabales* et cuneos manu
        Gestans aëna, etc.

[3] See Appendix VI : THE SINGLE EXTERNAL CIRCUMSTANCES AND PROCEEDINGS IN THE WORK OF CRUCIFIXION.

[4] *Ibid.*, No. 7.

to turn, of continuing fixed in an unnatural position of the body, from a maddening sensation of thirst, from a benumbing of the muscles, arteries, and nerves, advancing with exceeding slowness from the extremities to the centre of life, —all this can only be a matter of imperfect conception, not of trustworthy description. The very first of those terrible strokes of the hammer which, as a voice of judgment upon an ungodly race, " re-echoing in immensity and prolonged unto the last day,"[1] descended upon His sacred hands and feet, formed the beginning of a process of execution, than which anything more torturing and painful was hardly ever experienced. And *if* there were indeed modes of death more frightful, *if* anything more hellish still had been devised by Satan for the punishment of mankind which serves him: the Lord, who had lived the noblest and purest life here below, died the death of the cross as the most painful and most fearful of all. He, who knew no sin, endured the sufferings of that death designed for the worst of sinners, as the bitterest of all sufferings; the One pure and holy above all angels experienced these pangs more keenly than any single child of man would ever be able to experience them.

No testimony of unmerited hate is spared Him, who yet suffers as love itself. The painful tortures of the cross become for Him still more painful; because they fall upon Him, the Sinless One, as one rejected, as one who is righteously placed on a level with the worst transgressors, and has become a curse and object of aversion for all mankind. Not only must He see fulfilled that which was prophesied with regard to Him in Psalm xli. 9 : " He which eateth bread with me, hath lifted up his heel against me " (John xiii. 18); not only was the flight of all His apostles, not only was the denial of Peter (Mark xiv. 50, 66 ff.) mingled as a bitterly painful addition in His cup of suffering. In His examination He must see the representatives of His nation, as well

---

[1] Mackay, *The Glory of the Cross*, p. 43. Cp. what was said long before by Leo the Great, *Sermo* vi. *de Passione Domini*, c. 4 : Pendente enim in patibulo Creatore, universa creatura congenuit, et crucis clavos omnia simul elementa senserunt.

as the representatives of the Roman authority, testifying in melancholy rivalry against His holy and innocent cause. A murderer is demanded by the people in place of Him (Matt. xxvii. 16 ff.); and between two other murderers must He hang upon the cross, as one who is forsaken of men—nay, also of God Himself (Matt. xxvii. 38, and parallels). As an accursed one, an offscouring of all things, does He hang upon the tree of suffering: and yet He has become a curse only in order that He might become salvation and blessing to all; become as a sinner—yea, sin itself, only in order that He might be able to cancel the sins of all sinners.[1] Only to this end did He, the heavenly High Priest of the New Covenant, suffer Himself to be slain as a holy and spotless sacrificial lamb—though indeed as an atoning sacrificial lamb, as a sin-offering, like the victim on the great day of atonement—namely, that He might make all expiation for sin by means of sacrifice, henceforth for ever unnecessary, that He might comprehend in one *all* the sacrifices of the Old Testament ritual, sin-offering and trespass-offering, burnt-offering and peace-offering, meat-offering and drink-offering, in one ideally completing presentation of sacrifice; and remove them out of the way, in favour of that worship of God in spirit and in truth which henceforth takes their place.[2] Hated without a cause, as never any other on earth (John. xv. 25), He loves all—and not merely His own—with a love such as was never before displayed among men. He loves them with a love which delivers not only from temporal death, but also from everlasting destruction.

[1] Luther, *Comm. in Gal.*, c. 3, 13 (Opp. Lat., t. xxii. p. 20): Videamus nunc, quomodo in hac persona duo contraria concurrant. Invadunt eum non solum mea, tua, sed totius mundi peccata præterita, præsentia, et futura, et conantur eum damnare, sicut etiam damnant. Sed quia in eadem illa persona . . . est quoque æterna et invicta justitia, ideo congrediuntur illa duo, summum et maximum et solum peccatum, et summa, maxima, et sola justitia. Hic alterum cedere et vinci necessario oportet, cum summo impetu concurrant et collidantur. . . . Ideo necesse est in hoc duello vinci et occidi peccatum, et justitiam vincere et vivere. Sic in Christo vincitur, occiditur et sepelitur universum peccatum, et manet victrix et regnatrix justitia in æternum.

[2] Edgar, *Philosophy of the Cross*, p. 314 sqq.

No form of indignity is spared Him, which is connected with that mode of death in itself most shameful; and yet is His pillar of infamy and tree of the curse in the eyes of God the sacred altar of sacrifice of the New Covenant, the throne of dominion and the emblem of victory in the Messianic kingdom! Mockery and blasphemy, opprobrium and scorn, are more abundantly lavished upon Him than upon any crucified one. With the spittle of the ungodly is His countenance defiled (Matt. xxvi. 67; Mark xiv. 65); the purple robe, the sceptre, and crown, insignia of royalty, are mockingly thrust upon Him, in order to bring into derision His frank confession as King of the kingdom of God (Matt. xxvii. 28, and parallels). To the kingly purple robe of Pilate's warriors, Herod in contumely adds the glittering white raiment, symbol of His candidature for Israel's throne (Luke xxiii. 11). The combined mockery of both authorities, the Jewish and the Gentile, who as His persecutors have from being enemies become friends, accompanies Him up to the place of execution. Even while hanging on the cross He must support the ignominy of the accusing superscription above His head (John xix. 19, and parallels), the shame of nakedness and of the dividing of His garments by lot on the part of the rude mercenaries (Matt. xxvii. 35, and parallels),[1] the bitter vexation of the myrrh-draught presented by the hands of the executioners (Matt. xxvii. 34),[2] the raillery of the passers-by and of the priests and scribes standing near Him (Matt. xxvii. 39, 41 f.), and the reviling of one of the

---

[1] In what manner the brutal custom of stripping off and portioning-out the garments of those crucified might further supply the occasion for frivolous jests at the expense of the unfortunate beings hanging naked on the cross—or at best covered only with a cloth around the loins—is shown by a witticism of Artemidorus (*Oneirocreit.*, ii. 61): "To be crucified is a piece of good fortune for the poor, since he is *exalted* by the cross; but a misfortune for the rich, since he is crucified *naked*."—That the denudation of the *cruciarii* was not an absolute one, and that it did not take place in the case of all without exception, is shown in Appendix VI., No. 4.

[2] Hengstenberg, *Vorlesungen über die Leidensgeschichte* (Leipzig, 1875), S. 250: "Presented to the transgressors, the draught was a kindness; presented to incarnate righteousness in His sufferings, it was a severe and bitter indignity."

malefactors crucified at His side (Luke xxiii. 39). He endures all this as the Redeemer of the world, as the gracious High Priest of the Church purchased unto salvation with His blood, as the royal Victor over the powers of darkness, through whose sufferings—just where they reach the extremity of being forsaken by God, and of the gloomy night of death—the beams of His unquenchable life-sun breaking forth shed a radiance of glory. His death ensues as an event accelerated with miraculous rapidity, which—occurring within a few hours of the nailing to the cross—delivers at once from an existence otherwise continued, spite of wounds and tortures, through long wearisome days. He dies, being put to death as to the flesh, but made alive as to the spirit (1 Peter iii. 18), entering into Paradise in the power of an imperishable life (Heb. vii. 16; Luke xxiii. 43; Eph. iv. 8, f.), by the energy of His world-moving power and love obtaining even for His lifeless body on the cross protection from rudely mutilating ill-treatment and shelter in a secure resting-place (John xix. 31 ff.; Matt. xxvii. 57 ff., and parallels). He for whom was designed the end of a mean slave, of a common transgressor, dies the death of a king, testified to as a Divine kingly ruler even before His end by the prayer of the penitent thief, and in His end by the confession of the Roman centurion (Matt. xxvii. 54; Luke xxiii. 42), but yet more gloriously testifying of Himself in His last words upon the cross, the unspeakably consolatory legacy to His Church of the King of heaven now entering into glory, the sevenfold glorious proclamation of the near completion of His work of salvation.

In the SEVEN WORDS ON THE CROSS we see shadowed forth most gloriously and most profoundly that which was experienced by the God-man in the hours of His suffering, and that which this suffering signifies in relation to God and in relation to the world. They form the true point of culmination, the most touching and affecting expression of the Messianic self-consciousness, so far as the work of atonement is concerned. They are the superscription which *God*, for the faith of the Church, has placed above the Crucified One; even as Pilate's title was the *human* superscription for the outward eye of Jew and Gentile. To the seven petitions of the Lord's Prayer, as the sum of all praying and longing after truth, correspond the seven words upon the cross, as the sum of all truth itself.[1] They disclose to us immediately in a first series of cries of the heavily afflicted One—a sacred *tetrade*—the relations His sufferings bear towards humanity: to the totality of those combined against Him in hatred and mockery, whose raging does not prevent Him praying for them as the objects of His high-priestly work of expiation (Luke xxiii. 34); His relation to the one sinner who repents, whose blessed entrance into the heavenly kingdom He consolingly promises (Luke xxiii. 43); to those specially nearly connected with Him by the bonds of outward community of life, whose temporal well-being occupies His loving heart even amidst the most violent pangs (John xix. 26 f.); and, yet once more, to the totality of those who had risen up against Him, to the world of sinners, whose froward opposition He answers with nothing but a touching cry of grief, in which, still more than the longing for the mitigation of His bodily sufferings, seems to find expression the thirst for the salvation of the lost and erring. Introduced by this plaintive cry of thirst, His "last appeal to the sympathy of mankind,"[2] the second series of cries arising from the cross, the concluding *triad*, is now directed exclusively to God. He who—as the Atoner for sin, the Substitute bearing in place of others the weight of the Divine wrath, wrapped in the terrible gloom of being forsaken of God—pours forth, at the very hour when also an external darkness begins, to the terror of men, to veil the earth around, His cry of anguish and dismay; but hereby proclaims to us the unspeakably consolatory fact that the guilt has been expiated in our place,

---

[1] Mackay, *as before*, p. 31: As the seven petitions of the Lord's Prayer are the summation of all request, so these seven words are the summation of all truth, etc.

[2] "His last appeal to humanity." *Ibid.*, p. 144; cp. p. 150.

the price of redemption has been paid for us, unto the uttermost farthing (Matt. xxvii. 46 ; Mark xv. 34). Only for a little while endures the dread dismay of His desolation : then, not as one who has sunk into the depths of despair, but as one who has risen to the height of an ever indissoluble communion with God, He raises already the glorious cry of victory (John xix. 30), which, with the quieter language of prayer, out of the Psalter (Luke xxiii. 46 ; Psalm xxxi. 5), imdiately succeeding it, proclaims the completion of the august work of salvation. The speedy return of the Saviour who had entered Paradise, to the bodily tabernacle forsaken only for a short time ; the glorious arising of the faithful Shepherd who received power to take His life again, even as He had laid it down ; the proud succession of self-testimonies of the Risen One during the forty days of His glorious life ; the final entrance into the heavenly glory of the eternal throne at the right hand of God : all this is seen to be consolingly guaranteed in the last words of the Lamb of God offered up upon the cross, and prophesied too as the necessary consequence of His self-surrender unto death.

With the utterances of the Lord Himself are associated those of the disciples, by way of explanation and confirmation. We shall thus, in the second place, consider the cross and the death of the cross, *in the light of the Apostolic discourses and writings.*

B. *ACCORDING TO THE TESTIMONY OF THE APOSTOLIC DISCOURSES AND WRITINGS.*

If we contemplate the cross in this light, we see everywhere prominently apparent the same main line of thought with regard to the absolutely typical, the priestly atoning, and the kingly transforming and consummating significance of this centre of the redeeming activity of Christ ; yet in such wise, that the relations of this saving fact to its prophetic preannouncement under the Old Covenant on the one hand, and

to the life of the New Testament Church in the present
and the future on the other, are brought out much more fully,
and more in detail, than in the Gospels. And especially in
this is the Apostolic proclamation of the cross distinguished
from the Evangelic-Messianic, that *it everywhere and always
views the sufferings of the Lord upon the cross in the glorifying
light of that resurrection and exaltation to the right hand of
God, by which they were followed.* No Apostle speaks otherwise of the crucified Saviour, than as penetrated with the
sense of His mighty and loving presence, as the Lord of
Glory with the heavenly Father in the Holy Spirit reigning,
and returning to judgment upon the whole world. To be
" witnesses of the resurrection," they all alike regard as the
special task of their lives, the purport of their whole Apostolic
ministry. So already in the days of the Ascension and the
outpouring of the Spirit (Acts i. 22; ii. 32; iii. 15; iv. 33;
v. 32), so through all the stadia of the Petrine and Pauline
labour, up to the high-priestly ministrations of the Apostle of
love at Ephesus (Acts x. 40; xvii. 18; 1 Peter i. 3, 11; iii.
18 ff.; v. 1; Rom. iv. 25; viii. 34; 1 Cor. xv. 1 ff.; Rev. i. 5;
John xx. 30 f.) And in intimate connection with their
testimony concerning the power of the resurrection, do
they with one accord speak of the sin-expiating sacrificial
death, upon which this miracle of miracles served to impress
the Divine seal, of the bliss-giving mystery of that blood of
sprinkling, through which all who believe receive a cleansing
from their sins, and an entrance into everlasting blessedness.

It is true a deeper speculative penetration into the mystery
of redemption is still to some extent wanting in the discourses
of those disciples standing during the years immediately
succeeding the Lord's Ascension in the foreground of the
Apostolic history, a Peter, a Stephen, a Philip, a James.
They contemplate the death of Jesus, the holy Servant of
God, specially in its historical, rather than its soteriological-
doctrinal aspect (Acts ii. 23, 26; iii. 13 ff.; iv. 10 f.; x. 39),
and they lay stress less upon the inner necessity in connection
with the history of redemption, than upon the character of

His sufferings as predetermined in accordance with Divine revelation, and predicted in accordance with the testimony of Scripture (Acts ii. 23 ; iii. 18 ; iv. 28 ; v. 32 ; viii. 35 f. ; xv. 15 ff.) Even at a later period, some of the representatives of this form of primitive Christianity, still as yet bearing a preponderatingly Jewish-Christian colouring, remain without advancing beyond such standpoint of a less developed Christology. JAMES, especially, speaks indeed in his epistle of the kingly glory and coming to judgment of the exalted Saviour (James i. 1, 7 ; ii. 1 ; v. 8 f.) ; but of His priestly reconciling and expiatory work, He nowhere makes express mention. PETER, on the other hand, we see in his epistles, written without doubt a considerable period after his labours in Jerusalem, and not so very long before his death by martyrdom, not only delineating the history of the Lord's sufferings from their outward side, the salvation-bringing succession of suffering and exaltation (1 Peter i. 11 ; iv. 13 ; v. 1, 10), with wondrously penetrating power and vividness (ii. 21 ff.; iii. 18 ff.); but also developing the more profound bearings and import of the Messianic sufferings and death, as ideally fulfilling and taking the place of the sacrificial ritual of the Old Testament (1 Peter i. 2, 18 f.), as washing and cleansing away the sin of the world,—yea, as extending its operation of blessing even into the depths of the kingdom of the departed (1 Peter iii. 19 ff.; cp. also 2 Peter ii. 1 ; i. 16 ff.)

Yet more abundantly, and with more majectic exultation of faith (*plerophoria*), does the Apostle PAUL unfold the blessed contents of the gladdening mystery of the cross. For him, from his youth up a zealous Pharisee, who so long as he knew Christ only after the flesh, must necessarily receive the bitterest offence from His death on the cross (1 Cor. i. 23 ; Gal. v. 11 ; vi. 12), the word of the cross became the most vital centre of an animated testimony of faith, and of an ever self-consuming zeal of ministering love, from the time he saw the Crucified as the Risen One in heavenly glory. The cross of Calvary appeared to him henceforth as the foundation of all liberty and the beginning of all salvation and blessedness (Rom. x. 4; 1 Cor. i. 18 ff. ; ii. 2). It became for him "the lever which lifted the law out of its place;" the expiatory death of the God-man thereon accomplished, "the means of procuring a righteousness entirely new;" the Crucified One Himself the absolute and eternal reconciliation between flesh and spirit, between man and God,—yea, on this very account "the incarnate principle of sonship with God, the pre-existent man from heaven, by communion of Spirit with whom we become partakers of a new life from God."[1] With that wondrous dialectic acumen and plastic art of representation, which is without an equal in the circle of the Apostolic writers, he develops out of the one idea of the Saviour's death on the cross of the curse (Gal. iii. 13) the whole infinitely varied contents of his Christology, the whole "cross-wise formed relation of the deepest humiliation and loftiest exaltation of the two opposite natures."[2] The doctrine of the threefold import of the redeeming death as a death of the highest *exemplary* significance for our walk in the new obedience (Rom. v. 19; vi. 3 f. ; Gal. iv. 4 ; Phil. ii. 8, etc.), a death of high-priestly *atoning and reconciling* efficacy (Rom. iii. 24 ff.; v. 6; Gal. iii. 13 ; Col. ii. 14 ; 2 Cor. v. 18 ff.), a death of royal power of blessing and *everlasting salvation and peace-bringing* significance (Acts xx. 28 ; Ephes. ii. 13 ff. ; Coloss. i. 20 ff.; 1 Cor. x. 16; xi. 25) is presented by him, as regards its essence in perfect agreement with Peter, but yet much more deeply, with more abundant plastic power of the imagination, and with a much more imposing breadth of view. For Peter, it is the *tree* on which the Lord hung (1 Peter ii. 24; Acts ii. 23 ; v. 30 ; x. 39);[3] for Paul, the cross

---

[1] O. Pfleiderer, *Der Paulinismus* (Leipzig, 1873).

[2] Hamann, *Werke*, Bd. vii. S. 127 (edit. Rothe).

[3] Only once (in Acts iv. 10,—the address before the Great Council)—does Peter speak of the *cross* of Christ. . . . ὃν ὑμεῖς ἐσταυρώσατε ; in every other case he employs the less definite expression "tree," ξύλον. Conversely the latter term occurs in Paul only twice (Acts xiii. 29 ; Gal. iii. 13) ; elsewhere he always uses σταυρός.

which, pointing at the same time to the heights and the depths, the length and the breadth, formed the emblem of the infinite (Eph. iii. 18), to which ever again and again he refers as the centre and essence, the foundation and cornerstone of all certainty as regards salvation.[1] For Peter, too, the range of the influence of this redemptive suffering on the cross extends indeed down into hell beneath, and up to the region of the heavenly angels and saints above (1 Peter iii. 19 ff.; i. 12 [at the end of the verse]; comp. Eph. iv. 8 ff.; Col. i. 20 f.; Phil. ii. 9 ff.): but it is not depicted with equally predominating interest as with the Apostle of the Gentiles, as that which embraces all nations of the earth, as encompassing Jew and Gentile alike with its fulness of blessing, as laying the foundations of a covenant of grace which extends to the ends of the earth (Gal. iii. 28 ; Eph. ii. 11 ff.; Col. i. 20 ff.; iii. 11). On this very account Paul is so far from being ashamed of the Gospel of Christ in presence of the wise of this world, for this very reason he makes his boast so confidently and so fearlessly of his message, which is to the Jews an offence and to the Greeks a folly (Rom. i. 16 f.; 1 Cor. i. 23), because he has made the thousandfold experience that the arms stretched forth upon the cross are stretched forth in the same love alike to circumcision and uncircumcision, to Jew and Greek, Barbarian, Scythian, Bond, and Free, and that the power of compassion in the faithful Saviour's heart is able also to melt the obdurate resistance of unbelieving human hearts. It is more than an idealising of certain Old

---

[1] Even though the famous passage, Eph. iii. 18, which has been from ancient times so very frequently explained in reference to the cross, with its four ends, was *not* written with a conscious reference to this four-armed symbol of redemption—and any definite hint in favour of such reference is certainly wanting alike in the words themselves as in the context—yet it can assuredly be adduced as an indirect evidence for the majestic breadth and fulness of the conceptions regarding the history of salvation attached by Paul to the cross of Jesus. The "*metaphysical* greatness" of the love of the crucified Saviour is in the deeply affected mind of the Apostle, by virtue of his vividly enkindled imagination, regarded as a "*physical-mathematical*" greatness, "extending on every side" (Meyer).—On the *history of the exposition* of these remarkable words and of their Old Testament representatives, Job xi. 8, 9 ; Psalm cxxxix. 8, 9, see below, Appendix VII.

Testament religious ideas, more than a mysticism of subjective pious emotions of the heart, which is developed on the ground of this vitally experienced communion of salvation with the Crucified and Risen One. He "became the creator of a philosophy of history which has its centre in the cross of Christ,"[1] and the fundamental thoughts of this philosophy of history include the eternally unalterable norms of *all* true philosophy of history in general, the cognition of that "wisdom of God in a mystery, the hidden wisdom, which God ordained before the world unto our glory," and compared with which all the wisdom of this world, and of the princes of this world, is nothing but folly (1 Cor. ii. 6 ff.)

For the very reason that the idea of a comprehensive historic-philosophic speculation, starting from the cross of Christ as its centre, lies at the basis of the peculiar spiritual greatness of the Apostle of the Gentiles, and precisely because this very idea, so fruitful and so strongly marked by genius, is much less easily recognised in the other Apostles and New Testament writers, one might feel tempted to attach an absolute—rather than relative—importance to Paul, at the expense of his fellow-disciples; yea, even to extol him as strictly speaking the "spiritual creator of Christianity," to the genius of whom the Lord Himself, the lowly rabbi of Nazareth, does not attain.[2] But, apart from the fact that Paul would oppose to *this* attempt also to make an idol of his name, an indignant "What! was Paul then crucified for you?"[3] all such isolating of the Apostle of the Gentiles from his fellow-disciples is seen to be untenable. For the word of the cross is just as much their Gospel as his. If they otherwise denominate it, and clothe it in a series of ideas some-

[1] Carrière. *Die Kunst*, etc., iii. 1, S. 24.
[2] So notably E. v. Hartmann ("Das Christenthum Christi" in "die Literatur," 1874; also in his "Selbstzersetzung des Christenthums"), who regards the historic-philosophic speculation sprung from the genius of Paul, this beginning of all Christian philosophy and science whatever, as no doubt a falsification of the Christianity of Christ, but pays the tribute of greater admiration to the author of this falsification than to Christ Himself. Similarly also v. Hellwald, *Culturgesch.*, S. 389 ff.
[3] 1 Cor. i. 13. (Luther's version.)

what differing from his, yet—Apostles of the cross are they all, even as he. The writer, too, of the EPISTLE TO THE HEBREWS describes the ideal and exalted kingly high-priesthood of Christ in traits which in reality exactly correspond to the Pauline testimony of the Crucified and Risen One (Heb. i. 3; iv. 14 ff.; v. 1 ff.; vii. 1 ff.; ix. 14 ff.) And once at least he expressly makes mention of the sacred altar of this high-priesthood—an altar inaccessible for those servants of the law "who minister in the tabernacle"—and this in words which scarcely admit of a doubt that the altar of the cross on Calvary, the place of the for ever completed sacrifice of the Son of God, is thereby intended (Heb. xiii. 10).[1] JOHN, however, the disciple of love, who remained at the foot of the cross until the last breath of the Saviour, the eye-witness of that stream of water and of blood, which the spear-thrust in the side of the already departed One drew forth (John xix. 34; 1 John v. 6), in his animated testimonies concerning the blood of Jesus Christ as the propitiation for the sins of the whole world (1 John i. 7; ii. 2; iv. 10), extends in brotherly spirit the right hand of communion to the Apostle of the cross. Not only as Apostle and Evangelist, but also as the Spirit-anointed prophetic Seer of the New Testament, does he testify to the cleansing power of the blood shed upon Calvary, the blood of "the Lamb that was slain" (Rev. v. 6; vii. 14; xiii. 8; comp. i. 5; v. 9; xiv. 3). The sacred name of the Lamb, which, according to the symbolic description in Rev. xiv. 1; xxii. 4, shall shine resplendent upon the foreheads of the servants of God, what else could it be but the sign of the cross—the original and ideal of that prophecy of Ezekiel concerning the delivering

---

[1] For this explanation of the ἔχομεν θυσιαστήριον, κ.τ.λ., which since the time of Thomas Aquinas has gradually become the prevailing one, the fact is decisive that the author in what immediately follows comes to speak of the place of execution "without the camp," *i.e.*, without the City of God of the O. T. (ver. 11—13). Hardly thus can Christ Himself be intended as the spiritual altar of Christians (Mich., Stier, Thol., Hofm.) The reference to the Communion Table (Böhme, Bähr, Bisp., Ebrard) is certainly justified as a secondary application. Comp. Bengel, Bleek, De Wette, Delitzsch *in loc*.

Tau, the bright counterpart to the dark symbol of the beast upon the foreheads of the lost (Rev. xvi. 2; xx. 4)?[1]

Even more distinct than the doctrinal and prophetic testimony of the Apostles are their Church-founding labours and sufferings—sufferings which impress upon them in their totality, and not upon Paul alone, the stamp of heralds of the word of the cross. The taking up and bearing of the cross of Jesus in its literal, terrible reality—the "cross" being understood in the wider general sense of the *varia genera crucis* of Seneca—fell indeed to the lot of but few among them.[2] And cross-bearers of a type affording an everlasting model, glorious heroes in lowly following after the Crucified, were they all, even those who were not decked with the purple of the Martyr's death. Even though Paul, the man who thrice received forty stripes save one, thrice was beaten with rods, once was stoned, and more than thrice suffered shipwreck (2 Cor. xi. 24, 25), may have had a right above others to speak of himself as a bearer of "the dying of the Lord Jesus," or to make mention of his scars (2 Cor. iv. 10; Gal. vi. 17): in regard to their inner willingness and readiness of heart, they were all of them "bearers of the marks" in spirit and in truth; whom no saint of the following ages of Christianity, and none of those stigma-bearers of whom the Romish Church is so proud, even distantly approaches. The Apostolic Church is the true Church of the Cross, the prototype of all martyr-churches and communions of the cross in later Christian history. What it is to follow Christ upon the way of His passion, what it is joyfully to drink of His cup and to be baptised with His baptism, must for all ages be studied in this Church, and in this Church ever anew. Just as the right

---

[1] Compare Dorner, *Entwicklungsgesch. der Lehre v. d. Person Christi*, I. S. 291, not. 231.

[2] As being actually crucified, tradition mentions, in addition to Peter, who was nailed to the cross with his head downwards (Euseb., *H. E.*, iii. 1), also the Ap. Bartholomew, who is said to have been crucified and then flayed alive in Armenia or Albania, by order of Prince Astayages; and Philip, who it is alleged was bound to a cross and stoned at Hierapolis in Phrygia, under Domitian. (*Mart. Rom.*, Baronius, etc.)

apportioning of the preaching of the Crucified, the testifying to the kernel of the Gospel verity in full power, the victorious displaying and bringing forth of the banner of the cross, the banner which invites to enter the gates of salvation, is to be learnt from their records, and from their records alone.

One might attempt to present a grouping of the leading representatives of the Apostolate according to their several types of doctrine and other characteristic peculiarities, in such wise that they—the most prominent figures in the earliest communion under the cross—should also externally display the figure of a cross, and so immediately typify the sacrificial altar upon Calvary. Much might be said in justification of such a combining of the five principal types of the Apostolic individuality in teaching, according to which Peter would represent the foot, the firm root of the stem of the cross, John the towering, heavenward-soaring apex of the same, James and the author of the Epistle to the Hebrews (each of these in combination with his nearest spiritual kinsmen: the former thus with Jude and Matthew, the latter with Luke) the right and the left end of the transverse beam, while Paul would occupy the bright central position, at the point of juncture of the two arms.[1] We refrain, in order not to expose ourselves to the charge of being occupied with a mystic play of fancy without any scriptural basis, from a fuller exposition of this thought. Nevertheless we very decidedly maintain that the Church of the Apostolic age, together with its sacred

[1] Somewhat differently does F. Godet, in his interesting study on "the four principal Apostles," [*Studies on the N. T.*, Engl. tr.: Hodder and Stoughton, 1877,] group the four leading types of doctrine among the Apostles. He treats that of Peter, the Apostle of the *Doxa*, as the common ground and starting-point; from this point represents the opposition of principles between James and Paul, the Apostle of good works and the Apostle of the righteousness of faith, as developing itself; but John, the Apostle of the Divine life in love, as forming the crowning close of the whole. We miss in connection with this arrangement the due place of the author of the Epistle to the Hebrews, to whom in the history of the development of the peculiar doctrinal types of the New Testament, certainly no less degree of significance can be attached than, *e.g.*, to James. It seems to us, moreover, that for Paul must be claimed a more decisively central position than is the case in this arrangement of Godet.

records of revelation, was inwardly and in a spiritual manner consecrated with the mark of the emblem of redemption, and glorified by its lustre; and thus that no later age of Christianity has taught more purely and accurately concerning the signification of this emblem, or has exercised itself in a more hallowing and blessing-giving use of the same.

III.

The Cross of Christ in the Pre-Constantine Church and Theology.

IN the immediate post-Apostolic age, up to the end of the persecutions under Constantine, there is apparent, indeed, in many respects a diminution of the original purity and strength of the primitive Christian life in the Spirit. But yet there still glows, beneath the ashes of a mind and habit more conformed to the world, which has settled over it, the fire of the first love; and so often as the storms of persecution raise this veiling cover, or for a considerable period remove it, the original brightness shines forth clearly once more. The Church continues, thanks to the severity of the Divine discipline, in the fellowship of the sufferings of Christ; she on this account experiences and testifies most abundantly to the power of His resurrection (Phil. iii. 10). Christendom remains the community of the cross, her whole consciousness and life hallowed and glorified by the impress of the sacred symbol of redemption. Neither are there wanting fair fruits of this her life of faith and love—a life planted with Christ into a like death, and abundantly watered by the blood of her own martyrs. But they are fruits of modest and not always brilliant appearance—precious in the sight of God, but poor and contemptible in the sight of the world; not like golden apples of a restored Paradise, and yet in reality ripened upon the Tree of Life, anew conferred upon humanity. The bare, lonely, and leafless stem of the cross of Jesus—yet infinitely surpassing all the trees of this world in ever-enduring power of germination and fulness of life—

bore them and brought them to maturity. Not in the houses of kings, or the halls of the rich, or the gardens of the wise of this world, did the shoots and offsets of this wondrous tree bring forth such fruits; but in the huts of the poor and the lowly, the deserts far from the noise of cities, the subterranean meeting-places of those persecuted and hunted to the chambers of the dead. It is the Church of the martyrs and of the catacombs which presents to us these the first-fruits of the primitive Christian spirit, engrafting itself upon the life of ancient Greek and Roman civilisation. No wonder that they are redolent of the air of the catacombs, and that even a reading of the accounts of these battles and victories of the virgin Christendom, bleeding with a thousand wounds, merits to be called a cross for the spirit.[1]

The bearing of the cross of Christ, as of a yoke, gentle indeed, but yet deeply bending down and painfully wounding, forms the most salient characteristic of the peculiar life of primitive Christianity at this stage of its development. The whole life of the Church of the martyrs is an earnest conflict in the service of the Lord,—a conflict involving many an arduous struggle, and one which never presses on to victory save through much bloodshed. The service of the "Warrior of Christ," the *Agon Christianus*, as Augustine, on the ground of 1 Cor. ix. 25; 1 Thess. ii. 2; Phil. i. 30; 1 Tim. vi. 12; 2 Tim. iv. 7, etc., terms him, is no mere play, no light children's toil. Full many of these soldiers of God in the times of severe persecution, from Trajan to Dioclesian, followed the Lord literally to the cross, or even, like Peter, were crucified with the head downwards. This latter is expressly related by Eusebius of several Egyptian martyrs under Dioclesian, as, moreover, by the Roman Martyrologium (certainly a much less reliable authority) of the Cilician martyr Calliopius at Pompeiopolis (304), and of a youth of only fifteen years, named Venantius, under the emperor Decius.[2] That bishop

[1] Kahnis, *Blicke aus der Vergangenheit in die Gegenwart und Zukunft der Kirche:* Allg. ev. luth. K.-Ztg., 1874, No. 19.
[2] Euseb., *H. E.*, viii. 8; *Martyr. Rom.*, 7 Apr. and 8 May.

Symeon of Jerusalem, the son of Clopas, suffered martyrdom by crucifixion, under the emperor Trajan, at the age of a hundred and twenty years, is already testified by Hegesippus.[1] Eusebius states of Pionius that he underwent at Smyrna, in the time of Marcus Aurelius, first "nailing to the cross," and then "tortures in the flames." Of the pious female slave Blandina, at Lyons, under the same emperor, the epistle of the congregations at Lyons and Vienne relates that she was attached in the form of a cross to a block of wood, and exposed to wild beasts to be torn in pieces. Upon the Palestinean martyr Theodulus was also, according to the testimony of Eusebius, inflicted death by crucifixion.[2] As crucified, the Martyrologies besides speak of the bishop Asteios of Dyrrachium (under Trajan), St. Dionysius (as is alleged, under Hadrian), the erewhile soldier Alexander, who is said to have overturned a heathen sacrificial table in presence of the emperor Antoninus; Theodorus, who was, it is asserted, crucified in his military garb at Perga in Pamphylia (likewise under Antoninus). Farther, as belonging to the Decian-Valerian age of persecution: the bishop Nestor, at Perga (251), the Roman bishop Xystos, or Sistus II. (258); the pious couple, Timotheus and Maura, at Thebes in Egypt (circ. 250); Arcadius (as is alleged about 260). During the reign of Aurelian: Lucilianus at Constantinople, and Philomenus at Ancyra in Galatia. During the great age of persecution under Dioclesian: the brothers Marcianus and Marcus, in Egypt (it is asserted as early as 287); the deacon Apollonius, at Iconium; the aged Christians Agricola and Vitalis, at Bologna; the three boys, Asterius, Claudius, and Neon, at Ægæ in Cilicia; the two physicians, Carpophorus and Leontius, at Aquileia, both, as is alleged, nailed to the cross, and then transfixed with arrows; the Cilician parallels of these two, Cosmas and Damian, likewise physicians, and likewise upon the cross transfixed with arrows; Faustus, at Cordova, who is said to

---

[1] In Euseb., *H. E.*, iii. 32.
[2] Euseb., *H. E.*, iv. 15, 47; v. 1, 41 f. *De Martyrib. Palæst.*, xi. 24.

have been exposed to the same kind of martyrdom; the Laodicean martyrs Thalus and Trophimus; Vincentius, roasted upon a cross over the flames, at Valentia in Spain (already celebrated in song by Prudentius, in the fifth hymn of his *Peristephanon*); the Pontian Zoticus; the Spanish maiden Eulalia, at thirteen years of age; Benedicta, the daughter of a Gallic councillor, and the Syrian maiden Sempronia at Sibapolis. The accounts are not very definite concerning the time of the martyrdom of the Grecian sisters Martha and Mary, or of the Egyptian Lycarion, who likewise are said to have suffered death upon the cross.[1] Not a few of these alleged martyrdoms on the cross—to which a considerable number might still be added from the post-Constantine period of persecution,[2] had we not to regard the limits imposed upon us in the present chapter— are, perhaps to be looked upon merely as products of the imagination of a later age addicted to the reverence of the martyrs. Yet even in such creations of the mythology of the early Church and of the Middle Ages there exists, apart from the isolated instances of faithful historic reminiscence which they may include, the general and underlying view—in itself unquestionably a just one—of an extraordinary severity and cruelty in the times of the persecution of the early Christians, having many points of analogy with that in the sufferings of the Lord. As an indirect confirmation of our designation of the pre-Constantine Church as one, more than the Church of any later Christian epoch, characterised by a *painful* following of the cross, an *Ecclesia pressa et cruciata*, do these accounts also, albeit to a great extent legendary, thus at any rate retain their value.

---

[1] On the martyrs here mentioned, compare the splendid hagiologic work of the Jesuit Barth. Ricci: *Triumphus Jesu Christi crucifixi* (illustrated with plates by Adrian Collaert). Antv., 1614. See also Wessely, *Iconographie Gottes und der Heiligen*, and Stadler and Heim, in the *Heiligenlexicon*.

[2] Especially belonging to the time of the great Persian persecution of the Christians, under Sapores II. (343—380), in which, *e.g.*, the maiden Tarbula, sister of the bishop Symeon of Seleucia, as also another maiden, Gudelia, etc., are said to have been crucified. (Wessely, S. 212, 379.)

The more abundant the opportunity thus granted to these Christians of early times for practical exercise of the communion of suffering with their Lord, and the more joyful their readiness to enter into such school of suffering—a readiness which stamped upon their whole life, even in those times which were not, strictly speaking, times of persecution, the impress of a "dying daily," a "constant martyrdom,"[1]—so much the more spiritual in its nature remained their devotion to the Crucified, so much the less could a tendency to a false externalism and an ethnicising degeneration of their religious life already gain with them the upper hand. Of a properly so-called WORSHIP OF THE CROSS, a superstitious reverence for, or even idolisation of, the symbol of redemption at the cost of the devotion due to the Redeemer Himself, nothing is as yet to be perceived among them. The cross, as they know it, is "not something to be worshipped, but only something to be endured."[2] The crown and centre of their religious life is, no doubt, devotion to the crucified and risen Saviour; but this as essentially addressed to Himself, not to the instrument of His sufferings or to the single external circumstances of the Passion. They observe the Passover, the memorial of His sufferings and His resurrection, as the oldest and principal festival of the cycle of their Church Year. They observe Sunday, with the two days of *stationes* (religious assemblies),—Wednesday and Friday—of which the former was intended to recall to remembrance the betrayal on the part of Judas or the beginning of the Passion, the latter the death of the Lord or the culmination of the Passion—as prominent points in their ecclesiastical cycle of weeks. But to the cross as such, not one of their sacred days is as yet devoted. Even of processions and pilgrimages with uplifted station-crosses, of crucifixes as indispensable accompaniments of churches and

---

[1] Non solum effusio sanguinis in confessione reputatur, sed devotae quoque mentis servitus immaculata quottidianum martyrium est. Hieron., *Ep.* 108, 31. Comp. Cyprian, Non illi defuerunt tormentis, sed tormenta defuerunt illis. (*Ep.* 12, 1.)

[2] Non adorandae, sed sebeundae cruces. Minucius Felix, *Oct.*, 12.

altars, of the setting up of crosses at the entrances to houses or cities or villages, etc., there is as yet no word. In the houses of religious assembly of the Christians there would appear, indeed, to have been present here and there, as also perhaps in their private dwellings, simple figurative representations of the cross. But even this is only presumably to be inferred from the reproaches sometimes addressed to the Christians on the part of the Heathen, that they were "worshippers of the cross" (*crucis religiosi*), as from the replies of the Church Fathers to this charge. When Minucius Felix declares, in answer to the suspicion of Staurolatry: "We neither worship crosses, nor wish for them,"[1] he appears hereby, and still more decisively by the reference which follows to the trophies of the heathen, and their resemblance to a cross with a man attached to it, to deny that crosses or crucifixes were in religious use among the Christians. In substantially the same manner does Tertullian express himself, in an amplifying imitation of the arguments of Minucius with regard to the reproach in question, as well as the still more false and slanderous charge of the worship of an ass. The offensiveness of the latter accusation he throws back upon the Heathen with natural indignation, and with bitter scorn at the untruthful and self-contradictory nature of the statements in Tacitus (whose information with regard to the religion of the Jews formed the source of his calumniation). But with regard to the other point he says, "He who regards us as worshippers of the cross is himself equally guilty," referring to the images of Pallas and Ceres, and declares, in opposition to all adoration of these and similar material figures: "*If* we perchance have crosses (as objects of religious reverence), yet our worship is in reality addressed to the whole living God."[2] Neither from these justificatory

---

[1] Cruces etiam nec colimus, nec optamus. *Oct.*, c. 29.

[2] Nos, si forte, integrum et totum Deum colimus (*Apologet.*, c. 16). Comp. shortly before : Sed et qui crucis nos religiosos putat, consectaneus noster erit.... Et tamen quanto distinguitur a crucis stipite Pallas Attica et Ceres Pharia, quæ sine effigie rudi palo et informi ligno prostat? etc.—So in substance, *ad Nation.*, I, 12.

remarks of the Carthaginian apologete, nor from the wretched caricature scratched upon a wall by that heathen mocker in Rome, who represents the Christian Alexamenos as kissing his hand (comp. Job xxxi. 27) to the crucified ass-god,[1] is anything to be definitely concluded either for or against the supposition of a regular occurrence of figurative representations of the cross, or of the crucifix, in the worship of the Church about the beginning of the third century. The name *crucis religiosi* might very naturally be attached to the Christians, even without the existence among them to any great extent of such representations. Upon their earliest monuments of art, the cross as such—as we shall presently see—occupies at any rate no prominent position.

Only that invisible imitation of the symbol of redemption which consists of a blessing and consecrating marking of oneself with the four points of the cross—the practice of *crossing oneself* or CRUCESIGNATION (the representation of a *signum crucis transeuntis*, according to Gretser's expression)—appears to be definitely and clearly attested even as regards this early period. " At every step, at incoming and outgoing, at the putting on of one's clothes and shoes, at bathing, at table, at the kindling of the lights, going to bed, sitting down, and whatever we do, we mark the sign of the cross upon the forehead." Thus confesses Tertullian in his " Wreath of the Warrior,"[2] and when at the same time he appeals in justification of the pious custom to the time-honoured tradition of the Christians, he would seem to date its origin from a period scarcely any later than that of the Apostles. Of the passages Rev. xiv. 1 ; xxii. 4 (or Ezek. ix. 4) Tertullian does not make mention ; at least, in the apologetic treatise above adduced. But that these and similar words of Holy Writ had already very early given an impulse to the formation of the custom,

---

[1] With the derisive subscription : Αλεξάμενος σέβετε (= σέβεται) θεόν. Comp. Ferd. Becker, *Das Spottcrucifix*, etc. Breslau, 1866 ; Fr. X. Kraus, *die römischen Katakomben*, etc. Freib. 1872.

[2] *De cor. milit.*, c. 3 ; cp. c. 4, as also *ad uxor.*, ii. c. 5.

scarcely admits of a doubt. Accordingly Basil the Great does not hesitate to trace back the custom to Apostolic tradition, and already Cyprian, as well as the third book of the so-called Apostolic Constitutions, makes mention of it as a constituent part of those sacred actions connected with the sacrament of baptism, while the eighth book of the same liturgical codex (of somewhat later date) testifies to its practice in connection with the observance of the Supper.[1] Even the employment of the cross in connection with the expulsion of dæmons or healings of those possessed, as these had to be performed by the lower ecclesiastical office of exorcists, itself belongs in its first period to the time before Constantine. Of its effects the apologetes boast, as miraculous proofs of the power of Christianity in presence of the Heathen, who must themselves be witnesses of such events without being able to explain them. In speaking of these cases, express mention is made of crossing oneself—not, indeed, so early as Justin, Tertullian, Cyprian, or Origen, but yet—by Lactantius, who gives a detailed statement as to the power of the cross as signed upon the brow of the confessors of Christ, especially as to "how terrible this sign is to the dæmons, when they, adjured by the name of Christ, fled out of the bodies of which they had taken possession."[2] Yet without doubt those earlier writers were already acquainted with the application of the sacred sign in the work of exorcism. For as this plays an important part in very ancient rituals in the exorcism at baptism—a fact which is indirectly attested as early as the time of Tertullian[3]—so can neither the numerous references to its dæmon-expelling operation in Christian poets

---

[1] Basilius, *de spiritu S.*, c. 27. Cyprian, *ad Demetrian.*, 26 (trophæo crucis mortem subigere); *de unit. eccles.*, p. 116 (qui renati et *signo Christi* signati). *Const. Ap.*, iii. 117 (ἡ σφραγὶς ἀντὶ τοῦ σταυροῦ), viii. 12 (τὸ τρόπαιον τοῦ σταυροῦ). Cp. Augusti, *chr. Archäol.*, ii. 442, 730.

[2] *Inst. div.*, iv. 27. Comp. ii. 6; Justin, *Dial. c. Tryph.*, 85; Tertull., *Apol.* 23; *De cor. mil.*, 11; *De idolol.*, 11; Cyprian, *De idolor. vanit.*; Origen, *c. Cels.*, vii. 4.

[3] *De cor. mil.*, c. 3; also Cypr., *Ep.* 76 *ad Magn.* Comp. Augusti, *l.c.*, ii. 429 f.

and prose writers from the fourth century onwards,[1] nor the important part which it plays in the life of celebrated monkish Fathers and saints from the time of St. Anthony, and even, *e.g.*, in that of the apostate Julian,[2] be rightly understood otherwise than on the supposition of a use of it in such forms of adjuration dating back to the earliest centuries of the post-Apostolic age. Regarding the intrinsic credibility of the accounts in question, as well as regarding the moral and religious value of this thaumaturgy effected by means of crossing oneself, it is very difficult from the standpoint of the present development of Christian doctrine and life to form a just conception. The fearful tension of the opposition between the Græco-Roman idolatry and oracular manifestations—which precisely as a spiritual power on the point of expiring might once more develop mighty dæmoniacal

---

[1] *E.g.*, in Prudentius' *Hymn. in quadragesima:*

> Crux pellit omne crimen,
> fugiunt crucem tenebræ;
> tali dicata signo
> mens fluctuare nescit, etc.

Similarly in Sedulius' *Hymn. paschalis ad nocturnum*, str. 9:

> Tu hostis antiqui vires
> per crucem mortis conteris;
> qua nos signati frontibus
> vexillum fidei ferimus.

Compare also the lines of Gregory the Great: *Lignum crucis mirabile*. str. 3:

> Tu Christe rex piissime
> hujus crucis signaculo
> horis momentis omnibus
> munire nos non abnuas.

So also the favourite verse of prayer belonging to the later Middle Ages:

> O crux, ave spes unica!
> Hoc passionis tempore
> Piis adauge gratiam
> Reisque dele crimina.

Compare too Athanasius, *adv. Gentes*, c. 1; Cyril, *Catech.* 13; Epiph., *Hær.* 30, and farther patristic authorities in Gretser. iii. 20—26.

[2] Athanas., *Vita S. Antonii* (comp. Müller, *Athan.*, S. 395 ff.) Concerning the involuntary crossing of himself on the part of Julian the Apostate, by which he is said to have frightened away the dæmons brought into a temple at Athens by the spells of a goëte, see Theodoret, *H. E.*, ii. 3. Other stories of the cross in connection with the same emperor are told by Gregory of Nazianzus, *Or.*, iii. p. 70; iv. p. 112; Sozomen, v. 1.—(Comp. Grets., iii. 19.)

forces—and Christianity in its youthful freshness, pressing forward upon its career of victory with growing plerophory of faith, might render necessary on the part of the Christians many other modes of conflict than were known to later ages, might still impart (to that which in later ages more and more stiffened into an empty ceremony) in the majority of cases a substance and life energetically exerting itself, might hand down through a succession of generations the charismatic dominion over spirits granted to the Apostles (Luke x. 17— 20; 1 Cor. xii. 28), and thus bring it into combination with forms as yet strange, or at all events not common, in the Apostolic age, until at last under this modification too it ceased to be operative, and disappeared from the practice of the Church. For yielding anything of apologetic value, the domain of these phenomena seems, from the standpoint of the present day, hardly any longer to be adapted. Even the theology of Rome, which has a special interest in attaching considerable weight to the miracles wrought by virtue of external ecclesiastical ceremonies, and which also on this account sought most zealously in former times, in its polemics against the Protestants, to make capital out of these exorcisms by means of crucesignation practised in the early Church,[1] is in a position only very partially to overcome the manifold critical objections which are opposed to the supposition of the absolutely historical character of the said accounts. But in any case, what is here urgently called for in both directions—namely, that of an over-credulous acceptance of what is handed down, and that of an over-ready rejection of the same from a standpoint which denies miracles in principle—is a proceeding by the way of a cautious testing and a reserved judgment. In relying on the authority of the Fathers we may easily come to have too much of a good thing; on the other hand, it is also easier to suffer oneself to

---

[1] Gretser devotes to the exorcising, healing, and magically consecrating operation of the crucesignation (the latter feature, *e.g.*, in the endowing of the holy water with sanative qualities) no fewer than twenty chapters of his third volume: *De signo crucis transeunte.*

be led by the influence of modern conceptions and scientific prejudices to a one-sided doubting and impugning of the facts in question, than it is to manifest operations of faith and love similar to those of the Christians of the times from which these accounts date.

Thus much also is already distinctly apparent from that more ordinary, not thaumaturgical, practice of crossing oneself, observed in the Church of this period, that it was inspired and impelled by a very high degree of devotion to the redeeming death of the Saviour on the cross; and that the impulse to a constant confessing and consecrating presentation even of the outward symbol of this great fact of salvation was already powerfully active in the Church. The operations of this impulse one discovers also in another domain, on which has sprung up a not less interesting and far more abundant fulness of characteristic manifestations of the life of the Spirit among the early Christians. We mean the SEEKING FOR SO-CALLED "HIDDEN CROSSES" (cruces dissimulatæ) in the province of Biblical exegesis, or of an apologetic demonstration for the Messiahship of Jesus in connection with the sacred history. Every single instance of the existence of directly or indirectly cruciform objects mentioned within the compass of the Mosaic ceremonial legislation, or of the Old Testament history of salvation, yea almost every kind of wooden vessel or block of wood referred to within the limits of this history, is, by virtue of this impulse, explained as a significant type of the cross on Calvary. The pious investigators of Scripture are as it were drunken with the air of the cross. Side by side with that artificially typologising mode of proceeding which discovers the blood of the Lord in every scarlet-red or purple object, sees holy baptism reflected in every mention of water, however accidental, they leave nothing unobserved which seems adapted to indicate either the material or the form of the symbol of redemption. Both Apostolic modes of expression—that preferred by Peter, which brings into greater prominence the material side, and the Pauline one, which lays greater stress upon the form and appearance (comp. above, p. 102 f.), serve as guides to this tendency directed towards the greatest possible piling up of analogies. Even into the domain of heathen mythology and literature do they make occasional incursions, in order to augment the number of significant vouchers. As Plato is already cited (see above, p. 83) as prophesying of the salvation-bringing name of Christ, so must even the vine of Bacchus—this latter, it is true, as a plagiarism from the blessing of Jacob: Gen. xlix. 10 ff.—yield a typical reference to the cross, and the Sibyls themselves proclaim mysterious oracles relating to this very object.[1] In addition to these there are those analogies derived immediately from external nature about us, or from the business of daily life, as masts with cross-yards, ploughshares, spades, trophies, statues, flight of birds, swimming of fishes, and similar things, in which the form of the sacred symbol is seen to be reflected even beyond the pale of the history of salvation, as a testimony to all the world for the revealed truth.

The germs of this remarkable procedure in the multiplying of types appear so early as the literature of the Apostolic Fathers. It is true Ignatius of Antioch and Polycarp content themselves as yet with a practical-mystic exposition of the significance of the cross, without by an artificial allegorism importing ideas foreign to the subject.[2] But already Clement of Rome cannot resist interweaving with his exhortations to the Corinthians a fragment of the scarlet wool of Rahab, as a significant type of the blood of the Redeemer.[3] And with the author of the Epistle of Barnabas, written only a few years or decades later, the typology of the cross is already in luxuriant bloom, betraying, like the kindred allegoristic arts of the same author, its origin in the school of Alexandrine

[1] Justin, *Apol. maj.*, p. 89. Comp. *Orac. Sib.*, v. 257 ff.; viii. 245 (Sozom., *H. E.*, ii. 1).

[2] Ignat. ad Smyrn., 1 (ὥσπερ καθηλωμένους ἐν τῷ σταυρῷ τοῦ κυρίου 'Ι. Χρ.); ad *Trall.*, c. 11; ad *Ephes.*, c. 9 (ἀναφερόμενοι εἰς τὰ ὕψη διὰ τῆς μηχανῆς τοῦ 'Ι. Χρ., ὅ ἐστιν σταυρός, σχοινίῳ χρώμενοι τῷ Πνεύματι τῷ Ἁγίῳ), ad *Rom.*, 7 ('Ο ἐμὸς ἔρως ἐσταύρωται, κ.τ.λ.)—Polycarp, ad *Phil.*, c. 7: καὶ ὃς ἂν μὴ ὁμολογῇ τὸ μαρτύριον τοῦ σταυροῦ, ἐκ τοῦ διαβόλου ἐστίν.

[3] Clem., 1 *Cor.* 12.

Judaism, especially of Philo.[1] Here already the bramble bush, on which, according to Rabbinical tradition, the scarlet wool was placed on the Jewish Day of Atonement, as also the tree upon which, according to the same authority, it was placed at the killing of the red heifer, figure among the types of the cross of Christ. The same is the case with the fruit-bearing verdant tree, planted by the rivers of water, of the first Psalm, the glorious Trees of Life of Ezekiel's temple stream (Ezek. xlvii. 12), the blood-dripping wood of the Esra Apocalypse (4 Esra v. 5), the outstretched arms of Moses in prayer for the victory of his people during the battle with the Amalekites (Exod. xvii.; cp. Isa. lxv. 2), the serpent lifted up by Moses as a symbol of salvation (Num. xxi.), and finally the muster of the 318 servants of Abraham, the victor over Chedorlaomer and deliverer of Lot; this last by virtue of gematric interpretation, inasmuch as they interpret the letters I H T, representing the number 318, as indicating the name of Jesus and the symbol of the cross (T or +).[2]—Yet more luxuriantly is this mode of view developed in the Apologies of Justin Martyr. Alike as regards its material and its form, the cross is for him prefigured by a long series of Old Testament types. As typical with respect to its material are, in his estimation, not only the Tree of Life, but also the wonder-working rod of Moses, with which he divided the waters; the wood with which he sweetened the bitter waters of Mara, as well as the palm trees of Elim; Abraham's oaks of Mamre; Judah's staff given as a pledge (Gen. xxxviii. 18); Jacob's ladder, his staff, and his peeled poplar, hazel, and chestnut rods (Gen. xxx. 37, according to Luther's version); Aaron's almond rod that budded; Isaiah's rod out of the stem of Jesse (Isa. xi. 1); David's tree planted by the rivers of water (Psalm i. 3), and flourishing palm tree (Psalm xcii. 12), and not less his comforting "rod and staff" (Psalm xxiii.);

---

[1] On Philo's influence upon the exposition of Scripture on the part of the Greek Fathers in general, and more particularly of Barnabas, see E. Siegfried, *Philo v. Alexandria als Ausleger des Alten Testaments*, etc., Jena, 1874, S. 330 ff.

[2] Barnab., *Ep.*, c. 7, 8, 9, 11, 12. Comp. J. G. Müller's explanation on these places.

Elisha's wood with which he caused the iron of one of his disciples which had fallen into the Jordan to swim (2 Kings vi. 1—7); finally, also the wood of the delivering ark of Noah, the type of the Church.[1] Similarity of form with the cross he perceives—apart from such non-biblical objects as mast, ploughshare, human form, standard, military emblem, trophy, etc.—in the Paschal lamb, transfixed upon the spit, in Moses' hands uplifted in prayer, in the brazen serpent, in the horn of a unicorn, which the blessing of Moses (Deut. xxxiii. 17, according to the Septuagint) promises to Joseph, in the stretching forth of the hands on the part of the Lord towards His disobedient and gainsaying people, spoken of by Isaiah (ch. lxv. 2).[2] Most of these instances occur again in the later Fathers, but not without being augmented by one or other additional analogy. Thus Irenæus adds to the material types of the cross not only—by virtue of an antitypical interpretation, or by a special extension of the comparison of Paul, Rom. v. 12 ff.—the Tree of Knowledge, through which Adam sinned,[3] but also the ploughshares and sickles into which the prophet Micah foretells that the swords and spears shall be beaten in the Messianic age of blessing (Mic. iv. 2 f.) As a reference to the form of the cross does he regard, *inter alia*, the mention of the life of the people hanging before their eyes, in Deut. xxviii. 66.[4] Tertullian also observed in the Tau of Ezekiel (ch. ix. 4) a pre-reference to the sacred symbol of redemption; but, moreover, regards the wood borne by Isaac to his own altar of sacrifice, the ram taken from the

---

[1] Justin, *Dial. c. Tryph.*, p. 312 sqq., 367 sq.

[2] *Apol. Maj.*, p. 90 sqq. ; *Dial.*, p. 259, 317 sq., 338, 341.

[3] Iren. *adv. Hær.* v. 16 sq.—On the parallels to this antitypical parallelising of the Tree of Knowledge with the Cross of Christ, *e.g.*, *Evang. Nicod.*, c. 23 sq. ; Tertull., *adv. Jud.*, 13; Firmic. Mat., *de errore prof. rell.*, c. 25 ; Augustine, *Serm.* 1. c. 4 ; *Serm.* lxxxiv. c. 3, etc., comp. Piper. *Der Baum des Lebens*, "Ev. Kal." 1863, S. 54 ff. To the passages herein treated of must be added, Commodian. *Carm. Apolog.*, v. 324 sqq.

[4] The words Et erit vita tua pendens ante oculos tuos et non credes vitæ tuæ (in the original equivalent to saying "Thou wilt be in constant peril of thy life, and not believe in the preservation of thy life"), Messianically interpreted of the death of the Lord upon the cross : Iren., *adv. Hær.*, iv. 23 ; v. 18; comp. Tertull., *adv. Judd.*, 12 ; Cyprian, *Testimm.*, ii. 20 ; Lact., *Instit.*, iv. 18.

thorn bush and offered in place of Isaac, the wood (ξύλον), mentioned in Joel ii. 22, and Jer. xi. 19, and other things, as prophecies relating to the cross.[1] A like mode of interpretation prevails in Cyprian, especially in his " Testimonies (for the Messiahship of Jesus) against the Jews," in Commodian and Lactantius; it is occasionally found also in the Alexandrians Clement and Origen. Nevertheless the spiritualism of these latter with more difficulty admits of a quiet and persistent maintenance of such explanations as the only allowable and legitimate interpretations of the passages in question, and therefore occasions a frequent departure from the traditional view introduced by pseudo-Barnabas and Justin—a view which in the first place becomes strictly traditional only with the western theologians.[2]

However quixotic and uncritical much that is here mentioned may appear from the modern exegetical-scientific standpoint, yet it cannot be denied that an ardent love to the crucified Saviour and a devout absorption in the mystery of His redeeming suffering underlies it all; and that in this so powerfully acting impulse to discover typical points of connection with that which forms the centre and essence of all salvation, and to discover these in all epochs of the history of redemption, as also in the visible creation around us, there is to be seen an effort, in many respects praiseworthy, after a deeper and more connected intellectual apprehension of the Divine revelation of salvation, or, if you will, the first prerequisite for a philosophy of history from the Christian standpoint. The allegoric-exegetic tradition of the following epochs has to some extent outdone, in point of arbitrary assertion and unbounded play of imagination in this domain, even the Epistle of Barnabas with those its immediate successors. But also in the direction of the working out of

[1] Tert. *adv. Judd.*, 10—13; comp. *Apol.* 16; *ad. Nat.*, ii. 12; *adv. Marc.*, iii. 18 sq.

[2] Cyprian, *Testimm. ad Judd.*, ii. 20—22; *De zelo et liv.*, p. 261; Commodian, *Carm. Apolog.*, v. 222 sqq., 320 sqq.; Lact., iv. 18 sqq.—As regards Clement and Origen, comp. Diestel, *Gesch. des A. T. in der Kirche*, S. 34, 36 ff; Siegfried, *as before*, S. 343 ff., 351 ff.

deeper and purer conceptions as to the essential character of the history of salvation, as to the fundamental laws in the Divine government of the world, and at the same time as to the person and work of the Divine-human Redeemer, later ages have made notable progress, a progress however to which an important and lasting impulse was given in that study of the emblems and types of the cross which was made in the first Christian centuries.

As regards the earliest ART-ACTIVITY, too, on the part of the Church, there is felt a powerful impulse to the objectivising and plastic emblematisation of its devotion to the Crucified, without however, in this respect either, more than mere germs and incomplete beginnings at first making their appearance. On the one hand an aversion for all that reminded of the superstitious idol worship of the Heathen, on the other also the wish to preserve themselves as far as possible free from meriting the reproach of staurolatry, expressed in the mockery-crucifixes and similar forms, led the Christians to avoid all more decided steps in this direction. The ardour, too, with which the Gnostic sects, as the Valentinians (whose specially powerful æon, the all-embracing, immovably standing frontier-guardian of the world of light, Horos, bore also the name of "Stauros," and was symbolised by the cross) and the Ophites, occupied themselves in their speculations with the cross or the wood of life, as likewise the Manichæan doctrine of the Jesus patibilis, extended after the manner of a cross through the material,[1] all this might naturally contribute to enjoin upon Catholic Christendom the greatest possible reserve on this point, and might admit of pictorial representations of the cross, or even of the Crucified, only to the most limited extent. As regards the aversion for art on the part of the early Christians in general, the alleged entire absence of pictorial representations in their religious assemblies, the only very hesitating and emblematically concealed drawings

---

[1] Augustine, *contr. Faust.*, i. 32; Evodius, *De fide*, c. 28 (from the *Epist. fundamenti*). On the Ophites comp. what is said above, p. 87, note ². On the Σταυρὸς of the Valentinians, Henrici, *Die valentin. Gnosis*, etc., S. 179.

of the saints, which alone they had permitted to themselves, very exaggerated statements have been made, as well in polemical writings of early Protestant theologians against Rome, as in the text-books of the History of Art and of Church History—to the reducing of which to more modest dimensions the modern investigations in the catacombs, especially on the part of the indefatigable De Rossi, have contributed not a little. But though, for the Roman Christianity at least, the number of Christian figures and emblems, which are proved to date back to the second or third century, has been by degrees shown considerably to exceed the estimates formerly current, yet as regards the representation of the Saviour on the cross, the earliest art of the Church has in this respect, at all events, imposed upon itself the severest restraint. For according to the distinct evidence of the monuments, *crucifix figures, whether painted or plastic, are at this period*—as indeed in the two first centuries after Constantine—*as yet altogether wanting*. The earliest known instance of such a figure dates from the age of Gregory the Great: it is the crucifix presented by this pope to the Lombard queen Theodolinde, now in the Church of St. John at Monza. Of yet later date, perhaps belonging to the seventh or eighth century, does the only image of the Crucified which has been discovered in the Catacombs at Rome, that of San Giulio, appear to be. But it would also seem, as will be more fully demonstrated below, that the Christian art of the East did not, up to the beginning of the sixth century, venture upon representations of   crucified Redeemer. Without doubt, aversion for the punishment of crucifixion, as a mode of execution infamous and accursed in the extreme, which it is alleged was legally abolished and interdicted by an edict of Constantine—although probably this may have been the case only under one of his successors—also contributed in its measure to render the depicting of their Saviour as one hanging upon the tree of the curse, for the Christians of the first ages an impossibility. As the Good Shepherd, with the rescued lamb upon His shoulders, or even as Orpheus, as the vine, as a fish, as a lamb, or as otherwise emblematically represented, in accordance with the types found within or outside of the Bible, does He appear sufficiently often in the catacomb figures of the earliest centuries. But the cross remains constantly wanting, in these symbolic-iconographic representations, which in no case approach to the character of portraits. Not even the well-known combinations of the lamb with the cross, most widely diffused throughout the west, from the time of Paulinus of Nola, would appear to date back to a period as early as the pre-Constantine age. We need not therefore say that for such representations as that of the youthful Christ standing, with an ivory-adorned cross in His arms, upon the mountain of Paradise, or as that of the bust in which Christ appears with long hair and a cruciform Byzantine nimbus, no such early antiquity can be vindicated.[1] "The Church in those days, when her blood daily mingled with her tears, bore the death and cross of her Redeemer deeply enough in her heart without such things; what she needed was consoling and uplifting thoughts, and on this account they preferred to draw upon the walls of the subterranean city of the dead scenes which typified the infinite compassion, the inexhaustible love of the Lord, or the ultimate victory of the good cause, the triumph over the world and its persecutions. For the same reason, no scene of martyrdom was yet depicted,"[2] etc.

While thus the cross and crucifixion remained still foreign to the painting as to the sculpture of the pre-Constantine period in general, or the use of the cross in painting was confined to such merely decorative figures of the cross, or crosswise placed panels, as are displayed in the renowned ceiling-piece of S. Lucina, or the yet more beautiful one of S. Priscilla,[3] the sacred symbol of redemption plays, on the

---

[1] Stockbauer, *as before*, S. 133 ff.; F. X. Kraus, *Die christliche Kunst in ihren Anfängen*, S. 101 ff.

[2] Kraus, S. 104. Comp. the remarks throughout the section on early Christian paintings, S. 83 ff.

[3] Both ceiling-pieces—planned and executed on a like ornamental system as the heathen adornments of walls, ceilings, etc., of the same age (with wreaths of

other hand, a very important part in the ART OF MONOGRAM-MATIC WRITING among the early Christians, that profound mystical hieroglyphics which by means of simply interwoven name-signs served to express a comprehensive confession of faith in the Redeemer and His work. Inasmuch as this simple and transparently clear but deeply significant kind of cipher embraces in itself the very earliest expressions of Christian art, and inasmuch as in it the cross, in combination with the initial letters of the name of Christ, forms the most essential and primary object of the representation, *the whole Christian art-development may be traced back, indirectly, to the cross as its primary vegetative germ, or at least as one of its earliest impelling motives.*

It is remarkable that here too we meet with the same leaning upon pre-Christian heathen conceptions and symbols, as we saw was frequently the case in the domain of that seeking on the part of the Apologetes and Exegetes for hidden crosses. It is possible that all the oldest forms of the early Christian monogram (Figs. 63—66).

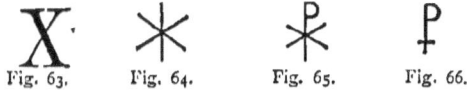

Fig. 63.   Fig. 64.   Fig. 65.   Fig. 66.

have been already occasionally employed on pre-Christian inscriptions or coins of Rome or the East; and have thus in their passing over to the use of Christians undergone a like change of signification in accordance with Christian ideas, as was the case in the domain of painting, *e.g.*, with the figure of an Orpheus, or, in that of sculpture, with that s^t an ancient rhetor or philosopher, which was transfo the Catholic community of the middle of third century into a statue of their venerated bishop and martyr, St. Hip-

flowers, cornucopias, leafy vine branches, little birds, winged genii, tritons, etc.), but bearing in addition specifically Christian symbols, such as especially the Good Shepherd—are represented and explained in the admirably illustrated, though certainly to a large extent uncritical and (particularly as regards its chronological data) wholly unreliable, work of the Abbot of Solesmes, Dom. Gueranger, *Sainte Cécile et la Société Romaine aux deux prem. Siècles* (Par. 1874), p. 284 sq. Comp. also Kraus, *as before*, S. 95.

polytus.[1]—The figure X, the simplest primary monogram, as initial letter in the name of Christ, and at the same time as a remote indication of the cross, occurring with especial frequency upon seals and rings, as upon grave inscriptions, had —at least as a numeral, *e.g.*, upon the monumental inscriptions of the famous tenth legion, at the same time also as simple adornment, perhaps only by way of ornamentation upon ancient Italian and Etruscan vase-covers,[2] etc.—already, within the limits of heathen art and epigraphics, played a part of which the Christians, so far as they made use of this sign, must not seldom be reminded. At any rate the specifically Christian sense which this cipher of the name of Χριστός (and Χριστιανός, Acts xi. 26) necessarily soon obtained, quickly enough pushed out the remembrance of those pre-Christian significations; so that the sign had already within the epoch under review become that characteristic main symbol of the religion of Jesus, with regard to which the emperor Julian once designated his efforts directed to the extirpation of this religion a "warfare with the X."[3] The sign ✳ also, an

Fig. 67.

X interwoven with the initial letter of the name of Jesus, in such wise as to result in a simple star form,—occurring for the first time as a Christian symbol upon a catacomb inscription, with the consular date of 268 (or perhaps 279),—appears to have been at least on some occasions already employed upon pre-Christian art-monuments; whether as a mere ornament once upon the under side of the bottom of an urn lasecca,[4] or as the most simple representation of a star, and in this case possibly with religious symbolic signification, as upon Phœnician coins, and even upon those of the pseudo-Messiah Bar-cochba and the emperor Julian, on

---

[1] Piper, *Mythologie der christlichen Kunst*, i. 42 ff. Comp. Kraus, S. 111 ff.
[2] Comp. ch. i., p. 18 ; as also Appendix I.
[3] *Misopogon*, pp. 99, 111 (ed. Paris, 1853).
[4] De Mortillet, *Le signe de la croix*, etc., p. 126.

which it displays the sign (Fig. 68). The sign (Fig. 69), combining in itself the two first letters of the name Χριστός,

Fig. 68.   Fig. 69.

attested as a Christian monogram for the first time by an inscription belonging to the year 298, the consular year of Gallus and Faustus, has likewise already passed through a previous heathen history. It occurs, perhaps as a name cipher of the master of the mint, already upon Attic tetradrachms, as well as upon certain Ptolemaic coins; so too, as we know, upon Bactrian coins of Hippostratus, belonging to the second half of the second century before Christ, as well as (without essential modification of form) upon silver coins of the Pontian king Mithridates, in the last century before Christ; lastly, upon a coin of the persecuting emperor Decius from Magnesia at the foot of Sipylus, where, in connection with a preceding A, it seems to be a sign of abbreviation for ἄρχοντος, just as it occurs besides as an abbreviation, *e.g.*, for Χρυσός, Χρόνος, in Greek inscriptions and manuscripts.[2] Finally, also the sign (Fig. 67), which is seen for the first time in the Christian West upon an inscription belonging to the year 355, as upon coins too of the emperor Valentinian I., but on the other hand must have been earlier in use in the East as a Christian monogram—since Ephraem († 378) designates it as one of the most frequently occurring and widely spread signs of this kind—and was current even in heathendom as an abbreviation of important significance. Upon coins of the Armenian king Tigranes, vanquished by Pompey, it appears to represent the first letters of the name of this ruler, or even of his capital, Tigranocerta (ΤΙΓΡ). In like manner it is found, assuredly only as a monetary

---

[1] Cohen, *Description des Monnaies Rom.*, t. vi., pl. xi. 46;—De Sauley, *Recherches sur la Numismatique Judaique* (Par. 1854), p. 166. Comp. Martigny, *Dictionn.*, p. 416; Stockbauer, S. 113.

[2] Münter, *Sinnbilder der Christen*, etc., i., S. 33. Lenormant, *Mélanges d'Archéologie*, iii. 195 sqq. Stockbauer, S. 86 f. Compare also what has been said above, p. 15.

cipher, without any kind of deeper significance, upon three coins of Herod the Great.[1]

That of the various points of contact with pre-Christian emblems here brought under notice, some are only of an accidental nature, must be admitted to be possible. On the other hand, there can be no question as to the heathen origin of the following signs, likewise also sometimes occurring upon early Christian monuments:

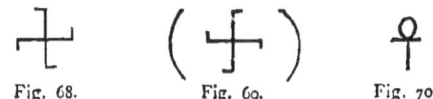

Fig. 68.   Fig. 69.   Fig. 70.

Especially often is there found the Swastika sign, alternating in the two forms here given. Sometimes it is an adornment of goblets, sometimes of other household service or utensils, sometimes of the graves of martyrs, sometimes of the garments of grave-diggers, etc. And indeed, according to De Rossi, this was at a very early period, in the second and first half of the third century, a particularly favourite form of the hidden indication of the cross, which later fell more into disuse.[2]

Some archæologists have sought to attach to it the significance of a monogram strictly speaking, *i.e.*, the abbreviated indication of a name or a group of names. Gori has explained it of the name Jesus, in the peculiar mode of writing it *Zesus*, with Z for J, which occasionally occurs. Others have looked upon the two Zs, supposed to be intertwined in it, as abbreviations of the well-known form of salutation, ζήσης (*vivas*), and accordingly claimed as the sense of their reduplication the plural ζήσητε, etc.[3] In the entire absence of authentic documentary evidence, these interpretations possess little value. What is certain is only that this sign, a very ancient and frequently occurring emblem upon heathen

---

[1] Garrucci, *I vetri ornati dei pr. Christiani*, p. 104; comp. Martigny, *Dictionn.*, art. "Monogramme du Christ," p. 414; Stockbauer, S. 87, 107; Rapp, S. 127. Compare above, ch. i., p. 16, note ².

[2] De Rossi, in the *Spicileg. Solesm.*, iv., p. 514; *Roma sott.*, p. 318. Comp. Garrucci, *l.c.*; also Buoranotti, Boldetti, and others, in Stockbauer, S. 92.

[3] Gori, *Symb. lit.*, in Stockbauer, *as before*.

monuments, of the East as well as of the West, was, on account of its resemblance to the cross, adopted by the Christians, and for a time (at any rate before the employment of the more accurate and complete representations of the cross), cherished and multiplied with affection. The same appears also to have been the case here and there with the Egyptian ansate cross; yet its occurrence upon Christian monuments earlier than the fourth century, or even before the discovery of a considerable number of ancient Egyptian figures of this kind at the destruction of the Serapeion under Theophilus, A.D. 390, can hardly be proved.[1] The lower half of the ansate cross, on the other hand, the T or St. Anthony's cross, as such unquestionably passed over into Christian usage at a much earlier date; whether precisely by reason of an imitation of ancient Egyptian characters, or on account of the resemblance, in itself sufficiently great, of the Greek and the Roman T to the form of a cross, may remain undecided. (See immediately below, and compare our copy of some early Christian catacomb inscriptions bearing this sign T as a monogram of the cross: Appendix V., No. 5.)

De Rossi, who designates the three figures here last treated of, as well as the monogram X, as *cruces dissimulatæ*, and in doing so certainly rightly indicates their general significance,[2] adds to the series of these hidden crosses yet another significant emblem, that of the anchor or anchor-cross:

Fig. 71.   Fig. 72.   Fig. 73.

Even Clement of Alexandria bears witness to the existence of this symbol as employed for the purposes of Christian ornamentation. He recommends to the ladies of his congregation to wear as an ornament besides the dove, the fish, the ship, the lyre, or the ship's anchor.[3] Especially upon early

---

[1] Rochette, *La croix ansée*, etc., pp. 306 sqq.
[2] De Rossi; in Pitra, *Spicel. sol., l.c.*
[3] *Civiltà cattol.*, 1857, v., pp. 731 sqq. Stockbauer, S. 130.

Christian signet-rings does it appear frequently represented, under one or other of the above forms, ordinarily the second of these, which with special distinctness expresses the emblematic reference to the cross. A gem, dating, it is alleged, from as early as the second century, evidently belonging originally to a signet-ring, displays an anchor placed between two fishes, a lamb, a dove, an image of the Good Shepherd, and a ship with a T-shaped mast. The cross in the form of a T appears upon it not less than three times; between all these figures are inscribed the letters of the word ἰχθύς.[1] In general the anchor appears in frequent combination either with the figure of a fish or with the name ΙΧΘΥΣ (= Ἰησοῦς Χριστὸς Θεοῦ Υἱὸς Σωτήρ). Whether, however, this combination, as is often assumed, is designed to express the sense of "Hope in Christ" (analogous to the frequently occurring formula upon early Christian grave-inscriptions: *Spes in Christo, Spes in Deo Christo*), or whether the emblem of the anchor is in every case to be referred to the simile of Heb. vi. 18, 19, and to be taken in the first place as an emblem of Christian hope, may be open to doubt. Raoul Rochette sees only the idea of salvation or blessedness in Christ expressed by the anchor, and De Rossi likewise thinks that the figure of the anchor is ordinarily and in the first place a *crux dissimulata*, a veiled allusion to the sign of the cross, while it comparatively rarely symbolised the idea of hope. The latter he considers to be the case where, *e.g.*, the proper names, such as Elpidius, Elpizusa, or Elpis, appear in combination with several figures of anchors,—cases which, for the rest, lose somewhat of their significance from the fact that sometimes also the names Agape, Agapetes, Agapetus, are met with upon the inscriptions on graves, accompanied with the symbol of the anchor.[2]

Much in the sphere of this primitive Christian monogrammatics and cross-symbolics may stand in need of satisfactory

---

[1] R. Rochette, *l. c.*, p. 223.

[2] R. Rochette, *l. c.*, p. 223; de Rossi, *Roma sott.*, ii. 318; and *De monumentis Christianis* ΙΧΘΥΣ *exhibentibus* (Par. 1855), p. 18; Martigny, *Dict.*, p. 32.

explanation by means of further researches. Some things, as, *e.g.*, the precise date of the origin of many an inscription or pictorial representation, or the special motives which led to the choice of this or that particular form, may perhaps never be divined with perfect certainty.[1] Be this as it may, so much—thanks to the efforts made in the exploration of the catacombs and the extraordinary results yielded from this source—so much is brought distinctly to light that, between these earliest germinal beginnings of the pictorial art among Christians and those typical-allegorical speculations of the Church Fathers in regard to all the history of redemption's having Christ the Crucified One as its aim, there exists a highly significant parallelism, and that this parallelism, especially as regards the striking prominence given to the cross in both domains of spiritual creation, presents really astonishing analogies. *The hidden crosses of the art monuments and inscriptions form a faithful copy or companion piece to the hidden crosses of the patristic typology and exegesis.* There underlies *both* forms in which this central main fact of salvation is emblematised one and the same glowing love to the Crucified One, one and the same ardently enthusiastic faith and hope in His gracious presence, one and the same confessor's courage, making glad to die, one and the same thirst for the bliss-giving communion of His sufferings. The impulse to the celebrating presentation and glorifying of the blessed mystery of redemption by the blood of Christ is, in in the one case as in the other, most powerfully active; it objectivises itself here as there in a multiplicity of more or

[1] It is only uncertainty as to the antiquity, that is to say the time of the earliest appearing of the single forms, which has prevented our treating in the present division of some farther monogrammatic figures, which *possibly* may have a pre-Constantine origin, although their most frequent occurrence belongs to the follow-

Fig. 74.   Fig. 75.   Fig. 76.   Fig. 77.   Fig. 78.   Fig. 79.

ing epoch. So the star-monograms (Figs. 74, 75), the forms (Figs. 76—78), and the combination (Fig. 79), and many others.

less chosen, forced, or artificial emblematisations ; it produces
there rhetorical and historico-philosophic, here iconographic
modes of presentation, which, with marvellous rapidity,
become traditional, and of which the increasingly favourite
character becomes evident from the putting forth of a multitude of fruitful germs, in which new and ever new variations
of one and the selfsame theme announce themselves. To
the full opening up of all these germs, the impulse towards
the increased multiplication of the symbolic forms, unquestionably present in a high degree of vigour, does not, within
the period of time now under review, succeed in attaining.
The pressure of persecutions, falling with heavy weight upon
the Church, sufficiently accounts for the fact that as yet the
stage of the *cruces dissimulatæ* was not really passed, either
in art or in the philosophy of history and Christological
speculation. As in the latter province there are still wanting
the daring genius and the lofty flight of thought of an Athanasius and an Augustine, so do the conceptions of the
Christian artists at first remain behind the abundant and
imaginative creations of a Paulinus of Nola and the no less
luxuriant splendour of the architects and plastic artists of the
Justinian age, not to say behind the much higher and more
glorious art products of the maturer Middle Ages. Even the
use made of the symbol of redemption remains for the time
being at the stage of modest rareness. A testimony of
brilliant religious acts or of magnificent missionary successes
of the Church the banner of the cross cannot as yet be ; and
the more so, since the custom of bearing crosses at the head
of processions, as towering banners or standards, visible from
afar, did not as yet exist. Everywhere does the outward life
of Christendom appear until now as a down-trodden one,
walking in lowly servant form ; everywhere is still breathed
the air of the catacombs; everywhere still flows martyr
blood. The Church of God held in the bondage of Egyptian
slavery, sighing beneath the oppression of Pharaonic persecutions, still waits for the delivering act of the new Moses,

---

[1] Eusebius, *De vita Const.*, i., 12, 19, 20, 38 ; ii., 51. *De laud. Const.*, c. 17, etc.

who, at the same time with her elevation to the victorious throne of freedom, had to lay the foundation for a more copious and independent development of her powers of life, a development, indeed, which was forthwith to degenerate also into manifold abnormal forms and excesses, and together with an abundance of glorious phenomena to bring to maturity also full many a baneful fruit of Heathenism and Judaism.

IV.

Constantine's Vision of the Cross.

AS THE STARTING-POINT FOR THE SENSUOUS EXTERNAL
ADORATION OF THE CROSS IN THE MIDDLE AGES.

THE dream-vision of Constantine before his decisive conflict with Maxentius belongs to the number of those facts of history in themselves small, but in their consequences affecting the course of the world, and therefore fraught with universal significance. Small we call it, because dreams with important bodings and higher suggestions are precisely in the life of the great and powerful of this earth so far from rare, that they are rather to be counted among the ordinary than the extraordinary events.[1] To such dream with Divine suggestion—analogous to those given under well-known circumstances to a Pharaoh, a Solomon, a Nebuchadnezzar, an Alexander, a Cæsar, an Innocent III., a Frederic the Wise,— does it seem that this fact, attested as to its essential contents by so many witnesses, must be reduced.[2] Lactantius, Ruffinus, and Sozomen, next to Eusebius the earliest and most trustworthy independent authorities regarding the event, speak only of a dream, in which the cross with the inscription,

---

[1] Compare the abundant illustrations furnished in Splittgerber, *Schlaf und Tod*, with the psychical phenomena accompanying the same, S. 98 ff., 132 ff.; as well as in Perty, *Die mystischen Erscheinungen der menschlichen Natur*, 2nd edn., ii. 353 ff.

[2] Lactant., *De morte persecut.*, c. 44; Ruff., *H. E.*, ix. 9; Sozom., i. 3. Only the first of these accounts: "Commonitus est in quiete Constantinus, ut cœleste signum Dei notaret in scutis atque ita prœlium committeret," could possibly be looked upon as in entire harmony with that of Eusebius. But "*in quiete*" is surely equivalent to "in sleep," and nothing in the words suggests an appearing of the cœleste signum Dei even before this sleep.

"In this conquer!" was displayed to him, and thus the Divine direction to exalt this symbol to a military emblem was communicated. The account given by Eusebius—beside which that of the uncritical later compiler, Gelasius of Cyzicus, can lay claim to no independent significance—represents this dream, indeed, as preceded by the objective and external appearing of a brilliant sign of the cross, visible in the sky at clear noonday, in connection with the before-mentioned inscription;[1] and attaches unusual weight to this statement by an appeal to the narrative given by the emperor himself, and confirmed by an oath. Yet even in this account the dream properly speaking plays the principal part. It is added—like one of those retrospective or epimethean dreams of which history notes no less a number having a high significance, than it does of the directly prophetic or promethean[2]—by way of explanation and confirmation to that vision. The Divine admonition, as yet uncomprehended on the ground of the vision, is repeated by Christ, appearing in the dream, and more nearly defined by the fact that the symbol beheld in heaven is to be imitated and employed as a banner in the impending conflict. Such later inculcation of the command already given by means of the vision itself could hardly have been necessary had the words "Τούτῳ νίκα" appeared, written with actual letters and distinctly legible, in the sky, above or beneath the figure of the cross. The extraordinary and wondrous sight would have been impressed much too ineffaceably alike upon the emperor as upon his warriors—who, according to Eusebius, were joint witnesses of the appearing—for it to be necessary that a subsequent dream by night should present it before him anew, and as it were interpret it. So too an external manifestation and sign in the sky, seen by a whole army at once,

---

[1] *De vit. Constantini*, i. 28 : Ἀμφὶ μεσημβρινὰς ἡλίου ὥρας, ἤδη τῆς ἡμέρας ἀποκλινούσης, αὐτοῖς ὀφθαλμοῖς ἰδεῖν ἔφη ἐν αὐτῷ οὐρανῷ ὑπερκείμενον τοῦ ἡλίου σταυροῦ τρόπαιον, ἐκ φωτὸς συνιστάμενον, γραφήν τε αὐτῷ συνῆφθαι λέγουσαν· τούτῳ νίκα. Again, c. 29 : . . . Ἐνταῦθα δὴ ὑπνοῦντι αὐτῷ τὸν Χριστὸν τοῦ Θεοῦ σὺν τῷ φανέντι κατ' οὐρανὸν σημείῳ ὀφθῆναί τε καὶ παρακελεύσασθαι, κ. τ. λ.

Comp. Perty, *l. c.*, S. 390 ff.

would hardly have passed unnoticed on the part of the great majority of contemporary heathen and Christian historians. That which Constantine really saw in the sky on the afternoon preceding that memorable dream-night, may perhaps have been a bright cloud-creation, bearing an approximate resemblance to a cruciform or labarum-shaped figure.[1] It is even possible that he saw nothing of this kind with his outward eye, but that—deeply moved by the critical nature of his position, and meditating intently on the most effectual way of securing the assistance of the Divine powers and the victory over his foes—he received a visionary impression, which presented before his inner eye the symbol of the Christians' God as the only true and victorious military emblem. The dream by night, by which this was succeeded, set the seal upon that which he had seen during the ecstasy. What in the former case was looked upon rather as a possible means of salvation and blessing, ripened in the latter case into a bold and vigorous resolve; it was withdrawn at once from the realm of bare possibilities, now recognised as a Divine necessity, and promptly carried into execution.

An explanation of these events, by which they thus become psychologically comprehensible—and such as may be supported by various points of analogy from the earlier and later history of the human soul-life[1]—by no means excludes the co-operation of the living God as the author of the dream, as well as of the preceding vision or ecstasy; but rather, regarded from the Theistic standpoint, renders absolutely necessary the supposition of such Divine co-operation and supreme origination. A providential bringing about of the resolution of Constantine, henceforth to fight under the symbol of Christ, must thus necessarily be supposed; and the more so, the

---

[1] Comp. the historic instances adduced by Gieseler in his "Church History" of the appearing of such cloud-crosses; *e.g.*, that one of purple colour, which was observed at Weimar about Christmas-time in the year 1517, and was regarded as a significant Divine portent.—A long chapter: *De apparitionibus ss. crucis*, of course almost entirely of a legendary character, is presented by Gretser, "De cruce," t. i., lib. iii., pp. 624—668.

[2] Splittgerber, *l. c.*, S. 152 ff.

greater the inner improbabilities under which the attempt to trace back this resolution to merely political considerations on the part of the emperor must labour, the more distinctly the great victory obtained by him over Maxentius was later by himself ascribed to the special kindness of the God of the Christians, and this indeed not merely orally on his part in conversing with Eusebius, but also much earlier in writing, viz., in the public archives, as well as in the edict of Milan of the year 313, and the more evidently the transition wrought in him from the time of this victory—a transition from a worshipper of Apollo and the other gods of the Roman state to a confessor of the religion of Christ—is seen to exclude for ever a permanent, formal, and complete relapse into idolatry. The great and powerful *effects* of this process of transformation (however regarded and explained), by virtue of which, from the time of the conflict with Maxentius, he appears as the declared patron and constant protector of the Christians, formerly—to say the least—treated with indifference, these great effects it is which absolutely forbid the resolving of the account of Eusebius into a mere legend, a subtilisation of the same into a myth without any actual kernel of reality. It is true the idea of an entire renewal, after the type of that of Paul at the entrance to Damascus, to which later Christian authors, as, *e.g.*, one so early as Theodoret, have sought to raise the effect of the Constantinean vision of the cross, is in painful opposition to the actual moral and religious comportment of the emperor during his subsequent reign. On this account an absolutely miraculous character cannot be conceded to the event which called forth his tranformation: to conceive of the labarum vision as an objective sign in the sky, perceptible at the same time for many, is impossible.[1] Still less indeed is possible that absolute

---

[1] Uhlhorn, *Der Kampf des Christenthums mit dem Heidenthum* (Stuttg. 1874) S. 328 ff., still maintains the objectively miraculous character of this event, adducing by way of parallel the star of the Wise Men (Matt. ii.) He expressly combats at the same time the merely psychological mode of interpretation, as well as the "natural" interpretation, by the supposition of a bright phenomenon in the atmosphere.

denial of everything of a supra-natural character to the fact, as one brought about by Divine providence—a denial according to which this fact would be a politically crafty invention of the emperor, confirmed on his part by an act of perjury; or at best a transforming and idealising version of that which popular rumour was wont to assign as the motive-cause of his attaching himself to the religion of the cross, adopted by him in order to please the Christians.[1] Neither are those heathen versions in which the account of the victory over Maxentius is current, in the rhetor Nazarius (321), and later in Libanius (389), of which the former represents heavenly hosts sent by the gods as hastening to the help of Constantine, the latter that the victory was obtained through the prayer of Constantine to the gods,[2] adapted to shake the credibility of the accounts, given by the Christian historians in essential harmony, of a divinely occasioned dream-vision of Constantine.

With the supposition of a dream-vision of providential origin, with regard to which we find ourselves in agreement with the majority of more recent critics,[3] does the circumstance also specially well harmonise, that the LABARUM standard introduced from the time of the victory of Constantine as an emblem of the Christian Roman imperial army (Fig. 80) by no means displays the character of an absolutely new invention, or that of the product of a directly Divine revelation; but that, on the contrary, the striking resemblance of this symbol to the frequently mentioned

Fig. 80.

---

[1] So substantially Spittler, Henke, Gibbon, Martini, Manso, Baur, Burckhardt. Keim does not go quite so far.

[2] *Nazarii Panegyric. in Constantin.*, c 14. Libanius, 'Ὑπὲρ τῶν ἱερῶν. ii., p. 160, Reiske.

[3] Mosheim, Schröckh, Augusti, Hug, Neander, Gieseler, Niedner, Gass, Kist, Koelling (*Geschichte der arianischen Häresie*, i., S. 70 ff.), Schaff, Heinichen, Mozley (Bampton Lectures 1865), etc. A dream, even though without higher providential causation, is Keim also inclined to suppose (*Der Uebertritt Constantins zum Christenthum*, 1863). Very cautiously and attractively is the whole question examined by Schaff in the *History of the Ancient Church* (S. 459 ff. of the German edn.), Koelling, as above. and especially Heinichen, in his excursus to Eusebius, *De vita Const.*, i. 28 (*Eusebii scripta historica*, 2nd ed., 1870, tom. iii., pp. 758—780.

monogrammatic figures upon more ancient coins of the East, seems to indicate a reflection on the part of the emperor on the relations of these characters to the monogram of the name and cross of Christ, as well as a bearing of this reflection upon his resolve to select the said symbol as his device. Whether now those abbreviations upon Egyptian, Bactrian, or Pontian and Asiate coins (coins of Asia Minor), representing the form (Fig. 81) in diverse modifications, may

Fig. 81.   Fig. 82.

have been present to his mind; or whether—what indeed has but slight probability—the sign (Fig. 82), sometimes figuring upon Attic tetradrachms, may have aroused his attention on account of its accord with the monogram of the Christians:

Fig. 83.   Fig. 84.   Fig. 85.

in any case it would appear that a harmonising contemplation, like that which had still earlier appropriated certain pre-Christian cruciform characters (Fig. 86) to Christian uses, or like that which later led to the adoption also of the sign (Fig. 87) on the part of the Christians, had been called into exercise in his case too. But among the symbols of this kind known to him, which he caused to pass before his

Fig. 86.   Fig. 87.   Fig. 88.

spirit's eye, none can have appeared to him so much a pregnant emblematisation of the essence of the Christian religion as the figure (Fig. 88), combining in the simplest manner the initials of the name of Christ with the sign of the cross, the profoundly suggestive double monogram of

Christ and the cross.[1] This symbol, with which he had certainly before become acquainted through occasional intercourse with Christians,[2] and which—on account of its twofold significance, and its points of contact with those secret signs of the East—might be expected to awaken special sympathy in a mind like his, prone as it was to a mystic syncretism, became to him the all-embracing expression of his enthusiastic self-surrender to the new religion, from the moment in which God had caused that vision beaming with bright radiance to arise before the eye of his mind, and as His sacred sign had enabled Constantine to recognise in it the significant emblem of His cause.[3]

In something after this fashion may the human and the Divine, subjective and objective, imaginative reflection and higher suggestion, have co-operated in bringing about that decision in the action of the great emperor, fraught with such momentous consequences, and exerting by its after-effects such a mighty influence through a long succession of ages— as the most immediate fruit and result of which stands his glorious victory over the heathen usurper. With whatever inner preparation the decisive step may have been accompanied, and whatever religious or even political considerations

---

[1] *De vit. Const.*, I. 31 : . . . δύο στοιχεῖα τὸ Χριστοῦ παραδηλοῦντα ὄνομα . . . χιαζομένου τοῦ ρ κατὰ τὸ μεσαίτατον. In the word χιαζομένου, even as in the well-known passage of Plato (*Tim.*, p. 36) as prophetically interpreted by Justin, there is an allusion to the hidden cross, which was supposed to be contained in the figure.

[2] Did Helena exert a preparatory influence upon Constantine previously to his accession to the Christian faith? Dieckhoff, Keim, Heinichen, and others contest this view, and rather suppose—on the ground of Euseb., *De v. Const.*. iii. 47, 2— that the Empress-mother was led to attach herself to Christianity only after the change in the faith of her son. But comp. Koelling, *as before*. S. 75, who with good reason reverts to the opinion, formerly prevailing, of the priority of Helena's conversion, and the incredibility or at least inaccuracy of the above-mentioned account of Eusebius.

[3] Important contributions towards demonstrating the fact that Constantine himself from the first traced this victory to the special aid of the Christians' God, are found also in Piper: "*Zwei Inschriften Constantins des Grossen,*" etc. Gotha 1875. It is there shown that, like the much-discussed *instinctu divinitatis* of the former inscription, so the *duce te* (scil., *Christo*) of the second, contains a direct reference on the part of the thankful emperor to the glorious event.

may have contributed to the bringing of it about, at any rate it was a step taken with full resolution, involving indeed no moral renewal of life and purification of heart, but yet a consistent attachment to the cause of the Christians' God, and maintained throughout with real enthusiasm. Hence, accordingly, the pride and pomp with which, in the first place, the outward sign and emblem of this cause was henceforth invested by the emperor, and glorified as a symbol of the religion called to dominion over the earth. A long gilded shaft, with a transverse rod intersecting crosswise its upper end, upon which was hung as a banner a square purple cloth, richly adorned with precious stones and gold embroidery, as well as with the likenesses of the emperor and his sons, formed the military emblem, or *vexillum*, destined to bear upon it the sacred sign witnessed in the sky, the *labarum* in the strict sense of the term—a vexillum differing from the ordinary military ensign of the Romans, not by its mode of construction, but only, as it would seem, by the special sumptuousness of its adornments. Above the transverse rod of this banner was fixed a golden wreath or crown, adorned with precious stones, enclosing the " sign of the salvation-bringing name," the monogram of Christ in the form of a P crossed by an X (or, what is the same thing, of an X transfixed in the middle by a P).[1] Fifty chosen warriors, the band of the Staurophoroi, had henceforth to encompass, and in turn to carry, this labarum ensign in all wars of the emperor. So in the war against Licinius, where it is said to have wrought new wonders of victory.[2] It remained the consecrated imperial banner of the Christianised Roman empire, even under the successors of Constantine. Of these only Julian the Apostate removed the monogram of Christ from above it, while Jovianus took care to have this restored.—Of the other military objects which Constantine adorned with the sacred monogram, Eusebius expressly mentions in the course of his description the helmet of the emperor ; Lactantius, however, the shields of his

[1] Euseb., *Vit. Const.*, i. 31 (see also above, p. 143, note [1]).
[2] *Vit. Const.*, ii. 7—9.

warriors. If the statement of the latter with regard to the form of this sign upon the shields is to be taken as literally exact,[1] it must be conceived of as somewhat differing from that of the labarum monogram, namely, as representing the figure (Fig. 89); yet these words are hardly to be pressed. At any rate, coins and other monuments of the time of Constantine ordinarily display the monogram in the form described by Eusebius, with the assuredly unimportant variation that some-

Fig. 89.   Fig. 90.   Fig. 91.   Fig. 92.   Fig. 93.

times the cross-pieces of the X entirely enclose the ear (or handle) of the P—which form (Fig. 90) would seem to be the earlier and more original one—and sometimes appear shortened, in such-wise that the said ear towers above the X, so that the form (Fig. 91), resembling the Bactrian labarum, results.[2] The diagonal figure (Fig. 92) is found for the first time upon coins of Magnentius and later emperors; it would seem no more than the form (Fig. 93), appearing at about the same time, 355 (once the monetary sign of the Jewish king Herod, cp. above, p. 130), to have been in official use under the first Christian emperors.—If upon many monuments of the time of Constantine there are given pictorial representations of the labarum standard as a whole, which in single particulars do not correspond with the description of Eusebius, e.g., represent the monogram not as above the colours, within the golden wreath, but upon the colours themselves; or place upon the colours, instead of the three imperial effigies, the words ἐν τούτῳ νίκα; or present the flag-staff alone, without banner or streamer upon it, crowned by the wreath with the monogram; these modifications are to be accounted for either by the special regulations of the emperor himself, or by the caprice of

---

[1] " . . . . . transversa litera X summo capite circumflexo Christum notavit." De morte persecut., c. 44. (Compare thereon Stockbauer, S. 100.)

[2] Comp. Orelli, Inscriptt. collect., vol. i., Nos. 1913, 1916 ff., 1922. Rapp, Das Labarum und der Sonnencultus, S. 116 ff.

the artists labouring in his service.[1] It remains uncertain what was the form and arrangement of these delineations of the "salvation-bringing sign" borne, according to a statement of Eusebius in the last book of his "Life of Constantine," upon all the weapons even of the private soldiers (iv. 21).

Moreover, it was not merely by diverse imitations of the monogram beheld in that vision that Constantine witnessed his confession of the religion of the cross. If we may trust the statements of Sozomen and Aurelius Victor, he at once decreed the abolition of crucifixion as a punishment in the now Christianised Roman empire. The accuracy of this statement is, however, open to considerable doubt. At any rate, from the time of that decisive victory he zealously practised the rite of crossing himself, the frequent signing of his forehead with the protecting symbol of salvation.[2] Immediately after that entry into Rome, which followed the defeat and death of Maxentius, he caused his own statue to be erected, as a sign of victory, upon the forum, with a spear or banner in the form of a cross in his right hand, with the inscription placed beneath, "Through this salvation-bringing sign, the true symbol of valour, I have delivered your city from the yoke of the tyrant."[3] Later, after his victory over Licinius, he had himself represented in a painting, at the entrance to his palace in Nicomedia, in full armour as the slayer of the dragon, his head adorned with the cross, and writhing at his feet a transfixed dragon;—so too there exists a copper coin of his, which displays the labarum (Fig. 94) standing upon a pierced serpent.[4] His coins, it is true, display also to a great extent heathen emblems: their impressions, upon which still frequently figure Fig. 94. Apollo with the sun-ball, sometimes also Mars, Victoria, or

[1] Martigny, *Dictionn.*, art. "Labarum," p. 359, where the more special evidences from Georgi, Bottari, Garrucci, etc., are adduced.

[2] Euseb., *V. C.*, iii. 2: τὸ πρόσωπον τῷ σωτηρίῳ κατασφραγιζόμενος σημείῳ.— On the precarious character of the statements of Sozomenus (i. 8) and Aurelius Victor (*De Cæs.*, 41) concerning the abolishment of the punishment of crucifixion, see above, p. 65.

[3] Euseb., *H. E.*, ix. 9 ; *V. C.*, i. 40.

[4] *V. C.*, iii. 2. Comp. H. Cohen, *Les monnaies Romaines*, vi. 160 ; Eckhel, *Doctrina num. vet.*, viii., p. 88.

the genius of the Roman people, whilst others appear adorned with the monogram of the Christians' God, reflect the strange Christian-heathen medley of religion which remained peculiar to his whole policy of government, a policy conditionated by his twofold position as protector of the Church on the one hand and Roman *pontifex maximus* on the other. One of his coins (with the reverse *Soli invicto Comiti*) places an equal-armed or Greek cross immediately beside the figure of the sun-god. And even at the consecration of Constantinople as his Christian residence a solemn procession was held, in which the statue of the emperor, holding in its right hand a goddess of Fortune, whose head was adorned with a cross, was enthroned, in place of Helios, in the chariot of the sun.[1] Significant, notwithstanding, is the absence of evidence for any kind of *entire relapse*, however temporary, into the state of heathenism —the constancy thus with which the policy favourable to Christianity was maintained by him during the last twenty-five years of his reign, from the time of his victory at the Milvian Bridge until his death; yea, the increasingly decided tone of his edicts, which—especially after he had learnt, in the circle of the Christian bishops at the Council of Nicæa, to feel himself " bishop of the external affairs of the Church " —sometimes almost assumed the character of oppressive and persecuting measures.

In this same later period falls the remarkable event which gave to the superstitious and idolatrous cross-worship of the Christendom of the Middle Ages perhaps a more direct impulse than the labarum vision itself, with its more immediate consequences: the PILGRIMAGE OF HELENA to the Holy Sepulchre (326), and the alleged *discovery of the true cross of Christ* on this occasion. The state of the facts regarding this incident is yet more difficult to discover, than with regard to that event happening fourteen years earlier, in which Constantine himself, as yet without his mother,

[1] Orelli, Inscr., *l. c.* Burckhardt, die Zeit Constantins, S. 461 ff., 474 f. That after 323 the emblems of the heathen sun-worship disappeared from the coins of Constantine, is ordinarily asserted (see *e.g.*, Gieseler, i. 1, 275), but hardly with good reason. Comp. Burckh., S. 391 f.

formed the central acting figure. If in the case of Constantine there is to be discovered, as a result of a proper critical mode of procedure, a genuine historic core to the traditions, frequently indistinct and mutually contradictory as they are, here, on the other hand, a careful testing of the sources appears to eliminate all element of fact, and to leave nothing but legend remaining. It is fatal to the tradition that Eusebius, the only contemporary witness, distinctly indeed reports Helena's pilgrimage, as well as that which she, and Constantine before her, had done for the clearing and adorning of the Holy Places in Jerusalem, but is utterly silent as to that which in later tradition formed the true point of lustre and main result of the whole journey —the discovery of the cross. It might perhaps be objected that the Bishop of Cæsarea, so severe and determined in his opposition to all kinds of image and relic worship, who in opposition to the desire of the Imperial Princess Constantia for a portrait of Christ launched forth into such strong expressions as "heathen custom," etc., would perhaps have intentionally passed over an event, however remarkable in itself, if he saw that from it might arise the germs of a dangerous superstition. But how could such an ardent admirer of that which Constantine had done from the beginning of his Christian period for the glorifying of the symbol of the cross, think it necessary to ignore precisely this latest and most remarkable contribution in the domain of the cross worship, on the supposition that he knew anything of it? How could he help hearing of the astonishing discovery in that Holy City so closely adjoining his own see? How could the pieces of the true wood of the cross which Helena presented, not only to the Church of the Holy Sepulchre, but also to the new Church of the Cross at Constantinople—how could the phylacterium which she caused to be made for her Imperial son,—how could the helmet and the bridle for his charger, which Constantine himself caused to be forged out of the nails of the sacred cross, in order to bring about a literal fulfilment (!) of the prophetic passage of Zech. xiv. 20,— how could all this escape the attention of so enthusiastic an encomiast of the gifts and powers of the cross as Eusebius?[1] And then we must take into consideration the serious contradictions and improbabilities in the accounts of the historians —partly of one, partly of from two to three generations later than the event—who do actually record it. Cyril of Jerusalem, the one least removed from the event († 386), appears to know something of the fact of the discovery of the cross ; but what he says in his Catecheses delivered at the Holy Sepulchre, amounts simply to this, that the cross of the Lord, still in existence, must be taken as a most certain proof of His resurrection. On the other hand, the letter of this bishop to the emperor Constantius, in which he enters more fully into the well-known details of the legendary history of this discovery, is certainly a forgery ; since Cyril is therein represented, at a time when he was beyond doubt still a semi-Arian (about 351), as already an orthodox Nicænist.[2] Of the next following authorities, Ambrose represents that the true cross of the Redeemer was distinguished from the two crosses of the malefactors buried with it, simply and without a miracle, namely by the title of Pilate found upon it.[3] Ruffinus on the contrary, as well as the three Greek continuators of Eusebius, relate that, since the title was no longer affixed to the wood, recourse was had, in accordance with the directions of Macarius Bishop of Jerusalem, to a Divine ordeal—the testing of the miraculous sanative power of the wood upon one dangerously ill, in order to establish the identity of the salvation-bringing sign.[4] That which the most copious of these historians, Sozomen, at the beginning of the fifth century, mentions simply as a rumour—viz., that a dead person was recalled to life by means of the new-found sacred cross—*that* his western contemporaries Sulpicius Severus and Paulinus of Nola are already able to relate with all definiteness of detail ; and

[1] Comp. *V. C.*, iii. 25 ff. (espec. c. 47, where the non-mention of the discovery of Helena appears most surprising), with the unmeasured terms of praise in which he commends the σωτήριον σημεῖον : *De laudib. Const.*, c. 9, 10.

[2] Cyrillus, *Catech.*, iv. p. 27 ; x. p. 91. As regards the spuriousness of the *Ep. ad Constantium*, see Gieseler, i. 2, 279.

[3] Ambrosius, *Orat. de obitu Theodos.*, p. 498.

[4] Ruffinus, *H. E.*, i. 7; Socrat., i. 13; Theodoret, i. 18 ; Sozom., ii. 1.

indeed the miracle of resurrection seems with them to have been directly substituted for the miracle of healing.[1] The position too of Chrysostom, who belongs to a somewhat earlier date, in relation to this tradition is apt to awaken serious distrust. While in one of his homilies he manifests a certain acquaintance with its contents, he asserts in another relating to the gospel of the penitent thief, that Christ did not leave His cross upon earth, but took it up with Him to heaven, whence—on His return to judgment—it will be displayed as the "sign of the Son of man." The fragments also of the cross discovered by Helena, which had quickly spread throughout the world, and are already referred to by Cyril, would appear not to have been unknown to him; but he can hardly have attached to the same any special importance, seeing that he as occasion offers expresses himself in so spiritualistic a manner upon the subject.[2]

The reality of the discovery of the true cross by Helena, already assailed by Dallæus, Salmasius, Witsius, and other Protestant critics of the seventeenth and eighteenth centuries,[3] must, in accordance with the above-indicated state of the argument, be pretty unconditionally surrendered. That which at all events remains as the core of the tradition—the fact, in itself not impossible, but yet one attested neither by Eusebius nor the Christian pilgrim of Bordeaux (333), of an excavation made at the command of Helena, and the lighting in connection therewith upon some ancient wooden blocks, in which it was thought the remains of the cross were to be recognised, and which may have given the first impulse to the presentation of relics which now followed—this, which is perhaps to be presupposed as the actual foundation of the whole, appears to be of so unsatisfactory a character, that one can scarcely avoid, in connection with the tradition as it now lies before

[1] Sulpic. Sev., *Hist. sacra*, ii. 49. Paulin. Nol.. *Ep.* 34 (11).
[2] Comp. Chrysostom., *Hom.* 35, *De Cruce et Latrone*, with *Hom.* 85 (84).
[3] Dallæus, *Advers. Latinorum de Cultus Religiosi Objecto Traditionem*, Genev. 1664. Salmasius, *Epp.* 3. *De Cruce. ad Bartholinum.* Witsius, *Miscellan. Sacra*, ii. 364. J. A. Schmid, *De Crucis Dominicæ per Helenam Inventione Diss.*, Helmst. 1714. More recent critical contestation see, *e.g.*, in Sybel und Gildemeister *Der heil. Rock v. Trier*, 1844, S. 15 ff.

us, bringing the charge of conscious deception and invention, to say nothing of unobserved and unintentional accumulation and reduplication of mythical elements. It is a result of historical criticism highly instructive and significant for aiding one to form a judgment on the whole province of the sensuous-external rites of worship in the Catholic Church, that the tradition concerning Helena's discovery of the cross, which underlies the worship of the cross in its more material form, *is critically far less supported than the tradition of Constantine's vision of the cross, which inaugurated the more harmless and ideal (merely typical) form of this worship.* There exists, we admit, inasmuch as this latter event served to introduce an effort after the greatest possible multiplying of copies of the sacred sign and objects of devotion, and thus also indirectly to inspire Helena with her desire to visit the Holy Land— there exists a notorious causal connection in the process of origination of the two traditions. But how much purer, how much freer from deception and delusion stands forth the earlier fact, as compared with that happening a decade and a half later, this is shown not only by the state of matters, as regards the sources of the said traditions, but also still more urgently by the long series of effects which have proceeded from the one event and the other. For as the roots, so the fruit! From the suggestion, given indeed naturally and physically, through dream or vision, but indisputably coming from God, by virtue of which Constantine raised the cross as the sign of his attachment to the cause of Christ, there has doubtless sprung up many a sensuous external addition to the worship of the Lord in the spirit and in the truth, but yet not that which is immediately and properly speaking idolatry. The alleged discovery of the cross on the part of Helena has been the source of a rankly luxuriant growth of superstition of the worst kind, the fruitful womb and tap-root of all the relic worship and abuses in the form of pilgrimages during the following centuries. From the former fact, of which the historic foundation is still faithfully and clearly reflected through the lightly concealing garb of legendary report, sprang the whole Christian art-tradition, in its more abundant and more powerful creations. From the latter event, hardly now to be separated from its mythic surroundings (*involucra*), yea, perhaps to be entirely regarded as a pure mythus, arises the succession of uncomely appendages and tasteless superstitious additions, which have most odiously disfigured the religious art products of the Middle Ages, and in part those of the present day, and have repressed for centuries the truly free, original, and ideal unfolding of the artistic power of creation. Constantine's vision of the cross has served as a starting-point for the sensuous realism of the cultic tradition of the Catholicism of the Middle Ages—a realism not indeed biblically correct, but yet æsthetically productive, and thus unquestionably historically justified—in a manner analogous to that in which the *materialism* of a sensuous tendency in the sphere of Divine service (cultus), which is neither biblically nor historically to be justified, conformed neither to Evangelical nor truly Catholic principles, appears to have been not, it is true, exclusively produced, but to a very important extent fostered, by the pilgrimage of Helena, with its incredible miracles. In point of time, as of origin and inner essence, the two events—that confined to the *seeing* of the figure of the cross, and that which proceeded to the *finding* of the wood of the cross—border closely the one on the other. And, as the latter could originate only upon the foundation of the former, so have also the two tendencies of the religious life of the Middle Ages, sprung from these and characteristic of them, the religious æthetic and the magic-superstitious or materialistic tendencies, ever been active only in close connection the one with the other. They present one continued succession of sensuous-external efforts, directed to the heathenising (paganising, partly also Judaising) of the Christian principle—a succession which we shall regard in the sequel as forming one indivisible course of development, without making any attempt at artificial distinction or separation of the more moderate realistic from the more broadly and grossly materialistic phenomena, yet with a natural division of the single spheres of Church life, in which these are specially active.

V.

The Cross in the Church of the Middle Ages.

IMMEDIATELY after the exaltation of Christianity to the rank of the religion of the Roman empire, the cross begins to act as a power, even as a mighty power. It pervades the whole Christian life of civilisation in all its ramifications, from the highest to the lowest grade of society. It becomes the sign under which, and by means of which, Christianity exerts its deeply penetrating and mightily renewing influences upon mankind, the emblem of the victorious exertion of her power on the part of the Church, in an outward and an inward direction. "The sign once abhorred by all," exclaims Chrysostom,[1] "the hated instrument of supreme punishment, has now become the most cherished and the most honoured of all,—one found with princes and subjects, with women and men, maidens and matrons, slaves and free. . . . Everywhere do you see it highly esteemed and held in honour: in the houses, upon the walls, and on the roofs, in towns and villages, at markets, on the highways, in deserts, upon mountains and in glens, upon hills and upon the islands and ships of the sea, on books and on arms, upon garments, on couches, at banquets upon golden and silver vessels, upon pearls and wall-paintings, upon the bodies of the possessed, yea, of diseased animals, in war as in peace, by day and by

---

[1] *Contra Judæos et Gentiles, quod Christus sit Deus*, c. 9 (Opp., t. i., f. 569 sqq.) —On the surpassing importance of the passage here adduced for the apologetics of the Early Church, comp. Förster, "Chrysostomus als Apologet," *Jahrb. f. deutsche Theol.*, 1870, S. 450.

night, in the dances of the merry and in the union of those who mortify themselves." The same Father, one of the most enthusiastic encomiasts of the cross as an everywhere triumphant power, elsewhere describes how the cross is now "borne (by all its confessors) upon the brow, not by private citizens only, but also by crowned heads, who wear it above their diadems."[1] He means by this, as is clear from similar expressions on the part of Augustine,[2] and as is besides confirmed by pictorial representations upon art monuments, not something like the custom of signing oneself with the cross (crossing oneself), but an actual impressing or suspending of the sacred symbol upon the brow, whether immediately, as the picture—not unsuspected, indeed, as regards its genuineness—of that fair youth upon the bottom of an early Christian drinking-vessel presents this, or as adornments of princely diadems, such as are worn in the effigies of Valentinian III. and his wife Licinia Eudoxia upon coins, such as are also worn in other imperial likenesses.[3] The cross, the bright surpassing ornament of the great ones of the earth, the highest grace of the imperial crown! What an advance since the days of Tertullian, who was able to speak only of the use of that invisible sign of the cross in the daily life of his fellow-Christians; but where he came to speak of the emblems of the Roman empire, its rulers and warriors, could at most only point to the presence of hidden crosses, as it were unsuspected and involuntary representations of the sacred symbol of redemption! No doubt, with the world-dominating position in which our symbol now appears, there is inseparably connected a varied externalisation of the idea, and an unreflecting mechanical or even magical superstitious

[1] *Exposit. in Psalm.* cix. (T. v., f. 259).

[2] Augustin., *in Psalm.* lxxiii., § 6: Jam in frontibus regum pretiosius est signum crucis, quam gemma diadematis. Comp. *in Psalm.* xxxii.; *Serm.* ii. 13.

[3] Martigny, *Dictionn.*, p. 186. In the same work (p. 188) is a representation of that exceedingly beautiful youth adorned upon the forehead with the equal-armed cross (Fig. 95) (with the somewhat enigmatical legend *Liber Nica*), after Boldetti, who assumes as indisputable the early Christian origin of this figure. More recent authorities, however, as Garrucci, regard it as of later origin.

Fig. 95

use of the cross itself. And if with the Christians of the age immediately succeeding Constantine, and onwards to the close of the fifth century, contents and form, or Christian spirit and external sign, as yet, for the most part, appeared combined in due proportion, yet in place of this early synthesis there appeared later a growing severance of these two elements. Only for a moment, and in constantly less satisfactory measure, do the advocates of an energetic reaction in the sense of a purer primitive Christian spirit succeed in their recombination. The two great halves into which Christendom divides itself from the time of Justinian and Heraclius—the rigid Byzantine school of the East, and that of the Germanic West, this last, spite of its union beneath the pastoral crook of the successors of Peter, fiercely agitated and torn with severe conflicts—participate pretty equally in this condition of secularisation and materialisation of their religious life. And no one of the great domains over which, on this side and on that, the formative and creative action of the Christian spirit extends, continues exempt from the effects of this endeavour after an external and sensuous presentation. All of them alike, those tendencies of Church life directed more preponderantly towards the outward, and those directed more towards the inward, render homage to the cross in that onesidedly objectivising and grossly realistic manner, sometimes even descending to the level of a pseudo-Christian fetichism, which is characteristic of the religious civilised life of the Middle Ages as a whole.

There are five main spheres of Church life in which, with a view to the unfolding on every side of the phenomena belonging hereto, we shall have to trace out the sensuous crossworship of the Middle Ages. In the field of the outward diffusion of Christianity, or in *Missions*, the power or influence of the cross makes itself felt. In the ritual of the Church, or in the *Cultus*, its majestic dignity is asserted. In Christian *Art* is unfolded its beauty, or the plenitude of its æsthetical bearings. In the inner and outward life of devotion of the monks and mystics, or in *Asceticism*, there is an after experience of the pains of the cross. In the *Religious Literature*, finally, especially of the *Mystics*, there is an attempt to fathom the fulness and depths of the idea of the cross. Each of these spheres again includes within itself a number of more special forms, into which the stream of devotion to the cross—as modified in a characteristic manner—is seen to flow. The greatest abundance of such forms is displayed in the domain of the artistic æsthetic glorifying of our symbol, in which altogether the branch of the religious life of the Middle Ages now occupying us has put forth its vegetative power most luxuriantly, but also in what is relatively the most normal, sound, and effective manner.

A. *THE EXERTION OF THE POWER OF THE CROSS IN THE MISSIONARY ACTIVITY OF THE CHURCH.*

As a subduing power the sign of the cross first appears in the missions of the Christendom of the Middle Ages. The missionising of the Church at this stage of her development bears essentially the character of conquest : it seeks by the conversion of whole masses, and indeed often enough by the method of forcible compulsion, by a mode of procedure advancing from without inwards, or but too frequently remaining contented with the outward, to bring about the subjection of the nations to the faith in Christ. The cross of Christ waves as a triumphal banner at the head of these expeditions of conquest on the part of the Church, the unbloody as the bloody ones. It is the indispensable requirement for the accomplishment of the preparatory as of the conclusive act of this missionary enterprise. It is regarded as the unvarying emblem of Christianity in its character of a missionising power upon earth, as the manifest symbol and vehicle of all the effort directed to the external diffusion of the kingdom of Christ, whether on the part of its spiritual servants or of its temporal patrons and vassals.

Characteristic in this respect is the emblem adopted by

the Christian emperors of the East and of the West from the end of the fourth century, which designates them as "ever augmenters of the kingdom," *i.e.*, as augmenters of the kingdom of Christ, as advancing the great work of the diffusion of the empire of the cross over the whole earth. The IMPERIAL GLOBE, a terrestrial globe crowned by an upright standing cross, the significant Christian counterpart to the ancient oriental symbol of the Venus' looking-glass or ansate cross (Fig. 96), of which it would appear to be a simple reversal — we first meet with upon coins of the

Fig. 96.   Fig. 97.

emperor Valentinian I. and of Gratian. And in the peculiar form (Fig. 97), where it is intertwined with the labarum monogram, it is found already upon a coin of Nepotianus, a nephew of Constantine, who reigned less than a full month (350). At first the emblem, of which the originally Christian signification is beyond doubt,—as it is also directly attested by Suidas in speaking of a statue of Justinian,—is as yet combined with heathen or semi-heathen symbols. For upon that coin of Nepotianus it is the goddess Roma (*Urbs Roma*), who holds the imperial globe in her hand ; while upon those of Valentinian and of Gratian, as upon those of Theodosius I., of Arcadius, and of Honorius, it is the goddess of Victory who does so. Theodosius II. is the first who causes himself to be represented as the bearer of the ball surmounted by the cross, and that in such wise that he appears as holding this in his left hand, and in his right a labarum standard. And only after Justinian I.—under whom, moreover, Victoria is still occasionally represented as the bearer of the cross-surmounted ball—does that mode of presentation become gradually the prevalent one, according to which *the labarum is seen to be entirely replaced by the later symbol of the imperial globe;* inasmuch as the bust of the helmed (or crowned) emperor holds in his right hand the globe surmounted by the cross.[1] Thus the warlike symbol yields to the more pacific one, the "emblem of victorious power" gives place to the more peaceful but yet more majestic emblem of the subjugation of the world through faith in the Crucified.[2]

It must not, however, be supposed that with this change the new Christendom became in reality an empire of peace. Neither in the hand of the Merovingian kings from Clotaire I., (511—561), nor of the western emperors from Charlemagne, nor in that of the Byzantine successors of Justinian or of other rulers of Eastern Europe, *e.g.*, of the Servian hero-king Stephan Dushan (about 1350), does the imperial globe indicate that those making use of it were "augmenters of the kingdom" only in a peaceful sense; any more than the other cruciform emblems upon the coins, diplomas, documents, etc., of these rulers imply that they engaged, as the protectors of Christianity, only in the works of peace.[3] Yea, even popes and bishops, who were wont from the time of the pontificate of Vigilius (538—555) solemnly to prefix the great Latin cross to their signature at the subscription, as also to distinguish themselves by the golden cross for the neck (ἐγκόλπιον, *crux collaria*), and later by the *crux gestatoria*, carried before them in their processions,[4] did not thereby protect themselves against the ever-recurring necessity of exchanging their spiritual ornaments for military harness, and armed, if not

[1] See the very accurate account (illustrated with engravings of the most important coins) given of the course of historic development, here briefly sketched, in the art. "Numismatique chrétienne" of Martigny, *Dict. des Antiqu. Chrét.*; also Stockbauer, S. 193 ff., whose statements, however, are less exact, *e.g.*, that Arcadius first represented the globe of the empire in the hand of Victoria.

[2] Comp. on the one hand Rapp, S. 134 of the *Abhdlg.*, on the other Suidas, in Stockbauer, S. 104.

[3] On different other points belonging to this subject (affixing the cross at the beginning of diplomas, from the fifth century; instead of the name of the subscription, from the sixth century; the blood-red crosses subscribed by the Byzantine emperors, green by their princes, gold-coloured by the kings of England, etc.) see Stockbauer, S. 123. On other things of a kindred nature: Martigny, p. 186 seq Comp. also Gretser's dissertation: "De globo crucigero"—(*De cruce*, tom. iii. l. i. c. 20).

[4] The latter distinction, at first belonging only to the popes, was from the time of Innocent III. conceded also to the patriarchs. and from that of Gregory IV. t all archbishops. See Augusti, *Archäol.*, i. 199.

with the sword, yet like Christian I. of Mainz with heavy battle clubs, to take the field. This tendency to transform the missionary work of the Church into a rude trade of war attains its climax in THE CRUSADES. The peaceful ploughshare of the Church is, in direct opposition to the prophetic description (Micah iv. 3 ; Isaiah ii. 4), beaten into the sharp spear, into the battle sword ; instead of the Saviour, Ares or Thor would seem to go forth in Christian armour against the hosts of unbelievers fighting under the banner of the crescent. But even here the sacred symbol of Christianity is active in a manner not merely destructive, even here it creates fresh and ever fresh forms of blessing-fraught labour in the service of Christ. The crusades call forth the SPIRITUAL ORDERS OF CHIVALRY, the order of the Knights of St. John as the first of these, and afterwards those organised upon this model;—a succession of valiant, self-forgetting hero hosts, resplendent also through works of ministering love, who, zealously cherishing at once the outer and the inner missionary principle of the Church, fight under the banner of the cross. The manifold fruitful reactions which, spite of the degeneration or stagnation of the majority which early ensued, proceeded from them, call for no further explanation on our part. And not merely as an instructive chapter of heraldry, as the "diplomatic staurology," the science of the crosses and stars of the knightly orders, have the various crosses of the knights of the orders obtained an abiding significance.[1] Their noble exemplar, the cross of the Knights of St. John, or Maltese cross (Fig. 98), is still, upon the battle-fields of the present day, in the form of the red cross of ministering love and Samaritan's compassion, as much beloved as it is, in the form of the iron cross of valour, terrible to the foeman, and gladdening and inspiring for the sons of the fatherland.

Certainly the original significance of the emblem, as aiming at the representation and diffusion of the name of Christ in missionary effort, has here been gradually lost sight of.

[1] Comp. Stockbauer, S. 123.

This symbol has, as it were, passed over into the domain of the world, has become entirely secularised in its character and effects, after it had already, in the Middle Ages, belonged half to the spiritual, half to the temporal domain. But yet, in those cases where it was subservient to the missionary principle, as the purely spiritual expression thereof, the cross of the Churches of the Middle Ages has repeatedly yielded results which lay claim to the possession of an exemplary value for every age of Christianity and its missions. The conquering missionary activity of the Christian Middle Ages too has frequently waged its victorious warfare by the power of the proclamation of the Gospel, has forced many a rude tribe to the acknowledging of Christ, more by the sword of the Spirit than by any outward force. And in the accomplishment of this, the symbol of the cross has played a very important part. The pious missionary priests and monks of the ancient British Church of the sixth to the eighth century —a Church so richly endowed with the apostolic gifts—who, either alone or in parties of the significant number of twelve, proclaimed the Gospel to the Celtic or Germanic tribes of Central and Western Europe, were wont as a rule to do so by going forth into the villages, gathering the people around a cross set up in the open air, and preaching to them the word of life.[1] Many a proud cathedral, many a cloister dispensing light and blessing in the darkest ages, many a bishop's see continuing to exist even to the present day, has sprung from the huts of hermits, of which the first beginning was formed by a simple cross made of the fresh boughs of trees, perhaps of twigs of hazel or branches of cornel wood, like that on which Gallus and Hiltibald were wont to hang their little caskets of relics.[2] And not merely the missionaries of the school of St.

---

[1] Beda, *Hist. Eccl.*, iii. 26. Comp. Ebrard, *Die iroschottische Missionskirche des 6, 7 und 8 Jhdts.*, S. 432.

[2] *Vita S. Galli*, in Mabillon. *Acta SS. O. S. Bened.*, t. ii., p. 223. (According as we here read, *virgam colurneam = colurnam*, or perhaps *corneam*—comp. Virg., *Æn.* iii. 22 : *virgulta cornea*—must we understand the hazel or the cornelian cherry to be the wood out of which Gallus plaited his cross.) Of the somewhat earlier Kentigern too (sixth century), his biographer Jocelyn relates that he erected crosses wherever he went in his journeyings. (Ebrard, *as before.*)

Patrick and Columba observed this custom; the Benedictines in the service of Rome likewise made use of the cross as their ploughshare for breaking up the hard hearts of the heathen. They too fought, though often it may be in a spirit but little evangelical, under the banner of the blessing-fraught symbol of redemption, the first solemn signing of which over the hosts of their catechumens (the so-called *prima signatio, primsigne*) on every occasion denoted the beginning of their work of conversion, the first preparatory occupation of a new mission field. Winfried and Ansgar, Brun of Querfurt, and Otto of Bamberg, went forth armed with the cross as their weapon upon their no less perilous than glorious wanderings among the heathen nations of their day. That which is related concerning the Franciscan John de Marignola of Florence, of about the middle of the fourteenth century, a bold pioneer of more recent attempts on the part of Rome at missionising among the peoples of India— namely, that surrounded by hosts of his new converts he had erected upon the point of a rock at Cape Comorin a large stone cross (having the arms of the Pope and a Latin and Indian inscription thereupon), and had anointed it with oil, and solemnly consecrated it, as a memorial of the blessing upon his labours in this region—is typically significant with regard to the whole missionary effort of the Romish Church in the Middle Ages—perhaps, also, even in more recent times. For if not entirely in this form, yet with rites and performances in general akin to these, have its messengers far and wide taken possession of provinces newly added to the kingdom of Christ, untroubled as to the manner in which these domains, thus externally conquered, were to be led to an inner and true appropriation of salvation in Christ. From the evangelical standpoint, this missionary work may be condemned as being too external, too mechanical and legal; we may reject the thought of its possible resuscitation in the present day as a monstrosity in glaring contradiction with the relations and requirements of our age; may regard conversions of whole nations at once as a thing no longer possible, and may therefore direct our efforts essentially to the winning of individuals or of comparatively small circles: yet with all this an ideal exemplary value, even for later ages of Christianity, cannot be denied to the labours of those missionaries who overran the heathen world during the thousand years which preceded the Reformation. And in the lustre of the cross which glorifies their heroic deeds, their sufferings, and their martyrdoms, we cannot refuse to acknowledge the light-giving operation, the "glory with unveiled face reflecting itself in us," of Him who is the effulgence of the glory of God and the perfect expression of His nature (2 Cor. iii. 18; iv. 4; Heb. i. 3).

B. *THE GLORIFYING OF THE MAJESTY OF THE CROSS IN THE CULTUS OF THE CHURCH.*

The different modes of the cultic application of the cross in the Church from the time of Constantine arrange themselves under three main points of view. They consist either in the use of the invisible cross drawn by the hand, or in the application of visible crosses or crucifixes in connection with religious acts, or in the observance of Church festivals in honour of the cross.

The custom which we have shown in Chapter III. to exist at any rate early in the second century of the Christian era, namely, of CROSSING ONESELF, now attains to an ever more widely extended significance. Even the most trifling occasions and objects of the outward life were rendered sacred by the invisible crucesignation, the Christian antitype of circumcision according to Augustine (*Serm.* 160). This sign is made upon the drinking vessel which is to be borne to the lips, upon the food to be enjoyed, as well as upon the mouth of a person sneezing;[1] upon forehead and breast at going to sleep and rising; upon the forehead also of soldiers in war,

[1] Sophronius, *Prat. Spirit.*, p. ix., Cotel. Gregory of Tours, *De Mirac. S. Martini*, i. 20.

immediately before the sounding of the signal for battle.[1] The magic exorcistic use is even transferred, from the proceeding with a view to restoration in the case of possessed persons, to an analogous process in the case of animals which have fallen sick.[2] It finds its application in the worship of the Church : at each prayer ; at the reading of the Gospel, when the whole congregation has to stand up and sign itself with the cross ; before the sermon, which the bishop or presbyter does not begin without invoking a blessing by making the sign of the cross; at the Trisagion, as in general on the mention of sacred names; sometimes also at the recitation of the Apostles' Creed, and especially on the acknowledging of the resurrection of the flesh. In the sacrament of baptism, a solemn marking of the forehead and breast of the candidate with the sacred sign, the *obsignatio fidei* or the *signaculum*, immediately introduces the baptismal act in the narrower sense, or the immersion (in the West from the fourteenth century, the sprinkling). In the East this crossing of the child presented for baptism thrice takes place, as does also the anointing with oil therewith connected ; in the West this takes place only once, but accompanied with a thrice breathing upon the mouth, as a sign of the communication of the Spirit (John xx. 22).[3] In like manner the signing of the cross takes place in connection with the sacraments of confirmation and of the anointing of priests, in each case in combination with acts of anointing. The most frequent use of the crucesignation is at the mass and the celebration of the supper ; for the right observance of the latter the priest

---

[1] Prudentius, *Adv. Symmach.*, ii. 712 :
  Hujus adoratis altaribus, et cruce fronti
  Inscriptâ, cecinere tubæ, etc.
Compare his *Cathem.*, hymn. vi. 129 :
  Fac, quum vocante somno
  Castum petis cubile,
  Frontem locumque cordis
  Crucis figurâ signes.

[2] Chrysostom, in the passage adduc above, p. 152. Comp. Pellicia, *Eccles. polit.*, iv. 190.

[3] Augusti, *Archäol.*, ii. 441 f.

repeatedly crosses, not only himself, but also the missal, the altar, the eucharistic elements before and after consecration, and finally the congregation at the benediction.[1] While the eighth book of the Apostolic Constitutions as yet only expressly prescribes a single crossing at the beginning of the sacred action, and while as yet the *Micrologus* of Ivo (about 1100) requires *either* one, or three, or fivefold application of the signing of the cross in the sacred oblation, but directly forbids a two or fourfold use of the same,[2] the various recensions of the Ordo Romanus gradually raise the number of crossings necessary for the mass canon from three to twenty-five. So many at least did Innocent III. appoint; but the later redactions of the Roman missal have brought the number to fifty-five in all, thus surpassing the Syrian liturgy (which prescribes thirty-six of them) by nearly twenty.[3]—The special manner and form too of the crossing gradually underwent different modifications, and gave rise to several sharply divergent ecclesiastical traditions. The ancient Church appears to have known no other mode than that of the marking of the brow, the mouth, or the other objects of crucesignation with one extended finger of the right hand.[4] In place of this, Greek Christendom in the lapse of time, eventually also in its leading Creed, the *Conf. orthodoxa* (Pt. I., Quest. 51), declared obligatory the custom of the so-called Greek crossing, according to which with the joined three forefingers of the right hand (while the little finger and ring-finger remain closed) first mouth, then breast, then right, and then left shoulder, must be touched. The

---

[1] Bellarmine, *De missa*, l. ii. c. 15: "Nam signo crucis se ipsum sacerdos consignat: item librum, altare, res offerendas et oblatas, denique populum, dum ei benedicit." Comp. already Bonaventura, *Expositio missæ*, cap. iv.

[2] For the symbolical reason: ". . . . . quia *semel* exprimitur ad essentiæ divinæ unitatem, *ter* ad personarum trinitatem, *quinque* ad quinque plagas Domini repræsentandas" (*Micrologus de observatt. eccl.* c. 14). Somewhat otherwise Bonaventura, *l. c.*

[3] See on this point Augusti, *as before*, S. 730 f.

[4] Sozom., *E. H.*, vii. 27; Epiphan., *Hær.* 30, 12 (of a certain Joseph: σταυροῦ σφραγῖδα τῷ ἀγγείῳ διὰ τοῦ ἰδίου δακτύλου); Cyril, *Catech.*, 13, sub fin.; Sophronius, *Prat. spirit.* ix.

schismatic denominations of the East depart to some extent from this practice : the Armenian monophysites, as well as the majority of the Russian Raskolnics, combine only index and middle finger, single sects of Russia the thumb, index, and ring finger in crossing themselves.[1] In western Christendom there prevails, from about the time of the eighth century, and under the special influence of the Benedictine monks,[2] the *Latin* rite of crucesignation, consisting in the touching of the forehead, breast, then the left, and finally the right shoulder with the open right hand. On the other hand, the *German* cross is also permitted here, which is drawn with the extended thumb of the right hand, upon which the index finger with the others falls transversely, the left hand resting at the same time upon the breast.—Further, there belong also to the different forms of the usual cross—the cross represented in actions—the early ecclesiastical custom of praying with uplifted or outstretched hands, as well as the custom, becoming general in the West since the beginning of the ninth century, of folding the hands. The former and earlier one was characterised by Fathers like Cyprian, Ambrose, Augustine, etc.; the other and later, by Pope Nicholas I. in his directions to the Bulgarians, as an imitation of the Cross of Christ.[3]

The manifold employment of this invisible or usual sign of the cross (*crux usualis, transiens*) is accompanied with a no less frequent employment of the visible or FIGURATIVELY REPRESENTED CROSS (*crux exemplata*). Crosses, simple or more or less ornamented, become, above all, an indispensable ornament of churches and their altars. " No one shall build a church, until the bishop has come and raised the cross there," is read in a capitulary of Charlemagne. Before this Roman laws of Justinian, and of emperors still earlier, had

[1] Merz, art. "Kreuz," " Kreuzeszeichen," in Herzog, viii., S. 57 ; Gass, *Symbolik der griechischen Kirche*, S. 184 f.

[2] Pellicia, iv. 191.

[3] Cyprian., *Ep. ad Fortunat.*, p. 276 ; Ambrosius, *De cruce, Sermo* 56 ; Augustinus. *De Trin.*, iv. 15 ; *De Civit. Dei*, x. 8 ; comp. also Prudentius, *Peristeph.*, Hymn. 6.—Also *Nicolai I. Papæ Resp. ad Bulgaror. consulta* (in Harduin, *Concil.*, t. v., p. 371).

contained similar ordinances.[1] "To set up the cross" (σταυρὸν πηγνύειν, *crucem figere*) becomes thus equivalent to "to lay the foundation of a church;" just as "to offer at the cross," or "before the cross," becomes equivalent to "to offer upon the altar," *i.e.*, "read mass." Besides the altar crosses, which were generally of silver or gold, and were sumptuously adorned with pearls or jewels, great crosses in the sanctuarium (chancel) at the east end of the church, or above the entrance (at the west) of the building, or on the triumphal arch (the so-called *crux triumphalis*), or finally upon the ambon of the lector, the reading-desk (hence the formula, *de cruce cantare*), served for the adorning of the house of God.[2] Great crosses, often colossally great, of wood or stone, were set up, not only in the churchyards, but also frequently at the entrances of towns or villages, by the highways and public places, in front of princely or private dwellings, in the court of monasteries, etc. From these great and prominent signs the localities in question obtained their names, as " Crossway," " Crossplace," " Cross-passage " (cloister), "Cross Hill," etc. [Comp. " Crouch Field," " Crouch End," " Pen-y-Groes," etc.] Under such public and always accessible crosses transgressors were wont especially to seek their asylum (*ad crucem confugere*); the ordeal of the cross-trial—*i.e.*, the trial how long one could stand with the arms outstretched crosswise, such as was imposed, *e.g.*, in charges of adultery upon both parties, the man and the woman—was wont to be made; and refractory monks or nuns were wont to undergo their penance of "standing at the cross" (*stare, vadere ad crucem*).[3] At the consecration of churches and churchyards, the cross played a prominent part; namely, at the consecration of graveyards, the solemn bearing in and setting up of the great principal cross; at the consecration of churches, the signing of the walls in twelve different places with the chrisma in the form of a cross, on the part of the consecrating bishop or abbot, as prescribed in the *Ordo*

---

[1] See the passages in Merz, S. 59.
[2] Augusti, *Beiträge*, i. 166; Merz, S. 58 f.
[3] Du Cange, *Glossar. man.*, sub voc. CRUX (judicium crucis); Augusti, *Handb.*, ii. 428 f.; Zöckler, *Krit. Geschichte der Askese*, S. 67 f.

Romanus.[1]—Presently there remains no Christian grave, no longer a coffin, without some kind of adornment in the form of a cross. The living, too, place themselves under the protecting influence of the sacred emblem in the most diverse ways; paint the same upon the walls of their houses and bed-chambers; adorn therewith doors, windows, the most varied household utensils; pave their very floors with crosses —at least in the East for a time, until the second Trullan Council forbade the objectionable practice;[2] wear upon the neck little crosses of gold, silver, etc. (often richly ornamented, and inlaid with relics), as amulets or phylacteries (*encolpia*), or put on, as the priests at the reading of the mass, sumptuous garments embroidered with great crosses, and such-like. As abundant sources for the impulses to, and models for, the development of Christian art, these last-named customs must again be spoken of in the following division—that on the history of art. Here we have still further to refer to some religious solemnities in which crosses play a prominent part. Thus to the Greek ritual for the consecration of the altar-cross, the σταυροπήγιον, an act of benediction to be performed at the setting up of new wooden altar-crosses, for which the eastern *Euchologium* prescribes a pretty complicated liturgy; so to the general adoration of the cross practised in the West on Good Friday, on which day the cross is presented upon the altar to receive solemn expressions of devotion in the form of kneeling before it, kissing it, etc.—a custom observed in the diocese of Milan, in accordance with Ambrose's liturgy, on each Friday during the whole passion season;[3] in like manner to that other Good Friday custom, according to which the cross was covered and let down into a vault, to be drawn up again as soon as Easter morning came; lastly, to the processions or supplicatory journeys,

[1] Et faciat episcopus crucem per parietes cum pollice suo de ipso chrismate in 12 locis. (*Ord. Rom.*) Comp. Du Cange, i. 1273.

[2] *Concil. Trull.*, ii., c. 73. Comp. Ruffinus, II. C., ii. 29; Cyrill. Alex., *contra Julian.*, l. vi., p. 196.

[3] Comp. A. Freibe, Der Karfreitag in der deutschen Dichtung, Gütersloh, 1877.

originally—as is shown even in their rise at Constantinople in the time of Chrysostom, about the year 400—nothing else than the triumphal bearing about of splendid crosses, accompanied with the singing of hymns; later also—with reference to the carrying about of the station-cross (*crux stationalis*), as well as other crosses and cross-banners, which formed the peculiar characteristic of these processions— called simply *cruces*, cross-processions,—bearing, moreover, special characteristic appellations (such as *cruces bannales*, processions within the boundaries of the parish; *cruces nigrae*, mournful processions, those taking part in then. being dressed in black, and the altar and pulpit draped in black, etc.), according to their special character and significance, and conferring upon the whole week after Rogation Sunday, the Ascension week, in which they were regularly held in great numbers, the name of "cross-week."[1]—Like the *crux usualis*, the *crux exemplata*, too, was modified in traditionally varying forms, among which the following are deserving of special notice: the "common cross" (*crux ordinaria*) of the western countries (Fig. 99); the "Greek," or equal-armed cross (Fig. 100); the double cross (also called patriarchal or Lorraine cross), and frequently to be met with as well among the Byzantines as in the West (Fig. 101); the papal cross, or

Fig. 99.   Fig. 100.   Fig. 101.

triple cross of the western lands (Fig. 102); the triple cross, or cross with eight ends, of the Russian sectaries (Fig. 103), of which the lowermost transverse bar is said to represent the footboard of the cross of the Lord; finally, the ordinary

---

[1] Du Cange, i. 1276. Luther, Sermon on Rogation Sunday (Works, Bd. 12, Seite 142). Comp. the author's *Geschichte der Askese*, S. 275; Merz, S. 59.—An interesting attempt to trace back most of the Christian processional celebrations to the previous heathen supplications of the nature of the Ambarvalia (in which, of course, the use of the cross would then form their specifically Christian element), is made by Pfannenschmidt, in Schenkel's *Allg. Kirchl. Zeitschrift*, 1872, S. 517 ff.

church cross of the Russians (Fig. 104), (with chains for fixing it to the cupola of the tower or to the ridge of the roof.)[1]

Fig. 102.   Fig. 103.   Fig. 104.

To the glorifying of the cross were also devoted several special ecclesiastical FESTIVALS of yearly recurrence, upon the origin and special signification of which there rests, it is true, a good deal of obscurity. The earliest appears to be that festival of the EXALTATION OF THE CROSS (σταυρώσιμος ἡμέρα or σταυροφάνεια; fest. exaltationis S. Crucis), which fell on the 14th of September. Western authorities, bearing date of the fifth and sixth centuries, as the Acta of the Egyptian ascetic Mary († about the year 400) and those of the Patriarch Eutychius of Constantinople († 582), explain it as having reference to the discovery of the true cross by Helena; some sources even, though it is true very late and very confused ones, date it back to Constantine's vision of the cross. At any rate, it had already existed for some time before the recovery by the emperor Heraclius (in the year 628) of the Holy Cross, stolen by the Persians under King Chosru II., at his conquest of Jerusalem in the year 614; as of course before its solemn re-erection in the Church of the Holy Sepulchre, undertaken by the same emperor three years after its recovery. The latter fact became henceforth the main object of the celebration, without however—in the East at least—pushing out

[1] Comp. Stockbauer, S. 123 f., where also prominence is given to the fact that the form (Fig. 105) is by no means an exclusively western one, but is, strictly speaking, the prevailing form among the Greeks (in a higher degree than Fig.

Fig. 105.   Fig. 106.

106). He appeals in proof to Didron, Annales Arch., v. 323.—On the Russian Raskonic cross, with its eight ends, compare also Ausland, 1874. No. 10, S. 193.

of view the older reference to the previous exaltation or glorification of the cross under Constantine and Helena. The ritual of the Russian Greek Church contains distinct allusions as well to the fact of the temporary removal of the cross by the unbelievers, and of the humble procession of penitents, in which Heraclius (at the instance of those who had been taken captive with the cross, and of the patriarch Zacharias who had been liberated by him) is said—barefoot and without crown or purple—to have borne the recovered relic upon his shoulders to the Holy Sepulchre, as well as to the miracles of the earlier legend of the discovery of the cross. Of that serious and humbling fact we are reminded by the vigils, accompanied with severe fasting, with which the celebration begins, amidst the chanting of now plaintive and lowly, now triumphant stanzas. The earlier legend, especially the miracle of the restoration of the dead person to life, which is said to have convinced Bishop Macarius of the genuineness of the discovery of Helena, is recalled to mind by certain symbolic actions in the principal religious service, in which the bishop, robed in full canonicals, holds above his head the great altar cross, wreathed with flowers and plentifully adorned, with it enters through the low and narrow northern door into the church (as though he were just emerging from the grave), then standing at the ambon holds the heavy burden for a considerable time above his head, while he alternately bends down under it, and then again triumphantly rises with it; and while at the same time the assembled multitude sings the Kyrie, now low, now with a loud swelling voice, etc.[1] In the West, where Pope Honorius I. († 638) is said first to have introduced it, there remained prescriptive only the reference to the later event; since the earlier, the DISCOVERY OF THE CROSS, had already here somewhat sooner received its special festival (*f. inventionis S. Crucis*), which falls on the 3rd of May. The first mention of this latter is that in the *Sacramentarium* of Gelasius I. († 496),

---

[1] See, on the whole subject, E. v. Muralt (Muravieff): *Briefe über den Gottesdienst der morgenländischen Kirche* (1838), S. 284 ff.

where already are given certain prayers, to be addressed to the Saviour who died upon the redeeming wood of the cross, Himself the true "wood (tree) of life and the Restorer of Paradise." Then it is mentioned in the *Sacramentarium* of Gregory the Great, the Martyrologium of Rheinau, of the eighth century, and other later sources. The fixing of its celebration on the 3rd of May remained, it is true, reserved for the Councils of Toulouse (1229), of Cologne (1281), Liége (1287), and an edict of Gregory XI. (1376).—A third festival belonging to this category is that one peculiar to the Eastern Church, the festival of the ADORATION OF THE CROSS observed at Mid-Lent, *i.e.* on the middle Sunday of the fasting season, which according to the Greek reckoning coincides, not indeed in point of time, but yet of signification, with the Mid-Lent of the West, the Sunday Lætare, as a resting-point in the midst of the deprivations and exertions of the Quadragesima—a *dominica refectionis*. The Synaxarion of the festival brings into prominence this its significance, in the words: "As the travellers who have passed over a long and rugged road and are exhausted by the effort, if they anywhere light upon a tree with shady foliage, rest awhile encamped (beneath it), and traverse the remainder of their journey as with renewed youth: so now also there has been planted by the holy fathers in the midst of the time of fasting and of the toilsome road and racecourse, the life-giving cross, which yields us comfort and refreshment, and renders the weary cheerful and equipped for further toil; .... for the Cross is named the Tree of Life, and it is so. As that Tree of Life was planted in the midst of the paradise of Eden, so have our fathers in God planted the cross in the midst of the sacred season of fasting," etc.[1] In like manner do Theodorus Studites, Theophylact, and Pseudo-Chrysostom express themselves in their sermons held on the day of this festival. As a sort of western equivalent for the adoration of the cross, which formed the object of this eastern festival, appears

[1] From F. Piper, *Ev. Kalender*, 1863. S. 72 f., where also extracts are given from he sermons of Theod. Stud., etc., presently to be mentioned.

moreover the custom already referred to of kissing the cross on Good Friday.—Only to the schismatic churches of the East, especially the Monophysites of Egypt and Abyssinia, as well as the Nestorians, belongs the festival of the *Hiding of the Cross*, concerning which Assemani has given more particular account in his Oriental Library.[1]

It was only to be expected that the Church, in the multiplication of the forms of its cross-cultus carried to so great an extent, should not be spared the necessity for defending this form of worship against Christian or non-Christian opponents. The orthodox Apologetics, addressed to those who called in question or reviled this reverence for the cross, advanced for the most part parallel with the defence of the employment of pictures in worship. It is directed sometimes against Jewish or Mohammedan censurers of *all* pictorial representation of sacred things, sometimes against the rigid Puritanism of iconoclastic parties in the East or in the West, sometimes against docetic, spiritualistic, or grossly sensuous heathen errors and abuses—such as were diffused by the Manichæans, the Paulicians, sometimes also the Armenians—in relation to the cross.

Against the JEWS the right of Christendom to the adoration of the cross was maintained, *i.e.*, by that Archbishop Gregentius of Taphar in Arabia, about the middle of the sixth century († 552), who held, in the presence of many thousands of Jews and Christians, a prolonged disputation with the learned Jew Herban on the truth of the Gospel—a disputation which, after an obstinate resistance on the part of the Jewish advocate and his adherents, is said to have ended in a brilliant victory over this man, and, as it is asserted, in the conversion and baptism of half a million Jews! The notes of the discussion contained in the extract show that Gregentius urged almost the same arguments, drawn from Holy Scripture and from history, against the genuinely rabbinical scepticism of Herban, as were employed, *e.g.*, by Tertullian and Cyprian in their writings against the Jews. A pretty long

[1] *Bibliothec. Or.*, T. iii., P. i. pp. 84. 96, 525 ; P. ii. p. 384.

series of typical Messianic prophecies, in which the cross appears as the great power for redemption, is adduced by him; with these, however, he mingles many an exceedingly artificial interpretation, *e.g.*, that of the plant *Sebek*, Gen. xxii. 13—*i.e.* the thornbush in which the ram was caught on Mount Moriah—as a direct type of the Tree of Life on Calvary, etc. When the Jew objects to this that his opponent applies the results of his learned study of Scripture in an entirely arbitrary way, just as it suits him, and wherever he so much as meets with a piece of useful wood (*utile lignum*) in the Old Testament, represents it at once as an emblem of the cross,[1] Gregentius protests against being supposed to regard only pieces of wood as types of the cross; rather is for him every lifting up of the hands, every military standard, every crossing of swords in war, and all such things, a prophecy having reference to the sacred symbol.[2] So, too, with later anti-Jewish apologetes, *e.g.*, with Peter the Venerable, do such forms of argumentation occasionally recur. In all the negotiations between Christians and Jews in the Middle Ages, the cross, as an object of aversion for the one and of reverence for the other, plays an important part. Appearings of the sign of the cross in the sky, as once in the time of Constantine, are said sometimes to have lent effectual support to the evangelistic preaching of the missionaries. Thus on the 18th March, 1415, while a Franciscan in Spain was preaching on the Lord's Supper, a cross, white as snow, is said to have appeared in the sky, and to have produced the instant conversion of a hundred and twenty Jews.[3]

The well-known subtilisation of the sufferings of Christ on the cross, on the part of the MANICHÆANS, into an emblem of "the universal suffering of the soul of nature and of mankind," also afforded to the Fathers, from Augustine down to the late Middle Ages, abundant occasion for apologetic

---

[1] Tu hîc in Vet. Scripturâ si utile lignum inveneris, hora est illud ut assimiles tuæ cruci, etc.

[2] Gregentii Tephrens. archiepiscopi disputat. cum Herbano Jud.—*Bibl. Patr. Maxima Lugd.*, t. vi., f. 1014 sq.

[3] Comp. Kalkar, *Israel und die Kirche*, S. 27.

expositions. Not less so the doctrine of the Neo-Manichæans or PAULICIANS, according to which Christ Himself is the all-animating cross: reverence for the wood of the cross, this symbol of the curse, thus to be rejected as heathen worship and pernicious idolatry. Side by side with this rigidly puritanic aversion for any and every act of reverence for the cross, there is said, however, to have existed in the very same sect the superstitious custom of placing wooden crosses upon persons dangerously sick, in order to heal them.[1] The standpoint, too, of the ARMENIANS of the eleventh and twelfth centuries appears to have been one of opposition to the cultus of the cross on the part of the orthodox, mingled at the same time with a certain grossly materialistic superstition. They maintained that the cross was sanctified only by being sprinkled with the blood of animal sacrifices: sanctity and claim to veneration did not belong to it in and of itself. They were accused not only of this reprehensible custom of smearing it with the blood of sacrifices, but also of the still more unbecoming practice of fastening three crosses together, and designating them, when thus bound, the Trinity.[2] To a Manichæan-Paulician origin must we, as it seems, ascribe the hostility to the cross on the part of the sect of the BOGUMILI, who, according to the "Panoplia" of Euthymius, "refused to the Divine cross, as the instrument of the Redeemer's death, its due honour;"[3] in connection, therefore, with whose trial before the Inquisition under Alexius Commenus (1118) the melodrama was enacted with the two piles for execution, of which the one, adorned with the wooden cross, was to be chosen by those who penitently submitted, as the place of burning, but which in reality proved the place of mercy. One sees a purified, mystic-evangelical, refined form

---

[1] Pet. Sicul., *Hist. Manichæor.*, p. 16 sqq.; Photius, *Contra recent. Manich*, i. 7.

[2] Isaaci Cathol. (circa 1145), Invectiva in Armenios (particularly against the assertion: unctione irrationalium victimarum, non ejus ipsius expressione, crucem sanctificari); *Bibl. max. Lugd.*, t. xx., f. 1243a. Comp. also, Incerti auctoris collectanea de quibusdam hæresibus, *ibid.*, t. xxvii., fol. 623 seq.

[3] Euthym. Zigad. *Panopl.*, tit. 23. No. 14. Comp. the *Oratio* of the patriarch Germanus, *in exaltat. vener. crucis, contra Bogomil.* (Gretser, *De cruce*, ii. 157 sq.)

of Bogumilism cherished somewhat later by the Constantinopolitan monk Niphon, under the Emperor Manuel Commenus, in combating the forms of the Church's homage displayed towards the cross, not this homage in itself. He approved only of that staurolatry which had reference to representations of the cross with the superscription, " Jesus Christ the Son of God," and on the other hand pronounced the reverence manifested towards crosses without this inscription a superstition, and ascribed the miracles wrought by the mere symbol of the cross to the operation of the devil.[1]—The influence of the Bogumili and their predecessors the Manichæans, Paulicians, and Euchites, made itself felt with considerable effect upon several western sects of the thirteenth and fourteenth centuries, particularly upon the adherents of PETER OF BRUIS and upon the Albigenses. Of these the Petrobrusians showed themselves the most extreme opponents of the reverence of the cross. According to their opponent, Peter the Venerable, they would not admit of adoration or even reverence in regard to the cross, but animated each other to break it in pieces and trample it under foot, and are even said to have held public *auto-da-fés* of collected crucifixes, and to have eaten the meat roasted over the flames in their religious assemblies on Good Friday, in contempt of the ecclesiastical regulations which enjoined fasting.[2] As Henry of Lausanne, the leader of his party after the death of Peter of Bruis, at once abolished these repelling extravagances, nay, even—as a token that we have to follow Christ the Crucified—had a cross banner carried before him in his journeyings from place to place; so also the Cathari or ALBIGENSES, of the twelfth and thirteenth centuries, by no means opposed all use of crosses or crucifixes in worship, but only that of the Romish church-tradition. Their crosses, as is objected against them in a lengthy polemical treatise by

[1] Leo Allatius, *De Ecclesiæ occident. et orientalis perpetua consensione*. Colon. 1648, ii., c. xii., p. 671 sqq.

[2] Petri Venerab. Ep. contra Petrobrusianos (in *Bibl. max. Lugd.*, t. xxii.) Especially the section, "Against their assertion that the cross of the Lord is neither to be adored nor revered, but rather broken into pieces and trodden under foot." (f. 1051—1057.)

Bishop Luke of Tuy (about 1230), were not four-armed, but three-armed (T-shaped); and if they depicted the Saviour upon them, they represented Him as nailed with three nails, not with four, thus with the feet placed the one over the other; in addition to which the practice was charged against them of making their representations of Christ, as of the saints, the Virgin, etc., not beautiful, as one might expect, but as ugly as possible. The counter-argument of Luke betrays many weak points. He takes his stand mainly upon tradition : first upon that of the Romish Church, which one must follow before all; then also upon that of the Greeks and Armenians. That the nails of the Crucified were four in number is evident from the existence of the four genuine nails, which are still (in his day) preserved, namely, in Constantinople, in Tarsus, in Nazareth, and at St. Denis near Paris, and have been seen and reverenced in these places by himself, the bishop, so greatly experienced in travelling. In like manner, the fact that there were four arms to the cross of Christ is shown on the authority of the Romish Church, which employs in its service only four-armed crosses, or else double crosses, with a smaller transverse ledge over the main transverse arm, to indicate the title of Pilate ; and whose most powerful Pope, Innocent III., in his sermons, has expressly declared himself opposed to the form with three arms. The fact, too, that a cross preserved in a monastery at Nicosia in Cyprus, alleged to be the genuine cross of one of the two thieves, has four arms, affords an indirect argument against the supposition of the Albigenses that the cross of the Saviour was shaped like a T.[1]—Farther than the Albigenses, namely, to the entire rejection of crosses and the practice of crossing oneself, did the WALDENSES proceed, and that not alone in their later stage of development, in which they assumed an attitude of decided hostility towards the Romish Church. Against them the Church practice was defended by Everard of Béthune in Artois (about 1200), in his clumsily written and fiercely pole-

[1] Luc. Tudens. adv. Albigenses, ii.. iii., in the *Bibl. max. Ludg.*, t. xxv., p. 195 sqq.

mical work *Antihæresis*.[1]—Of the English LOLLARDS, finally, the adherents of the doctrines of Wicliff in the fifteenth century, it is related that they entirely and radically rejected the ecclesiastical veneration for the cross, therein proceeding farther than Wicliff, who approved of a moderate use of pictures and crosses in worship, so long as this was preserved free from idolatry.[2] Picus of Mirandola, also, in one of his celebrated nine hundred theses (of the year 1484), denied the claim of the cross to veneration; but later retracted this denial as an error, and even cherished during the last years of his life an ardent desire himself to travel the world over, the cross in his hand, in the character of a missionary.

The most vigorous discussions in favour of, and in opposition to, the Catholic tradition regarding the cultic use of the cross, had already taken place at the time of the IMAGE CONTROVERSY. The Iconoclasts of the East, after Leo the Isaurian—to whose position in relation to this question later opponents of the orthodox custom, as the Bogumili, expressly appealed—utterly rejected as idolatry all reverence of images; but approved of the erection and religious use of crosses (without the image of Christ thereupon). Thus Leo the Isaurian caused to be set up, in the year 730, in place of the celebrated image of "Christ the Surety" above the brazen gate of the imperial palace at Constantinople—destroyed at his command—a cross with a subscription, composed in Iambic trimeters by the iconoclast Stephanus, to the effect that the emperor had erected, in place of the dumb and lifeless figure of earthly material sullied with colours, represented as Christ, the glorious symbol of the cross, the boast of the gates of "believing princes."[3] The Council of the Iconoclasts, more-

[1] Also under the title, Contra Waldenses; see *Bibl. max.*, t. xxiv., f. 1560, spec. cap. 17 : "Quod crux dominica veneranda sit."
[2] Lechler, *Johann Wiclif*, i. 555 ff.; ii. 317, 319.
[3] Ἄφωνον εἶδος καὶ πνοῆς ἐξηρμένον
Χριστὸν γράφεσθαι μὴ φέρων ὁ δεσπότης
Ὕλῃ γεηρᾷ, ταῖς γραφαῖς πατουμένῃ,
Λέων σὺν υἱῷ τῷ νέῳ Κωνσταντίνῳ
Σταυροῦ χαράττει τὸν τρισόλβιον τύπον
Καύχημα πιστῶν ἐν πύλαις ἀνακτόρων.

Comp. *Theod. Studitæ opp.*, Ed. Sirmond., f. 136.

over, under Constantine Copronymus (754), directed its anathemas indeed against every form of image-worship, but not against the ecclesiastical use of crosses, any more than against that of relics or against the invocation of Mary and the saints. The decrees of the second Nicæan Council (787), restoring the worship of images, therefore—just as the theological argumentations of a John of Damascus, in the Fourth Book of his great dogmatic work, which lie at the foundation of these decrees—proceed upon the recognition of the fact of the reverence devoted to "the venerable and life-giving cross" as something established and unassailable, and demand for the images of Christ and of the saints exactly the same sanctity and reverence as for this.[1] And the orthodox apologetes for iconodulia, with special emphasis Theodorus Studites, again and again object against their heretical opponents, as an act of gross inconsistency, that while they admit the cross as an object of reverence, they do not in the same way admit the images of the Saviour.[2]—In many respects different is the position parties assume in relation to the question of the reverence for the cross in the image controversies of the West. Here there pretty early arises a strong middle party, represented by the Frankish theologians of Charlemagne and his successors, who approve neither of the iconoclasm of the East nor the iconodulic tendency of the popes, but demand in regard to images, as well as to crosses, etc., a sober evangelically moderate use in worship. But here also we meet with an extreme iconoclastic tendency, of which the spokesman, Bishop CLAUDE OF TURIN († 839), opposed as idolatrous, not only the reverence of images, but also its hagiological background, the invocation of saints; and extended his polemics not merely to relic-worship and the making of pilgrimages, but also to the ecclesiastical

---

[1] 'Ορίζομεν . . . . . παραπλησίως τῷ τύπῳ τοῦ τιμίου καὶ ζωοποιοῦ σταυροῦ ἀνατίθεσθαι τὰς σεπτὰς καὶ ἁγίας εἰκόνας . . . . . καὶ ταύταις ἀσπασμὸν καὶ τιμητικὴν προσκύνησιν ἀπονέμειν. (See the Acts of the Council, in Mansi xiii. 877.)

[2] Theodori Stud. Antirrhetic. adv. Iconomach. lib. tres. Also his Orat. in adorat. crucis med. quadrages. (*Bibl. max.*, t. xiv., p. 900 sq.)

use of the cross. This genuine precursor of the puritanism of the Reformation, caused the wooden or stone crosses to be removed from all the churches of his diocese. In justification of this proceeding he objected against the defenders of the reverencing of the cross that—since they would have us reverence the cross, because Christ had hung thereon—in order to be consistent they must also reverence many other things, with which Christ had come in contact : thus mangers, because as a child He had laid in one ; stones, because His grave was formed of one ; virgins, because a virgin had borne Him ;—yea, asses, for riding upon an ass had the Lord made His entry into Jerusalem ! Moreover the Lord had bidden us *carry* His cross, not worship it; and for this very reason did the opponents demand its worship, because they were averse to the taking up and bearing of the same, whether externally and bodily or in spirit and in truth.[1] It ought to have been easy for the champions of orthodoxy to reply in a becoming manner to these attacks, in which the element of a pretty rough banter outweighs to some extent that of the evangelical seriousness becoming a question of such importance ; especially since so distinguished a theologian as Archbishop Agobard of Lyons, who agreed with Claude in his objections to the ecclesiastical use of images, expressed himself in a moderate, a conciliating way, and one essentially conformed to the ancient ecclesiastical tradition.[2] Yet, in reality, their arguments leave much to be desired. Thus Dungal, of Pavia, opposes to the supposed contemner of the incarnation and enemy of the cross of Christ nothing better than a one-sided and moderately clumsy demonstration on traditional grounds. Bishop Jonas of Orleans, on the other hand, who is able to bring into the field counter-arguments drawn from Biblical sources in greater abundance, displays just as little tact in their handling as he does moderation in

---

[1] Claudii Apologet. excerpt., in the *Bibl. max.*, l.c., p. 197 sqq., immediately before Dungal. respons. adv. Claud. (p. 204 sqq.)

[2] Agobardi Lugd. lib. contra superstitionem eorum, qui picturis et imaginibus sanctorum adorationis obsequium deferendum putant (*Bibl. max.*, t. xiv. p. 286 sqq.), cap. 19.

his replies to the objections of the opponent. He directs his polemics with special zeal against the remark of Claude about the ass as being entitled to equal importance as an object of adoration as the cross. To this assertion he opposes a reference, in itself entirely apposite, to Gal. vi. 14, as showing that the apostle gloried not in the ass, but in the cross. He wearies the reader, however, by the excessively long time he occupies over the expression assailed, as well as over the reply to it, and moreover errs in the passionate and unseemly attacks he makes upon the person assailed, whom eventually he even—in quoting certain lines from Ovid and from Virgil —compares to the drunken Silenus, fallen from his ass.[1] Another contemporary writer, the deacon Amalarius of Metz, in the chapter of his work on " the churchly office" which treats of the adoration of the cross, opposes the assaults of Claude mainly with the history of miracles, *e.g.*, with the account of the victory of the Anglo-Saxon King Oswald in consequence of the erection and adoration of a cross, as drawn from Bede's " Church History." Nor does he neglect to point to the fact that, as opposed to the numerous miracles wrought by the cross, nothing is known of any that were performed by the ass of Christ.[2] All intelligent appreciation of the really profound and true in the argumentation of Claude—namely, of the proposition that the cross of Christ is not so much externally to be reverenced as rather to be borne—is wanting in pretty equal degree to all these apologetes of the Catholic traditional standpoint. As regards the later centuries of the Middle Ages, we shall be in a position to point out, especially among the Mystics (see sec. 5 of this chapter), a considerable number of those theologians for whom, while they continue to agree generally with orthodox tradition, there is by no means wanting the endeavour after a profounder appreciation of the idea of the cross.

[1] De cultu imaginum, ii. p. 186 (in *Bibl. max.*, t. xiv.)
[2] Amalarii Metens., *De Eccles. Officio*, i. c. 14 ; de adoratione sanctæ crucis.

c. *THE UNFOLDING OF THE BEAUTY OF THE CROSS IN ECCLESIASTICAL ART.*

No one of the various directions, in which the Church of the Middle Ages carries into execution the glorifying of the sacred symbol, appears so well justified, and has shown itself in an equal degree productive, as that belonging to the sphere of artistic formation and creation. In the domain of art were to be brought out the most abundant and most permanently valuable treasures,—to be brought out for that life of devotion which is intent upon the glorification of the cross. For the cross, once the epitome of all that is odious and execrable, belongs in itself to the most effective motives of æsthetic conception, to the purest and noblest sources of artistic production and enjoyment. Definitely that form of the terrible implement of the Carthaginians and Romans, the four-armed long cross—with regard to which we may suppose, with an especially high degree of probability, that it was employed in the crucifixion of the Redeemer—includes in its lowly but severe simplicity the germs from which have sprung the most significant representations, and those which lay most hold upon our feelings. It appears as closely allied to one of the most charming and captivating polygonal figures, that of the many-rayed star; but it is a "star with diminished rays." It signifies a renouncing of all glittering and splendour,—yea, a restriction of the element of radiance itself within the barest conceivable limits. The cross "from its very nature presents the element of extension in a manner which is specific indeed, but at the same time as much as possible simple and measured; on which account it bears great resemblance in those cases where there is an equal length of the stem with that of the two arms (thus in the case of the 'equal-armed cross')—to the star, to which at the same time it presents an absolute contrast: for the extension is here reduced to the smallest proportion of bulk and of limbs, and is restricted to the severest indentity of forms." The

[1] K. Köstlin, *Aesthetik* (Tübingen, 1869), S. 415 f.—Comp. in general the whole of his instructive chapter, S. 380 ff.

same is the case with the kindred relation of the cross, specially the oblong (Latin) cross, to the figure of a tree, or of the human form standing with outstretched arms. While it appears as a star deprived of its lustre, as it were impoverished, so does it at the same time present a resemblance to a leafless tree, a tree deprived indeed of all its crown, save what is represented by two bare main branches; or to a human frame shrunk into the most indigent proportions, the skeleton of the upright standing human form—in either case an image of mighty strength, but also of most unrelaxing severity and of joyless and lifeless rigidity. The long or high cross "presents in the most decided manner the opposition of the cross-form to all animated expansive organisations: it is like a tree of which only the stem and two main branches remain alive; and these branches, moreover, have been curtailed in their extension, and have become deadly rigid in a regular and rectangular form of extension; it appears in the world joylessly mourning." And this hard and severe form loses nothing that is essential to it, even though we regard it from the point of view of those inorganic formations which are familiar to us from our youth up; if thus we compare it in the first place to those mineral crystal forms which bear resemblance now to one, now to another of its modifications. It is and remains rigid, from the very fact that it is "a specific inorganic form," without any inner life and without any sign of life of its own. "It produces the impression of the intersection of one body by a second, and, with this, of a violent interruption of the continuity of its parts. In the equal-armed (Greek) cross the impression produced is certainly at the same time that of four bodies proceeding from a common centre in different directions: the thought of having before one a pierced body does not thus here present itself so exclusively or so powerfully as it might otherwise do; and the more so because the regularity of this cross-form, so easily taken in at a glance, imparts to it something of a mildness of character. But in truth even this form is not entirely free from a certain appearance of harsh interpenetration."[1]—In spite of this its sharp and hard character, which suggests to the thought a deadly weapon, the soul-piercing sword of Symeon (Luke ii. 35), what fulness of the most sublime, yea the most lovely elements of beauty, is to be evolved from this typical form, so soon as one is intent upon restoring to the star its rays, to the tree its foliage, upon animating the rigid skeleton by clothing it with flesh and blood! The symbol of the most melancholy desolation and desertion has become, through the sacred body of the God-man who hung upon it, a scene of peacefulness, of salvation, and of life, acting with irresistible power of attraction upon thousands and thousands. In place of sorrow and gloom, there beams forth joy and transport from the painfully hard and angular scaffold of wood which was erected by the prince of this world to be a gallows; since the Prince of Life, by His bleeding and dying thereon, has consecrated it to be the gladdening sacrificial altar of the New Covenant!

As a symbol which in the first instance denotes energy, strength, triumph, victorious breaking through from death to life, has the cross above all become an effective motive in ECCLESIASTICAL ARCHITECTURE. Its application to this object appears to be hardly less ancient than the custom itself of erecting independent places for the religious meetings of the Christians. We know at any rate the inner and outward arrangement of those churches of the pre-Constantine period for which in general the second book of the Apostolic Constitutions prescribes an oblong form, and a position turned to the east,[2] though with too little of exactness for us to be able to determine very definitely whether, and to what extent, the form of the cross was already consciously applied in their construction. But thus much is unquestionably evident, that from the time of Constantine—with whom begins a more vigorous and more varied architectural activity on the part

---

[1] Köstlin, *l. c.* [The word employed is *Durchsetzung*. A stone is said to be "durchsetzt" when it is penetrated with another fossil, or with metallic particles.]
[2] *Constitt. Apostl.*, ii. 57.

of the Church—the form of the cross becomes the constant ground-form on which ecclesiastical buildings are constructed. Whether, then, this emperor added to the other modes of gratefully glorifying imitation of the salvation and victory giving sign, as these were devised by him, also the designed adoption of cruciform plans as the basis of construction in one or other of his numerous church edifices ; or whether, what is indeed more probable, his architects conceived more or less instinctively the thought in question, and, by means of a modified working out of certain ancient Roman typical forms, carried it into execution ; in any case, many churches, even of those belonging to the Constantinean epoch, clearly present the cross as the typical form of their inner construction. To the Byzantine style of church building, with the quadratic form which underlies it, are typically related those octagonal or round churches,[1] of which, according to the express and credible testimony of ancient authorities, Constantine erected several—the Church of the Holy Sepulchre in Jerusalem, Helena's Church of the Ascension on the Mount of Olives, the one built in the form of an octagon at Antioch. In the style of the oblong basilica, the precursor of the Romanesque and Gothic church structures of later time, were many of his churches in Rome constructed, as well as some in the East—thus in Tyre, in Bethlehem, in Mamre, and also one in Jerusalem, not far from the Church of the Holy Sepulchre.[2] The first of these (all of which we have to conceive of as churches or chapels of the sepulchre, formed after the construction of the cylindrical monuments of tombs among the Romans) were conformed to the model—distinctly enough perceptible from the inside, at any rate—of the equal-armed or Greek cross ; the latter, by

---

[1] Kreuser, *Der Christliche Kirchenbau* (Bonn, 1851), i. 13 ff., 34, 38, and elsewhere, is decidedly inclined to regard Constantine himself as the author of the plan and peculiarities of construction of the churches erected during his reign. He especially traces back, in accordance with early Roman tradition, numerous basilicas at Rome to this emperor, which can hardly date from his time. Comp. Gregorovius, *Gesch. Roms im Mittelalter*, i. 87 ff., who recognises with certainty only St. John's in the Lateran as a creation of Constantine.

[2] Euseb., *H. E.*, x. 4 ; *Vit. Const.*, iii. 37, 41, 43, 51 sqq.

virtue of a transept intercepting the nave at right angles immediately before the apsis, were conformed to the model of the lengthened or Latin cross. In the case of some of these ecclesiastical edifices of Constantine and the Constantinean age, the form of the cross seems to have been rendered strikingly prominent, even externally, since contemporaries and later writers expressly indicate the cruciform character of these structures; so in the case of the Church of the Apostles at Constantinople—displaying indeed a mediate form between the Byzantine and the Latin style of architecture—which was later rebuilt under Justinian.[1] But even where the form of the cross did not stand in external and bold relief, it continued nevertheless to present the fundamental type to which the internal disposal and arrangement was conformed ; for, on account of the position of the altar in the apsis, the most easterly part of the nave, lying nearest to this, at all times claimed, as the natural place of assembly for the communicants, to be regarded as a privileged spot, and, where it was not, as a transept, shut off from the space in front, yet was assuredly always looked upon as an especially important middle space, as it were of an ideal transverse arm of the cruciform building. In short, even in the domain of the history of architecture, and here also with respect to the form of the basilica, after the time of Constantine at least, the saying of an ancient author retains its universal truth, that " the Cross forms the foundation of the Church." [2]

The quadratic style of architecture, which has remained almost exclusively prevalent in the East, from the time of Justinian further developed into the BYZANTINE DOME-STYLE, retained the equal-armed cross as the ground-plan for the interior of the church, surrounded as it was by quadratic walls of enclosure ; later, however, in its most characteristic church and chapel edifices,—namely, those of the Russian Church,—has brought out the form of the cross

---

[1] See Gregory Nazianzen, *Somn. de Anastasiæ Eccles.*. 2, 16, 60. Procopius, *De Ædif.*, i. 4.

[2] Σταυρὸς ἐκκλησίας θεμέλιος. pseudo-Chrysost., *Or. in venerab. Crucem* (in Chrysost. Opp., ed. Montfauc., t. ii. p. 822).

also externally in the overarching and roofing. The five slender cupolas, resplendent with gold, under the influence of Mohammedan-Tatar ideas for the most part of bulbiform construction, with which the majority of Russian churches are covered, regularly form a Greek cross—whether it be a direct, rectangular cross, or an oblique cross, after the type of the *crux Andreana*—of which the centre is represented by the main cupola, towering high above the point of intersection of the two transverse arms of the ground-plan. So far as churches of this form of construction deserve to be called beautiful, they owe this mainly to the maintaining and vigorous carrying into effect of the cruciform principle. The interior, especially when regarded from the centre, for this very reason always leaves the impression of refreshing harmony; whether this harmony of the four cross-aisles of equal dimensions, into which one looks, is contemplated in majestic proportions—as, *e.g.*, in the Hagia Sofia, at Constantinople,—or, owing to more modest relations of space, is perceptible only in the form of the delicate and lovely. Viewed also from without and at a distance, these churches appear always beautiful, so long as those five cupolas rise above them in the form of the cross. Where—as in the case in many churches of Greece, and in general in the southern districts of eastern Christendom—some other order of arrangement than the cruciform is employed, *e.g.*, the ranging of a number of cupolas in a line upon the front of the building; or where, as in the case of many of the older churches of the Russian empire, an arbitrary accumulation of cupolas or towers, to the number of nine for instance (as upon some of the churches of Moscow), or to eleven (as upon the church of St. Sophia at Kiev), or to a still greater number (as again upon some of the churches of Moscow), has obtained, there the impression of harmonious beauty is regularly sacrificed; the denial of that which is in principle the typical and normal form receives its own punishment in the rise of a greater or less degree of tastelessness and stiffness.

Entirely similar is the development of the ecclesiastical

architecture in the West, where, after a passing influence of the Byzantine cupola-style in the age of Justinian (churches of Ravenna, later at Venice, Aachen, etc.), the oblong basilica form has asserted for itself a prescriptive predominance. Owing to the fact that the design of the Latin cross, which from the time of Constantine was inseparably associated with this fundamental form, becomes in increasing measure distinct and animated, two new independent orders of architecture are successively formed from it—the Romanesque and the Gothic—of which the glorious play of form becoming ever more abundant and luxuriant, seems in its gradual rise, especially if we distinguish an earlier and a later Gothic as relatively independent types, to reproduce the course of development of the ancient Greek architecture, with its succession of Doric, Ionic, and Corinthian orders of pillars. *The cross is the centre and crown of all these genetically related creations.* It forms the impelling primary force which successively operates as a creative power in the profoundly serious and severe figures of the circular arch style; as in the conceptions of the pointed arch style, with ever bolder flight soaring heavenwards, and at the same time ever putting forth more abundant and more elegant forms. Already in the time of the pre-Romance basilicas, under the Merovingian or Carolingian rulers of France, in single ecclesiastical or monastic buildings, which may be looked upon as the more direct precursors of the Romanesque and Gothic edifices, the cruciform principle breaks vigorously through the oblong encompassing walks, which would enclose it and force it back into the interior. They are the cross-basilicas, whose erection upon the design of the salvation-bringing symbol of redemption is expressly brought into relief, as being the aim of their founders. So it is with that of Bishop Namatius at Clermont in Auvergne (*circa* 450), which Gregory of Tours describes as one of the largest and most splendid of its time; that of King Childebert, of the year 555; that built by the abbot Fulrad of St. Denis (784); also one erected at Fulda under the emperor Louis the Pious (completed 819), one erected by Bishop Udalrich

(† 973) upon the churchyard of St. Mary at Augsburg, etc.,[1] Upon the monastic buildings, too, of this age is the type of the cross in various ways outwardly expressed. The five Vosgian monasteries under the abbot Hildulf of Medianum, comprised according to Columban's rule in one, Bodomünster, Medianum, Stivagium, Sennones, and Juncturæ, called as a whole Moyen Moustier (*Monaster. medium*), or St. Hildulph, formed together one great Latin cross.[2]

More gloriously, indeed, and more perfectly than in these edifices of the basilica epoch, which certainly still present many signs of clumsiness and sudden transition—edifices for whose more exact description, too, the necessary points of connection are, owing to the destruction of the monuments in question, or the erection of later structures over them, for the most part wanting—does the architectural simplicity and fecundity of the idea of the cross become apparent, from the moment when (at the close of the ninth century) the basilica form appears as raised to the ROMANESQUE, and therewith —by virtue of a perfect mastery over those ancient heathen elements still to some extent prevailing in the former—as entirely and thoroughly Christianised. That which henceforth supports and penetrates the whole fabric of the house of God as a fundamental principle of its construction, is the thought, not of parallel lines, but of diverging lines which intersect each other crosswise ; in which the opposition between sensuous and spiritual, between earthly and heavenly, but also the removal of this opposition by means of the redeeming work of Christ, is seen to be reflected.[3] "The intervenient character of the Middle Ages appears nowhere more beautifully than here, where ancient tradition is penetrated and informed by the new Germanic spirit, where the lengthwise arrangement of the interior with a view to the altar in the basilica, and the central arrangement in the Byzantine

---

[1] Greg. of Tours, *Hist. Franc.*, ii. 16. Mabillon, *Annal. O. S. B.*, i. pp. 121, 459 ; ii. pp. 251, 423 ;'iv. pp. 139, 247. Gretser, *l. c.*, ii. c. 12.

[2] AA. SS. Boll., t. iii. Jul., p. 218, No. 59.

[3] Comp. Schnaase, in Carrière, *Die Kunst*, etc., iii. 2, S. 166.

dome-structure, are blended in one organic whole, and the opposition of strength and weight is reconciled in the vaulting, which still continues the upward direction of the pillars in the roof itself which combines them and is borne by them."[1] In two directions does the oblong Latin cross appear in its action as the all-conditionating master-design of the Romanesque, and later also of the Gothic or Germanic, style of architecture. Once in a horizontal direction, as the figure of the *ground-plan*, formed in the well-known manner from the five squares of the Greek cross by the addition of a sixth (Fig. 107). But then also in a perpendicular, upward-tending direction, namely, as the overarching network of the *cross-vault*,—this construction, so marvellously ingenious and yet so simple, by means of mutually intersecting semicircular vaults,—which reposes upon the supporting pillars, as the proud crowns of the forest trees upon their stems. But not merely do these great structures, regulative of the foundation and the finishing of the whole, display the form of the cross. The principle of the mutually intersecting lines of the planes dominates in a truly organic manner the very details of the building. Every single panel of the cross-vault, consisting of four spherical triangles united together at the extreme points, is an imitation of the figure of the cross. Every pillar appears in its ground-plan or transverse section "starlike as a cross, with rounded-off wings and ornamental gradations between them." Cruciform, moreover, are the gracefully arranged centre pillars of the circular windows, as in another manner the ornaments too of the rosette above the main entrance. The form of the cross is displayed finally also by the towers completing the edifice above and outwardly, as well in the single ones in the manner of their roofing with so-called cruciform roofs, as by their number and order of arrangement; which (especially where, as upon the cathedrals of Spires, Worms, Mainz, Bamberg, four or five of them appear

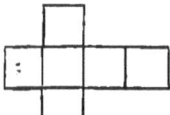
Fig. 107.

[1] Carrière, *as before*, S. 180. Comp. his *Aesthetik*, ii. S. 69 ff.

grouped together; or where, as upon the churches of Laach, Hildesheim, Limburg, six or seven of them appear thus arranged) in a similar manner represent the figure of the Latin cross, as do the cupolas upon the Russian churches that of the Greek.

With more animation, and at the same time with more elegance, than the Romanesque cathedrals—many of which, in their reproduction of the form of the cross, displayed immoderately colossal proportions, such as, *e.g.*, the great church of the monastery at Clugny, with its two cruciform choirs, the one towards the east and the other towards the west; or the cathedrals of Languedoc, with their high side-aisles surrounding the whole building, even to the cross-arms of the choir—do the GOTHIC churches represent the cruciform principle in the abundant fulness of its characteristic power of production; in the delicate spires or pointed turrets regularly ornamented above with cross-flowers, which crown the pillared buttresses as well as the projecting roofs or dormers (*Wimberge*) of the roofing; in the network of girdles and ribs, by which the panels of the cross vaulting appear as at the same time adorned and supported; in the ornamentation of the high pointed windows, displaying ever more glorious star-like, radiated, or rose-shaped figures, and yet never untrue to the fundamental idea of the cross; in the transverse section of the pillars, likewise ever attaining to more and more complicated rosette forms, and yet also on their part firmly retaining the characteristic figure of the cross, etc. Indeed it would appear that, like as the peculiar characteristic which distinguishes an animal or vegetable organism is even preformed in the minutest of the countless cellular structures out of which it is composed, so here the design of the cross, after which the whole was constructed, has been imprinted even upon the single component elements. The whole building presents itself, in its harmonious oneness, as a marvellously transparent embodiment of a profoundly Christian idea. In order to become conscious of this its consecration with the seal of the Spirit, its being born of believing and loving self-surrender to the

Crucified, there is need neither for raising the glance to the crosses which crown the spires, nor of excavating from below the foundation-stone marked according to ancient traditional prescription with the sign of the cross![1] Neither is there need to have recourse to forced and monstrous hypotheses, as that which would see in the whole of the Gothic cathedral an external representation of the crucified Saviour, and in the two towers of the west front a likeness of the nails in His feet! A simple glance at the ground-plan of the glorious creations, as well as at the execution—so strictly conformed to law, and yet so free and full of animation—of their idea, even to the most delicate elaboration of detail in the ponderous masses of stone, suffices to bring to light the deeply Christian character of their meaning, and to lead us to recognise in them true culminating points of human art production, points of culmination not to be attained otherwise than upon the wings of enthusiastic devotion to the crucified and risen Son of God.

But also to the architecture of the RENAISSANCE, which, as early as the close of the Middle Ages, especially in Italy, arose partly in combination with the Gothic, partly in rivalry therewith, the idea of the cross does not remain alien, although this has strictly speaking no connection with its fundamental idea. For this modified revival of the architectural forms of the Classic ages, which " opposes to the rhythm of movement in the Gothic a harmony of geometrical and cubic proportions, a rhythm of masses," bears to the core a worldly character : it originates in civil architecture, and is only conventionally adapted to ecclesiastical forms and requirements. Nevertheless, even in many of the ecclesiastical edifices belonging to this order the Latin cross prevails, in combination with a cupola over the centre of the transverse arms, and a light broad nave throughout the length of the building; some, as the cathedral of Certosa near Pavia, with its splendid façade and lofty elegant cupola tower, and the cathedral of St. Paul in

[1] Durandus, *Rationale div. off.*, i. 1 : . . . . primarium lapidem, cui impressa sit crux, in fundamento ponere.

London, are veritable masterpieces of that nobler architecture of the Renaissance for which the cross serves as a model. Some few of these, notably the gigantic pile of St. Peter's, which has been regarded with so much wonder and has exerted so great an influence, have received as their basis the form of the Greek cross, and not without beneficial effect. And amongst the decorations of their walls, for the greater part derived from antique models—often tasteful, but often on the other hand thoroughly tasteless—as well as upon the exceedingly large tympans, formed upon the models of antiquity, the cross occupies a not unimportant place. Yet the cross always appears here as an accessory, not necessarily belonging to the total construction, but rather externally fitted to it; which may indeed be entirely omitted, but which, in proportion as it is set aside or struck out of the list of influences here at work, leaves the whole structure deprived of its churchly and spiritual character, and on that very account deprived of its salt and its savour. There is thus repeated here also in the art of the West the same history of the degeneration into the gracelessly stiff and odious—arising from the abandonment of the cruciform style of architecture—which we met with in an analogous manner, if with variously modified effects, in the ecclesiastic structures of the East. The worst fruits of this process of degeneration, but just germinating and displaying its feeble beginnings at the close of the Middle Ages, have been reaped only in the experience of modern times.

As the architecture, so has further the Christian PLASTIC ART opened a wide field of animating conceptions (*motifs*) to the artistic endeavour directed towards the glorification of our emblem. The history of ornamented crosses and of crucifixes forms one of the most interesting chapters of the history of art in general during the Middle Ages. It may, however, as one of the best explored domains in this sphere, be treated by us with comparative brevity; so that only the most important and at the same time most characteristic products of this type of Christian art are here brought into relief.

It has already been observed by us, in speaking of the incipient stage of Christian art in the pre-Constantine age, that crucifix figures properly so called, plastic or painted representations of the cross with the Redeemer hanging thereon, dying or dead, remained still unknown to the two centuries immediately succeeding Constantine. A sacred reserve prevents the Christians as yet from making the highest object of their devout hoping and longing, the Prince of Life wrestling in the death-conflict, the immediate object of artistic reproduction. Only timidly and with hesitation does art rise, over many preparatory stages, to the daring height of this venture. The lowermost of these preparatory stages consists in the production of symbolically and beautifully ORNAMENTED CROSSES, especially of those to be borne at the head of processions (*cruces stationales*), thus churchly imitations of that which Constantine in his Labarum had created for the military domain; in like manner also sumptuous crosses serving for the adornment of altars or fonts. As the earliest instance of this kind must that cross, wrought in gold and richly adorned with variegated precious stones, be regarded, which Constantine caused to be erected, as the most significant "bulwark of his empire" upon the roof of a porch of his palace in New Rome.[1] The silver processional crosses of Chrysostom before mentioned (*circa* 400) attach themselves immediately to these. Further, the renowned station-cross, from the baptismal chapel in the cemetery of Pontianus on the Via Portuensis in Rome, of simply symmetrical oblong form, ornamented upon the stem and arms with inlaid jewels in considerable number, some of them of a square, some of a round form; the stem set with gracefully executed roses, of which eight bloom on the right-hand side and eight on the left; the transverse beam furnished with two burning lamps, under which are suspended by golden chainlets the Greek letters A and ω (Rev. i. 8).[2]

---

[1] φυλακτήριον αὐτῆς βασιλείας (Euseb., *V. Const.*, iii. 49).

[2] Represented first in Bosio's *Roma sott.*, p. 131; and afterwards frequently, e.g., in Martigny, art. *Croix*, p. 187; in Lübke's *Vorschule z. Stud. der Kirchl. Kunst*, S. 125 (5º Aufl.), etc.

The whole does not correspond, it may be, in every respect with the requirements of our modern artistic taste; but at any rate it produces the impression of that which is deeply solemn, of dignity and loveliness. Dating from the end of the fifth century, it represents one of the earliest plastic symbolisations of the cross in its character as the Tree of Life. It ranges itself with those representations, adorned mainly with emblems derived from the vegetable kingdom, wreathed with branches of palm, olive, or laurel, as well as with flowers, of which several are still in existence—just as Paulinus of Nola († 431) had them brought into his churches, and describes them in his song:

> "Lo, flowers and wreaths surround the exalted cross,
> And with the blood of the Lord is it reddened, the cross.
> Hovering doves above it bear witness that the harmless and gentle
> Shall surely discover the way to the kingdom of heaven."[1]

Numerous other modes of ornamentation early arise side by side with this drawn from the vegetable kingdom. Thus the wreathing with stars, as in the case of several crosses in the churches of Ravenna; the crowning of the upper arm of the cross with a diadem of jewels, as in the case of the golden cross-lamp (said to be T-shaped) in Paulinus' church of St. Felix; the employment of the monogram with or without A and ω, or even these letters alone, as is likewise the case upon Paulinus' cross-lamp; also Fig. 108. the adornment with a bas-relief medallion, representing scenes from the Old Testament history, the image of the Good Shepherd, etc.; the embellishment with small portraits finely elaborated in crystal, as upon the superb cross of the empress Galla Placidia, set with more than two hundred precious stones, which displays in a wonderfully executed circular figure of this kind her own portrait, together with that of her sons Valentinian III. and Honorius; finally, the combination of a greater number of medals, as in the case of the remarkable richly ornamented episcopal cross of Ravenna, alleged to be the work of the bishop Agnellus, consisting

[1] From Augusti, *Beiträge*, i. 167 f.

of twenty coins combined in a cruciform arrangement, with busts of his predecessors in the episcopate.[1] The so-called *encolpia* too (ἐγκόλπια), simple gold crosses or neck crosses for wearing as amulets upon the neck, with only intrinsically valuable ornamentation (*i.e.*, with pieces of some kind of relics) belong to this class. So also the hollow gold crosslet with a ring upon it, discovered so early as the seventeenth century in the cemetery of the Vatican; in like manner the hollow cross, with inlaid fragments (splinters) of the true holy cross, and a few hairs of St. John the Baptist, with which Gregory the Great once presented Reccared, king of the West Goths, etc.[2] A second preparatory stage towards the crucifix is formed by THE CROSS COMBINED WITH THE SYMBOL OF THE LAMB, a combination very frequently presented in sculptures as upon paintings of the fifth, sixth, and seventh centuries, which in itself also was executed in various manners. Either the lamb appears standing under the blood-red cross, as in the descriptions written by Paulinus of the churches at Fundi and Nola;[3] or the lamb, lying or standing on the ground, bears the lance-like long cross as a banner upon its shoulder; or it rests, as a sacrificial lamb, according to Rev. v. 6, upon an altar under the cross; or it appears upon an altar-like hill beneath the cross, pouring forth its blood from the neck into a cup;[1] or the cross (like that Vatican cross described by Cardinal Borgia, a present of the emperor Justin II. (565—578), bears on its uppermost point and at its foot busts of the Redeemer, whilst in its

---

[1] For the cross-lamp of Paulinus, Paulin., *Nat.*, ii. pp. 660, 665 sqq. The medallion cross of Ravenna, Ciampini, *Vet. mon.*, ii. tab. 14. The sumptuous cross of Galla Placidia, Odorici, *Antichità cristiane di Brescia illustrate* (Brescia, 1845). See also Martigny, *as before*. Stockbauer, S. 127 ff. Buse, *Paulin, Bischof v. Nola und seine Zeit*, ii. S. 77 f.

[2] Gregor. M., *Epp.*, l. ix., No. 22: *ad Recharedum Visigoth. Regem*. Comp. Bosio-Aringhi, *Roma subterranea* (1671), p. 115; as well as the instructive article *Encolpia*, in Martigny, p. 232 sq.

[3] "Sub cruce sanguinea niveo stat Christus in agno,
    Agnus, ut innocua injusto datus hostia leto, etc."
                                    Paulinus, *Ep.* 32 *ad Sever.*
triumph., p. 616, and *Roma sott.*, passim.

middle hangs a lamb; or the mosaic-like delicately executed figure of a lamb is placed in the midst of the cross.¹—A third preparatory stage to the representation of the crucifixion, in point of time perhaps not later than the preceding, but rather running side by side therewith, is displayed by THE CROSS IN COMBINATION WITH THE IDEAL FIGURE OF CHRIST, likewise in various modifications. Sometimes Christ stands, in the form of a youth of surpassing beauty, with flowing locks, upon the hill of Paradise, from which burst forth the four streams (? emblem of the four Evangelists), in his right hand holding a slim Latin cross of about his own height, which is adorned with pearls.² Sometimes there appears a vacant cross, surrounded (1) by a monogram (Fig. 109), suspended above it; (2) by an empty grave depicted under it, with the two seeking women and the Christ who appears to them, thus a representation of the resurrection ; (3) by the twelve Apostles, divided into two groups, six standing on the right-hand side of the cross and six on the left. Sometimes further—as upon the celebrated oil-phial from the catacombs now in Monza, sent by Gregory the Great to Theodolinde, queen of the Lombards, instead of the martyr relics she had sought—a living verdant foliage-cross, symbol of Christ as the bliss-giving Tree of Life, forms the centre of a larger group, among the figures of which are specially to be observed two boys adoring the cross, the crucified thieves at the right hand and the left, the sorrowing Mary, and Peter equipped with the two keys, etc., and above all these a bust of Christ enthroned within the nimbus of the cross between the sun and moon.³ Sometimes, finally, as upon other similar oil-phials at Monza and elsewhere, the representation of the Redeemer as crucified in this or that particular manner is left out, but yet indicated as necessarily presupposed in the scene,

Fig. 109.

¹ Borgia, *De cruce Vatic.*, p. 19 sqq. Comp. the frontispiece to that work, representing a cross with an inlaid figure of a lamb (*crux vermiculata*), from Ravenna.
² See the beautiful representation of the sarcophagus of Probus († 395), in Stockbauer, S. 143.
³ Plates in Martigny, p. 190 ; Stockbauer, S. 145.

specially by the depicting of the two crosses of the malefactors ; or, instead of the naked body of the dying Saviour, there is introduced, as in a representation in the church of St. Apollinaris at Classe in Ravenna, belonging to the year 675, a bust of Christ upon the cross, placed at the point of intersection of the two beams.[1]

The latter of these representations, displaying a sacred shrinking from direct representation of the crucifixion, date from an age in which on the part of a number of Christian artists, at first among those belonging to the Eastern Church, this shrinking was already overcome, and the transition was accomplished to the crucifix figures strictly so-called. The earliest plastic crucifix still in existence, which came to Monza as a present from Gregory the Great to Theodolinde, on the occasion of the birth of her son Adulowald, and has been preserved there till the present day in the coronation church of St. John, is notably the work of a Greek artist, and characteristic of the type of crucifix figures which came into vogue in the East from the time of Justinian.[2] It represents Christ—arrayed in a sleeveless tunic, or colobium, His face youthfully bearded, His head (surrounded by a nimbus of rays) slightly inclined to one side—hanging still living upon the cross, with His feet nailed side by side to a rather large footboard ; upon the title above the head the letters I C X, and under the transverse arms of the cross inscribed in Greek, somewhat abbreviated, the words " Behold thy son " and " Behold thy mother," which the Lord addresses to the figures of Mary and John, represented (greatly reduced in size) as standing at the ends of the two arms. Above the whole, upon the border of the upper cross-arm, are depicted sun and moon, the sorrowing witnesses of the Redeemer's death, henceforth occurring upon most figures representing the crucifixion.[3]

---

[1] Didron, *Annales archéolog.*, t. 26, livr. 3 (1869). Gori, *Symb. lit.*, iii. 221.

[2] Gregory the Great, *Epp.*, l. xiv. 11, 12. An engraving thereof in Didron, *l.c.*; and Stockbauer, S. 160.

[3] On the sun and moon (sun's disc and lunar crescent) as frequent symbolic figures of the representations of the crucifixion in general during the Middle Ages, see Piper,*Mythol. und Symbolik der Christl. Kunst*, i. 2. 137ff., 153ff., 178ff., 699ff.

Most of these peculiarities are to be observed in connection with the other plastic crucifix figures, as also the painted ones, of Byzantine origin, dating from the seventh and following centuries. Only the tunic early disappears, giving place, in consequence of the influence exerted by a painting of Anastasius Sinaita (*circa* 600) and other Syrian representations, to a mere cloth around the loins, which leaves the upper part of the body entirely naked, and covers only the lower part of the person from the navel, together with the upper parts of the legs down to the knees. Not in quite so stereotyped a manner as in painting is the Byzantine art tradition fixed in the preparation of plastic figures of the crucifixion in metal, stone, ivory, and wood. Yet even in regard to these, the well-known ecclesiastical ordinances, which became prescriptive as regards the former, especially the 82nd canon of the Trullan Council of 692, which forbids the representation of Christ in the form of a lamb, thus expressly legitimating the depicting of the Crucified in human form,[1] as well as the principles which prevailed after the victory of the orthodox over the opponents of images, exerted too their characteristic influence. This influence made itself felt especially in the fact that henceforth painted representations of the crucifixion

[1] The true sense of the remarkable and much-discussed words of this canon: Ἐν τισι τῶν σεπτῶν εἰκόνων γραφαῖς ἀμνὸς δακτύλῳ τοῦ προδρόμου δεικνύμενος ἐγχαράττεται . . . . κατὰ τὸν ἀνθρώπινον χαρακτῆρα καὶ ἐν ταῖς εἰκόσιν ἀπὸ τοῦ νῦν ἀντὶ τοῦ παλαιοῦ ἀμνοῦ ἀναστηλοῦσθαι ὁρίζομεν, is certainly open to dispute. An absolute prohibition of every kind of figure of Christ under the likeness of a lamb appears not to be expressed thereby, rather is it intended only to apply to those representations of the Saviour under the form of a lamb which depict also John the Baptist as he points to Him with the finger (John i. 29, 36), which are designated as shadowy types unworthy of the time of the πλήρωμα νόμου, or of grace and truth, and as therefore to be avoided. Thus much, however, is clear, that, in opposition to such representations, the depicting of the crucified Saviour in the actual form of a man (κατὰ τὸν ἀνθρώπινον χαρ.) is recommended and insisted on as the normal ecclesiastical type. It cannot be inferred from the canon either that there was no crucifix proper in existence before 692, or that after that time the representing Christ under the form of a lamb was without further qualification anathematised in the East, and altogether disappeared from ecclesiastical usage there—with which the expressions of approval with regard to certain figures of this kind, on the part, *e.g.*, of John of Damascus, *Orat.* iii. *de Imagin.*, are in conflict. Comp. Augusti. *Denkw.* xii. 124 ff.

became of much more frequent occurrence, and were more elaborately executed—in their application to churches, bookcovers, manuscripts, etc.—than sculptured crucifixes, which latter, just because of their comparatively rare occurrence, remained less affected by the slavish constraint of theory and conformity to the appointed model, which expresses itself in the paintings. Remarkable for their comparatively original character are among others that formerly the breastcross of Louis the Pious, having come from Jerusalem in 799 as a present to Charlemagne;[1] the cross of victory of the emperors Constantine VII. Porphyrogeneta, and Romanus II., splendidly adorned with enamelled work and precious stones, of the year 950, now in the cathedral of Limburg on the Lahn;[2] the crucifixion scene upon a panel of the Pantaleon gates of the church of St. Paul in Rome, executed in brass at Constantinople about the year 1070; several Russian crosses, or at least crosses belonging to the treasures of Russian churches, wrought in gold or ivory, and dating from the fourteenth, fifteenth, and sixteenth centuries; an iron cross of a construction in many respects peculiar, recently discovered by the English traveller the Rev. H. F. Tozer, in a church of the island of Crete : about eighteen inches high, hollow inside, and containing within it a piece of wood which is alleged to belong to the true cross, above the Crucified bearing not the ordinary I C X C, but the letters I N R I, and so forth.[3]—In much greater number and variety do plastic crucifix representations arise in the ECCLESIASTICAL ART OF THE WEST from the seventh century. Until the time of Charlemagne the Byzantine influence very markedly exerts itself upon their formation, whether as relic crosses serving as encolpia or phylacteries, or as greater station crosses, church crucifixes, etc. From the time of Charlemagne the western art-tradition in our domain begins to display an independent

---

[1] Kratz, *Der Dom zu Hildesheim*, S. 16. Stockb., S. 176, 186.
[2] F. ausm. Weerth, *Das Siegeskreuz der byzant. Kaiser Constantin VII., Porphyrogenitus, und Romanus II.*, etc., erläutert. Bonn, 1866.
[3] The account of the discovery appears in *the Academy* of 27th Feb. 1875.

bearing. Yet this its individual character, as opposed to the influences from Byzantium, still continuing to exert themselves with considerable force, appears not to have fully established itself before the end of the eleventh century. About the year 1050, on the occasion of the ecclesiastical controversy between Leo IX. and the Patriarch of Constantinople, Michael Cærularius, the difference in the mode of representation prevailing on either side—now clearly defined and deliberately adopted—was at length formulated in this wise, that the Greeks represented Christ upon the cross as dying, the Latins on the other hand as living; on which the former grounded the reproach that their opponents represented the Lord "not in a natural appearance, but contrary to all nature," and these again the accusation that the Greeks in a certain manner made a representation, not of Christ, but of an Antichrist.[1] With full decision indeed does no other but the Frankish and German art of the following centuries hold to this conception of the Crucified, as only " put to death as to the flesh, but made alive as to the spirit" (1 Peter iii. 18); whilst the Italian remains under the continuing influence of the Byzantine school, and on this account does not rise to such original and varied creations in this domain as those of its more northerly neighbours. As important trophies of the latter may be mentioned, among others, the celebrated relief of the "Extern Stones" near Horn in the district of Lippe, of the year 1115, a very early and still rude attempt at a representation of the descent from the cross, formed with considerable freeness and boldness, not without the consultation of Byzantine models—remarkable especially on account of its depicting the soul of the dead Redeemer as that of a child, which God the Father, hovering over the cross, and holding a cross banner, takes up to Himself;[2] diverse altar or station crosses with rich adornment in gold, filigree, and precious

[1] More on this controversy between Cardinal Humbert, as the representative of the Romish tradition, and the Patriarch Michael, see in Hefele, *Conciliengesch.*, iii. 737; comp. Gieseler, *KG.*, ii. 1. 387.

[2] An engraving, *e.g.*, in Becker's "Charakterbilder aus der Kunstgeschichte," S. 216.

stones, *e.g.*, a late Romance one in the Mauritius church at Münster, a similar one in ivory in the cathedral at Bamberg; a bronze cross with elaborate plastic pedestal in the Soltykoff collection at Paris (twelfth century); a cross in the cathedral at Regensburg (Ratisbon) belonging to the early Gothic age (thirteenth century), especially richly adorned with precious stones, remarkable from the fact that Christ is represented in the middle of it, sitting and teaching with an outspread Bible upon His knees. The simply beautiful image of the Crucified One between John and Mary, in baked clay, upon the altar of the church at Wechselburg (middle of the thirteenth century), also deserves being brought under notice; so the passion-scenes of the altar-work at Triebsee in Pomerania—this crown of all the masterpieces of Gothic sculpture.[1]

The works of PAINTING in the Middle Ages belonging to this province display in general the same course of development as the sculpture crosses, with which moreover, especially in the earliest centuries, they appear—by virtue of their peculiarity as figures of mosaic, enamel, or filigree-work—most intimately allied. The earliest and simplest attempts in this sphere join hands as it were with the most delicately wrought and complicated figures of early Christian monogrammatics, side by side with which their production for a while proceeds. The star monograms (Figs. 110, 111), of the time of

Fig. 110.   Fig. 111.   Fig. 112.   Fig. 113.   Fig. 114.

the sons of Constantine; the somewhat later forms (Figs. 112, 113, 114),—the last, as a combination of the Latin cross with the name of Christ, X, a specially direct precursor of the crucifix figures;[2] the anchor crosses and palm crosses

---

[1] Kugler, *Kl. Schriften*, i. 796 ff. Otte, *Handb. der kirchl. Kunstarchäologie*, 4e Aufl., S. 111, 696.

[2] Comp. Le Blant, *Inscriptions Chrétiennes* (Paris, 1856), i. p. 37, No. 227; as well as Stockbauer, S. 119, 156 f.

(Figs. 115, 116), and so forth,[1] show in this primitive Christian hieroglyphic art, the budding impulse to an æsthetically corresponding emblematic representation of the mystery of redemption, as having reached a stadium of development at which the transition to the representation of the Crucified in images,

Fig. 115.   Fig. 116.

strictly so called, involved but a single step. That also this step was made with hesitation, is evident from that which has been above observed as to the different preparatory stages to the plastic crucifix figures. For these preparatory stages partly precede, partly advance for a time side by side with, the earliest painted representations of the Crucified One; notably the images of a lamb in combination with the cross, with doves, with the four streams of Paradise, as Paulinus of Nola introduced them into his churches, were partly plastic, partly executed in mosaic painting. In like manner in the later phases of development of the representation of Christ under the form of a lamb, or also in combination with the cross, there were besides plastic executions in relief, etc., those too in mosaic painting. Of such kind were the representations of the lamb for slaughter upon the altar under the cross in the Cosmos and Damian's church of Pope Felix IV. (524—530), as also in the old church of St. Peter; as well as that of the cross, surmounted by a bust of Christ, in the church of San Stefano, belonging to the seventh century; as likewise in other churches of Rome, Ravenna, etc. That primitive type, too, of the Byzantine crucifixes[2]—of which the cross of Theodolinde in Monza is the earliest plastic example which has been preserved to the present day, and that painting of Anastasius Sinaita, as well as a painting by the Syrian monk Rabulas, probably somewhat older still (upon a manuscript of the Gospels of the year 586, now exist-

---

[1] The latter form asserted to be of frequent occurrence upon the graves of martyrs, as well as upon so-called blood-phials.

[2] Either graphic or plastic representations of the Saviour on the cross.

ing in Florence), present the earliest examples in painting—
was, as is clear from the close agreement of these very examples, a common one for the plastic art and for painting.
Paintings in mosaic, or on enamel, on glass, as also wall paintings, were from the beginning of the seventh century just as
frequently, or rather for the East, since the conclusion of the
image controversies, much more frequently, fashioned in accordance with this prescriptive type, than sculptures in ivory,
metal, stone, or wood. And these eastern paintings of the
crucifixion gradually stiffened to the type of the most rigid
legal constraint of ecclesiastically dictated tradition; in suchwise that the main and characteristic peculiarities of the
Crucified and His surroundings—the nimbus of the cross, the
bearded face of the dying Saviour, inclined as it is a little
to one side, the somewhat broad footboard, with a twofold
nailing of the feet thereto—the malefactors on the right hand
and on the left, John and Mary in like manner; beneath the
cross the skull of Adam, which, according to legendary tradition, lies buried here, etc.,—recur without any important
variation, and, at least in the adornment of churches, must
have been executed most mechanically in accordance with the
prescribed rules of the painters' handbook of Mount Athos,
ascribed to Manuel Panselinus in the eleventh century.[1]

Very much more freely and productively was the painting
of the West able to develop itself, as in general so also in
our special domain. If at the same time Byzantine artists
continue frequently active in the West—particularly in Italy
—until after the commencement of the twelfth century, as
instructors and refiners of the taste, yet the diversity of the
ideas embodying themselves in the western paintings representing the crucifixion surpasses in a very high degree that
of the eastern ones. Influenced for a while, among other
agencies, by the highly original but fantastic and monstrous
representations of Irish and Ancient British painters,[2] the

[1] Didron, *Manuel d'Iconographie Chrétienne Grecque et Latine, Trad. par Durand.* Paris, 1845.
[2] A characteristic representation of such an Irish drawing of the crucifixion, belonging to a St. Gall MS. of the 10th century, is given in Stuckbauer, S. 198.

Frankish and German crucifix painting, from the time of the Carolingians, begins gradually to put forth a whole series of peculiar accompaniments of the scene of the crucifixion, in which are reflected, as it were broken into many colours, partly the legendary creations, partly the theological and christological speculations, of ecclesiastical scholasticism. The Redeemer, depicted until the thirteenth century for the most part perfectly living and without any painful expression of countenance, appears, according to the example furnished by Charlemagne in his mosaics at Aachen, generally clothed in a purple dress, sometimes arrayed in a kingly crown, the cross frequently conceived of as the Tree of Life, and therefore represented as the natural trunk of a tree, unhewn and of a green colour.[1] Instead of the surroundings suggested by the Gospel narrative, among which, in addition to John and Mary, the centurion Longinus is also a favourite figure, to the study of which special affection is devoted, there arise frequently new personalities of symbolical significance, or else allegorical figures—sometimes death and life, sometimes the Church and the Jewish synagogue, sometimes the head of Adam, sometimes a serpent, sometimes a cup at the feet of the Crucified, for the collecting of the blood flowing from His side; in like manner sun and moon indicated in various modifications above the same, etc. Fresh licenses of a peculiar nature are assumed by the school of painters of Middle and Upper Italy—a school which gradually attained to an independent development from the time of the thirteenth century. Giunta of Pisa represents the Saviour as hanging upon the cross, already dead, and around Him six weeping angels flying. A figure of unknown origin, in the chapel of St. Silvester at Rome, of the year 1248, represents Him as hanging upon a fork-shaped cross, with arms bent upwards in the figure of a Latin Y.[2] Cimabue († 1300) introduces into the ecclesiastical art tradition the placing of the feet one above the other, as being

---

[1] On the cross represented as the Tree of Life, see Piper. *Ev. Kal.*, 1863, S. 86 f., and the engravings 3 and 4 belonging to S. 84.
[2] Comp. above, ch. i. b., p. 65.

fastened by only one nail to the stem of the cross, this mode of placing them having been shortly before contemned and opposed as Albigensian and heretical—an innovation which, spite of the visions of St. Brigitta († 1373), expressly testifying to the nails through the feet having been two in number, pretty quickly obtained the ascendency over the opposite opinion and custom.[1] From the time of Fiesole the "soul-painter" who produced works of wondrous depth and feeling in his representations of the Crucified One († 1455) on the one hand, and John of Eyk († 1470) on the other, increasing solicitude is directed to the depicting of a sorrowful expression in the face of the suffering Redeemer, now as a rule crowned with thorns; as too an increasingly touching and affecting mien is imparted to the figures of John, of Mary, and of the Magdalene, standing at His feet, frequently with the result that no longer the Crucified One Himself appears the main figure of the whole group, but rather these witnesses of His death, especially the two Marys, assume this character. —In the representations too of the resurrection of the Lord, belonging to the later Middle Ages, do modes of conception in many respects peculiar with regard to the death of the cross and its theological significance play their part. Thus the Risen One, as a rule hovering above the open rock sepulchre and the guards who are sleeping beside it or fleeing in terror, pretty regularly holds in His hand a cross banner, the emblem of His triumph over the powers of death. Exceptions to this mode of presentation which became general in the Italian painting, especially from the time of Giotto, but already frequently occurred even earlier in the German art, are comparatively rare. In proof of the extraordinarily far-reaching influence exerted by the idea of the cross upon the ecclesiastical art products of the Middle Ages in general, this mode of representing the resurrection also is at any rate very instructive and significant.

If we add to that which has already passed under con-

[1] See Appendix VI., No. 7; and comp. what has been before remarked on the controversial writings of Lucas Tudensis against the Albigenses.

sideration also the extensive field of the representations of the crucifixion in the wider sense, especially the tablature of the Passion, with its combinations of numerous scenes from the history of the Lord's sufferings; and if we consider that precisely within the sphere of this passional painting, or painting of altar tablets, the art of the expiring Middle Ages—as well Germanic as Netherlandish—wrought its pre-eminently thoughtful and affecting products, we are certainly justified in concluding that the painting too of the Middle Ages has presented its contributions in rich abundance to the glorifying of the cross, or, conversely, that upon its products also there has passed from the devout contemplation of the sacred emblem and instrument of redemption a specially powerful inspiring and fructifying influence. Entirely in the same degree as the ecclesiastical architecture and sculpture of the Middle Ages, the painting does not indeed show itself dominated by the idea of the cross as its impelling vital force and central guiding motive in all artistic creations; much too is wanting generally to its attainment within the period under review to the full development of its creative powers and to the true maturity of its productions. But to a great extent it maintains the same prominent significance even within this sphere of art; and that manifestation so instructively prominent in architecture and the plastic art, in accordance with which definitely the most intensely religious, the most deeply Christian conceptions of the artist appear as almost without exception matured beneath the cross and aglow with the flame of devotion to the Crucified, proves itself also almost equally without exception true in the domain we have just contemplated.

As a peculiar province, effecting the transition from the graphic or plastic art to the poetic, or rather simultaneously calling into requisition both modes of artistic invention, we have further only to mention a form of the artistic glorification of the cross now extinct—*i.e.*, entirely fallen out of use—although one greatly cultivated in the Middle Ages. We mean the application of the cross-form as groundwork for acrostic and other artistically arranged compositions of a religious ascetic import, or, briefly, the Latin devotional POETIC COMPOSITION IN THE FORM OF A CROSS. The earliest known example of this remarkable species of art, belonging half to the domain of poesy, half to the domain of graphic emblematisation, we owe to Hrabanus Maurus, the brightest star of the intellectual firmament of Germany in the latter part of the Carolingian age. It is a poem in hexameters, divided into twenty-eight sections or figures, composed "To the praise of the sacred Cross," at all events while he was yet a simple monk of the convent at Fulda, before his elevation to the abbacy thereof, and thence to the archbishopric of Mainz —as indeed the art exercise in question presupposes the abundant leisure of conventual retirement and freedom from time-consuming earthly engagements. A mention of Alcuin, the instructor of Hraban, occurring in the poetic preface to the composition, might seem to favour the supposition that it was composed during Alcuin's lifetime, thus before 804— perhaps during the stay of about a year on the part of the youthful Fuldensian monk with Alcuin in Tours, or shortly afterwards. But the likeness of the young Emperor Louis the Pious already prefixed to the poem in the early manuscripts, and further, the existence of a later added dedication of the poem to Pope Gregory IV. (827—844), as well as the statement of the Fuldensian annals of the year 844, that two monks of the said convent conveyed the work to Rome, to the successor of this Gregory, Sergius II. (844—847),—all this combined renders probable the supposition of a later date of composition, most likely at the beginning of the reign of Louis the Pious. The twenty-eight divisions or hexameter-groups of the poem are constructed in such-wise that one part of the letters, without injury to the connection in other respects, yields alone a special sense, which refers to the virtues and glories of the sacred cross. And indeed these separate letters (in the manuscripts and editions ordinarily printed in red, and enclosed by red lines) form on each occasion a cross of simpler or more complicated structure; simplest in the third figure, where great uncial letters—each enclosing within itself several smaller ones—yield together the crosswise interpenetrating words *Crux* and *Salus*,—

<pre>
     C
     R
   SALVS
     V
     X,
</pre>

more complicated in other divisions, where, *e.g.* (as in the fifth), four squares, each containing an hexameter, surround a cross, likewise composed of hexameters, as emblems of the four corner-stones of the house of God, namely the Patriarchs, Prophets, Apostles, and Martyrs; and many other similar arrangements. The elements combined by means of the separate red letters sometimes too form hexagons or other geometrical figures, out of which the form of the cross arises; occasionally also delicately shaped blossoms, symbolic animal forms or angel figures—denoting the cherubim and seraphim, as well as the animals of the Evangelists—finally some few times also figures of human shape, as in section i. the Saviour Himself standing with outstretched arms; in the last section the poet kneeling in lowly adoring position beneath a cross, as well as upon the dedication page in the front the heroic form of the emperor Louis, with the shield in the left hand, and a long cross-spear in the right.—Not quite so excessively artificial and idly toying, but yet like the other presupposing a considerable labour of thought and an ingeniously computing art of drawing as of composing, appears the poetic glorification of the cross, constructed upon a principle in many respects diverse from that of the previous work, by the seraphic doctor of the Franciscan order, St. Bonaventura († 1274). The frontispiece to his edifying treatise consists of "the Tree of Life," followed by the explanations added in the preface to this treatise. An exceedingly large leafy tree, in the conformation of its boughs and branches representing a triple cross (with three pairs of transverse arms ranged one above another), bears upon each of its twelve main branches—as it were the spiritual leaves or fruits of these branches—four verses, having reference to the characteristic features and conditions of the life of Jesus, and describing successively His Divine origin and walk, His suffering on the cross, and His glorification. The object of the whole lucid presentation, at once graphic and poetic, is according to the statement of the author to afford to the disciples who desire to be crucified with Christ (Gal. ii. 20) guidance to an intimate, living, and loving contemplation of His sufferings. To this end he had gathered out of the forest of the Gospel, in which the life, sufferings, and glory of the Lord are fully treated of, a "bundle of myrrh" (Cant. i. 13), and had in such-wise arranged that which was gathered, "by means of a figurative tree, that in the lowest branches of this tree the origin and life of the Redeemer should be described, in the middle ones His sufferings, and in the uppermost His glory." And in truth "there stand upon the first series of branches, alphabetically arranged on either side, four inscriptions; so also upon the second and the third; upon every branch hangs a fruit, so that they appear like those twelve fruit-bearing boughs of the Tree of Life" (Rev. xxii. 2). As a dodecade thus do the eulogies of the crucified and risen Saviour appear, consisting on each occasion of four verselets, and growing in the form of fruitful branches out of the Tree of Life. The *first* of these celebrates "the glorious origin of the Saviour and His sweet birth;" the *second*, the lowly walk of His condescension; the *third*, the dignity of His perfect virtue; the *fourth*, the fulness of His overflowing compassion; the *fifth*, His confidence in the peril of suffering; the *sixth*, His patience under injuries and revilings; the *seventh*, His steadfastness under the pains of the bitter cross; the *eighth*, the victory obtained by His death-conflict; the *ninth*, the newness of His resurrection with its wondrous gifts; the *tenth*, the exalted ascension with its spiritual graces; the *eleventh*, the righteousness of the future judgment; the *twelfth*, the eternity of the Divine kingdom. As examples of the twelve strophes, each consisting of four lines, and throughout rhyming by means of the final syllable, *us*, may here be cited:

No. 1:
Jesus origine præclarus, quia
Jesus { ex Deo genitus,
præfiguratus,
emissus cœlitus,
Maria natus.

Jesus glorious in origin, because
begotten of God,
prophetically heralded;
sent from heaven,
born of Mary.

No. 2:
Jesus humiliter conversatus, quia
Jesus { conformis patribus,
Magis monstratus,
submissus legibus,
regno fugatus.

Jesus of lowly walk, because
like unto the fathers,
proclaimed to the wise men,
made under the law,
banished from His kingdom.

No. 7:
Jesus constans in cruciatibus, quia
Jesus { spretus ab omnibus,
cruci clavatus,
iunctus latronibus,
felle et aceto potatus.

Jesus steadfast in sufferings, because
mocked by all,
nailed to the cross,
associated with the thieves,
receiving as His drink vinegar and gall.

No. 8:
Jesus victor in conflictibus, quia
Jesus { Sol morte pallidus,
translanceatus,
cruore madidus,
intumulatus.

Jesus victorious in the death-conflict, because
as the sun in death turned pale,
with the spear transfixed,
with plenteous drops of blood bedewed,
in the sepulchre entombed.

On the trunk of the tree beneath the crown stands, as the comprehensive programme of the whole, the strophe:

O crux frutex salvificus,
vivo fonte rigatus,
Cuius flos aromaticus,
fructus desideratus.

O cross, salutary stem,
by living fountain watered,
whose blossom is full of fragrance,
whose fruit is longed for.

Devotional reflections in prose then explain in the little book itself the contents of the 12 × 4 lines of verse; so that these recur as superscriptions to the forty-eight chapters of the tractate, while the contents of the whole form one continuous meditation on the history of the Lord's life, with specially detailed consideration of His sufferings on the cross. The ascetic value of these treatises is more considerable than the poetic value of the delicately playing rhymelets or the artistic value of the designing of the frontispiece, carried out after the manner of a genealogical tree: for the very clumsy and tasteless way in which this is executed in some of the manuscripts and editions of Bonaventura's works he himself cannot, of course, be held responsible.[1] At all events, the composition taken as a whole is not in point of originality of conception inferior to Hraban's "Praise of the Cross." As a creation of the mind inbreathed by the ardent spirit of devotion of the seraphic doctor and his "first companions," does the little book maintain a distinguished place among the products of the mystic literature of an edifying nature in the Middle Ages. The graphic-poetic artistic form herein employed, which is also here and there reproduced by later authors—as, *e.g.*, by Picus of Mirandola in his *Staurostichon*—suffers indeed from a certain externality akin to a play upon words, but nevertheless merits not from a religious æsthetic point of view to be so severely judged, as for example the carefully modelled drawings of figures with which, somewhat later, Raymond Lull thought of demonstrating to his disciples the mysteries of the natural, the logical, and the moral domain. Here too it is devotion to the Crucified, the bringing to bear of every single element of poetic and rhetorical diction upon the Divine-human centre and crown of all Christian consciousness alone, which determines the relative value of the whole, and is in a position to make amends to a certain extent for the presence therein of an element foreign to our modern views and tastes.

We shall contemplate in the last place the purely poetic forms of the artistic objectivising and glorification devoted to the cross.

The POETRY OF THE CROSS of the Middle Ages forms too an exceedingly interesting domain, a domain including in

[1] Comp., *e.g.*, the illustration prefixed to the said tractate (*Lignum Vitæ*, pp. 423—432) in the Lyons edn. of Bonaventura's works, i. p. 423; similar, though somewhat better, that in the Venice edn. (Venet. 1754, tom. v., p. 393). On two ancient illustrations in a MS. of the Psalter in the Brit. Museum (*Cod. Arundel.* 83), comp. Piper, *Ev. Kal.*, 1863, S. 87 f., who gives here a brief analysis and characterisation of the tractate.

itself no small diversity of particular forms, and presenting within the same many an art product of permanent worth. We do not disconnect the contemplation of it from that of the graphic and plastic branches of art directed to the same end, for this reason only, that it appears on many points to present an exact analogy to these in their peculiar features; and because its separation from them by devoting to it a special chapter would not render sufficiently apparent the close interchange of operation which, as already has been shown in the remarks upon the graphically illustrated Latin poetry of the cross, and as will be further evident from the remarks on the passion plays, exists between some of its characteristic forms and the corresponding modes of the plastic art activity.

The LYRICS OF THE CROSS, under which head we may range pretty nearly the whole extensive province of the composition of passion songs, together with the hymns or prayerful effusions having reference to the Holy Cross, its spiritual and miraculous gifts and properties, extends in its earliest productions far back into the time of early Church history. It is true the original type of all Christian hymn poetry, the hymn of Clement of Alexandria to the Redeemer, does not yet present the idea of the death of the cross in its central significance; it displays at best a certain nearer kinship with the hymnology of the cross in later times, in this respect, that he piles up a luxuriant abundance of the symbolically significant names and glorifying attributes of the Redeemer, with which on the one hand he recalls to our mind the Orphic hymns of classic antiquity (which possessed generally for him a typical character), with their combinations of manifold names, *e.g.*, of Zeus, of Aphrodite, etc., and on the other becomes himself a pattern for later poets or mystic devotional writers in the Church, who delight in similar allusive accumulations of names or attributes of God, of the holy Virgin, of Christ, and more especially of Christ crucified.[1]

So, *e.g.*, Hrabanus Maurus at the beginning of the poem before spoken of. *De laudibus S. Crucis* (Fig. 1), where altogether there are combined sixty-six

But several early Christian Greek poets of the period immediately succeeding Clement already afford contributions to the lyric glorification of the Redeemer's passion or of His cross. As the earliest indeed must we regard the unknown author of that prophecy of Christ's advent in acrostic hexameters, placed in the mouth of the Erythræan sibyl—a prophecy which Constantine the Great, so early as the time of the Council of Nicæa, adduced in his address to the assembled fathers as a marvellous testimony for revealed truth, and whose thirty-four verses represent by their initial letters the names, "Jesus Christ, Son of God, Saviour, Cross."[1] At some distance follows Gregory Nazianzen with some of his poems, e.g., a hymn to Christ on the Paschal festival, a "driving away of the evil one (through the cross) and a calling upon Christ;"[2] later, in the seventh century, the patriarch Sophronius of Jerusalem with his hymn, "to the glorious cross,"[3] celebrating the wonders of the cross belonging to the Church of the Holy Sepulchre—the cross carried away by Chosroes and restored again by Heraclius; as moreover several other Greek poets whose names are unknown.[4] The Syrian Church too of the fourth and fifth centuries, rich in song, yields important contributions towards the glorifying of our object, in its peculiarly luxuriant, abundantly figurative mode of representation; it celebrates the cross now as the heavenly ladder, now as a bridge for passing over into the heavenly kingdom, now as a rudder for life's little bark, etc. The highest soaring and most daring flight in this order of poetry is made by Cyrillonas in his poetic "homilies on the Paschal festival," in which the cross is lauded as, *inter alia*, the all-closing bar opened by Christ, the key of the kingdom of heaven and of the graves, the mill grinding the precious wheat

encomiastic names of Jesus; nineteen more than Pope Damasus, for instance, had combined in one of his *carmina*.

[1] 'Ι. Χ. Θ. Υ. Σ. Σ. (= Ἰχθύς Σταυρός.) Vid. *Constantini Orat. ad Sanctor. Cœtum*, c. 18 in *Eusebii scripta histor.*; and comp. *Orac. Sibyll.*, viii. 217 sqq.

[2] Ἀποτροπὴ τοῦ Πονηροῦ καὶ τοῦ Χριστοῦ ἐπίκλησις, Carmin. var., No. 21, in *Opp. Greg. Naz.*, ed. Colon. 1690, t. ii. p. 94. Comp. Carm. 61 ad Nemesium.

[3] Εἰς τὸν τίμιον σταυρόν, in Daniel, *Thes. Hymnolog.*, iii. 36.

[4] See, e.g., Daniel, *as before*, p. 134, Τροπάρια. *Ibid.*, Πρὸς Χριστὸν σταυρωθέντα.

of the body of Christ, the high-towering vine bearing the sweet cluster Christ, the sacred altar of the nations.[1] To an offensive degree of turgidity are these laudations of the cross carried in the homilies of Isaac of Antioch, on Adam and Christ, on Christ and the two malefactors, on virginity as the fruit of the cross. "Christ," it is here said, *inter alia*, " had ascended the cross and bore us anew, in order that the dragon might not bite us; up upon the wood he laid His young ones, that they might not be trampled by the foxes. . . . . Dying, He bowed Himself in pains, and bore us upon the cypress tree, in order that the basilisk might not destroy us. As the stork upon the summit of the cedar made He His nest far away from the serpent, ... the crown of thorns upon His head placed He as a wall around His nest; He gathered therein the nations, whom He had borne afresh by His sufferings, that they might remain in quiet, and that the hawk might not force his way to them to rend them," and so forth.[2] The LATIN POETRY OF THE WEST has not indeed preserved itself entirely free from similar departures from the standard of good taste, yet its abundance of noble and sterling products of this nature is relatively much larger. Its productiveness in this domain moreover extends from the times of Ambrose and Prudentius through all the centuries up to the time of the Reformation. From a period so early as the fourth and fifth centuries a few not unimportant contributions are to be specified: the Ambrosian Easter Hymn *Ad cœnam agni providi*, not indeed composed by the celebrated Bishop of Milan, but yet at any rate belonging to the most ancient of the so-called Ambrosian hymns;[3] several Passion Hymns and Easter Hymns of Prudentius, and amongst these the Quadriagesimal Hymn *Cultor Dei memento*, of which the laudation of the

---

[1] G. Bickell, *Ausgewählte Gedichte syrischer Kirchenväter, Cyrillonas*, etc., (Kempten, 1872), S. 37 ff., 46 ff. Comp. Zingerle, "Proben syrischer Hymnologie," *Tüb. Theol. Quartalschr.*, 1873. iii., espec. S. 473.

[2] Zingerle, "Ueber und aus Reden von zwei syrischen Kirchenvätern über das Leiden Jesu." *Tüb. Theol. Quartalschr.*, 1870, i. S. 92 ff.

[3] Only four of the so-called *Hymni Ambrosiani* were composed by Ambrose himself. See A. Ebert, *Gesch. der christlich-lateinischen Literatur*, i. 171 f.

demon-expelling operation of the symbol of the cross has been already dwelt upon by us; several of the same kind by Sedulius, as, *Hymnum dicamus Domino*, as also *Rex æterne, Domine*, and others; several poems by Paulinus of Nola, at the same time active for the glorifying of the cross in the domain of architecture, sculpture, and painting; also the hymn usually ascribed to Cyprian, but in reality proceeding from the pen of his contemporary Paulinus, "of Passover or the Cross," in sixty-nine hexameters, as well as another hexameter poem, *De passione Christi* ("Quisquis ades, mediique subis in limine templi," etc.), current under the name of Lactantius, but which can only be of considerably later origin; not less the epigram "upon the Holy Cross," by the African grammarian Calbulus, about the year 500, and so forth.[1] Its time of splendour is celebrated by the earlier Latin hymnology during the second half of the sixth century in the compositions of Gregory the Great (*Rex Christe, factor omnium*, and *Lignum crucis mirabile*—the latter a song for the celebration of the festival of "the Invention of the Cross"), and still more in those of VENANTIUS FORTUNATUS, Bishop of Poitiers († about 600). This latter merits above all other poets of earlier western Christendom to be designated simply the Singer of the Cross. His pious intercourse with the Thuringian princess and Frankish queen Radegonde (widow of Clotaire I.), foundress and abbess of the cloister of the Holy Cross near Poitiers, inspired him with various songs of praise for the emblem and instrument of redemption, songs which belong to the most glorious products of spiritual composition of any age. Partly too may these have been occasioned by the present of a relic consisting of a fragment of the True Cross, sent by the emperor Justin II. to Radegonde, for which Fortunatus was charged to compose a lengthy poetical epistle of thanksgiving.[2] At any rate they are of incomparable beauty, and this indeed is the case not only with the two Passion hymns,

---

[1] Ebert, S. 413. Augusti (*Denkw*. ii. 135) and Stockbauer (189 f.) ascribe the poem *De pass. Christi* to Venantius Fortunatus.

[2] So conjectured, not without probability, by Ebert, S. 509.

especially well known, and spread far and wide by later hymnals, *Pangue lingua gloriosi* and *Vexilla regis prodeunt*, but also with the morning song *Crux fidelis, inter omnis* (intended for recitation at morning prayer, after the *Benedicamus*, the seven-lined strophes alternating with " Crux fidelis," and closing with " Dulce lignum " as a refrain), as finally with the glorious distichs " upon the cross of the Lord," *Crux benedicta nitet*, etc., in which the conception of the cross as the Tree of Life, which runs through all these songs, attains its fairest and most touching expression :

" Thou shinest, hallowed Cross, whereon Christ did hang in the flesh,
And in His own blood our wounds healed.

Mild in pitying love became He an offering for sinners ;
Holy Lamb, Thou snatchedst us out of the jaws of the wolf.

Here with pierced hand redeems He the world from destruction,
Bars in His own death, gracious, to death itself the way.

To this with bloody nails was fixed the hand
Which Peter from death, Paul from transgressions drew forth.

Wondrous fruitfulness ! O thou sweet, glorious tree of the cross !
Fruit such as none else e'er bore, bears thy deep-laden bough.

Again from the scent of the fruit arises revived the departed,
Returns from the dark grave to life again restored.

None smites the heat beneath the loved shade of the cross,
Nor moon by night, nor yet by day the sun.

Shining, stand'st thou planted beside life's flowing waters,
Spreadst, with flowers adorned, kindly thy leaf crown.

Between thine arms hangs clinging the vine-stock,
Which yields forth the wine most precious, darkling with hue of crimson."

Each following century has its poetry of the cross of greater or lesser significance to display. To· the eighth belongs Bonifacius, who, in his acrostic hexameters entitled *Ænigmata*, describes the principal virtues of the Christian as ten golden apples, growing upon the stem of the cross of Christ as the true Tree of Life, and opposes to these the ten vices as fruits of the fatal tree of pestilence of which Adam once ate. To the ninth century belongs—in addition to Hraban's artistic composition before referred to, as moreover

[1] From the German rendering of Pachtler, in Bässler, *Auswahl altchristl. Lieder* (Berlin, 1858), S. 64.

some single hymns of Theodulf of Orleans († 821)—a series of distichtic poems of Scotus Erigena, versified prayers, paræneses or lyric descriptions, sometimes having reference to the cross, sometimes to the Crucified One Himself, His Descent into Hades, His Resurrection, and Ascension, in many of their parts of no small poetic value; so that the gifted precursor of the later scholastic and mystic speculation takes, by virtue of these compositions, a position not altogether subordinate among the intellectual poets of the Middle Ages.[1] For the close of the tenth and beginning of the eleventh century we may mention Fulbert of Chartres, one of the most influential of the immediate precursors, or rather founders, of the scholastic tendency of thought († 1028), among whose works there exists a poem in hexameters, not without value, "De s. cruce."[2] In the eleventh century our order of poetry is further represented by Peter Damiano († 1072) in some of his *Carmina*;[3] in the twelfth, pre-eminently by St. Bernard with his seven hymn-prayers, transfused with ardent love, to the limbs of Christ's body, which have been translated into German by Paul Gerhardt, as also Adam de St. Victor, author of the hymn *Laudes crucis attollamus;* in the thirteenth, Bonaventura with his glorious "song of praise (*Laudismus*) of the Holy Cross:" *Recordare sanctæ crucis*, his brief but fervent *horæ*, or short prayers for the canonical hours, on the passion of the Lord and the pangs of Mary, as also several other highly poetic glorifications of our object, which—apart from his *Lignum vitæ*, of which we have before treated—he has left behind him; about the beginning of the fourteenth, Jacoponus, the singer of the *Stabat mater*, or the sequence of the seven pangs of the blessed Virgin ; further on, in the fourteenth and fifteenth centuries, also a succession of more or less well-known composers of sequences and hymns, whose passion-songs form important and in many cases exceedingly affecting

---

[1] A further examination is devoted to his merits with respect to this class of poetry in Appendix VIII.

[2] His hexameter *Carm.* 12, *de S. Cruce*, we give in Appendix VIII.

[3] Comp. *Petr. Dam. opp.*, ed. Paris, 1642, tom. iv., p. 6 sq.

accompaniments to the passion-pieces of the contemporary painters. Yet close to the very edge of the expiring Middle Ages, Sebastian Brant composed, under the influence of the newly revived classical science and art, his "wreathlet of roses, plaited out of the flowers of the life and sufferings of Jesus, and entwined with blood-red roses of compassion," fifty verses in Sapphic metre, to which—spite of the to some extent word-playing and toying nature of their contents— an independent poetic aspiration cannot by any means be denied.[1] Truly beautiful and touching also is the ode "On the Cross of Christ" (*Crux ave, præsignis arbor*) of Jacob Montanus of Spires, whose life extended even to the age of the Reformation.

In addition to this copious abundance of lyric elegiac— partly also epigrammatic or didactic—glorifications of the Cross, there early arose a not less considerable number and diversity of epic compositions. The epic poetry of the cross coincides essentially just as much with the legendary compositions touching the Tree of Life, as does its lyric poetry with the hymn poetry of the Passion. Long even before Venantius Fortunatus sang his magnificent songs of praise to the cross as the resplendent Tree of Life laden with precious fruits, were the germs of that legend-poetry of the wood of the cross, so luxuriantly developed in the later Middle Ages, already present. Their earliest traces are lost in the Gnostic circles of the second century of our æra. The apocryphal Gospel of Nicodemus, unquestionably influenced by the speculations of this circle, in its second part, which describes with true poetic boldness of conception Christ's descent to Hades, not only places the redemption by the cross in significant antitypical opposition to the once deadly operation

---

[1] See the same in Wackernagel, *Das deutsche Kirchenlied*, i. S. 252. In the same work, S. 226 ff., will be found Sebastian Brant's "*Rosarium ex floribus vitæ passionisque domini nostri J. Christi consertum,*" etc. etc., as also in great part the other hymns of the Middle Ages mentioned by us. Those omitted by him will generally be found in the collections of Daniel or Mone. For a worthy translation of many of the most celebrated among them, see the Mediæval Hymns and Sequences of Dr. John Mason Neale, Lond., 1851.

of the Tree of Knowledge in Paradise—"Come with me," says the Lord as He leads forth Adam out of the prison, "all ye who have died through the wood which this man hath touched: all of you I make alive again by the wood of the cross," etc.—but it has also already the tradition of the Tree of Life in Paradise, and of the "oil of compassion" trickling down from the same. For this oil, so it goes on to relate, the patriarch Adam when he had fallen sick sent his son Seth in vain to the gate of Paradise; the latter here received from the Archangel Michael, instead of the desired miraculous remedy, a consoling prophecy in relation to Christ the Son of God, who after 5500 years should come down to earth, and who would then anoint and heal the suffering father of mankind with the desired oil. In connection with this ingenious legend, which lies before us in later apocryphal documents wrought up in a form yet somewhat more complicated, there arise at an early period also some other legendary traditions, developed out of the antitypical parallels of Adam and Christ, or of the fall and redemption (Rom. v. 12 ff.) So especially the alleged fact of Adam's being buried on Golgotha, at the place over which the cross of Christ was raised,—a tradition of Jewish origin, already mentioned by Origen, and later by Athanasius, Epiphanius, Chrysostom, and others, which obtained a footing far and wide in the Eastern Church literature and art-tradition of antiquity and the Middle Ages, as also—spite of the adverse judgment pronounced upon it by Jerome[1]—with many authors of the West. The same also was the case with the tradition, attaching itself still more immediately to the primitive Christian typology of the Tree of Life, of the descent of the wood of the cross from the Tree of Knowledge; thus of the

---

[1] *Hieronymus in Matt.* xxvii. 33; *in Eph.* v. 14. Comp. Oreg., *Tract.* 35 *in Matt.* (27); Athanas., *Serm. in pass. et crucem Domini*, c. 12; Epiphan., *Hær.*, 46, 5; Chrysost, *Hom.* 85 *in Joann.* (19, 17). See in general: Piper "Adams Grab auf Golgatha," *Ev. Kal.*, 1861, S. 17 ff., and the illustration there given, of a remarkable artistic representation of the cross on Golgotha, to which the head of Adam buried beneath is looking up, from an ivory tablet in the museum at Darmstadt.

fabrication of the instrument of salvation out of the very wood, in connection with which the first sin which wrought the ruin of the human race was perpetrated—a tradition first appearing as to its central thought in the "Anagogic meditations on the work of the six days" of Anastasius Sinaitica (about 650), and later zealously espoused and developed by western narrators of legends from the twelfth century downwards; first, Canon Lambert at St. Omer, about 1120; then Peter Comestor, 1170; Herrad of Landsperg, 1175; Gervasius of Tilbury, 1212; and Jacobus de Voragine, in the "Golden Legend," about 1280.[1] Principally out of these elements, but partly also out of mythically confused reminiscences of the discovery of the cross by Helena, and the exaltation of the cross by Heraclius and their accompanying wonders, as also finally out of echoes of Celtic or Germanic traditions concerning the Tree of the World (see above, p. 21), transplanted into a Christian soil, is the legendary material composed, which has grown especially from the time of the twelfth century into such luxuriant forms—a material wrought up, at first epically, but ultimately also dramatically, in the long series of legends of the cross-wood both in poetry and prose, from the Anglo-Saxon poets Caedmon (Kaedmon), and Kynewulf, to Calderon's "Sibyls of the East" and "Dispute of the Trees about the Kingship." The earliest and simplest of the products belonging to this order are (like the last, which for the most part draw out of an abundant store, and dispose with particular freedom of the material), the most poetically valuable. Between the two extremes lies much that is thoroughly tasteless, wildly fantastic, displeasing from its clumsiness of form, affording in general as little satisfaction to the æsthetic as to the religious sense. In Caedmon's Genesis, the profound "prelude of Milton's epos at the threshold of English literature," as it has been fittingly termed,[2] the idea of the Tree of Knowledge, planted by Christ in Paradise, as type or progenitor of the delivering tree of the Cross, stands forth as yet simply and distinctly,

[1] This latter popularised by Longfellow. [2] Carrière, *Die Kunst*, etc., iii. 2, S. 143

in pristine freshness and purity, from among the multitude of apocryphal additions of later times. The first-born Son of God Himself relates :

> "I had placed there in Paradise a new
> fruit-tree with branches, so that apples bore
> the fruit-tree's boughs : and ye both ate there
> the glittering fruit, as the malignant one bade you,
> the minister of hell . . . .
> Then I was grieved, that the work of my hands
> should endure the fetters of the prison house.
> . . . . It was for you
> when me upon the cross' stem the warriors pierced
> with spears upon the gallows and me that youth did thrust,
> and I came upwards to the eternal gladness
> to the holy Lord, into the heavenly kingdom," etc.[1]

In Kynewulf's "Christ" too are to be found remarkable echoes of the tradition of the cross-tree, in its earliest and simplest form. The cross appears in this glorified to the ideal form of the king of all the trees of field and forest, the life-diffusing world-tree, like the ash Yggdrasill. The description of the scene already alluded to by Caedmon, how all the other trees begin to weep around this their king, the tree of the cross, presents glorious traits which remind us of the ancient Germanic legends of Baldur. "The cross of our Lord stands exalted before all peoples, the shining token, the beaming tree, bedewed with blood, the pure dropping blood of the King of heaven ; its bright radiance it sheds upon all creation," etc.

> "Yea the trees also knew, who created them with blossoms,
> many and not few : when the mighty God
> upon one of them was lifted, where for the salvation
> of the dwellers upon earth he endured torments full severe,
> a death full of suffering for the people's weal.
> Then stood with bloody tears of the trees many a one
> rolling down beneath the sky red and thick :
> their sap was turned to blood. This they cannot tell,
> the farsighted dwellers upon earth,
> how many *there* were moved, which yet could not feel."[2]

Other beautiful renderings of the same legendary material

---
[1] Grein, *Dichtungen der Angelsachsen*, etc., i. 143 f. (out of "Christ and Satan," the so-called second book of Caedmon).

[2] Grein, i. 180 f. Comp. also Fr. Hammerich, *die älteste christliche Epik der Angelsachsen*, etc. (From the Danish of Michelsen.) Gütersloh, 1874. S. 87.

are afforded by *Scò hâlge rôd* ("The Holy Cross"), the prophetic visionary composition of an unknown Anglo-Saxon monk of Caedmon's school—a composition which introduces the sacred wood of the cross, the glorious tree of victory itself as speaking, and makes it relate how it was not only a silent witness of the Passion, but also a deeply feeling sharer of the same. "I trembled, but the Lord embraced me; yet I was not permitted to bow me to the earth, to fall into earth's bosom, but I must stand fast. As a cross was I raised; I lifted up the rich King, the Lord of heaven, I might not bend. They pierced me with dark nails, they mocked us both together. I was entirely covered with blood, shed out of the side of the man after he had breathed out his spirit," etc.[1]—Of the Christian Epic poets in the sphere of Old High German literature, Otfried of Weissenburg belongs to our province, who in the beginning of the fifth book of his "Krist" glorifies the salutary token of victory in the cross with traits of partially the same nature as those of his Anglo-Saxon predecessors. But into many also of the most fruitful and abundantly cultivated domains of *secular* legendary lore of the Romance and German Middle Ages has the cross-legend forced its luxuriantly prolific shoots. Even if we should exclude the Niebulungen Sagè—although even the red cross which Krimbild marks upon the cloak of Siegfried in order to point out the one vulnerable place in his back, affords a significant note of accord—yet we surely at any rate find in the legend of the Holy Grail an offshoot from the legend of the wood of the cross: that blood-red, passing fragrant corallite, or grail-stone, which Wolfram of Eschenbach—in the Parcival—characterises as the "food-bestower" of the Templars (*Templeisen*) of Salvatierra, and the demon-expelling power of which is in old authors expressly derived from the circumstance that it, the red corallite, often exists in the form of a cross.[2] In the German Friedrichsagè[3] two trees

---

[1] Grein, ii. 140 ff.; comp. Jos. Bach, *Dogmengesch. des Mittelalters*, i. 84 f.
[2] So the Liber de natura rerum cited by Vincentius of Beauvais in the *Speculum naturale*, viii. c. 57.
[3] The legend of the German emperor FREDERICK (Frederick II. 1215—1250),

play an important part, which are unmistakably derived from
the cycle of legends concerning the wood of the cross : the
pitiful dry tree which grows in the Holy Land, and is
called the tree of victory; and the ash-tree upon which the
emperor, after he has come down from the mountain, hangs
his shield while he musters his summoned host (*heriban*, levy
of all capable of bearing arms in defence of the country)
around him for the great decisive conflict. Dante's Divine
Comedy too glorifies the two trees of Paradise. The poet
under the guidance of Virgil finds the Tree of Life in the sixth
circle of the mountain of Purgatory, where the souls of the
penitents, under the influence of the oft-repeated cry, " Blessed
are they that hunger and thirst after righteousness," in self-
consuming longing ever encompass the sweetly fragrant
heavenly food of the fruits of this tree, because, as they exclaim:

"because for the tree *that* impulse fires us,
which brought Christ gladly thither to the cross,
on which his precious blood our shame atoned."

As a sublime heavenly counterpart to this tree of the mount
of purification, which affords to those surrounding it the
agonising raptures of Tantalus, there then appears in Paradise
that gigantic and brilliant cross of radiance in the sphere of
Mars, which is formed by the blissful spirits of those who
fought and fell in the Crusades for the cause of Christ.[1]—
Among the numerous poetic products of the narrower circle
of the legends of the cross-tree, in which the sending of Seth
for the oil of compassion, the transplanting of a slip from
the Tree of Knowledge from Paradise to Jerusalem—where
accordingly the cross was framed from the trunk which grew
out of it,—also the building of Solomon's temple, the Sibylline
prophecies of the Queen of Sheba, and other similar fantastic
embellishments appear as of particular significance, does the

who was popularly believed to have been enclosed in the Kyffhäuser Mountain,
whence his return was earnestly looked for by the German people about the close
of the Middle Ages. This expectation may now be regarded as in some sense
realised by the establishment of the Protestant empire of the Hohenzollern, the
neighbours and kinsmen of the Hohenstaufen.

[1] *Parad.*, 14, 124 ff. ; comp. *Purgat.*, 22, 131 ff.; 23, 67 ; 24, 116 f.

Middle Low German poem (of the fourteenth or beginning of the fifteenth century), "*van deme holte des hilligen cruzes*," edited by E. Schröder, on account of its no slight artistic value, merit a place of special prominence.

There is also, finally, a DRAMATIC POESY OF THE CROSS, most closely allied to the Epic by the community of its material, but which certainly did not within the period of the Middle Ages ripen to such a fulness of important products as the other. The drama of the cross coincides essentially with the passion play—this lyrico-dramatic objectivising of the fundamental and central facts of salvation, closely allied to the liturgy of the mass, and originally held exclusively in the Church and the language of the Church, *i.e.*, in Latin—which only gradually from the time of the thirteenth century assumed a separate place as an independent act of the religious service of the Church, and, together with the plays on Corpus Christi day, in celebration of the miracle of Transubstantiation, became the principal form assumed by the spiritual drama. The legendary tradition of the descent of the wood of the cross upon Calvary from the trees of Paradise occupies, in these plays too, an important place. More particularly in the *Complaints of Mary*, or "Disputes between Mary and the Holy Cross," one of the earliest and simplest forms of the more serious order of spiritual drama, is this material handled for the most part with enthusiastic zeal and with telling effect. In one of the old English Complaints of Mary, edited by Morris, Mary accuses the cross of being a false tree; unjustly and altogether without reason had it destroyed the pure fruit of her womb, her sweet bird, with the deadly draught that only the children of Adam had to drink; whereas no stain of the guilt of Adam attached to her Son. "Cross, thou art my Son's cruel stepmother," cries she in her anguish, "so high hast thou hanged him that I cannot even kiss his feet! Cross, thou art my deadly foe; thou hast beaten my bird blue!"

> "Cros, þou holdest hym hiȝe on heiþe,
> Hys faire feet I may not kysse ;
> * * * *

Cros, I find þou art my fo,
My brid þou berist beten blo ;
Among þes folys frawdys."

To which *Sancta Crux* replies : "Lady, I owe to thee my honour; thy glorious fruit, which I now bear, makes me beam with red blood. Not for thee alone, no, to save the whole world, blossomed this fair flower in thee. . . . Christ's blood gave me baptism, when in red streams it spread itself over me, the tree fashioned of cypress and olive wood.

'Crystis blood ȝaf me bapteme
Bystreke I was with red streme,
Whan Jesu bled vpon a beme
Of ciprefse and Olyue.'

Thou wast crowned queen of heaven because of the child which thou hast borne. I shall one day appear as a bright relic at the day of judgment; then shall I take up my complaint for thy holy Son, on me innocent put to death." By such discourse is Mary reconciled to the cross ; she gives it a kiss, and henceforth manifests her love towards it.[1] Farther, elaborated dramatisings of the material under review, not merely confined to a colloquy like this, have also been mentioned in considerable numbers in the literature of the Passion Plays and Mysteries of the expiring Middle Ages. So in that Silesian passional of the fifteenth century recently edited by Birlinger and Crecelius, which represents Christ as dying on the same wood which was the instrument of Adam's sin ; in the French mystery of the same century, brought out by Jubinal, in which the sending of Seth, the son of Adam, to fetch the oil of compassion out of Paradise, appears also to form part of the representation, but with the peculiar modification that the consoling promise of Adam's eventual healing is given, not to Seth, but to Adam himself, and Seth, instead of the oil he had sought, takes with him out of Paradise a small branch from the Tree of Knowledge, with the direction

---

[1] Dispute between Mary and the Cross, in R. Morris, *Legends of the Holy Rood*, (Lond. 1871), Append. p. 197, 8. Comp. the somewhat more extended poem of the same nature from another MS., *ibid.*, pp. 131—149.

to plant the same upon his father's grave.[1] Similarly also in the Belgian mystery play of the seven joys of Mary (exhibited at Brussels in 1444), in which the incident of the planting of the branch of the Tree of Knowledge upon Adam's grave, in order that one day the healing and delivering wood of the cross might spring forth therefrom, is likewise brought prominently into the foreground.

As having attained to the true maturity of artistic completion, and being freed from the ineptitudes and incongruities attaching to it—especially of frequently burlesque additions and tasteless buffooneries, — and moreover as developed on the technical side in a satisfactory manner, does the Dramatic Poetry of the Cross appear only at a period considerably beyond the confines of the Middle Ages, in Calderon († 1687), the Shakspere of the spiritual drama. His "Sibyla del Orient" forms the most richly stored collection of the various legendary elements connected with this subject, for the purpose of transforming in the light of a genuine dramatic art the one whole formed out of them. Disposing freely and with genius of the apocryphal legendary lore, the poet takes as the central point of action a point somewhere between Adam and Christ, in the history of Solomon and of his intercourse with the "Prophetess of the East," the Queen of Sheba. Thus, looking back upon Paradise and forward upon Calvary, is developed the history of that salutary wondrous wood which, cedar, palm, and cypress at once, is recognised and adored by the wise prophetess as an image of the Holy Trinity, and as destined one day to be the instrument of salvation for all mankind; which—because it will not fit in into the building of Solomon's temple—must serve as a bridge over the brook Cedron, but even there too is recognised by the queenly possessor of the prophetic spirit, and now inspires her to make her glorious prediction with regard to the erection of the New Testament house of God, as also with regard to Christ, the "youth whose diadem is

[1] Birlinger and Crecelius, *Altdeutsche Neujahrsblätter für* 1874, Wiesbaden, 1874. Jubinal, *Mystères inédits du XVe siècle*, t. ii., p. 16 sqq. Freibe, *as before*.

woven out of reed and thorns, and in place of leafless roses is adorned with drops of his own blood." " Marvel not," she says to Solomon with regard to the wondrous triple wood,

> "that it to-day from thy
> Proud building is excluded,
> Since for a higher temple's use
> God it reserves and consecrates.
> O already it seems to me, I see
> How upon its neck doth cling
> Another and far fairer structure ;
> For life informs the building."[1]

In several others also of the *autos* or religious tragedies of Calderon does the legend of the Cross as the Tree of Life play a prominent part : so in the "Dispute of the Trees about the Kingship," in " Poison and Antidote," " Life a Dream," and " Orpheus." The legendary cycle, too, which has reference to the fate of the cross at the time of Chosru and Heraclius has received an independent moulding in one of his dramas, "The Elevation of the Cross." And, besides this, he has added in the " Devotion to the Cross" an entirely original composition—as to its material absolutely new, or at least appearing in the writings of no poet or author of note. Calderon, in consequence of all this, became the true hero of the dramatic poetry of the cross : he occupies the same towering, all-eclipsing position among the representatives of this poetic genre, as Venantius Fortunatus among the lyric poets of the cross. It is true some of his pieces, more especially that last named, are pervaded by a spirit of one-sided externalism in the religious devotion to the Christian symbol of salvation—an externalism suggesting to the mind the fetichism of the heathen—which can, as such, hardly be any longer termed Christian. And because of this his one-sidedness and of his errors, in which to a certain extent and in a somewhat different manner his great countryman and contemporary Lope also participates, shall we have occasion to return to him once more in the study of the post-Reformation age. Here it was a question, in the first place, only of

[1] From the German translation of Calderon by v. d. Malsburg. Comp. Carrière, *l. c.*, iv. 429 f.

rendering justice to his historic position, as forming the crowning close of the poetry of the cross-legends as this developed itself from the early Middle Ages, and more particularly as regards its assumption of the dramatic form. It was a question of rendering apparent the fact that in this domain of art too, as in all the others—that of music alone excepted, which does not within the space here under contemplation attain to any very high stage of development—the idea of the cross has called forth a considerable number of original creations, and even that it has very essentially contributed *immediately to the production and bringing to maturity* of the highest results which the *Christian art* of the Middle Ages *has been able in any province to achieve*, whether in those provinces before under review or in that we have just contemplated.

D. *THE AFTER-EXPERIENCE OF THE PAINS OF THE CROSS IN ASCETICISM.*

All the confessing and glorifying of the Christian symbol of salvation which has hitherto passed under notice starts primarily and essentially from the presupposition of the honour due to the same as a triumphant and widely prevailing power. It is the *gloria crucis*, to which we see rendered —sometimes with regard to the outward exertion of power proceeding from it, sometimes more with reference to the radiance streaming from it, and transforming the realm of the Church's devotional acts as of her artistic creations— the tribute of enthusiastic homage on the part of Christendom. But beside this *gloria crucis*, the *dolor* or *tristitia crucis* is not forgotten; only that, in harmony with the spirit of the Middle Ages, a sensuous experience, proving, or after-sensation of the very pains of the crucified Redeemer, rather than an inner and spiritual conception of them, is aimed at. It is not so much a lively presentation of, or sympathetic entering into, this suffering, as it is A DIRECT REPRODUCTION OF THE SAME IN ONE'S OWN BODY, which is sought by the ascetics of the Middle Ages with regard to the suffering of the Saviour on the cross. It is a comparatively rare thing for the authors of the monastic rules, the preachers, or ascetic writers, to rest content with enjoying a devout and profound self-absorption in the mystery of redemption by the method of silent meditation or contemplation,—to which category belongs, *e.g.*, a silent meditation of three days in the solitary cell upon the sufferings of Christ, prescribed by Gualbert of Vallombrosa to those newly received into his order (a sort of prelude to the "spiritual exercises" of the Jesuits); in like manner the saying of an Albertus Magnus, that half an hour of devout meditation upon the sufferings of the Lord would obtain more merit than a whole year of penance![1] The tendency truly conformed to the spirit of the age does not, in the ascetic domain, content itself with such more harmless mode of realising the nature of the Passion as belongs only to the sphere of inner conception. It demands a more palpable accomplishment of the entering into the communion of Christ's sufferings; it desires to see His wounds and sufferings as much as possible represented even externally in the body of the devout penitent.

The early fathers of Christian monasticism in the East, of the fourth and fifth centuries—Anthony, Hilarion, Macarius, etc.—as yet know evidently nothing of such rushing upon a sensuous-external conformity to the body of Jesus' sufferings, upon a grossly literal accomplishment of the "being crucified with Christ," or of the stigmatism (Gal. ii. 20, vi. 17). We read in Palladius, Ruffinus, Theodoret, Cassian, and other admirers of their ascetic deeds of heroism, much indeed about their fasting and watching, their living without shelter and in solitude, their self-mortification by means of wretched clothing, continuance in burning heat or severe frost, etc.; but of such violence done to the body as should serve to impress upon them externally the stripes and wounds of the suffering Redeemer there is no word. Even of the scourge there is made at first only a judicial executive use, for

[1] See the author's *Kritische Geschichte der Askese*, S. 314 f.

the chastising of disobedient subjects, in the community of these Egyptian or Syrian monastic fathers. Self-flagellation remains entirely foreign to the Eastern ascetic practice of the first six to seven centuries. The alleged proofs advanced from the writings of Nilus, a disciple of Chrysostom in the fifth century, or of John Climacus († 606), for its occasional occurrence at that early period, are wanting in all real demonstrative force.[1] Self-flagellation is an invention of western ascetics, a product of the Benedictine order in its later development, intent upon increasing the severity of its strict mode of life, as this begins only in what is properly the dark period of the Middle Ages, about the year 1000. It appears developed in the bosom of this order and in that of the Camaldulensian order about the middle of the eleventh century, in the time of Peter Damiano and Hildebrand, to a more than heroic degree of perfection in the systematic maltreatment of one's own body; to become in later times an exercise legally prescribed or at least recommended for the ascetic praxis of the greater number of the monastic orders, generally with a considerable relaxing of that unnatural excess of severity represented by the heroes of the scourge of the time of Hildebrand.

Even earlier than the rise of this principal form of self-mortification—which comes only incidentally under notice in connection with our subject—another form, akin to this, had been greatly practised on the part of western ascetics: a form in which the tendency to the real and immediate representation in the sphere of the bodily life comes forth with special distinctness. It is the terrible penance of self-crucifixion by means of a painfully wounding impression of the sign of the cross upon the back or other parts of the body, or else by the carrying about of heavy crosses of wood or metal, which wound the person by means of sharp nails, etc. We meet with this for the first time in the case of Radegonde († 587), the pious widow of the Frankish king, whose ardently enthusiastic devotion to the cross showed itself productive,

---

[1] *Ibid.*, S. 38 f.

not only in the sphere of art and poetry, by calling forth creations of abiding value—such as more particularly the glorious hymns of Fortunatus—but also in that of ascetic practice. She is said to have sought, by means of placing a brazen cross heated over glowing coals upon different parts of her body, in one of her meditations upon the Passion, immediately to realise to herself the pain of the Crucified. The example thereby afforded did not, it is true, find so many imitators as the acts of intrepidity on the part of the heroes of the scourge before referred to; yet the history of monasticism and of the saints embraces in every successive century some single instances of a like practice of mortification. So that of the English abbess, the princess Editha, contemporary with Dunstan in the tenth century, who countless times scratched the symbol of the cross upon her forehead with large sharp nails; that of the Dominican prior, Volvandus or Volandus of Strasburg († after 1230), who in the same manner drew it upon his breast; but above all that of Suso, the most rapt and ardently loving of all the mystics of the preaching order († 1365), who, in the days in which he still treated his body with unsparing severity, was not content with graving, by means of his sharp writing-style, the letters I H S upon his breast, near to the heart, but was wont besides to hang a wooden cross of a foot in length, and of proportionate breadth, transfixed with thirty pointed nails, upon his shoulders, and by the frequent pressing of the many sharp points (daily twice or three times, sometimes oftener) into his flesh, to "administer discipline to himself"—an exercise which he acknowledges having continued during a period of eight years.[1] Of the practice, too, of carrying heavy wooden crosses, which one occasionally meets with in ecclesiastical antiquity as a more harmless custom of essentially symbolical significance—*e.g.*, among those Egyptian hermits whose coming forth with such burdens upon their shoulders was, according to Cassian, only ridiculed, not regarded with de-

---

[1] Further details in the history above cited, S. 65 f.

vout admiration[1]—does the impulse of sickly or half-crazed ascetics of the Middle Ages, an impulse ever fertile in the invention of new tortures, make a real mortification of the body, and one inflicting pain, even to the forcing of blood. To this do penitent pilgrims in particular not seldom submit themselves, whether in consequence of a penance expressly enjoined upon them, as the Bohemian abbot Bozethecus of Sasowa (about 1086), or voluntarily, as the Byzantine Nicholas Peregrinus about 1090, or Raymond Palmarius, of Piacenza († 1200).[2] Even in the age of the Reformation, it is said that Peter of Alcantara, the Franciscan saint († 1562), bore up a high and steep mountain an excessively heavy cross formed of beams, in order to plant the same at its summit, whereby he caused, not only his sweat, but, through the wearing of a rough garment of Cilician goat's hair next his skin, his blood too to trickle down in streams. The kindred order of barefooted Carmelites, the creation of Theresa and John of the Cross, is said to have made the dragging about of such heavy crosses, combined also with a crowning with thorns and imposing of flagellations upon oneself, a special form of penance for its members, and to have characterised the act (usually performed in the refectory of the monastery in presence of the assembled occupants) by the name of *Ecce homo*.[3] Without making use of this name, but in reality aiming at the same result, namely, the most complete and all-sided representation possible of Jesus as the Man of Sorrows, a depicting of the Passion in a terrible living form, did the flagellants also proceed—not only the isolated hermits, in accordance with the precepts of Romuald and Peter Damiano, but also those socially united in the great pilgrimages of the fourteenth and fifteenth centuries. The holding up of the hands crosswise

---

[1] Cassian, *Collat. Petr.*, viii. 3.

[2] To the instances mentioned in the author's *Gesch. der Ask.*, S. 70, add that of the abbot Bozethecus, who, at the command of the bishop of Prague, had prepared for him, and bore on his shoulders to Rome, a crucifix as broad and as long as himself. Comp. *Mon. Germ. Scr.*, t. ix., p. 149 sqq.

[3] *Gesch. der Askese*, as above.

during repeated intoning of the penitential psalms, thus the recitation of psalms in the posture of a cross (after the example of Moses, Exod. xvii.) ; further, recitation of psalms with frequent metanœas or genuflexions, *i.e.*, prostrations to the ground ; finally, psalm recitations, or rather psalter recitations (the singing through, and indeed the repeated singing through of the whole psalter), accompanied by the simultaneous infliction upon oneself of the most numerous and most painful strokes of the lash : these three forms of undergoing penance, pursued alternately with inexhaustible zeal and astonishing endurance, form the masterpieces of ascetic dexterity and valour for which Dominicus the Mail-Clad became celebrated. The crosswise spreading out of the arms in connection with a penitential smiting of the breast ; a scourging even to blood with implements of torture whose cords bore—crosswise driven through their thick end-knots—sharp and long spikes ; finally, prostration to the ground with arms outspread crosswise, accompanied with the singing of the verse,

"Jhesus der wart gelabt mit gallen,
Des süllen wir an ein criuze vallen,"

form moreover the characteristically prominent manipulations of the flagellant hosts of the time of pestilence and famine, 1349-1350, on account of which these were named "Cross-brethren" or "Cross-flagellants" (*Crucifratres, Cruciflagellatores*). This sensuously copying representation or imitation of the sufferings of the Crucified One is, in the one case as in the other, maintained as the highest standard of conception by which the form and mode of performing penance can be regulated in detail. Here too, it is customs originally harmless, essentially only of figurative import, and entirely unadapted for producing acute pain, much less the laceration of the body—like the above-mentioned practice of standing in the attitude of the cross, with outstretched hands in penance (the *stare ad crucem*), or that of taking one's food at the cross by way of punishment (at the pillory-cross in the court of the monastery, the *comedere ad crucem*), or that of the smiting of the breast crosswise, as a sign of violent penitential grief (the cross-formed στερνοτυπία, also *palmata* or *pectoris tunsio*)—customs occurring only in the earlier stages of development of the western monastic discipline, from which those more violent and excentric forms of the sensuous imitation and representation of the pain of the Redeemer on the cross have gradually been developed.[1]

The passionate endeavour after a sensuous conformity to the Redeemer's body of crucifixion appears as having attained to the form of most acute disease, although of a disease by no means transitory, but rather continuing as an epidemic for more than six centuries in several communities of the Romish Church, in the five wounds of St. Francis and the members of his order who emulated him, as also of the Dominicans and other monastic societies. STIGMATISATION, the most systematic and favourite form of sensuous imitation of the passion of Christ, sprung from a stupidly literal apprehension of Gal. vi. 17, and consisting of the production of four bleeding prints of the nails upon the hands and feet as well as a still greater wound in the side of the ascetic, is regarded either as a supranaturally wrought fruit and consequence of the ascetic endeavour, or as a special element in this endeavour itself, *i.e.*, as a spontaneous result or natural effect of the effort after more perfect conformity to the body of Christ's sufferings. In the former case it is looked at in the light of a miraculous reward of grace, with which the Saviour crowns the constant longing for perfect conformity to the effects of His passion, as a charisma similar to those raptures or ecstatic conditions of another kind frequently related in the legendary history of the saints, namely, visions, miraculous experiences of hearing, taste, or smell, mystic exaltations, floatings in the air, phenomena of flying, etc.; or even akin to the grace of tears, this effect of continued penitent contemplation of the blessed mystery of Christ's wounds, already playing an important part in the life of the early monastic patriarchs of the East.[2] To this view of the

[1] *Gesch. der Ask.*, S. 51 ff., 67 ff., 261 ff.
[2] *Ibid.*, S. 354 ff. Comp. W. Preger, *Geschichte der deutschen Mystik im Mittelalter*, i. 55 ff., 60 ff.

phenomenon as a charisma, exclusively reckoned orthodox in the Romish Church, the Protestant theory which would explain it from natural causes, and would thus relegate it to the province of the ascetic action itself, is in irreconcilable antagonism only when it asserts a violent infliction of the wounds by the hand of the ascetic himself, thus—as again not long ago by Virchow in his discussion of the case of Louisa Lateau— presupposes a deliberate act of fraud, whether on the part of the stigmatised person himself or on that of the directing and controlling spiritual advisers or friends.[1] This rationalistic, or rather materialistic, explaining away even of the last remains of a supernatural character belonging to this phenomenon has it is true an important point of support in the fact of frequent unmaskings of alleged cases of stigmatisation as the acts of hypocritical impostors,—a circumstance of so much the greater import from the fact that such cases of pseudo-stigmatisation or of impositions of a like kind are equally ancient, and some of them even more ancient, than the fact belonging to the last years of St. Francis, typically prescriptive and preparatory to those stigmatisations alleged to be genuine. Already two generations before this fact Archbishop Eustathius of Thessalonica († 1194), in accordance with his sober and almost evangelical reformational zeal against the senseless ascetic extravagances of the monks of Mount Athos in his time, censures too the hypocritical juggling of the same after the fashion of dervishes or fakeers, *e.g.*, the scratching of themselves with knives, nails, or files, smearing of the body (on the edge of the coat of mail, rings or chains surrounding it) with blood, and other similar abuses.[2] A stigmatisation, strictly so termed, after the manner of that of St. Francis, is said to have been feigned by a nun at Zell near Constance, about the time of the opening of the Council of Constance;[3] whilst a century later the

---

[1] Virchow, *Ueber Wunder* (address at the Breslau assembly of Natural Philosophers, Sept. 1874), S. 11.

[2] Observations of Eustathius of Thessalonica on the Monastic Estate. From the Greek (into German) by G. L. F. Tafel (Berlin, 1847), S. 30 f.

[3] [Assembled Nov. 1, 1414.]

Dominicans at Bern sought by means of deception, and at the same time with the employment of violence, to make a stigmatised person of a poor imbecile tailor. At a yet later period there arise, sometimes among the Jesuits, sometimes among the Carmelites, sometimes among the members of other orders, similar instances of a cruel use made of infatuated penitents as the victims of a pretendedly miraculous marking with the five stigmas. As regards the means too employed in connection with such acts of deception, history furnishes many particulars. Of stigmatisations "with the rouge-box," the noble Spanish mystic Luis de Leon († 1591) has to tell us, as a form of hypocrisy practised by monks and nuns in his day. The demoniacal nun Eustochio, at Padua, is said to have employed needles for the piercing of her hands and feet, and a sword for causing the wound in her side. A little bottle filled with blood, kept concealed in the bed, formed for the pseudo-stigmatised Angela Hupe, of Boke in Westphalia, who was afterwards detected, the means of effecting the bleedings in her hands and feet, given out as miraculous, etc.[1] Nevertheless an attempt at tracing back *all* the cases of stigmatisation occurring in the history of the monks and saints, from eighty to a hundred in number, from the time of St. Francis († 1226), to a grosser or more refined form of deception of the characteristic nature above instanced, can hardly prove successful. Chloride of iron and supho-cyanide of potassium—the means lately recommended by a Swiss professor of chemistry as specially adapted for producing intense "bleedings or blood-sweating" on any part of the body at pleasure—could hardly have been known or accessible to a single one of those bearers of the stigmas who are still living, amounting according to the statements of chaplain P. Majunke to the number of at least eight or ten.[2] With regard to the

---

[1] See the author's paper "Louise Lateau, die belgische Stigmatisirte," in the *Beweis des Glaubens*, 1875, S. 8, and the proofs there given.

[2] Majunke ("Louise Lateau, ihr Wunderleben," etc. Berlin, 1874, S. 102 ff.) mentions, after the enumeration of a greater number of other female bearers of the stigmas during the nineteenth century (who are now dead), as *perhaps* still

numerous representatives of this strange phenomenon who lived at the time when alchemy was still flourishing, or even earlier, the suspicion of the application of such modern chemical products is of course inadmissible. But, apart from this, the personal character of a Francis, a Katerina of Siena, a Coleta, a Lidwina, a Mary of Mörl, and generally of most of the persons adduced as cases in point, absolutely precludes the supposition of a gross fraud, such as a scratching or tearing open of the wounds repeated in cold blood every Friday. A violent producing of the wounds on the part of the stigmatised person might in itself and at their first appearing, in a moment of sacred frenzy or in the blissful agony of a transport superinduced by an excess of the intensive contemplation of the passion, perhaps not be irreconcilable with the religious-ethical character of these persons. But never can the charge of deliberately applying artificial means for effecting the constant maintenance or regular periodical recurrence of the bleeding of their stigmatic wounds be brought home against them. This constant or periodical recurrence of the bleeding or smarting of their wound-prints, especially on a Friday, related as characteristic with regard to the majority of those thus stigmatised, demands some other explanation than that offered by the supposition of a direct and systematically practised self-infliction. And in reality all that is reported with regard to the most important symptoms in the different bearers of these marks accords at least equally well, if not far better, with the psychico-pathological explanation which at once and most naturally presents itself—an explanation which sees in the phenomenon a diseased condition of body superinduced

living (?), Crescentia Nierklutsch in the Tyrol, and Dorothea Visser at Gendringen in Holland ; farther, as certainly still living, Palma of Oria in Naples, Helena of Bolavatta in India, Vitaline Gagnon in Canada; to which he adds the names of three others, less known (at Bordeaux, at Grenoble, and at San Francisco). To these would the case of the Bohemian Franziska Pschera at Scheibenradisch, lately published in the Austrian papers, naturally form an addition. On the other hand, Dorothea Visser is spoken of by Majunke himself in the second edn. of his work (S. 117) as not really presenting a genuine case of stigmatisation, while doubts are expressed by him also with regard to Palma of Oria.

by an extraordinary excitement of the emotions of the soul, and manifesting itself also in unwonted corporeal phenomena —than with that downright materialistic explanation, by virtue of which every case of stigmatisation would properly belong in the first place to the annals of a police court. The specially frequent occurrence of the phenomenon in connection with persons of the female sex, to which sex at least five-sixths of the stigmatised persons known to history belong, eminently favours the pyschico-pathological mode of explanation. Whether then we accept as the main ground of our explanation the supposition of suppressed monthly purifications or some other hysteric conditions, or start from the general fact that in women the susceptibility for religious excitement and the warmth of emotions and affections is markedly present, at any rate all that can be in any way referred to this category harmonises remarkably well with the supposition in question, while the rigidly materialistic explanation is, in presence of the fact of the so frequent occurrence of the phenomenon in the case of women, and those as a rule exceedingly weak and delicate women, involved in contradictions of every kind. Nor does the circumstance that this phenomenon was unquestionably, at least up to the close of the Middle Ages, almost entirely confined to members of one or other of the two rival mendicant orders, either the Franciscan or the Dominican, by any means necessitate the assumption of gross acts of fraud, originating in the desire of advancing *per fas et nefas* the interests of one's own order; but, on the contrary, equally as the phenomenon itself, is accounted for in a manner preeminently satisfactory, by the psychological mode of explanation. In like manner does the regular recurrence of the bleeding of the stigmas, at the times specially consecrated to the devout contemplation of the Lord's passion, find in this mode of regarding the phenomenon its fittest means of explanation. Ardent meditations on the passion, repeated every Friday,—accompanied perhaps for a considerable time by such violent mortifications or "disciplines" as those undertaken by Radegonde with her burning cross of metal, or by Suso with his nail-covered cross of wood, or by St. Brigitta and similarly by De Guyon with melted wax dropping down upon the bare skin,[1]—may as a rule have formed the preliminary step to the physico-somatic affections, of which the perfect outcome finally manifested itself in the permanently sickly condition of the stigmas—a condition of disease which, especially as respects its peculiar periodical manifestations of bleedings (those continuing without interruption are much more rare), is, so far as these present themselves in the experience of women, one specially admitting, yea almost imperatively demanding, the calling to our aid of the hypothesis of an abnormal hysteric condition, brought about by the progress and tendency of the religiously excited psychical life.—What at any rate further tends to recommend this mode of solution, which, however modified in its application to particular instances, in every case places the central point of the whole enigmatical phenomenon in the intensified psychical functions, especially in the plastically formative power of the imagination, is the fact that, apart from the judgment of so many critics of the different Protestant confessions in later and most recent times, it is also substantially advocated by a considerable number of unprejudiced Catholic inquirers. Thus, not only in the thirteenth century, Jacobus de Voragine, the author of the "Golden Legend" († 1298), as in the following century Petrarch, farther on Peter Pomponatius, Agrippa of Nettesheim, and others, have favoured this hypothesis of the imagination either with more immediate reference to the stigmas of St. Francis alone, or in its wider application, but also among Catholics in more recent times it has received the adhesion, *e.g.*, of Fehr, Mahler, Alf. Maury, Perty, Warlomont.[2]

[1] On the two latter see the author's *Gesch. der Askese*. S. 20.

[2] The proofs in *Gesch. der Ask.*, S. 361 f.—The last named of the above authorities, Dr. Warlomont of Brussels, makes use in his *Rapport médical*, issued at the request of the Brussels Medical Academy, on the case of L. Lateau (Brux., 1875). of the expression " nevropathie stigmatique " as a designation characteristic of the sickly phenomenon in question.

A more thorough examination of this remarkable phenomenon, concerning which we have expressed ourselves more fully elsewhere,[1] does not enter into our plan. Only as the point of culmination and systematic outcome of the sensuous asceticism of the cross of the Middle Ages, in its development increasing in intensity from century to century, must the condition of stigmatisation be here taken into account, and must again be briefly returned to, in common with some nearly related phenomena of kindred origin, in our consideration of the post-Reformation epoch. What our decision must be as to the religious value of the phenomenon, is apparent from the remarks we have already made, to which we add only the excellent observation of that admirable theosophist J. Fr. von Meyer, in his brilliant and profound dissertation on "the Cross of Christ."[2] "There have been men, even down to recent times, who had so firmly impressed upon themselves the image of the Crucified, that they have received the wish and the gift of experiencing something of the wound marks of the Lord in their body. Even though this had not been demonstrated by facts, we should regard it as possible by means of a lively faith, to which through the enkindling of the imagination all things are possible. Nor do we wish to censure this childlike pious desire. *But it is a greater grace to experience spiritually and in reality, that which Christ endured for us bodily in the flesh.* That miracle of the senses is in itself transitory; but the spiritual miracle of inner union and renewal is eternal and abiding: the suffering of the Lord is here too presented to us in a copy."

E. *THE SOUNDING OF THE DEPTHS OF THE CROSS IN THEOLOGY, ESPECIALLY IN THE MYSTICAL THEOLOGY.*

"Bodily exercise profiteth little; but godliness is profitable unto all things, having promise of the life that now is,

---

[1] Comp. the author's dissertation, "Ueber wahre und falsche Askese," in Vilmar's *Past.-theol. Blätter*, ii., S. 77—88.
[2] *Blätter f. höh. Wahrheit*, Bd. ii., S. 444 (of the smaller collection).

and of that which is to come." "Though I bestow all my goods to feed the poor, and though I give my body to be burned, and have not love, it profiteth me nothing."[1] The worthlessness of sensuous ascetic performances of the nature of those contemplated, as seen from these and similar utterances of Holy Scripture, compared with a true and spiritual following of the Crucified and Risen One, by no means remained a thing wholly unknown to the Church and Theology of the Middle Ages. Warnings against the perils of a spurious humility and self-chosen spirituality of angels, arising from the unsparing treatment of the body, yea, of a being puffed up in the fleshly mind, resound through all the stages and stadia of its literature. Of the fact, too, that neither the Lord in speaking of the taking up of His cross, nor Paul, by "the bearing about in the body the dying of the Lord Jesus," or "the mortifying of the members which are upon the earth," or by "the marks of the Lord Jesus," or by the "keeping under his body and bringing it into subjection,"[2] etc., has any reference to a bodily and external following of the sufferings of Christ, is widely acknowledged in a confession true at the core. The purer spiritual apprehension of the idea of the following of Christ on the cross, in accordance with the teaching of the Gospel, thus appears as not having died out: it appears nevertheless, it is true, almost everywhere most strongly alloyed with sensuous-ascetic principles and doctrines. The theological representatives and advocates of the prevalent views of the religious morals seek as a rule to recommend both at the same time as valuable, and even as necessary: the literal and the typical and ideal, the sensuous and the spiritual apprehension and carrying into effect of the Divine injunctions which have reference to the crucifying of the flesh and the mortifying of the old Adam. As prominently influential teachers and ethical lawgivers in the domains in question do the representatives of the *Mystical* theology more especially appear, alike in its more learned form as near akin

---

[1] 1 Tim. iv. 8; 1 Cor. xiii. 3.
[2] 2 Cor. iv. 10; Col. iii. 5; Gal. vi. 17; 1 Cor. ix. 27.

to Scholasticism, as this developes itself more particularly in the Romance lands of south-west Europe, as in its more popular form, as this attains to its particularly vigorous growth on German soil. But then they are able least of all to deny the principles of the abstract ignoring and contemning of the rights of the bodily factor in the sphere of the Christian moral life—principles derived from their highly esteemed and much-admired codex of legislation, the collection of the writings of pseudo-Dionysius the Areopagite, a codex actually invested with almost the authority of revelation. Even in their sermons and writings they speak most emphatically in commendation of a one-sided restraint upon the lawful emotions of the sensuous nature: approving, yea admiring, judgments upon the most unnatural and extravagant acts of violence done in ascetic self-discipline, and frequently at the same time also upon the most external and morally worthless forms of creature-idolising superstition or a mechanically legal service of works, go in their case strangely hand in hand with evangelically genial dissuasives from such excesses, as well as often with surprisingly temperate and intelligent representations of the real nature of the following of Christ in its essentially spiritual character. This unnatural juxtaposition of purer evangelical knowledge and a sickly legal or even hyper-ascetic spirit of zeal characterises the utterances of the theology of the Middle Ages in general, alike of the mystical as of that not mystic in the narrower sense, so far as they relate to our subject. The great extent to which even the less strictly mystical theology too is influenced by the fundamental conceptions and principles of Mysticism is as a rule very clearly marked just where it is a question of estimating the value of ascetic endeavours and modes of conduct; so that a sharp line of separation between mystics and non-mystics appears here in general to be hardly possible, and very many a scholastic or practical churchly theologian will consequently have to be ranged under the point of view of a representative of mystic ideas in the wider sense of the term.—Thus we shall meet with a long succession of witnesses by their lives in the Church, from the Fathers of the fourth and fifth centuries down to the immediate precursors of the Reformation Age, in whom an external homage rendered to the cross or a grossly sensuous asceticism of the cross is found to co-exist, without being brought into any real harmony, with a deeper apprehension of the idea involved in the Christian symbol of salvation. The recognition of the infinitely higher importance of the spiritual following of the cross above the merely external will indeed meet us here and there ; but neither special clearness and consistency in the theoretical or practical turning to account of this knowledge, nor the going forth of an influence to any extent far-reaching and continuous from it to the Christian ethic life of society, will be at all perceptible within the limits of the pre-Reformation Age.

Among the CHURCH FATHERS of the period from the fourth century to the eighth, or of the time from Eusebius and Lactantius down to John of Damascus and Alcuin, those of the EAST dwell with special interest and fulness upon the external dominion and glory of the once abhorred and lightly esteemed symbol of the cross, of which they are never weary of celebrating the triumph, and turning to account this triumph in apologetical or polemical interest, in opposition to the enemies of the faith. With Chrysostom, the most ardent panegyrist of the cross, and the one of loftiest flight,[1] vies in this respect Cyril of Jerusalem, who in his thirteenth *Catechesis* more especially, in meditating upon the words of the creed, " Crucified (dead), buried," displays a sublime enthusiasm in his laudation of the cross as the mighty bulwark of grace for the poor and lowly, the weak and sick, the symbol of victory for believers, and the terror of evil spirits.[2] Athanasius, too,

---

[1] Comp. above, p. 152 ; as, besides the principal passage there given from the *Serm. contra Jud. et Gentiles quod Christ. sit Deus*, especially the two discourses *De cruce et latrone* (Opp., t. ii., p. 403 sqq., 411 sqq.), and the preceding, *De cœmeterio et cruce* (p. 397 sqq.) The *Serm. in venerab. et vivificam crucem* is notoriously spurious ; cp. below.

[2] *Catech.* xiii., sub fin.; comp. also the similar although shorter disquisitions in *Cat.* iv.

comes under this head, in whose writings there frequently occurs, *inter alia*, that which was also a favourite idea of Chrysostom, namely, that the exaltation of Christ on the cross served for the purifying and sanctifying consecration of the region of the air, this scene of action of the demons (Ephes. ii. 2; Luke x. 18), who however also advances much that is more profound and of greater ethical importance in his meditations on this subject; thus the beautiful thought that the dying Saviour on the cross presented in and with His Spirit, to the heavenly Father, as His members, the whole number of those children of men made alive in Him.[1] Further, the two Gregories, Basil the Great, Cyril of Alexandria (in his defence of Christianity against the assaults of Julian), Ephraem, and the later Syrians, as Isaac of Antioch and Cyrillonas, of whose excessive laudation of the cross in their poetic discourses we have already spoken above. All the encomiums conceived and circulated by these earlier writers are comprehended in one, and almost outdone by the luxuriant turgidity of the typologies, the play on symbolic numbers, and the rhetorical flourishes of Anastasius the Sinaite, in several of his works composed about the middle of the seventh century, especially the "Anagogic Contemplations on the Six Days' Work."[2] More sober, and more of a nature to remind of Chrysostom, Athanasius, and the three Cappadocians,[3] is that which is advanced by John Damascenus in praise of the glorious symbol of redemption, as also in justification of the adoration presented to it in the orthodox Church.[4]—Occasional beautiful appeals from the outward form to the inner reality,

---

[1] *De Incarnatione Dei Verb. et contr. Arianos:* comp. the similar passages in Chrysost., *De cruce et latr.*, i. and ii. The apologetic import of the cross of Christ, as a power triumphant over all hostile efforts of demons, as in the world of men, is several times insisted on by Athanasius, in a manner entirely similar to that in which it was afterwards by Chrysostom, *e.g.*, Λόγ. καθ' "Ελληνας, c. 1.

[2] Anogogic. contemplatt. in Hexaëmeron, lib. xii. (in the *Bibl. max. Lugd.*, t. ix., f. 871 sqq.). As also his 'Οδηγὸς ζωῆς (Viæ dux, *ibid.*, p. 817 sqq.); his Διάλεξις κατὰ Ἰουδαίων, κ.τ.λ.

[3] Basil of Cæsarea, † 379, his brother Gregory of Nyssa, † abt. 396, and his friend Gregory of Nazianzus, † 389.

[4] *De fide orthod.*, iv. c. 12, p. 265 sq.

from the rhetorical apologetic to the deeper ethical bearing of the homage rendered to the cross, are to be met with in all these Fathers. They almost all warn against forgetting, in the imposing exterior of the emblem, its serious and profound significance—in the cross, the Saviour Himself who hung thereon. They warn against ever approaching Him who was nailed to the cross, the holy sacrificial Lamb of God, adored and glorified by the angels of heaven, in any other manner than with fear and trembling, in sacred awe and reverence. They insist on an inner purification of heart through the power of the cross: "If the inner man is full of evil thoughts, one may be on Calvary, or on the Mount of Olives, or at the monument of the Resurrection, and yet be far removed from receiving Christ into the heart, as far as though one had never professed His name."[1] Even in the rankly fanciful panegyrics of those Syrians one meets here and there with more refreshing portions, which prove that a more earnest, evangelically pure and sober devotion to the Crucified was not unknown to them either, but rather formed the essential foundation for all that which they composed or spoke in glorification of the symbol of redemption. Thus Balæus (about 430), in his fifth panegyric upon Acacius of Berœa, represents this venerable bishop in the evening of his life as confessing in prayer: "To Thee did I crucify my life, because I was mindful of Thy cross; to Thee did I stretch forth my hands, because I saw Thine extended upon the tree. Thy reproach did I hear, and despised my glory; Thy spitting upon did I remember, and constrained myself unto bearing and enduring; for the raiment's sake which they put upon Thee, did I despise costly clothing. Since I thus desired to honour Thy reproach by the poorness of my garment, so do I enwrap myself in Thy glory."[2]

Among the WESTERN FATHERS there arises, in accordance with their more practical bent of mind, the element of

---

[1] Gregory of Nyssa, *Ep. ad Ambrosium et Basilissam* ; comp., for what precedes, Chrysostomus, *De cœmeterio et cruce*, § 3 (t. ii., p. 401, Opp.), and Cyrillus, *Catech.* xiii. *l.c.*

[2] Bickell, *Ausgewählte Gedichte syrischer Kirchenväter*, S. 102.

surrender to the Crucified One in spirit and in truth comparatively much more strongly; although even they occasionally fall into the panegyric tone of the Orientals, and make use of the traditional hyperboles in the domain of the allegoric typologic glorification of the sacred symbol, as if in rivalry with their Eastern brethren. AMBROSE, in his two sermons on the cross, dwells with manifest delight on this brilliant outward aspect of the cultus of the cross. Thus, when he sees the all-embracing extent of the redemption proceeding from the cross on Calvary, expressed in the arms pointing to the four quarters of the heavens,[1] or when he describes the salutary overshadowing operation of the Tree of the Cross upon the believers gathered around the Redeemer. Yet he also frequently lays stress upon the fact that not the symbol consisting of wood, but the sacred body of the Redeemer hanging thereon, is the object of the devout reverence of the Christian, and that "if a man consecrates himself devoutly to the passion of the Saviour, he is not thereby delivered up to death, but the work of death is in him healed and taken out of the way."[2] The like is the case with AUGUSTINE, who repeatedly insists with emphasis upon the ethically typical significance of the sufferings of Christ upon the cross, and warns against a false and superstitious confidence in the external power of this sign. "God demands active fulfillers of His salutary signs, not painters or depicters of them; if thou bearest the sign of the humiliation of Christ upon thy brow, bear the following of His lowliness and humility in thine heart!"[3] JEROME too, although it is true he praises the ardent self-surrendering devotion to the cross displayed by his pious friend Paula, who, "prostrate before the cross, was wont to adore the Lord, as though she saw Him (bodily) hanging thereon;" yet warns in connection therewith, in tones not dissimilar to those of Gregory of Nyssa (*see above*), against

---

[1] Comp. Appendix vii.

[2] Ambros., *Serm.* 55, 56: De Cruce.

[3] Factorem quærit Deus signorum suorum, non pictorem. Si portas in fronte signum humilitatis Christi, porta in corde imitationem humilitatis Christi, *Serm.* 32. c. 13. Comp. *Serm.* 302, c. 3, etc.

the errors of a one-sided external cultus in this domain. "Only to those who bear their cross in truth, and daily rise with Christ, does it avail anything to visit the scenes of the Crucifixion and Resurrection. Let him who says, 'The temple of the Lord, the temple of the Lord,' suffer the Apostle to say to him, 'Ye are the temple of the Lord, and the Holy Ghost dwelleth in you.'" From fanatical hyperasceticism, too, and hot-blooded aspiration for martyrdom, he emphatically dissuades. "Not merely the shedding of one's blood is reckoned to us (by the Lord) as martyrdom, but the undefiled religious service of the pious mind is a daily and ever-enduring martyrdom."[1]

To the most important contributions which the ascetic literature of the earlier Church has made to our subject belong the Passion Sermons of LEO THE GREAT.[2] They glorify the cross of the Lord in a tone of sublime enthusiasm, yet without the excesses of high-sounding phraseology or inflated rhetoric; zealously bringing into relief the typological correspondences with the typical in the Old Testament, together with the other symbolically significant features, without becoming wearisome by an excess of allegoristic references; everywhere having due regard to the practical point of view, without repeating the language of a sickly and unnatural asceticism. The cross is celebrated as the true altar of sacrifice, proclaimed beforehand by the voice of prophecy, on which "the blood of the spotless Lamb of God washed away the old hereditary sin; where Satan's adverse yoke of dominion was broken; where humble lowliness triumphed over proudly exulting arrogance," etc. It is "the alone true source and firm foundation of the hope of Christians," the sacred place of execution, whence the exalted Redeemer "drew heaven and earth into a communion of grace with Himself," the fountain of all blessings, the "ground of all gracious gifts; that by which the weakness of believers is

---

[1] *Ep.* 108 *ad Eustoch.*, c. 31 ; *Ep.* 49 *ad Paulin.* Comp. also the author's monograph on Jerome, S. 459.

[2] *Serm.* lii.—lxx. : De Passione Domini (pp. 198—278, Opp.).

turned into strength, reproach into glory, death into life."
At the cross we have to comprehend the wondrous mystery
of the paschal sacrifice; after the image of Him, who out of
love became like unto our deformity, to be formed anew ; to
Him, who out of our poor dust prepared to Himself his body
of glory, to raise ourselves ; to be turned aside by nothing
temporal from pressing forward in the imperial road to glory.
He therefore who, assailed by the power of lusts, is in danger
of quitting the way of obedience and truth, let him fly back
to the cross of the Lord, let him nail the motions of his
corrupt will to the wood of life, let him with the prophet im-
plore of the Lord : " Nail (to it) my flesh by thy fear ; for I
am afraid of thy judgments!"[1] The Cross of Christ is
alike the means of grace (*sacramentum*) of the Divine revelation of salvation, as the pattern (*exemplum*) for animating us
to a pious mind and conversation; as it delivers us from the
yoke of the bondage of death, so does it also confer upon us
power to follow the Crucified One. "If thus a conflict should
be imposed on us against the pride of this world, against the
lust of the flesh, or against the arrows of the heretics, let us
never enter into the conflict save as armed with the cross of
the Lord!"[2]—That which affects us most agreeably in these
sermons of a Romish Pope is the almost utter absence of
references to the miserable outward forms of the traditional
Catholic cultus of the cross, as this prevailed far and wide
even at that time : to reliquary crosses, fragments (splinters)
of the true cross in Jerusalem, miracles wrought by means of
the cross, etc. As far as this spiritual conception and defence
of the fundamental truths of salvation is concerned, Leo still
walks essentially in the footsteps of Augustine, his theological teacher and exemplar. In GREGORY THE GREAT,
however, hardly a century and a half later, there already
meets us, spite of the Augustinism in principle and form even

---

[1] Ps. cxix. 120, according to the LXX. : Καθήλωσον ἐκ τοῦ φόβου σου τὰς σάρκας μου, κ.τ.λ. (*Vulg.*: Confige timore tuo carnes meas.) *Serm.* lxx. c. 4.
[2] The last propositions from *Serm.* lxxii. : De Resurrectione Domini, ii., cc. 1, 4.

of this Church Father, a considerably more external and
material mode of treating the article of the Cross, on its
theoretical and practical sides. Where he speaks of the
mysteries of the Cross as the final end and culminating
point in the development of the history of Redemption, his
discourse is seldom free from an exuberant typological turgidity. From a devout use of relics of the cross and other
kinds of relics he looks for extraordinary salutary effects,
wrought inwardly and outwardly upon the life of Christians ;
the adoration of the Cross is regarded by him as a means for
deliverance from the bonds of sin.[1] Christ's redeeming work,
completed on the cross, he represents indeed, as to the thing
itself, in harmony with earlier writers—*e.g.*, Leo among others
—although in much cruder language—as a deceiving of
Satan, a being taken on the part of the devil on the hook of
the Incarnation.[2] Even his magic hierarchical theory of the
sacrament of the altar, as an unbloody repetition of the
bloody offering of Calvary by the hand of the priest, is
closely connected with this his proneness to a sensuous
external way of looking at things.

In the theology of the MIDDLE AGES proper, the views
represented severally by Leo I. and Gregory I., the deeper
and more spiritual one of the former and the more sensuous
one of the latter, hold each other substantially in equipoise.
The official ecclesiastical tradition, cherished and maintained
by Scholasticism, in the West as in the East, from the
twelfth century downwards, leans strongly in favour of the
sensuous external mode of interpretation, while the deeper
Augustinian-Leonine conception lives on mainly within the
circles of the Mystics. As stern or even decided opponents
of the magic-superstitious tendency do the latter hardly ever
show themselves. Entire rejection of the external cultus of
the cross was regarded from the time of the violent assault on

---

[1] Comp. also the miraculous histories communicated by him, as to the magically
healing, delivering, or converting effect of the cross or cross-symbol ; *e.g.*, *Dialog.*
l. i., c. 10 ; l. ii., c. 7.

[2] *Moralia in Job*, ch. i. 33.

the part of Claude of Turin, and still more from the time of the Petrobrusians and Waldenses—to whom reference has been already made—as heretical. As the whole ecclesiastical system of the veneration of saints, images, and relics, so do also the symbol of the cross and crucifix, remain altogether unassailed on the part of the Mystics in all the influence of their position in the religious and secular life of the people. Bolder spirits, arising with a freer energy, as, e.g., in the East, the celebrated Archbishop Eustathius of Thessalonica—a man less indeed of a mystical than of a Biblical-practical bent—in the West, Meister Eckart, oppose no doubt the unbridled excesses of asceticism and the silly confidence in the mechanical and frequently pharisaic-hypocritical practices of monkery, but never speak a word against the ecclesiastically sanctioned means for the quickening of devotion or for the advancement and guidance in an ascetic direction of the penitential impulse.—How rankly an esentially external, superstitious, self-righteous (*werkheilige*) *theologia crucis* has flourished and bloomed, in the EAST especially, since the triumph over the iconoclastic tendency, is made manifest by the sermons, preserved in considerable number, of a succession of exalted dignitaries of the Byzantine Church, in which the audience is exhorted to the observance now of this, now of that festival in honour of the " venerable and life-giving cross." Gretser has contributed a respectable number of such sermons on the festivals of the cross—in Greek, accompanied with a Latin translation—of which not a few had remained unknown until his time, in the second volume of his oft-mentioned work.[1] Small as is their theological value, that is yet very instructive, and characteristic of the spirit of the devotion of the East in the Middle Ages in general, and of the history of the development of our subject in particular, which is said by a Nicetas the Paphlagonian, Andreas of Crete, Joseph of Thessalonica,

---

[1] *De Cruce*, tom. ii., in quo varia Græcorum auctorum encomiastica monumenta Græco-Latina de SS. cruce continentur, nunc primum ex variis bibliothecis eruta, c.et. (Ingolst. 1600).

Theophanes Cerameus, the Presbyter Pantaleo, the Patriarch Xiphilinus, the Patriarch Germanus (II.) of Constantinople, the Emperor Leo the Philosopher, etc., in praise of the most sacred cross. It is an exuberant luxuriating in the gush of encomiastic utterances and the most high-sounding attributes possible—similar to that in the verses of the preaching Syrians of the fifth century—which is here to be perceived: much tickling of the ears, but little touching of the heart, expresses in general the impression produced by them. An "invincible panoply of Christian folk, a brazen wall over which no robber can climb, an immovable tower against the enemy, the rejoicing and the crown of angels, the discomfiture and shattering of all evil spirits, the offence and debasement of the Jews, the refutation and condemnation of the heathen,"—in these and yet other high-sounding encomiums does that Nicetas Paphlago (*circa* 880) speak of the sacred symbol.[1] But that which is most high-flown in connection with this subject is afforded by a homily, falsely ascribed to Chrysostom, but assuredly belonging only to the Middle Ages, "on the venerable and life-giving cross, and on the fall."[2] "Wilt thou learn the power of the cross," it is there said *inter alia*, "and the encomiums due to it, then listen: the cross is the hope of Christians, the resurrection of the dead, the leader of the blind, the confidence of the desponding, the way of the wanderers, the avenger of the wronged, the staff of the halting, the solace of the poor, the bridle of the rich, the humiliation of the arrogant, the penitence of the disorderly, the token of victory over the demons, the defeat of the devil, the instructor of children, the abundance of the needy, the steersman of the mariner, the haven of the shipwrecked, the rampart of the besieged, the father of the orphans, the protector of the widows, the judge of the unrighteous, the pillar of the righteous, the repose of the dis-

---

[1] Serm. in exalt. venerab. Crucis, in Combefis, *Auctar. biblioth. Gr.* I., p. 440 sq.

[2] Pseudo-Chrysost. Sermo in venerab. ac vivif. Crucem, in Opp. Chrys., ed. Montfauc., t. ii., p. 820 sqq.

tressed, the guardian of the little ones, the head of men, the goal of the aged, the light of those sitting in darkness, the majesty of kings, the humanity of barbarians, the liberty of slaves, the wisdom of inexperienced, the law of those in anarchy, the promise of the prophets, the proclamation of the apostles, the glory of the martyrs, the discipline (*ascesis*) of the monks, the chastity of virgins, the joy of priests, the foundation of the Church, the security of the world, the destruction of idol temples and altars, the dispersing of the odour of the fat (in offerings), the offence of the Jews, the condemnation of the ungodly," etc.

The WESTERN ecclesiastical literature, too, has its panegyrics upon the symbol of redemption, but these are generally restrained within the limits of moderation and good taste. ODILO of Clugny († 1048) appeals in devout prayer to the Crucified: "To Him, in whose name the knees of all in heaven, on earth, and under the earth do bow, do I humbly confess my guilt, to Him, the Father of all spirits, both those on earth and those in heaven; and command thee, ancient enemy of our race, Turn away from me thy secret devices and thine evil machinations! For with me is the cross of the Lord, whom I constantly worship; it is my tower of resort, my way, and my strength, the invisible standard, the banner of love which knows no defeat, which expels all evil, which scatters before it all darkness! By its power I will walk the way to heaven; it is to me life, to thee, O arch-enemy, death! The cross of our Lord be my ornament and glory; His blood remain my true redemption!"[1]—Prayers, or contemplation or paræneses of a like character are moreover found among countless other ecclesiastical writers from the time of the Carolingians to the Reformation. Some specially touching prayerful meditations belonging to this order (*Orationes*) are contained in the works of ANSELM of Canterbury, the founder of a deeper, more ethically matured, and purer conception of the mystery of the redeeming death of

---

[1] Odil. Cluniac. abb., Orat. in crucem adorand., in *Bibl. Patr. max. Lugd.*, t. xvii., f. 653.

Jesus, in the midst of an age only too much given to an external or magical and superstitious mode of regarding the subject. "Hail," it is said in one of them, "hail, glorious, precious wood, which the Creator Himself has sanctified by His contact! through heaven and earth beams thy radiance, through the ages is its brightness shed; yea, hell itself is lit up with it. . . . . What tree is to be compared to this wood? Christ Himself is here blossom and fruit, fragrance and perfume, leaf and crown. Be then to me also the very Tree of Life, open to me the gate of Paradise, and unite me to Him who hung upon thee, unto all eternity!"[1]—With Anselm vies ST. BERNARD in fervent adoration and ascription of praise to the cross. Several of the allegorical and moral contemplations or *sententias* upon our subject most favourite in later times come down from him, or are at least ordinarily taken from his writings. Thus that of the robber spirit which underlies our dread of the cross; for if we were not thieves or robbers, we should not fear the cross. In like manner that of the four ends or arms of the cross as emblems of the four Christian virtues: love, long-suffering, hope, fear of God (or, otherwise, abstinence, patience, wisdom, humility.)[2]

A sententia recurring with special frequency, and wrought out in various ways, in these ascetic meditations upon our subject, those of Bernard included, is that of the two equally authorised modes of bearing the cross of Christ—the sensuous, consisting in the mortification of the body, and the spiritual, which was carried out by a devout contemplation of the Crucified, or even by compassion towards one's neighbour. "In two ways may we take up the cross; either in that we afflict the body by mortification and abstinence, or that by

---

[1] *Orat.* 42. Comp. also *Orat.* 41, and especially *Orat.* 43. the most powerful of these meditations on the cross.

[2] Bernard. Meditat. in passion. et resurrect. Domini, c. 6. (*Opp ed Mabill.*, t. ii., f. 507 sq.). Comp. De S. Andrea apost. Sermo ii. (t. i., f. 1066). The Sententia : Quare timent homines crucem? Quia latrones sunt : Si latrones non essent, crucem non timerent, is found also in the writings of Bernard's contemporary, Drugo of Ostia (*Bibl. max.* t. xxi., f. 332). But it must certainly be original in Bernard's writings.

compassion we make the sufferings of our neighbour our own." Something like this reads the sentence to which currency was first given by Gregory the Great, one which exceedingly often, and indeed almost regularly, recurs in the expositions of the Gospels during the Middle Ages, at the passage Matt. xvi. 24 (and parallels, Mark viii. 34 ; Luke ix. 23),[1] which moreover is found adopted among the instructions addressed by Pope Nicholas I. to the newly converted Bulgarians, in answer to their questions and difficulties,[2] and also pretty frequently repeated by others, *e.g.*, by Odilo of Clugny in the second book of his Collations, by Bonaventura in the beginning of his tractate on the "Wood of Life," and in various other passages from his writings.[3] The "seraphic Doctor," BONAVENTURA, the enthusiastic admirer of St. Francis and his wound-marks, belongs in all respects to the most zealous of those panegyrists of the cross, who not only lavish encomiums upon the outward symbol of redemption, but also insist upon the inner or moral significance of this symbol. His method, it is true, is often characterised by a certain verbal play, and the employment of manifold partitions of more or less ingenuity, artistic schematisms, typological figures, generally adopted from earlier writers, especially from Bernard, yea, here and there by his approvingly citing and even reproducing such florid descriptions as that of pseudo-Chrysostom as given above.[4] In a chapter of the " Compendium of Theological Truth " ascribed to him— according to others, proceeding from the pen of Thomas of

---

[1] Duobus modis crucem Domini bajulamus, cum aut per abstinentiam carnem affligimus, aut per compassionem proximi necessitatem illius nostram putamus. So Greg. Max., *Hom.* 37 *in Evang.*, and entirely similarly *Hom.* 32. Of later writers comp., *e.g.*, Bede, *in Matth.* xvi. 24 (*Opp. ed. Basil.*, t. v., f. 70). Christ. Druthmar *in Matth.* xvi. 27 (*Bibl. max.*, t. xv.) ; Anselm on Matth. xvi. (*Opp.*, t. i., p. 89) ; Zacharias Chrysopolitanus, *In unum ex quatuor*, i. (*Bibl. max.*, t. xxi.), etc.

[2] Nicolai Resp. ad Bulgar., c. 7 (in Harduin *Concill.*, t. v.)

[3] Odilo, Collat. l. ii. (t. xvii. *Bibl. max.*, f. 285). Bonavent., *Pharetr.* l. iv., c. 7 ; *Dicta. Sal.*, Tit. vii. c. 4, etc.

[4] *Pharetr.* l. 4 (Opp. t. i., p. 108). Comp. *Exposit. missae*, c. 4 (Opp. t. ii., p. 80).

Aquino, but at any rate composed more in the style of Bonaventura—which treats of the cross of the Lord, the three operations of the instrument of suffering on Calvary are first enumerated, namely, the sentence executed thereupon, the shame thereon endured, and the salutary fruit of redemption thereby obtained (*supplicium, opprobrium, pretium*). Then follows the enumeration of twenty-four types of the cross, taken partly from the Old Testament, partly from the New; then that of the seven last words of the Redeemer, accompanied with brief practical application; then an explanation of the four arms of the cross, as having reference to the four virtues of love, humility, obedience, patience, or to the four benefits wrought by Christ—the opening of heaven, the destruction of hell, the communication of graces, the forgiveness of sins; finally, an allusion to the four species of wood or trees out of which, according to the legend, the cross of the Lord was put together.

"Palm, cedar, cypress, and olive, the trees of the cross." [1]

More free from externalism, more indifferent in regard to traditional forms and formulas, and altogether of a more spiritual character, is that which is taught by the tertiarian Franciscan nun ANGELA OF FOLIGNO, of somewhat later date than the preceding († 1309), a favourite authoress with all subsequent Quietists and Mystics, in her "Theology of the Cross of Jesus Christ." True resignation under the sufferings and afflictions imposed by the Lord is here declared to be preferable to all self-elected penances and mortifications. "The heavenly Physician surely knows incomparably better than the sick and disordered human being, as to what mortifications or trials are best adapted to purify and raise the soul. The self-chosen exercises of penance and denials are only too often subject to vain self-complacency, whilst those coming upon us by the disposal of Divine providence, if we

---

[1] Crux Domini palma, cedrus, cypressus, oliva, with the mystical reference of the cedar to the *altitudo contemplationis*, the cypress to the *fama bonæ opinionis*, the palm to the *fructus justitiæ*, the olive to the *lenitas misericordiæ*. (Compend. Theol. Veritatis, l. iv., c. 16, p. 773, t. ii., Opp. S. Bonavent.)

bear them with true patience and submission as coming from God's hand, are veiled indeed before the eyes of men with the appearance that we must bear them of necessity, ... but in reality are to be embraced with all heartiness, as favours afforded to us by our supreme physician and Saviour, out of pure love for our everlasting salvation."[1] From the writings of these venerated churchly and monastic authorities of the eleventh century to the thirteenth, especially those of Bernard and Bonaventura, partly also from those of Angela of Foligno, does the popular GERMAN MYSTICISM of the last period of the Middle Ages principally derive the material of the conceptions, partitions, and turns of discourse, on the ground of which it continues to develop our article, alike on the theoretic-contemplative as on the practical ascetic side. An increasing operation of its speculation upon the idea of the cross, and upon the influence of this idea in practical life, with the effect of rendering that idea itself more spiritual and profound, one can hardly fail to recognise. Even in the case of BERTHOLD OF REGENSBURG, the venerated preacher of the Franciscans in the times of the Interregnum († 1272), do the paræneses admonishing to the taking up and bearing of the cross of Christ assume a tone unusually hearty, and popularly warm and fresh. In the beautiful sermon on the cross of the Lord, "Von dem hêren Kriuze,"[2] he treats first of the saint whose day it was (22nd July), Mary Magdalene, whom he compares to the moon, while the blessed Virgin Mary, who mourns with her at the cross, is like the sun,—the former, an image of the light of night with its spots, as it were tears of penitence for sin, the latter an image of the gloriously beaming light of day. The depicting of the blessedness and glory which a Mary Magdalene, too, enjoys with the Lord in heaven, prepares the way for a description of the last judgment. At that time, Christ the Judge of the world will receive no one into favour, who does not appear

---

[1] B. Angelæ de Fulignio Passus Spirituales, etc., c. 10 (in *Vita B. Angelæ, auct. Arnold.; AA. SS.*, 4 Jan.). Comp. Tersteegen, *Leben heiliger Seelen*, Bd. ii., St. 5.
[2] Pfeiffer, *Berthold von Regensb.*, i. 537—548.

before Him laden with a cross of some kind. " Dar bringet
San Peter sîn kriuze ; sô bringet einer sin houbet, daz ist im
abe geslagen in dem dienste unseres herren ; sô bringet der
guote Sant Andrēs sîn kriuze ; sô bringet der guote San
Bartolomēus sine hût uf im ; sô bringet der guote San
Laurencius sinen róst; sô bringet der diz, sô bringet der daz.
Alse si eht die martel geliten hânt, sô habent sie ir kriuze
volleistet. ' Owê bruoder Berhtold, wie geschieht danne den
die keine martel liten ? ' Die müzent ouch ir kriuze tragen
oder sie enkoment niemer in die freude unser herren mê."[1]
For, it is now further shown, many thousand saints are blissful in the kingdom of heaven, who had never endured a
martyrdom, but who none the less were saved, because they
were able to point, in place of their martyrdom, at least to a
"cross with four places (ends)," *i.e.*, the spiritual cross of
following Jesus in the four main virtues,—the same spiritual
cross which had also brought Mary Magdalene to heaven,
though she was " never tortured in martyrdom." As the four
virtues which form the "places" or arms of this spiritual
cross, he designates, freely adapting the language of S. Bernard, that of faith (above), that of love (on the right hand), of
hope (on the left), and of *staetikeit*, or patience, which last
forms the upholding stem and firm foundation of the others :
" Daz ir mit diesen drin tugenden staete sult sin." In ingenious and frequently animating, sometimes even enchaining,
descriptions of this tetrade of virtues does he then proceed to
the close of the sermon. Especially in regard to hope and its
demoniacal opposite, evil *zwîvel* (doubt), this sin of sins,
does he excellently discourse.—Marked by greater regard to
the essential import, freer from the allusive externalities of the
allegorical moral tradition, and more directly testifying from

---

[1] " Then St. Peter brings with him his cross ; another brings his head, which
was cut off in the service of our Lord ; good St. Andrew brings his cross ; good
St. Bartholomew brings his skin (scalp), good St. Lawrence his gridiron ; one
bringing this and another that. As they have endured martyrdom, they have
accomplished their cross. ' But what happens then to those who have suffered no
martyrdom ? ' They, too, must bear their cross, or they will never come (with the
others) into the joy of our Lord."

an independent profound apprehension and experience of the Christian mysteries, is the teaching of Meister ECKART concerning our subject. And yet, with all the spiritual innerness of his religious views and conceptions, he detracts nothing of its objective fundamental world-renewing significance from the sacrifice of the eternal Son of God upon the cross. He lays, however, just because he places the central point (centre of gravity) of the work of salvation *essentially in the Divine doing*, but little stress upon man's endeavour after virtue ; and forms a decidedly unfavourable judgment alike of external mortifications and of a self-imposed cross. He declares those to be asses, who think they can attain to spiritual poverty and resignation by means of fasting and penances ; for "it is far better to esteem a rational work than a bodily work." A denying, perceiving, and combating of cherished sinful inclinations "is more becoming to thee, than though thou shouldst fast at the same time from all nourishment." Ascetic "peculiarity in clothing, in food, in words or gestures," he designates as something to be shunned. Not less does he warn against the externalism of confiding in "the dead bones" of relics, in pilgrimages, and other superstitious rites of cultus.[1] Much in his expressions regarding this subject is very nearly related to the " Cross-Theology " of the but little earlier Angela of Foligno. Yet it appears doubtful whether the German provincial of the Dominicans could already have received intelligence of the writings of the Italian nun of the third order of St. Francis.—Similar to the doctrine of Eckart is that which is proclaimed by TAULER, who also warns against the self-made myrrh, against hairy shirts and cilices, which can surely bring no peace ; and of those two modes of bearing the cross, the ascetic-mortifying and the spiritual-ethic, displayed in compassion and self-sacrificing love to one's neighbour, commends the latter as by far the more excellent.—SUSO too, the severe self-torturer even unto blood, rises in his later years to a purer and more just

---

[1] W. Preger, *Gesch. der deutschen Mystik im Mittelalter*, i. (1874), S. 450 ff. ; cp. 426 f.

recognition of the true value of those external exercises once zealously practised. He confessed to having been withdrawn from his excessive rigours, and directed into the "reasonable school of true inner resignation," the only true art and mode of cross-bearing, by an unmistakable and emphatic manifestation of God Himself.[1]—A non-German representative of the mystic theology, who, however, is inwardly closely related to the German school of Mystics, ST. BRIGITTA, belongs to the number of the most ardently loving adorers of the cross of Christ: she is wont on this account seldom to be depicted otherwise than as near a cross, or as adorned with one. The self-torturing cruelty of the experiments with the dropping of wax, before mentioned, in connection with her Friday meditations on the Passion, did not even in her case prevent the rising to a more spiritual apprehension of the nature of the grace of the Crucified One, yea, to the acknowledgment, " Even though man should suffer his body to be a thousand times put to death for God's sake, yet he avails nothing to make satisfaction to God for a single sin, to answer God on a single point. All is pure grace—therefore always do good works, but reckon them always as nothing," etc. As the expression of a truly pure and decidedly evangelical knowledge, these and similar utterances of the Swedish visionary are certainly not to be regarded; since again exhortations to the " meriting of the kingdom of heaven with good works," and such-like, also proceed side by side with them. But on the mystery of the cross, the " main and central point of all her observations," she has nevertheless breathed many a profoundly thoughtful and touching utterance, which shows that she had learnt not merely outwardly to contemplate and sensuously to depict that wondrous " interpenetrating of the righteousness and compassionating love of Him who, as the pelican, nourishes His young with His blood," but also in the depth of her heart to know and experience it.[2]

The most glorious confessions, in the sense of an earnest

[1] M. Diepenbrock, *Suso's Leben u. Schriften*, S. 42 ff., 287 f.
[2] Hammerich, *St. Brigitta*, S. 244 f.; comp. S. 222.

theology of the cross, ennobled and sanctified by a penetration into the depths of Christian experience, are to be found in connection with the three great Mystics of the fifteenth century: GERSON, THOMAS À KEMPIS, and STAUPITZ; in the case of each of them, it is true, with a minting peculiarly his own. Of JOHN GERSON, the most learned of those theologians of the Middle Ages, who combined to the full extent the scholastic and the mystic tendency of mind and mode of teaching, it can hardly be asserted with justice, that, as a preponderating man of intellect, he contributed "publicly to transmit the interest in Mysticism only in the way of a theoretical recognition and nominalistic discussion of the conditions of the intuition of God."[1] The honourable title of a *Doctor Christianissimus* belongs to the venerated Father of the Council of Constance, so far as he is a mystical theologian, in reality, and indeed mainly, on account of the decision with which he maintains aloft the revealed objective grace manifested on the cross, and exalts this above all his scholastic and mystical speculations.[2] His sermons, and especially his Passion sermons, exhort to a lowly and penitently confiding fleeing to the Crucified, who endured all that He did endure on account of our transgressions, and who also will not reject the worst sinner that approaches Him longing for salvation. "Thou sayest, I have done nothing good, have wrought nothing in order to please God, how can I approach the cross? Draw near to it, nevertheless, and obtain for thyself good, in becoming united with Him in faith, in hope, in love. And if thou repliest,

---

[1] This is the opinion of A. Ritschl (*Die christl. Lehre v. der Rechtfertigung u. Versöhnung*, i. 113), who, however, does but scant justice to this towering theologian, or to the merits of the Mystics of the last centuries of the Middle Ages in general, for the advancement of evangelical knowledge and preparing the way for the Reformation. See the author's review of his work, *Bew. des Glaubens*, 1875, March part, S. 145.

[2] Compare, for instance, the beautiful distichs (from the treatise *De elucida', scholastica theologiæ mysticæ* in Schwab, Joh. Gerson, S. 374):

    Conscius est animus meus, experientia testis:
    Mystica quæ retuli dogmata vera scio.
    Non tamen idcirco scio me fore glorificandum:
    Spes mea crux Christi, gratia non opera.

My sins are too great, too scandalous, for thee to dare to approach it, I say to thee: Nevertheless, draw near to the cross; for where sin is great, the compassion is yet greater. Art thou in want of purification? Here is the fountain. Needest thou pardon? Here is the throne of grace!"[1] In statements such as these, and similar ones—for besides them, it is true, his sermons sometimes present unrefreshing subtleties, *e.g.*, as to the re-assumption of the blood of Christ, the conflict of the archangel Michael with Lucifer, etc.— Gerson manifestly stands very near to the recognition of the truth made in the Reformation of the sixteenth century. He extends the hand to Luther equally much as does Huss, in whose condemnation he took a prominent part, or as any one of those other witnesses of the truth in his century, designated as in the narrower sense Reformers before the Reformation. In many respects he reminds us, moreover, of the moral allegorising practice of the earlier Mystics. So in the explanation of the four ends of the cross, of the virtues or functions of the mortifying of sin, the forsaking of earthly goods, the suppression of sensual desires, and the denying of one's own will; but also in his exhortations to discretion in ascetic zeal, in warnings such as, "Poor raiment and cilicium often enough conceal beneath them the worm of pride," etc.[2]—THOMAS À KEMPIS, alike in his sermons and meditations as in the "Imitation of Christ" (for the actual proceeding of which from his pen, the recent investigations of Hirsche have, in our opinion, afforded decisive proof), knows no other way to light than that of the cross. This he understands, no doubt, in the sense, as well of an external mortifying, as of a spiritual contemplative following of the Lord. As a strict ascetic, he does not, for instance, speak contemptibly of the severe crucifying of the flesh of the "friends of God;" he describes to his novices this *crux monachorum* as something which is deserving, if not of direct imitation, yet of all admiration. But only because

---

[1] *Expos. in pass. Domini*, Opp. t. iii., p. 1195.
[2] J. B. Schwab, *Johann Gerson*, 363, 768 f., 712; cp. 393, 395.

in the midst of their self-mortifications the consolation flowing from the wounds of the Crucified becomes their portion in most abundant measure, because they taste " the hidden honey from the rock, because the oil of compassion trickling down from the blessed wood of the cross refreshes them." Enthusiastically does he describe the glory of this Tree of Life, the implanting of which in the heart is the best remedy, the strongest weapon, against all deadly assaults of the devil. He teaches his pupils to recognise poverty conjoined with humility as the sweet root of this tree of the cross, labour and penitence as its bark, compassion and righteousness as its two main branches, truth and doctrine as its precious leaves, a sense of honour and modesty as its blossoms, sobriety and self-restraint as its fragrance, chastity and obedience as its beauty, faith and hope as its far-shining splendour; finally, salvation and everlasting life as its glorious fruit. " No forest produces such a tree; even Solomon's gardens bring to maturity no plant of like healing virtue and like balmy odour. It is the most fruitful tree, blessed above all the trees of Paradise,—the vine with Divine fruit, the fertile olive tree, the fig tree, rough without, but inwardly sweet as honey, the glorious palm, which is rightly called the bearer of Christ, because Jesus bore it upon His shoulders, and because then, set up upon Mount Calvary, it bore Jesus."[1] More soberly, but in a manner not less affecting, and not less enthusiastically, does he speak of the beatitudes of the cross, as the true " royal road " to heaven, in the *Imitatio Christi*. The word of the Lord concerning the taking up of His cross sounds severe to many, he observes, but yet more severe will one day sound to them the curse of the Judge on account of the despising of His cross. . . . . " Why dost thou hesitate to take up the cross? In it is salvation, in it life, in it defence against the enemies, in it the infusion of heavenly sweetness, in it power of the soul, in

---

[1] *Sermon. ad Novitios*, esp. P. iii. S. 1: De cruce quotidie tollenda, S. 1, 7, 9, 10. Comp. also of the Meditations or *Conciones*, esp. Med. 23: De cruce Jesu, quam pro nobis ipse portavit; also Medd. 24, 27.

it joy of the spirit, in it perfection of virtue and sanctification. *There is no salvation of the soul, no hope of life, save in the cross.* .... No other way leads to life, to the true inner peace, but that of the cross, and of daily dying with Christ; for not in a multitude of sweetnesses and consolations consists our merit and the salvation of the soul, but in the patient bearing of severe assaults and afflictions." In short:

"Cross is for the true monk life and the gate of heaven."[1]

—More evangelically again does JOHN STAUPITZ, the most immediate precursor of the Reformation among all the German Mystics, know how to speak of the true advantage and use of the cross. In his tractate concerning the love of God he severely rebukes the self-righteous, work-holy endeavour of those who would by their own virtue and good-doing obtain for themselves God's approval, for wishing "to allure Him with their piety, as one allures the hawk to the bait." It is to take away from the compassion of God its due precedence, and to carry soiled rags to the market, in order to pay for gold with dirt. "We experience so much the more confidence in God, in proportion as we have learnt to despair of ourselves, rely not at all upon our own powers, but look to the cross of Christ alone." "Look to the wounds of Christ," cried he once to Luther, assailed with bitter reproaches of conscience; "behold His blood for thee shed; from this the atonement will shine forth to thee."[2]

Somewhere at the standpoint of this last and noblest representative of the German mystical school stand the strictly so-called Reformers before the Reformation, the direct prophetic precursors of the evangelical principle of acceptance. In the writings of JOHN WESSEL, in particular, the salutary fact of the redeeming death upon the cross, as laying the foundation of all our hope, is with great clearness

---

[1] Vita boni monachi crux est, et dux paradisi —*De imit.*. iii., c. 56—one of those unintended hexameters of which, as Hirsch (*Prolegom.* to a new edn. of the *Imit. Chr.*, 1873) has shown, some are frequently to be met with in Thomas à Kempis.

[2] Ritschl, *as before*, S. 114 f. Comp. Plitt, *Gesch. der evang. Kirche bis z. Augsburger Reichstage*, i. 39.

and living conviction placed in the centre of all soteriological-ethical contemplations. " It is in truth meet and right," says he, " that we should glory in the cross of Christ ; for from it most shines forth our whole Christian dignity. Through it is given us a firm confidence and earnest of this our dignity, the possession of which has first been made known, and most firmly guaranteed to us by the cross."[1]—Not quite so exclusively as with Wessel does the centre of gravity of that activity which makes salvation ours appear with SAVONAROLA to be placed in the objective grace which brings salvation. The churchly means of grace and sanctification, the traditional forms and rites of Christian asceticism, stand higher in favour with the Florentine Dominican preacher, than with the spiritualistically inclined Netherlands precursor of a Zwingli and a Calvin. In his "Triumph of the Cross," a work of genius in the form of a comprehensive apology for Christianity, it is preponderantly the external side of the mystery of redemption, the victorious power—constraining the mighty ones of the earth, and putting to shame all the philosophers —and the world-wide mission of the revelation of God in Christ, to the glorifying of which he directs his endeavour. He begins with the representation of the all-prevailing power and the all-obscuring glory of the Saviour, under the figure of a triumphal procession of the ancient Roman type. The thorn-crowned Saviour rides gloriously through the world, sitting enthroned high upon a four-wheeled chariot, conquering the world by no other weapons than by the sight of the miracles He displays before it. In His left hand He holds the cross (encircled with the glorifying light of the Holy Trinity), together with the other instruments of His passion ; in His right, the book of the two Testaments. At His foot stands the cup with the host upon it, around Him vessels with water, wine, oil, balm, and the other symbols of the sacraments. A step lower than Christ sits His mother, the holy Virgin ; beneath her, again a stage lower, are to be seen the bones of the blessed martyrs, in urns of gold, of

[1] *De magnitudine passionis*, c. 42. Comp. Ritschl, S. 116 f.

silver, of crystal, or urns adorned with jewels. In front of the triumphal chariot advance the patriarchs and prophets of the Old Covenant, immediately before it the apostles and evangelists. It is surrounded by countless saints and doctors of the Church, with books in their hands; it is followed by a countless number of converts from among the Jews and Greeks, among the Latins and barbarians, whilst the hosts of the enemies of the cross opposing the procession are resistlessly scattered.[1]—The highly poetical description, characterised by an abundant rhetorical splendour, is perhaps indebted for some of its characteristic features to the profoundly suggestive painting of Christ by Fiesole in the San Marco Church, or at least to this among other influences;[2] but on the other hand it reminds also of many of the most brilliant poetic word-paintings in the *Divina Commedia*, especially of that of the victorious chariot of the triumphant Church, which Dante beholds near to the mountain of purification, drawn by Christ Himself in semblance of a griffin.[3] The more serious, mystic-ascetic aspect of the idea of the cross retires in this brilliant exordium, as indeed throughout the entire treatise, very much into the back-ground. In a passage of the extended proem, where the writer is speaking of the historic testimony of Christ to His Divine power and wisdom, he shows in an interesting manner in what the folly of the cross, the application of one of the most unimposing, and apparently unlikely means for the attainment of the greatest and most glorious of all aims, consisted.[4] That

---

[1] Hieron. Savonarolæ Triumphus Crucis, sive de veritate fidei, lib. i., cap 2: *De triumpho Christi*.

[2] Piper, *Einl. in d. monument. Theol.*, S. 679.

[3] Comp. the author's address: *Das reformator. Lehrstück vom Kreuze*, etc.— Evang. K.-Zeitung, 1874. No. 67, S. 519.

[4] *Triumph. Cruc.*, ii., c. 14: Quodsi crucis horror et opprobrium una cum subsannationibus, sputis, alapis, verberibus ac tormentis, quæ moriens passus est Christus, considerentur: nihil hac cruce magis tetrum aut stultum, antequam Chr. cruci figeretur, poterat inveniri. Per ipsam vero Chr. orbi terrarum maximam contulit et indidit sapientiam, ut omnis Christiani professio docet et experientia quotidiana testatur. Ergo præcipua et Divina est in Christo sapientia, etc. (p. 152 s. ed., Lugd. Bat. 1633.)

which is afterwards said in the apologetic dogmatic review of the most important doctrines of the faith—composed essentially upon the foundation of Thomas Aquinas, but reminding here and there also of Raymond of Sebonde—concerning the passion as the greatest of the mysteries of the humanity of Jesus, is inadequate, and offers hardly anything remarkable. That Savonarola had penetrated into the depths of the cross, and knew how to testify thereof in a powerfully effective manner, we learn from very many sections of his other writings and sermons, especially that glorious chapter of his little book "On the Simplicity of the Christian Life," which sets forth how, in the contemplation of the Crucified, the highest transports of joy are made known to the Christian, and the view is opened into the deepest wondrous depth of the Divine love, etc.[1] The prevailing point of view from which he regards the symbol of redemption is without doubt the one expressed in the vision of the victorious chariot—that of triumphing over the anti-Christian powers. He dwells manifestly with greater preference upon the *gloria crucis* than upon the *ignominia crucis*. Even where he treats of the latter, his position in regard to it is not the truly free, confidingly trusting, and actively cheerful one of the evangelical Christian. A strongly legal bent and an ascetic rigour not seldom, as in the case of Thomas à Kempis, bordering on the diseased, show that with him such a complete subduing of the monkish element by the evangelical Reformed, as was the case with Luther and the other fathers of the Reformation who had proceeded from the bosom of the mendicant orders, had not taken place; although, by virtue of an apprehension of the principle of justification by faith which was in its essence sound, he approached very near to them, and on many points reproved the degeneracy of the Papal Church as severely as any of the Reformers before the Reformation, with the exception of one only.

The mode of apprehending our subject represented by the last-named theologians, especially by Thomas à Kempis and

[1] *De simplic. vitæ Christianæ*, v. 15.

Savonarola, is typical for the nobler and better Middle Ages in general as compared with the true form of life of the Christian community as restored by the Reformation. The highest that the development of the life of Western Christendom was able to produce up to the beginning of the sixteenth century was men whose testimony concerning Jesus the Crucified, and concerning the power of this testimony of the cross, was related to that of Luther much as the prophetic testimony of John the Baptist was related to the Messianic testimony of Christ. The depths of the mystery of the cross were recognised and sounded by them; but in consequence of a loving diving into those depths there cleave to them wounds and bruises which do not suffer their devout consciousness to penetrate to perfect liberty and serenity in Christ. The art of dying with Christ they understand, but the art of rising again by the help of His Spirit remains for them more or less strange; they experience abundantly the "fellowship of the sufferings" of the Lord, but the "power of His resurrection" (Phil. iii. 10) attests itself only imperfectly in their teaching and life. Between a sickly asceticism and an enthusiastic idolising of the Romish ecclesiastical ideal, with its manifold externalisation, and its forms of degeneracy partly of a work-holy, partly of a superstitious nature, does the piety of these times in general oscillate ceaselessly to and fro: an indecision which makes itself felt in a characteristic manner, even in the innermost centre of the Christian-believing consciousness, in the position of the heart towards the crucified Saviour. For sometimes the impulse to a loving embracing and inner experience of the sensation of His wounds manifests itself with such intense fervour and such overpowering force, that the pious devotionalist is smitten as with incurable sickness, and remains incapable of truly free and fruitful labour in the service of the Lord. Sometimes, on the other hand, it is only the external side of the central fact of salvation, the significance of the cross as the towering, widely swaying banner of the Church militant, as the victorious emblem of Constantine, upon which they fix the eye, and by which they are fired with an enthusiasm producing more and more only an external churchliness, but not true Christianity. *The desire to possess the cross at the same time in each of these forms and expressions—as a humbling cross of suffering, and as a cross of magnificence, glittering with gold and precious stones—prevails with all men of this time and tendency, even the most advanced and enlightened.* Where the recognition of the irreconcilableness of these two forms of confession to the Crucified forces its way into decided clearness, there it is at once over with the peaceful remaining of the man who has struggled into such recognition any longer within the Church; there the necessity arises, even without taking the field with iconoclastic fanaticism against the cross as an external object of devotion, as did Claude of Turin and Peter de Bruis, nevertheless, for a rupture with the existing Church communities. The rejection in principle of the ecclesiastical adoration of the cross impels, as the example of the Waldenses shows, with inexorable force to the formation of sects. Only a cautious shrinking from drawing the last practical conclusions, as is the case with Meister Eckart, and in another manner with Wessel, with Staupitz, and some others of these representatives of a decidedly spiritual conformation of the idea of the cross, is able to retain externally the bond with the Romish Church. That neither the unnatural rigours of ascetic self-castigation, nor the superstitious confidence in these or those sensuous representations of the Crucified One, express the true sense of the following of the cross demanded by Christ; that the one and the other of these forms of devotion represent deviations from the genuine and original form of truth for Christian piety, this the Reformation first brought into living recognition within wider circles, and, moreover, to a permanently blessing-fraught practical effect.

·

VI.

The Cross in the Theology and Church of the Reformation.

WITH the radically altered position assigned in the Reformation to the *principle* on which salvation is obtained, there stood in necessary connection an essentially new conception and treatment of the *symbol* of salvation. The nature of the change and renewing which this underwent we shall have to designate as a SPIRITUALISING. For the cultus rendered to it by the Christendom of the Middle Ages was of a one-sidedly sensuous character. Not merely that which it undertook for the testing of the power of the cross upon the field of missions, for the glorifying of its dignity and greatness by liturgical acts, for the unfolding of its æsthetic fulness of ideas in works of plastic art and poetry, bore a preponderantly selfish, yea partly superstitious materialistic character: even its penetration into the interior of this profoundly significant emblem, its attempts at a more earnest experience and more ethico-theological presentation of the idea of the cross, showed themselves more or less strongly affected by this tendency to the externalisation and materialising of that which the Divine Founder of Christianity had revealed as essentially spiritual precepts and truths. It is a severe judgment which is passed upon the Church of the Middle Ages, especially the Papal Church, but it is not untrue: "The more in it the cross came into use in its manifold forms and symbols, so much the more did true evangelical faith in

Christ the Crucified also disappear. The more the cross of Christ became outwardly represented, the more did it become inwardly an offence and folly to men. The Catholic Church reminds us in this respect of those Christians who speak too much of their spiritual experiences, make too much ado about it, so that at last they talk themselves out, and utter brilliant sayings with very little solidity in them."[1]

What was needed was to oppose to this extreme externalisation, which had befallen not only the practical cultic handling of the subject, but even the conception of the cross itself, before all things, a spiritualising purification and critical regeneration of its idea. In opposition to the one-sided and exuberant *theologia gloriæ*, into which the following of the Crucified had degenerated in almost all the domains of life and of teaching, even that of asceticism not excepted, it was necessary to set up a new and genuine *theologia crucis*, drawn from the depths of the life-giving word of God. And this process of renewal and spiritualisation might not remain a merely external one. Not merely what Scripture in truth TEACHES concerning the cross of the Lord, was it necessary to bring to the remembrance of the Church and of all the world: it must also be exemplified in a new and better way than before, how one LIVES under the cross as scripturally apprehended and experienced. It must be alike theologically demonstrated, and in a practical Christian manner proved in the life—before friends and foes, in presence of the one-sided encomiasts of that which was ancient in the Church, as in presence of the alienation from all that is Christian and churchly, making its presence felt in wider and ever wider circles—in what the true confession of Jesus and His cross consists, and what FRUITS it produces.

A contemplation under three points of view will serve to make us acquainted with the efforts and accomplished results of the Reformation Church and its theology in our domain.

[1] Herzog, *Theol. R. E.*, viii. 60 f. (Supplementary words of the editor to H. Merz's Art. "Kreuz.")

We have to see how in the first place the idea of the cross is traced back by the testimony of the Reformers and their theological successors to its pure and evangelical primary form ; how in the second place this article of the cross, purified and spiritualised in accordance with the principle of the Reformation, is maintained and brought into operation, as well in the sphere of worship as polemically against the advocates of the sensuous cross-cultus of the Romish Church ; finally, what influences proceed from the new scriptural and more spiritual apprehension of the symbol of salvation to the domain of the artistic and scientific—especially the philosophic scientific—creation. Another attestation and verifying of the idea of the cross restored in the Reformation, namely, that in the practical ethical life of the Church, especially in its missionising (converting and educating of peoples) at home and abroad, must, as forming that part of its task in greatest measure yet incomplete, having still to realise the greater number of its problems in the future, become the subject for an independent examination in a closing chapter.

A. *THE SPIRITUALISING OF THE IDEA OF THE CROSS BY THE THEOLOGY OF THE REFORMATION.*

As opposed to the tendency of the pre-reformational theology, aiming either exclusively at the glorification of the cross in accordance with the Romish ecclesiastical tradition, or at least at the combination of such external glorification with an inner and purer cultus of the cross, LUTHER declares himself a "theologian of the cross" simply, *i.e.*, a representative of the theology which enters with full decision into the following of the Saviour in the Biblical sense. "The cross of Christ," he says in his exposition of the sixth Psalm, "is the only instruction in the word of God, the absolutely pure theology."[1] As early as the time of the Heidelberg Dispu-

[1] Crux Christi unica est eruditio verborum Dei, theologia sincerissima. *Operatt. in Psalm.* vi., ver. 11.

tation (1518) he expressly gives in his adhesion to this *theologia crucis*, in opposition to the *theologia gloriæ* of the Romelings, who, in their high-soaring endeavours after an intelligent contemplation of God, upon the invisible or intellectually apprehended phase of His existence, ignore precisely that which is at hand and visible, by which God has revealed Himself in Christ—His back (*posteriora*), *i.e.*, His humanity, weakness, yea, the folly of His cross—and thereby, as well as by their aversion for the lowly following of the Lord in suffering, prove themselves "enemies of the cross." " The *theologus gloriæ* calls the evil good, and the good evil; the *theologus crucis* calls things by their true names, that is, he fails not to recognise the God concealed in suffering and humiliation, but as a true friend of the cross " calls the cross good, but the works of the law worthless: for by the cross are these works brought to nought, and the old Adam is crucified; which last, on the other hand, is by works first thoroughly built up." In short, only "in Christ the Crucified is found true theology and the right knowledge of God."[1] In harmony with this programme of his course as a Reformer, put forth at the very outset of that course, does he repeatedly declare himself in his later writings and sermons against the external religiously and morally worthless cross-worship of the Papists. He reproves the clergy in the papacy, who "rather bear the cross of Christ in silver than in the heart and life." " They have made it in silver, since it is thus good to bear, and does not pain; yea, it sells its kisses and blessings, and has become to them a servant profitable for their pleasure. But into the heart must the dear cross not come, must also have nothing to do with their life." These convenient Christians say, with all the appearance of sanctity, Christ's

---

[1] *Disputat. Heidelberg.*. Thes. 19—21; with the explanations appertaining thereto. (Opp. ad Reform. histor. spect., t. i., p. 399 sq.) The expression *posteriora Dei*, employed in the twentieth thesis (. . . qui visibilia et posteriora Dei per passiones et crucem conspecta intelligit), is an emblematisation of the revelation of God in creation, taken from Exod. xxxiii. 23. in accordance with the language of the earlier Mystics, and occurs, *e.g.*, with Tauler, and even with Sebast. Frank and others.

cross is better than their own, and for this reason pass by their own cross, which they were bound to take up and bear after Him, "that they might full honourably bear His, yea, even reverence and worship it as an idol!"[1] To the same effect is also his zealous protestation against the abuse of dedicating churches to the wood upon which Christ hung, and showing to it other outward signs of reverence, in gold, silver, and precious stones. "Now that one should wish to trample the sacred cross under foot is also not good. That one should revere it is indeed excellent; but that one should fall down before it, dedicate churches to it, make the soul's salvation dependent upon it, this is not well."[2] "The worldly wise," it is said in another place, "call it bearing the cross when one encloses a fragment of the holy cross in a golden cross or monstrance, and when the priest puts on a cope, puts a stole round his neck, and then carries the same silver or golden cross about the church, gives it to the people to kiss, that they may offer pennies. O the folly! For the sake of avoiding such jugglery and idolatrous error I would burn the holy cross to powder, if I had a piece of it. For Christ says not (Matt. x. 38), Take my cross! but, thy cross, and bear it; let my cross be, on which I have suffered much shame. See that thou also thus suffer on thine, which is laid upon thee. . . . . Thus thou hast what it is to bear thy cross, to lift up the cross of Christ, or find the same. A thing which consists not in offering, kissing, or frequenting the holy cross, but in everywhere with patience receiving and enduring unjust treatment."[3]

That Luther's rejection of the outward cross-worship of ecclesiastical tradition was no such radical and fanatical one, that he would not have willingly retained certain more harmless and simple uses of the same, is well known. It will besides be further referred to below, in treating more specially

---

[1] *Pred. am hl. Dreikönigstage.* Erlangen edn., Bd. x., S. 397.

[2] *Pred. am Tage der Kreuzerhebung.* Bd. xv., S. 455 f.

[3] *Sermon vom Kreuz und Leiden* (held 1522). Bd. xx., S. 318 f.; comp. also the sermon under the same title belonging to the year 1531. Bd. xvii., S. 40 ff.

of the practices in this respect observed in worship by the Protestants and their opponents. Here we have more immediately to complete the series of those of his utterances which belong to the theological development of the article of the cross in its dogmatic and ethical aspect.—There are *two kinds or stages of the cross*, thus does he frequently teach, namely, the ordinary suffering imposed by the Lord upon men, which does not deserve the name of a suffering for Christ's sake, or cross in the narrower sense; and the true cross, severe suffering on account of the testimony of Christ, combined with reproach in the sight of the world, yea, with apparent abandonment by God. "By the cross of Christ," he continues in the sermon last cited, "you are not to understand this or that wood on which Christ hung; but the cross of Christ is the reproach and great ignominy which Christ innocent endured. If I lie in bed and am sick, or if one on account of his transgression is put to death by fire, water, or sword, this is not the cross of Christ; but infamy and persecution for righteousness' sake is the cross of Christ. Therefore must true Christians be branded as heretics, as transgressors, they must be condemned, despised, and judged of every one, so as to become a dishclout to every one; even as the prophet speaks in Ps. xl. 18 [17], 'I am a solitary one and utterly poor,'[1] as though he would say, The whole world has forsaken me, and I stand here all alone, regarded by no man, but rather by every one despised and contemned." Similarly in another place:[2] "That is also a cross, if I stand and suffer, and have none to console me; but that is after all only a poor cross. But if I stand and suffer, and all people sing thereat, and dance, and say, That was well deserved, yea, he deserved much more—as was done to the apostles: this is the right and true cross, thus to be forsaken, both by men and by God; that is to find the true cross; and when it is now found, one must also exalt it, not as the Emperor Heraclius or as the stationists, but by thanking and praising

---

[1] Ich bin ein einziger und ganz arm.
[2] *Pred. am Tage der Kreuzerh.*, Bd. xv., S. 460 f.

God on account of it, etc. .... So also our cross, while we still remain therein, is indeed more infamous than the wheel or gallows; but when one has thus in faith borne it, it becomes so delicious as Christ's cross now is; and as His is now manifest, so will ours also become manifest."[1]—Especially in this latter form—one of particular severity and heaviness, as a testimony by suffering for Jesus' sake, imposed by God Himself, and accompanied by infamy in the sight of all the world—is the cross a characteristic badge and NECESSARY ATTRIBUTE of Christianity, in Christians as a whole and as individuals. It is the "sign and watchword of all Christians." It is for us all "a certain mark and sign that we belong to the kingdom of God." No one who will belong to this kingdom may be ashamed of it: all who will be Christians must bear this burden imposed upon them by Christ. "When the kingdom of Christ approaches, the cross follows immediately upon it: God's anger and the cross are for us an (indispensable) exercise in faith."[2] The whole life of the Christian is indeed "nothing else but a life of faith, of love, and of the holy cross—a walk wherein one ever advances from faith to faith, from love to love, from patience to patience, and from cross to cross."[3] "Therefore does also the Euangelion bear its device, which Paul gives to it, 1 Cor. i. 18: *Verbum crucis*, a word of the cross. He who will not have the cross must also be without the word. It is true, nothing more lovely were to be found in heaven or on earth than the word without a cross. But it would not remain long to our humour, since nature is not able to bear for long together mere pleasure and delight: as the saying is, 'Man can endure everything except good fortune,'" etc.[4] In general, "where God's word is preached, accepted, or believed, and brings forth fruit, there the dear holy cross also cannot long be a-wanting; pray let no one think that he will have peace,

---

[1] Similar also are his observations on Gal. v. 11, 12 (*Comm. maj. in Ep. ad Galat.*).

[2] *Works*, Bd. xv. 186; vi. 265 f., 427 f.; xx. 43, 317 f.; xxxviii. 14.

[3] Sermon on penitence and the sacrament, (*Kirchenpostille*, Bd. xi. 171.)

[4] "To the Christians at Augspurg," (Letters of the year 1523, Bd. liii. 226.)

but rather that he must stake everything that he has on earth: goods and honour, house and home, wife and child, body and life."[1]—Thus does the cross accordingly belong to the number of the essential and necessary marks of true Christians. The treatise, "Von den Conciliis und Kirchen" (1539), mentions expressly as a seventh and last sign (or sacrament in the wider sense) of the " Christianly holy people," in addition to the word of God, baptism, the supper, keys, spiritual office of preaching and prayer; also, "the salutary mystery (Heilthum)[2] of the sacred cross, that it (this people) must inwardly bewail all affliction and persecution, every kind of assault and evil (as the petition of the Lord's prayer is), from the devil, world, and flesh; must be exposed, terrified, outwardly poor, despised, sick, weak, suffering; .... and the cause thereof must alone be this, that it cleaves firmly to Christ and the word of God, and thus also for Christ's sake suffers (Matt. v. 10)."[3]

And not only does Luther speak often and much of the necessity of the cross for all Christians; he expresses himself also equally often and at large on its object and its salutary fruit.—As the OBJECT of the cross he brings into prominence in the first place the advancement of the individual in the life of faith, and in loving devotion of himself to the Christian fellowship: "that it may impel and constrain us unto believing, and extending the hand the one to the other." Further: "that our faith become approved and manifest for the world, that other people also be stirred up to believe, and we also be lauded and praised." Further: "to this end also is the holy cross good, that one thereby quell sin; when it thus whispers to thee, the enticement loses its power over thee, be it envy, hatred, anger, or other sin. To this end has God imposed upon us the holy cross, that it may impel and constrain us to flee to Christ, and to seek grace and help in

---

[1] *Catech. maj.*, third chapter, p. 473, 65 M.
[2] *Heilthum* = salutare mysterium.
[3] Bd. xxv. 375.—Of the indispensable necessity of the cross for the Church, he treats further in *Comm. maj. in Ep. ad Gal.*, t. iii., p. 60 sq.

Him."[1]—As the MEANS whereby the cross attains to its main end in the quelling of sin, does the Commentary on the Epistle to the Galatians adduce faith, hope, the sword of the Spirit—in general, the whole armour of God. "One knows the mode of this crucifixion: the nails, which through the grace of God penetrate deeply, and hinder the flesh from following its desires and lusts, are the word of God, Eccles. xii. 11," etc.[2] And this cross *ought* to hurt the old man; it is meet that it should painfully wound him, in order to withdraw him from the service of sin. "The cross ought to be so constituted as to give pain; ought not to be self-chosen (as the Anabaptists and all work-righteous ones teach), but to be laid upon us. . . . . For the devil, a mighty, evil, crafty spirit, hates the children of God. In addition to this, the cross serves for the exercise of faith, for the correction of the word; item, to quell the remaining sin and pride. Yea, a Christian can just as little dispense with the cross as with food and drink."[3] Even from that which has been already cited, it is evident in what the salutary FRUIT and effect of the cross consists. "God casts us into the midst of the fire of assaults, sufferings, and tribulations, by which we are to our very end cleansed and proved; in order that thus not only sin should be the more mortified the longer we live, but also that faith might become approved and increase, that we become from day to day more certain of our cause, grow in the understanding of Divine wisdom and knowledge, that Scripture becomes ever brighter and clearer for us, in order so much the more powerfully to admonish our own, and to reprove the gainsayers, by wholesome doctrine."[4] Next to these main effects, consisting in the preservation from sins, approvedness in the faith, upholding in the spirit of prayer, and advancement in Christian experience and wisdom, it is

---

[1] Bd. li. 343, 465; lii. 160.
[2] *Comm. in Gal.*, anno 1519, (Vol. xxiii. of his Latin works,) p. 441 sq.; *Comm. maj.* (ib. p. 55.)
[3] *Feine chr. Gedanken der alten hl. Väter*, etc., 1530. (lxiv. 298-300.)
[4] On 1 Pet. i. 7. (Second Exposition, Bd. lii. 24.)

specially also the consolation experienced in suffering with Christ, the blissful nature of a communion of sufferings with the Lord, which is brought forward as the fruit and reward of patient following of the cross. "The cross of Christ consists indeed in the afflictions which the Church endures *for Christ's sake*. He who touches her touches the apple of Christ's eye; and of a truth the head experiences more acutely and more quickly that which is done to it, than do the members. So then does Christ, our Head, when we suffer as His body, make these our afflictions His own, and suffers with us."[1] "Christ sanctifies by His contact all sufferings and tribulations of His believers: he who does not suffer, clearly shows that he does not believe, and that Christ has not made over to him His sufferings. If, however, any man will not bear the cross which God imposes on him, no one will compel him—he may certainly go and deny Christ; yet let him in doing so know that he has no fellowship with Christ, nor part in any one of His blessings."[2]

We have been more liberal comparatively in the quotation of these sayings of Luther having reference to the article of the cross, than we felt called to be in the contemplation of his spiritual predecessors; for the very point here under examination is wont as a rule to receive but slight notice, even in the more comprehensive presentations of the doctrinal characteristics of the great Reformer. This point has, for instance, been only incidentally touched upon here and there, not examined more at length, by Harnack and Köstlin in their works on Luther's theology, as likewise by Luthardt in his tractate on the ethics of Luther.[3] Of the declarations too of

---

[1] Ergo crux Christi generaliter significat universas Ecclesiæ afflictiones, quas propter Christum patitur (Act. ix. 4). Qui autem illam tangit, tangit pupillam oculi sui. Sensus subtilior et velocior est in capite, quam in reliquis membris corporis. . . . . Sic Christus, caput nostrum, afflictiones nostras suas facit, et patitur, cum nos, corpus ipsius, patimur.—*Comm. Maj. in Gal.* vi. 14.

[2] *Feine chr. Gedanken.* lxiv. 299. Comp. also Bd. iii. 412 f.; viii. 1000 f.; xv. 336 f.

[3] Occasional allusions of this nature, *e.g.*, in Köstlin, *Luther's Theologie*, ii. 545; in Luthardt, *Die Ethik Luther's in ihrem Grundzügen* (Leipzig 1867), S.

MELANCTHON which have reference to this subject, which, as regards their essential import, are at least closely akin to those of Luther, it cannot be said that in modern presentations of the history of dogmas or of the history of ethics they have met with the notice or appreciation due to them. Melancthon devotes a merited attention to the doctrine of the cross —as in general in pretty numerous passages of his writings, so in particular in those masterpieces which, as being of a specially classical character and historic importance, have become doctrinal standards in his Church. As he had already, in his " Unterricht der Visitatoren an die Pfarrherren " (1528), brought into relief the importance of this article by the setting apart of a special chapter, "Von Trübsal," to the consideration of this subject, so does he in the twenty-sixth article of the Augsburg Confession enumerate, among those doctrines which, in opposition to the externalisms and refinements of the scholastic doctrinal tradition, are specially salutary and necessary, immediately after the article of faith that of the cross.[1] He there emphatically declares, in opposition to the reproach of the adherents of Rome, to wit, that the Protestants, like Jovinian of old, denied the necessity for serious discipline and crucifixion of the flesh: the matter will "be seen from their writings to be very different. For they have always taught concerning the holy cross, that Christians ought to suffer ; and this is a true, earnest, and not feigned mortification."[2] The same thought occurs again in the corresponding place of the apology for the Augsburg Confession,[3] where moreover the necessity for a patient bear-

57.—An old tractate of Sidel, *Tröstliche Abhandlung Luther's von Leiden der Christen* (Halle, 1725), not accessible to us, appears substantially to consist only of those *Feine chr. Gedanken* of the year 1530. Similar to the above presentation, though not so complete, is the treatment of the subject in the author's address delivered at Berlin in 1874, "Das reformatorische 'Lehrstück vom Kreuze," etc. (*Evang. K.-Zeitung*, 1874, No. 47 ff.)

[1] Latin text : *de cruce ;* Germ. text : "vom Trost in hohen Anfechtungen."

[2] Semper enim docuerunt de cruce, quod christianos oporteat tolerare afflictiones. Hæc est vera, seria et non simulata mortificatio, variis afflictionibus exerceri et crucifigi cum Christo. (p. 57, 31 M. ; cf. p. 56, 15.)

[3] Art. xv. : *De traditionibus humanis*, p. 213, 45 M.

ing of the cross and of affliction is mentioned amongst the Christian duties of the first rank, such as the fear of God, love, faith, confiding in the Lord ; where the Church is designated as the kingdom of Christ and of His quickening Spirit, either manifest or "hidden under the cross;" where cross and affliction (similarly as often in the writings of Luther) are represented as the indispensable mark of the Christian, as a burden of necessity to be borne ; from which, so certainly as God imposes it, "the power of keys can set no one free or quit. Niemanden frei, los absolviren kann."[1] That enumeration too of the cross among the sacraments in the wider sense, which we observed above in Luther's treatise "Von den Conciliis und Kirchen," one meets already in Melancthon's Apology. In addition to prayer and alms, cross and affliction are instanced as acts or experiences of the Christian, which, because they "also have God's promise," might be reckoned among the sacraments. Although, according to another passage of the same Confession, they "do not merit reconciliation to God, but are thank-offerings, when those who are reconciled (versühnet) bear and endure such afflictions."[2]

In a connected manner, and even to a certain extent in systematic order, does Melancthon develop the theses relating to this subject in the chapter of his great dogmatic work which bears, in the editions of the second epoch of this work, (those from 1535,) the title: "Of afflictions, or the bearing of the cross;"[3] in those of the third epoch (from 1543), "Of sufferings and cross."[4] The motive for the insertion of this *locus* he expressly denotes as existing in the circumstance already mentioned by him on the occasion of his treating of the article of the Church, namely, that the Church of Christ is essentially of a spiritual nature, as well as the statement in particular "that the Church in this life is subject to the cross

---

[1] Art. iii., p. 117, 46 ; Art. iv., p. 155, 18 ; Art. vii., p. 196, 57 ; 197. 59 sqq.
[2] Art. viii., p. 204, 16 ; Art. xxiv., p. 263, 67.
[3] De afflictionibus seu de cruce toleranda.
[4] De calamitatibus et cruce.

and afflictions."[1] This fact of the subjection of the Church to the cross forms accordingly the proper theme of which the whole section treats. And indeed there are in the yet briefer elaboration of the locus, as it is presented in the editions of the second epoch, in the main only four doctrines, which he briefly expounds with a view to rendering apparent the necessity and the Divine aim in the fact spoken of.

1. We do not suffer accidentally, but in accordance with God's design, or at least permission.

2. God does not impose His sufferings upon us in order to destroy us, but in order to call us to repentance; so that afflictions are, properly speaking, signs of His favour and compassion.

3. Instead of displaying ill-humour or grief, the suffering Church has to exercise herself in obedience and patient submission to the will of God; and this for the following reasons:—

(*a*) On account of the sin still present in the flesh of her members;

(*b*) Because she must in suffering become conformed to Christ, her head;

(*c*) Because sufferings for Christ's sake form the true spiritual sacrifices of praise, which God desires.

4. A main object, for the sake of which God sends us sufferings, is that of affording us a stimulus to exercise in faith and prayer,—with which the training to sincere patience, steadfastness, meekness, resignation, etc., as a further aim in the Divine ordaining of suffering, is immediately connected.[2]

In an enlarged form does our article appear in the *Loci* of the third epoch, where it immediately precedes, and is preparatory to, the chapter which treats of prayer. Those four Divine aims or designs in the ordaining of cross and afflictions are here also again enumerated, though in a somewhat altered

---

[1] Cum dictum sit, Ecclesiam in hac vita subiectam esse cruci et afflictionibus, visum est adiicere quædam de hoc loco, etc. (*Loci comm.* secundæ ætatis, p. 528 sqq. Opp. ed. Bretschn., t. xxi.)

[2] *l.c.*, pp. 528–534.

order of succession (in such wise that No. 4 appears transposed before No. 3), and moreover augmented by a new element : the reference to the fact that God, precisely when He most severely chastens, promises His help as immediately at hand, together with alleviation and deliverance from the ill. This point appears placed in the midst of the others, so that the whole pentade of Divine aims in suffering now forms the succession : 1. no accident, etc.; 2. call to repentance; 3. nearness of the Divine help under the heaviest cross ; 4. exercise calling forth faith and prayer ; 5. exercise in patience and lowly obedience.—This pentade of Divine salutary aims, in which the Christian is able to recognise equally many grounds of consolation or means of blessing (*remedia calamitatum*), is preceded by a decade of grounds for the phenomenon that the Church is unquestionably subject far more than the children of this world to suffering and affliction. This fact, so incomprehensible for the children of the world, and for the most part employed by those philosophers who fall back only upon earthly knowledge and wisdom [1] for deducing the most perverted consequences, is explained, according to Melancthon, on the following ten grounds :—

1. The children of God have their part like others in the general depravity of our race.

2. It is meet that the chastisements and judgments of God should begin with the members of His household.

3. The devil directs his assaults particularly and especially against them.

4. Those whom God loves He chastens above others.

5. The sufferings of the pious have to serve as salutary exemplifications of doctrine for others.

6. The same are at the same time indirect proofs for a retribution in a better state of existence, pledges for a reward beyond the grave.

7. They serve for bringing into conformity with Christ, and with the sufferings of Christ.

---

[1] The representatives of that materialistic wisdom, quæ defigit oculos in materiam, nec de hominibus aliter quam de pomis aut violis aut rosis cogitat.

8. They serve, even where they are not chastisements for known and definite sins, for the purging away of such imperfections—still cleaving to the saints—as a false sense of security, impure thoughts in the heart, vain self-reflection, doubts, etc.

9. They are designed to make manifest that saints serve God out of pure obedience for His own sake.

10. They are intended to show that not carnal might and power, but the invisible strength of Christ, which is mighty in the weak, rules the Church.

A third scheme, devoted to the classification of sufferings generally, according to their nature and aim, concludes the whole instructive treatise. All suffering of men is reducible to four kinds, develops itself in the four species, which differ from each other in degree:

1. *Punishments* properly so called, merited corrections, τιμωρίαι.[1]

2. *Trials*, or sufferings of a testing character, δοκιμασίαι,—serving for the calling into exercise of faith and zeal for prayer, in time of prosperity; but also for the advancement of virtue, watchfulness, courage, etc., in adversity.

3. Sufferings for a *testimony*, μαρτύριον, *confessio*, — by means of which no sin whatever finds expiation, but, as in the case of Abel, Isaac, Jeremiah, the prophets who were put to death innocent, Paul, and other apostles, etc., only the certainty of Divine truth is attested and the higher value of the "life beyond," as compared with the earthly life here staked against it, is made manifest.[2]

4. *Redemptive* sufferings, λύτρον,—for the expiatory bearing of the punishment incurred by a sinful humanity; a kind of suffering undertaken solely and alone by Christ, the sinless

---

[1] For which expression some of the later dogmatists among the Lutherans, *e.g.*, Hebenstreit, Baier, and Hollaz, of the Reformed Coccejus, Heidegger, prefer employing the synonymous παιδεῖαι. (Comp. Ritschl, *Lehr. v. d. Rechtfertig.*, etc., iii. 33.)

[2] . . . . testimonia, quibus ostendunt se, cum veritatem vitæ anteferunt, serio sic sentire de Deo, ut docent ac vere statuere nequaquam fabulosam esse doctrinam evangelii; testantur item restare aliam vitam et aliud judicium post hanc vitam. (p. 954.)

Son of God and Son of man, for the enduring of which no ordinary sinful child of man is able.

Even apart from this scale of the kinds of suffering of the cross, the introduction of which into the dogmatic-ethic doctrinal tradition of our (Lutheran) Church belongs in itself to the meritorious services of the gifted *Præceptor Germaniæ*, the reasonings of the *Locus* to which we refer present not a little that is instructive and worthy of careful attention. Thus, among other things, an admirable description of the essential character of Christian patience, in opposition to the bearing of heathen heroes and philosophers under calamity, a bearing wanting in all true steadfastness. So also an exposition, worthy of all consideration, of the manner in which we have to suffer in the service of the Church, and for the Church: free from selfish zeal, hatred, or envy; standing forth for the pure doctrine with dignified seriousness and calm spirit, etc.[1]—The Lutheran dogmatists of the sixteenth and beginning of the seventeenth century, who after Melancthon's example retain our article as an integral part of the Church's system of doctrine, show themselves entirely dependent on him. They alter but little, and nothing that is essential, in the mode of treatment introduced by him; any instances of perfecting that which was contributed by him they are not able to present. The theological "Examen," or Compendium, composed at Helmstädt by TILEMAN HESSHUSIUS, the well-known controversialist, places the gradation of the different kinds of sufferings at the head of the chapter "von Kreuz und Trost;" and reduces them at the same time—in accordance with the method of abbreviating and excerpting pursued throughout—from a tetrade to a triad, inasmuch as he comprehends in one Nos. 2 and 3 the sufferings of the nature of a trial and the sufferings for a testimony.[2] LEONHARD HÜTTER'S *Loci Communes* place

---

[1] Non dimicandum est de privatis affectibus, non prætexendæ publicæ causæ odiis privatis et livori, sed veræ et necessariæ doctrinæ puritas graviter et sedatis animis defendenda est. (p. 952.)

[2] Tilem. Hesshusii Examen theologicum, continens præcipuos locos doctrinæ christianæ. Helmst. 1587. (p. 438, Loc. xxi.: *De cruce et consolatione.*)

in like manner the main kinds of suffering first, but with the retaining of Melancthon's number of four. On the nature and significance of the sufferings as a trial, as also of the sufferings for a testimony, they discourse pretty fully, and offer many useful contributions in addition; *e.g.*, the proof that the so-called trials are never merely and simply trials, but also in some way chastisements for sin; in like manner do they afford an instructive disquisition concerning true and false witnessings by suffering, and especially the glittering semblance of martyrdom on the part of schismatics and heretics. The examination of the causes of sufferings appears in Hütter enlarged by all sorts of polemic and scholastic additions; it begins with the refutation of the errors advanced by the Epicuræans, Stoics, Calvinists, Astrologists, Apocalyptists, the stricter (materialistically disposed) Aristotelians, concerning the true causes of sufferings; then distinguishes general grounds—the fall, God's righteousness, compassion, pedagogic wisdom—and special grounds, resolving the latter again into such as serve to explain the sufferings of the ungodly, and such as serve to explain the sufferings of the godly. The special grounds for explaining the sufferings of the godly are developed in the form of ten points, which resemble the corresponding decade in Melancthon's writings, although deviating from them on some single points, and here and there also presenting something new which is of real value.[1] Somewhat enlarged also appears the chapter on the consolation of Christians in suffering; Melancthon's pentade of consolatory grounds here having become an octade, which are clearly elucidated by means of passages of Scripture cited, and in part also by argumentation in the form of syllogisms.[2] With Hütter

---

[1] So, *e.g.*, under No. 10 a good critique of the Romish conception of the sufferings of martyrs as actual satisfactions or expiatory redemptive sufferings (λύτρα) after the example of Jesus; as well as of the abuse of the passage, Col. i. 24 (of the *adimpletio defectuum passionis Christi*), to which Bellarmine had recourse for the purpose of defending this view.

[2] L. Hutteri, *Loci comm. theologici*, Viteb. 1619, loc. xxx.: De cruce et calamitatibus sive afflictionibus humanis. (pp. 933—948.)

(† 1616) already comes to a close the succession of those Lutheran dogmatists who assert for the article of the cross a fixed place in the system of the *Loci Communes*. Even as Chemnitz, in his expository lectures on the *Loci* of his teacher, Melancthon, devoted no attention to the section treating of this subject, as in like manner the dogmatic labours of Ægid. Hunnius do not know the doctrine of the cross and afflictions as a special chapter of the Protestant system of doctrine, so is this doctrine altogether wanting in most of the dogmatic systems from the beginning of the seventeenth century, such even as the particularly comprehensive and highly esteemed work of John Gerhard. Yet QUENSTEDT († 1688) still thought well to incorporate in his armour-clad doctrinal edifice of the "Didactic-polemic Theology" a locus, *De cruce et de probatione vitæ*, strongly seasoned with dialectic additions in accordance with the then prevailing scholastic taste, which he placed in immediate proximity to the section treating of faith, of prayer, and other means for appropriating salvation.[1] Some smaller compendiums, too, in part belonging to a still later period, concede, in praiseworthy return to the precedent given by Melancthon, a special chapter to the doctrine of the cross. So the "Geistliche Deutungen allerhand weltlicher auserlesener Historien" of JOH. MOLLER (1650) and the "Ordnung des Heils in Tabellen," composed by the venerable practical expositor of the Bible, CHRISTOPH STARKE in 1734, which as a thirtieth article—between that of Good Works and that of Prayer—treats pretty fully of "das Creutz."[2]

The early disappearing of our article from the Lutherandogmatic systems of doctrine, at least from the specially distinguished and influential ones, may be a matter for regret, and—as an indication of a too exclusive value at-

---

[1] *Theologia didactico-polemica* (Viteb. 1691), part iv. cap. 10. (p. 346 sq.)
[2] Joh. Moller (Past. in Dirschau) *Allgori · profano-sacræ, d. i. geistl. Deutungen*, etc., Jen. 1650. (Thl. i., c. 27.)—Chr. Starke (then not as yet at Driesen, where he died in 1744, but still at Neunhausen): *Ordnung des Heils in Tabellen*, etc., Königsberg 1734. 4° (S. 58).

tached to the theoretical or intellectual side of saving truth, in distinction from its practical moments—a thing to be censured.[1] Yet we must not forget, in connection with this phenomenon, that at all events valuable contributions towards its development have been afforded in the form of special treatises, even on the part of those Lutheran teachers of the Reformation age and the period immediately succeeding it, who do not concede to it a place in the organic unity of the Church's doctrinal system. This they effected more particularly by means of practical hortatory or consolatory tractates. Of such parænetic monographs upon our theme we possess several of eminent value from the pen of Brenz and Urbanus Rhegius, the two Swabian reformers. JOHN BRENZ composed in the years 1527, 1528, soon after the commencement of his spiritual functions at Swabian Hall, and as it seems with a view to the supplementing of his two catechisms published at about the same time, a group of four little tractates ("Etlich Tractetli"), all of them having reference to our subject. The first of these, "How the wood of the cross is to be lopped, and to be most softly handled," pursues in a popularly original manner the thought that we must learn not to flee the cross of the Lord, in itself knotted, unplaned, and hard pressing, but to "lay hold of it in the softest place, that it may not be too heavy to bear—auf dass es nit zu schwer werde zu tragen." And indeed "the cross becomes for us smooth and planed, if we see in Christ our future redemption and resurrection. If now by faith we see the Son of God hanging on the cross, we see also on the cross the resurrection (Urstend) and Easter Day. Then is there joy in sorrow, life in death, glory in reproach, *in labore requies*. . . . . The world cannot take that grip: it is blind, knows not how to say anything of the crucified God: it thinks it will seize the cross at the softest place; but it sees not the

[1] Comp. Ritschl, *as before*, iii. 156, who censures the phenomenon in question as a "mutilation of the Lutheran dogmatics," and seeks to explain it from the predominating "stress laid by Melancthon upon the articles of faith as the main characteristic of the Church."

Son of God before its eyes, and accordingly finds nothing else but hurt, ruin, loss. But a Christian sharpens his eyes, thinks not so much of the cross as of the Son of God (of the Word), in whom is found a gain a hundredfold more than is lost. There is no need of argument upon this point: if one finds the Son of God upon the cross, he finds a store of all good things. .... In short, let a cross come how it may, in body, or possessions, etc., so is it always at top and bottom most hard and almost unplaned; but in the middle part, where the Son of God hangs, it is most smooth and most soft." The second tractate, "For what cause prosperity and adversity are sent;" as also the third, "How one should stand towards things indifferent, such as Church customs which are called ceremonies;" and not less the fourth, "Of sufferings and Divine Providence," are devoted to the treatment of the same subject. In a specially elaborate manner does the last develop the evangelical grounds of consolation, by which we are to be raised and strengthened under cross and affliction; and this on the basis of the eighth chapter of the Epistle to the Romans, which, in the leading points of its argument, is practically expounded and applied.[1] The special attention which Brenz in particular devoted to our subject is manifest also from the chapter "Of cross and sufferings," inserted in the Brandenburg-Nürnberg liturgy of the year 1532, which was compiled mainly under his co-operation, as well as from the corresponding section of his larger catechism, of the year 1551.[2]—Of URBANUS RHEGIUS, several writings of the period of his labours as Lüneburg superintendent (1530—1536) bear upon our subject: a consolatory letter to the Christians at Hildesheim, a tractate on the "medicine of the soul" (Medicina animæ),

---

[1] The first three of the "Etlich Tractetli durch Joh. Brentz Ecclesiasten zu Schwebisch Hall geschrieben" (1528) are furnished in the (German) work of J. Hartmann, "Life and Selected Writings of Joh. Brenz" (Elberf. 1862), S. 322 ff. Of the fourth he furnishes, S. 131, a pretty complete epitome. The first two Tractetli appear also in Klaiber's *Evangel. Volksbibliothek*, Stuttg. 1868, Bd. ii., S. 24 ff.

[2] Hartmann, *as before*, S. 138, 154, 288.

and especially a "Trostbüchlein" to the Christians at Hanover, against the raging and blaspheming of the Papists—"wider der Papisten wüten und lestern," Wittenb. 1536.[1] In the last-named writing, the high value of which has been pointed out with becoming emphasis by Uhlhorn in his biography of Urban, it is shown how God in His leading of the pious ever most closely links together the three things: the Gospel, the cross, and the consolation of redemption. Everywhere He extends to them the heavenly ladder, upon which the Christian, who will not remain in the world, and with it be exposed to the judgment, has to climb up. This ladder has seven rounds, which, counted from below upwards, are: the gospel with the sacraments, faith, confession, cross, patience, experience (inward proof), and hope—to which God then adds, as an eighth and concluding upward step, His Divine deliverance or eternal life.[2] The central or middle position in the succession of the seven steps to be climbed represents, according to Urban, the cross, of the "immense utility" of which he treats with special fulness and minuteness. "Mark what a treasure lies hidden under the cross, which the world cannot see, namely, sanctification. We are by the cross finely meetened for sonship, in that this world loses its charm for us, and the future one is loved, and we desire it from our heart; for by the cross God impels us to a life of penitence. . . . . The cross makes cheerful, watchful, circumspect, vigorous, and serious Christians; but nothing

---

[1] Also in Latin: Consolatio in omni genere afflictionum et scala ad vitam coelestem, electis Christi membris in Hannovera, in *Opp. Urb. Rhegii*, Norimb. 1562, fol. 423—438. *Ibid.*, fol. 412 sqq., the Medicina animae; and fol. 381 sqq., the Libellus consolatorius electis . . . . Chr. membris in Hildesheym.

[2] This ladder of eight rounds is graphically presented at the close of the tractate, in the following manner:—

Liberatio ab omnibus malis: vita æterna	. . . .	H. 8.
Spes. Sperare gloriam post afflictionem s. crucem	. .	G. 7.
Probatio. Experiri quod Dei promissio vera sit .	. .	F. 6.
Patientiam sub cruce præstare, perdurare	. . .	E. 5.
Crucem propter Christum suscipere	. . . .	D. 4.
Christum ore et factis confiteri	. . . . .	C. 3.
Credere. Agnoscere peccat. in nobis et gratiam Dei	. .	B. 2.
Audire Evangelium Christi, Sacramentis Eccles. uti	. .	A. 1.

but prosperous days without the cross make snoring, uncircumspect, idle, lukewarm Christians, in whom seriousness dies out, and with whom the evil spirit can do what he will; for they lie there defenceless, pray not, do nothing, care nothing, as though there were no longer any necessity. While, after all, for a Christian no greater danger and necessity can arise than carnal security; for he soon altogether forgets God and himself, so that he lives on as the beasts, and asks after nothing more than this temporal state. Therefore is the cross as necessary for a Christian as food and drink." To the question of the great importance of this exercise and purification by means of the cross does he return at each of the following stages. Even at the seventh, that of hope, he observes, " If, then, the hope of Christians is not put to shame, there must also certainly follow help and consolation here under the cross, and after this affliction everlasting joy and life ; and he who unceasingly looks upon this reward becomes courageous and manly to ascend these steps."[1]

On the part also of several Lutheran theologians of the time of the Reformation the high significance of the cross as a divine measure for education, and a most important factor in the ethical development of Christians as a whole or as individuals, is duly appreciated. Thus in ANDR. OSIANDER'S " Consolatory Treatise, drawn against the Ungodly Assailants of the Word of God out of the three first Petitions of the Lord's Prayer," in LAZ. SPENGLER'S " Consolatory Christian Direction and Medicine under all Adversities," also in JUSTUS JONAS' plea for the marriage of priests, against the episcopal vicar of Constance, Joh. Faber, in which the necessity in particular of learning to know the cross of Christ and its sweetnesses from the experiences of married life is excellently brought out. In like manner in DAV. CHYTRAEUS' brief introduction to theological study (Rostock, 1558), where the cross is adduced as the tenth and last, but not on that

---

[1] A pretty complete epitome of this work in Uhlhorn, *Urb. Rhegius*, S. 270—274.

account least important, characteristic mark and means of forming the true theologian.[1] Some corresponding reflections upon our subject are also found in the *Meditationes sacræ* of JOH. GERHARD. That which he teaches in No. 41 of these meditations—Christ's suffering *for* all, *from* all, *in* all; in addition, the thought of the greatness of the heavenly reward, of the Exemplar of all saints, of the inner sweetness and blessedness of the cross itself, etc.—offers, it is true, no fully equivalent compensation for the absence of the article of the cross in his system of doctrine, but it nevertheless abounds in truly refreshing and consolatory suggestions, and by no means merits the severe judgment of Ritschl, who thought himself justified in characterising the contents of this chapter as an "exceedingly frigid reflection."[2] As the thoughtful and pleasing character of these Meditations of Gerhard on the cross, temptation, and patience[3] carries us back to the writings of Thomas à Kempis, so has it many points in common with the corresponding chapters in the "True Christianity" of the contemporary JOH. ARNDT, and further shows the numerous precious fruits of the later ascetic literature of our subject. We refer, for example, only to the heart-refreshing passion sermons and meditations of a Herberger, Joh. Heermann, M. Hyller, H. Müller, Hedinger, Rambach, Steinhofer, Lütkens, Lassenius, etc.; to the books for edification published under the title of "School of the Cross or of Consolation" (or of "School of the Cross" alone, or of "School of Patience," or "School of Conflict," or "Kreuz, Buss, und Betschule," etc.) by a Wudrian, Olearius, Müller, Kegel, Weidner, M. Fr. Roos, etc.; finally, and above all, to the classic productions of that master, properly so called, of this evangelical cross and con-

---

[1] *De Studio Theologiæ recte inchoando*, Rostoch., 1558 (1572). Comp. Th. Pressel, *Dav. Chytræus*, S. 15 f., and, as concerns the work of Justus Jonas, *Adversus Joh. Fabrum pro conjugio sacerdotali* (1523), the work by the same author, *J. Jonas*, S. 52.—On the writing of Osiander, above referred to, W. Möller, S. 274 f.

[2] *Lehre v. d. Rechtfertigung*, iii. 158.

[3] Comp., besides *Med.* 41: Fundamenta patientiæ Christianæ; also *Med.* 40, De utilitate tentationum; as well as *Med.* 42, Quomodo vincenda tentatio. De perseverantia, in Scholz' edition of the *Meditatt. sacræ*, and of the *Exercitium pietatis* (Gütersloh, 1863), p. 162 sqq.

solation literature, CHR. SCRIVER; specially the fourth or paracletic part of the "Soul's Treasure," Gotthold's "Bed of Sickness and Victory," together with several of the most valuable and thoughtful of Gotthold's "Emblems."[1] A more detailed reference to this literature would lead us—not indeed away from our theme, but in its prosecution beyond the limits of our special task. The names mentioned will suffice emphatically to remind of the abundant treasures our Church has accumulated in this domain, so extraordinarily conducive to the furtherance of the whole Christian life. They will serve to render manifest the fulness of salutary Christian fruits, ripened under the steadfast perseverance and progress of our fathers in Christ upon that lowly but victory and triumph-yielding path of the cross, which the chivalrous champion and protector of the German Reformation once chose, when, "untroubled about his coronet," he uttered the manly declaration, "I will acknowledge my Lord, whose cross is more to me than all the power of earth!"[2]

To the theology and Church of the REFORMED CONFESSION it certainly cannot be objected that it has been wanting in joyful readiness and steadfast courage for entering upon this path of the cross. Yet the position assumed by it in relation to our article appears to be one differing in many respects from that of the doctrinal tradition of the Lutheran Church. CALVIN'S *Institutio* presents, in its later and enlarged editions, a pretty comprehensive section, *De crucis tolerantia*, placed in the editions from 1559 downwards, between the chapter "On Self-Denial" and that "On the Contemplation of the Life to Come," and brought into specially close relation with the former; in such wise that the bearing of the cross appears as a constituent part in the work of self-denial, or a special form and mode of the same.[3] The tone of the

[1] As, *e.g.*, No. 136: "The Christian without a Cross." [Further references to the German literature of the subject will be found at this place in the author's own work.]

[2] John the Constant, when he was in the act of subscribing his name to the Augsburg Confession. (Comp. Schmidt, *Melancthon*, S. 201.)

[3] De crucis tolerantia, quæ pars est abnegationis. In the editions after 1559, lib. iii., cap. 8; previously (after 1545), lib. ii., c. 21, §§ 15—25.

argumentation therein presented is—in essential difference from that in the parallel chapters with Melancthon and his successors—not so much one of dogmatic expounding and consolatory edifying, as rather of earnestly exhorting, warning, and the enforcing of ethical rules and precepts. The paraenetic element preponderates over the paracletic to a very high degree. The whole section, which attaches itself to the ten exhortations to self-denial in the preceding chapter, comprehends in itself altogether eleven paræneses:

1. We must regard all trouble of this earth as a communion of the sufferings of Christ, or as a taking up of His cross;

2. We are to be lowly under the thought that, while Christ indeed suffered only and alone out of free obedience to the Father's will, no one of us suffers without guilt;

3. We are to learn from tribulation patience, and from patience experience, and from experience hope, Rom. v. 3, 4;

4. We are to regard all sufferings as salutary measures of God, to exercise us in obedience, and to try our faith as gold is tried in the fire (1 Pet. i. 7);

5. We are to recognise, from the obstinate resistance of our flesh to God's salutary discipline, how necessary it is to be exercised in the bearing of the cross;

6. We are to recognise in all sufferings the sign of the corrective fatherly love of God towards us, as His sons, not bastards, Heb. xii. 7 f.;

7. We are to esteem suffering for the sake of Christ and His righteousness, not as loss or shame, but as the highest honour, Matt. v. 10 f.; Acts v. 41;

8. We are to bear our cross with joyful gratitude towards God, to fight at all times valiantly against being overcome by the sense of pain;

9. We must be on our guard against the unnaturally rigid and rugged contempt of pain and death displayed by the Stoics, but rather follow the example of Him who wept with those that wept, as also the pattern given by the Apostle, 2 Cor. iv. 8—10;

10. We are to avoid also the extreme of despairing under affliction, following the example of a Peter, who for God and Christ's sake suffered himself to be girded and led whither he would not, John xxi. 18;

11. We are to learn in general, in opposition to the false and fatalistic-proud firmness of the philosophers, that true Christian patience through which the bitterness of the cross is succeeded and assuaged by true spiritual joy.

It produces to some extent the impression of harsh legality that these statements, however much of a paracletic character they may contain in themselves, yet almost without exception bear the form of precepts, exhortations, or warnings, that thus the *debet, decet, oportet*, etc., present therein a much greater number than do the applications of consolatory promises. The following chapter too, that on the contemplation of the life to come, bears this preponderantly parænetic, rather than thetically expository and paracletic, character. Yet the latter beautifully closes with a reference, equally hortatory as consolatory, to the bliss-giving power of the resurrection, which is exerted in us in and with the communion of the sufferings of Christ: "Then first triumphs in the hearts of believers the cross of the Lord over Satan, the flesh, sin, and the ungodly, when their eyes are directed to the power of His resurrection." (2 Thess. i. 6, sqq.) Important enlargements upon our subject are presented also in Calvin's treatise "On Offences" (*De scandalis*), with its affecting exhortations against the fear of the cross or the shunning of the cross. In like manner in his homilies on the principal Old Testament mine of doctrine on the cross of suffering, the book of Job, particularly on ch. xix. 17—25 of that book.[1]

Besides Calvin, it is specially PETER MARTYR VERMIGLI, among the Reformed Theologians, who devotes a more particular attention to the article of the cross of suffering as a salutary means of discipline on the part of God in His training and sanctifying operation upon the godly. His tractate "Of the Bearing of Cross, Afflictions, Flight, and

[1] Comp. Stähelin, *Joh. Calvin*, ii. 266 f., 426 ff.

Banishment," forms the twelfth *locus* in the evangelical system of doctrine, composed out of his writings after his death; preceded by that "Of the Christian Life," and followed by that "Of Prayer and the Intercession of Christ."[1] The treatment dwells, after advancing a number of reasons why God is wont to impose cross and afflictions, with special minuteness upon the distinction between those sufferings, on the one hand, which we have drawn upon ourselves or have imposed upon ourselves by an act of our own will, and that cross and suffering, on the other hand, imposed upon us by God. A patient bearing of the latter he declares to be infinitely more important, more salutary, but at the same time more difficult, than any self-chosen battling with our desires, even supposing this to be carried on with unsparing strictness and severity. In like manner are the noted virtues of heathen heroes and philosophers—firmness, self-denial, valour, etc.—far surpassed by the corresponding virtues of Christians; while the apostolic "rejoicing and glorying in tribulations" is something entirely foreign to the world of heathenism. For Christians' sufferings are only a means of advancing them upon the course of ethical perfection. "They are as the Red Sea, in which Pharaoh perishes, but Israel is delivered; for with the ungodly they call forth despair; with the godly, the certain assurance of salvation."

To Calvin and Peter Martyr attach themselves in part the leading representatives of the Dogmatic-ethic doctrinal tradition of the Reformed Church subsequent to them. Yet that neglect into which our article begins to fall in the teaching of the Lutheran Church, even in the generations immediately succeeding Melancthon, here makes its appearance if anything still earlier, and to a larger extent. To this contributes not a little the fact, which has its root in the essential characteristic of the Reformed Church itself, that *the polemic against the external cross-worship of the Romish tradition appears to a great number of distinguished teachers of*

[1] Petri Martyris, *Loci Comm. Theologici*, Basil., 1580. Tom. i., p. 1193—1212, De cruce et afilictionibus perferendis, ubi etiam de fuga et exilio.

this Church, and particularly several among the Reformers, as Zwingli, Farel, Beza, etc., *something of far greater importance and necessity than the conceiving of sufferings and trials under the point of view of the following of Christ, or of the cross imposed by Him*. This circumstance leads over to the contemplation of a second principal moment in the modern or post-Reformational development of our subject.

B. *THE TRANSFORMATION OF THE CULTIC USE OF THE CROSS IN ACCORDANCE WITH THE REFORMATIONAL SPIRITUALISING OF ITS IDEA, AND THE CONTROVERSIES WITH THE ROMISH THEOLOGIANS RELATING THERETO.*

In relation to the prevalent sensuous external conception of the idea of the cross and of its place in worship on the part of the Western Church, the representatives of the evangelical Theology and Church might occupy one of two positions. They might, in following the precedent of the pre-Reformers and Mystics of the Middle Ages, lay indeed a preponderating stress upon the spiritualised idea of the cross in the sense of Matt. xvi. 24, and yet for that reason deal sparingly with the sensuous honouring and glorifying of the symbol of salvation in connection with traditional rites of worship; thus they would reject and set aside only the worst forms of excrescence upon this domain, the absolutely contra-scriptural, idolatrous, heathenish. Or they might go to work in a more radical manner, and regard the whole province of a devotion cultivated through the medium of external signs and material representation from the point of view of idolatry, of that deifying of the creature forbidden in the second commandment of the Decalogue; by which the standpoint of a Claude, of a Peter de Bruis, and the Waldenses, is returned to, and the use of material crosses in worship is altogether banished.

At the milder and more conservative standpoint did the LUTHERAN Church place itself. Luther we saw above, simultaneously with his zealous opposition to the misplaced "external reverence" shown to the cross, giving utterance to the declaration, "That any should wish to tread even the sacred cross underfoot, were not good. *That one honours it, is indeed as it should be* (fein)," etc. In harmony with the spirit of this declaration is his whole theoretical and practical bearing in relation to this question. Decidedly as he warns against superstitious pilgrimages to crosses alleged to be endued with miraculous powers, adoration of splinters of the true cross, and such-like practices, as foolish " delusion and conceit," yea, as "nothing but error and idolatry;" indignantly as he exclaims, in opposition to the advocates of these superstitious doctrines and rites, " Therefore I would that all crosses were overthrown, which have thus exuded sweat and blood, whence have arisen the pilgrimages and bawling which have wrought so much error and misery;"[1] yet he will not on that account hear of a radical abolishing of all religious use of pictorial representations of the cross or of the Crucified ; yea, he expressly puts in a word in favour thereof. "Although I do not entirely reject images, and *specially the figure of the crucified Christ*," he says in one of his sermons on the day of the discovery of the cross. In accordance with the principle "that images and Sabbath are matters of freedom in the New Testament," does he regulate also his bearing towards crosses and crucifixes, alike in the exercise of his personal piety as in his influence upon the religious customs and institutions of the Lutheran community.[2] As he chooses as the arms of his seal a (white) rose, with (red) heart and (black) cross thereon,[3] so does he wish that every Christian father of the family of the evangelical communion should " in the morning, when he gets out of bed, bless himself with the holy cross," and after that pray his "*Das walt Gott*," etc. In like manner, he does not speak contemptuously or with condemnation, but rather with approbation, of the custom descended from the Papacy of saying "Benedicite, gratias,

[1] Sermon on the Day of the Elevation of the Cross (Erl. edn.), Bd. xv., S. 459.

[2] Sermon on the Day of the Invention of the Cross, Bd. xv., 334. Letter "To the Christians at Strassburg" (1524), liii., S. 275.

[3] Köstlin, *Luther, Sein Leben und seine Schriften* (1874), i., S. 22.

and other blessings morning and evening," as also of the "childish practice of blessing oneself,[1] when one sees or hears something dreadful and terrible." So does he by his sermons of the days of the invention and elevation of the cross sanction the retention of these high days in the festive cycle of his Church, and no less lays the foundation for the other religious applications which crucesignation and the cross have found in Lutheran lands ; for the use of altar-crucifixes and crosses in connection with funereal processions ; for the employment of the *crux usualis* in the benediction at the close of the service, in the act of baptism, in the consecration—not indeed of holy water, oil, salt, tapers, and such-like, but yet—of the bread and wine in the Lord's supper.

The polemic against the sensuous cultus of the cross in the Romish Church plays, in correspondence with this essentially conservative tendency, no specially prominent part either with Luther or the other fathers and founders of the Lutheran Reformation. It is ordinarily entirely wanting in such sermons, devotional writings, or dogmatic-ethical dissertations as are specially devoted to the contemplation of the cross in the spiritual sense. Neither Luther's sermons " Of Cross and Sufferings," nor the writings of a Brenz, a Rhegius, etc., bearing on this subject, nor Melancthon's *locus* thereon, contain critical excursions upon this field of polemics. The earliest attempts in the domain of Church History at contesting the right of the Romish adoration of the cross display a temperate and conservative bearing. The Magdeburg centuries still frankly acknowledge the existence of a religious use of the cross even in the period immediately succeeding the Apostolic age. They admit that from the well-known passage of Tertullian, where it speaks of the reproach of worshipping the cross brought against the Christians, it seems to follow that they then already possessed figures of the cross, whether in their places of religious assembly, or at

---

[1] Lat. text : "ut sese cruce vel precatiuncula muniant." *Catech. maj.*, p. 399, 74 Müll.

home in their private dwellings.[1] In M. CHEMNITZ' critique upon the Council of Trent (1573) is a sharper polemic first waged in the direction referred to. The cultic use of crosses in the places of assembly of the pre-Constantine Christendom is here throughout decidedly contested, and the age of crucifixes strictly so called—*i.e.*, figures of the cross with the form of the suffering Saviour upon it—is dated back to a period not much earlier than the time of the second Trullan Council; since the canon of this Council bearing upon the question speaks of such representations as only recently having come into use.[2] As Chemnitz notoriously falls into a hypercritical exaggeration upon this point,[3] so does his argumentation upon the whole subject contain much that is open to exception, and which has been refuted by later researches in the province of the earliest history of Christian worship and art. The impulse given by him to a more exact historico-critical examination of the domain in question must, however, be recognised as an indisputable merit. It has borne, among friends and foes, important fruits in the form of further controversies upon the disputed point, and has thus cleared the ground for a more thorough investigation of the whole subject.

The REFORMED Church took up from the first, in the person of her founders and earliest theological representatives, a position sternly antagonistic, not only to the worship of images, but also to the adoration of the cross. The stormy scenes of renewed burning of images, which play a leading part specially in the history of the Reformation in Switzerland, brought to destruction, along with many useless images of Mary or the saints, also many an artistically valuable

---

[1] *Centur. Magdeb.*, iii. c. 6 : "Crucis imaginem seu in locis publicorum congressuum, seu domi privatim Christianos habuisse, in eodem libro (*Apolog.*, c. 16) indicare videtur Tertullianus; ab hoc enim Ethnici Christianis objiciebant, quod ' crucis religiosi ' essent."

[2] *Exam. Concil. Trid.*, lib. iv., p. 779 sqq. (edn. Preuss). Especially advanced and assailable is the position : Observandum vero est, imaginem Christi crucifixi, h. e. sicut canon loquitur, figuram seu speciem humanam repraesentantem humiliationem, passionem, et mortem ipsius, istis primum temporibus circa ann. Dom. 690 coepisse fieri et in Ecclesia collocari.

[3] Comp. above, ch. iii. p. 125. Further in Augusti, *Archäol.*, iii. 577 ff.

representation of the crucified Saviour, or many a fair Passion picture. By the "Conjurors' Tables," which ZWINGLI declared must be abolished, in order that the Pope might no longer have his posts in the Church, were notoriously to be understood altars with altar-images, thus works of art of the latter kind; and no other is his meaning by the term "storks' nests," which must be burnt, if we would have no storks upon the house.[1] Even as Zwingli, does CALVIN, too, express himself with inexorable severity—a severity tempered by no declarations in other places—against all and every kind of religious use of images, as incompatible with the ten commandments, and necessarily leading to idolatry. His disquisition thereon in the *Institutio* falls into a like hypercriticism with regard to ecclesiastical use of images in general, as did Chemnitz with regard to the antiquity of crosses and crucifixes; for he ventures simply and without qualification to deny the presence of images of any kind in Christian churches during the first five centuries.[2] Similarly as Calvin, did also FAREL and BEZA declare themselves against every use of images and crucifixes for religious purposes. The former composed a treatise "On the true Use of the Cross of Jesus Christ" (1560),[3] the bluntly anti-Romish argumentations of which form a remarkable contrast to the sermons or treatises of a Luther, a Brenz, a Rhegius, etc., on the same theme. Of the cross in the spiritual sense, and the duty of patiently bearing the same, there is no syllable throughout this little book. The whole is a mail-clad controversial treatise against the idolatrous worship of the cross on the part of the Romish Church, of which the unscripturalness and inconsistency with the principles and practice of the earliest Christians is set forth not without exegetic and patris-

[1] See especially his statements at the second Zurich controversy (Oct. 1523) against images and the mass, Christoffel, *Huldr. Zwingli.*, S. 107 f. Comp. also the chapter De statuis et imaginibus, in the *Commentar. de vera et falsa relig.*, 1525. On acts of violence against crosses, as well before that disputation (Nich. Hottinger) as after the same, comp. Christoffel, S. 108, 124.
[2] *Inst. Rel. Christ.*, lib. i., c. 11, § 13. Comp. lib. iv., c. 9, § 9.
[3] Published anew by Felix Bovet (Geneva, 1865): *Du vray usage de la croix de Jésus Christ*, par Guillaume Farel, suivi de divers écrits du même auteur.

tic learning. Every attempt to have, or honour, or still more worship, crosses or crucifixes apart from Christ, or by means of them to seek to work miracles, is condemned as idolatry. "The Saviour Jesus, as the Gospel teaches to know Him, and as we are by the Holy Ghost made partakers of Him through the sacraments, is the true Christ, whom the man who has once come to the knowledge of Him can neither forsake nor deny. But the Christ known by means of images, crucifixes, and signs of the cross is not the true Christ; He preserves neither from the denial of His name, nor from the service of Antichrist."[1] The manner in which the mischief and injury inflicted upon Christianity by the pretended discovery of the cross on the part of Helena is censured, in which the "proud and presumptuous folly and stupidity"[2] of the Romish apologetes of the sensuous cultus of the cross is lashed, in which the inconsistency of restricting the idolatrous cultus only to the cross and the nails, and not extending it, for instance, to the Lord's crown of thorns, is reproved, in which the pilgrimages, now to this cross, alleged to be endued with miraculous powers, now to that, are ridiculed, vividly reminds one of the fiery spirit of a Claude of Turin.[3]—Of BEZA belongs in particular to this place his tolerably sweeping vote given against the adoration of the cross, on the occasion of his conference with the Würtemberg Lutherans, as Jac. Andreä and others, at Mömpelgard, in the year 1586. Although he agreed with his Lutheran opponents to this extent, that he disapproved of the violent removal and destruction of images, and conceded their permission, as that of organs and instrumental music, as things indifferent; yet he expressed himself with severity against the use of images as a means for advancing the Church's devotion, and maintained that pictorial representations of the crucified Saviour had from of

---

[1] .... Mais celuy qui est cognu par les images, par les croix, et par les signes des croix, n'est point le vray Christ, et n'empesche point de renier Christ, et de recevoir et servir l'Antechrist. (*l. c.*, p. 158.)

[2] P. 139: bestise et asnerie tant orgueilleuse et outrecuidée, etc.

[3] *L. c.*, p. 16 sq., 68 sq., 141 sq., 143. 145 sqq.

old been found more to injure than benefit the religious life of the Church, and to lead many to idolatry.[1]

Even as late as the seventeenth century, iconoclastic excesses were practised here and there by the more zealous representatives of this cultic Puritanism of the Reformed Church. The court preacher of Friedrich V. of the Palatinate,[2] Abrah. Scultetus, soon after Friedrich's coronation as king of the Bohemians (end of 1619) reformed the Castle Church at Prague, by causing the images to be violently removed therefrom. In defence of his thesis, "All images should be put away from churches; all altars, tablets, crucifixes, and paintings, because they are idolatrous and have their origin in the Papacy, are to be entirely and utterly abolished," he published at the beginning of the following year the sermon, "A brief Scriptural Report of the Idol Images in the Christian Church at Prague," which he afterwards had to vindicate under the pseudonym of Theophilus Mosanus, against animadversions on various sides, and among these particularly the "thorough counter-report to Abraham Scultetus' supposed scriptural report of the idol images," of the Lutheran Balduinus (Wittenberg, 1620).[3]—Outside of Germany, too, the rugged principles of the Reformed Church, with regard to the use of images as something anti-Christian, have repeatedly led to the practical as well as the literary renewal of the iconoclastic conflicts of the eighth and ninth centuries. Well known are the attacks made upon images by the French Huguenots at Valence, Rouen, Orleans, Lyons, and elsewhere, with regard to which, not only Calvin, but also Condé, felt it necessary publicly to express disapproval; as in like manner the devastation by the adherents of the Reformed Church in Belgium, about the year 1566, of churches in that

---

[1] *Acta colloquii Montisbell.* (Tubing., 1594), pp. 400 sqq., 417, 420 sq. Comp. Piper, *Einleitung*, etc., S. 690.

[2] [Son-in-law of James I. of England, and ancestor of the present Royal Family.]

[3] *Theophili Mosani Vindiciae, oder Gründliche Rettung der kurzen und Schriftmässigen Predigt, so Abrah. Scultetus . . . gethan.* Hanaw, 1620.—On the whole controversy, comp. Pfaff: *De eo quod licitum est circa picturam imaginum SS. Trinitatis et personarum Divinarum.* Aug. Vindel., 1749, No. 36 sqq.

land, amounting (as is alleged) to four hundred in number. The history of the Scottish Reformation, too, is not free from similar stormy scenes, to which on some occasions, moreover, crosses in particular fell victims, without calling forth on the part of Knox any other than humorous remarks with regard thereto. In England the few minute points, in which it was thought well to retain the use of the sign of the cross in the liturgy of the Episcopal Church, especially its application in the sacrament of baptism, gave rise to fierce literary controversies between Anglicans and Presbyterians.[1]

Of greater importance than these controversies, carried on within the bosom of the evangelical confessions themselves, from which neither scientific research nor even the interest of Christian piety could hope to derive real profit, was the learned polemic waged with respect to images and crosses between the theological representatives of Protestantism and those of Rome from the time of the Tridentine Council. In this were deposited the fruitful germs of a series of vigorous researches in the domain of the earlier history of the cultus and art of the Christian Church, *yea even those to a certain extent impelling to the creation of the whole Christian archæology as a science*. The assaults directed by Flacius and Chemnitz from the standpoint of the Lutheran Church, by Calvin and others from that of the Reformed, against the renewal of the ancient, uncritically corrupted, and heathenised tradition by the ecclesiastical legislation of the Council of Trent, were first met on the Romish side—if we except the unimportant controversial productions of an Eisengrein, an Arn. Meermann, etc.—by BELLARMINE, in his great polemico-dogmatic work (1582 ff.), and BARONIUS, in his Annals of Church History (1588 ff.). Both represented the traditional principle with like onesidedness as did the others the Reformational-critical; they come therefore into collision with historic truth, to an extent corresponding with that of the others in the opposite direction. Bellarmine accordingly seeks, on the one hand, to

---

[1] Soldan, *Gesch. des Protestantismus in Frankreich*, ii., S. 33 ff. Fr. Brandes, *John Knox*, S. 152, 180. Schoell, art. "Puritaner" in Herzog, 12. 364.

date back as far as possible the origin of Christian painting and of the Church's use of images, by the assertion that even from the time of Christ Himself there existed three authentic likenesses of Him; and, on the other hand, to represent the homage presented to the cross in the later Church (from the time of John Damascenus) as mere *Dulia*, not *Latria*, and thus as much as possible to deprive it of its offensive character. Baronius, again, places his critical investigation at the service of the most degrading superstition, one devoted to the worship of relics. He defends, *e.g.*, as genuine the wooden crib of the Saviour preserved in Rome, champions the reality of the discovery of Helena and the genuineness of the relic-crosses of a Gregory the Great, and thereby calls forth the adverse criticism of his Protestant opponents.[1] Specially do controversies and investigations begin to concentrate upon our subject from the time when JUSTUS LIPSIUS in Louvain († 1606)—not to be regarded as a narrow-minded apologete of the Romish traditional position, but rather one who from time to time offered to the less temperate advocates of this position occasion for attack upon his sceptical-critical mode of proceeding—imparted by his three books "Of the Cross" the first impulse to a more philologically exact treatment of the archæology of the history of the Lord's passion, and, by giving currency to expressions such as *crux immissa, commissa, decussata,* etc., distinguished himself as the legislative creator of a peculiar terminology for this domain.[2] Partly as carrying to completion this preparatory work of Lipsius, partly as a reply to the attacks of Protestant polemical writers, directed against the Romish doctrines or traditions regarding the cross, as those of Joh. Marbach, Rud. Hospinian, Lambert Danæus, Francis Junius, etc.,[3] did the Jesuit JAMES GRETSER (born at

---

[1] *Baronii Annal. Eccles., e.g.*, ann. 599, No. 26; 603, 14; 604, 4, etc.—Comp. Bellarmine, *Disputatt. de controv. fidei*, iv. 2; on this latter also Perrone, *Prælect. Theoll.*, vi. § 163.

[2] *De cruce libri*, iii. Antverp., 1595; Amstel., 1670; Vesal., 1675, and elsewhere.

[3] Comp. Gretser's reply to these opponents in the *Mantissa* appended to the first vol. of his work *De Cruce* (No. 11: Apologia pro S. Cruce advers. Franc. Junii cavillationes), as well as in the third vol., lib. iii.: Advers. tres S. Crucis

Markdorf in South Swabia, 1562, died professor at Ingolstadt, 1625) undertake, in his voluminous monograph upon the cross, a comprehensive historic-archæological and dogmatic-polemical vindication of the traditions of his Church relating to this subject.[1] The whole controversial material bearing on the question is treated by him, especially in the third edition of his work, now swollen to the dimensions of three stout quarto volumes,[2] with a thoroughness and completeness, for his age, really exhaustive of the subject. The work opens with a dissertation upon the cross of the Lord, its nails, footboard, title, etc., in which he for the most part bases his conclusions upon the researches of Lipsius, but to a great extent also corrects or supplements these researches in accordance with the prescribed standard of Romish tradition and legend. This is followed by the historic-apologetic consideration of the pictorial representations of the cross and crucifix in ancient and modern times. As a third book there is added, at least in the second bulky edition, a collection of the different appearings of miraculous crosses as heavenly signs, according to ancient as well as modern tradition. Book fourth further pursues the miraculous effects of the symbol of salvation, by means of a special study of the cross described with the hand (the *crux transiens*) and its magic powers. Book fifth, forming a point of attachment with the mystic and ascetic literature of earlier and later times, treats of the spiritual cross, in the sense of Matt. xvi. 24. To these

calumniatores, Hospinianum et Danæum Calvinianum, Marbachiumque prædicantem Lutheranum (p. 257 sqq.).

[1] *Jacobi Gretseri, S.J., De Cruce Christi rebusque ad eam pertinentibus, libri* iv. Ingolstadii, 1598 (2 vols. in 4to).—As appendices to this first vol. afterwards appeared: 1600, a *tom.* ii., *in quo varia Græcorum encomiastica monumenta Græco-Latina de SS. Cruce continentur, nunc primum ex variis bibliothecis eruta,* etc.; and, 1605, a *tom.* iii., *quinque libris comprehensus, quorum* 1. *est de nummis crucigeris*; 2. *de cruciatis expeditionibus*; 3. *de usu et cultu S. Crucis, contra hæreticos*; 4. *hymn. et encomia Græcorum et Latinorum de cruce continet*; 5. *Paralipomena ad. t.* i.

[2] Ingolst. 1608 (here the first vol. especially very thick, enlarged to more than double its original size).—In the complete edition of Gretser's works (Regensb., 1734—1741) the three tomes *De Cruce* form the first three of the splendid series of seventeen fol. volumes.

there is added a comprehensive apparatus of learned supplements, excurses, mantissas, etc., occupying the last two of those three quarto volumes, and containing a great number of documents in prose and poetry (in part before unpublished) belonging to the devotional literature of the cross (sermons and hymns), as also pictorial representations and descriptions of the cross, as occurring upon early Christian coins and inscriptions, a detailed history and apology for the crusades, and many similar things. The diligence in compiling displayed in connection with this colossal work merits in reality the admiring recognition bestowed upon it by men like Petavius, Muratori, etc., and the more so, in that but few of the aids then at all accessible for the prosecution of this investigation have escaped the keenly observant eye of the learned Jesuit. As, for instance,—though not in a position to avail himself of the results of the researches of his Roman contemporary Bosio († 1629) within the catacombs—he has to some good effect availed himself of that which an Occo (1579) had effected just before his time for the numismatics of the Roman imperial age. Of scientific criticism there is not, it is true, a trace to be found upon any point in his work. His research moves only in the direction of compilation, never in that of sifting and elucidating. Even the most absurd legends and miracle-histories he asks his readers confidingly to receive, provided they accord with his apologetic aim and interest. Staurolatry in the strict sense of the term, the adoration of the cross as a worthy, yea absolutely necessary, object of Christian devotion, he feels himself called to teach and preach—he who was born on a Good Friday, and from his youth up has been filled with ardent enthusiasm for the sacred symbol! The cross of Christ is for him "a real Divine power, invested with dominion over heaven, earth, and hell," a dispenser "of long life for them that love it, but of a life exceedingly short and of sudden end for its foes and contemners."[1]

[1] Vere enim crux Christi cœli, terræ, Erebique, et vitæ necisque potens et Domina est, figura omnium perfectissima et absolutissima, longævæque datrix vitæ, si crucem ames, brevissimæ autem, si spernas eamque amplecti recuses. (Lib. i., c. 43 *sub fin.*)

Partly side by side with Gretser, so that he had an opportunity of turning their labours to account, partly following in his footsteps and defending or supplementing that which was set forth by him, was our subject treated by the following writers: Augustine Fivizanius, Alfons Ciacconius, Giacomo Bosio (uncle to the renowned explorer of the catacombs, Antonio B.), Ricci (Collaert), Daniel Malloni, Cornelius Curtius, Barthold Nihusius (Niehues), Nicquet, Joseph Maria Carraccioli, Francis Quaresmius, and other Romish theologians, from the end of the sixteenth to about the middle of the seventeenth century. Their labours consist in part of monographs of more modest dimensions, in which, as, *e.g.*, in the tractates of Niehues and Curtius, where the disquisition turns upon the nails, or, as in those of Nicquet and Carraccioli, upon the superscription (the τίτλος) of the Lord, one or other special point of the *archæologia crucis* is discussed; in part of works of more imposing calibre and more sumptuous execution, to which order belong in particular the dissertations of G. Bosio and Bartholom. Ricci, entitled after the precedent furnished by Savonarola "the Triumph of the Cross"—the latter of these a hagiological *édition de luxe*, embellished with numerous engravings by Adrian Collaert, devoted to the description of the sufferings of Catholic martyrs put to death upon crosses of all ages, down to modern times.[1] In point of critico-scientific value, most of them cannot even be considered to stand on a par with the work of Gretser. Some, as those of Malloni and Quaresmius relating to the wound-marks of Christ, appear to have been limited in their circulation to Italy alone, and to have speedily fallen into oblivion, for the reason that no scientific value whatever attaches to them.[2]

---

[1] *Triumphus J. Christi crucifixi, cum iconibus martyrum.* Antv. 1614. Comp. above, ch. iii., p. 112.

[2] Dan. Malloni, *Elucidationes in stigmata D. n. J. Christi.* Venet. 1606. Francisc. Quaresmius (Guardian. Hierosolymit. et commissar. Terræ S., t. 1660): *De quinque vulneribus D. N. J. Christi, varia, pia, et luculenta tractatio.* Venet., 5 tom. in fol. (!), 1652.—On the other above-mentioned contemporaries or successors of Gretser, see the account of the literature at the close of the Preface.

On the Protestant side, opposition was raised to the Romish glorification of the cross and the sensuous idolatrous cultus rendered to it on the part of the Catholic Church from the time of Constantine downwards: in a more comprehensive and systematic manner by CONRAD DECKER in his "Romish Staurolatry" (1617), in part also as early as the time of JOH. ARNDT, in his treatise "Of the right Use and the Abuse of Images" (1596), directed mainly against the members of the Reformed community in Anhalt; later by Baudis, Wildvogel, and other German Lutheran theologians;[1] with a more special tendency, and with reference only to single points, by the learned Reformed polemicists of the seventeenth century, specially by SALMASIUS († 1653), in his three letters on the Cross, addressed to the Danish Court Physician Bartholinus —letters in which the story of Helena's discovery, the traditions concerning the nails of Christ, the resting-block and footboard of the cross, etc., are subjected to a severe critical handling;[2] farther by DALLÆUS († 1670), whose comprehensive polemical work on the degenerate cultus tradition of the Latins devotes a separate book to the sensuous cultus of the cross, in which the origin of this cultus only *after* the age of Constantine is demonstrated with an almost excessively lavish application of acumen and learning;[3] nor less so by the learned brothers SPANHEIM; Ezekiel († 1710), author of a discourse or treatise on the Cross of the Lord, published in Latin, as afterwards in French, in 1655; and Frederic († 1701) author (1686) of the apology for Dallæus' critique on the Roman image-worship—an apology directed against the

---

[1] Conr. Deckeri, *De staurolatria Romana, libri* ii. Hanov. 1617. 8vo. (Thus published in Germany, not—as wrongly supposed—at Rome.)—John Arndt, *Iconographia: gründlicher und christlicher Bericht von Bildern*, etc. (1596).—Andr. Baudis, *Crux Christi ex historiarum monumentis constructa.* Viteb. 1669.—Chr. Wildvogel, *De ven. Signo Crucis.* Jen. 1690.

[2] De cruce, epistolæ tres ad Bartholinum. (In Th. Bartholini, *De latere Christi aperto diss.,* 1646—comp. the *De cruce Christi, hypomnemata* ii. of the latter, Havn. 1651.)

[3] *Adversus Latinorum de cultus religiosi objecto traditionem, libri* v. (Tom. ii., pp. 704—799, ed. Genev. 1665.)

Catholics Maimbourg and Noel; in like manner also by Witsius, and many others.[1]

With the dawn of the eighteenth century the examinations devoted to our subject begin to assume a more pacific character. The polemical interest begins to fall behind the historic archæologic. Catholics, Lutherans, Reformed, devote themselves to a joint labour, or at least to a calm and passionless rivalry, in the investigation of the art monuments, church customs, etc., of the early Christians and of the Mediæval Church ; amidst which a not inconsiderable portion of sound study falls to the lot of our subject. It is the time in which, on the part of the Catholics—leaving out of account the further prosecution of Bosio's explorations in the catacombs by Fabretti, Boldetti, Bottari, Marangoni, etc.—a Muratori made the cross of Nola, Phil. de Venutis that of Cortona, Paciandi the crosses and crucifixes of Ravenna, Stephen Borgia the Vatican and the Veliternian cross, Giorgi, Gori, and others the monograms of Christ, the object of learned monographic representations ; while on the Protestant side, e.g., the primitive Christian monogram was treated of by Mencken, Helena's finding of the cross by J. A. Schmid, the early ecclesiastical custom of crossing oneself by Fulda and others, a gilded crucifix of great value for the history of Christian art by Joh. E. Imm. Walch, etc.[2] The way is thus prepared for the investigation of our own age, so much more plentifully supplied with apparatus and aids, as well as so much more abundant in results of many-sided importance, the age of the brilliant labours of a Münter, Piper, Zestermann, Rochette, Didron, Garrucci, De Rossi, etc. That the deeply stirred interconfessional polemic of the century of the Reformation has directly prepared the way for these endeavours of most recent times, by supplying the first impulse to the scientific examination of the materials in question, is, in the bulk of cases, no longer to be recognised from its

[1] Ezech. Spanheim, *Discours sur la croix de notre Seigneur*. Gen. 1655.—Fr. Spanhemii, *Historia imaginum restituta, contra Nat. Alexandrum et Lud. Maimburgium*. Lugd. Bat. 1686.—H. Witsii, *Miscellan. sacra*, ii. 364.

[2] See the account of the literature at the close of the Preface.

tendency and nature. Yet even to the present day the Italian and French archæologists of the Romish confession proceed with regard to certain chronological questions (estimate of the antiquity of particular inscriptions, figures, monograms, etc.), to some extent in a different manner than the Protestant Germans. Just as in other respects too, *e.g.*, as concerns the æsthetic estimate of this or that ancient Christian or Mediæval work of art, there are still to be recognised aftereffects of the confessional difference, by which our special domain too is affected to an important extent.

Even within the bounds of Protestant Christianity, controversies as to the use or non-use of the sign of the cross in worship have continued in some measure to our own time. As about the middle of last century the practice of the Lutheran Church on this point had to be defended in divers ways as good and praiseworthy, in opposition to the attacks of the Reformed theologians (*e.g.*, by J. J. Chr. Fulda in a Leipzig dissertation, 1759),[1] so even in the present century did CLAUS HARMS of Kiel once allow himself to be betrayed into a recommendation of the use of the sign of the cross in place of prayer, a recommendation wanting in the necessary sobriety and of questionable catholicising tendency, for which he was more than once called to account. "Do not," he once exclaimed to his hearers, "do not in the hour of temptation depend upon words or thoughts alone! Do more, and defend yourselves with the holy cross. Powers of assuaging does the holy cross bring with it . . . . The world does not always leave us time to think of our devotions, . . . but a moment is gained to make a cross," etc.,—an utterance at all events not to be characterised as without qualification, and in every respect genuinely Lutheran, which has been, moreover, even within the most recent times, and within the circle of Lutheran theological literature itself, frequently the subject of unfavourable criticism.

---

[1] See, on the Reformed side, E. H. Zeibich, *Diss. de signo crucis e templis nostris eliminando.* Viteb., 1735, on the Lutheran, J. Jul. Chr. F(ulda), *De crucis signaculo, Christianarum precum comite destinato.* Lips. 1759.

c. THE IDEA OF THE CROSS IN MODERN ART, RELIGIOUS POETRY, AND SPECULATION.

Modern Christian art has in part remained unaffected by the purified and spiritualised idea of the cross introduced at the Reformation, in part been more or less powerfully influenced thereby. The former is, as might be expected, in a special degree the case with the art of the Romish Church. Yet even she very energetically favours, till towards the middle of the seventeenth century, in some of its principal domains, and particularly that of painting, with results of some importance, that tendency of a nobler renaissance which is inwardly akin to that of the Reformation, and may be regarded as the normal development of the truly sound and great ecclesiastical productions of the Middle Ages. That which Fiesole and Van Eyck introduced in its fundamental principles in the middle of the fifteenth century, the tendency to mystic idealisation and vigorous expression of the truly human in the representations of the Passion, was first able to bring forth its ripened fruits in full maturity only in the two following centuries. The triumphs of the cross in the domains of architecture and sculpture, which fall entirely within the Middle Ages; are now succeeded at the threshold of the new age by a brilliant series of corresponding triumphs on the field of painting. The period from Rafael to Murillo includes within itself the highest and best which ecclesiastical art has yet produced in the form of painted representations of the scene of the Crucifixion, and of the Passion. Catholic masters of Italy, Spain, and the Netherlands vie, in their profoundly penetrating symbolisation of the mystery of redemption, with the Protestants of Germany and Holland. With a Rafael, Correggio, Guido Reni, Rubens, etc., do Albert Dürer, L. Cranach, Hans Holbein the younger, and P. Rembrandt dispute the palm of the cross. To the creations justly most celebrated in this domain belong: a representation of the Passion by Bernardino Luini, disciple of Leonardo da Vinci; a descent from the cross, or a mourning over the body of

Christ by Mary Magdalene and John, of Fra Bartolomeo; a similar one, producing a deeply moving effect, by Daniel di Volterra; a Christ on the cross, represented with face upturned to heaven, as victor over grave and death, by Michael Angelo; a sepulture by Perugino, the teacher of Rafael; also by Rafael himself a cross-bearing (markedly imitated from a woodcut in Dürer's great Passion, thus a work of kindred spirit with that of the earliest and noblest master of German-Protestant art), as also a sepulture, a glorification too of Constantine's victory through the sign of the cross in the battle at the Milvian Bridge; further, by Correggio, the celebrated thorn-crowned head of Christ upon the handkerchief of Veronica, the only serious picture of this master, but also his best; by Titian a crowning with thorns, and a sepulture; by Tintoretto a crucifixion scene, remarkable for its excessively affecting pathos, verging indeed upon an unhealthy straining after effect; by the two Caracci, as well as by Guido Reni, celebrated representations of the thorn-crowned and crucified Christ, among which, particularly the crucifixion scene of the latter, preserved in the gallery of paintings at Bologna, is justly famous for its simply majestic and yet touching expression. Side by side with these products of the Italian schools of painting stand on the same level several works of great Spanish masters: Zurbaran's Mary and John at the sepulchre of the Lord; Alonso Cano's Christ on the cross; the bewailing of the body of Jesus taken away, by the same master; above all, Murillo's embracing of the feet of the Crucified by St. Francis in the transports of religious enthusiasm. Several of the creations, too, of the Brabant school of the seventeenth century, having reference to our subject, are no less masterpieces of the first rank. So Rubens' descent from the cross, in the Cathedral at Antwerp—of all the works of that highly gifted master indeed the most perfect; Anton van Dyck's lamentation over the body of Christ; by the same master, Christ bearing His cross, the crucified Saviour, and others. As regards the number of their successful efforts, the representatives of the Protestant art of Germany and Holland are not, it is true, able to rival these coryphæi of the later Catholic art, but as regards the intrinsic value of their productions they are fully on a level with them. In many respects they even surpass them; especially in point of simple dignity, inner sense of truth, the avoiding of false pathos, and a disturbing straining after effect. In proof we may adduce Dürer's Christ the Crucified in the bosom of the Holy Trinity; by the same master, the Saviour crowned with thorns sitting mourning upon a stone by the way, in the greater series of woodcuts upon the Passion; by the same, a colossal thorn-crowned head executed in woodcut; the crucifixion, by Lucas Cranach the elder (Luther and Cranach himself standing at the foot of the Crucified); the crucifixion, by Holbein the younger, "one of the most classic and majestic productions of German art." Rembrandt's "descent from the cross," a worthy companion to that of a Rubens, renowned for its wonderfully effective distribution of light and shade, and particularly on this account a powerful "northern counterpart to Correggio's southern brightness in his miracles of colour."[1]

It is evident from this brief glance round, which might easily be extended to the compass of a considerable gallery of pictures characteristic for the history of the art, how modern religious art still continues to be dominated by an irresistible attraction to the grace-diffusing foundation fact of salvation, yea, how precisely its greatest exponents have laboured to place their greatest and best at the feet of the Crucified. The action and reaction, too, between the Protestant and the Catholic art-execution, as it shows itself specially fruitful, and presents itself in its higher necessity upon the particular domain before us, is admirably illustrated by several of the instances afforded in the above survey. Even a Rafael is able to learn something from the vigorous profundity of a Dürer; and, conversely, the Germans and the Netherlanders need in our domain of art less than in any other to withdraw from the influence of the Italian style, in order to give ex-

Carrière, *Die Kunst*, vi. 356; comp. 205, etc.

pression to their innermost religious feeling. The common love to the Saviour, the strong attraction to the Crucified, preserves them on this domain, amidst what is in other respects an often wide divergency of their tendencies, in a remarkable manner at one with each other.

This relation exists, so long as the renaissance of a nobler order and tendency in Catholic art prevails, or at least still continues to present itself. From the time of the predominating of the *spurious* renaissance, that of the unnaturally stiff or *baroque* style of the Jesuits—which began to spread with the close of the sixteenth century, at first in the domains of architecture and sculpture, but in the course of the seventeenth extended its sway over that of painting too—the possibility of a friendly advance of a freer and purer evangelical art-taste side by side with that of the Romish art-schools has altogether ceased. The latter turn away more and more from the ideal of the Christ at all, to devote their principal attention to one-sidedly Romish ecclesiastical ideals, representations of the assumption or immaculate conception of Mary, of the glory of the pope crowned with the triple crown, and that of his cardinals, as well as that of the countless host of church saints of both sexes. "Saints impaled, roasted, flayed, in whom the fanaticism of the Inquisition expresses itself," more and more replace the august heavenly form of the Crucified. St. Sebastian, bound naked upon a tree, and pierced with countless arrows; St. Lawrence, roasted upon the gridiron; St. Bartholomew, flayed alive; in like manner those put to death on crosses of different forms—crosses of St. Andrew, inverted crosses of St. Peter, malefactors' crosses, etc., as Collaert drew them for Ricci's Triumph of Jesus Christ the Crucified: these are the favourite figures of this rudely naturalistic school of art, surrendering itself as it does to the cultus of masses of flesh, of the baroque, the crass, and the horrible, in the studies of which there remains scarcely so much as a corner to spare for simply beautiful and faithful representations of the Redeemer.—A genuine evangelical art keeping clearly before it its principle and its tasks, could certainly never have entered along with Rome upon the course of this tendency to the utterly stiff and distorted Spanish style. But yet, as having ceased to be inwardly free and transparent, being held down by unfavourable outward relations, and led away from its true aim, the religious activity even of our own (Lutheran) Church for more than a century, fell, too, to no small extent, into the same melancholy errors. This is clearly testified by the outer and inner condition of our places of worship, from the time of the Thirty Years' War until after the middle of last century, and in particular is shown by numerous examples from the condition of the altar-crucifixes, passion-paintings, etc., belonging to that period. It is only in the present century, simultaneously with the purifying renewal of Roman Catholic art proceeding from an Overbeck and a Cornelius, that in Protestant Christendom also an artistic creation of higher beauty, of rarer severity of form, and fresher fulness of life, has begun to flourish—a creation in the products of which it is true, the majestic figure of the Crucified no longer in the same degree forms the all-dominating central and culminating point as with the venerable German masters of the period of the Reformation, but yet in principle maintains the same position as with them,[1] and is apprehended and treated in a manner in harmony with the purified evangelical conceptions of the essence and kernel of salvation.

A connection of close community, or at least relations of near affinity, exists too in the domain of modern spiritual MUSIC, between the nobler and better productions of the Romish Church and those of the Evangelical. Of a musical glorification of the cross in the literal sense we cannot of course speak. But the Crucified One and His passion have become, for the entire development of the musical art in modern times, a motive of predominant importance, essentially as much so as in former times for that of architecture, sculpture, and painting. A series of glorious

[1] Compare. e.g., Gust. König's Psalm pictures to Psalm xxii., Cornelius' great cartoon of the Crucifixion, in the Ludwigskirche at Munich; also Thorwaldsen's Entry of Jesus into Jerusalem, and the Cross-bearing, etc.

creations, from Palestrina's *Improperia* and Allegri's *Miserere* down to Bach's Passion of Matthew and of John, to Händels *Messiah*, to Graun's cantata "The Death of Jesus," and to Beethoven's *Missa solemnis*, clearly enough demonstrate this fact. Protestant ecclesiastical art has on this domain too learnt much from the Romish masters and exemplars. Its noblest and best, indeed, it owes to the pristine vigour of its own power and to the immediate descent into the purifying depths of evangelical truth and fulness of life. To Luther, and his friends Georg Rhau and Hans Walter, as well as the succeeding creators and promoters of the Lutheran Church Song (Eckart, Stobäus, Crüger, etc.), do a Bach and a Händel, the great masters of the first rank in the domain of Oratorio and Passion Music—the Dante and the Milton of music, as they have been admirably termed—owe a more immediate incitement and a richer fulness of profound ideas, than to their Italian predecessors.

To the POETIC glorification of the cross, too, did the post-Reformational Romish Christendom yield many a truly beautiful contribution ; so long as the Jesuitical spirit had not yet entirely stifled its nobler and better consciousness and endeavour, an endeavour closely akin to that of the Church of the Reformation. Testimonies for the justice of this assertion are furnished on the one hand by the Latin hymns and sequence poetry of the sixteenth and seventeenth centuries, to which alike many classically learned Protestant poets, as many belonging to the Papal Church, have contributed the fruits of their leisure. Among these are some writers of no small eminence, such as the Jacob Montanus of Spires before referred to, Eobanus Hessus, Zacharias Ferrerius, Antonius Muretus, Wolfgang Ammonius ; as in the seventeenth century Mezler, author of a "Consolation by the Wisdom of the Cross," in Latin verses,[1] and the Munich Jesuit JAMES BALDE († 1668), who overshadows them all, the greatest religious composer of Latin poetry in modern times, who made not only the blessed Virgin, but also the suffering and dying Saviour,

---

[1] *De Consolatione Staurosephiæ*. Carmina. Constant. 1650. 16mo.

the object of prolonged meditations of a highly poetic character, especially in his "Philomele, oder sterbende Nachtigall" (1644). To this place, on the other hand, belong the Italian or Spanish compositions of some of those noble, evangelically minded spirits, who, although through the adverse nature of outward circumstances or the constraint of the Inquisition they were retained in the bosom of the Romish Church, were yet from their heart attached to the Gospel, or in any case were not far removed from the purer evangelical knowledge. What can be more thoughtful and lovely than the sonnet of VITTORIA COLONNA, which celebrates the healing and protecting power of the Tree of Life?

> The ivy, reft of that support in climbing,
> On which she leans so fondly in ascending,
> Tremblingly sways in place of upward tending,
> Feels herself earthward drawn, and lies reclining.
>
> The soul, which charmed by sense, deception pleasing,
> Lets the earth drown pure thoughts and impulse higher,
> Must wrestle in unsatisfied desire,
> In rise and fall, weak, helpless, and unceasing—
>
> Till in the Tree of Life at last abiding,
> Upon whose stem of safety upward soaring,
> Close linked in root and crown to this for ever,
>
> She sees—raised high, on firm support confiding—
> The Father, who for endless life in glory
> First made her, and whose grace does now deliver.

The sonnets of MICHAEL ANGELO, the man of genius, friend of this gifted, pious, and noble daughter of Rome, give forth to no small extent the selfsame tone. As a man of eighty-one years he breathes out the ardour of his believing trust in the Crucified, in a confession which from beginning to end might be sung by a son of the Evangelical Church:

> My life, in its small bark so frail and slender,
> Has crossed the storm-lashed waves unto that haven
> Where, for good deeds and bad with which 'tis laden,
> A full account to God it must needs render.
>
> Now can I see my heart, in strong endeavour
> For idolised art, with warmest ardour burning,
> Has taken up sore burdens, without learning
> That man's poor work is vain and foolish ever.

> But what to that vain love a charm can offer,
> Now that I see a twofold death impending!
> The one's at hand, the other near, and never
>
> Can brush or chisel yield calm peace unto the spirit
> *Which seeks His love, who to the cross descending*
> *Outspread His arms, up to Himself to raise us."*

Still more abundant is the Spanish religious poetic literature of the sixteenth century in songs of special beauty bearing upon our subject. Who does not know that wonderful sonnet, which certainly with justice is ascribed, not to Ignatius Loyola or Francis Xavier,[1] but to ST. THERESA, the reformer of the Carmelite order and profound mystic writer:

> I love Thee not, dear Lord, for thought of gaining,
> Nor for desire of heaven's eternal glory;
> Nor could I, from the dread of hell's dark story,
> Renounce the hope of earthly joys obtaining.
>
> It drew me, Lord, the sight of Thy deep anguish,
> The shame, the pain, for me which Thou wert bearing,
> Thy suffering form which cruel nails were tearing,
> Thy wound-marked limbs, which then in death did languish.
>
> It was Thy love alone, dear Lord, that drew me:
> Were there no heav'n, I would be Thine for ever,
> My heart would fear, though hell existed never.
>
> Thou, Lord, and Thou alone, couldst win me to Thee;
> If what I hope for were no more remaining,
> Yet still my love to Thee should know no waning.

The Spanish lyric poets of the cross, to which belong, besides Theresa, especially her spiritual son and disciple, John of the Cross, the singer of the four glorious canciones of the "holy flame of love" (Llama de amor viva), as also the man endued with almost the evangelical spirit of the Reformation, Luis de Leon,[2] form the immediate connecting link to the great masters of the DRAMATIC glorification of the cross in the seventeenth century. With these last, however, the limit

---

[1] As is done by the R.C. convert Hugo Lämmer [and in the English hymnals], on the testimony of some Jesuit authorities of doubtful value. (*Cœlestis Urbs Hierusalem.* Freib., 1866, p. 57.)

[2] Comp. the author's dissertation Petrus v. Alcantara, Teresia v. Avila, und Johannes vom Kreuze, iii. (*Ztschr. für die gesammte luth. Theologie,* 1866, i., S. 57 f.), as well as Wilkens, *Fray Luis de Leon,* S. 178 ff.

of that which an evangelical Christian heart can regard as beautiful, or can employ as an impulse to a devout aspiration towards the Redeemer, is already attained.[1] Apart from the rankly luxuriant maze of legends, of late formation and wide divergence from Biblical truth, into which they lead us, the moral character of their compositions is only in part such as can be brought into harmony with the principles of evangelical ethics. Of the "Discovery of America," the only piece by the lively, genial, inexhaustibly productive LOPE DE VEGA at all bearing upon our subject, we can scarcely any longer say that the cross is therein glorified in a truly worthy manner, and one in accordance with the worship of the Lord in spirit and in truth. It is only the thaumaturgic side of the symbol of the cross, to which the effective closing scenes of this drama appear to be devoted: the banner of the cross, raised in accordance with truly Romish, and particularly Jesuitical missionary practice, in the midst of the Indians, testifies its power to the hosts of the multitude looking on in wondering childish ignorance, by countless miracles, and thus aids in introducing their baptism, with the administration of which the succession of the triumphs of Columbus comes to a close.—Hardly a single one of the pieces devoted by CALDERON to this subject affords to the Protestant reader who is endowed with a finer critical organ any pure and entirely satisfactory enjoyment. In the "Visionary of the East" it deeply wounds us that, in order to obtain a perfectly corresponding factive prediction of Christ's crucifixion between the two thieves, King Solomon shows himself gracious and just, only after the manner of an ordinary barbaric tyrant: of the two condemned men, whose pardon is sought of him by the Queen of the East, through the adoration of the miraculous wood of the cross transported and caught up to God, he sets the one indeed free, but causes the other, in an entirely arbitrary manner and without reference to his deserts, to be executed. The "Exaltation of the Cross" is rich in specially effective scenes, which present nothing offensive to the Evangelical

[1] Comp. the examples given above, ch. v., p. 210 ff.

Christian consciousness; but that the holy cross, finally, can be taken from the Persians only by treachery, and that such treachery as perpetrated against the Infidels should appear in the light of a benefit and noble deed, can scarcely be spoken of as satisfactory. In the " Devotion to the Cross," the most artistic and most finished in point of form of all Calderon's Dramas of the Cross, the symbol of salvation appears entirely in the character of a fetich to the Church, the external adoration of which secures impunity even for the worst transgressions. It is the religion of rude Italian or Spanish banditti which is here glorified. Eusebio, the robber, murderer, and violator of maidens, is represented as pious after his fashion, because he has from his youth up worn a cross upon his breast, because he plants crosses upon the graves of those murdered by him, because he has taken a vow to kneel before every cross by the wayside, etc. It must therefore be a cross-shaped plank by which he is saved from the impending danger of destruction in a shipwreck. And when, finally, as he is pursued on account of his deeds of rapine and murder, he casts himself down bruised and mangled over a rocky precipice, it is again a cross standing there, the very one beneath which he once came into the world, which as it were embraces him with its delivering shadow, and by its mere vicinity obtains for him the blessed death of the penitent thief, even without confession. The first confessor who comes up after his death digs his body out again from the earth which covers it, and by a miracle restores him again to life, to confess before the wondering multitude, " My sins are more in number than the motes in the sunbeam, but devotion to the cross has delivered me before God's throne!" Whereupon he receives the absolution of the Church, then anew to die.—In presence of so crass an apotheosis of the Romish superstitious degeneration and corruption of Christianity, all attempts at defence from the religiously or æsthetically idealising point of view remain superfluous and useless.[1] " It is a glorification

---

[1] On such an attempt, compare the article, Die Andacht zum Kreuze, in the *Ev. Kirchenzeitung*, 1875, Nos. 15, 16, in which a valuable contribution is offered to the religious æsthetic appreciation of the poem as a whole.

of heathenism within the bosom of the Catholic Church, the execution of which is marked by high poetic power"[1]—more cannot be said in favour of the piece. Only the fact that the poet has elsewhere repeatedly given expression to a purer and more worthy conception of the Christian salvation and symbol of salvation, may serve to qualify our judgment upon his moral bearing on the whole. It can also hardly be asserted — inasmuch as such an open confession of heathen doctrines and sentiments on the one hand was ventured on by him only on this single occasion, and on the other has remained more or less foreign to the rest of the poetic literature of modern Catholicism—that the aforesaid composition ever became typical for any considerable number of similar utterances on the part of his own Church. The spirit of Jesuitism, which like a parasite growth of deadly nature gradually sucks up and stifles the nobler life of Romish Christendom, has it is true in the domain of prose literature diffused similar and in many respects more baneful poison, by means of its destructive moral principles. In the domain of poetry, however, it has been preponderantly only an affected dulness and the tastelessness of learned conceits, not morally destructive doctrine and heathen wisdom, which has proceeded from it.

Nothing of special eminence has been produced by the Evangelical Church, either in the dramatic or the epic glorification of the symbol of redemption. MILTON'S great Biblical epics of the history of redemption touch only incidentally upon the domain of the history of the Lord's passion ; even in the "Paradise Regained" it is not the redemptive sufferings of the Lord which form the central point of the presentation, but rather His temptation. It is otherwise with KLOPSTOCK'S "Messiah," which in the strict sense deserves to be called an epic-poetic glorification of the Passion. But only in single ones of its executions does it present that which is really great and beautiful: regarded as a whole, it appears hardly of equally harmonious beauty and perfection as many of the better odes of the poet, *e.g.*, that to the Redeemer.—The true field of

[1] Hase.

Evangelical Christendom, so far as it undertakes in singing to proclaim the praise of the crucified Saviour, lies in the province of spiritual lyrics. The German Lutheran Church-song, and within this most specially the Passion song, the lyric-elegiac glorification of the dying Saviour, and of the fulness of consolation and of life flowing forth from His wounds, indicates the culminating point of the development hitherto attained by the Christian Church at all in the domain of hymnology. In it lives again the incomparable beauty and power of the Psalms of David, new-born of the Spirit of revelation shed forth without measure, and wonderfully invigorated and made young again by the bliss-giving communion with the Risen One, livingly present in the midst of His suffering Church. Though the Italian, the Spanish, the Latin lyric poetry of the cross of the modern Romish Christendom be able to reproduce the highest and most glorious efforts of the poetry of the ancient Church and the Middle Ages on our theme; though in the odes of a John of the Cross and a Theresa the ardent devotional glow of a Francis or a Jacoponus be worthily revived; though the elegant and yet heartily tender and heavenward-soaring strains of a Balde may perhaps rise to the height of the poetic effusions of a Prudentius or of a Venantius Fortunatus, yet what has been sung in praise of a crucified Saviour's love, and of the evangelical solace brought by it in suffering and in death, by Valentine Herberger, Joh. Heermann, and Paul Gerhardt, by Justus Gesenius, Joh. Scheffler (Angelus Silesius),[1] Gottfried Arnold, Wolfgang Dessler, Benjamin Schmolck, Zinzendorf, and others, far surpasses all the efforts of the great singers of the Middle Ages and of the Early Church. It ascends to the

---

[1] We believe ourselves justified in placing this profound and loving singer too in this connection, spite of his secession to the Romish Church as early as 1653. For as a German evangelical composer of hymns he preserves unimpaired, with all the severity of his polemics as a convert, and notwithstanding the close relation in which he stands to the Quietistic mysticism of Molinos, Madame de Guyon, etc., the position of an adherent of the Silesian Lutheran school of poetry. [A graceful translation of one of Scheffler's Hymns of the Cross appears in the *Family Treasury*, Feb. 1877.]

height of the most glorious products of the psalm-poetry of the Old Covenant ; it lays claim to a significance absolutely œcumenical, and one transcending and soaring above all the limits of mere Protestantism. It has already proved itself, by its passing over into the language and melodies of so many a non-German nation, in so victorious a manner, to be a living treasure of Christian solace, surpassing in point of inner wealth anything of the kind in other languages and literatures, that in reality only the religious lyric poetry of the Old Covenant offers fitting points of comparison for it. It is worthy of notice that, of all kinds of Protestant spiritual hymn composition, that whose crown and centre is formed by the cross and the Christian consolation flowing forth therefrom, has hitherto shown itself the one most richly endowed with vitality, most abundantly furnished with an imperishable productive power. The objectively confessing, fresh, and jubilant song of a faith exulting in victory, which characterises the epoch of the Reformation, appears already to have ceased to be heard with the very beginning of the seventeenth century; to the ardent songs of sanctification of the pietistic epoch, neither the preceding nor the following age has been able to present any equal of its kind. But tender passion hymns, breathing forth faith and love, consolatory confessions to the Crucified as the solid ground of all our consciousness of redemption, and the alone true solace under all suffering, have been—from the earliest commencement of German evangelical psalmody among the Hussites in the fifteenth century—composed and ever again composed, substantially without any other break than the short one of the vulgar-rationalistic epoch (1770—1820). The full and pure classicalness of diction of the singers of " O Lamm Gottes unschuldig," " O Haupt voll Blut und Wunden,"[1] " Ein Lämmlein geht," etc., " Herzliebster Jesu," " Wenn meine Sünd' mich kränken," and similar hymns, has certainly never returned after that gloomy period of decadence and apostasy ; as it

---

[1] [An English translation, beginning, "O sacred Head once wounded," is familiarly known.]

had indeed even before given place to poetry of another kind and tendency. But this later pietistic Moravian and mildly supranaturalistic poetic composition, which preceded the rationalistic or revolutionary age, of the school of Schmolck, Gotter, J. Andr. Rothe, Gellert, Hiller, has been in all essential features again equalled, if not on every point, yet certainly in the domain now specially occupying us, by the spiritual singers of the nineteenth century, such as Knapp, Spitta, Sturm, Gerok, etc. In opposition to any possible doubts as to the accuracy of this assertion, it suffices to remind of the glorious strophes of an Albert Knapp:

Eines wünsch ich mir vor allem andern,	One thing I long for more than all beside,
Eine Speise früh und spät;	Morning, night, 'tis food for me;
Selig lässt's im Thränenthal sich wandern	My joy will e'en in this sad vale abide,
Wenn diess Eine mit mir geht:	If this one thing present be.
Unverrückt auf Einen Mann zu schauen,	To look with constant loving gaze on Him,
Der mit blut'gem Schweiss und Todesgrauen	Who with bloody sweat and eyes with trembling dim,
Auf sein Antlitz niedersank	Prostrate on the ground did sink
Und den Kelch des Vaters trank.	And the Father's deep cup drink.
Ewig soll er mir vor Augen stehen,	Yes, He shall ever stand before my eyes;
Wie er als ein stilles Lamm	Like a Lamb I see Him there,
Dort so blutig und so bleich zu sehen,	So pale and bleeding, as He slowly dies
Hängend an des Kreuzes Stamm;	On the cross so hard and bare.
Wie er dürstend rang um meine Seele,	I see Him wrestling for my sinful heart,
Dass sie ihm zu seinem Lohn nicht fehle,	That it of His reward might form a part.
Und dann auch an mich gedacht,	Of me thinking as He cried,
Als er rief: es ist vollbracht!	"It is finished!" ere He died.

To the height of Heermann's or Gerhardt's, or Gesenius' Passion poesy, these lines may not perhaps attain: but with the best which was sung during last century, *e.g.*, by a Hiller or a Tersteegen, they are unquestionably on a level. May the raging of the storms of revolution, which have lately once more burst in upon the German Protestant Christendom, break against the faithful confession of its singers—who, thank God, notwithstanding a thinning having taken place in their ranks for a time, have not yet again died out—without being able to deprive the Church of the blessing, in the form of spiritual blossoms and fruit, which has proceeded and still does proceed from them.

We attach immediately to this contemplation of the modern poetry of the cross that of the MYSTIC AND THEOSOPHIC SPECULATION upon our subject; for, apart from the fact that its representatives are in many respects at the same time distinguished representatives of the spiritual poetry, there exists between the two provinces a close and many-sided relationship. Similarly as in the lyrical poetry or hymns of the cross, so is—on the part of those who pursue this form of speculation—the objective side of the mystery of redemption by the Crucified most closely associated with the subjective. To blend as much as possible into one the Christ for us and the Christ in us, is the main practical aim of this tendency; just as the proof, by means of natural philosophy or by the philosophy of history, that the mystery of the cross is the key to the enigma of enigmas, the centre of all natural and spiritual existence, forms its great theoretical problem.

In the ROMISH Church of the period immediately succeeding the Reformation, endeavours of the latter kind still recede comparatively into the background. The mystic contemplations on the mystery of the passion of Christ bear a preponderantly practical ascetic character, in which sometimes the advancement of a devotional self-absorption in the contemplation of the form of the suffering Saviour, beheld objectively in the spirit—even though accompanied with the employment of aids to the senses—is the predominating aim; sometimes the recommending of a passive resignation of oneself to the following of the Lord's sufferings, and the voluntary taking up of the cross imposed by Him. The objective side of the devout contemplation of the passion is fully developed with special care in the "Spiritual Exercises" of LOYOLA. Almost two entire weeks out of the four weeks' course of meditation —the third and greater part of the fourth week—are in them seen to be devoted to the Sufferings of Christ; whilst only one week is appointed for meditation upon Creation, the Fall, and Sin with its consequences, and again only another week for meditation on the Exaltation of Christ, and His living omnipresence in the Church. Several religious societies of later origin—*e.g.*, the congregation of the Passionists, founded by Paul of the Cross 1725, which prescribes to its novices a ten days' meditation upon the history of the Passion before receiving the vow of their profession—further cultivated this method of devout contemplative self-surrender in an independent manner;[1] while the congregations belonging to the later development of the order of Jesuits notably devote themselves, in a systematically arranged meditation, to the adoration of the "most holy sacrament of the altar," or of the sacred heart of Jesus.—The subjectively spiritualising operation of the contemplation of the Passion, the suffering with Christ and for Christ, comes into play with special force in the mystic authors of the sixteenth and seventeenth centuries. Thus with ST. THERESA, who is never wearied of exhorting her nuns to the believing embracing of the cross, to a willing entering upon the path of the cross as the best of all paths, to the overcoming of all timid shrinking from the bearing of the cross, and who depicts with sacred ecstasy the "bitter-sweet suffering" of being crucified to this world after the example of Paul (Gal. vi. 14)—in which the soul "is suspended and suffers, as it were stretched out crosswise between heaven and earth, without help coming to it from any side whatever." All this, not without also from time to time recalling to mind the virtues of the sign of the cross made with the hand in the religious services or in daily life, and discussions raised upon the question, *e.g.*, whether this or the holy water is the more efficacious for the driving away of evil spirits.[2] A like encomiast and lover of the resigned

---

[1] Comp. Fehr, *Allgem. Geschichte der Mönchsorden*, etc., ii., S. 57; as also Pins a Spiritu Sancto, *The Life of St. Paul of the Cross*, London, 1868.—In the regulations and practice of several societies of the modern Romish Church which are named after the cross, the feature of the devout contemplation of the Passion recedes more into the background. So among the "Daughters of the Sacred Cross" of Marguérite Senaux (1625), the congregation of the "Daughters of the Cross" (1640), the Belgian "Daughters of the Sacred Cross," founded by Priest Habets at Liége (1835), the "Sisters of St. Andrew, or of the Cross," a foundation of Mdlle. Béchier, in the diocese of Poitiers (1806)—societies having almost exclusively practical aims—comp. Fehr, ii., 319 f., 322, 389.

[2] "Life of St. Teresia, written by herself" (Bd. i. of the German redaction of

following of suffering in the service of Jesus is Theresa's disciple JOHN OF THE CROSS, whose heart was never free, save when persecutions and afflictions afforded him the opportunity of proving the fitness of his monastic name, who in all respects upheld his maxim, "Either to suffer, or to die!" (*aut pati aut mori*); who indeed in the objective meditation on the Passion presented extraordinary manifestations, even to the calling forth of stigmatic phenomena upon his body, *e.g.*, as is asserted, at one time an abscess upon his knee, with five wounds arranged in the form of a cross, etc.[1] To this category belongs also LUIS DE LEON, who, when on account of his outspoken evangelical sentiments he must journey to the prison of the Spanish Inquisition, obtained as a favour an image of the Crucified, one of the holy Virgin, a scourge, the Holy Scriptures, as well as the writings of St. Augustine and other spiritual men, and then, as he afterwards thankfully acknowledged, " learnt in this school of the cross, beneath the cross of the Lord, to form an intimate acquaintance with the Scriptures, and to refresh himself therefrom, as a traveller by a delicious draught from a spring."[2] Of those belonging to a later time who represent this Quietistic-ascetic Mysticism of the cross, we have, in addition to Mich. Molinos, Madame de Guyon, Fenelon, etc., to make special mention of ANGELUS SILESIUS. The most effective possible transposition of the Jesus for us into a Jesus in us, the greatest possible spiritualising and living appropriation of the blessings of salvation obtained on Calvary, forms one of the principal and leading thoughts of the profound sayings in his " Cherubinischer Wandersmann."

The cross on Calvary cannot deliver thee,
Except in thine heart it firmly planted be.

---

her works by Gall. Schwab, Sulzbach, 1831), ch. 31, comp. chaps. 11, 15, 20, 22, 27 ; also "Way to Perfection," ch. 18, at the beginning ; "Soul's Fortress," v. 2, vi. 1, 9, vii. 3. (Bd. iii. and iv. with Schwab.)

[1] Lechner, *Leben des heil. Johannes v. Kreuze* (Regensburg, 1858), S. 223 ff.; 228 ; cp. 227 f., as well as my already cited (p. 317) dissertation in the *Zeitschrift f. luth. Theologie und Kirche*, 1866.

[2] Wilkens, *as before*, 272, 278 f.

> No death more glorious than that a life doth bring,
> No life is nobler than that from death doth spring.
>
> 'Tis true indeed God wills thee salvation to receive :
> If thou believ'st He will without thy will, thou dost
> too much believe, etc.

The endeavour after a *theoretical* fathoming and elucidation (by means of natural philosophy and the philosophy of history) of the mysteries of the cross, as the centre of revelation and key to all earthly and heavenly wisdom, preponderates among the Mystics of PROTESTANT Christendom. We may associate with these some of those remarkable enthusiasts of the Reformation age, with whom indeed no formal attachment of themselves to the Lutheran or Reformed Christendom took place, but who were nevertheless inwardly nearer thereto than to the Church of Rome and its doctrines.—AGRIPPA, of Nettesheim († 1535), the author of the "Vanity of the Sciences," the "Hidden Philosophy," and other books of sententious, yet confused, cabalistic mystic wisdom, is greatly occupied with the sign of the cross as to its deeper import. He calls it, as it presents itself in its regular fundamental form, as equal-armed Greek cross—consisting of four squares placed around a fifth, which is situated in the middle, (Fig. 117)—the "solid fortress of all strength," and ascribes to it secret miraculous virtues.[1] With him many points of contact are presented, as in general, so specially in these thoughts on the cross, by SEBASTIAN FRANCK, a native of Donauwörth († 1543); only that in his writings the ethical side of the philosophy of the cross comes out more strongly, in a manner not seldom according with Luther's, although his pantheistically inclined spiritualism and subjectivism early felt itself repelled by Luther's objectively ecclesiastical bearing; and Luther, on the other hand, on one occasion warned against the fanaticism of Franck, as that of "the devil's own and dearest blasphemer." In essential harmony with Luther does Franck say, "The cross alone is the theology of Chris-

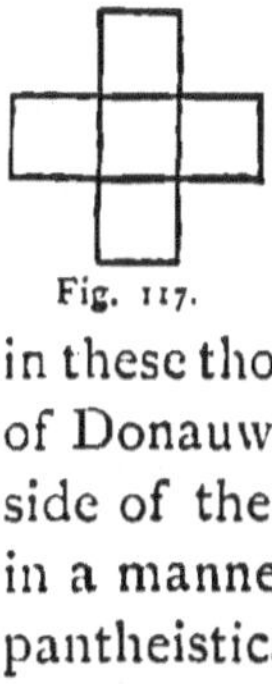

Fig. 117.

---

[1] *De Occulta Philos.*, lib. ii. Comp. Carrière, *Die Weltanschauung der Reformationszeit*, S. 109.

tians, and death the only way to life."[1] He speaks of the distinction between the theology which will see " God's back parts" (Exod. xxxiii. 23), and that which will behold Him face to face; precisely as Luther of the relation of the *theologia crucis* to the *theologia gloriæ*. Only the way of the cross and of affliction leads, according to him, to the depths of the knowledge of God. The " Thaw or Cross " he calls " the true key of David, which alone can open the closed book of Scripture." "Only those who bear the sign of this cross and affliction upon their brow (Ezek. ix. 4), *i.e.*, who in their life publicly bear and testify to the crucified Christ, open this book," etc.[2] His frequent and formal references to the Thau of Ezekiel are explained from the adoption of some cabalistic elements into his speculation, in which, moreover, his contemporaries of kindred spirit, Agrippa and PARACELSUS († 1541), went much farther than he. The former especially by elaborate, but certainly extremely inflated and misty contemplations on the wonder-tree, or tree of life, of the ten sephirs; the latter by the mixing up of yet more numerous cabalistic conceptions and expressions in his quixotic alchemistic reveries.[3]

Upon the teaching of these fanatical spirits of the Reformation Age, as well as the more spiritualistic Valentine Weigel († 1558), who more nearly approximated to the doctrinal views of the Lutheran Church, is built up the Theosophy of JAK. BÖHME, the profound shoemaker of Görlitz († 1624), in whose conceptions—the fruit of a clairvoyant genius, but often

[1] " Allein das Kreuz ist der Christen Theologey, und der Tod allein der Weg zum Leben."

[2] See the treatise which appeared in 1539, "The closed book, sealed with seven seals, which no man can rightly open but those to whom the Lamb belongs, and who, marked with the Thaw, belong to the Lamb," as well as the excerpts from the same given by E. A. Hase, *Sebastian Franck von Werd, der Schwärmgeist* (Leipzig, 1869), S. 151 ff. Comp. also the selections there made. S. 230—239, from several other writings of Franck, as " Die Guldin Arch " [the golden ark], Paradoxes, etc., under the heading, " The way of the holy cross, of hope, and the love of God."

[3] Comp. Rocholl, *Beiträge zu einer Geschichte deutscher Theosophie*, S. 47 ff. Carrière, *as before*, S. 110 ff. Harless, *J. Böhme und die Alchymisten*, S. 38 ff., 46 ff., 57 f.

confused and fantastic in their nature—a pretty important part is assigned, *inter alia*, to the cross. In his earliest writings, *e.g.*, the "Aurora," the staurosophic element remains as yet more in the background; whilst in the later ones, particularly the "Three Principles of the Divine Essence," the "Threefold Life of Man," the "Signatura rerum," "Psychologia vera," "Election of Grace," and the "Mysterium magnum," he returns ever afresh to his favourite thought of the ✠ form in the fourth form of nature, or of the ✠-birth out of fire, water, acerbity, etc. Thus it is said among other things in the "Three Principles," on the occasion of explaining the essence of the first and second Principles, or God and the Divine nature, "And yet there is no essence separable *from* the others, but all things the one *in* the other entirely one essence; and every form or birth takes its own form, power, operation, rising, from all the forms. And the whole birth taken altogether retains now especially four sorts of form in its birth, as the arising, descending, and then through the revolving wheel in the acerb *essentia*, the transverse going out on both sides, like a ✠, or, as I might say, they proceeded from the point, towards the east and west, the north and the south. For from the stirring, moving, and arising of the acerbity in the lightning-flash is formed a ✠-birth; for the fire ascends upwards, and the water goes downwards, and the essentia of the asperity crosswise."[1] In a somewhat different manner is the cross explained in the *Psychologia vera* as the mystic ground and centre of all unseen things. The cross ✠, as shown in the table illustrative of that which is here explained, passing through the two concentric circles, which denote the highest principles of the Divine nature, is said to represent " the persons of the Godhead, as they are divided in the eternal unique descent." The *eye*, drawn through one of the lines or angles of this cross, denotes "each one a world; that to the left the great dark world, that to the right the world of

---

[1] J. Böhme's sämmtl. Werke, von K. W. Schiebler. Bd. iii., S. 17; comp. S. 342 f.

light." The *heart* in the angle of the cross "denotes the foundation or centre of the Godhead."[1] The reference of these profound but obscure speculations to cabalistic sources receives special light from a picture, contained in the *Magnum mysterium*, of the triple cross, with the three crowns hanging over it, unquestionably a free imitation or speculative continued development of the mysterious Tree of Life of the ten Sephiroth, which, in the explanation appended thereto, is explained as "a revelation of the Holy Trinity, the same to be recognised in the figure and likeness of all visible things."[2] Greatly, however, as this quixotic staurosophy, founded on the ideas of natural philosophy, seems to have formed one of the leading subjects for speculation with him, especially in the later epochs of his development, Böhme is nevertheless also well acquainted with the ethico-mystical side of the doctrine of the cross, the Cross-theology in the sense of an Angela of Foligno, an Eckart, a Suso, and others, as is shown, *i.a.*, by his utterances upon the suprasensuous life, in his "Way to Christ." "The cross of our Lord Jesus Christ, with the mockery of the world which hates thee, that thou must learn to love and to accept for the daily exercise of thy penitence; so wilt thou ever have cause to hate thyself with the creature, and to seek that everlasting rest in which thy will can repose."[3]

By Böhme's Philosophy of the Cross, to which John Arndt, the author of the *Wahres Christenthum*, as well as Joach. Betkius, the censorially strict separatist and enthusiast († 1663), at least on their ethico-ascetic side, pretty nearly approached,[4] were the later mystics and theosophs of both confessions, the Lutheran and the Reformed, and even several of the Roman-

[1] *Ibid.* vi., S. 25 f. Comp. also Bd. vi., 28, 269 ff., 463, 486 f.

[2] *Myst. Magn.*, cap. 30.

[3] Bd. i., S. 134 f. Comp. also *Myst. magn.*, c. 48. (v., 384 ff.) The sacrifice of Isaac as a type of the true spiritual self-crucifixion of man.

[4] Joh. Arndt, "Lehr und Trostbüchlein vom Glauben und heiligen Leben," 1620. (See also above, p. 307.) Joachim Betkius, *Mysterium Crucis, oder Erinnerung derer Geheimnissen und Krafft des Creutzes Christi*, etc., Berl. 1637. Frankf. 1646. Also by the same, *Göttliche Leidensgemeinschaft wahrer Christen mit ihrem Haupte*. Amsterdam, 1660.

Catholic communion influenced. In the fantastic speculations in natural philosophy among the later ROSICRUCIANS—*i.e.*, not that alchemistic-sophistic secret compact of J. B. Andreä († 1614), which was merely invested with an air of mystery, and which is said to have existed contemporaneously with Böhme, but those of the alchemistic enthusiasts of the beginning of the eighteenth century, to the number of which Duke Ernest Augustus of Saxe Weimar belonged, and for a time also John Conrad Dippel and others, the cross as the secret fundamental power of creation plays an important part. By means of an absurdly whimsical etymology, the name Rosenkreuz, *rosea crux*, is derived from *ros*, dew, and *kreuz*, cross, and on this account a high degree of significance and activity for the chemical operation is ascribed to the actual dew of heaven, and so forth.[1]—Upon the basis of such and kindred speculations also rests the work, long highly prized and zealously read in mystic-theosophic circles, "the Mystery of the Cross of Jesus Christ and His Members."[2] This book, which appeared anonymously in the original French edition of 1732, is the work of the Mystic DOUZE-TEMS, a countryman and spiritual kinsman of Madame de Guyon, la Combe, Poiret, and other representatives of the then flourishing Mystic Quietistic school. With remarkable alchemistic speculations on the cross—as the supposed result of a combination of the triangle of fire △, which (as is asserted) denotes the Trinity, with the triangle of water ▽, which is said to denote grace,

Fig. 118.   Fig. 119.   Fig. 120.

goodness, kindness, and, combined with the former, results in

[1] Harless, *as before*, S. 115. (On the authority of the work which appeared in 1742, "Theosophic heart-devotions, addressed to the one supreme Jehovah," by Ernst August, Herzog zu S.-Weimar.)

[2] Mystère de la Croix (affligeante et consolante, mortifiante et vivifiante, humiliante et triomphante) de Jésus-Christ et ses membres. Ecrit au milieu de la Croix dedans et dehors par un Disciple de la Croix de Jésus. Achevé le 12 d'Aout, 1732. Nouvelle Edit. (xxiv. 390 pp.), à Lausanne, 1791.—Appeared also in German, Leipzig, 1782.

Figures 118, 119, and finally 120,—this author combines profound thoughts on the wisdom and folly of the cross of Jesus, on the true resignation in the bearing of inner and outward afflictions, trials, and assaults. "We err," he writes *inter alia* on this subject, "when we regard the adversities and afflictions to which the world exposes us as the true cross of Christ. They are crosses, but they are not the true cross. The true cross consists in inward penitence, in the constant mortification of our own flesh, of our own will and the fleshly love of self and of the creature, that we may live only in the spirit; in the following of the meekness and the lowliness of heart of Jesus, which deeply humbles our natural pride and anger; in bidding a final farewell to our own I, with all which belongs not to God, and which draws us from Him, even as Jesus once did this." To such a perfect delivering up of self to God only he attains who utterly renounces his own doing and working, and allows the Lord alone to work all things upon us and in us. "We must cease to act, in order to be only receptive; die, in order to attain to the true life; wither and decay, in order to become afresh verdant in God. It is the Lord who will fight for thee; thou hast only to rest and be still. He who in this way passes with resignation through the painful hell of the inner cross, is a true member of the body of Jesus Christ, the head and commander of the great host of cross-bearers. In short, our whole life must be a life which for us constantly dies, and a death which for Jesus constantly lives."[1] The peculiar beauty and persuasive power of this and similar sections suffers considerable diminution and interruption from the reveries of natural philosophy before alluded to, on the composition of the cross out of the triangles of fire and of water, as well as from alchemistic speculations of a character still much more odd, as to "the miracles of the cross in outward nature;"[2] and partly also from fanatically unevangelical doctrines, such as that of purgatory as the epitome of the "crosses after this life," of the restoration

[1] Pp. 100, 112, of the French edition.
[2] *L.c.*, p. 259 sqq.

of all things, and of the rejectable character of the dogma of justification through faith alone as an abuse of the cross of Christ in the interests of a false liberty, and of an indolent fleshly indulgence.[1]

Spite of these instances of onesidedness and caprice, the ideas of this French theosoph have met with a lively approval on the part of later representatives of the same intellectual tendency, and down to the most recent times have called forth manifold declarations of a like kind. Their after-operation is manifest in not a few of the characteristic conceptions of the French theosoph ST. MARTIN, as well as of the Strassburg mystic F. R. SALTZMANN († 1820), the author of the tractates still held in high estimation in many theosophic-ascetic circles, entitled " Glances into the Mystery of the Decree of God," " Religion of the Bible," " Spirit and Truth, or the Religion of the Initiated," etc.,[2] a man who received his impulse from St. Martin. Even in the writings of FRANZ VON BAADER, this kind of staurosophic speculation still continues to flourish. A certain endeavour to rid it of its wildest and most uncritical alchemistic outgrowths cannot fail to be observed in connection with his teaching; yet in point of fact he does not succeed in freeing himself from the well-known vagaries of the theosophy of a Paracelsus, a Böhme, or a Douze-Tems. Like a genuine fire-philosopher (*Philosophus per ignem*), as he loves to designate himself, he explains the cross as the symbol of fire, inasmuch as this is the centre of the ternary of water, air, and earth. The cross is for him " centre and ternary, root and perfection of all things."[3] In the concluding observation to his treatise on lightning as the father of light, it is said, " *Per ignem* signifies, as is well known, also *per crucem;* because the cross everywhere implies the tetrade (Father—decussation), as is already implied by

---

[1] Ch. ix. : De l'abus des croix, et surtout de celle de Jésus (p. 157 sqq.) Comp. ch. xi. : Des Croix après la mort ; and Ch. xv. : De la Croix victorieuse et triomphante de Jésus-Christ (pp. 310—340).

[2] See, *e.g.*, the " Blicke in das Geheimniss," etc. (Strassburg, 1810), S. 168 f.; "Relig. der Bib." (Strassb., 1811), S. 279 ff.

[3] Werke, herausg. v. Fr. Hoffmann, etc., Bd. xii., S. 343; cp. S. 191.

the numeral hieroglyph (Figs. 121 or 122)." In the lectures on the Philosophy of Religion he observes, manifestly pursuing J. Böhme's line of thought (see above), " In the cross of

Fig. 121. Fig. 122. Fig. 123. Fig. 124.

nature, consisting of four forms, the Word is born. This cross, Fig. 123, or also Fig. 124, is the proceeding forth of the lightning from above, the downward precipitation of the startled asperity, and the dividing of the sting or going out to the two sides."[1] Yet more fully does he develop this idea in a passage of his Philosophy of Society, in which he is treating of the just "insight into the connection and inseparableness of the law of reaction with that of subordination," and showing how "only in the midst of them, as the four quarters of the world or cardinal points, everything which is may be comprehended as existing." " This double law," so he teaches here, " is indicated by the figure of the quarternary (Fig. 125), or, what denotes the same thing, the cross ┼ ; with which cross the ancients were wont always to imply the middle or centre. This cross accordingly has a deeper significance than most theologians are able to assign to it from the merely historical standpoint ; even as this cross in the figure 4 reminds of the Pythagorean tetrade, and presents the key to the right understanding of all nature. For in this cross, or quarternary, the rising or beginning falls in d, the setting in e; the former gives, the latter receives; while a and b, the *dextrum* and the *sinistrum*, in the most universal significance react, *i.e.*, represent the active and re-active principle as the expansive and contractive, in their co-ordination and even in their opposition. Our later German natural philosophers have apprehended this latter law of co-ordination in an abstract manner and without that of subordination, and have therefore not been able to

[1] *Vorles. über relig. Philos.*, i. 217. Comp. *Ueb. den Blitz*, etc., Werke, Bd. ii., S. 46.

advance beyond a polar dualism."[1]—No one can fail to perceive that, in these attempts at the vindication of the cross as the fundamental principle of all true philosophy of nature, Baader was following an illusory Will-o'-the-wisp derived from the earlier alchemistic school of theosophs, and one which led him into the byways of a lamentable obscurity, which was never to be brought into harmony with the methods of the natural science of the present day, and if it did not destroy the possibility, yet made much more difficult for him the effort, of attaining to a profitable turning to account and rendering fruitful the idea of the cross, even for those provinces where its application is in reality perfectly legitimate, particularly that of the philosophy of history and speculative dogmatics.— On the ethical side of the idea of the cross, he has presented us with many excellent lessons; *e.g.*, on the fact that "the Christian is not less a cross to the world than the world is to him;" that "the insipidity and worthlessness of most moral teachings in modern times arises from the fact that they take away from the seriousness and pain of the birth to the moral life, from the cross, the decussation, *i.e.*, from the very main thing;" as also that "Cross and sadness is not to be separated from the joy of love, because man must one day come forth again with sadness from that into which he entered with joy;" and not less on the "cross of speculation, the pang and reproach of intellectual poverty," etc. etc.[2]

The German evangelical theosophy from the middle of last century has for the most part refrained from that method of natural-philosophic speculation upon the cross, which was pursued by Baader with special zeal, but not with equal profit as regards the results, while on the other hand it has applied itself with a diligence so much the more productive to the ethical treatment of its subject, and the treatment of it in

[1] *Vorles. über Societätsphilos.*, herausg. v. Fr. Hoffmann. WW., Bd. xiv., S. 104. Comp. also the treatise cited at the close of this passage, "On the Pythagorean Square in Nature, or the Four Quarters of the Globe," Tüb. 1798. (WW., Bd. iii., especially S. 267, 326.)

[2] *Speculat. Dogm.*, Bd. ix., 10 ff. Comp. *Firm. cognit.*, Bd. ii., 184, 302; *Sätze aus der erot. Philos.*, iv. 178; also letters, Bd. xv., 528, 541, 568, etc., etc.

accordance with the philosophy of history. To this category belongs a series of profound and oracle-like utterances on the part of HAMANN, the gifted and witty Magus of the North, namely, several of his "Crusades of the Philologist," which essentially seek to vindicate as the only true and sound wisdom that same theology of the cross for which Luther had already fought. Upon the banner of this hasty collection of twelve essays (1762) "sparkles that symbol of offence and folly, in which the smallest art-critic with Constantine overcomes, and carries out the oracle of judgment unto victory." Crusades to the East, new military-critical expeditions in the service of the Divine Logos, *Croisades à la moderne*, are to be the means "for restoring to life the dead language of nature."[1] For "the tyrant and sophist *Usus* can be disarmed by nothing but the æsthetic obedience of the cross," by bringing to light that "æsthetic secret of fair nature, which is called in the shepherds' stories a stone of the wise, in dissections shame, but in experience the dear cross—a *noli me tangere* for chamberlains and for algebraists."[2]—Admirably does he speak of the necessity for the cross of suffering in order to the spiritual weal of man. "The sweets of life lose their taste for the first who easily accustoms himself, and long continues, to use bitter and sour draughts. In the cross, as our religion terms it in the language of beautifully suggestive figure, there lies a great enjoyment of our existence and at the same time the true spring of our most hidden powers."[3] With regard also to the dogmatic import of the atoning sacrifice upon Calvary in relation to the history of redemption, we owe to him profoundly suggestive and forcible utterances, such as that on "the symbolic connection or affinity between the earthly thorn-crowns and the heavenly starry crowns," on the "crosswise effected relation between the deepest humiliation and highest exaltation of two opposed natures," on "Calvary as the last triumph of the extraordinary legislation over the Law-

---

[1] Werke, herausg. v. Roth, ii. 293, comp. 495; iii. 355 ; also iv. 156.
[2] *Ibid.*, vi. 31; iii. 410 f.
[3] Letter to Reichardt, vi. 257.

giver Himself," on the world-redeeming deed of that man "who, as a God of the living and not of the dead, brought forth an universal tincture of immortality against the sting of death, after a victory of right and of might over the most universal law of nature, and out of the carcase and skeleton of the destroyer and despot brought food and sweetness for the *nutrimentum spiritus;* that peace might be prepared upon earth, by the rejection of an evil and adulterous progeny, to the contentment of the whole human race, the restoration of the lost son, but also as the latest prelude to the glorious and terrible resurrection and the consummation of the universe for glory in the highest."[1]

In the case of OETINGER, the Magus of the South, contemplations of this kind retire more into the background. By virtue of his relations to Zinzendorf and his "blood-theology,"[2] the blood of Christ, or also the flesh and blood of the Lord, as the heavenly virtues and means of grace by which "all things are to be brought to the true corporeality," and God with His glory to make His abode in the creature, appears for Oetinger of far greater importance than the cross, the historic means of accomplishment and outward symbol of this process of spiritual-bodily transformation.[3] On the other hand, several adherents of that profound pneumatic-realistic school of "Würtemberg Theologians," as they were wont to term

[1] *Flieg. Brief an Niemand den Kundbaren.* Bd. vii., 117. Comp. *ibid.*, 125, 127.

[2] With regard to this, specially in its more rugged and exccentric type (of the "time of spasmodic malformations") comp. *i.a.* the saying handed down on p. 486 of Spangenberg's " Apologetische Zeitschrift" (1752), "Thus the crucifixion has not effected the work, *but the blood-shedding upon the cross ;* . . . they must not exclude the blood-sheding from the Passion, but make it the principal circumstance, otherwise they are in error." Further, the notorious Wound-litany of the year 1744, etc. See in general Plitt, *Zinzendorf's Theologie,* ii., S. 196, ff.; also S. 69 ff.; as well as, with regard to the occurrence in a somewhat milder form of the same teaching concerning the blood and wounds of the Saviour even in those writings belonging to a period prior or subsequent to that of the sickly misconceptions, Plitt, i., 291 ff.; 295—297 ; iii., 63, 64 f.

[3] *Theology from the idea of Life, etc.* (German by Hamberger, Stuttgard, 1852.) Comp. also the artt. " Cross," " Blood of Christ," and " Shedding of the Blood of Jesus," in his *Bibl. Wörterbuch,* edited by Hamberger.

themselves after JOHN ALBERT BENGEL, have admirably expressed themselves with regard to our subject: especially on the value and significance of the cross of suffering imposed by Christ, as also upon the mysteriously attractive and spiritually transforming power which proceeds from the cross of the Redeemer as believingly contemplated and embraced. To those sayings of Bengel himself which fall under this head there belongs a series of the most suggestive reflections in his *Gnomon* to the New Testament; such as that on Matt. xvi. 23, according to which on the one hand the cross is an offence to the world, but on the other hand also the world-shaped opposite to the cross is an offence to Christ; or that on 1 Cor. i. 24, "If we have overcome the offence of the cross, the whole mystery of Christ is for us clear and plain." In like manner other beautiful presentations of the fruit and value of sufferings for the disciples of Christ, such as "The good cannot thus be made hereditary; it must pass through the cross and be proved," etc.[1] Glorious is that which MAGN. FRIEDR. ROOS brings out in his "Brief Exposition of the Epistle to the Galatians" (on ch. v. 24) concerning the bliss-giving effect of the spiritual attractive power of the crucified Saviour, concerning that mysterious "communion through faith with Jesus in His cross, which is experienced, but cannot be explained." "For," so he further expounds, "the view of the crucified Saviour, beheld in the light of the Holy Ghost, makes upon the soul such an impression that it has henceforth an antipathy or hostility, but also a subjugating power, against the flesh and its desires; because this impression remains, and the view of the crucified Saviour is very often repeated. Here is the fountain of true sanctification, here the foundation of true liberty."[2] Where too he is treating of the "inner making one's own, or appropriation, of the cross," and the deliverance from the curse of the law thereby to be wrought, and not less where he is explaining Paul's "being crucified unto the world,

[1] Cited in Osk. Wächter, *Joh. Albrecht Bengel*, Stuttg. 1865, S. 45. Comp. also S. 323, 544 f.
[2] *Kurze Auslegung*, etc. (Tubing. 1784), S. 124 f.

and the world unto him," does he testify of deeply-felt, livingly-experienced truths ; as also in so many contemplations and prayers of his "School of the Cross" already mentioned before.[1] Not far removed from this circle of thought are also LAVATER and JUNG STILLING, the representatives of a peculiarly profound spiritual medicinal mode of teaching in relation to the effect of the redeeming death of Christ (as consisting in a mysterious inoculation of remedial powers of life into the organism of mankind, grievously diseased and as it were suppurating).[2] So also MENKEN, the thoughtful and suggestive expositor of that section of the Epistle to the Hebrews which treats of the perfect atoning sacrifice of the kingly High Priest, Christ (viii.—x. 12), as well as the typical narrative of the brazen serpent lifted up by Moses (Num. xxi. ; Joh. iii. 14), in which latter he seeks to point out an image of Satan, inasmuch as he was vanquished by the Lord upon the cross, thus a prophetic emblem of the idea of the atonement (which, according to his peculiar conception of it, is the rendering unsinful of the human nature by the victorious combating and overcoming of sinful flesh, in the person of Jesus upon the cross). Not less so R. STIER, an almost equally zealous opponent of the Church's doctrine of satisfaction as was Menken, yet differing from the latter in this respect, that he does not conceive of the Crucified as one-sidedly and alone a bearer of the Divine love, but as also at the same time a revealer of the Divine wrath, His death on the cross thus a sealing of this wrath, a terrifying form of threat and example of punishment.[3] Finally, J. FR. V. MEYER, who adhered more closely than the writers before mentioned to the fundamental idea of the doctrine of satisfaction handed down in the Church, but in connection there-

---

[1] *As before*, S. 30, 133 f.—*Kreuzschule oder Anweisung zu einem Christl. Verhalten unter dem Leiden*, with an appendix of prayers for special occasions. (7th edn., Stuttgard, 1875.)

[2] For them both comp. Ritschl, *Lehre von der Rechtfertigung*, i. 553f.

[3] Of Menken, see especially *Ueber die eherne Schlange*, etc. (partic. S. 385 ff. of the edn. of 1858.) Of Stier, *Andeutungen für gläubiges Schriftverständniss*, 1st Samml. (1824), S. 375, 2nd Samml. (1828), S. 24 ff.—Comp. Ritschl, *as before*, S. 557 ff, 567 ff.

with laid a main stress upon the reflection and reproduction, in the crucifying of sin in the penitent believer, of the act of expiation accomplished by the Lord upon the cross. That which he discourses concerning the necessary connection of the inner crucifixion of sinful humanity with the absolutely typical and in its essential character pure and liberating crucifixion of the Redeemer, belongs to the most vigorous and arousing teaching which modern evangelical theosophy has ever produced on this subject. The (spiritual) crucifixion of mankind is for him a "natural consequence of its present sensuous state and its suprasensuous prospect. It is a necessary requirement of its blissful continuance in an intransitory world, the true world of God; thither hath Christ opened the way for mankind through suffering, thither must it follow Him through suffering." It is true the crucifixion of the sensuous nature or the old man necessary in order to enter into this eternal world of God can never be effected by our own power: neither the practice of strict morality nor the endurance of ascetic rigours contributes in reality anything to its accomplishment. "This power to kill and to make alive belongs to God alone, even as the physical birth and physical death depends upon Him. But the instrument, which renders the sensuous man first desirous of another life, and then gradually ripened for it, is suffering of whatever kind. It impels him to the Mediator of both worlds proclaimed to him in the faith, it renders for him his faith in the Mediator precious and indispensable, and thus continues in the same faith to bind him ever more and more closely to Him who, by the meritorious power of His suffering, has rendered it for him a true benefit, an infallible means of the new birth, and (as such) much more easy to endure. Not only does he see in the much greater pangs of the Lord, the only Just One, a consolatory example, but he also knows that this Righteous One, who has made atonement for his unrighteousness, has thereby in the shortest and most sublime manner annihilated this unrighteousness, and calls forth in him the most perfect powers by the making of him a sharer of His own afflictions," etc.[1] The demand that this inner judgment of crucifixion upon the old man be carried out with all severity and consistency, without any kind of yielding to the sensibility of the old nature and its shrinking from suffering, and without any feeble and hesitating standing still at half-way to sanctification, is made by Von Meyer with great distinctness and earnestness. "You know it is impossible that suffering should cease to be suffering; the cross does not look for men without feeling. .... Annihilation of our impure, sinful, and foolish self, and Divine renewal, yea, a becoming one with God, is the design and mystery of the cross."[2] But to the severity of such a judgment to be executed upon the old man corresponds also the blessedness of the reward of grace awaiting the patient cross-bearer. He who is in the true spiritual sense crucified with Christ "will not be willing to exchange his lot with any one who stands beneath and mocks him, however noble and prosperous he (this mocker) may be. *He will not come down again, but through*—nicht wieder hinunter, sondern hindurch—and hears evermore in his smart the sweet words of immovable firmness, 'Verily I say unto thee, This day shalt thou be with me in paradise!' For those who are beneath must sooner or later follow him, and the longer it is deferred for them owing to their resistance, so much the more painful for them will the piercing of their hardened mind become. Besides, the Redeemer, with whom the suffering one dies, sweetens for him this inner death, and so it comes to pass that the suffering alternates with great pleasantness, and the languishing and desolation with unspeakable refreshings."[3]

It may be that not all these deductions of the noble Frankfort theosoph rest to an extent absolutely equal upon a solid Biblical foundation. Particularly the reference arising, towards

---

[1] Das Kreuz Christi—*Blätter für höhere Wahrheit.* (Smaller edition, Bd. ii., S. 438 ff.; espec. S. 441 f.)

[2] *As before*, S. 442 f.—Here is then added the passage already above cited (ch. v. 4, for ex., p. 239) on the merely relative value of bodily mortification and stigmatism.

[3] *As before*, S. 445 f.

the close of the passages here cited, to a continued activity of
the converting, purifying, and redemptive power of the Cross
of Christ, even in the world beyond death, during an intermediate condition between death and the final state, may
seem to involve a questionable tendency to purgatorial-
apocatastatic expectations, similar to those earlier developed
by Douze-Tems and others; with the supposition of which
tendency the chiliastic conception of the future of the kingdom of Christ, which is very clearly apparent at the close of
the treatise, is also perfectly in harmony. These questionable
sides, however, of Meyer's treatment of our subject, must
at any rate not be suffered to prevent our duly appreciating
the many excellences of the same; it must especially not
close our eyes to that point on which Meyer with more
vigour and clearness, even than Bengel, Roos and others, in
their teaching concerning the Cross, advances beyond the
contemplations and doctrinal presentments, devoted to the
same subject on the part of earlier writers. We recognise
this advance at once in the very clearly perceptible victory
over that misty element of alchemy and natural philosophy,
which to a great extent still darkens those contemplations of
Baader falling under this head,—an element which Meyer,
however, even if he in other respects cherished it to a certain
degree, at least never allowed to exert a disturbing influence
upon his profoundly thoughtful and earnest staurosophic
conceptions. But we recognise also, on the other hand, as
an important advance on the part of Meyer, more or less
too already in some of his immediate predecessors or contemporaries, such as Roos, Menken, Stilling, etc., that he
duly prizes that wondrously effective, mysteriously irresistible,
power of attraction, exerted by the cross of the Lord, in living
intercourse with the devout believing soul, *in its high significance for the inner life of the redeemed, and for their advancement in the path of sanctification.* This laying stress upon the
cross of Christ, in respect of its importance for the article of
sanctification and moral perfecting is met with, though only
sporadically here and there it may be, in the sermons and

writings of other Lutheran teachers of earlier date; *e.g.*, it is hinted at in the prose compositions of Scriver, Hollaz, Spener,[1] as likewise in spiritual song, the hymns of G. Arnold for instance, "O Durchbrecher," "Richtet auf des Heilands Leiden," yet nowhere is this importance exemplified with the definite emphasis and earnest consistency as here. Melancthon's classification of the various kinds of suffering in accordance with their approximation to the true cross; that which was advanced by Luther on different occasions, in the same direction; the powerfully stimulating teachings and exhortations of a Brenz, a Rhegius and others on our topic, had, with all their wealth of ideas, and their mighty power of consolation, yet left more or less untouched the point we are now considering: the increasing interpenetration of the objective and the subjective factor of the *Theologia crucis*, the turning to account of the idea of the cross in the interest, not merely of the doctrine of justification, but also of sanctification, and of the endeavour after moral perfection. And to have filled up this very gap in the earlier reformational doctrinal tradition, or at least to have pointed out with convincing emphasis the necessity for filling it up, is the no small merit of the evangelical theosophs of the close of the eighteenth and beginning of the nineteenth century, particularly of Meyer, in whose articles on the cross, here somewhat at length passed under review, the ideas of this school are brought to a specially clear and vigorous development.

The same ideas, or at least ideas closely resembling these, are to be met with also in the works of various Protestant theologians, of the most recent times, not belonging to the class of theosophs; and remarkably enough, *not only* in those of the representatives of the positive tendency, such as THOLUCK in his "Doctrine of Sin and of the Reconciler," as well as in several of his discourses; THEREMIN in several places of his justly prized collection of sermons, entitled "The Cross of Christ;" E. SARTORIUS in his "Doctrine of

[1] See particularly his glorious discourses, "The Cross," in his "Evangelischer Glaubenstrost," 1695.

Holy Love;" BECK in various of his "Christian Discourses;" occasionally also SCHOEBERLEIN, WUTTKE, and others.[1] Several also of the more distinguished representatives of the modern liberal theology have recognised the high importance which attaches to the doctrine of the cross of the Lord, and —so far as the more or less rationalistic presuppositions which they cherish with regard to the objective side of Christology permitted them—have sought to develop this doctrine in a dogmatic-ethical manner. Thus SCHLEIERMACHER, in two places of his Doctrine of Faith, treats of the attractive power of the Crucified One, and of the quickening operations which proceed from Him; while DE WETTE, in harmony with his symbolic-æsthetic mode of contemplating the subject, is intent on presenting the higher significance of "Christ on the cross, as a type of the human race purified by self-sacrifice;" and the Jena theologian, RUECKERT, depicts in its sin-slaying and sanctifying power the responsive love awakened by the communion of faith with the Crucified, not without tokens of his being himself under the power of this love.[2] The attempt has recently been made to draw the net gain from the presentments of these latter, as well as from the earlier theological tradition, on the part of A. RITSCHL, in his great work on "The Christian Doctrine of Justification and

[1] Tholuck, *Die Lehre von der Sünde und dem Versöhner*, 1823, also in several of his sermons on the Passion [the latter translated by Professor Park.] Theremin, *Das Kreuz Christi*, Berlin, 1828—1841. Sartorius, *Die Lehre von der heiligen Liebe,* Stuttg. 1861. J. T. Beck, *Christl. Lehrwissenschaft*, 1841, Pt. i.; *Christl. Reden*, in various passages. Besides these, also Wuttke, *Christl. Sittenlehre*, ii. 235 ff., 298 ff. Schöberlein, *Die Geheimnisse des Glaubens*, 90 ff., 136 ff. To this list also belongs the collection of sermons by Langbein of Dresden (*Das Wort vom Kreuze*, 4 vols., Leipz. 1857 ff.), the work of F. W. Krummacher while in Potsdam (*Der Leidende Christus* [eighth edn. of Engl. tr.: " The Suffering Saviour,"] Berlin, 1854), H. Dalton (*Pred. über die 7 letzten W. am Kreuze*, 1871); also those of the English theologians often cited by us above, McCheyne Edgar (*The Philosophy of the Cross*, 1874), A. B. Mackay (*The Glory of the Cross*, 1874), and others. Of French evangelical theologians, *e.g.*, E. de Pressensé, *The Mystery of Suffering;* Cæsar Malan, *The True Cross*, etc.

[2] Schleiermacher, *Der Christl. Glaube*, ii. 15, 94 ff., 3te Aufl. De Wette, *De morte J. Christi expiatoria* (1813), pp. 192, 256 sqq. Rückert, *Theologie*, 2 Bde., 1851. (Comp. Ritschl, i., S. 537.)

Atonement," a treatise, which, spite of its many one-sidednesses and unjustified attacks upon the churchly standpoint of belief, has nevertheless done a real service—and one to which by no means the lowliest place is due in the series of its varied instructive and meritorious disquisitions—by the thorough way in which the writer has drawn renewed attention to this whole domain, and illustrated its high importance for the theoretical and practical labour of the Church and of the Church theology of the present day.[1]

[1] *Christl. Lehre von der Rechtfertigung*, etc., iii., 166 ff.; 334 ff.; 454 f.; 549 ff. We shall have occasion below to refer more particularly to some of the specially characteristic utterances among those here cited.

VII.

The Cross in the Present and Future of the Church.

WILL the many-thousand-voiced chorus of Christian witnesses to the truth, whose songs of praise devoted to the cross of the Lord have, in that which we have hitherto written, passed, at least in some of their most characteristic notes and forms, before our spirits' ear and eye, now at once have to cease its activity? Can the series of the nobler and more significant of the phenomena and endeavours falling under this head be regarded as having attained to its definitive historic close; so that, after drawing the *facit* from the development up to this time, the religion of the cross may at once be borne to the grave, and the idea of a dominion over the world on the part of the Christian symbol of salvation henceforth be spoken of only as a romantic fantasy of bygone ages?

Some things in the course of development of the cultus of the cross in the Church, so far as it has already passed under our observation, might indeed seem to lend countenance to opinions and expectations of the nature here indicated. From the fact that the sensuous staurolatry of the post-Constantine age encountered an opposition of increasing strength, and that precisely on the part of the noblest and most advanced living witnesses of Christianity, so early as towards the close of the Middle Ages; that afterwards, at the time of the Reformation, there begins an increasing spiritualising and refining of the idea of the cross, which advances, in the Reformed

communion with pretty considerable rapidity and even with
impetuosity, in the Lutheran more slowly and with only
partial success, to the almost entire abolition of the sensuous
factors in the cultus of the cross : from this gradual replace-
ment of the *crux materialis* by the *crux spiritualis*, at least in
the worship of the Protestant ecclesiastical community, one
might feel tempted to draw conclusions in favour of the
supposition, that a complete laying aside of the last remains
of the external religious use of the Christian symbol of
salvation awaits us in a no very distant future. Yet
further considerations in the same direction may have to be
taken into account. Thus especially the fact that a state
of mind extremely inclined to escape from the cross, nay,
extremely hostile to the cross, animates the great mass,
particularly of the so-called cultured classes of our day ;
that the cry of Voltaire, " Ecrassez l'infame," has become
pretty much the war-cry of many thousands, and that precisely in Germany; that the decidedly negative answer given
by Strauss, professedly in the name of public opinion, to the
question, Are we any longer Christians? is in reality hailed
with joyful bursts of applause by countless representatives of
that public opinion ; and that the " self-dissolution of Christianity "[1] predicted by the pessimistic allies of the optimistic
Strauss, best corresponds to the wishes and expectations of
these thousands of anti-Christian worshippers of the " Zeitgeist" (spirit of the age). We certainly live in a time when
with all earnestness the question may be pondered in
Christian lands, whether the grave-yard is not to be replaced
by the furnace of cremation, the sepulchral cross by the
mortuary urn. What Goethe once sang as a wayward youth,
in his more thoughtless days, when the petulance of Martial
sometimes counted with him for a higher and better canon
than true poetic refinement and classic dignity—namely, in
the notorious Venetian epigram—this confession of the great

---

[1] [Title of an unhappily popular infidel work by Ed. v. Hartmann, of which the first edition appeared at Berlin in 1869. Six editions of it were called forth within five years. See above, p 104, note.]

poet, frivolous as it is, if not blasphemous, has borne only too rank fruits of imitation in the circle of latter poetic copiers and idolisers. And not that they were ever composed, the insolent verses of the revolutionary heaven-stormers of young Germany, such as those in Herwegh's "Call to arms": "Tear the crosses out of the earth, let them all be turned into swords! God in heaven will excuse it," or in Rob. Prutz's "Kreuz und Rosen" (1862):

> "Nur mir kein Kreuz aufs Grab gesetzt,
> Sei's Holz, sei's Eisen oder Stein !
> Stets hat's die Seele mir verletzt
> Das Martyrholz voll Blut und Pein :
>
> Dass eine Welt so gottbeseelt,
> So voller Wonne um und um
> Zu ihres Glaubens Symbolum
> Sich einen Galgen hat erwählt.
> * * * *
> Drum nicht das Kreuz mir auf das Haupt!
> Pflanzt Rosen um mein Grab herum ;
> Die Rose sei das Symbolum,
> Dran eine neue Menschheit glaubt ! "—

not that anything of this kind has been composed in the German tongue, but that it has been circulated with the approval of thousands upon thousands in Germany, and that the sentiment and mode of thought which expresses itself therein has become the publicly acknowledged spiritual patrimony of powerful parties in the state life of the present day: this fact is certainly such as to awaken in minds of little faith the delusion that within a period of no great length the last hour of Christianity will have struck, that there will at least soon be no longer room for speaking of a profession of the religion of Jesus the Crucified on the part of our people and land.

The bearing too of the Romish Church, numerically the most powerful branch or stem of Christendom, in relation to the question before us is only too much such as to lend support to such fears as are here indicated. The Romish Church clings tenaciously to the sensuous-external and superstitious cultus of the cross of the Mediæval phase of the development of Christianity, without essential modifications of any kind. It is a significant and characteristic utterance which Pio Nino, the ominous *Crux de cruce* of the prophetic succession of Popes in the pseudo-Malachi,[1] is said to have addressed to the renowned spiritualist Home after his accession to Catholicism. " This is our magic wand," he is reported to have said, on extending to him a crucifix to kiss.[2] Crucifix and sign of the cross are in reality, with the Romish Church, still only conjuring means, to which magic effects of the most diverse nature are ascribed. In respect of the truly displeasing frequency of the application of the sign of the cross in the majority of her liturgical acts, the ostentations and challenging part which she has lately again assigned to her procession crosses and pilgrimage crosses in the favourite "explosions" of the ultramontane popular feeling in France, and similar displays, the Church of Rome may still claim above others the right to be designated the Church of the Cross, *i.e.*, of the external adoration of the cross. Dr. Pusey is perhaps justified in the reproach he brings against her, of having gradually ceased to be a Church of Christ and become a " Church of Mary," and in the words of earnest warning in which he points out to her the danger, that sooner or later "the collapse of her baseless system of doctrines as to the prerogatives of Mary may bury with itself in its ruins the belief in Christ."[3] But with the Mariolatry is also most closely connected the staurolatry; as also the adoration of the body of Christ in the sacrament of the altar, as well as the latest bosom child of the Jesuitically degenerate cultus tradition of this Church—the delicately toying devotion to the sacred heart of Jesus—are nothing else but particular secondary forms of the idolatrous-supersti-

---

[1] Comp. what Bishop Hefele wrote as late as 7th July, 1875, upon the papal chief, after having, it is true, in the meantime made humble submission to him: " *Crux de cruce*; after he has lost the temporal power, he will now also desolate the Church."

[2] Perty, *Die mystische Erscheinungen der menschlichen Natur*, ii. 41.

[3] Eirenicon: or the Church of England a portion of Christ's one Holy Catholic Church, etc., Oxf. and Lond., 1866, i., p. 258.

tious adoration of the external symbol of redemption. Let any one also think of the superstition, partaking of the nature of fetich-worship, practised by the Roman populace of the city and province, under the inducement of the most lavish proclamations of indulgence, and consisting of the kissing of certain sacred crosses of wood or iron, more especially on Good Friday;[1] of the bewildering theatrical display at the Good Friday celebration in St. Peter's Church, at which a great suspended cross, lit up with three hundred and sixty-five tapers, is gazed upon and adored. Let him in like manner call to mind such apologetic products of modern Ultramontanism as the apotheosis even of the most childish of the miracles of the cross, the defence even of the most quixotic legends of the thaumaturgic operations of the crucifix—*e.g.*, that of the oft-repeated flight through the air of St. Joseph of Copertino [† 1663] to a crucifix of wood suspended high upon the wall, a flight explained on the ground of "mystic attraction"—as is done in the "Mystik" of Görres and in similar writings.[2] Let him ponder over the stigmatic manifestations of the present day, and the use to which they are put in the interests of ecclesiastical politics, on the part of our Ultramontanes, who know how to attach even to the stigmatisation of a Louise Lateau of Bois d'Haine "a significance in the German Church conflict"! Let him meditate on the continued existence even of that much ruder form of the ascetics of the cross once flourishing in the Middle Ages, which we became acquainted with as a self-mortification by the dragging about of heavy cruciform planks of wood, a practice which the Swiss traveller Keller quite recently saw actually exemplified in the West India island of Trinidad, in the case of Moxos Indians, converts of Jesuit missionaries, who in the processions with difficulty dragged about excessively heavy wooden crosses, chained to the naked leg[3]—a strange living monument and relic of those renowned

---

[1] Hase, *Protestant. Polemik*, S. 557, 570.
[2] Görres, *Mystik*, ii. 520 ff.; comp. Perty, *as before*, 413.
[3] Keller Leuzinger, *Vom Amazonas und Madeira*, Stuttgart 1874.

Indian missions of the Society of Jesus, the successes of which were in reality due to the alternate use of the cross now as a rod and now as a magic wand!

The Romish Church is in general a church of anachronisms; on that account the anachronisms too of the kind just indicated in its practice of the present day cannot surprise us. Nor can we, on the other hand, feel surprise if the wilder currents of the spirit of the age surge passionately against its obstinate maintenance of such ideas and customs of the Middle Ages, and let no small share of their hostility also be expended upon other churches fighting under the same banner, all unconcerned about their essentially different way of life and mode of fighting. Whether the Lutheran Church is any longer to be permitted to retain her religious use of the cross, confined as it is to the noble proportion of primitive Christian simplicity, whether she is not presently to be forced to conform to the rite of the severer type of the Reformed Church in this domain, on this question may the "culturkämpfer" (champions of culture) of the present day—the longer continuance of their mixing up in the internal affairs of the ecclesiastical confessions being presupposed—very soon be inclined to raise very serious discussions. And with the prohibition of the signing of oneself with the holy cross, still defended with manly courage by Cl. Harms, with the holding up to ridicule of the characteristic practices of early Lutheranism, such as that of the morning and evening blessing still admired with affectionate reverence by Leopold Ranke, they would then hardly rest satisfied. Behind the culture champions of to-day stand mocking and fiercely grinning those of the future, who will only be satisfied with a fresh rehearsal of the crusades of wild megæras against the images of Christ in schools and churches which came into play under the Paris commune. For to this they are impelled, these disciples of the "New Faith," proceeding as they do beyond Strauss himself. His deliverance to the effect that "the humanity of the present day, with its love of life and action, can never be any longer contented with the emblem of the cross, the harsh embodiment of the Christian world-shunning and passivity,"[1] they thankfully accept; but of his exhortations to tolerance and moderation his in other respects docile scholars will hear nothing. That which heathen Japan once compelled the professors of the religion of the cross within the range of its authority to do, that may the legislation of degenerate sons of Christendom, perhaps before any very lengthened interval of time has elapsed, dictate to the steadfast confessors of faith in Jesus. *L'abolition des pratiques injurieuses au Christianisme* would then yet again, as once in the not exactly glorious history of the commercial relations between Holland and Japan, have to form an aim of slow and toilsome attainment for the politics of protecting powers favourable to the Christians.

We are here depicting no unreal creation of the fancy, no erl-king or spectral form devoid of flesh and blood. The more than ferocious hostility to the cross on the part of the hundreds of thousands of the members of the *Internationale*, is a factor with which the Christian politician of our day must necessarily reckon. It is also very much a question which current will at first obtain the upper hand, whether that of the more peaceful Straussians, who would content themselves with imposing that "blockade" already predicted by Schleiermacher, that "complete starving out of all science,"[2] or, on the other hand, that of the communistic ultras, prepared for storming all that is sacred. In any lengthened continuance of the reign of terror of these latter which threatens us, perhaps at no very distant day, certainly no rational person will be found to believe. But when it has raged itself out, the wild hurricane, to whom will the further future then belong? Will the honest and decided disciples of Strauss then have the domain which used to be called Christian or churchly to dispose of; or will it once more be only the "Half," and not the "Whole,"[3] to whom we must look for the building up

[1] Der Alte u.d. Neue Glaube, etc., S. 93.
[2] See Schleiermacher's letter to Lücke, *Theol. Studien u. Kritiken*, 1829, S. 489 f.
[3] ["Die Halben und die Ganzen" is the title of a work published by David Strauss in 1865, which is directed against the standpoint of Schenkel.]

and extension of the religion of the future? Will it be gifted members of the new Deistic-church of Herr Richard v. d. Alm for instance, men inclined to retain the cross in their churches—not indeed as emblematic of redemption, but yet as a "primeval symbol expressing the direction of the four cardinal points, the universe, infinity in relation to space," and to retain this symbol alike in the form of a statue crowned with ivy, as of a solemn act of crossing made with the finger at the close of the service?[1] Or adherents of that Union which, spite of its radical mode of proceeding against every form of church dogma, once sang at the Turnhalle in Berlin (1869) the verse:

> "The edifice of all worlds in ruin sinks,
> The heavens themselves do pass away,
> The cross of Christ must stand"?

or perhaps future European partisans, gathered from among reformed Jews and ex-Christians, to the standard of the eloquent advocate of the Brahmoists of India, Keshub Chunder Sen, who, in one of his addresses inspired with the idea of human culture, characterised "the love of our enemies and self-denial after the example of Christ as the prime condition of human prosperity in Europe as in Asia," and spoke of the cross on which Jesus died as the mirror and powerful incentive to a life in such a spirit?[2]

A Christianity remodelled on the reform plans of these latter parties would perhaps be preferable to the irreligion— pure and simple—of the Straussians, or of the professors of the absolute Monism à la Häckel. Were it only conceivable that such an intermediate form between humanistic cultus of the spirit of the age and the following of Christ could be proved to be tenable, or that religious communities capable of exerting the power of life could proceed therefrom! But

[1] Rich. v. d. Alm, *Theologische Briefe an die Gebildsten der aeutschen Nation.* 3 Bde., Leipzig, 1862.
[2] "Jesus Christ, Europe and Asia;" address of Keshub Chunder Sen.—*Protest. K. Ztg.*, 1874, Nos. 10 and 11. On the high esteem in which the emblem of the cross is held on the part of the adherents of the Brahmo-Somaj faith, comp. also *Contemp. Review*, Aug., 1870, p. 70.

it is precisely this possibility which we must call in question. Between the attraction to the service of the world and the cultus of the Zeitgeist on the one hand, and the attraction which draws into the service of the Crucified on the other, a stable middle-position can never be attained. The attraction to the Crucified, where it is really present, will constantly prove itself stronger than that to the world and to conformity to the world. Whatsoever therefore there is that is Christian in those tendencies of the "half" will, especially under the pressure and impression of the conflicts with the "whole" enemies of Christ, become entirely Christian and churchly. The cross of the Redeemer will still exert its attractive power (John xii. 32) upon many of the strong ones who come too near to Him. It will become for many a one a corner-stone on which he is dashed to pieces, but will also prove itself for many others a powerful lodestone which irresistibly draws him into the bliss-giving communion of life with the Three-one God. An indistinct wavering or double-hearted wish to form a compact between cross and world, between the Spirit of God and the spirit of the age, between the Christian principle of faith and the modern principle of culture, is in any case possible only so long as one clings to the delusion that there can be a faith in the Crucified, which is not at the same time a faith in the truly and bodily Risen One! Long ago has its annihilating sentence been pronounced upon such a delusion, long ago has Paul called out in thunder-tones of judgment to those who would rock themselves to sleep in deceptive fancies of this kind, " If Christ be not raised, your faith is vain : ye are yet in your sins. Then they also which are fallen asleep in Christ are perished (lost) ! " There is no true entering into the communion of the sufferings of the Lord, which is not at the same time a living, powerfully convincing recognition of the power of His resurrection ! Boast if you will of the "purely human emotions," the genuinely human tenderness and depth of feeling which the impression of the Crucified One, contemplated as the Ideal Man—who has died, but after all *only* died, for the idea of humanity—is able to produce; remind us if you will of the testimony once given even by a Diderot, in the circle of Baron Holbach, for the irresistibly attractive power and touching effect of the Gospel account of the sufferings and death of Jesus; point us to the judgment of a Devrient upon the passions-spiel of the Oberammergau (1850), or to the recent flocking of thousands of Berliners, among them also numerous children of the world, to the exhibition of E. v. Gebhardt's painting of the Crucifixion, as a representation bringing out the human side of the Passion with unwonted effect, and on this very account producing a deep impression upon others![1] If by these instances it is sought to prove the necessity that, in order to produce living faith and loving self-surrender to the Saviour, a purely human view and presentation of His passion to the exclusion of all conceptions of His Divinity, is what is demanded; then, in order to maintain this position, one must surrender himself to the strangest infatuation, an infatuation which a passing glance, *e.g.*, at Diderot and the frivolous materialistic spirit which, spite of that confession of the power and beauty of the Bible, (*de ce diable de livre!*) dominated him to the end of his life, ought sufficiently to dissipate. It was something more than purely human dignity in suffering and death, which beamed forth to the youthful Zinzendorf (1719, at Dusseldorf) from the grief-stricken visage of Correggio's *Ecce Homo*, and rendered him throughout the whole of his career of abundant activity a confessor of the life-maxim, " I have but *one* passion : it is He, only He ! " The first steps on the path of following the Crucified One may be successfully made by one who perceives in Him only the Crucified, the man perfected in death, and still continuing to live in spirit. But so soon as the more difficult part begins, so soon as after the sweet we have also to taste the bitter fruit of the cross, so soon as we are called seriously to experience the communion of the Saviour's sufferings, and in addition to the sufferings of purification and discipline we have also manfully and victoriously to endure the sufferings

[1] Comp. v. Leixner-Grünberg, in the *Protest. K. Ztg.*, 1874.

of testimony, true *martyrium* in Melancthon's sense of the term, then becomes manifest the powerlessness of the one trusting only in the man Jesus of Nazareth, and not also in the eternal Son of God; then appears the insufficiency of that standpoint which denies the everlasting redemption brought in through the heavenly high-priesthood of the God-man— appears in the most pitiable manner and with ruinous effect for those misled by this view.

The humiliation of the Lord upon the cross, and His exaltation to Divine glory, the suffering humanity and the victorious Divinity, belong of necessity inseparably the one to the other, like the two halves of one ring. It is a piece of one-sidedness to wish to have, enjoy, and cultically exalt, solely and alone the glory of the Crucified One, as we saw done by the Christendom of the early and middle ages, after the example of Constantine and Helena. But it is no less a one-sidedness to emphasise exclusively and alone the lowly condition of the Crucified One, and accordingly to assign to the Church, the spiritual body which He forms to Himself out of mankind, a participation only in the sorrowful and shameful lowly side of His redeeming work.

"If we die with Him, we shall also live with Him;
If we suffer, we shall also reign with Him." (2 Tim. ii. 11, 12.)

It is an unalterable fundamental law of the kingdom of God that after suffering follows glory: they that mourn shall be comforted (Matt. v. 4; 2 Cor. i. 7; Rom. viii. 17; 1 Peter i. 11). Only a one-sidedly spiritualistic, or rather rationalistic, theological would-be wisdom, can wish to attenuate the *gloria crucis*, the divinely fair converse and necessary counterpart to the *ignominia crucis*, into something abstract and beyond the grave (Jenseitigkeit); in such wise that it should signify in relation to Christ Himself a spiritual continuance of life in the idea of love which is effective among His followers, or in some kind of spiritualising and deification *a parte post*, however this may be conceived of; in relation to the Church, on the other hand, a remaining constantly subject to cross, shame, and humiliation on this side the grave, without any other hope of any kind than that of consolation and deliverance in the world beyond. This would be to depart widely from that which the Reformers wrote concerning the cross as a salutary and highly necessary corrective for the Church in her earthly condition. It never entered their minds to represent the empirically present actual connection between the Church and the cross as a logically necessary one, and one absolutely essential to the weal of the Church in all time, and thus to declare the cross to be an inalienable attribute of the Church, a *nota ecclesiæ* of the same rank as Word and Sacrament are declared to be in Art. 7 of the Augsburg Confession. It was not the intention of Luther to assert anything of this kind, when, in the treatise "Von den Conciliis und Kirchen," he enumerated, as the last of the main features or characteristic marks whereby the "Christianly holy people" of the Church is to be recognised, also the "salutary mystery of the holy cross;" nor had Melancthon anything similar before his mind, when in the development of the article of the cross in his Loci, he took as his starting-point the favourite thesis, "that the Church in this life is subjected to the cross and afflictions" (ecclesiam in hac vita subiectam esse cruci et afflictionibus), or when, in the Apology, he declared such an enlargement of the notion of " sacrament " to be possible, that eventually also cross and afflictions, as also alms, prayer, etc., might be comprehended under it.[1] Only in its degenerate form, as present among the Anabaptists, as a "worldly kingdom" composed exclusively of pious and holy citizens—not in a milder and more spiritual conception, as a kingdom of freedom and prosperity, after the times of oppression and trouble—is the exposition of the chiliastic idea (as this is derived from Rev. xx.) rejected by the 17th Art. of the *Augustana*. The "ultimate deliverance from all afflictions," which Melancthon in an important passage of his Loci holds forth as the prospect of the oppressed and suffering Church,[2] is by no means con-

---

[1] *Apol. Conf.*, Art. xiii., p. 204 M. Comp. above, p. 279 of our exposition.
[2] Deus, quum punit, promittit auxilium et mitigationem malorum et liberationem; . . . liberet Deus suam Ecclesiam tandem ex omnibus miseriis. (*Loc. tert. ætat.*, p. 946 Br.)

ceived of as an abstractly spiritual and future one (jenseitige). Ecclesiastical pessimism receives no kind of support from the testimony of the Reformers in their teaching; either by that which they have taught concerning the Church, or by their teaching concerning the cross. " The Church is for them a bearer of the cross, is as an earthly Church always a crossbearer; but not in the sense that they conceived of the cross of the Lord which she is called to bear exclusively as the instrument of suffering and brand of shame, so that she may not also temporarily, yea even in a certain sense always and constantly, receive a part too in the glory and victory of the Crucified One! Only an exceedingly one-sided ecclesiastical subjectivism could rest content and feel satisfied with such a condition of the Church, in which her form of the cross—even when this arises from a melancholy want of spontaneity and enslavement by the power of the State—should be regarded as a normal condition, and voted permanent. If any one would permanently force upon the Church such condition of unfreedom (and we are here speaking in the first place of the Evangelical Church [as distinguished from the Romish], and particularly that of Germany), then precisely the duty of energetic resistance against such violence would be that cross which the Lord imposed upon her, not with a view to consign her to everlasting and hopeless continuance in such conflict, but in order to lead her, tried by such steadfast combating and suffering, to victory and peace. . . . There are inalienable rights and interests of the Church which it behoves her to maintain with treasure and blood, with body and soul, and *not* to maintain which is the true shunning of the cross and hostility towards it; even though a Church deprived of those rights may at the first glance appear poorer and more conformed to the cross, than one asserting the possession of them. The Church as evangelical, as having her appointed place under the cross of Christ, may suffer and bear much for Jesus Christ's sake; she may allow herself to be deprived of everything—everything except her confession! He who touches her confession, does not seek to impose upon her some specially heavy and painful cross; he aims at her life. As opposed to such assaults, not endurance and patience, but energetic self-defence, is a sacred duty."[1]

We repeat here these thoughts, presented elsewhere a year ago, because the opinion that a condition of suffering, consisting in a continued spoliation of her goods and an increasing limitation of her free activity, is for the Evangelical Church something naturally to be expected, and scarcely involving an act of injustice against her, is an opinion not only most extensively diffused in our day among those who cherish hostility towards the Church, but also greatly favoured and countenanced by the advances of ill-judged advocates of the Church's interests. When, for instance, a distinguished and on many points meritorious theologian like A. Ritschl, while on the one hand laying emphatic stress—as we have above thankfully pointed out—upon the high significance of the article of cross and suffering in the total organism of evangelical doctrine, and while he would have a greater place than hitherto has been the case in our works of Dogmatics and Ethics conceded to the truth "that the Christian occupies an exactly opposite relation towards the cross of suffering to that of the natural man," as also to the enjoining of the virtues of Christian patience, humility, power in prayer, etc., yet, on the other hand, endeavours, after the manner of a really extreme Christian subjectivism, to hold apart and separate Church and Kingdom of God, and in opposition to the positive churchly theology—against which he brings the reproach of hierarchical schemings and ecclesiastico-political agitation, ill-guided pastoral zeal, coursing with the name of God in the domain of public life, the calling forth of a churchliness which loves to display itself in the market-place, and other evil things of a like nature—recommends an essentially unfree, oppressed condition of the Church, and one in which she is incapable of powerful independent action, in her relations to the modern

---

[1] The Article of the Cross in the doctrine of the Reformers in its significance for the Evangelical Church of the present day.—*Evang. K. Ztg.*, 1874, No. 48, S. 533 ff.

temporal powers, and in particular contests her right to the unrestricted maintenance of her confession, and in the domain of doctrine either recommends or demands the most serious concessions to modern infallible science:[1] there is to be perceived in all this a view of that which is obligatory and necessary for the Church of the present day, which we certainly are not able to enrol in the class of sound Church political counsels; with regard to which we believe, on the other hand, that, while cautiously entertained, it may be able to contribute something to the weal of evangelical Christendom, yet, in the hands of clumsy workmen, it is in a position with equal ease to exert a truly disintegrating effect upon the Church's faith and life. From the standpoint of a speculative rationalism, most seriously departing from the teaching of the Church in regard to the doctrine of God and Christ, as also to that of sin,—from this standpoint to preach to the congregation repentance, and to lead it more deeply into the cross, seems to us hardly practicable; the protest which will be raised by those who decidedly espouse the interests of the Church, against such action, we believe to be in all essential respects justified.

We are certainly persuaded that our Church will have at first to be more deeply immersed in the baptism of sufferings than heretofore, and to be kept in the school of the cross for the gathering of yet more abundant and precious experiences than she has yet made. The compass of that which she has to experience and to learn with regard to the *crux spiritualis*, appears to us by no means exhausted yet. But we must be permitted to express decided doubts—the analogy of the personal experiences of the individual Christian equally forbids the supposition in question, as do the contents of the saving promises of the word of God—as to its being *only* progress in the knowledge and experience of the *ignominia crucis*, without any consolatory and refreshing enrichment in such experiences as the *gloria crucis* affords, which awaits the Church in the

---

[1] See the author's review of Ritschl's work, in the *Beweis des Glaubens*, 1875, S. 146 f.

more immediate future. The wounds which the Lord inflicts, He knows also how with healing hand to bind up; He suffers no temptation to overtake His people, without having made trial of their strength to endure it. Yea, He turns their sufferings immediately into Divine glory; He transforms them, in proportion as He stirs them in the fining-pot of affliction, from glory unto glory. " There yet remaineth a rest to the people of God :" in this consolatory promise of that apostolic man who knows how to testify in a manner glorious beyond that of others concerning the fruits of the atoning sacrifice of the new covenant, presented upon the altar of the cross, is contained a still more special consolatory promise. After the bitter side of the communion of suffering has been tasted by the Church of Christ, the sweet, the preciously refreshing side of this same communion will be brought to her for her full experience. After sounding the depths of the cross of suffering, the bright rays of the cross of glory will be contemplated by her anew, in fairer lustre than before.

The cross of Christ is no object exclusively of the historic past. It has still a future upon earth, a great and glorious future, even though it may not appear great in the outward sense of those for whom that which is great and glorious in the kingdom of God is in any case something strange and incomprehensible. We are not thinking immediately of the last, the eschatological future, which is predicted in the word of the Lord (Matt. xxiv. 30) of the appearing of the sign of the Son of Man in heaven. Something of the nature of a far-beaming revelation of the might and majesty of the cross of Christ, the symbol of redemption, the sacred altar of sacrifice of the new covenant, irradiating as a lightning flash the whole surface of the globe, seems in reality to be here predicted. That mysterious word of prophecy is in much too close contact—especially in that which is fore-announced as the terrifying effect of the majestic heavenly appearing, in the "mourning of all the tribes of the earth"—with the twofold Johannine proclamation of that which will one day take place, when they shall look "upon Him whom they have pierced" (Rev. i. 7; John xix. 37; comp. Zech. xii. 10), for the reference in "the sign of the Son of Man" to the cross, or at least to the passion of Jesus, His humiliation in shame, agony, and death, to be lightly overlooked. Nor is there anything at all strange in the circumstance that, according to this supposition, Christ makes mention aforehand of His cross, while He has not yet suffered crucifixion; for in those exhortations also, so abundantly attested and probably several times uttered, namely, to the taking up of His cross (Matt. x. 38, xvi. 24, and parallel places), the Lord spoke of this as the instrument of His death, already long before that death itself. Nevertheless the indefinite character of the expression, "Sign of the Son of Man," leaves it uncertain whether we have to think of a cross in the proper and externally visible sense, such as a great brilliant cross of cloud, or a cross of streaming radiance, far transcending in glory and awe-inspiring majesty that once beheld by Constantine. The interpretation which specially commends itself to the majority of the Fathers, as also to a considerable number of modern theologians—that which sees in this passage a reference to such majestic cosmico-symbolic manifestation of the instrument of salvation—has certainly more in its favour than the (Judaising) interpretation of the expression as having reference to some event of history which has already taken place, *e.g.*, to the human form which as is alleged appeared to Titus in the Most Holy Place on the night of the destruction of the Temple. Yet, on account of the manifold significance of the term "Sign of the Son of Man," it seems to us the wiser course not to look for a direct appearing and manifestation of the cross, but to regard as the sense and import of this word of prophecy some assurance, amounting to immediate recognition (given as in a lightning-flash to all men upon earth), of the truth of the revelation of God in Jesus the Crucified—thus some kind of Divine confirmation of the *via crucis* as the only way of salvation, of a nature to inspire with dread and trembling the unbelieving world.[1]

[1] Further in the Appendix IX.: THE SIGN OF THE RETURNING SON OF MAN, MATT. xxiv. 30.

Not this eschatological event heralding the last times have we now before our mind, when we assert for the cross in the further development of the Church a great future. The cross, as a symbol alike of the outward confession as of the lowly following of Jesus, as the infinitely profound and pregnant symbol of the religion of truth, the significant central position of which in the totality of the Divine plan of salvation is attested by a typico-prophetic previous and preparatory history of an eminently providential character, and of undeniably teleologic design,[1] this cross has still within the earthly historic course of the world a highly important mission to fulfil, in which the synthesis of those two one-sided exertions of its influence in the past history of the Church—that preponderantly directed only outwards, during the period from Constantine to Luther, and that preponderantly only of an inward nature, from Luther to the present time—will be represented and realised. It is mainly three domains of the life of the Christian Church in which the idea of the cross, on the one hand as the evangelically purified conception, and on the other as the (in the genuine and nobler sense) catholic conception, completed and enriched, thus the idea of the cross restored to its early-Christian and apostolic fulness, will have to develop its fruit-bearing activity. First of all and in a special sense it will have to prove, far more abundantly and powerfully than heretofore, its SANCTIFYING efficacy in its operation upon and in the religious-ethical life of Christians as individuals. The extraordinary conflicts, toils, and perils with which in the present time the Christian standing appears to be beset and harassed on every side; the abundance of the questions, of a theoretical and a practical nature, now awaiting their solution at the hands of those engaged in the service of the Lord and of His Church; the character of a restlessness and business distraction, wrought up to the highest pitch of tension, attaching in consequence thereof in increasing degree to life even in Christian circles, a "life at high-

[1] See above, ch. i., A and B, especially the concluding observations, pp. 29 f. and 69 ff.

pressure," as it has been fittingly termed;—all this renders necessary a far more vigorous exertion of the endeavour after sanctification and the proof of a living faith, than the bearing of the representatives of evangelical churchliness has hitherto as a rule displayed. In the midst of the perplexing many-sidedness of the Martha services, such as the extraordinarily active life of the present imperatively demands of the Church, the devout and contemplative mind of a Mary, directed to the one thing needful, must not be denied; rather must this grow and wax strong precisely in the same degree as the other.[1] Extraordinary times call for extraordinary measures. We do not propose the adoption of measures akin to those of a hyper-ascetic superstitious staurolatrous Ultramontanism, nor of measures after the pattern of those employed in the American or British Methodistic agitations and revivals. So far as immediately concerns the want of life and salvation in the *German* Protestant community, we desire only an energetic drawing of the practical consequences contained in any case in the principle of justification of our Church; a reviving and fruitful re-vindication of authority for the reformational article of the cross of the Lord in its deep significance for our whole character, as living, loving, and suffering in the service of Christ; increasingly abundant and more fruit-bearing experiences in the sphere of that mysteriously bliss-giving attractive power which flows from the Crucified One, this real treasure of our Lutheran mystic-ascetic literature, the precious pearl which glistens forth to us in G. Arnold's love-inspired verses:

> Liebe, zeuch was in dein Sterben,
> Lass uns mit gekreuzigt sein,
> Was dein Reich nicht kann ererben;
> Führ ins Paradies uns ein![2]

Of the helpful impulses which are afforded us in relation to

---

[1] Comp. Edgar, *The Philosophy of the Cross*, p. 269 f.; and in general the whole instructive chapter, "The Cross the Instrument of Sanctification," p. 256 ff.

[2] O Love, embrace us in Thy dying
Let all in us be crucified
That cannot in Thy kingdom shine;
Lead us into Paradise.

this endeavour on the part of foreign representatives of living Christianity, we both may and ought most thankfully to avail ourselves, though never to the neglect of the Christian duty of earnest trying of the spirits and the exercise of a safer judgment thereupon in accordance with God's word.

The second domain of the Church's life upon which we hope to behold anew, in the nearer or more distant future, great triumphs of the cross of Christ, is that of MISSIONS, Home as well as Foreign. We cannot regard the successes of the cross as a missionary power as being as yet by any means exhausted; and for this reason, that its successes in the sphere of Christian personal sanctification, the indispensable foundation and pre-requisite for a fruit-bearing and sound missionary activity among unbelievers at home as well as in the heathen world, are as yet far from exhausted, and that a glance at the present condition of the Christian and extra-Christian nations suffices to show that the work of the chosen witnesses, upon whom is incumbent the proclamation of the grace of the Crucified and Risen One before every creature, is as yet far from having attained its close. Any other kind of diffusion of the kingdom of grace, within and without, than that which takes place beneath the cross, and through the power of the cross, appears however for us inconceivable. Rationalism, even in its most ethically purified and idealised form, as this is represented by the modern speculative school of Germany, has no undertakings worth mentioning, not to speak of any kind of success in the field of missions, which it can point to. And this simply because it knows not the full power of the cross; because it either has not experienced, or has experienced only in the feeblest measure, the heart-transforming, life-renewing, sinner-converting efficacy of that grace proceeding from the Crucified and Risen One, that wondrous effect of the heavenly fire which melts away even the most obdurate pride, that "alchemy of the Holy Ghost,"[1] as a recent writer upon our subject ventures to call it; and for this very reason experiences nothing of the impulse to testify to others the

---

[1] Mackay, *Glory of the Cross*, p. 283.

blessedness of this experience. Only the circles which have placed themselves wholly, with their confessing, teaching, and life, under the cross; only the much-despised and contemned pietistic orthodox circles, covered over and over again with Langhansian[1] venom and scorn, only the mission circles in the strict sense of the term are wanting neither in the missionary spirit and zeal, nor in missionary success. Without their activity, ever quickened and kindled anew at the feet of the Crucified, the work of extending the kingdom of God would long ago have come to a standstill. Let any one criticise and censure the method pursued by them as he will; let him call in question their enthusiasm as unsound, or at least ill-guided; let him agree with Schleiermacher's witty remark on the British friends of missions, who "made use even of the wood of the cross as masts for their gain-seeking voyage of life," or join in any similar bonmots; the fact remains none the less, that the power and self-sacrificing courage for works of rescuing love to sinners, as this is required for the great mission problem at home and abroad, will be found only among those who go forth as lowly bearers of the cross of Christ, who by intimate communion in prayer with Him know how to draw forth the power of that faith which "never permits us to sit at home in pleasant and easy repose, and see the champions of the cross, consecrated by the great sacrifice of the Lord, striving unto blood with the enemy for the victory."[2] It is moreover objective views and considerations, founded on the nature of the aims of Christian missionary labour, as also on the character of the heathen whose conversion is sought, which have long convinced, not only the theologians of the Church, but sufficiently large-hearted and enlightened statesmen too, of the adaptation and worth of the missionary work consecrated by the cross, and of this only.

---

[1] [Langhans, a radical theologian of Switzerland, whose name is associated on the Continent with a bitter hatred of the mission work, which he seeks to cover with ridicule and scorn. The reader may be able to find a parallel case in our own land.]

[2] *The Perfect Man; or, Jesus an Example of Godly Life.* By the Rev. Harry Jones. London, 1870.

A British Parliamentary Commission issued in 1856, of which Mr. Gladstone was one of the members, came to the conclusion —as the result of the most thorough investigations, based upon evidence derived from all mission-fields far and near—that not the application of external means of civilisation, but the preaching of Christ crucified, is the true agent for raising barbarous tribes to a higher stage of culture, and even "that by the preaching of the word of the cross of Christ, and by this only, do the heathen obtain a true susceptibility for the outward ennobling of life."[1] The Christian circles of England and America might teach much that is salutary, in this domain too, to us Germans, especially our statesmen and Church politicians, if we would only learn! In the often too mechanical employment of measures which have been adopted with success in one case or other, and then have come to be regarded as infallible, errors may no doubt frequently have been committed among them also. The excessive expectations too which have been cherished in connection with the use of these means, the occasional falling into a fanciful and uncritically confident expectation or intoxication with millennial prospects of the future, may likewise be censurable.[2] In its totality, however, that which is accomplished on this side in the form of sacrifice made for the cause of the Crucified retains its full claim to our admiration; and the only true effect we German evangelical Christians can experience in presence of these magnanimous deeds of our British and American kinsmen (*i.e.*, of kindred race: Stammesverwandten), stands written in Heb. x. 24: παροξυσμὸς ἀγάπης καὶ καλῶν ἔργων.

A third and last series of salutary results we look for from the future more earnest cultivation and more abundant de-

---

[1] "Missions, their Place and Work in the Present Day," from the Danish or H. Kalkar. (*Allgem. lit. Anzeiger f. das evang. Deutschland*, 1873, S. 183.)

[2] As instances, comp. Mackay, *as before* (p. 281 ff.), as especially Edgar, p. 340: "Under the cross the hopes of the believer bloom into tropical luxuriance; we feel there that we cannot expect too much. We feel that the perseverance of the saints is only a necessary corollary to the crucifixion. We feel there that all doubt regarding our salvation is presumption and impertinence," etc.

velopment of the idea of the cross in the direction of the restoring an increasingly close, more true, and solid communion between the members of diffcrent branches and divisions of the kingdom of God. The IRENIC, the peace-making activity of the cross, is not the least important, even in our days. This should be earnestly and with one accord sought, above other tokens of the favour of our heavenly High Priest, by all His confessors; especially at a time in which melancholy denominational strife within co-operates with the assaults of enemies without for the ruin of the Church, and a deplorable splitting up into parties, of those who by the manifold community of their interests are called to be one, furnishes only too powerful arguments in favour of the apparent truth of the assertion made by one of their own more distinguished prophets, that Christianity is undergoing a process of self-dissolution. The cross of Christ alone will be able to silence this lamentation, to close these smarting wounds. We do not favour any essentially untruthful endeavours after peace, based upon merely superficial overlooking of differences, in place of a thorough reconciliation of opposites. We are as far from advocating misty compromises made on the part of faith with unbelief, as we are from pleading in favour of absorptive projects of union, which would fail to render justice to the good claim of historic confessions, or of rabid schemes of a comprehensive national Church. For the evangelical Church of Germany in particular we desire and call for the endeavour after such ordering of its internal relations, as shall assure the maintenance in its integrity of the fundamental form of its ecclesiastical order and type of doctrine, as shall not consign to the grave the Lutheran character of the German Church of the Reformation, but preserve, strengthen, and aid it to the full development of its peculiar gifts and distinctions. We do not make this demand out of confessional obstinacy, or by virtue of an unjustifiable "estimate of one's own wares;" but only out of love to real ecclesiastical peace, the prime condition of which is, not suppression, but maintenance and loving solicitude for the historic forms the life of the Church has assumed, especially when these forms have been approved and attested by a particularly abundant charismatic fulness of its powers and gifts. In the cross, in the common self-surrender to the crucified and divinely exalted Son of God, was the true union of Christians of every confession long ago guaranteed and sealed.[1] It is therefore only necessary that time and space be allowed them for the increasingly pure conception and more powerful experience of the "salutary mystery of the holy cross," which forms their most precious patrimony, in order that the outward presentation of their communion of life may make unimpeded progress to a blissful joy of all faithful confessors of the truth.

It would assuredly be sad, and unhappily only too just a ground of triumph for the enemies of Christianity, if the most pregnant symbol of the spiritual union and communion of all Churches should, through the combined operation of unbelieving and hypocritically pretending or superstitious powers of the age, be prevented from exerting its pre-eminently pacific effect in presence of the still existing divisions within the Church. What if, when there has long remained no single doubt more as to the might of the word of the cross to resolve into blissful harmony even the strongest contrasts, among the representatives of a divinely enlightened Christian view of the world, whether theologians or philosophers; when in particular the alone effectual remedy, and the alone true reconciliation and peace-making for the sickly over-tension of one-sided tendencies of the age to optimism or pessimism, in the ecclesiastical or extra-ecclesiastical domain, has been recognised in the cross of Christ,[2] solely and alone the

---

[1] Luthardt, *Apologet. Vorträge*, ii., S. 121: "There is *one* place in which all Christians find themselves in spirit one—that is THE CROSS. In this is to be found the spiritual unity of the Church." [Comp. the sentiment expressed in the profoundly spiritual hymn of Hugh Stowell: "From every stormy wind that blows," etc.]

[2] See on this point Luthardt, *as before*, iii., 176, 195; Kahnis, *Luth. Dogm.* recast 1874). i. 466 f; Kuyper, *Der Modernismus*, edited (in the German trans.) by

inflexible obduracy of churchly-confessional (denominational) parties should offer an insuperable resistance to the reconciling power which flows forth from this salutary mystery! We do not regard this as possible. We have confidence in the inner power and truth of the Gospel of the Crucified One to assert victoriously its peace-making, healing, and reconciling power on this side also. It will do this so soon and in the same proportion, as all churches have become in perfect truth Cross-churches, churches under the cross, communions confessing and cherishing that genuine *theologia crucis* in which there is no guile, which calls the good, good, and the bad, bad, spite of all dissembling arts of a truth-corrupting *theologia gloriæ*. The power of the blood of the Crucified, which makes peace in heaven as upon earth (Col. i. 20), cannot be always resisted, even by the self-seeking separative tendencies and party contentions within the bosom of the Church Militant. As the last enemy, death will be destroyed: at the time when this takes place, all other enemies will have been made the footstool for the Lord's feet (1 Cor. xv. 25). When at length the sacred blood of the Crucified flows in unhindered power and freshness through the life-veins of all the members of His body, through all the branches of the mighty far-shadowing tree of Christendom, the crown of this tree will put forth in glorious unity and wondrously harmonious splendour its leaves, blossoms, and fruit. And though the stem should be greatly weather-beaten and almost withered, a fresh top without corrupt or faded branches will flourish in the splendour of Christ, the eternal Sun of Righteousness, as in the days when He first visited us, the gracious dayspring from on high. That remains not less true for the whole Christian Church than for each of its members, which one most richly endowed with grace of the psalm-singers of the New Covenant uttered beneath the cross:

Riggenbach, S. 33 f. ; comp. J. H. Fichte, *Die theistische Weltansicht*, 1873; and the programme of the Catholic philosopher Katzenberger of Bamberg, *Das apriorististische und das ideale Moment in der Wissenschaft*, 1874, S. 42.

Das weiss ich fürwahr. und lasse	This I know indeed, and never
Mir's nicht aus dem Sinne gehen :	Suffer it to leave my mind,
Christenkreuz hat seine Maasse	That *our* cross must have its measure
Und muss endlich stille stehn.	And at last an end must find.
Wenn der Winter ausgeschneiet,	Winter snows must be expended.
Tritt der schöne Sommer ein ;	Summer then comes fair and bright ;
Also wird auch nach der Pein,	Thus shall suffering be ended,
Wer's erwarten kann, erfreuet.	Who can wait shall see the light.
Alles Ding währt seine Zeit	Things of earth their time endure,
Gottes Lieb in Ewigkeit.	But God's love is evermore.

Call it Chiliasm if you will, the transferring of the consolatory hope of the individual Christian, expressing itself in this confession, to the domain of the whole Christian Church. There is besides the fanatical also a well-founded Chiliasm, based upon the promises of God's word, and indispensable for the thriving of the life of the individual Christian, as for that of the Church at large. The expectation of such deliverance, consolation, and glorification of the suffering Church, as leaves her still a Church standing beneath the cross, falls under the ban of no orthodoxy as measured by the ancient standards. The profounder self-absorption in that mystery of godliness which is without controversy great, and into which the angels desire to look, will ever afresh call forth and quicken again the consolation of the Church's witnesses of the truth in all ages, the consolation in the confession of which a Flacius and a Spener join hands: THE HOPE OF BETTER TIMES.

APPENDIX.

I.

ON THE PURELY ORNAMENTAL USE OF THE SYMBOL OF THE CROSS ON PRE-CHRISTIAN MONUMENTS.

(Comp. p. 17 f.)

THE majority of cruciform figures to be observed upon the monuments of pre-Christian and extra-Christian art are of religious symbolic import. Only of rare occurrence, and comparatively recent origin, or of doubtful character, are those cross-symbols presenting themselves upon ancient art implements or inscriptions, to which notoriously *no* reference to religious conceptions or customs attaches, but which, like the hieroglyphs already alluded to on page 4, are characters of only accidentally cruciform type, or as adornments of art-works or implements bear only a decorative significance, and appear employed, whether in unthinking imitation of certain actual religiously significant cross-symbols, or in a purely arbitrary manner, as moments of artistic presentation.

On some of the latter symbols we have already treated in the text. Thus on the figure ┼, which, in connection with stars or with a half-moon, appears upon ancient Gallic or ancient Spanish coins—*e.g.*, upon a coin of the ancient Iberian city Asido, and here *possibly* is without religious import (see p. 19); in like manner (p. 18) on the sign ⚥, upon a silver vase of Cære: hardly a religious symbol, but probably—since it is depicted on the hindquarter of a horse—a koppa, ϙ, developed from motives of decoration into the figure of a circle or mirror, with a cruciform handle (Venus' looking-glass); or perhaps also a combination of the signs ϙ and ┼ (⊕), of which the latter, the cross-shaped Phœnician Tau, is sometimes found inscribed upon the hind-quarters of horses upon ancient pictorial representations (*see* Raoul Rochette, in the frequently cited dissertation De la croix ansée, etc., *Mem. de l'Acad. des Sciences*, xvi. 2, p. 320; as well as the illustration, pl. i., No. 32); as too the ancient Orientals were wont to burn upon their camels (on the neck or hind-quarter), and equally so upon their slaves, the cruciform Tau symbol (according to a statement of the Arabic lexicographer Firuzabad, which is followed by Freytag in his Arab.-Lat. lexicon, and Gesen. *Lexic. man. Hebr.*, sub voc. וְם ; comp. Rochette, *l.c.*, p. 324). The religious import of these signs, ⊕, ┼, or ♀, supposing such import to have been originally present, appears, at any rate in the later period to which the representations and accounts in question belong, to have been no longer preserved in tradition, and the symbols themselves thus to have become arabesques maintained without regard to their signification. Thus also probably the signs ⊕, ⊕, , ┷, etc., frequently occurring upon ancient Italic (Etruscan or præ-Etruscan) vases; occasionally also upon buckles, pommels of daggers, and other ancient art products, brought to light in the central European fields of research.[1]—Yet more certainly do the cruciform figures of the tattooing practised by many of the South Sea Islanders fall entirely without the circle of religious symbols. The purely decorative character of these marks cannot well be doubted; although to the custom of tattooing, as to all *hiero*glyphics in general, a religious significance primarily attached. Comp. below, p. 376.

To some remarkable cases of the merely ornamental employment of the cross upon pre-Christian monuments of Rome, of the last century of the Republic and the beginning of the Imperial Age, attention has been drawn by the renowned Roman archæologist DE ROSSI, as also on the foundation of De Rossi's researches by the French writer EDMOND LE BLANT. According to the *Iscrizioni doliari* of Marini, preserved in MS. in the library of the Vatican—a work, apart from the translation of his preface, printed in tom. vii. of Ang. Mai's *Scriptorum veterum nova collectio*, as yet unpublished— there are found, in the midst of a considerable number of early Christian inscriptions with cruciform symbols, monograms of Christ, etc., also some manifestly heathen inscriptions, which likewise present under various forms the symbol of the cross. Thus there is found

[1] Comp. p. 18.

upon a brick, taken from the catacomb of St. Hermes (in cruciform arrangement of the letters, which appear to have been imprinted with a seal):

☦ FIG PLOTINAE AVG ☦

Marini long ago pronounced in favour of the pre-Christian character of the ornamental cross symbol which stands at the beginning and the end of these words; and De Rossi remarks, in confirmation of this view, " In truth, in order to recognise in these and similar characters, which often occur in ancient inscriptions upon bricks, unequivocal expressions of the Christian symbol of redemption, one must descend to a much later age than that of the Empress Plotina." That Plotina, the wife of Trajan and adoptive mother of Hadrian, to whom by the latter emperor a temple was consecrated after her death (Dio Cass., 68. 5; comp. Plin., *Paneg.*, 83), was in secret a Christian, can scarcely hardly have made use of the sign ╅ as indicative of her Christian profession; since the use of the same as a Christian symbol be assumed. Yet even had she been so, her contemporaries would belongs only to a considerably later age (see, *e.g.*, the seal inscription of Theoderic, King of the East Goths; also furnished by De Rossi and Le Blant:

☦ REG DN THEODERICO BONO ROME).

Unquestionably, even as the crosses of this inscription, are the names upon ancient coins and vases, placed in the form of a cross, pointed out by Garrucci (vid. *Revue Archéologique* 1866, i., p. 90 sq.), to be regarded as products of heathen and not Christian art, and, on this very account, as purely ornamental figures, wanting in any deeper symbolic character. Thus, a full half-century before the Christian era, Cossutius Maridianus, a master of the mint in the service of Julius Cæsar, inscribed his name in the form of a cross, in order as Garrucci supposes, to present an allusion to the *Julium Sidus*, the planet Venus, frequently depicted under the figure of a cross. Similar names, arranged crosswise, are to be found upon certain ancient earthen vases, belonging to an age scarcely less early (in Camurrini, *Iscrizioni di vasi fittili*, p. 18, n. 33; p. 58, n. 361):

SE
SOTER
ST

LI
CRVSANTVS
TI

In like manner, of heathen and not Christian origin appears the inscription upon a brick in the Museum at Wiesbaden, the work of a tile- or brick-maker, Sempronius Heron, employed by the XXII. Legion, which was stationed in Upper Germany:

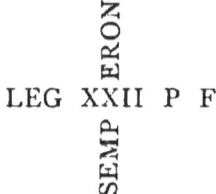

The vertically placed abbreviation of the name Sempronius Eron intersects the appellation of the legion (Legio XXII. primigenia fidelis). But just as little as the predicates bestowed upon this latter can be supposed to contain an allusion to its Christian faith, can, as it seems, the whole cross-wise arrangement of the letters lay claim to any religious significance. "Ces sigles, pas plus que le dauphin sur lequel elles sont imprimées, ne doivent être regardées comme des signes de religion." (Garrucci, *l.c.*) Comp. in general Le Blant, in the *Rev. Archéol.*, 1872, p. 126 sqq.

However remarkable the instances here adduced of a merely ornamental application of the symbol of the cross in the pre-Christian art and epigraphics, they yet greatly recede into the background, in point of number and importance, before the much more frequent instances of a manifest and indisputably religious character of cruciform figures and emblems upon the monuments of antiquity, as also of the heathendom of later epochs. Where these figures were turned to account for the embellishment of the instruments of daily life, *e.g.*, coins, hafts of swords or daggers, buckles, etc., and even of urns or vases not designed for the cultus of the dead, and on this account were multiplied in considerable numbers, as it were manufactured wholesale, there the religious significance originally attached to them was early lost sight of, and by the purely decorative application in course of time entirely pushed aside and obscured. But, as all emblematic writing among all nations originally bore an hieroglyphic or hieratic character (see Wuttke, *Die Entstehung der Schrift*, i., Leipzig, 1872; and the article on this work "Tattooing," in "Ausland," 1873, S. 48 ff., 72 ff.), as in general every product of art and all technical skill was in its rudimentary beginning called forth and directed by the patriarchal or priestly labours of the earliest pathfinders of human culture, so here too an analogous origin to the class of symbols under review cannot be disputed. GABRIEL DE MORTILLET, in the work already frequently cited by us, "Le Signe de la Croix avant le Christianisme" (Paris, Rheinwald, 1866), has certainly erred in entirely leaving out of account the possibility of the non-existence or the existence *no longer* of religious references in the numerous signs of the cross upon early Italic and ancient Celtic vases, urns, chests for the ashes, horn-books, dagger and sword hafts, coins, etc., examined and described by him. But when, on the other hand, the editor of the *Revue Archéol.*, ALEXANDRE BERTRAND, in a notice of De Mortillet's book, in vol. xiv. of this Review, p. 447, scouts the idea of a religious-symbolic significance to the pre-Christian cross in general, and consequently claims for it throughout, and invariably, only an ornamental character, he manifestly falls in doing so into a no less culpable extreme of an opposite kind. It is not the axiom figuring at the head of the work criticised by him—" Des la plus haute antiquité la croix a été employée comme symbole, comme emblème religieux" (De Mortillet, Préface, p. ii.)—which merits to be condemned as a "radically false idea" (pensée fausse a priori), "resting upon no solid basis;" but only the uncritical and one-sided manner in which De Mortillet seeks to endow with a religious symbolical meaning *every* ancient cruciform sign *without exception*, and moreover the mystic confusedness and indefinite character of the views he entertains with regard to the alleged widespread and primitive secret cuitus of the peoples among whom these signs are found. For since the places where the objects marked with crosses were discovered are said in almost every case to contain *only* such symbols of the cross, but no idols, etc.,—an assertion, moreover, wanting in all solid foundation, and having a show of truth only in relation to a very limited domain of the antiquities under review,—De Mortillet, too hastily generalising, will assume that the cruciform figures are primeval emblems of a purified cultus, relatively free from idolatry, and one thus appearing to be the direct precursor of Christianity. "La Croix a donc été, dans la haute antiquité, bien long-temps avant la venue de Jésus-Christ, l'emblème sacré d'une secte religieuse qui repoussait l'idolâtrie" (p. 174). Against this concluding proposition of the researches of De Mortillet, Bertrand should have directed his polemics, not against the more generally stated and in itself unassailable thesis of the high antiquity of the cross as a religious symbol, from which De Mortillet took his start. Of a sect for the rest free from idolatrous rites—nay, even an anti-idolatrous sect of pious worshippers of the cross, or

Staurolatræ, which might be regarded as a special forerunner of Christianity—there is no trace whatever in the history of ancient civilisation and religion. The one-sided monumental proof for the existence, such as De Mortillet seeks to afford, suffers, apart from its being formally inadmissible, from serious difficulties, gaps, and objections of a material kind. Many even of the Etruscan monuments, for instance, on which De Mortillet specially relies, present distinct allusions to the worship on the part of their authors of various forces of nature and dæmonic powers; whilst in the case of many other monuments of heathendom—which, however, are ignored by M. de Mortillet, we know not whether designedly so—especially those of Ulterior and Citerior India, America, etc., the closest connection between their symbolics of the cross and well-known forms of idolatry is patent upon the very surface.

The hypothesis of a merely ornamental application of the sign of the cross, at certain later stages of the development of heathen civilisation and art, unfortunately overlooked by De Mortillet, to the no small prejudice of his otherwise so meritorious investigations, finds too an important support in the fact that the form of the cross, although only finding a comparatively rare expression in nature without (see on this above in the text,p. 38 ff.), is yet one of pre-eminently æsthetic influence, and in itself invites and urges to artistic reproduction. Thus, even without the reflection that the Saviour of the world died thereupon, the cross, as the energetic opposition to the simple horizontal line, the in principle deadly enemy of the serpent coiling inert upon the earth, the noble, severe unification of the beaming star, is one of the most powerfully inciting motives to plastic art activity. (See above in the text, chap. v., p. 180 ff.) It must indeed appear strange if human art production had never and nowhere before the advent of Christianity into the world, received this symbol, so attractive, and so naturally presenting itself, into the number of its more favourite devices. That this acceptance originally took place, not without the co-operation of religious factors—nay, was principally determined by such factors, appears to us beyond doubt. But for after-times there has certainly been left here and there to profane art-activity an application and multiplying of this symbol. The drawing of sharply defined boundary lines between the earlier religious. and this later secular, purely ornamental representation of cruciform characters, would naturally form one of the most difficult tasks of archæological investigation; if even we might assign it at all to the domain of solvable questions. Precisely this, however, seems to us—apart from single cases, where *either* the merely decorative *or* the purely cultus-symbolical character of the figures in question is expressed with documentary clearness—to be impossible.[1]

II.

EARLIER AND LATER OPINIONS WITH REGARD TO THE SYMBOLIC MEANING OF THE EGYPTIAN ANSATE CROSS.

(To pp. 3 and 37.)

WITHOUT in any way mixing ourselves up with the problems of Egyptian philology or archæology, for the solution of which only those specially qualified can be pronounced competent, we present here a general view of the principal of the numerous conjectures with regard to the true meaning of the *Crux ansata*, which have been advanced on the part of earlier and later investigators.

That the sign ☥ is equivalent to "Life," *i.e.*, expresses the linguistic value of the ancient Egyptian and Coptic *anch* ($\bar{a}n\chi$) = "Life, existence" (Champoll., *Diction. Égyptien*, p. 329 : exister, vivre) is directly attested by the well-known incident in connection with the destruction of the Serapeum under Theodosius I., and is now generally acknowledged. There is still a question, however,

---

[1] The bearing on our subject of the crosses discovered by Schliemann (Nov. 1876) in the supposed tomb of Agamemnon at Mycenæ, must depend greatly on the age to which these crosses belong ; and this is a point not yet fully decided. Mr. Percy Gardner says, in a letter in *The Academy*, of April 21, 1877, "Dr. Schliemann has spoken of bone buttons covered with gold leaf. These certainly occur in great quantities, and seem to have been used in the adornment of weapons, as well as to form a centre to the crosses of gold laurel leaves which were found. These plated bone buttons are mostly either rounded or else lozenge-shaped, and of large size, some being two or three inches across. The gold leaf which covers the buttons bears patterns which appear to be engraved ; the bone beneath bears the same pattern as the gold laid over it. These patterns are the Svastika or fire-drill, with nails in the angles, small crosses, and interlaced wave or scroll devices. At first sight they have a strangely modern look, and, on reflection, this look is seen to arise from the exact regularity of the lines of the patterns, their neatness, and the careful balance of part against part," etc. Later, in a letter dated Athens, April 6, 1877, he remarks on certain rings of beaten gold found in this tomb : "I do not believe that any one looking at them by themselves would have imagined them to belong to a nascent, but rather to a declining or expiring art. In merit they are about on a level with the Roman coins of Gallienus or Constantine."

as to what more sensuous and concrete notion underlies this metaphysic-ideal meaning; in other words, what external sensuous sign the figure ☥ was originally and in itself designed to express.

1. The earliest attempt at solution is that handed down by Macrobius, *Sat.*, i. 20, who takes the staff, with the eye or circle upon it, to be an image of Osiris, or *the sun*.—To this our view developed above, p. 2, in accord with Rapp and Zestermann, immediately attaches itself. It is a question indeed whether the said words of Macrobius really relate to the sign ☥, and not rather to the hieroglyph ☉, or perhaps the sign 𓇳 "sunlight," "brightness." (Comp. Brugsch, *Hieroglyph. Gramm.*, S. 128, 137.)

2. Lipsius, *De Cruce*, i. 8, regards the sign as that of a T (tau) with a ring or handle at the top, but confesses that he does not know anything with certainty as to the significance of this ansate Tau: Certe in obeliscis, qui inde Romam vecti, sculptum sic vidimus: ☥, cum anulo tamen vel ansula superne, nec satis solide scio ad quam rem aut usum. As "ansate Tau" do also many later writers designate the sign, *e.g.*, Münter (*Religion der Babylonier*, S. 98). Comp. also the appellation usually bestowed upon it by the English numismatist, Sir R. Payne Knight—crux circulo dependens. (*Num. vet. in mus. Rich. P. Knight asservat.*, p. 165, and frequently elsewhere.)

3. As *Key*, emblem of revelation, or of the Divine fertilising power of nature opening the treasures of the soil, specially, therefore, of the river Nile (hence "KEY OF THE NILE"), the emblem was interpreted by the majority of archæologists of last century; comp. Letronne, *Mém. de l'Acad. des Inscript.*, etc., xvi. 2, 261. The purely hypothetical character of this interpretation, which still finds advocates in Bellermann (*Ueber die Scarabäen-Gemmen*, Köln. Progr. 1820, i., S. 20 ff.), and Grotefend (in Böttiger's *Amalthea*, ii., S. 101), is shown by Wilkinson, *Manners and Customs of the Ancient Egyptians*, iv. 341, who properly urges the fact that this symbol appears most rarely bestowed on the Egyptian monuments precisely upon the god Nile (Hapi-mou), whereas we ought certainly to expect it would form his regular attribute.

4. The Roman archæologist P. Ungarelli would see in this symbol a one-legged *sacrificial table* with a sacred vase upon it; he retained, however, in harmony with Champoll., Rosellini, etc., the signification

of "Life." See his *Interpretat. obeliscorum Urbis*, pp. 5, 6. Hieroglyphica ejusdem (vocis) figura formam exhibet mensæ sacræ fulcro innixæ, cui vas quoddam religionis indicium superpositum est. With justice does R. Rochette (*Mém. de l'Acad.*, *l. c.*, p. 287) reject this interpretation as unsatisfactory: "Je ne doute pas qu'on ne puisse en proposer une, sinon plus certaine, au moins plus plausible et plus heureuse."

5. As a *phallic* symbol would already some one or two of the earlier archæologists interpret this sign; *e.g.*, Jablonsky (*Panth.*, i. 258, 287), Nork (*Etym.-symbol.-mythol. Realwörterbuch*, ii. 390, who sees in it the emblem of Venus barbata), and others; comp. also Petit-Radel, *Monuments antiq. du Musée Napol.*, t. iv., pl. 56, p. 116. Of more recent writers, this view is advocated, among others, by Uhlemann (*Aegypt. Alterthumskunde*, iv. 143). . . . . According to the same authority (iv. 209), our (planetary) sign for Venus is an hieroglyphic figure, which even among the ancient Egyptians syllabarically expressed the goddess *Anuke* (Venus), even as *ank* expressed "vita" and *nok* "potens."—As a circumstance favouring this interpretation might be urged the fact that the staff- or tau-formed lower part of the figure occasionally displays a *conical* form: thus upon a very ancient fragment of inscriptions from the fourth pyramid (of the time of Mycerinos), on which the sign has the form ☥, in like manner occasionally upon Phœnician monuments, where it sometimes presents the same form, sometimes the similar form ♀. Comp. on the whole subject Rochette, *l. c.*, pp. 291, 325, 374, with his illustrations upon his pl. i., 10, 34, 35. This scholar, however important in many respects this frequent recurrence of the conical conformation of the lower half of the figure may appear for him, is nevertheless far from sharing the view that the ansate cross is a phallus symbol; any more than he is led, from the fact that it sometimes forms the figure ⳨, to hazard the conjecture that it signifies properly an altar of sacrifice with the flame burning thereupon; cp. *l. c.*, pp. 323, 347.

6. A very artificial and complicated mode of interpretation is that of FELIX LAJARD (author of " Recherches sur le culte de Venus," etc.), developed in his learned but somewhat confused treatise, *Observations sur l'origine et la signification du symbole appelé la croix ansée* (Paris, 1847). According to his theory, mainly having respect

to the Asiatic forms of the ansate cross (Assyrian, Persian, Phœnician), and less to the Egyptian forms, the sign is to be regarded as an abbreviating or simplifying presentation of the mythological sign *mihir*, of frequent occurrence upon Assyrian-Babylonian and Persian monuments. Like this mihir-sign, it would represent the Divine trias of the Assyrians and Persians; (1) the highest Divinity or Eternity; (2) Bel or Ormuzd; (3) Astarte or Mithras; for it includes in itself, in addition to the circle the symbol of eternity, indications also of the characteristic attributes of each of the two other Divinities. It is thus, corresponding to the character of this sacred trias of gods, a symbol of Divine renewal and transformation, and is on that account specially depicted at the representation of solemn initiations into mysteries.—This interpretation, although at first not altogether unfavourably commented on by many archæologists, *e.g.*, by Rochette, in the *Mém., l. c.*, p. 381; by A. A. Layard, *Nineveh and its Remains* [p. 301 of the German edition], very quickly, on account particularly of the almost unanimous opposition of the Egyptologists, fell into discredit, and may now be regarded as pretty generally abandoned (although Stockbauer, S. 94 f. of his "Kunstgesch. des Kreuzes," still uncritically assents to it).

7. Different Egyptologists, *e.g.*, Brughsch (Grammat., S. 133), assign the symbol to the category of those hieroglyphs which represent "Bands, bandages, knots, clothing." To what extent definine points of support for this view are to be obtained from Egyptian sources, is unknown to us.

III.

PARADISE, ACCORDING TO EARLIER AND MORE RECENT OPINIONS.

(To p. 44.)

How much has already been written on the position and constitution of Paradise! A complete historic notice even of the purely Christian-theological literature on this subject would call for a work to itself. And what compass such work might easily attain, even though mainly designed to subserve the interests only of the history of dogmas and of bibliography, and less those of dogmatic or natural philosophic speculation, is seen from the enormous calibre of such monographs of the two last centuries, as, *e.g.*, that of the Coccejan J. Marck in Leyden (*Historia Paradisi illustrata*, Amst. 1705, extending to 885 quarto pages !), that of the vigorous Lutheran apologete Th. Chr. Lilienthal ("History of our First Parents in the state of Innocence," in German, Konigsberg, 1722, 8vo), that of the learned Catholic Thom. Malvenda (*De Paradiso voluptatis*, Rom. 1605, 4to), Nichol. Abram (De fluviis et locis paradisi, contained in the collected works of this Jesuit: *Pharus Vet. Testamenti s. sacrarum quæstionum libri* XV., Paris, 1648, fol.), C. Joh. Golinus (*Edengraphia, s. descriptio Paradisi terrestris*, Messanæ, 1649, fol.); or the works partly of Protestant, partly of Catholic authors, which UGOLINO has received into the 7th vol. of his *Thesaurus Antt.* (*e.g.* John Hopkinson, Descriptio Paradisi, 1594; Steph. Morinus, Dissertatio de Parad. terrestri; Dan. Huetius, Tractatus de situ Parad. terrestris; Joh. Voorst, Diss. de Parad.) Even in our own century bulky treatises have been composed upon the subject. Most confusedly has it been treated by Joh. Schulthess ("Paradise, the Terrestrial and Super-terrestrial, Historic, Mythic, and Mystic, with a Critical Revision of the general Biblical Geography" [in German], Zurich, 1816, 8vo), most learnedly by Bertheau ("The Geographical Views underlying the Description of the Position of Paradise in Gen. ii. 10—14; a contribution to the History of Geography [German], Göttingen, 1848); most lucidly and instructively by Th. Pressel (art. "Paradies" in Herzog's *R. E.*, Bd. xx., S. 332—377).—Spite of the immense amount of information to be obtained from these works on the exceedingly numerous opinions and theories advanced by earlier or later writers upon the subject, it may not be unacceptable to our readers if we nevertheless furnish here some supplementary data. We aim in doing so mainly at briefly indicating the present state of the controversy, as this has been modified during the most recent period, under the influence of the ever-increasing number of the representatives of *natural science* who have for some time past taken part in the said discussions.

For a part of the theologians of the Early Church and the Middle Ages the question as to the probable site of Paradise must have appeared altogether an idle one; since they removed it entirely from earth and placed it in the heavenly world, and, on the ground of 2 Cor. xii. 2—4, identified it with the "third heaven." In opposition to this their fundamental view, based as it was upon an allegoristic-spiritualistic subtilising of the historic-concrete idea of Paradise, derived from the writings of Philo, first introduced by Origen into churchly speculation, and later advocated by Ambrose and Scotus Erigena; the greater part of the Fathers placed Paradise indeed upon this earth, but in an absolutely inaccessible locality, forming the transition to the other world, which they supposed to lie either in the distant East (Theophilus of Antioch, *ad Autol.*, ii. 34), or beyond the torrid zone in the south (Tertullian, *Apol.*, c. 47), or beyond the earth-encircling ocean (Basil the Great, Gregory of Nazianzus, Gregory of Nyssa, Cosmas Indicopleustes), or beyond insuperable mountains (Moses Bar-Cephas, *Tract. de Paradiso*, of the tenth century). Others, dissatisfied with the indistinctness of this fantastic mystical theory, distinguished an earthly and a heavenly Paradise, the former of which they assigned to some locality on earth no longer to be determined with certainty; so Justin Martyr, Methodius, Jerome. While the schoolmen remained preponderantly inclined to that mystic mingling of the earthly and the heavenly Paradise, the theology of the Reformation, from the time of Luther, contended with decision for the concrete-historic and earthly-real character of the Biblical Paradise, as admitting the possibility of historic investigation. It still observes, indeed, in some of its representatives, a half-and-half spiritual attitude; inasmuch as it regards the position of Paradise, conceived of as a geographically defined locality, as effaced by the changes produced upon the surface of the globe in consequence of the fall, and still more of the flood, and therefore undiscoverable; so Luther (*Enarrationes in Genes.*, 1524, and freq.), Dav. Clericus (Notæ ad Sansonis Geographiam Sacram, in Ugolino's *Thes. Antt.*, t. viii.), Gilb. Burnet (*The Sacred Theory of the Earth*, London, 1681), Hardouin (De Situ Paradisi terrestris—*Opp. sell.*, 1709), Hadr. Reland (De situ Parad. terr., in *Dissertt. miscell.*, t. i., 1706); whom several more recent writers have followed, as K. von Raumer (Palästina, 1840), F. de Rougemont (History of the Earth, 1856), Baumgarten, and, to some extent, Delitzsch (in their commentaries on Gen. ii. and iii.) The majority, however, of the Reformational and post-Reformational theologians firmly maintain the identity of the Garden of Eden described in Gen. ii. 10 ff. with some known region of the earth, consequently the topographical determinability of Paradise. In attempting to determine its position they generally employed as a means of doing so the four streams, Pishon, Gihon, Phrat, and Hiddekel, mentioned in the passage. And in this case the suggestion was a most natural one, of taking the two last-named rivers, as factors recognised with certainty and beyond dispute, as the starting-point for more nearly defining; and consequently pronouncing Mesopotamia, or some other special district of the Euphrates-lands, to be the Paradise of the Bible. In this way Calvin, in his Commentary on Genesis—and those who follow him either unreservedly or with unimportant modifications, as Francis Junius, Joh. Hopkinson (*as above*), Jos. Scaliger, Hugo Grotius, J. H. Hottinger, Joh. Voorst, Sam. Bochart, Steph. Morinos, Athan. Kircher, Dan. Huetius, and in later times J. E. Silberschlag ("Geogonie," Th. ii., Berlin, 1780) and others,—came to the conclusion that the region of the mouths of the Euphrates, or of the *Shatt el Arab*, which in some way, as by assuming the existence of a number of alleged former canals, it was sought to represent as consisting of four streams, is to be identified with the Mosaic Paradise. A view which has lately found again in Pressel (Herzog's *R. E.*, as before) a warm and acute defender, who rests his argument on a much better exegetical foundation than that of the earlier writers. Others, for whom the interpretation of the four "heads" (*rāshim*, v. 10) in the sense of "arms," "mouths of a river," necessary in support of this view, appeared less suitable, but who, nevertheless, believed the well-known names Phrat and Hiddekel are to be followed as guiding stars, placed Eden at the *sources* of the two Mesopotamian streams, thus in Armenia. To this land, however, in order to show that the Pishon and Gihon rose in moderate proximity, some other conterminous region was added; whether Colchis = Chavila, neighbour to it on the north (so, after Reland, A. Calmet, J. Jahn, Rosenmüller, Tuch, Keil, Kurtz, Delitzsch, De Rougemont, etc.), or the uplands stretching out from this region eastwards, as far as the Paropomisan Mountains, the birthplace of the Oxus (? = Gihon), in which latter case it would appear that eventually also the Jaxartes or the Indus (Pishon) might be brought into the list; thus first J. Dav. Michaelis (in the supplement to his *O. T. with annotations*), then A. Th. Hartmann (*Aufklärungen über Asien*, 1806), Hammer (in the *Wiener Jahrbb.*, 1830), Knobel (*Commentary on Genesis*, 1852), and others. Many advocates of the latter view lay stress upon the alleged mythical character of the whole Biblical account of Paradise and the Fall, and thereby approach the mythological interpretation attempted with various modifications by Herder, Paulus, Schelling, Gunth. Wahl, Eichhorn, Buttmann, Gesenius, Ewald, Sickler, Redslob, Bertheau, and others. Moreover, even of these some at least think in general of a definite land as the *regio Paradisi*, denoted, even though in indistinct outline, by the Biblical tradition. Thus Herder thinks more especially of Cashmere; Buttmann and Ewald, each in a peculiar manner, of India (whence the latter supposes the tradition to have wandered to Farther Asia, and here in consequence to have been supplemented or interpolated by the addition of the names Phrat and Hiddekel to the Pishon and Gihon, *i.e.*, to the Indus and Ganges); G. Wahl and Sickler of the high table-land between the Euphrates and Oxus, or the region of the Caspian Sea, etc. Only Paulus, Eichhorn, Gesenius, and substantially also Bertheau (for whom the Pishon = Ganges, while the Gihon = Nile, and yet he maintains that the Garden of Eden is to be sought in the remote north !) give up all attempt at finding a clear and definite geographical conception in the background of the narrative, and thus take for granted the absurdity of its contents. Similarly also within a very recent period Jul. Grill (*The Patriarchs of Mankind; a Contribution to the Foundation of a Science of Hebrew Antiquities*, ii. [German] Leipzig, 1875, S. 164 ff., 242 ff.), who strongly urges the mythical character of the Jahvistic description of the site of Paradise, as passing out of the domain of concrete geographical presentations; but yet fancies he can trace a dim reminiscence of the lands of upper India as once the cradle of the Semitic race. For alike the names Chavila (= Capila, Campila) and Cush (= Kuça) point to India, as also the river name Pishon, which certainly denotes the Indus, as Gihon the Nile, or perhaps also the Ganges; so that thus in one respect Ewald's hypothesis with regard to the account of Paradise approaches particularly near to the truth; in another respect that of Bertheau does so.—Substantially almost the same results are arrived at by the investigations of Dr. Joseph Kuhl, rector of the Catholic Progymnasium at Jülich (*Die Anfänge des Menschengeschlechts und sein einheitlicher Ursprung* [Early History of Mankind, and Unity of its Origin], Bonn 1875, S. 113 ff.) For him Hindoo Koosh is the mountain of Paradise ("Aram-Aryana"); the Pishon denotes in his estimation the Indus, the Gihon, the Nile, etc. He too accordingly supposes a mythic disturbance of the original form of the tradition, in consequence of which "we are deprived of the possibility of recognising in Eden a definite geographical locality."

For all the theologians or orientalists hitherto mentioned, the four streams of the Garden of Eden form the principal, nay for many of them almost the exclusive means of direction in their conjectures with regard to its position. To somewhat different views have those come who have regarded these four rivers as only an element of the second rank for the determination of the region of Paradise, and on the other hand have made the natural products of the Garden of Eden, its trees of life, its gold, bdellium, etc., in some case seven its supranatural guardians, the cherubim, the gnomons of prime significance for its discovery. By considerations of this sort were Grotius and Burnet influenced, when the former recognised in the flaming swords of the cherubim an allusion to burning naphtha (frequently occurring in the neighbourhood of the Euphrates lands), the latter to the glowing heat of the torrid zone. For the Königsberg theologian Hasse ("Discoveries in the Field of the Earliest History of the Earth and of Man" [German], Königsb. 1801,) the supposed identity of the *b'dolach* (Luther, *bdellium*) with the amber of the Baltic lands became a decisive motive for placing Paradise upon the coast of the Baltic, and definitely in Prussia, whose "claims as an amber land to have been the Paradise of the ancients," he sought, particularly by the help of the Eddic mythology, expressly to maintain. On the other hand, Credner (in Illgen's *Zeitschrift f. Hist. Theologie*, 1836, H. 1) was led, in part by asserted points of contact between the history of Paradise and the legends of classic antiquity, in part (more specially) by the fable of the golden apples of the Hesperides, to place the Hebrew "garden of delight" in the far west, in the Canary Islands, and to resolve the four streams into the all-surrounding Okeanos!

Without always losing themselves in such quixotic adventures as these, but certainly also without treating the Biblical tradition less contemptuously—either as leaving it entirely out of consideration, or degrading it to the level of a mere myth—have very recently a number of *historic-anthropologic* or *natural philosophic* inquirers attempted to solve the question of Paradise by the indications belonging to the province of natural history which are to be taken into account. The four rivers remain, as belonging to the supposed mythological clothing of the narrative, for the greater part entirely unnoticed by these natural-philosophic seekers after Paradise; yea, the problem is ordinarily only one of the determining, or rendering more or less probable, the region whence the diffusion of the human race over the earth proceeded. Of course it would be only advocates of the anthropological Monogenism who take part in this discussion. For those who espouse polygenistic theories, whether they are based on an anti-Darwinistic foundation (as in the school of the North American anthropologists, Morton and Agissez), or even favour at the same time the Darwin-Häckel doctrine of man's descent from apes (as, *e.g.*, Vogt, Schaafhausen, Ed. Reich—"Der Mensch und die Seele," Berl. 1872, S. 56 ff.—to which latterly also Darwin himself approaches), the question as to the centre of creation or the primitive hearth of the history of civilisation necessarily ceases to have any meaning.—Within the literature bearing on this topic we encounter a moderately great diversity of mutually contradictory views.

1. In favour of a TROPICAL LAND in general, without nearer definition of the locality in which it is to be sought, does the Austrian linguist and ethnologist, Fr. Müller, express himself—on p. 37 of his *Ethnographie* (Vienna, 1873), a work composed from an essentially Darwinian point of view.

2. In favour of EQUATORIAL AFRICA, whose slender-nosed species of apes, the gorilla, etc., appear to him the most probable immediate forerunners of man, Darwin has expressed himself in the sixth chapter of his "Descent of Man" (London, 1871, vol. i., p. 199). The same view does Huxley appear to espouse (*Evidence as to the Place of Man in Nature*, 1863); since for him also the gorilla and chimpanzee are the direct precursors or progenitors of man.—It is remarkable that in favour of this locality a decided Christian believer and resolute opponent of Darwin's theory contended with the greatest warmth, nay sacrificed his life to the restless endeavour after its empirical verification. David Livingstone sought with indefatigable zeal during his last great journey after the discovery of *four* mighty streams, taking their rise from one mountain (west of Tanganyika Lake), of the existence of which he had heard by report, and in which he hoped to find the true sources of the Nile, as described by Herodotus, ii. 28, but *also* the rivers of Paradise. Comp. Stanley, *How I found Livingstone*, p. 454 sqq., 618, 626, 714.

3. *Either* Central Africa, and if here the well-watered region of the sources of the Nile, *or* Citerior India, with its luxuriant vegetation, its abundance in other respects of the products of nature, and its many mighty streams, is declared by Oscar F. Peschel, in his [German] article "On the Position of Paradise," (*Ausland*, 1867, No. 47; and also in his "New Problems of Comparative Geography" [German], 1869), to be the most probable cradle of our race.

4. LEMURIA, a now submerged southern continent, between Citerior India and New Holland on the one hand, and Madagascar (as also Ceylon) on the other, the former existence of which it was first sought to render probable on the part of the English zoologist Sclater, who was followed too by Huxley, Hooker, Bonwick (*Origin of the Tasmanians*, Lond. 1870), also Peschel, *as above*, is supposed by Häckel to be the starting-point whence the "twelve species of men" gradually spread over the present surface of the earth. (*Natürliche Schöpfungsgeschichte*, 3rd edn., 1872, S. 321; 619 ff.) To this

hypothesis, founded partly upon the geography of animals and plants, partly upon alleged "chorologic" facts, adhesion has been given in the main by Oscar Schmidt (1873), F. v. Hellwald (1874), Alb. Heine (1872), Thomassen (1872), the anonymous author of "Racenlehre und Geschichte" (in the *Ausland*, 1872, No. 49), and many others.

5. The sunken ATLANTIS of Plato—not, however, as having existed between Europe and America, but as a continent or large island formerly situate in Oceania—is declared by the American who writes under what is probably the *nom de plume* of George Browne, in his strange book, of apparently humorous design: *Palæorama* . . . . (Erlangen, 1867) to be the Paradise whence early mankind first spread over America.—Yet within recent times scientific men of note have seriously pleaded, on the ground of the evidence of natural science (that of a platæonologic nature, as also that derived from the geographical distribution of plants), in favour of the actual existence of an Atlantis in the tertiary period; but as lying between central America and Europe, in the Atlantic Ocean: so Fr. Unger, *Die versunkene Insel Atlantis*, 1860; as also Oswald Heer, *Die Polarländer*, S. 21 ff. Comp. also the [German] work of Alex. Braun, "On the Significance of Development in Natural History," 1872, S. 34.

6. AMERICA have different philologists and naturalists, both of the Old World and the New, sought to prove to be the primary home of the human race; generally in connection with the supposition of an immigration of the inhabitants of Europe, Asia, etc., over the Aleutian islands and north-east Siberia. So Bernard Romans (in Smith-Barton, *New Views*, p. vi.); J. Klaproth, *Aria polyglotta*, p. 322; Gobineau, Essai sur l'inégalité des races humaines, i. 371; ii. 347; and others. Comp. Rauch, *Einheit des Menschengeschlechts*, S. 269.

7. The POLAR LANDS of the north, *e.g.*, GREENLAND, are regarded by Ph. Spiller, in his popular works on Cosmogony (1871, 1872), as the probable birthplace and earliest limit of the dispersion of mankind: for the reason that the lofty mountain lands and the polar regions, after a sufficient cooling down, must first have been habitable," etc.

8. EUROPE, and indeed Southern Europe in the post-pliocene or diluvial age (in which the necessities of the glacial period had gradually compelled the higher classes of animals, formerly most abundantly nourished by the rankly luxuriant vegetation of the miocene and pliocene epoch, to have recourse to *labour* and to the preparing of such rude products of art as the earliest implements of stone and of bone, belonging to the period of the mammoth and

rein-deer), is stated by Moritz Wagner, in opposition to Darwin's Africa-hypothesis, to be the true Paradise of the primeval ape-like ancestors of our race; as the place where that wonderful metamorphosis took place, "which, after the incalculably long ages of an exclusively animal life, at last raised the stupid anthropoid to the thinking anthropos" (in the *Ausland*, 1871, No. 24, S. 558 ff.)— Specially *Styria*, in the later tertiary period, or in the time of the peat-formation, immediately preceding the glacial period, when a peculiarly rich and luxuriantly developed plant life must have flourished in that region, is taken by F. Unger as the site of Paradise, the primal abode of mankind : *Das Alter der Menschheit und das Paradies*, Vienna, 1866, S. 62 ff.—Proceeding only from a linguistic standpoint, and having before his mind not so much the whole of mankind as rather only the Indo-Germanic race, J. G. Cuno (in his "Researches in the Domain of Ancient Ethnology," Th. i., *Die Skythen*, Berl. 1871,) seeks to prove that *Central Europe* is the primal seat and starting-point of the earliest life of civilisation. To this view a qualified assent is given by F. Spiegel (*Ausland*, 1871, No. 24; the same, 1862, No. 41), who moreover adduces the authority of Latham (1854), Benfey (1868), Laz. Geiger, and the American Whitney as favourable to this hypothesis, in opposition as it is to the ordinary assertion of the movement to the Indo-European culture having originated in Central Asia.

9. In favour of Central Asia or the Asiatic Highlands as the primeval dwelling-place not merely of the Arian family, but also of the whole human race, there still arise authorities of distinction, alike in the province of natural philosophy and the science of language as of theology and philosophy. Thus, as an opponent in particular of that Benfey-Cuno assertion of a Central European origin to the Aryans, A. Höfer, "Die Heimath des indogermanischen Urvolks" (in *Kuhn's Zeitschr. für Sprachwissensch.*, Bd. xx., S. 379), and H. v. Wolzogen, "Der Ursitz der Indogermanen" (*Lazarus' und Steinthal's Zeitschr. für Völkerpsychologie*, 1874, i.) So farther K. Chr. Planck, who maintains that specially the "central table-land of Asia," this " most concentrated and colossal elevation on the face of the earth," is to be regarded as the original abode of the human race. (*Wahrheit und Flachheit des Darwinismus*, Nördlingen, 1872, S. 175 ff.) Similarly the Danish writer on the Philosophy of History, C. Henrik Scharling, who maintains that " the cradle of mankind is to be sought where Persia and India impinge upon each other, between the mountain chains of Beloor-tagh and Hindoo-Koosh." (*Humanität und*

Christenthum, p. 84 of vol. i., German edition, Gütersloh, 1874). In like manner, Ernst von Bunsen (*Die Einheit der Religionen*, etc., Berl. 1870, S. 14 ff.), who thinks of the region of the sources of the Oxus and Indus, north of the Himalayas, or the "plateau of Pamer" [to the north-west of Tibet], as the place where—it is true as early as the tertiary period—mankind came into being, and lived through its paradisiac childhood. So also Supdt. O. Wolff, who, like the preceding writers, is induced, mainly on account of the alleged agreement of the earliest traditions of all inner-Asiatic nations, to place alike Paradise and Mount Ararat, or the apobaterion of the ark of Noah, at the Pamer-plateau and the Beloor mountains," this "most elevated centre of Higher Asia." (*Alt-testamentl. Studien und Kritiken*, i., 1874, S. 8, 28 f.)—That which has been manifestly overlooked in connection with assigning so northerly and so elevated a position to Paradise—the fearful severity of the cold in this region, by which an English expedition in 1874, consisting of Messrs. Trotter, Biddulph, Gordon, etc., was almost frozen upon the gigantic snowfields of the Pamer table-land, and could pass through them only with the loss of the skin of the nose—this has Prof. George Gerland, in the first vol. of his "Anthropologische Beiträge" (Halle, 1874), more carefully taken into account, inasmuch as he decides in favour of *the more southern part of Central Asia*, and specially the land south and south-west of the Himalayas, as the original home of the human race. In support of his position he has specially availed himself of the instances in the geographical distribution of plants which point to this region as the native land of most of the plants of culture, and particularly of the cereals, this main "lever in the development of civilisation"— instances to which certainly a special weight must be attached in the deciding of this question. Comp. Zöckler's notice of the said work, in the *Beweis des Glaubens*, 1875, Feb., p. 108 ff.

After not only every quarter of the globe, and almost every zone on earth, has thus been fixed on by the hypotheses of the modern seekers after Paradise, but even besides this certain primeval (?) continents have been new created for this express occasion, opinion seems within the most recent period to incline to return to that view, an especially favourite one with the theologians of the age immediately following the Reformation (Calvin, Grotius, and their successors), which places Paradise at the mouths of the Euphrates and Tigris—thus seeks it where, according to Biblical as well as ancient Babylonian documents, also "Ur of the Chaldees" (Gen. xi. 28), the ancestral land of the Abrahamides was to be found. For at the present time the voice of a distinguished geographical explorer has been powerfully raised :

10. In favour of NORTH-EASTERN ARABIA, INCLUDING THE SOUTHERN REGIONS OF THE EUPHRATES. The Paris Academician Vivien de St. Martin, in his *Histoire de la Géographie* (Paris, 1874), p. 529, espouses this view—partly on account of grounds of probability of an ethnological and natural-scientific nature, partly because he believes the Pishon of Genesis is indisputably to be recognised in a large intermittent stream of central and north-east Arabia, discovered by Consul Wetzstein (1865), which in former times constantly emptied its waters into the Lower Euphrates (close below its junction with the Tigris), and even now is said at times to flow through the whole peninsula in that direction towards the north-east.—The learned reasoning with which, *e.g.*, Pressel (Herzog, *as before*) seeks to prove the lower district of the Euphrates to be the true site of the Biblical Paradise, would thus—supposing the hypothesis of St. Martin to be well founded—at any rate receive important support. The British Assyriologist, too, A. H. Sayce, has adopted the opinion that this central-Arabian tributary stream of the Shatt el-Arab is the fourth river of Paradise ; but identifies this with the Gihon of Genesis, whilst he believes the Pishon is to be recognised in the Pasitigris [in Chaldæa]. (*Academy*, 20th March, 1875.) In opposition to all this, there remains, it is true, the exegetical difficulty that not the lower course, or mouths, but the sources ("heads") of four mighty streams must have been found in Paradise ! In presence of this statement of the text, which hardly admits of any qualifying explanation, an abandoning of the attempt to point out any definite narrowly circumscribed locality as the site of the former Garden of Eden—the position of which must, however, be assigned to Southern Asia in general—appears the only wise and appropriate course with regard to the matter. [The cumulative evidence in favour of No. 9 of the above positions would nevertheless appear to be exceedingly strong, if we may suppose the LAND OF EDEN—whence (the water) was divided and became four river-sources—to have been coextensive with the whole elevated tract between the sources of the Euphrates and Tigris, on the one hand, and those of the Indus and Indian Hyphasis (identified by Haneberg with the *Sutlej*), on the other. The GARDEN EASTWARD IN EDEN is then to be sought to the west of the Punjab. —TR.]

IV.

AGAINST THE ASSERTION OF AN ENTIRE IRRELIGIOUSNESS ON THE PART OF CERTAIN NATIONS.

(To p. 48.)

THE assertion that there are savage nations who are without any kind of religious feelings, conceptions, or rites—in other words, that the *argumentum e consensu gentium* is to be struck out of the list of proofs for the reality of the Divine existence and of immortality—has found numerous advocates in England and France during the period of Deism and naturalistic scepticism. It was specially LOCKE who, in connection with his denial of the existence of innate ideas, gave the impulse to the investigation of the ethnologic-culture-historic material collected by early and later travellers, with the object of obtaining direct evidence for the entire absence of religious and moral conceptions among many wild tribes. When (in his *Essay concerning Human Understanding* [1690], i. 3, § 9) he "ransacked" the travels of the French traveller in Brazil, De Lery (1580), the accounts of a Peter Martyr and Garcilaso de la Vega on the customs of the American Indians, the statements of a Vossius, a Lambert, a Gruber, and others, about the wild tribes of Africa, Asia, etc., "in order to relate to us how the Mingrelians without any reproach of conscience buried their children alive, and how the Tupinambos believe that by revenge and an unstinted devouring of their enemies they will merit Paradise" (Alb. Lange, *Gesch. des Materialism.*, 2nd edn., 1873, i., p. 306; comp. J. B. Meyer, *Philos. Zeitfragen*, p. 284), he was concerned it is true only with the proving of his favourite proposition of the absence of innate *moral* ideas. The polemic against the demonstrative force of the *arg. e consensu gentium*, that historico-ethnologic or national-psychologic proof for the existence of God already formulated by Cicero (*Tusc. disputt.*, 1. 13 : Porro firmissimum hoc afferri videtur, cur deos esse credamus, quod nulla gens tam fera, nemo omnium tam sit immanis, cujus mentem non imbuerit deorum opinio. Multi de iis prava sentiunt; id enim vitioso more effici solet : omnes tamen esse vim et naturam divinam arbitrantur."—Comp. also *De legg.*, i. 8, and *De nat. deor.*, i. 17 : . . . intelligi necesse est deos esse, quoniam insitas eorum vel potius innatas cognitiones habemus ; de quo autem omnium natura consentit, id verum esse necesse est) was farther from his mind than that against the universality and innate character of certain nations and principles of morality. Nevertheless, the contesting of the national-psychological proof of the existence of God on the part of later assailants of revealed religion, as Hume, Condillac, Helvetius, the French Encyclopædists, and the modern Materialists, for the most part attaches itself to Locke's doctrine of sensations, and in many cases appeals expressly to his authority. Among the more recent materialistic advocates of the thesis of an absolute irreligiousness of many peoples are principally to be mentioned: Louis Büchner (*Kraft und Stoff*, S. 186 ff.; also, *Der Gottesbegriff und dessen Bedeutung in der Gegenwart*, 1874); K. Vogt (*Vorless. üb. den Menschen*, 1863, i., S. 293 f.); Sir John Lubbock (*Prehistoric Times*, p. 564; and *Origin of Civilisation*, p. 138); Sir Samuel Baker, the renowned explorer of the Sources of the Nile (*The Albert Nyanza*, i., p. 246; also "Races of the Nile Basin," in *Trans. of the Ethnolog. Soc.*, vol. v., p. 231); Moritz Wagner ("Neueste Beiträge . . . . in the supplement to the *Augsb. Allg. Ztg.*, 1873, No. 92); as well as Osc. Schmidt (*Descendenzlehre und Darwinismus*, Leipz. 1873, S. 279 ff.) It is significant that to these assailants of the universality of religious conceptions among all nations there may be opposed—apart from the number, by no means small, of positive-theological or idealistic-philosophic investigators, who have expressed themselves in an opposite sense— also a series of antagonists belonging to the province of natural science or philology, who may be accused of anything but a prejudice in favour of orthodoxy, nay some of whom belong to a decidedly Darwinistic or even materialistic school. We mention here only for example, Ad. Bastian (*Die Völker des östl. Asien*, Bd. vi., pref., S. 1 ff.; also "Der Mensch," etc., iii. 208); A. de Quatrefages ("Unité de l'espèce humaine," in the *Revue des deux Mondes*, 1861, Avr., p. 654 sqq.); G. Lejean (*Rev. des d. Mondes*, 1862, Avr., p. 760); Theod. Waitz (*Anthropologie der Naturvölker*, Bd. ii., S. 72 ff.); G. Gerland, the continuer of Waitz' *Anthropologie* (vi. 796 ff.), as also in his own *Anthropol. Beiträge* (1874, i. 2076 ff.); G. Fritsch (*Die Eingeborenon Südafrikas*, 1872, S. 57, 197, 265 ff.); Max Müller (*Introduction to the Science of Religion*—see above, p. 48; also in his presidential address before the Aryan section of the Lond. Congress of Orientalists in 1874, see *Report*, etc., p. 21); Osc. F. Peschel (Völkerkunde, 139—273); E. B. Tylor ("Early Hist. of Mankind and Civilisation," i. pp. 411—419 [of the Germ. edn.]) Even F. v. Hellwald has, as already before in several articles in the "Ausland," so quite recently in his "Culturgeschichte" (p. 24 ff.), treated the question whether there are really any tribes without a conception of religion as for the present at least an open one, and has expressed himself with regard to it with cautious reserve. "Against the assertions of travellers that a people has no religion, we must arm ourselves with double precaution:" a people devoid of a religion is properly speaking "a chimera, equally as a future without a religion" (p. 32); "one must be on his guard against believing in so-called atheistic peoples, so long as their language has not been accurately investigated" (*Ausl.* 1870, p. 1038); yea "ethnology teaches us that the existence of peoples without a religion is to be denied with almost positive certainty." (*Ausl.*, 1875, p. 100), etc.

From the naturalistic standpoint the question has received the most intelligent treatment on the part of Tylor, *as above*. He takes as the "rudimentary" or "minimal definition" of religion, not, *e. g.*, a developed notion of God, with belief in a future judgment, worshipping of idols, offering of sacrifices and kindred rites, but merely the presence of a "belief in spiritual beings." Of this belief in spiritual beings—which essentially also Darwin (*Descent of Man*, i. 55) regards as the minimum of religiousness, and which Tylor designates by the term "animism," a term occasionally earlier employed by him, although then generally in another connection—he does not indeed assert with full and positive decision that every existing tribe actually possesses it, or must necessarily possess it. But yet he feels himself constrained on the ground of an enormous cumulation of testimonies, to admit "that belief in spiritual beings *is found among all lower races, with which we are sufficiently intimately acquainted;* while the assertion that such belief is wanting is confined to ancient tribes, or more or less imperfectly described modern ones" (p. 419). It is certainly not impossible, so he reasons, that a people should one day be discovered, which—as, according to the testimony of many travellers, certain tribes exist without any acquaintance with language or with the use of fire (?)—is wanting in any kind of religion. But "if it is a question as to facts, we must say that hitherto these tribes have not been found" (p. 412). Tylor points to a multitude of cases in which, too hastily and without sufficient acquaintance with the manners and peculiarities of the tribes in question, the presence of any traces of religious convictions has been denied to certain tribes; whereas afterwards a more accurate observation has clearly enough demonstrated the presence of these traces.

According to the testimony of J. D. Lang, who has devoted himself to explorations among the inhabitants of QUEENSLAND, Australia, the aborigines of this district are to be regarded as absolutely without religious ideas; and yet the baselessness of this assertion may be demonstrated even from that which this writer himself adduces concerning the belief of the said tribes in an evil spirit, Budyah, the offering of men and other sacrificial rites in order to placate him, his appearing under the form of a serpent, his speaking through the voice of thunder, etc., etc. Similarly as regards the assertion of Moffat that the BECHUANAS showed no trace of belief in immortality; where the statement immediately preceding, that the Bechuana word for shades or manes of the dead is "liritj," is in contradiction with this view: in like manner is it the case with the assertion of Don Felix de Azara that certain SOUTH AMERICAN tribes, as the *Payaguas*, etc., possessed no religion at all—an opinion sufficiently refuted by the *data* supplied by this traveller himself. If also, Tylor maintains, missionaries have frequently ventured on asserting an absolute irreligiousness of this or the other of the more degraded tribes visited by them, it was because the peculiarities of the tribe in question either had not been thoroughly enough studied by them, or because their aims at conversion had led the savages purposely to conceal from them their religious conceptions and rites. Baker's assertion of an absolute atheism on the part of the DINKAS, SHILLUKES, NUEHRS, KYTSHES, BOHRS, and other tribes of the White Nile, rests simply and solely upon a too superficial acquaintance with their customs, and leaves out of consideration that which earlier travellers like Kaufmann, Brun-Rollet, Lejean, and others have communicated with regard to the religious conceptions and sacrificial rites of these very peoples (pp. 413—418).

To these instances, selected by Tylor as typical for the others—instances of the refutation of assertions of entire irreligiousness by the results of later more accurate research—we may add the following. The DAYACKS on Borneo were declared for a time by Rajah Sir Jas. Brooke to be downright atheists, until after having obtained a more accurate knowledge of them he was compelled to recall this opinion as erroneous. (Lubbock, *Orig. of Civilis.*, p. 227.)—Against the assertion frequently advanced, and even most recently repeated by Moritz Wagner, *l. c.*, that all religious conception is wanting to the aborigines of the AUSTRALIAN continent, a number of significant facts in evidence of the contrary have been of late furnished by missionaries,

travellers, and others, and have been collected *inter alios* by Gerland.
(Waitz' *Anthropol.*, vi. 786 ff.) That among these he instances a
case not in point—that, namely, of the tribes west of the Liverpool
Range, who "ascribed everything in nature which they were unable
to explain themselves to devildevil," and who thereby manifest the
effect of contact with some English missionaries [? or sailors] or
other—does not in the least deprive the other facts collected by him
of their convincing power, and by no means calls for the ridicule
which Osc. Schmidt and Alb. Lange, separating the passage entirely
from its connection, have directed against Gerland's whole argument.
Comp. also the contributions of Quatrefages (*as above*) on the belief
of the Australians in immortality and in demons, especially those of
the aborigines in the neighbourhood of Sydney, who have a belief
not only in Wanguls (water-nymphs) and Balumbals (wood-fairies),
but also in a good spirit named Coyan, and an evil spirit named
Potoyan; comp. further the account given by Dr. v. Schweinitz,
Bishop of the Moravian Church, at the meeting of the Evangelical
Alliance in New York (1873), of the baptism of Nathaniel Pepper
in 1860, as the first-fruits of one of the most degraded tribes of
Australian aborigines in the colony of Victoria, and the subsequent
conversion and baptism of about a hundred other members of this
tribe. Another case of proof recently being afforded of the inaccuracy of that which has been asserted as to the total irreligiousness of the aborigines of Australia is that mentioned by Max Müller,
in his address at the London Congress of Orientalists before
referred to (Report, p. 21). The most degraded tribe of the Kami-
larois in the extreme north-west of New South Wales is acquainted,
according to the testimony of Sir Hercules Robinson, the Governor
of the colony, not only with a supreme Divinity, *Bhaiami*, ("Creator,
Maker,") but also with a subordinate Divinity, *Turramûlan*, as
mediator through whom the revelations of that god are made to men,
etc.—The tribes of KOHLS too, in Bengal, have in like manner been
repeatedly represented as without any kind of religious ideas beyond
a vague superstituous dread of demons. Even in missionary circles
this view was to some extent shared : the missionary Jellinghaus
entertained it for a while, until—in part from information obtained
from an adherent of the Brahmo-Samoj sect, but principally as a consequence of his own better acquaintance with the language of the
Kohls—he was led to another opinion, and learnt to recognise as the
true character of the heathenism of these tribes, not so much an absolute denial of God, as rather an "*ignoring* of God (Rom. i. 28, 31)

in the homage rendered to the forces of nature, and to mysterious demoniacal powers by incantations and magical rites," etc. (*Allg. Miss. Ztschr.* 1874, pp. 29, 63); comp. also L. Nottrott, *Die Gosnersche Mission unter den Kohls*, 1874, p. 57).—For the correction of the statements of Baker as to the alleged absolute irreligiousness of the Nuehrs, Dinkas, and other CENTRAL AFRICAN tribes, one ought to compare the *data* furnished by Georg Schweinfurt and Ernst Marno in various places of their works of travel having reference to these parts, *e.g.*, what is related by Marno (*Reisen im Gebiete des weissen und blauen Nil*, Vienna, 1874, p. 343 ff.), concerning the circumcision practised among the Nuehrs, their belief in the evil spirit Nyeledit—with which name too they denote alike the Supreme Being and their favourite ox—on their rain-making, magical arts, etc.—The statements of many earlier writers with regard to the HOTTENTOTS and CAFFRE peoples of South Africa, contesting the presence of religious conceptions among these tribes—among others also on the part of several missionaries, as Campbell and Van der Kemp, as moreover to some extent Moffat—have reference as such only to the want of the idea of a *personal* God, and not to the absence of all conceptions of spiritual powers, of a continued existence after death, of magical arts, etc. But even these call for a supplementing and correcting in many respects; partly from more recent works of travel, partly from the accounts of later missionaries, as Livingstone, the Hermannsburg and Berlin missionaries, etc. (Comp. in gen. Waitz, *Anthropol.*, ii. 167 ff., 342 ff.; also Fritsch, *Die Eingeborenen Südafrika's*, pp. 57, 98, 197, 231, 337 ff., who contests the existence of developed ideas of God, not of religious conceptions and religious customs in general, among these peoples.)—As respects the absolute irreligiousness said to exist among the different savage tribes of SOUTH AMERICA, especially in the wilds of the Amazon district, upon which—among others—Moritz Wagner has recently laid such great stress, we must remind the reader of that which so well-qualified an observer as Prince Max von Wied has testified of even the rudest of these tribes as exhibiting certain traces of belief in suprasensuous powers. (Comp. Müller, *Amerik. Urreligionen.*) That too which is related by Spix and Martius, Wallace, Bates, and Burmeister, does not appear to be of a nature to prove that these peoples are absolutely atheists; they too acknowledge that the conception of a thunder-god, a rain-god, and a certain hope of immortality exists among these barbarous peoples. (Baumstark, *Christl. Apologetik auf anthropologischer Grundlage*, Frankfort, 1872, i. 266 ff.)

Further, in order to a just appreciation of the religious belief of many rude nations—reduced to the minimum of Tylor's "animism," and thus at times presenting the appearance of an absolute atheism —we must duly take into account the fact that our present stock of knowledge, with regard to the spiritual and moral life of uncivilised nations, nowhere extends back to the original condition of these peoples, but everywhere presents the result of the manifold and far-reaching changes which have taken place in their condition. Changes, however, of any other kind than those of a debasing and degenerating tendency can hardly be supposed within the sphere of savage life. *Even the traces which are still to be found of religious emotions or ideas regularly bear a character of ruin, pointing back to earlier, more abundant developments;* as not less, too, the structure of their languages manifests the most distinct indications of a disorganisation, breaking up, and running wild having taken place. Instructive instances of such degeneration in the structure and vocabulary of the language, as well as in the religious consciousness of the people, are afforded, *e.g.*, by the BECHUANAS of South Africa, among whom Moffat, during his lengthened missionary labours, had an opportunity of immediately observing the gradual impoverishment of the vocabulary—for example, the falling into oblivion of the word previously in use, *Morimo*, "He who is in heaven, God." (*Missionary Labours and Scenes in South Africa*, Lond. 1842.) The same is the case with regard to those in our own close proximity, the GIPSIES, who have not seldom been characterised by more superficial observers as absolutely without a religion—so still by Charles G. Leland, *The English Gipsies and their Language*, Lond. 1873— whereas those who have made more thorough research into the constitution of their language and customs have, on the other hand, come more nearly to results such as those formulated by Mr. Groome, in a lecture on the Gipsies before the Anthropological Union at Göttingen in 1873: "Although the religion *is now reduced almost to nil*, yet we meet here and there with words which indicate *the presence of an earlier belief;* e.g., *duvel*, which signifies both heaven and God," etc., etc.—Interesting instances of a degradation traced to have taken place in tribes formerly of greater civilisation and refinement, are adduced by the Duke of Argyll in his "Recent Speculations on Primeval Man" (Lond. 1869), directed against Lubbock—particularly the case of the ESKIMO in the North, and the PESHERAHS, or inhabitants of the Tierra del Fuego, in the South, neither of which tribes, it is evident, was created in its present inhospitable place of abode, but driven thither out of warmer regions, and entered with this its expulsion upon its present morally sunken and degraded state. The same, too, is to be said of the BUSHMEN, the VAN DIEMENSLANDERS, PAPUAS, etc. (Further in the article of Zöckler on "The Lubbock-Argyll Controversy," in the *Beweis des Glaubens*, 1871, S. 464 ff.)—The NORTH AMERICAN INDIANS have been shown, by John D. Baldwin, the American archæologist, to be a deeply degenerate race, forming a mournful contrast with their ancestors of far higher civilisation, the Moundbuilders of the Ohio valley. (*Ancient America, or Notes on American Archeology*, New York, 1872.) With him is also in substantial agreement Albert J. Mott (in his Lecture on the Origin of Savage Life, before the Liverpool Liter. and Philol. Soc., 6th Oct., 1873); as is Alf. Russ. Wallace (*Academy*, Jan. 17, 1874).

On the part of the *theological* opponents of the thesis of an original irreligiousness of all mankind, and of the continued occurrence of absolutely irreligious tribes (tribes absolutely devoid of religion), the argument here under review, of a degradation which has ensued in the course of historic development, is generally urged with stronger and more emphatic accentuation than is wont to be the case on the part of the representatives of natural science. Yet even as regards the point of view of natural science compare the works before cited of Quatrefages and Gerland; also Alb. Wigand: *Der Darwinismus und die Naturforshung Newtons und Cuviers*, i. 337 ff. We refer the reader in general to Luthardt: *Apologetic Lectures*; Lüken, *Die Traditionen*, etc. (S. 3 ff.); Rauch, *Die Einheit des Menschengeschlechts* (S. 57 f.); Delitzsch, *System der Apologetik*, 1869 (S. 51 ff.); Zollmann, *Bibel und Natur* (223, 230 ff.); Baumstark, *Apologetik* (i. 176 ff., 248 ff., 266 f.); M'Cosh, *Christianity and Positivism*, New York, 1871 (p. 138 f.); J. Ch. Scholl, *L'Islam et son Fondateur*, Paris and Neuchatel, 1874 (p. 286).—Among the more recent *philosophic* opponents of the proposition of which we have been treating, we may specially mention Ulrici (*Gott und die Natur*, 2nd edn., 1867, S. 758 ff., as also *Gott und der Mensch*, ii., S. 427), Carrière (*Die Kunst*, etc., Bd. i., 1863, S. 46 ff., 107 f.), J. B. Meyer, *as before*, Froschammer (*Einleitung in d. Philos.*, etc., 1858, S. 220 ff.; *das Christenthum und die moderne Naturwissenschaft*, 1868, S. 317 ff.), K. Chr. Planck (*l. c.*, S. 162 ff.; 200 ff.), Joh. Huber ("Ethnographische Berichtungen"—extra sheet to the *Augsb. Allg. Ztg.* 1873, No. 126). The last-named article, a rejoinder to the contesting of the universality of religious ideas, previously attempted on the part of Moritz Wagner in the same journal, is very instructive. He convicts the learned traveller of a want of independence and reliance in his judgment upon the one-sided representation of Sir John Lubbock in the "Prehistoric Times," etc., as also of various minor errors in details. With regard to almost all the tribes claimed by Wagner as devoid of religion, he shows, generally as a result of a closer inspection of the sources, cited indeed by Wagner, but not by him examined with sufficient exactness, that they are in truth by no means destitute of all traces of religious conceptions: thus, with regard to the Eskimo, the Indians of the Amazon and the Abiponians, the inhabitants of the Tierra del Fuego, the Bari negroes and other Central African tribes, the Bushmen, etc.—While the theologians lay special emphasis upon the element of the degradation, these their philosophic allies lay the main stress upon the absolute universality of this *basis* of religious thought (*Anlage*). While, for the former, the imperfect traces of religiousness in the consciousness of the rudest tribes appear as poor remains of the primary condition of bearing the image of God, now lost or intentionally destroyed, as obscure *reminiscences* of a former Paradisiac communion with God, they appear for the latter as significant *germs* of a higher capacity for development, pointing to a specifically supramaterial essence in mankind. In the repelling of the assertion of the materialists that mankind has its origin in the beasts, both concur. In this fact lies also that which serves as foundation and support to the position, taken by us in the text, of a connection of the pre-Christian cross symbols and practices with regard to crucifixion with the primary religious consciousness of mankind.

V.

IS IT POSSIBLE THAT CHRIST WAS CRUCIFIED UPON A THREE-ARMED CROSS (T)?

(To p. 68.)

THE opinion that the Roman cross of punishment, at about the beginning of the Imperial Age, was a CRUX COMMISSA, formed like a T; that thus Christ too suffered upon such T-shaped or three-armed cross—as this form is frequently displayed in earlier pictorial representations of the crucifixion, especially of the Flemish and Cologne school of painting, as also on the well-known altarpiece of Luc. Cranach at Weimar (of the year 1553), and at a still earlier period the so-called Lothar cross, a peculiarly elaborated metal crucifix of the tenth or eleventh century, in the treasury of the Aachen cathedral (Stockbauer, p. 256)—has already been subjected to a more exact test by J. Lipsius, vol. i., capp. 8—10, of his monograph *De Cruce*, which closes with the result that the supposition of the crucifixion of the Lord on a four-armed cross (CRUX IMMISSA) has better evidence, and in general a stronger degree of probability in its favour; especially since—even *if* the cross of the Saviour had been a three-armed one—the form of a *crux immissa* with four ends or arms must result from the placing of the title (Matt. xxvi. 37, and parallels) above His head. (*Ed. Vesal.*, 1675, p. 47 : Tamen sunt qui de commissâ seu de Tau forma contendunt; nec damno, etsi dissideo: quia et illi si titulum superne addis, efficere atque imaginari possis quaternos istos fines.")—The question even in the present day in reality still shapes itself essentially after this fashion. Some expositors or biblical archæologists have even recently defended the T shape of the cross of Calvary, *e.g.*, Winer (*Realw.*, art. "Kreuzigung"), Keim, in his "Geschichte Jesu von Nazara," Bd. iii., S. 413 f., and in the smaller edition of the same work (Zurich, 1873), S. 340, as well as Grundt, art. "Kreuz," in Schenkel's *Bibel-Lexik.;* comp. also Tholuck, "Die Kreuzigung," in Piper's *Ev. Kal.*, 1861, S. 70. But that which is advanced by them is altogether insufficient to invalidate the very weighty and numerous considerations in favour of the four armed cross, presented specially by Zestermann, i. 27 ff., 36 ff., with the approval of Stockbauer, Degen, and others. Although even that which is maintained in favour of its four-armed construction cannot be termed right off demonstratively (apodictically) certain, and removed beyond the possibility of all further doubt.

For the *three*-armed construction, or T form, have been adduced:

1. Various expressions of Church Fathers, who understand the Greek letter T, ordinarily inasmuch as a numeral it denotes the number 300, as a typico-symbolic equivalent (or hieroglyphic) of the cross of Christ. So Barnab., *Ep.*, c. 9 extr., where the number of Abraham's servants, 318, expressed by the letter-signs IHT, is explained as a type of Jesus and His cross ('Ιησοῦς, σταυρός); so further Clem. Alex., *Strom.*, vi., 4, 11; Ambrose, *De fide ad Grat.*, i. 3; Augustine, *Serm.* 108 *de temp.;* Paulinus, Ep. xxiv. 23, and other

places, in which sometimes this very interpretation of the 318 servants of Abraham is repeated, sometimes a mystic-prophetic sense having reference to the cross appears to be attached to the 300 warriors of Gideon, the victor over the Midianites, and even to the 300 cubits' length which, according to Gen. vi. 15, the delivering ark of Noah was to receive; thus finally also Tertull., *adv. Marc.*, iii. 22; Origen, *Hom. in Ezech.*, ix. 4, where the Taû inscribed upon the foreheads, in the well-known passage of Ezekiel, is understood as a prophecy having reference to the Crucified One.[1]—No one of these patristic utterances, however, speaks of more than a mere *resemblance* of the sign T to the cross (Tertull., *species* crucis; Paulinus, *figura* crucis; Augustine, *similitudo* crucis; Clem. Alex., τύπος τοῦ κυριακοῦ σημείου), or that it prophetically *denoted* the cross. There is nothing, however, in their statements to lead to the supposition that the cross was *exactly represented* by the T, any more than those familiar parallelisings of the cross of Christ with the wood borne by Isaac to the place of sacrifice, or with the staff of Moses, or with the rod of David, or with the wood of Elisha (2 Kings vi. 1—7), etc., are intended to indicate anything of an accurate nature concerning the form of the cross on Calvary.

2. The humorous remark of Lucian in his Δίκη φωνηέντων (i. 61), above mentioned in the text, p. 67, which, as being based upon the generally acknowledged and widespread form of the T, certainly affords a somewhat greater degree of probability in favour of a general distribution of the three-armed cross in the imperial age of Rome, than do those patristic citations.

3. The expressions of Seneca, *Consol. ad Marc.*, 20, and Josephus, *B. J.*, v. 11, § 1, likewise already treated of by us, which testify *in general* to a diversity of forms in the ancient instruments of execution and of torture, thus of *cruces* in the wider sense; but thereby certainly afford us no information of a more special kind in favour of the T form as a particularly favourite or prevalent one.

4. An indication of Paulinus of Nola in No. 27 of his poems, according to which the Christian painting of the first centuries was wont to depict the cross of Christ mainly in one of two ways: as a *five*-ended figure with several stems, in the monogram of Christ ⳨,

or as a two-ended ("double-horned"), one-stemmed figure in the cross

---

[1] [Gesen. and the older lexicographers would find the root *tav* in 1 Sam. xxi. 13. But the reading (from *tuph*) followed by LXX., Vulg., and (appar.) Luther, is beyond doubt the true one. Cp. Thenius *in loc.*]

proper, which latter again may either resemble the mast with the sailyard ✝, or else the Greek letter and numeral T.

> "Forma crucis gemina specie componitur, et nunc
> Antennæ speciem navalis imagine mali,
> Sive notam Græcis solitam signare trecentos
> Explicat existens, cum stipite figitur uno,
> Quaque cacumen habet transverso vecte jugatur."—(v. 612—616.)

This poetic description testifies to the T form of the cross as employed, side by side with the ✝ form, in the Christian iconography and painting of the fourth and fifth centuries; for hardly can the poet intend to imply in a less exact manner that the second of the two comparisons, coupled by *sive*, was in point of fact identical with the first, as Zestermann (i. 41) seems inclined to suppose. Paulinus too would seem (according to *Nat. Fel.*, v. 660—665 seq.) to have himself made a T-formed golden cross as a lamp for his Church of St. Felix (see above, p. 193, and comp. Muratori, *Antiq. Diss.*, xxi.) But on the question whether the T form was also employed, along with the ✝ form, as a Roman instrument of execution, no kind of direct information is to be gained from these verses.

5. Some instances of iconographic representation of the cross of Christ, furnished by De Rossi from *early Christian grave inscriptions* in which it is represented by the sign T, instead of the ✝ sign, which is here also more usual; so upon a marble slab of the cemetery Callisto:

IRE ✝ NE IN PACE;

upon another:

ΑΦΡΟΔICIC
T

Similarly upon a tombstone preserved in the Vatican museum:

T AGAPIS ☧ Α

(Comp. De Rossi, in the *Bullet. arch. Christ.*, 1863, pp. 53, 82; Pitra, "De titul. Christ. Carthag.," in the *Spicileg. Solesm.*, iv., p. 527.)—That of which Paulinus testifies in those verses as being an early Christian art-custom, is directly confirmed by these inscriptions. But here again the T cross is attested by these monuments only as an occasional and comparatively rare product of Christian art or iconography, *not as a Roman instrument of execution*. Comp. above in the text, Chap. III., p. 124.

6. [Ernst von Bunsen, *Das Symbol des Kreuzes*, S. 215, appeals to the representation of the heathen caricaturist (see above, p. 115). According to Bunsen, "the crucified one here appears bound upon a headless or Tau-cross, the feet resting upon a transverse beam; above the head, *not as a prolongation of the cross*, is to be seen a perpendicular rod, to which the accusation was affixed, in accordance with a custom universally prevalent."—In the footnote he refers the reader to Dio Cassius, liv. 3—a passage which merely says of a certain slave that he was led through the midst of the ἀγορά, accompanied by a written declaration of the cause for which he was to be executed, and after that was crucified. It contains no reference to the upright rod in question.]

More than a certain distant possibility of the three-armed form of the cross of Christ cannot be shown from all this. The arguments, on the other hand, for its four-armed shape are weightier and of a more convincing character.

1. As an instance of a biblical-exegetical kind may be adduced the *superscription* over the head of the Crucified, expressly attested by all four Evangelists (τίτλος, John xix. 19; αἰτία, Matt. xxvii. 37; ἐπιγραφή, Luke xxiii. 38; ἐπιγραφὴ τῆς αἰτίας, Mark xv. 26). This *might* certainly be affixed to the transverse beam of a T cross— though hardly, indeed, without then giving it the appearance of a ✝ (see above). Yet more naturally should we be led to suppose that the upper end of the long beam of a four-armed cross, where it rises above the transverse beam, was regularly employed for the affixing of this superscription. If the latter was placed upon a small board (σανίς, Socrat., *H. E.*, i. 17; πίναξ, Euseb., *H. E.*, v. 1. 44), or upon a tablet whitened with plaster or chalk (λεύκωμα, Sozom., *H. E.*, i. 17; λευκὴ σανίς, Niceph. Callisti, comp. *Etym. mag.* and Suidas), then it was unquestionably identical with the inscribed tablet [the Schuld-Tafel of Bunsen, *as above*], which the *cruciarius* had, according to the prevalent custom, to bear suspended from his neck to

the place of execution. (Comp. further Suetonius, *Domit.* 10 ; Dio Cassius, liv. 3.) And precisely in this case would it be most natural to hang the same cord—by which this tablet had before been fastened round the neck of the malefactor—after his being nailed to the cross, upon the upper beam of the cross which rises above the transverse arms.

2. A series of *Patristic testimonies* distinctly and unequivocally represents the cross of Christ as four-armed, having four ends or "horns" pointing to the four points of the compass. These testimonies divide themselves into two categories:

(*a*) *Indirect* or *figurative descriptions*, based on certain resemblances to things which present the form of a four-armed cross; *e.g.*, a mast of a ship, a man with outspread arms, the praying Moses (Exod. xvii.), the vexillum, the Paschal lamb roasted on a spit, etc. So Justin, *Apol.*, i. 55 ; Tertull., *ad Nation.*, i. 12 ; comp. also Tertull., *Apolog.*, 12, where, moreover (as, too, in Minuc. Felix, *Octav.*, 29), the inner frames of the models for the statues of the gods, the trophies and military banners are compared to crosses ; so also pseudo-Jerome, *Comm. in Marc.*, c. xv., where, too, the bird cleaving the air, and the man or fish swimming through the water, are added to these comparisons. Under this head, too, fall the expositions of the apostolic words, "that ye may be able to comprehend with all saints what is the breadth, and length, and depth, and height" (Ephes. iii. 18), which is explained as a reference to the cross, on the part of Gregory of Nyssa, *Or. I. in Res. Dom. ;* pseudo-Jerome, *l. c. ;* Ambrose, *Serm.* 56 ; and Augustine, *Comm. in Ps.* 103 ; *Tractat.* 118 *in Joann.; Ep.* 120, etc. Comp. Appendix VII.

(*b*) *More direct descriptions*, which, even though proceeding from comparison with objects of nature or products of art, yet bring into prominence the four-armed conformation of the cross of Christ, not merely by way of allusion, but also in circumstantial, distinct delineation, generally indeed conceiving of the resting-block, or *sedile*, fixed to the lower part of the long beam as a fifth end or "horn." So Iren., *adv. hæres.*, ii. 24, 4: "Habitus crucis fines et summitates habet quinque, duos in longitudine, duos in latitudine, et unum in medio, in quo requiescit, qui clavis affigitur." In like manner, Justin, *Dial. cum Tryph.*, c. 91, where the comparison is with the unicorn, and the horn of this animal is parallelised with the upper end of the long beam, rising above the transverse arms ; Tertull., *adv. Jud.*, c. 10 (where, in like manner, that form of comparison is made use of) ; [Apollinarius of Hierapolis (cent. 2), as cited in the *Chron. Paschale*,

p. 5, " upon the *horns* of the unicorn."] Firmicus Maternus, *De errore profanarum religg.*, c. 22 ; and pseudo-Cyprian (or Victorinus), in his *Hymn. de Pascha.* :

" Arboris hæc species uno de stipite surgit
Et mox in geminos extendit brachia ramos,
Sicut plena graves antennæ carbasa tendunt
Vel cum disjunctis juga stant ad aratra juvencis."

3. *Two testimonies of later Fathers* absolutely exclude the T form : they admit only that cross to be a faithful representation of the cross of Christ, in which the long beam rises above the transverse beam. Gregory the Great, *Moral. in Job.*, c. 39 (*Opp.* i., p. 990 c) says, " Notandum vero est, quia iste trecentorum numerus in litera T continetur, quæ crucis speciem tenet ; *cui si super transversam lineam id, quod in cruce eminet, adderetur, non jam crucis species, sed ipsa crux esset.*" Almost verbally the same Isidore of Seville, *Comm. in Judic.*, c. 5.

From these testimonies results at least the following consideration, that the sphere of conception of the Fathers was dominated almost exclusively by the ┬ form of the cross of Christ, as established by Christian tradition ; and that from the time of Gregory the Great the T form was no longer recognised side by side with it, as was still the case in that poem by Paulinus of Nola. An absolutely certain decision in the question, whether the cross of Christ can really have been of no other form than such four-armed one, does not indeed result from this *consensus patrum*, of however great importance this may appear. For the force of the biblical testimonies, adduced under No. 1, is in no case entirely irresistible ; and no one of the Fathers mentioned, not even those belonging to the second century—pseudo-Barnabus, Justin, Irenæus, etc.—stood so near to the events of the Passion, or derived his knowledge from such clear and direct evidence of eye-witnesses, as to exclude all possibility of doubt regarding the trustworthiness of any part of their statements.

If Zestermann (i. 27 ff. ; ii. 7 ff.) proceeds further, and maintains generally that among all civilised nations of the first century before Christ exclusively four-armed crosses were in use — thus seeking to cut off all possibility of an execution of Christ upon a *crux commissa*—he seems to us to attempt to prove too much, and on that account to prove *nothing with certainty*. It may be the expressions *crux* and *patibulum* in the Roman authors from the time of Cicero regularly denote the four-armed cross; but we cannot at least deduce from the fact that Curtius makes use of the expression "crucibus affigere" in speaking of Alexander's execution of 2,000 Tyrians, or that Justin represents the Egyptian rebels (*circ.* B.C. 200) as crucifying, "patibulis suffigere," the voluptuous royal wives (Curt., iv. 4, 17; Justin, 30, 2), that these writers "*could not be thinking* of any other instrument of execution than the four-armed cross." [Although it is difficult to understand how the term *suf*figere, so frequently employed by Cicero and others in connection with the cross, could properly be used in speaking of execution upon a T cross.] Even if these and other Roman authors of the silver age, or an age yet later, were not able to conceive of any other than the four-armed cross as employed on such occasions, yet nothing follows from this with regard to the modes of crucifixion actually practised among those pre-Roman or extra-Roman peoples. Equally as the Scythians, Assyrians, Persians, etc., might—according to the more or less indistinct evidence of an Herodotus and other ancient classics—make use *either* of upright posts, *or* of three-armed *or* four-armed crosses (and Zestermann, *as above*, himself admits that we can attain to no degree of certainty, with regard to these earlier nations, in determining the form of their instruments of death), so also may a diversity in the form of the cross be claimed in the case of the Macedonians, the Egyptians of the Ptolemaic age, the Syrocusans, etc.; the more so, since the oft-cited utterances of a Seneca and a Josephus attest even for the beginning of the Roman imperial age the occasional employment of "cruces non unius generis, sed aliter ab aliis fabricatæ." ([1])—In all this, indeed, the conclusion of the authority to whom we have already often had occasion to refer, Lipsius (with his predecessors, *e.g.*, already J. Scaliger, in the *Thesaur.*, *temp.* 1658; and, in recent times, De Rossi, in Pitra, *Spicil. Solesm.*, l.c.), receives its justification; since

---

[1] We concur generally in the strictures of E. Friedrich (*Bonn. Theol. Litbl.*, 1875, No. 17 ff.) upon Zestermann's argt. Only this scholar appears to us to err in maintaining that σταυρός in earlier Greek had *only* the signification of stake, while he claims for the Latin *crux* the original signification *only* of cross in the narrower sense: stake with transverse beam upon it. For us at least, so far as *crux* is concerned, the derivation we have before given, from çram, "dolore vexari," appears to be the only admissible one. And for that wider sense of *crux*, according to which the pointed stake (pale), the *furca*, and other instruments of torture, can be denoted by it, Seneca, *Consol. ad Marc.*, 20, gives an unequivocal testimony, the force of which Friedrich vainly seeks to set aside. [For the

he had mentioned the three forms, of the *crux immissa, commissa,* and *decussata,* as forms of the Roman judicial cross alleged to coexist with each other : of the last-named form, however, he entirely disposed, and limited the second to a minimum of use, nay represented its employment as nowhere traceable with perfect certainty. *In this way, accordingly, the employment of the* CRUX IMMISSA, *as by far the most generally prevalent main form of this instrument of execution in the Roman empire about the time of the rise of our religion, appears to be proven.*

VI.

THE SINGLE EXTERNAL CIRCUMSTANCES AND PROCEEDINGS IN THE WORK OF CRUCIFIXION.

(To p. 93 ff.)

As regards the details of the matters now falling under examination, we must refer the reader to the well-known works of JUSTUS LIPSIUS (with his supplementers, SALMASIUS, BARTHOLINUS, NIHUSIUS, CURTIUS, etc.), GRETSER (*De cruce,* lib. i.), MERILLIUS (*Notæ philoll. in pass. Christi,* Roterodami, 1693), BYNÆUS (*De morte Christi,* lib. iii., 287 sqq.), KIPPING (*De cruce et cruciariis,* 17), JAHN (*Archäologie,* ii. 2, 369 ff.), FRIEDLIEB (*Archäologie der Leidensgeschichte,* 1843), LANGEN (*Die letzten Lebenstage Jesu,* 1864), STEINMEYER (*Die Leidensgeschichte des Herrn,* etc., 1868), KEIM (*Geschichte Jesu von Nazara,* iii. 290 ff.), ZESTERMANN, DEGEN, FRIEDRICH, etc. We give, for the complementing of that which has been remarked in the text, a brief notice of the principal acts belonging to the infliction of the punishment of the cross in the order of their succession ; and in doing so we direct our attention mainly to the literary controversies regarding the more obscure and difficult questions.

author's derivation of *crux,* as also for the probability of its having a Celtic origin, see p. 53, note. According to Bunsen, *l. c.,* S. 84, note ¹, the signification alike of *staurós* and *crux* is " Scheiterhaufen ;" but this meaning resolves itself into that of "stake," as above : unless (as would appear to be the case) he intends to include the signification of *funeral pile.* The funeral pile, however, was not called *staurós* or *crux,* but *pyre* or *rogus.* The Celtic root CROC (or Crog) appears most distinctly in the Italian form *croce.* The noun *croes,* on the other hand, may be a derivative from *crux.*—TR.]

The *Roman* mode of proceeding—alone of interest for the single incidents of the Gospel history of the Passion—included the following successive acts:

1. The *scourging* or *beating with rods*, at once inflicted as a matter of course, after the passing of the sentence, by way of introduction to any form of execution whatever (Valer., Max. i. 1, 6; Dion. Hal., ix. 48); in the case of slaves, with scourges (flagellis), thus as *flagellatio* strictly so called, in the case of free men, with rods (virgis, fustibus): vid. *Dig.*, xlviii. 19, 10: "Ex quibus causis liber fustibus cæditur, ex his servus flagellis cædi jubetur." The person who was to be scourged was deprived of his upper clothing and bound to a post or pillar, such as existed at every appointed place of judgment, of which too some were wont to be set up in camps in front of the prætorium. Comp. Plaut., *Bacch.*, iv. 6, 24:

"Abducite hunc
Intro atque adstringite ad columnam fortiter," etc. ;

also Cic., *Verr.*, v. 5, 10; *p. Rab.* iv., 13; Liv., viii. 7; Gell., *Noct. Att.*, x. 13, etc. The order for the scourging was given by the judge in the words "I, lictor, deliga ad palum,"[1] or "I, lictor, colliga manus" (Liv. *l.c.*)

2. *The journey to the place of execution*, uniformly accomplished amidst numerous outrages inflicted upon the condemned by the soldiers who were to act as executioners (therefore; in crucem rapere, Cic., *Verr.*, v. 64, 166 or, ad crucem trahere, etc.), was moreover for the sake of greater contumely directed through the most populous streets and squares (Dio Cass., liv. 3). The delinquent appears regularly to have been led *bound* to the cross (Chariton, iv. 2, p. 66, d'Orville-Reiske), his offence being proclaimed by a herald going before, or by the bearing in front of him of a *tablet* inscribed with the cause of the execution (Lamprid., *Alex. Sev.*, 22, 35), or even by the malefactor himself bearing this αἰτία or τίτλος, *causa, titulus* (πίναξ, σανίς,—see above, Append. V., p. 405) suspended from his neck (Suet., *Calig.*, 22; *Domit.*, 10; Dio Cass., liv. 3; Euseb., *H. E.*, v. 1, 44.)—On the *bearing of the cross* by the condemned, see above, p. 93, note [1].

3. The *setting up of the cross* upon the place of execution, regularly situated outside the gate of the camp or city (Plaut., *Miles Glor.*, ii. 4), ordinarily upon a hill or eminence visible from afar, took place

---

[1] [In this sense, too, *not in that of binding upon a cross of execution*, is to be understood, *e.g.*, the σταυρῷ προσδήσας of Dio Cass., xlix. 22.]

according to the earlier practice at executions beforehand, so that the cross (with or without the transverse beam) was already standing there when the *cruciarius* arrived: vid. Cic., *Verr.*, v. 66, 169; *p. Rab.*, 4. Later, however, this was done only immediately before the execution, as is shown by the phrases σταυρὸς πήγνυται (Plut., *Tit.*, c. 9), καταπηγνύναι σταυρόν (Joseph., *B. J.*, vii. 6, § 4), *crucem ponere* (Juven., 6, 221). As regards the necessary fixing with pegs, comp. Herod., ix. 120: σανίδα προσπασσαλεύειν. If the cross had a considerable height, as was the case with that of transgressors of rank, and in other single instances (*e.g.*, in that of Cartalo, Justin 18, 7; cp. Justin 22, 7; Suetonius, *Galba*, 9; Artemidorus, i. 76; ii. 53, 102; as in that of Haman, Esther v. 14), the pegs driven in at the foot were not of course sufficient; it needed then other special supports. For the lowness of the cross of Jesus testifies the stem of hyssop (John xix. 29).—A *standing* cross of execution, or gallows, appears to have been only exceptional with the Romans: comp., *e.g.*, Polyb., i. 86, 6; Diodor., xxv. 5, 2. As a rule, every cross was an individual instrument of death, to be dragged by the malefactor condemned to it to the place of execution, there to stand until the body hanging thereupon had fallen to pieces (Hor., *Ep.* i. 16, 48: "Non pasces in cruce corvos;" Lucan., *Pharsal.*, vi. 543; Prudent., *Perist.*, xi. 67; Cic., *Tusc.*, i. 43); or, according to the milder custom often practised from the time of Augustus, until the body was given up to the relatives of the deceased for sepulture, and the cross thus left bare was then cut down. (Quintil., *Decl.*, 6, 9: "Cruces succiduntur, percussos sepeliri non vetat;" comp. *Dig.* xlviii. 24, 1.)

4. The *divesting of the person to be crucified of his garments*, then the nailing of him *naked* to the cross, was an almost universal rule. See the remark of Artemidorus, already adduced in the text (p. 96, note [1]), as well as the direct testimony of the Evangelists: Matt. xxvii. 35, and parallels. That which is told us about Cartalo's crucifixion in full priestly attire (Justin, xviii. 7), seems to have been an exceptional case, brought about by special circumstances; and equally so that which Tacitus relates (*Hist.*, iv. 3) with regard to a slave of Vitellius. If the well-known cross of mockery of the palace of Alexander Severus [222—235] bears a figure clothed with a short tunic or frock, it *may* certainly be inferred therefrom that slaves, for instance, whose garments at any rate had no particular value, often escaped being nailed naked to the cross. (Comp. Becker, *Das Spottcrucifix in den Röm. Kaiserpalästen*, 1863, S. 38 ff.) But directly attested in the classics is neither this custom, nor the practice

assumed to exist by Langen (*l. c.*, p. 304), according to which at least a cloth around the loins was regularly left to the crucified for the covering of his body. See, against this supposition, Zestermann, ii. 34.

5. The *lifting up* (drawing up) *to the cross.*—The affixing of the person to be crucified regularly took place upon the cross already erected, not—as is represented in earlier and later paintings, *e.g.*, the renowned crucifixion scene of Rubens at Antwerp, so Kaulbach's "Nero" (the latter with reference to the martyrdom of Peter)—upon the cross while yet lying on the ground, before its erection. Against this latter supposition see already Lipsius, ii. 7. Decisive for the fact of the *cruciarius* being lifted up to the cross (whether as already attached to the *patibulum*, as no doubt in the earlier time was the case, or without it, as was certainly the prevalent custom from the beginning of the last century before Christ) are the expressions, *in crucem tollere, crucem ascendere, in crucem excurrere*, or the Greek ones ἐπιβαίνειν τοῦ σταυροῦ, ἀναβαίνειν ἐπὶ τὸν στ. Plaut., *Mostell.*, v. 1, 12; Cic., *Verr.*, v. 6, 12; v. 66, 169. Chariton, iv. 3, 5; v. 10, 6; Josephus, *B. J.*, vii. 6, § 4; Lucian, *Peregr.*, 45; the name too of *crucisalus*, "cross-dancer," "cross-leaper," which the slave Chrysalus gives himself in grim jest, Plaut., *Bacch.*, ii. 3, 127. Even that *patibulum ascendere* in Prudentius, *Peristeph.*, x. 641; likewise the "in crucem elevari" of Augustine, *Tract.* 3 *in Joann.*, as well as other similar passages in Church Fathers (Iren., ii. 24, 4; Justin, *Dial.*, c. 91), have a certain demonstrative force against the hypothesis of an attachment to a prostrate cross.—As *means* for the raising of the *cruciarius*, already Lipsius supposed the use of *ladders* (*De cruce*, ii. 8, note), but, in addition to this, in special cases also a drawing up with *ropes*. Both methods of raising may indeed have obtained side by side: no early author expressly mentions them, but both appear so natural, and so much what we might expect, that valid objections to the one or the other of them can hardly be raised. The passages adduced by Marquardt (*Röm. Alterth.*, v. 194) and others in favour of the supposition of a drawing up with ropes, namely, Plin., *H. N.*, 29, 4, 57; Euseb., *H. E.*, v. 1, p. 131; Firmicus Matern., *Astron.*, vi. 31, fol. 179, [Ignat., see above, p. 120, n. 2] are not of a force absolutely demonstrative, at least do not by any means exclude the occasional use of ladders too in cases of crucifixion. Moreover the words of Firm. Mat.: "patibulo suffixus in crucem crudeliter erigitur," are critically not entirely beyond suspicion as to their genuineness; cp. Zesterm., S. 39. But granted these passages

prove with sufficient certainty the use of cords, they do not on that
account deprive of their clearness those other passages which imply
an ascending by means of ladders, to which category belong also
in particular several expressions like *in crucem excurrere, crucem
ascendere,* ἀναβαίνειν ἐπὶ τὸν σταυρόν, etc.; comp. especially the
remarkable story of that Chæreas (in Chariton, iv. 3, 5), who has
already mounted the cross, and is about to be nailed to it, when
he suddenly receives a pardon, and is addressed in the command
κατάβηθι, upon which he ruefully "comes down," etc. We believe
therefore that both assertions are of a one-sided kind: that to the
effect that ropes *exclusively* were employed in raising the *cruciarius*
(Salmasius, Friedlieb, Langen, Marquardt, Keim), and that requiring
ladders for absolutely *every* crucifixion (Zesterm., Degen). We must
fall back upon the thoroughly intelligent statement of the case on
the part of Lipsius (*Not. ad lib.*, ii., c. 8, p. 210)—a statement which is
in contradiction with no hint of the ancients,—" Et sane de scalis,
apponere eas pæne necessarium videtur, utique ad erectam crucem.
Quomodo alias subduxeris, aut fixeris? Etiam de funibus sunt quæ
suadeant," etc. (Comp. also the two illustrations there given, of
which the one represents a cruciarius as drawn up with ropes, the
other as being taken up by means of ladders.)

6. The *preparatory fastening by means of ropes and resting-block.*
For the preparatory attaching of the person raised or drawn up to
the cross, there were *at any rate* certain ropes employed; and of
these ropes, as well as the knots tied with them, some passages in the
Classics and Fathers make express mention, namely, Lucan, *Phars.,*
vi. 543 sq. (the Thessalian enchantress Erichtho tears asunder the
ropes and knots of the crucified ones with her teeth); Plin., *H. N.,*
28, 4, 11 (the superstitious bearing about as a charm of a cord or
nail of one who had been crucified); and Hilar. Pict., *De Trin.,*
x. 13 ("Sed forte penduli in cruce corporis pœnæ et colligantium
funium et adactorum clavorum cruda vulnera sint timori! Et
videamus, cujus corporis homo Christus sit, ut suspensa et nodosa et
transfossa carne dolor manserit!")—Besides these ropes, of which
at least those attaching the breast to the cross must have remained
after the nailing of the hands and feet, because they had to protect
the body from falling forward, there also served for the preparatory fixing of the body the sitting-block (πῆγμα, *sedile*), that "*fifth*
projecting end*" of the four-ended cross, of which Irenæus makes
mention, *Hær.*, ii. 24, 4 (" habitus crucis fines et summitates habet
quinque, ... et unum in medio, in quo requiescit, qui clavis

affigitur"), which Justin Martyr, *Dial.*, c. 91, compares to a forth-springing horn on which the crucified, as it were, *rode* (Καὶ τὸ ἐν τῷ μέσῳ πηγνύμενον ὡς κέρας καὶ αὐτὸ ἐξέχον ἐστίν, ἐφ' ᾧ ἐποχοῦνται οἱ σταυρούμενοι); comp. also Tertull., *ad Nation.*, i. 12 ("Sed nobis tota crux imputatur, cum antenna scilicet sua et cum illo sediles excessu"), as well as that relief from the catacombs at Rome, (in Münter, *Sinnbilder*, etc. . . . . . *der alten Christen*, ii. Str. 28,) which confirms by the evidence of the monuments the existence of this *sedile*. (See also Stockbauer, *l. c.*, p. 37).[1] An alleviation of the painful position of the crucified one was certainly not that which was aimed at in providing this resting-block—since this might rather contribute to increase the suffering of the slowly dying one—but only for the gaining of a firmer hold before and during the nailing, as well as to prevent a falling down from the heavy weight of the body.—Whether lower down than the sedile, or even *instead* thereof, a *board* was placed for the feet of the crucified (ὑποπόδιον, *suppedaneum lignum*), was a question pretty warmly disputed among Christian archæologists at the beginning of the seventeenth century. Lipsius (ii. 10, p. 95 sqq.) leaves it undecided whether we are to give credit to the statement of Gregory of Tours (*De glor. martyr.*, c. 6) touching the existence of such a footboard upon the cross of Christ. Gretser (i. 29) defended its existence, by an appeal to those passages of Justin, Irenæus, etc., which he sought to interpret of the alleged hypopodium; as well as to ancient Christian paintings, which represent the feet of the crucified as resting upon such board. On the other hand, the historical character of the same was contested by Salmasius (*Animadverss. in Eusebii, H. E.*), Jac. Bosius (*De cruce triumphante*, Antv. 1617, lib. i., c. 6), and Bartholinus (*De cruce hypomn.*, i. 28 sqq., 54 sqq.), against which latter writer again Barthold Nihues (*Ep. de cruce ad Bartholin.*, p. 199 sqq.), and Cornelius Curtius (*De clavis dominicis*, p. 228 sq.), contended for its historical character. Since Gregory of Tours († 595) is in reality the earliest witness for the hypopodium, since, too, Christian art is acquainted with it only after the beginning of the seventh century—comp. the two representations of the crucifixion given by Stockbauer (p. 124 and following of his work), of which the one, belonging to the year 586, is still without the *suppe-*

---

[1] Friedrich, *l. c.* [in which he is anticipated by PEARSON, *Expos. of the Creed*, art. iii., chap. iv., p. 316, of Walford's edn.], seeks to interpret also the expression *acuta crux*, in Seneca, *Ep.* ci., of the *sedile;* whether rightly so, appears to us doubtful.

daneum, whereas the other, of an origin nearly a hundred years later, has one—we must decidedly range ourselves on the side of the opponents of the Gretser-Nihues view. Stockbauer justly remarks (p. 39) that the suppedaneum was invented after art had, on æsthetic grounds, ceased to depict the sedile, as a compensation, in order that one might not be obliged to represent the body of the crucified in a physiologically and mechanically inconceivable position. It was thus "merely an artifice, in order to give to the crucified body a position possible to the eye."

7. *The nailing to the cross.* That the preparatory binding to the cross with cords was followed by a nailing thereto is attested by the expressions *affigere, suffigere cruci*, προσηλοῦν, the distinct mention of the nail-prints : Luke xxiv. 39, John xx. 20 (comp. Iren. ii. 24, 4; Paulinus of Nola, *Poëm.*, 24, 455); also by the fact that Xenophon of Ephesus (iv. 22) speaks of the Egyptian mode of crucifixion, consisting in merely binding on with cords, as something strange and unwonted; as well as by the fact that the poet Ausonius in his *Cupido cruci affixus* (v. 56 sq.), where he describes the binding of the god of love to a myrtle-tree, furnishes similar indirect evidence in favour of nailing as the usual mode of crucifixion.[1]—On the exceedingly large and strong *beam nails* (Hor., *Carm.* i. 35; Cic., *Verr.* v. 21), of which the Romans made use in this terrible form of execution (see above, p. 93). That with such nails (or spikes) not only the hands, but *also the feet*, were pierced, these last thus not merely bound with cords (as was assumed by Clericus, on *John* xx. 27; Dathe, on *Psalm* xxii. 17; Herder, Von Ammon, and with special zeal Paulus, *Memorab.*, iv. 36 ; *Comm. z. d. Evangg.*, iii. 764 ff.; in like manner also Winer, *De pedum in cruce affixione*, Leipz. Progr. 1845; *Realw.*, art. "Kreuzigung;" and, with some hesitation, Schleiermacher, *Leb. Jes.*, S. 447, Chr. J. von Bunsen, Lücke, and others),[2] is shown by the direct biblical evidence of Luke xxiv. 39

---

[1] [That the nailing, too, invariably accompanied the crucifixions in various forms inflicted by the Roman soldiers in mockery, even as the scourging invariably preceded them, is shown from JOSEPHUS : Μαστιγούμενοι . . . ἀνεσταυροῦντο . . . Προσήλουν δὲ οἱ στρατιῶται δι' ὀργὴν καὶ μῖσος τοὺς ἁλόντας, ἄλλον ἄλλῳ σχήματι πρὸς χλεύην.—*B. J.*, v. 11, 1.]

[2] E. v. Bunsen, S. 33, expresses doubt as to whether *even the hands* of the Saviour were nailed. He speaks of the cross "upon which Jesus was crucified, and upon which cross drops of blood must have fallen on the nailing of his hands, unless these were bound, as ordinarily in crucifixions by the Romans." He accordingly interprets Luke xxiv. 39, 40, of the marks of the bound (fettered) hands and feet. "Only John xx. 25—27 refers unequivocally to the nailing ;" which—as the

—with which John xx. 20—27 is not in contradiction, since on the ground of decorum the wounds in the feet would not be mentioned;[1] as further by the testimony of Justin M. (*Dial c. Tryph.*, c. 97), of Tertullian (*adv. Marc.*, iii. 19 : Foderunt inquit manus meas et pedes, *quæ propria atrocitas crucis*), of Hilary (*Tract. in Ps.* 143), of Augustine (*in Ps.* 39), and other Fathers ; finally, by that of an ancient classic of decisive weight, by the passage in the *Mostellaria* of Plautus (ii. 1, 12).

> " Ego dabo ei talentum, prius qui in crucem excucurrerit ;
> Sed ea lege, ut offigantur *bis pedes*, bis brachia,"

which—as is shown from the double nailing—*presupposes* the existence of the nailing of the feet and hands *as a universal custom ;* but by announcing a twofold nailing of the feet too, menaces with the threat of an unwonted severity in the infliction of this terrible punishment. This passage, rightly interpreted, renders it at the same time preponderantly probable that the nailing of the feet, as a rule, took place by means of a single iron nail or spike of great strength, driven in common through the two feet placed the one above the other. It thus farther aids us in the decision of another archæological controversy of ancient date—that, namely, as to whether three or four nails were employed in the crucifixion : see above, p. 175 f. of the text. A right conclusion is formed on the *general* question as to the nailing of the feet (especially in opposition to Paulus) by Hengstenberg, Hug, Bähr, Neander [Engl. ed. of *Life of Jesus*, page 464, note], Langen, Keim, Ehrard, Meyer, Fr. X. Kraus, Zestermann, Degen.— With regard to the controversy as to there being *one* or *two* nails inserted *in the feet*, the more probable opinion—in opposition to that of *two* nails being employed, a view defended by many in earlier and later times, as pseudo-Cyprian (*De passione*), Ambrose, Augustine, Ruffinus, Theodoret, Gregory of Tours, the Anglo-Saxon Aelfric, Pope Innocent III., Luke of Tuy, St. Brigitta, Gretser, Corn. Curtius (*De clavis dominicis*, Vesal. 1675, ed. alt.), also Meyer (*on Matt.* xxvii. 35), Martigny (*Dictionn. des antiquités chrét.*, p. 192), Langen (*Letzte Lebenst-J.*, S. 319), Münz (" Zur Gesch. des

---

authenticity of the fourth gospel is very decidedly rejected by this writer—amounts in reality to no evidence beyond that of a highly questionable tradition. But compare the " Insertum manibus chalybem " of the Roman poet—a contemporary of St. Paul. (Lucan., *Pharsalia*, vi. 547.)

[1] [Nor was there any necessity that the Saviour should thus enumerate His wounds : it was enough for Thomas to recognise the *reality* of the pierced hands and side.]

Kreuzes," *Katholik*, 1867, S. 577), F. X. Kraus (*Beiträge zur Trier'schen Archäologie*, S. 18), Degen, etc.—according to which only *one* nail was used for the feet, thus *three* nails in all, is maintained by Gregory Nazianzen (Γυμνὸν τρισήλῳ κείμενον ξύλῳ λάβων, *Chr. patiens*, v. 1466), Nonnus (ἄζυγι γόμφῳ. *Paraphr., in Joann.*, c. xix.), Anselm of Canterbury (*Medit. X. de pass. Chr.*), Walter v. der Vogelweide (in Lachm., S. 37), the early English writing ANCREN RIWLE (in Morris, *Legends of the Holy Rood*, p. xx.), the Albigenses of the Middle Ages (see the polemics directed against them by Luke of Tuy: *De altera vita, c. Albigg.*, lib. ii. 222 sqq.), Daniel Malloni (*Elucidationes in Stigmata D. N. J. C.*, Venet. 1606—opposed by Curtius, *l. c.*), most recently by Keim (iii. 416, who, however, is not quite decided, but admits there *may* have been a separate nailing of each foot), Zestermann (S. 47); also Canon Farrar (art. "Cross," in *Smith's Dicty. of the Bible*).—On the position of *Christian art tradition* in relation to this controversy— in the earlier Middle Ages decidedly favouring the supposition of a twofold nailing of the feet; but from the time of Cimabue and Margaritone (cent. 13) inclining to the representation of the feet as placed one over the other, and pierced by a common nail—comp. Martigny, *l. c.*; Piper, *Einleitung in die monumentale Theologie*, S. 620; Stockbauer, S. 159, and elsewhere; also Morris, *l. c.*, p. 19, where reference is made to an interesting copper crucifix belonging to the twelfth century (in the Soltykoff art collection), which displays only *one* nail through the feet.

8. The *attaching of the title* above the head of the crucified, mentioned by all four Evangelists, and that as something naturally in course; not as an extraordinary occurrence, but as something taking place at all crucifixions. See above, in the text; also the passages from the classics cited under No. 2 of this excurse, which attest, not indeed expressly, but yet indirectly and by that which they presuppose, the affixing of the title at the head of the cross. Nor can it be distinctly inferred from Chrysostom, *Hom.* 85 *in Joann.*: οἱ γὰρ λῃστῶν (σταυροὶ) τίτλους οὐκ εἶχον, that —contrary to the custom in other instances—no superscriptions were placed over the malefactors on the right and left hand of the Lord; for Chrysostom rested his reasoning only on the silence of the Evangelists with regard to the titles above the malefactors' crosses; an argument to which in itself no demonstrative value can be attached. (This in opposition to Zestermann, S. 48.) Comp., moreover, Grets. i. 26—28, as well as Nicquet, *De titulo S. Crucis*

diss. (in *Authores de cruce*, 5 tom., 12mo, Lugd. Bat. 1695); Alberti, *De inscriptione crucis Chr.*, Lips. 1725; Altmann, in *Tempe Helv.*, iv. 662 sqq.

9. The *watching* (guarding) of the crucified, to prevent their being taken down by friends, certainly was regularly observed. Not only is this attested by the Evangelists, but also, *e.g.*, by Cicero, *pro Rabir.*, iv. 11; Petron., *Sat.* 111; Quintil. *Decl.*, vi. 9.—On the milder practice, obtaining from the time of Augustus, which rendered a prolonged watching unnecessary, was in harmony with the corresponding principles of Mosaism (see Deut. xxi. 23; Josh. x. 27), and partly on this very account, and in order not too greatly to shock the religious prejudices of the Jewish people, was followed by Pilate in the case of the Lord, comp. what has been already said above, No. 3 [and Josephus, *B. J.*, iv. 5, § 2].

10. The *accelerating of death by the breaking of the legs, or by the thrust of the spear.* Since death on the cross was ordinarily exceedingly slow, sometimes even only resulted from hunger after a hanging of several days' duration (Euseb., *H. E.*, viii. 8), or from the laceration of the flesh by beasts of prey (comp. what was said above, in the text, p. 51), and at any rate only ensued amidst acute agonies (Seneca, Ep. ci.: tabescere inter supplicia, et membratim perire, et per stillicidia emittere spiritum), there were also occasionally certain lenitives to the terrible lot of the crucified applied by the Romans. Thus not only the rendering insensible by the giving of wine mingled with myrrh—a custom not mentioned in the classics; thus only a specially Jewish practice: comp. Langen, *as before*, S. 300; Wetstein on Mark xv. 23—but also, more particularly, the breaking of the legs (σκελοκοπία), in order to bring about death more rapidly; a barbaric custom on other occasions also employed as a particular mode of execution (independently of crucifixion), comp. Plaut., *Asin.* ii. 4, 68; Seneca, *de Ira*, iii. 32; Suet., *Aug.* 67; *Tib.* 44, but which in the case of one thoroughly exhausted by crucifixion and wearied of life might almost be regarded as a benefit. Origen (*in Matt.* xxvii. 54) attests the custom as a συνήθεια τῶν Ῥωμαίων. Less common appears to have been that other practice, mentioned also by Origen, *l. c.*, and applied in the case of Christ, of a thrust with a spear in the side, in the place of the breaking of the legs. (John xix. 31 ff.) Yet compare, with regard to this, too *e.g.* Plin., *H. N.*, xi. 45; Quintil., *Decl.* vi. 9; and see in general Lipsius, *De cruce*, ii. 14; not. in lib. ii. 10; Friedlieb, *Archäol.*, S. 164 ff.—Against the

assertion on the part of Strauss and Weisse of the unhistorical character of John's account of the breaking of the legs and of the spear-thrust (comp. too Keim, iii. 509 ff.) see specially Ebrard, *Wissensch. Krit. der Evang. Geschichte*, 3rd edn., 732 ff.

VII.

HISTORY OF THE EXPOSITION OF THE PASSAGE EPHES. iii. 18; AS COMPARED WITH JOB xi. 8, 9, AND PSALM cxxxix. 8—10.

(To p. 103.)

JAK. GRIMM (*Deutsche Mythol.*, ii. 758, 2nd edn.) believes that his theory of the ancient Germanic myth of the world-tree Yggdrasill being transferred during the Middle Ages to the cross of Christ, " would fall if the same exposition of the wood of the cross (as symbolical representations of the tree of the world, which extends in its uppermost boughs to heaven, in its roots to the nether world, in its branches to the ends of the earth) could be proved out of earlier African or Eastern fathers;" but doubts as to the possibility of adducing such proof. That this doubt—with the removal of which the supposition of a pre-Christian origin to the world-tree of the ancient Germans, however, by no means loses its support (see above in the text, p. 21)—is not warranted, may easily be shown by an abundance of patristic testimonies for the interpretation of the cross as a kind of world-tree, specially for the referring of its four extremities to the four relations of space—above, below, east, and west. We have already (Appendix V.), in harmony with Zestermann, adduced a number of these utterances, as instances in favour of the probability that the historic cross of Christ was of four-armed construction. Here we would in particular point to a series of reasonings, belonging alike to the patristic as to later theological literature, in which the said symbolical meaning in reference to the cross is attached to the words of Paul, ἵνα ἐξισχύσητε καταλαβέσθαι σὺν πᾶσιν τοῖς ἁγίοις τί τὸ πλάτος καὶ μῆκος καὶ βάθος καὶ ὕψος (Ephes. iii. 18), or also to their Old Testament types, Job xi. 8, 9 (" heights of heaven is it; what canst thou do? deeper than the nether world; what canst thou know? Longer than the earth is its measure, and broader is it than the sea,") and Psalm cxxxix. 8—10 ("If I ascend up into heaven, Thou art there; if I make my bed in hell," etc.)

As concerns Ephes. iii. 18 more immediately, Gregory of Nyssa appears to have been the first among the Greek fathers to interpret of the cross the allusion in this passage to the four directions in space. After he had, in the *Orat. catechet. magna*, c. 32, explained the deeper significance of the four-armed conformation of the cross by the statement that "He who in His passion hung extended thereon unites and combines in Himself the whole universe; inasmuch as, by means of Himself, He gathers together the most diverse creatures into one accord and harmony" (ὅτι ὁ ἐπὶ τούτου ἐν τῷ καιρῷ τῆς κατὰ τὸν θάνατον οἰκονομίας διαταθεὶς ὁ τὸ πᾶν πρὸς ἑαυτὸν συνδέων τε καὶ συναρμόζων ἐστὶ, τὰς διαφορὰς τῶν ὄντων φύσεις πρὸς μίαν σύμπνοιάν τε καὶ ἁρμονίαν δι' ἑαυτοῦ συνάγων) . . . . "in such wise that every creature looks up to Him, and surrounds Him, and by Him is connected with other creatures in every direction"—he continues, "For the contemplation of this Divine mystery (*lit.* Divinity) we must not merely be guided by the hearing (by listening to His word), but our eyes too must instruct us in the sublime truths. On this account the great apostle Paul initiates the people of the Ephesians into such mystery; inasmuch as by his instruction he enables them to comprehend what is the depth and the height, and the breadth and the length," etc.; upon which there follows an interpretation of the passage Phil. ii. 10 f. with reference to the same mystery of the four dimensions of the cross. Similarly in *Orat. i. de resurrect. Christi.* "Not without reason," he here says, "'does the holy eye of the Apostle perceive the figure of the cross;" upon which he proceeds to show pretty circumstantially how the mention of the height (ὕψος) indicates the uppermost end of the cross; that of the depth, the lower; that of the length and breadth, the two extremities of the transverse beam; and how, on account of the significance of these four extremities of the cross, pointing to the four ends of the world, the cross of the Lord merits in truth to be called a "bond of all things," σύνδεσμος ἁπάντων.—From the Nyssenian this mode of interpretation passed over to a series of later fathers of the Eastern Church ; *e.g.*, to Anastasius Sinaita, who from our passage, as well as from the similar one, Ephes. iv. 8—10, developed his mystic-quixotic etymology of the name σταυρός = στὰ εὖρος (*Viæ Dux*, c. ii. de etymolog : σταυρός, crux = στὰ εὖρος, *sta latitudo ; στάσις καὶ εὖρος ἤγουν μῆκος καὶ πλάτος*, longitudo et latitudo : nam latitudo appellatur εὖρος. See *Bibl. Patr. Lugd.*, t. ix., f. 818 sqq.); also to John of Damascus (*De fide orthod.*, iv. 12); comp. also Maxim. Conf., *Liturg. Expos.*, c. 2 sqq.—A modified form of this interpretation is advocated too by those more sober exegetes of the Greek Church, such as Chrysostom, Theodoret, Œcumenius, Theophylact, who see indicated here—not indeed the cross immediately and *per se*, but yet the redeeming work of Christ. (Chrysostom, τὸ μυστήριον τὸ ὑπὲρ ὑμῶν οἰκονομηθέν. Œcumenius, the redemption by Christ was determined from all eternity [μῆκος], reached forth unto all [πλάτος], extends by its power into hell [βάθος], and is by the exaltation of Christ raised above all heavens [ὕψος], etc.)

Of Western Fathers, Ruffinus is the first who comes under this category. In § 14 of his *Expos. in Symb. Apost.*, he remarks: "Docet apost. Paulus illuminatos esse debere oculos cordis nostri, ad intelligendum quæ sit altitudo, latitudo, et profundum. Altit. ergo, et lat., et prof. descriptio crucis est, cujus eam partem quæ in terra defixa est, profundum appellavit," etc. He was followed by Jerome, who in his commentary on the Ep. to the Ephesians (*Opp.*, t. vii. 1, p. 603, Vall.) interprets the *altitudo* of the Pauline passage of the angel world, the *profundum* of the nether world, the breadth and ength of the middle space between the two, and then continues "Hæc universa in cruce Domini nostri J. C. intelligi queunt. . . . . Nec mirum si crux Christi universa possideat, quum etiam si quis crucifixus fuerit cum Christo eandem habeat protestatem,"—namely, because he then knows what is the lowest and the highest, the length and the breadth, etc.

With special minuteness of detail does Augustine apply himself in several places to the bringing out of the mystic references to the cross contained in Ephes. iii. 18; to which references he at the same time gives a moral application, of the main duties of Christians—of love, or activity in good works; of patience, or endurance to the end; of the hope of everlasting blessedness; and the profound contemplation of the mysteries of Divine grace. Thus he says of Christ, in *Serm.* liii. *de verb. Matt.* v. (*Opp.*, t. v., c. 317): "Non frustra ergo crucem elegit, ubi te huic mundo crucifigeret. Nam latitudo est in cruce transversum lignum, ubi figuntur manus : propter bonorum operum significationem. Longitudo est in ea parte ligni, quæ ab ipso transverso ad terram tendit. Ibi enim corpus crucifigitur, et quodammodo stat; et ipsa statio perseverantiam significat. Altitudo autem in illo ligno est, quod ab eodem transverso sursum versus ad caput eminet; et ea significatur supernorum expectatio. Ubi profundum, nisi in ea parte, quæ terræ defixa est? Occulta enim est gratia et in abdito latet. Post hæc si comprehenderis hæc omnia, non solum intelligendo verum etiam agendo—tunc jam extende te, si potes, ad agnoscendam agnitionem caritatis Christi supereminentem scientiæ," etc. Entirely similarly also *Ep.* 140 (*Opp.*, t. ii., c. 446 sq.); *in Joan., cap.* xix., *tract.* 119 (t. iii. c. 801); *in Ps.* ciii.—From Augustine this mode of interpretation, alike objective as subjective, by which on the one hand the many-sidedness and immeasurableness of the Divine compassions, and on the other the fulness of the Christian virtues, is found indicated in the four relations of height, depth, length, and breadth, passes over to the majority of the Western theologians who succeeded him; *e.g.*, to Cassiodorus, Gregory the Great (*Lib. sacramentorum*, p. 86, tom. iii., *Opp.*, ed. Bened.) pseudo Bede,[1] Thomas Aquinas—here and there with peculiar deviations from Augustine's moral interpretation. Comp., for instance, Bernard of Clairvaux, in pseudo-Bonaventura (*Pharetr.*, lib. iv., c. 10): "Circumire possum, Domine, cœlum et terram, mare et aridam, et nusquam inveniam te, nisi tantum in cruce: ibi dormis, ibi pascis, ibi cubas in meridie. Crux enim tua fides est, cujus latitudo charitas, longitudo longanimitas, altitudo spes, profundum timor," etc.—A specifically ascetic interpretation of the four relations is given in the pseudo-Anselmian book *De mensuratione crucis* (in *Anselmi Opp.*, ed. Colon. 1573, tom. iii., p. 311 sqq.; in Migne, t. ii., p. 290 sqq.), which would refer the depth to humility, the height to the duty of praising and loving God above all things, the breadth to the obedience of faith, the length finally to the enduring nature of self-surrender to the Lord: "Debemus ergo habere cruciatum, eo quod non tantum humiliamur ut debemus, et hoc est profundum crucis. . . . Sublimitas crucis est cruciari pro eo, quod te ad plenum laudare non possumus et amare. . . . Latitudo autem crucis est fidelitas semper spiritum crucians et dilatans, ut omnen hominem subjiciat tuæ laudi ac servituti. . . . Longitudo autem crucis tuæ toti vitæ nostræ debet commensurari, ut quamvis consideremus tecum esse jucundum et te in domo tua laudare et in abysso tuæ dulcedinis absorberi: tamen non tædeat nos portare crucem tuam, scilicet in misera hac vita pro tuæ laudis augmento."—The learned Romish exegesis of more recent times delights in gathering together all the different modifications of this mystic interpretation, and in like manner in characterising them as admissible. Thus Cornelius a Lapide (*Comment. in omnes D. Pauli epistolas*, p. 496 sqq.) approves in the first place of all the different modes of interpretation *not* directly applying these words of

---

[1] On the non-genuineness of the *Comm. in Epp. Pauli*, handed down in Bede's works, cp. K. Werner, *Beda der Ehrw.* (1875), S. 185.

the Apostle to the cross; thus (1) the referring of them to the extent of the redeeming work of Christ—Chrysostom, Theod., Oecum., etc.; (2) to the all-filling Godhead of Christ—Ambrose, Greg. Magn., Anselm, Bernard, Thomas Aq.; (3) those to the spiritual measurements or fourfold perfections of the Church of Christ—Jerome, Greg., Anselm, etc.; (4) the anagogic, having reference to the infinite fulness of glory of the heavenly (*jenseitige*) Kingdom of God—Anselm. Besides these interpretations (of which he prefers the first-mentioned as the *sensus maxime genuinus*) he discusses minutely, and in the main also approvingly, those interpretations which refer these words to the cross; among which again he declares admissible the objective mystical and the subjective mystical or moral modification of Augustine, yet, along with these, also the ascetic-contemplative one of the before-mentioned pseudo-Anselmian writing.—Similarly, yet entering less into details, Estius, and the bulk of those Romish exegetes who proceeded according to the traditional allegorical method. The Lutherans, on the other hand, for the most part return to that interpretation of the passage of the immensity or unfathomableness of THE MYSTERY OF GRACE favoured by Chrysostom, Theodoret, and others. Thus, *e.g.*, Salom. Glassius (*in Dom.* xvi., *p. Trin.*, p. 503): "Mathematicam instituit Apostolus et secundum quatuor dimensiones dilectionem Christi quasi metitur.... Verum mensuratione ista ἀνθρωποπαθικῶς instituta ejusdem immensurabilitatem et immensitatem in rei veritate indicat, quasi dicat: altior est coelis, profundior mari, latior latitudine terrarum, longior omni tempore, utpote in omnem æternitatem durans." Similarly Calov (*Bibl. illustrata*, t. iv.), who cites this passage approvingly; so also the writers adduced by Calov as authorities, C. Hemming, Osiander, Ægidius Hunnius. In like manner the Reformed theologians, Beza, Piscator, Zanchius, Crocius, etc.; as well as a series of modern Protestant exegetes; as Rückert, Olshausen, Baumg.-Crusius, Harless.—A few theologians of more recent times return to that interpretation of the reference to the four dimensions—closely allied to the foregoing—of the LOVE OF GOD; an interpretation which in earlier times found advocates in Theodorus of Mopsuestia and Chrysostom (the latter favouring it *along with* the view above spoken of), and later in Erasmus, Vatablus, Grotius, S. J. Baumgarten, Flatt; whilst many, more in harmony with the context, have maintained that the more definite conception of the LOVE OF CHRIST to us is that which is aimed at in this allusion to the four dimensions of its greatness: so Castellio, Calvin, Calixt, Zachariä, Morus, Storr, Rosenmüller, Meyer, Braune [in Lange's series], the last named again with a more express indication of that which is intended by the four dimensions of this love of Christ (namely, that it stretches in its *breadth* over all the nations of the earth, extends in its *length* through all times, that it *descends* into the depths of human sin and misery, and that it *raises* all to Divine glory); while others, as Meyer, reject all such nearer explanation. To this interpretation in reference to the greatness of the saving love of Jesus towards His Church, now the one most generally accepted in scientific-exegetic tradition, that earlier mystical application of the words to the cross does in point of fact approach very nearly, inasmuch as this cross can here certainly come into contemplation only as the pregnant symbol of the love of the Lord towards His people. The context, it is true, affords by reason of its comparative indefiniteness no ground for speaking of the cross of Christ in particular, any more than the Kingdom of Christ, or the Church (the spiritual temple of God), as definitely and expressly intended by the Apostle as the object of the measuring in the four directions. Comp., in regard to this latter interpretation, yet further the words of Luther (*Serm. on Ephes.* iii. 13—21; Erl. edn., 9. 280), "That I know, and am assured, that wherever I may go, Christ is there, and reigns there and in all places—wherever there is length, or breadth, or depth, or height; be it temporal or eternal," etc.; as also Heinsius, Homberg, Wolff, Bengel, Michaelis, Koppe, Stier, and V. Hofmann.

Several other texts of Scripture, like this passage of Ephesians pointing to the four relations in space, of height and depth, length and breadth, have also sometimes been interpreted directly of the CROSS OF THE LORD. So, besides Phil. ii. 10 f. (comp., *e.g.*, Ruffinus, *Expos. in Symb.*, l. c., and Augustine in some of the passages already cited) specially the above O. T. utterances, Job xi. 8 (cp., for ex., pseudo-Bonavent., *Pharetr.*, l. c.; Thom. Aqu., as also Everard of Bethune, *Contr. Valdenses*, c. 17, etc.), and Psalm cxxxix. (138), v. 8 f., where *e.g.* Gregory of Nyssa (*Orat.* i. *de resurr. Christi*), Augustine, and Cassiodorus, in their commentaries on the Psalms, have sought to trace out an allusion to the cross.

Without any special reference to one or other of these passages have the four dimensions in space been pretty often, and that even down to the most recent times, brought into mystic relation with the cross. To this class of references belong in antiquity—in addition to Ambrose, *De Cruce, Serm.* 56; Firm. Maternus, *De errore prof. religg.*, c. 22; pseudo-Jerome *in Marc.* 15, and Basil.

Magn., *Comm. in Isai. c.* 11—specially the celebrated verses of Cœlius Sedulius, often cited by the apologetes of the Romish cultus of the cross, alike in the Middle Ages and in modern times (*Carm. pasch.*, lib. iii.):

> " Quatuor inde plagas quadrati colligit orbis.
> Splendidus auctoris de vertice fulget Eous ;
> Occiduo sacræ labuntur sidera plantæ ;
> Arcton dextra tenet, medium læva erigit axem.
> Cunctaque de membris vivit naturæ creantis,
> Et cruce complexum Christus regit undique mundum."

In recent times, contemplations of this kind have presented themselves in special abundance in the writings of theosophic authors, as Douze-tems (*Myst. de la Croix*, ch. xiii. : des merveilles de la Croix dans la Nature extérieure); F. v. Meyer (*Blätt. f. höh Wahrheit*, viii. 145 f. : "The cross points upwards and downwards, to the right and to the left ; its fourfold direction indicates the universe (*das All*), to which it flows in, and from which it flows forth. Its summit rises to the throne of the Godhead, and its roots extend into the nether world. Its arms stretch forth from the rising of the sun to the setting of the same, from pole to pole. Heaven and earth are in it united, in it satisfied ; the most opposed is in it reconciled and made one"); Saltzmann (*Der Rathschluss Gottes*, etc.), p. 168 f. : "The figure of the cross forms two lines, of which the height and depth, breadth and length, extend to the ends of the creation and intersect each other in the centre, where the life of all creation is situated," etc.; Baader, *Societätsphilos.*, S. 104;[1] comp. "Briefe," vol. xv., S. 54 of his works. Under this head, too, falls a passage in Oetinger's *Theol. ex idea vitæ*, etc. (§ 126, p. 278, of Hamberger's Germ. edn.), where it is said in relation to the mysteries of the Tree of Life in Paradise, " Morning, evening, midday in Paradise did foreshadow these dispositions ;"—according to Hamberger (*l. c.*) "a very obscure passage ;" but one which immediately receives its light so soon as one thinks of the four dimensions of the world in the passages Job xi. 8, Psalm cxxxix. 8, Ephes. iii. 18, of which beyond doubt Oetinger was thinking.

[1] See above, p. 342.

VIII.

Joh. Scotus Erigena and Fulbert of Chartres as Singers of the Cross.

(To page 216.)

To the products of Latin Christian poetry, which may be looked upon as furnishing evidence of a specially convincing nature in favour of the assertion frequently made by us, that the CROSS OF THE LORD had inspired many even of those poets less distinguished as such to the bringing forth of many truly beautiful creations, belong those versified prayers which Joh. Scotus Erigena dedicated to his royal patron Charles the Bald, and which are given in the edition of his theological works (in Migne's *Patrol.*, Ser. ii., t. 122, p. 1221 sqq.) Among those *distichous* poems which form the first series of the poetic attempts of the gifted scholar and profound thinker, it is specially No. I., *De Christo crucifixo*, and No. II., *De cruce*, partly also those pieces treating of the Descent into Hell and the Resurrection, Nos. IV.—VI., which present remarkably fine contemplations and descriptions—such as take their place pretty much on equality side by side with the best of that which has been bequeathed to us by the other singers of the cross of the same century, Theodulf of Orleans or Hraban.

In the first-named poem (forty-one distichs) the poet begins with a comparison of the profane muse of classic antiquity with that of the holy Christian singers; thus he rises to the contemplation of the Crucified:

> " Nunc igitur Christi videamus summa tropæa
> Ac nostræ mentis sidera perspicua.
> Ecce crucis lignum quadratum continet orbem,
> In qua pendebat sponte sua Dominus
> Et Verbum Patris dignatum sumere carnem,
> In qua pro nobis hostia grata fuit," etc.

He then expatiates in praise of the Crucified as the giver of every good and perfect gift, and then implores such gifts in rich abundance upon his kingly ruler.

The poem *De cruce* (thirty-six distichs—*l.c.*, p. 1223 sqq.) presents at its commencement many points of accord with the conception, frequently presenting itself also in the prose works of Erigena (comp. Christlieb, *Erig.*, S. 391 f.), of a salutary operation of the work of redemption, not only upon the angels, but even upon the lower creation on earth : animals, trees, waters of the sea, winds, etc. :

> " Aspice præclarum radiis solaribus orbem
> Quos crux salviflua spargit ab arce sua.
> Terram Neptunumque tenet flatumque polosque
> Et si quid supra creditur esse procul.
> Dum revocat miseros humanæ gentis ab imo,
> Cuspide tartaream percutit ipsa Stygin.
> O crux alma, nites ultra Seraphim Cherubimque;
> Quod est, quod non est, te colit omne super.
> Te Domini rerum, Virtutes atque Potestas,
> Ordo colit, medio jure tenendo locum. . . . . .
> Te πνύξ nostra * dehinc justo modulamine laudat,   [* Ecclesia.
> Per te Christiferam namque redempta fuit," etc.

There now follows a detailed description, comparatively at any rate somewhat *too* detailed, of the miracle-working rod of Moses, as a type of the wood of the cross ; as well as in general of the miracles wrought in the time of Moses as types of those of the New Testament. From the mention of the brazen serpent, the poet in the twenty-fifth distich suddenly springs over to the subject of Mary Magdane, longingly seeking the Risen One. He thus addresses her :

> " Desine cæparios * meditare cernere vultus :   [* κῆπος, hortus ;
> Vivus adest Dominus ; quem gemis, ipsa vide.   *vid.* John xx. 15.
> Tersa pios vultus cursim solabere fratres :
> Evangelistes prima beata vale !—
> Christe, Dei Verbum, Virtus, Sapientia Patris,
> Sanguinis unda tui, qua madat ara crucis,
> Nos purgat, redimit, solvit, vitamque reducit,
> Electisque tuis præstitit esse Deos."

Of contents in part similar is No. IV., *De resurrectione*, where likewise the typical parallel with the miracles of the Mosaic period is specially worked out :

> " Festinans populus Ægypto hunc sumpserat agnum,
> Sanguine conspergens limina nota domus.
> Hic fons, virga, petra, cœlestis fulgor obumbrans,
> Serpens et manna, nubs, via, panis, aqua :
> Talia sæpe Dei jussu sub tempore facta
> Æternum Dominum significare suum."

Among the compositions of the same nature belonging to the second or *hexameter* series, specially No. I., *Christi triumphus de morte ac diabolo*, merits a distinguished prominence. Here the victory of the Crucified is celebrated, *i. a.*, by a complaint put into the mouth of

Satan, of which the pathos occasionally rises to the flight of a higher poetic inspiration, *e.g.*,

> "Me victum video, fugitivum sedibus atris;
> Quæ nova lux oritur, quam nunquam ferre valebo?
> Nunc mea regna ruunt passim, loca nulla tenebris:
> Sentio me captum, pavidum vinclisque ligatum.
> Eheu, quis me congreditur? Quis fortis in armis
> Audax committit mundi cum principe bellum?
> Illene confixus ligno septusque sepulcro,
> Quem rex Herodes sprevit summusque sacerdos
> Ruptus non timuit damnare Caiphas,
> Addictus morti, Romano principe cæsus?
> Hoc egomet feci, fateor, totumque peregi;
> Me stultum latuit virtus humilisque potestas.
> Hunc si cognossem, σταυρῷ non penderet unquam:
> Corporis humani servilis forma fefellit."

At length, deceived out of his dominion on earth, he resolves to betake himself to the only place of refuge still left to him:

> "Unum confugium superest, solamen et unum:
> Est antiqua domus mortis noctisque profundæ,
> Judaicum pectus, vitiorum plena vorago,
> Fraudis et invidiæ semper possessio larga. . . .
> Illic confugiam, gentilia pectora linquens,
> Odibilis Christo dominabor gentis avaræ;
> Omne meum virus fundam blasphema per ora,
> Ligno suspensum Dominum regnare negando."

But, untroubled about these new hostile designs of the Evil One, the Church of Christ has extended itself over the whole world, and ceases not to extol Him and the Holy Trinity in its songs of praise.

The comparative insignificance at other times attached, in the theological speculation of Erigena, to the concrete facts (in the history of redemption) of the death of Jesus, His descent into Hades, His resurrection, etc.—subtilised into the abstract as this significance is wont to some extent to be—is at any rate in these compositions brought into relief with a distinctness such as is only rarely met with in connection with the Christian thinkers of the Middle Ages. Comp. J. Bach, *Dogmengesch. des M. A.*, i. 295 f., where stress is rightly laid (in opposition to Christlieb) upon this their dogmatic importance.

To these compositions of Erigena there appears akin in point of form and contents an hexameter poem, *De sancta cruce*, which with some other Latin verses (hymns, prose compositions, prayers, etc.) is found among the writings of FULBERT of Chartres († 1028): *vid.*

Migne, *Patrol.*, Ser. i., t. 141, c. 345. We give here at least the first and last ones of the thirty-seven hexameters :

> " Vexillum regis venerabile cuncta regentis,
> O crux sancta, micans super omnia sidera cœli,
> Mortifero lapsis gustu, quæ sola reportas
> Antidotum vitæ, fructum suspensa perennem :
> Te colo, te fateor venerans, te pronus adoro.
> Christus principium, finis, surrectio, vita,
> Merces, lux, requies, sanctorum doxa, corona,
> Pro servis Dominus redimendis hostia factus,
> In te suspendens * per lignum toxica ligni   [* *leg.* suspensus.
> Purgavit, clausæ reserando limina vitæ."

The twelve concluding lines contain the petition for preservation and purification from the defilement of the seven or eight principal vices :

> " Protege nos jugiter ventosæ laudis ab aura,
> Et nobis dignas confer tibi solvere grates.
> Invidiæ maculam de mentibus ablue nostris,
> Infundens nobis ignem cœlestis amoris ;
> Iræ compescens stimulos fac nos patientes,
> Tristitiamque fugans, in damnis spem retinentes.
> Crimen avaritiæ nobis dona fugiamus,
> Ut pietatis opus placitæ tibi ferre queamus ;
> Ingluviem ventris nos vincere sobrietate
> Luxuriæque luem casto concede pudore,
> Ut per te mundi, per te quoque viribus aucti,
> Constanter vitam studeamus adire supernam."

IX.

THE SIGN OF THE RETURNING SON OF MAN.—Matt. xxiv. 30.

(To p. 362.)

THE earliest, or certainly one of the earliest, of those who maintain that the σημεῖον τοῦ υἱοῦ τοῦ ἀνθρώπου is to be referred to the Cross of Christ, does the unknown author of the homily *De consummatione Mundi et de Antichristo*, current under the name of Hippolytus, appear to be : ". . . Oritur ab Oriente usque ad Occidentem signum crucis superantis splendorem Solis, denuncians adventum et apparitionem Judicis," etc. (*Bibl. Patr. Lugd.*, tom. iii., p. 257 G.) This writer was first followed in the West by Hilary of Pictavium, who—in his commentary on Matthew (c. 26)—describes in lofty and powerful discourse the glorious coming of Christ, and in doing so speaks *inter alia* of the "light upon the tree, which sheds its lustre upon all," (lucens universis lumen in ligno). In like manner Jerome (*Comm. in Matt.* xxiv.), who however leaves the choice open between interpreting it of the cross, or of some other banner of victory: "Signum hic aut crucis intelligamus, ut videant (juxta Zachariam et Joannem) Judæi quem compunxerunt ; aut vexillum victoriæ triumphantis." In the genuine writings of Augustine there is found no interpretation in this sense of the passage in question—*Serm.* 130 *de Tempore* is pseudo-Augustinian, an excerpting translation of Chrysostom's *Homil. de cruce et latr.*

In the East, it is, after Ephraem (*Orat. de adparitione crucis tempore judicii*), Cyril of Jerusalem (*Catech.*, xv., p. 521 c. in tom. iv. *Bibl. Patr. Lugd.*), and the author of the eighth book of the Sibylline Oracles,—which interprets the passage (Psalm xcvi. 10, LXX.) *Regnabit Dominus a ligno* of the appearing again one day of the cross as a sign of triumph in the sky (*Sibyll.*, viii. 245 sq.) —specially CHRYSOSTOM, who in several passages of his writings advocates this view. More briefly does he express himself with regard to it in his homilies upon Matthew, where he only deduces the conclusion that the sign of the cross, beaming more brightly than the sun, will appear at the Parousia to the reproving conviction (πρὸς ἔλεγχον) of the unbelieving Jews ; like the wounds which the Lord will manifest to them in His body. (*Hom.* lxxvii. *in Matt.* ; tom. vii., *Opp.*) More at large, and with much greater dogmatic explicitness, does he treat of this one day reappearing of the cross in *Hom.* ii. *de cruce et latrone*, § 4 (*Opp.*, tom. ii., p. 417), where he is daring enough to represent the Lord as *not having left on earth at all* the Cross on which He suffered, *but having taken it up with Him into heaven :* βούλει μαθεῖν πῶς καὶ βασιλείας σύμβολον ὁ σταυρὸς καὶ πῶς σεμνὸν τὸ πραγμά ἐστιν; οὐκ ἀφῆκεν αὐτὸν εἶναι ἐπὶ τῆς γῆς, ἀλλ' ἀνέσπασεν αὐτόν, καὶ εἰς τὸν οὐρανὸν ἀνήγαγε. Πόθεν δῆλον τοῦτο; μετ' αὐτοῦ μέλλει ἔρχεσθαι ἐν τῇ δευτέρᾳ παρουσίᾳ, κ.τ.λ. He then describes, in detail, how sun, moon, and stars are eclipsed by the far-shining radiance of the cross, how the host of angels and archangels bear in triumph the resplendent symbol before the Lord, and how the terrors of judgment fall upon all the tribes on earth at the sight of it, and on looking upon the Crucified and Risen One.— This intrepretation of Chrysostom is generally followed by the later exegetes of the Greek Church, specially closely by Euthymius Zigademus (*in Matt.* xxiv) : Σημεῖον αὐτοῦ λέγει τὸν σταυρόν, λάμποντα τότε τοῦ ἡλίου πολλῷ φαιδρότερον· ἐκεῖνος μὲν γὰρ σκοτισθήσεται, οὗτος δὲ φανήσεται. τίνος δὲ ἕνεκεν ὀφθήσεται; ἵνα ταράξῃ προηγουμένους μὲν τοὺς Ἰουδαίους, εἶτα καὶ τοὺς Ἕλληνας, ὅσοι τῷ χριστῷ τὸν σταυρὸν ὠνείδιζον, καὶ ἵνα γνῶσιν, ὅτι αὐτὸς οὗτος κάτεισι Θεὸς ὤν.—Similarly, only more briefly, already Theophylact.

The theology too of the Middle Ages, and the religious poetry of the West, frequently adopts the conclusions of Chrysostom or of those his predecessors in poetry and prose. That which is sung in Anglo-Saxon measure in Kynewulf's "Christ," v. 1100 ff., of the judicial majesty of the Lord at the last day (Grein, *Dichtungen der Angls.*, i. 178 f.) :

> "He will recompense then,
> severely take again for all this,
> *when the red Cross set up shines,*
> *above the nations all glittering, in place of the sun,*
> to which then fearful, by wickedness undone,
> the black sinners look up with awe," etc.;

that which the unknown monkish composer of *Seó hálge ród* describes in an entirely similar manner at the close of his poetic vision (Grein, ii. 144; Bach, *Dogmengesch. des M. A.*, i. 85) ; that which is advanced in the same sense in the *Expositt. in Evangelia* of the Venerable Bede († 735), at the exposition of Matt. xxiv., all shapes itself in accordance with an unvarying tradition, recurring in most of the descriptions of the eschatological events on the part of the more distinguished representatives of the Latin theology of the Middle Ages. Comp., *e.g.*, the *Prognostic. rerum futur.* of the Archbishop Julian of Toledo (or Pomerius, † about 690), lib. iii. c. 5 : " Domino de scendente de cœlis, præcedet exercitus angelorum et archangelorum, qui signum illud triumphale, crucis vexillum, sublimibus humeris præferentes, divinum regis cœlestis ingressum terris trementibus nunciabunt," etc. (*Bibl. Patr. Lugd.*, t. xii., p. 605.) Similarly Peter the Venerable of Clugny († 1156), in his *Epist. contra Petrobusianos* (*ib.*, t. xxii., f. 1055 H.), in which the sect of Peter de Bruys, hostile to the use of the cross, is threateningly reminded of that appearing one day of the *crux Domini:* " Fulgebit in cœlo, ut discant terrigenæ non posse sibi conscensum esse ad cœlos, nisi per ipsam ; et agnoscant filii hominum non nisi per ipsam se posse fieri socios angelorum. Non est igitur honoranda ab hominibus, quæ angelicum eis honorem præparat ? Non est glorificanda mortalibus, quæ immortalem eis gloriam præstat ?"—Thomas Aquinas (*Cat. Aur.*, in

Matt. xxiv.) looks for a manifestation of the cross as the judicial act in condemning the ungodly at the last judgment ; and Thomas à Kempis opens the section of his *Imitatio Christi* which exhorts to the entering upon the *via regia crucis* (lib. ii. c. 12) with a warning reference to the eventual appearing of that symbol of salvation despised by men at the act of judgment, when none but the servants of the cross, the lowly followers of the Crucified, will appear with joy before His judgment-seat.—In the Romish *Officium S. Crucis*, too, allusion is made to the appearing again of the cross one day : " Hoc signum crucis erit in cœlo, cum Dominus ad judicandum venerit." Many Catholic theologians also of more recent times defend the referring of the σημεῖον τοῦ υἱοῦ τοῦ ἀνθρώπου expressly to the cross. So Salmeron, who (as already earlier Thomas Aquinas, *Opusc.* ii., c. 244) speaks of the other instruments of the Lord's sufferings as appearing with the cross in the sky ; Jansen, who speaks not of the material cross of Calvary itself as becoming visible at the Parousia, but (as already some earlier writers, *e.g.*, in the pseudo-Anselmian *Elucidarium*) merely of some kind of representation thereof ; Maldonatus, Cornelius a Lapide, etc. (Compare the latter on Matt. xxiv.)

This reference of the σημ. τ. υἱ. τ. ἀνθρ. to the Cross of Christ did not pass over to the exegetical tradition of Protestantism. Luther, in his sermons upon the Advent-pericope, Luke xxi. 25—36, interprets the signs in the heavens there spoken of, in regard to catastrophes of nature of every kind, and mentions on one occasion as belonging to them, *inter alia*, " much stranger forms of rainbows and other signs, cross, two or three suns, shooting stars, comets following each other, fiery skies, blood-red suns," etc. ; but yet in all this remains as far as possible from the early Church conception of the sign of the Son of Man, as the cross of Christ, concealed for the time being in heaven, and one day in glorified form appearing in the sky. (ERL. EDN., Bd. i., S. 112.) John Brenz (*Comm. in Matt.*) supposes the signum filii hominis to be = " filius hominis ipsemet, ea forma qua ascensurus est in coelum," etc. Calvin (*in Matt.* xxiv. 30) inclines to regard the sign of the Son of Man as the Son of Man Himself, as He, the once lowly one, will come again upon the clouds of heaven. Farel (*Du vray usage de la Croix de J. Christ,* p. 135), expressly polemicises against the interpreting the passage with reference to the cross ; appealing to the *Op. imperfect. in Matt.*, in which Christ Himself is represented as the sign of the Son of Man, and this indeed as the result of a much more probable interpretation than the well-known one of Chrysostom which became traditionally accepted. The great bulk of the Protestant exegetes of the first two centuries after the Reformation leave it altogether undetermined what is to be understood by this σημεῖον of Matt. xxiv. 30. Only some few decide in favour of the ancient churchly interpretation of the cross; so, in the Reformed Church, Clarius (see *Critici sacri*), and, on the Lutheran side, Joh. Gerhard. The latter opposes, indeed, that grosser form of the traditional conception, according to which the material cross of Calvary is itself to form the subject of the miraculous appearing in the sky. (So, *e.g.*, Thomas Waldensis, *De sacram.*, tit. 20, c. 158; Gregory de Valentia; Bessæus; Joh. Osorius; Blasius de Viega, etc., etc.) But against the more ideal supposition of an immense cross of light appearing in the sky he has no serious objections to bring. "Nec injuria quis cogitare possit, crucem adparituram tanquam fontem omnis gloriæ, quæ in die judicii piis obtinget, quia Christi in cruce passio et ignominia est summa piorum gloria." (*Locorum theol.*, tom. xix., p. 271; cf. 283: ed. Cotta.) In the Berleburg Bible, too, there is manifest a certain inclination to the old churchly interpretation, although this is greatly spiritualised: "Godly antiquity explains this of the sign of the cross, which indeed is the real characteristic of all true members of Christ; in reproach, denial and dying to all things. .... Yet in connection herewith it is to be observed that the ancients understood the sign of the cross not as a separate thing—das Zeichen des Creutzes nicht als eine particularität—as though Christ would have a wooden cross in His hand. .... (Rather): "The Son of Man will bring the sign of His former lowliness with Him in His glory."—Within the most recent times single orthodox expositors of Scripture have declared again in favour of the realistic sense advocated by Chrysostom: so, *e.g.*, the Calw Handbk. of Biblic. Expositn. (2nd edn.); and A. W. Assmann, Das Evangel. des Ap. Matthäus (Kassel, 1874), H. ii., S. 74 ("an enormously large cross," etc.)

Of the divergent interpretations we give here only the principal ones.

(*a*) The sign of the Son of Man is explained to be properly speaking a victorious banner, and not the cross itself. So, besides Jerome, *as above* (see p. 430), specially pseudo-Augustine, *Serm.* 130 *de Tempore:* " Sicut imperatorem regalis pompa præcedit .... sic Domino de cœlo veniente angelorum cœtus et archangelorum multitudo illud signum portant humeris excelsis et regalem nobis adventum nunciant," etc.

(*b*) As a *miraculosa quædam stella*, similar to that which was seen in the constellation Cassiopea in 1572-73, was this sign regarded by Ægidius Hunnius in his Commentary on Matthew. (Comp. Joh. Gerhard, *l. c.*) Some writers too of recent times suppose a star of miraculous character, an eschatological counterpart to the star of the Magi, to be here intended: *e.g.*, Fleck (*De regno divino*), H. Olshausen (*Bibl. Commentar*), also F. Bleek (*Synopt. Comment.*), who see an allusion to the star which "shall arise out of Jacob," Num. xxiv. 17 ; whilst exegetes of the period of the earlier supranaturalism and its conflict with rationalism, as Elsner and Homberg, see the natural phenomenon of a comet to be here indicated.

(*c*) Of the *Doxa* of the returning Messiah did Origen think (*Tract.* xxx. *in Matt.*) as the Sign of the Son of Man. So in substance also Bengel in his *Gnomon*: ". . . . Signum, coll. Marc. xiii. 26, 4, est pompa advenientis Filii hominis, qui ipse mox adspiciendus dicitur h. l."—Similarly, but more vague and undetermined, De Wette (" a sort of Shechina "), and Meyer ("a light-phenomenon, the first radiance of the Messianic doxa ; perhaps becoming ever more radiant and glorious, until the Messiah Himself comes forth from it in His glory "). Entirely the same as Origen again, J. P. Lange : "Why not the Shechina or δόξα of the Messiah himself? The splendour of the appearing in general to be distinguished from the personal appearing itself," etc. Simil. V. Hofmann in his "Schriftbeweis," ii. 2, 585.

(*d*) The Messiah, or Son of Man Himself, is intended by the "Sign of the Son of Man," according to the *Op. imperfect. in Matt.*, as also Brenz, Calvin, and Farel (see above), substantially also according to Starke, *Synops. ad h. l.*, who sees indicated by this expression either the Son of Man Himself, or at least the "powerful manifestation that He has risen from the dead, and has received power over all things." Comp. also Wolf and Storr (*Opusc.*, iii. 36), who suppose a genitive of apposition (the sign, namely—or which consists in—the Son of Man), Fritzsche, who makes it a genitive of the subject (" miraculum quod Jesus revertens Messias oculis objiciet "), Morus, Rosenmüller, Ewald, and others.

(*e*) An apparition resembling a man, which is said to have been seen during a whole night in the Most Holy Place of the Temple, at the time of the destruction of Jerusalem, would Rud. Hofmann ("Die Wiederkunft Christi und das Zeichen des Menschensohnes," Leipzig, 1850), following a Jewish fable of Ben-Goria, see indicated by the σημεῖον. See on the other hand Meyer *ad loc.*

(*f*) A strange apocalyptically misinterpreting, and yet spiritualistically subtilising exposition (rightly lashed by Calov and others) attempted by Grotius, with the approval of Polus in his *Synopsis:* the sign of the Son of Man is identical with the white horse in the Apocalypse (Rev. xix. 11), and this in turn denotes the pura evangelicæ doctrinæ prædicatio! For of this Christ is supposed to prophesy in our passage: "post tot corruptelas mirâ quadam efficaciâ eam restituendam esse, per ministerium illorum testium, qui venturi sunt in spiritu Mosis et Eliæ."

(*g*) Schott, Kuinoel, and some others, seek to identify that which is spoken of in the preceding verse (v. 29) with the "Sign of the Son of Man;" thus to subtilise this latter entirely into the indefinite.

(*h*) Some kind of sign not more nearly determinable, which also might possibly be regarded as something entirely different from the Sign of the Son of Man (as something "which a man may behold without knowing that with this the manifestation of the Son of God begins"), would Stier see indicated in this passage. (Comp. also Olshausen *ad loc.*)—Rightly has it been remarked by Von Hofmann (*l. c.*), in opposition to these last-mentioned interpretations, which refine away every concrete sense of the expression, that in any case some sign, as to the connection of which with the historic appearing of the Crucified and Risen One no doubt is possible, must here be intended; "since at least at the sight thereof the wailing of the generations of men not looking for Jesus, not expecting Him, at once begins." Compare our previous observations in the text.

INDEX.

	PAGE
Adoration of the Cross, Festival of the	170
Agobard, Archb. of Lyons (816—840)	178
Agrippa of Nettesheim, Mystic writer (d. 1535)	238, 327
Alba Longa, Vases of	19
Albigenses (cent. 12 and 13)	174, 228
Albertus Magnus (d. 1280), Saying of	228
Alcuin, Abbot of Tours (d. 804)	206
Alexius I., Emperor of the East (d. 1118)	173
Ambrose, Bishop of Milan (d. 397)	148, 164, 213, 245
America, Pre-Christian Cross in	24, 25
Anastasius Sinaiticus, Syrian monk (d. about 650)	197, 219, 243
Ancient British coins, bearing a cruciform emblem	19
Andreas of Crete	249
Andrew, St., Cross of	65
Angela of Foligno, Italian nun (d. 1309)	254
Angelus Silesius, Christian poet and mystic (d. 1677)	321, 326
Ansate Cross of the Egyptians	1, 131
„ „ of Buddhistic India	9
„ „ Significance of the	2, 15
Anselm, Archb. of Canterbury (1093—1109)	251
Anthony, St., Egyptian ascetic (d. 356)	117
„ „ Cross of	65
Antoninus Pius, Roman emperor (138—161), Persecutions under	111
Apollinaris, St., Church of, in Ravenna	196
Apostolic Church, The, a model for all subsequent ages	107
Apostolic constitutions (end of cent. 2, to cent. 4)	116, 163
Aquino, Thomas Count of (d. 1274)	265
Armenians (cent. 11 and 12)	164, 173
Arndt, John, of Anhalt, writer of *True Christianity* (d. 1621)	290, 307, 330
Artemidorus (fl. time of the Antonines) on the mode of crucifixion	96 n.
Assyrians, Crucifixions among the	55
Athanasius, Bp. of Alexandria (d. 373)	242

438　　　　　　　　　　　INDEX.

	PAGE
Attic coins, bearing a cruciform emblem	15
Augustine, Bp. of Hippo (d. 430)	153, 161, 164, 172, 245
Aurelius (Marcus Aurel. Antoninus, 161—180), Persecutions under	111
Aurelius Victor, Latin historian (fl. 358)	65 n.
Aurungzebe (d. 1707), Buddhist temple destroyed by	13
Babylonian-Assyrian crosses	6
Bach, Joh. Sebastian (d. 1750), Passion music of	315
Bactrian Labarum Cross	15
Balæus (abt. 430), Prayer recorded by	244
Balde, James (d. 1668), Poems of	315
Baronius, Cæsar, Cardinal (b. 1538, d. 1607)	302
Bartholomeo, Fra., Italian painter (d. 1517)	311
Basil, Bp. of Neocæsarea (d. 379 or 380)	116, 243
Beda Venerabilis (d. 735)	431
Beethoven, Ludwig v. (d. 1827), Passion music of	315
Bellarmine, Robert, Cardinal (b. 1542, d. 1621)	302
Bengel, Joh. Alb. (d. 1752)	338
Bernard, Abbot of Clairvaux (d. 1153)	216, 252
Berthold of Regensburg, Franciscan monk (d. 1272)	255
Beza, Theodore, Theologian of the Reformed Church (b. 1519, d. 1605)	300
Boehme, Jacob, German mystic (b. 1575, d. 1624)	328
Bogumili (cent. 12)	173
Bonaventura (d. 1274)	207, 216, 253
Borgia, Stephen, Cardinal (d. 1804), Researches of	194, 308
Bosio, Antonio, the Columbus of the Catacombs (d. 1629)	305
Bozethecus, Bohemian abbot (about 1086)	231
Brant, Sebastian (d. 1520), Passion poetry of	217
Brenz, John, Lutheran theologian (d. 1570)	286
Brethren of the Cross (cent. 14)	232
Brigitta, St., Swedish ascetic (d. 1373)	204, 238, 258
Buddhists, Northern, Belief of in a western paradise	11
Caedmon, monk of Whitby (d. abt. 680), Poems of	219
Calbulus, African grammarian (fl. abt. 500)	214
Calderon, Pedro, Spanish dramatist (d. 1687)	225
Calvin, John (b. 1509, d. 1564)	291, 299
Cano, Alonso, Spanish painter (d. 1665)	311
Caracci, Annibal (b. 1560, d. 1609)	311
„　　Louis (b. 1555, d. 1619)	311
Carolingian Age (751—987)	186
Carthaginians, Crucifixion among the	50, 52, 58
Cassian, John, Abbot of Marseilles (d. abt. 440)	228, 230
Charles the Great (Charlemagne, d. 814)	164, 177

INDEX.

Chemnitz, Martin, Lutheran theologian (d. 1589)	298
Childebert, King of the Franks (511—558)	186
Chosroes II., King of Persia (590—628)	168
Christian art in the Early Church	124 ff.
„ (or Latin) Cross, The	68
„ „ „ Typical form in Church architecture	184—189
Chrysostom, John, of Constantinople (d. 407)	149, 152, 243, 250
Chyträus, David, Luth. theologian (d. 1600)	289
Cimabue, Italian painter (d. 1300)	203
Claude, Bp. of Turin (d. 839)	177
Clement of Alexandria (d. abt. 220)	123, 131, 211
Climacus, John (d. 606)	229
Clotaire I. (511—561)	157
Colonna, Vittoria, Marchioness of Pescara (d. 1547)	316
Commodian of Gaza, Christ. poet (cent. 4)	123
Constantine (d. 337), His Vision of the Cross (27 Oct., 312)	137 ff.
„ Change in the conduct of, from this time	139, 146
„ Cross erected by	192
„ V., Copronymus (741—775)	177
„ VII., Porpyrogenitus (911—959)	198
Corpus Christi, Festival of (first enjoined 1264)	223
Correggio, Antonio, Italian painter (d. 1534)	311
Cranach, Lucas, Germ. painter (d. Oct. 16, 1553)	312
Cross, The, Impression produced by the form of	181
„ „ in later Christian Song	315 ff.
„ „ represented as the Tree of Life	193, 203, 207
„ „ Words of Christ upon	97
Cross of Malta	7, 158
Crosses afforded an asylum for transgressors	165
„ were not directly depicted on early Chr. monuments	224
Crucesignation	115, 161
Crucifixes, Introduction of (sec. half of cent. 6)	125
Crucifixion, Deeper import of the punishment of	51, 75
„ as represented by the Heathen caricaturist (beginning of cent. 3)	115
„ Practice of, abolished by the Christian emperors	65, 145
„ of Christ, History of the	92—97
Crucifixions of early Christians	110 ff.
Cruciform figures of the Assyrians, etc.	7
Crusades (1096—1291)	158
Crux, Probable derivation of the term	53 n., 408
„ commissa	66
„ decussata	65
„ immissa	68
„ transiens or usualis	115

440 INDEX.

	PAGE
Cruces dissimulatæ	119 ff., 131
,, ,, Motive which urges to seek these	123, 133
,, stationales	167, 192
Cyprian, Bp. of Carthage (d. 258)	116, 123, 164, 214
Cyril, Bp. of Alexandria (412—444)	243
,, Bp. of Jerus. (348—386)	148, 242
Cyrillonas, Syrian Christian father (fl. abt. 400)	212, 243
Dallæus or Daillé, John, Theolog. Ref. Ch. (d. 1670)	307
Damasus I., Pope (366—384)	211 n.
Damiano, Peter, Cardinal Legate (d. 1072)	216, 229, 232
Dante Alighieri (b. 1265, d. 1321)	39, 222, 264
Decius, Rom. emperor (249—251), Persecutions under	110 f.
De Wette, W. M. L. (d. 1849), his conception of the import of the death of Christ	344
Dioclesian (C. Valerius Diocletianus, emperor 284—305), Persecutions under	110 f.
Discovery of the Cross (*Inventio S. Crucis*), Festival of the	169, 214
Dominicus, Mediæval ascetic	232
Douze-Tems, French mystic (wrote in 1732)	331
Druids, Cruciform emblems among the	15
,, Tree of the Cross among the	20, 77
Dürer, Albert (b. 1471, d. 1528)	312
Dushan, Stephen, King of Servia (d. abt. 1350)	157
Easter Island, Colossal statues on	22
Eckart, Meister, Germ. Domin. monk (d. 1329)	257
Eden, Site of	36, 44, 392
Edict of Milan (313)	139
Editha, English ascetic (cent. 10)	230
Egyptian coins, bearing a cruciform emblem	15
Egyptians, Crucifixions among the	54
Encolpia	157, 194
Ephraem Syrus (d. 378)	129, 243
Epiphanius, Bp. of Constantia in Cyprus (d. 403)	86, 87, 163, 218
Epistle to the Hebrews, Author of, on the death of Christ	105
Erigena, John Scotus, Scholastic theologian (d. abt. 874)	216
Euchites, Later (cent. 11)	174
Eusebius, Bp. of Cæsarea (d. 338)	136, 137, 144
Eustathius, Archb. of Thessalonica (d. 1194)	234
Eutychius, Patr. of Constantinople (d. 582)	168
Exaltation of the Cross, Festival of the	168
"Extern Stones" near Horn	199
Farel, Wm., Swiss Reformer (b. 1489, d. 1565)	299

Feet, Nailing of the, in crucifixion - - - - - - 204, 415
Felix IV., Pope (526-530) - - - - - - - - 201
Fiesole, Giovanni da (d. 1455) - - - - - 204, 264
Flacius, Matthias, Lutheran theologian (d. 1575) - - - - 302
Fragments of the True Cross - - - - - - 149, 194, 198
Francis of Assisi (b. 1182, d. 1226) - - - - - - - 235
Franck, Sebastian, Germ. mystic (d. 1543) - - - - - 327
Frederick II., Emp. of Germany (1215—1250) - - - - 221
Frederick V., Elector Palatine (d. 1632) - - - - - - 301
Fulbert, Bp. of Chartres (d. 1028) - - - - - - - 216
Fulda, Monastery of (founded 744) - - - - - - - 206
Furca, as an instrument of punishment - - - - - - 63

Galla Placidia (consort of Theodosius the Great), Cross of - - 193
Gallus (d. 640), pupil of Columba, founded the monastery of St. Gall
in 614 - - - - - - - - - - - - 159
Garcilaso de la Vega (b. 1530, d. 1568) - - - - - - 23
Gelasius I., Pope (492—496) - - - - - - - - 169
Gerhard, John, Luth. theologian (d. 1637), on the Christian's cross - 290
Gerson, John (d. 1429) - - - - - - - - - 259
Giotto of Florence (d. 1336) - - - - - - - - 204
Giunto Pisano (fl. 1210—1236) - - - - - - - 203
Gnupson, Erich, Missionary journey of - - - - - - 26
Gothic architecture, Prevailing idea in - - - - - - 189
Gozzo, Large crosses on - - - - - - - - - 7
Gratian, Rom. emperor (367—383) - - - - - - - 156
Greek, or St. George's, Cross - - - - - - - 17, 168
Gregentius, Archb. of Taphar (d. 552) - - - - - - 171
Gregory I. (the Great), Pope (590—604) - - 67, 125, 170, 214, 247
„ IV., Pope (827—844) - - - - - - - - 206
„ VII. (Hildebrand), Pope (1073—1085) - - - - 229
„ of Nazianzus (d. 389 or 390) - - - - - 212, 243
„ Bp. of Nyssa (d. abt. 396) - - - - - 243 f.
„ Bp. of Tours (573—595) - - - - - 161 n., 186
Gretser, James, Jesuit critic and archæologist (d. 1625) 115, 118, 249, 303
Gualbert of Vallombrosa (cent. 11) - - - - - - 228

Hadrian, Rom. emperor (117—138), Persecutions under - - - 111
Hamann, Joh. Georg, Mystic theologian (d. 1788) - - - 336
Händel, Georg Friedr. (d. 1759), Passion music of - - - 315
Harms, Claus (d. 1855), favours the practice of crucesignation - 309
Hebrews, Crucifixions among the - - - - - - 55 ff.
Helena (d. abt. 328), Pilgrimage of, to the Holy Sepulchre in 326 - 146
„ „ Her discovery of the supposed wood of the cross 151
„ „ Church of the Ascension built by - - - 183

	PAGE
Henry of Lausanne (d. 1147 or 1148)	174
Heraclius, Emp. of the East (610—641)	168, 169
Herod I., Coins of	130, 144
Herrera, Span. historian (d. 1625)	23
Hesychius (fl. 380)	62
Hilarion, Palestinean monk (d. abt. 371)	228
Hilary, Bp. of Poitiers (d. 367)	413, 416, 429
Hildebrand (v. Gregory VII., Pope)	229
Hiltibald, deacon (cent. 7), companion of Gallus in missionary work	159
Hippolytus, Bp. of Portus on the Tiber (d. 235)	65 n.
Holbein, Hans (d. 1554)	312
Honorius, Emp. of the West (395—423)	156
Honorius I., Pope (626—638)	169
Hrabanus Maurus (d. 856)	206
Hütter, Leon., controversial theologian (d. 1616)	283
Iconoclasts, Council of the (754)	177
Ignatius, Bp. of Antioch (d. under Trajan)	120
Image controversies (726—869)	176
Impalement, Practice of	55, 59, 62
Indians (East), Stone crosses among the	9, 10
Innocent III., Pope (1198—1216)	163, 175
Irenæus, Bp. of Lyons (d. under Septim. Severus, A.D. 202)	122
Isaac of Antioch, Poetic homilies of	213, 243
Isidore of Seville (d. 636)	67, 82
Jacobus de Voragine, author of "The Golden Legend" (d. 1298)	219, 238
Jacoponus, Christian poet (d. 1306)	216
Jaina sect, Antiquity of the	11
Jerome (d. 420)	181, 218, 245
John, St., on the death of Christ	105
„ Order of (instituted 1099)	158
John de Marignola (cent. 14)	160
„ of Damascus (d. 756)	177, 243
„ of the Cross, Spanish ascetic (d. 1591)	231, 317, 326
Jonas, Justus, Germ. Prot. Reformer (d. 1555)	289
Jovianus, Rom. emperor (d. 364)	143
Julian, Rom. emperor (361—363)	117, 128, 143
Julius Firmicus Maternus (fl. 340)	407, 412
Jung Stilling, Germ. pietist (d. 1817)	339
Justin II., Emperor of the East (565—578)	194, 214
Justin Martyr, Christian apologist (fl. 150)	116, 120, 121
Justinian I. (the Great), Emperor of the East (527—565)	164
„ Declension in the character of Christianity from the time of	154

INDEX. 443

	PAGE
Justinian I., Digests of	70
„ Form of the Labarum under	156

Kempis, Thomas à (d. 1471) - - - - - - - 260
Kingly significance of the death of Christ - - - - 91
Klopstock, Friedr. Theoph. (d. 1803), The *Messiah* of - - - 320
Kynewulf, Anglo-Saxon poet (b. abt. 725, d. towards the close of
 the cent.) - - - - - - - - - - - 220

Labarum cross, Pre-Christian form of the - - - - - 16
 „ „ Origin of the - - - - - - - - - 17
 „ „ of Constantine and his successors - - - 140 ff.
Lactantius, Firmianus (d. abt. 318) - - - 116, 123, 136, 143
Las Casas, Barthol. de, Span. missionary to S. America (d. 1566) - 23
Lavater, J. G. C., Swiss theologian (d. 1801) - - - - - 339
Leo I., the Great, Pope (440-461), Passion sermons of - - - 246
 „ IX., Pope (1049—1054) - - - - - - - - 199
 „ III., the Isaurian, Emperor of the East (717—741) - - - 176
 „ VI., the Philosopher, Emperor of the East (886—911) - - 250
Leonardo da Vinci (d. 1520) - - - - - - - - 310
Licinius, Victory of Constantine over (323) - - - - 143, 145
Lipsius, Justus, critic and archæologist (d. 1606) - - 63, 66, 68, 303
Lollards (cent. 14) - - - - - - - - - - 176
Lope de la Vega, Span. poet (d. 1635) - - - - - 226, 318
Louis the Pious, Emperor of the West (814—840) - - 186, 198, 206
Loyola, Ignatius, founder of the order of Jesuits (d. 1556) - - 324
Lucas of Tuy, Span. bishop (cent. 13), opponent of the Albigenses - 175
Luini, Bernardino, Ital. painter (d. after 1530) - - - - 310
Luis de Leon, Span. poet (d. 1591) - - - - - - 235, 326
Luther, Martin (b. 1483, d. 1546) - - - - - 270, 295, 357

Macarius, Bp. of Jerusalem (age of Constantine) - - - 148, 169
 „ Egyptian anchorite (d. 390 or 391) - - - - - 228
Magnentius, Rom. emperor (350—353), Labarum of - - - 144
Manichæans (arose abt. 270) - - - - - - - - 172
Manuel Commenus, Emperor of the East (1143—1180) - - - 174
Martyr, Peter (d. 1526) - - - - - - - - - 23
Mediæval poetry of the Cross - - - - - - - 211 ff.
Melancthon, Philip (b. 1497, d. 1560) - - - - - 278, 357
Menken, Gottfried, Christian mystic (d. 1831) - - - - - 339
Merovingian age (511—751) - - - - - - - 157, 186
Meyer, J. F. v., Christian mystic (d. 1848) - - - 239, 339, 342
Michael Angelo (b. 1474, d. 1564) - - - - - - 311, 316
Milton, John (b. 1608, d. 1674), Biblical epics of - - - - 320
Milvian Bridge, Battle of the (28th Oct., 312) - - - - - 140

INDEX.

	PAGE
Minucius Felix (fl. abt. 220)	114
Mithridates (d. B.C. 63), Coins of, bearing a cruciform emblem	15, 129
Monogrammatic writing in the pre-Constantine Church	127
Montanus of Spires, Ode of	217
Murillo, Barth. Steph., Span. painter (d. 1682)	311
Nicæa, Council of (325)	146
,, Sec. council of (787)	177
Nicetas the Paphlagonian (fl. abt. 880)	250
Nicholas I., Pope (858—867)	164, 253
,, Peregrinus, ascetic (abt. 1090)	231
Niedleben, Monuments of, belonging to the Bronze age	20
Nilometer, The	4
Nilus, disciple of John Chrysostom	229
Odilo, Abbot of Clugny (d. 1048)	251
Oetinger, Friedr. Chr., mystic theologian (d. 1782)	337
Origen, Eastern Church Father (d. abt. 253)	81, 116, 123
Osiander, Andreas, Lutheran theologian (d. 1552), on the sufferings of Christians	289
Oswald, King of Northumbria (d. 642)	179
Otfried of Weissenburg (cent. 9)	221
Palladius, Bp. of Helenopolis in Bithynia (401—431 circ.)	228
Palms of Solomon's Temple	44
Paracelsus, Swiss mystic (d. 1541)	328
Patibulum, Form of the	63
Paul, St., Testimony of, as to the import of the death of Christ	101 ff.
Paulicians (arose abt. 657)	173
Paulinus, Bp. of Nola (d. 431)	65 n., 148, 193, 214
Persians, Crucifixions among the	60, 61
Perugino, Pietri, Ital. painter (d. 1524)	311
Peter, St., Testimony of, to the import of the death of Christ	101
Peter Comestor, French ecclesiastic (d. 1188)	219
,, Martyr, writer on Spanish affairs (d. 1526)	23
,, Martyr Vermigli, Ital. Prot. Reformer (d. 1562)	293
,, of Alcantara, Span. Franciscan monk (d. 1562)	231
,, of Bruis (died by violence, 1130)	174
,, Pomponatius, Ital. philosopher (d. 1525)	238
,, the Venerable, Abbot of Clugny (d. 1156)	172, 174
Petrarch (d. 1374), Opinion of as to the origin of stigmatisations	238
Picus, Joh., Count of Mirandola (d. 1494)	176, 210
Poets of the German Reformation	321
Priestly significance of the death of Christ	90
Prometheus, Punishment of	53

INDEX. 445

	PAGE
Prophetic significance of the death of Christ	89
Prudentius, Christian poet of Spain (d. after 404), Passion hymns of	213
Quaresmius, Italian resident in Jerusalem (cent. 17)	306
Quenstedt, Lutheran theologian (d. 1688)	285
Radegonde, Frankish queen (d. 587)	214, 229, 238
Rafael (Raffaello da Urbino, b. 1482, d. 1520)	311
Raymond de Sebonde, Span. philosopher (d. 1432)	265
„ Lull (d. 1315)	210
„ Palmarius (d. 1200)	231
Reccared (acceded to the Catholic faith 589), Cross presented to	194
Religious significance of the infliction of death punishment	47 ff.
Rembrandt, Paul (d. 1669)	312
Reni, Guido, Ital. painter (d. 1642)	311
Resurrection, The, of Christ, the point from which His death was viewed	100
„ „ „ Mediæval representations of	204
Rhegius, Urban, Lutheran theologian (d. 1541)	287
Romans, Crucifixions among the	60
Romanus II., Emperor of the East (959—963)	198
Roos, Magn. Friedr., Germ. mystic theologian (d. 1803)	338
Rosicrucians, mystics of the beginning of the 18th cent.	331
Rubens, John Paul, Flem. painter (b. 1577, d. 1640)	311
Ruffinus, Ecclesiastical writer (d. 410)	21, 136, 148, 228
Runic crosses, Antiquity of	21
Saint Victor, Adam de (cent. 12), Paschal Hymn of	216
Salmasius, Claudius, Protestant controversialist (b. 1596, d. 1653)	307
Savonarola, Jerome, Ital. Reformer (d. at the stake 1498)	263
Schleiermacher, Friedr. E. D., "the German Plato" (d. 1834), Aspect of Christ's death apprehended by	344
Schliemann, Discoveries of	14, 379
Scriver, Chr., Germ. devotional writer (d. 1693)	291
Sedulius, Rom. poet (fl. 450), Paschal Hymns of	214
Serapeion, Destruction of the	2, 131
Sergius II., Pope (844—847)	206
Serpents, Worship of	73
Sistus, bishop and martyr (d. 258)	111
Sophronius, Patriarch of Jerusalem (cent. 7)	163 n., 212
Southern cross, Constellation of the	38
Sozomen, Eccles. historian (d. after 443)	65 n.
Spanheim, Ezek. and Fred.	307
Spener, Ph. J., German pietist (d. 1705)	343
Starke, Chr., Germ. expositor (d. 1744)	285

INDEX.

	PAGE
Statue, taken for that of Hippolytus	127
Stauros, Derivation of the term	61 n.
Staupitz, John (d. 1524)	262
Stier, Rudolf, Christian mystic (d. 1867)	339
Stigmatisations, among the Romish ascetics	233
Sufferings, The, of Christ, always to be viewed in the light of His exaltation	100
Suidas, Greek lexicographer (cent. 11)	156
Sulpicius Severus, ecclesiastical historian (end of cent. 4)	148
Suso, ascetic and mystic (d. 1365)	230, 257
Swastika or Svastica Cross (Fig. 23), Significance of the	10, 31, 130
„ Appearance of, upon Etruscan urns	18
„ „ „ Scandinavian monuments	20
„ Influence of, upon the character of Indian architecture	13

Tau of the Prophet Ezekiel	80
Tauler, John, of Strassburg, mystic theologian (d. 1361)	257
Tertullian, Church Father (fl. 195)	81, 114, 115, 122, 153
Theodolinde, Lombard queen (acceded to the Catholic faith 587)	125, 195, 196
Theodoret, Bp. of Cyrus in Syria (d. 457)	228
Theodorus Studites, Abbot of Studium (d. 826)	170, 177
Theodosius I., the Great, Emperor (378—395), Coins of	156
„ II., Emperor (402—450), Coins of	159
Theodulf, Bp. of Orleans (d. 821), Hymns of	216
Theophylact, Archbp. of Bulgaria (d. abt. 1112)	170
Theresa, Span. Carmelite nun (d. 1582)	231, 317
Thirty Years' War (ended 1648), Decay of Christianity during the	314
Thor, Hammer of	20
Tigranes (d. B.C. 55), Coins of	129
Tintoretto, Italian painter (d. 1594)	311
Titian, Venetian painter (b. 1477, d. 1576)	311
Trajan, Rom. emperor (98—111), Persecutions under	111
Tree of Knowledge, The	9, 12, 219
„ „ „ relation of to the cross of Christ	75
„ Life	8, 42, 87
Trent, Council of (1545—1563)	298, 302
Trullus, The, in Constantinople, Second Council of (691 or 692)	166, 197

Valentinian I., Emperor (364—375)	129, 156
„ III., „ (425—455)	153, 193
Valerian, Emperor (255—259), Persecutions during the closing period of	110
Van Dyck, Anton, Flemish painter (d. 1641)	311
Van Eyck, John, of Bruges (cent. 15)	204
Venantius Fortunatus, Bp. of Poitiers (d. abt. 600)	214

INDEX. 447

Victor, St., Adam ae, Christian poet (cent. 12) - - - - 216
Vigilius, Pope (538—555) - - - - - - - - 157
Volterra, Daniel di, Italian painter (d. 1566) - - - - - 311
Volvandus of Strassburg, Dominican prior (d. after 1230) - - 230

Waldenses (beginning of cent. 12) - - - - - - - 175
Warka, Clay coffins found at - - - - - - - - 8
Wessel, John, of Groningen (d. 1489) - - - - - - 262
Wicliff, John, of Lutterworth (d. 1384) - - - - - - 176
Winfrid, or Bonifacius, native of Kirton, Devonshire, evangelist and
    martyr (d. 755) - - - - - - - - 160, 215
Wood of the Cross, Legends regarding the - - - 217, 218, 222
Words of Christ upon the Cross - - - - - - - 97 ff.
Worship of the Early Church directed to the person of Christ - 113

Xiphilinus, Patr. of Constantinople (d. 1075) - - - - - 250

Yggdrasill, World Tree of Scandinavian mythology - 21, 219, 419

Zinzendorf, Count Nicholas L. von, Moravian leader (b. 1700,
    d. 1760) - - - - - - - - - 321, 337, 355
Zurburan, Francis de, Span. painter (d. 1662) - - - - - 311
Zwingli, Ulric, Swiss Prot. Reformer (b. 1484, d. 1531) - - - 299

www.ingramcontent.com/pod-product-compliance
Lightning Source LLC
Chambersburg PA
CBHW051855300426
44117CB00006B/404